Contents

Poems of Pilgrimage

Miscellaneous Poems

Imitations, etc.

THE VARIORUM EDITION OF THE COMPLETE POEMS OF THOMAS HARDY

THE Variorum Edition OF

THE Complete Poems OF THOMAS HARDY

EDITED BY

James Gibson

M

THE VARIORUM EDITION OF THE COMPLETE POEMS OF THOMAS HARDY

ISBN: 0 333 23773 0

The Variorum Edition first published in 1979 by
MACMILLAN LONDON LIMITED
4 Little Essex Street London WC2R 3LF
and Basingstoke
Associated companies in Delhi, Dublin,
Hong Kong, Johannesburg, Lagos, Melbourne,
New York, Singapore and Tokyo

Typeset by
WESTERN PRINTING SERVICES LTD, BRISTOL

Printed and bound in Great Britain at
THE PITMAN PRESS, BATH

List of Manuscript Illustrations

Introduction

FIFTY YEARS after his death Thomas Hardy's status as one of the very greatest of English writers, both as novelist and poet, is indisputable. It is remarkable, therefore, that among the flood of critical and biographical works which his writings have led to there has been so little examination of his texts. The need to present, with all possible accuracy and completeness, what the writer actually wrote is so indispensable a part of our understanding, and provides so valuable an insight into the creative mind at work, that it must be the hope of all those who admire Hardy's writing that what Professor R. L. Purdy did for Hardy bibliographical studies in the 1950s will be done for Hardy textual studies in the next decade. This variorum edition of the *Complete Poems* is a first contribution to those studies.

Three factors have contributed to the neglect which has occurred so far. The first of these is that his work has been in copyright. This will change significantly on 1 January 1979 when almost all Hardy's published work will enter the public domain. The second is Hardy's whimsical humility, which derived amusement from belittling his own craftsmanship and giving the impression that his writing was dashed off without much care. This book will add to the evidence that he was, in fact, a conscientious and painstaking craftsman, meticulous almost to a fault. The third factor is closely associated with the second. Not only was it far too widely believed that Hardy's texts were not worth studying, but there has also been an inadequate realisation of how large and rich a quantity of material has survived in spite of Hardy's known sensitivity about his texts, and in spite of the famous Max Gate bonfires. When variorum editions of the novels are available, they will certainly provide one of the wealthiest of all sources for the study of a great writer at work.

Although there remains a great deal of material to be studied in any examination of Hardy's poetical texts, it is to be regretted that so few of his earliest drafts have survived. His reticence was such that he was not accustomed to leave the birthpangs of his poems for others to experience. What evidence there is of the earliest stages of creation is limited to a handful of rough drafts, most of which are to be found in the Dorset County Museum. At this stage, it is necessary to define some of the terms which I shall be using. A 'rough draft' is a manuscript which is clearly an early working and which pre-dates any printing. A 'fair copy' is a manuscript which is a late working, probably dates from near the time of the first printing of the poem, but which may be later, and which may have a number of revisions, some of which may have occurred after the first printing. The 'collected manuscripts' are those fair copies which were bound up, according to Hardy's wishes, in eight books of verse corresponding to the eight published books; and an 'extra manuscript' is one which is not so bound up.

We may never know how many extra manuscripts there were, but it has been possible to identify one hundred and fifteen. Some were presented to friends, some were kept by the editors of journals in which they had been published, some survived as rough drafts because Hardy died before he could destroy them, others were auctioned in aid of the Red Cross. The Dorset County Museum collection of thirty-one is the largest, the University of Texas has seventeen, and the University of California at Berkeley eight. These fifty-six manuscripts, together with another thirty-four in the possession of other institutions and individuals, have been checked. Of the remaining twenty-five, three are reported by the Plymouth Public Library to have been destroyed in the Second World War, a few have disappeared without trace, while about fifteen are owned by private collectors who have not let me see them. Mr Frederick B. Adams, Jnr, has the largest collection. He has, I believe, nine, but I have been refused permission to check them because, not appreciating the monopolistic conditions which prevail in some fields of American scholarship, I omitted when I began my research to reserve for myself access to manuscripts whose whereabouts were well known and required no intensive research. Mr Adams has, however, been so kind as to tell me that if he could allow me to see them they would add 'little grist to your mill'. The extra manuscripts contain many interesting insights. One of the most valuable is the manuscript of 'The Two Tall Men' (see p. 832), now in the Colby College Library. This is an early version of 'The Three Tall Men' (834), and it illustrates both the large amount of rewriting that might take place, and Hardy's ability to take an early poem and develop it in such a way that the new poem is deepened in feeling and irony.

Of the thirty-one extra manuscripts in the Dorset County Museum twenty may be regarded as fair copies, the remainder as rough drafts. The earliest of the rough drafts, and in some ways the most important, is 'Song' (see p. 700), which is written on a single leaf, probably torn from a diary or notebook, and headed 'June 22. 1868'. This was eventually to become the poem 'Retty's Phases' (765), published in *Human Shows* almost sixty years later. It well illustrates Hardy's habit of sitting on a poem for many years before revising and publishing it. It will be seen that the amount of revision in the rough draft is substantial, and that at this stage he seems to have known that there were to be seven stanzas, even though two stanzas are but fragments and one stanza has not a single word. Alternative wordings are written in for consideration alongside his first thoughts. This draft certainly confirms Hardy's remark to Edmund Gosse that 'Many of the poems were temporarily jotted down to the extent of a stanza or two when the idea occurred, and put aside till time should serve for finishing them – often not till years after.' Of the other rough drafts, eight are of poems which appeared in the posthumous *Winter Words*, and it is probable that they would have been destroyed like their predecessors if Hardy had survived. They show that he used any piece of paper that happened to be available for his rough drafts. One is reminded of the blue paper sticking out of his pocket on that memorable day when he first met Emma Gifford in 1870, a piece of paper which 'proved to be the MS. of a poem, and not a plan of the church'. The rough draft of '"A Gentleman's Second-Hand Suit"' in the Dorset County Museum is written on the verso of a stockbroker's letter and application form for an Ealing Corporation issue of five-per-cent stock. Irony was never far away from Hardy! The amount of revision in these rough drafts is substantial, with insertions, deletions and alternatives (in ink and pencil) thronging the page. They show how industriously Hardy worked away on his texts when they were at this stage. In *Good-Bye to All That* Robert Graves quotes Hardy as saying, 'Why! . . . I have never in my life taken more than three, or perhaps four, drafts for a poem. I am afraid of it losing its freshness.' If we accept the accuracy of this – and we may wonder about the freshness of poems worked on over a large number of years (and surely Hardy would never have said 'it losing') – most of these Dorset County Museum rough drafts seem likely to be second drafts.

Although there are comparatively few extra manuscripts, there is an abundance of collected manuscripts, 917 to be exact. Hardy was impressively meticulous about collecting together his fair copies, and for each of the eight books of verse, from *Wessex Poems* (1898) to *Winter Words* (1928), there is an accompanying bound-up volume of manuscripts. Every poem in the eight books of verse will be found in manuscript in the bound-up volumes, with the exception of 'Childhood among the Ferns', which, sadly, is missing from *Winter Words* and is in the possession of Mr Frederick B. Adams, Jnr. These eight books of manuscripts were presented to the following institutions:

Wessex Poems	The Birmingham City Museum and Art Gallery
Poems of the Past and the Present	The Bodleian Library, Oxford

Time's Laughingstocks	The Fitzwilliam Museum, Cambridge
Satires of Circumstance	The Dorset County Museum, Dorchester
Moments of Vision	Magdalene College, Cambridge
Late Lyrics and Earlier	The Dorset County Museum, Dorchester
Human Shows	Yale University
Winter Words	The Queen's College, Oxford

The collected manuscripts are more interesting than is generally realised, for two reasons: first, because they contain many uncancelled variants found nowhere else, and, secondly, because they contain enough revision to give us a valuable insight into Hardy's mind at work. The revision is, of course, heaviest in the early volumes, and markedly less in the later volumes, but in total it is considerable. At first sight it is surprising that Hardy did not write out clean copies for presentation purposes, but, apart from the work involved in doing this, he may well have thought that there were strong arguments for presenting his fair copies, and that is what these bound-up collected manuscripts are. He wrote these final drafts on sheets of good-quality paper of uniform size, having probably had, as early as the 1890s, the idea that one day they would be collected together. The poems in *Wessex Poems* are on slightly larger paper than the poems in the other seven volumes, all of which are on paper approximately 8″ × 10″. From *Time's Laughingstocks* onwards the paper used was almost all made by A. Pirie & Sons. This can be ascertained from the watermarks, which have the additional interest that many of them contain the year of manufacture. The fact that the sheets vary within a book – that is to say that in *Human Shows* one sheet is marked 1906, fifteen sheets are marked 1913, five 1914, sixty 1920, and 116 bear no year at all – may eventually help to date more precisely some of the poems written on them.

The first six volumes of collected manuscripts, from *Wessex Poems* to *Late Lyrics and Earlier*, were the printers' copy-texts for the corresponding first editions. They are marked with type-setters' names, castings-off and calculations, and even signature letters which can be matched with the first editions. A few of these manuscripts are those which had previously been sent to journals, as is evidenced, for example, in 'The Revisitation', which has not only Hardy's signature at the end, but also contains beneath the revisions the version which had previously appeared in *The Fortnightly Review*. It is remarkable what good condition such sheets are in after having been through the hands of not just one printer but two. *Human Shows* and *Winter Words*, too, may have been set up from their corresponding manuscripts in the bound-up volumes, but the evidence is by no means so clear. Writing to Macmillan on 11 February 1928, Florence Hardy said:

> The volume of poems [*Winter Words*] is being typed, but very slowly as the typist can only come for half every day. I wonder whether it would be a good plan if I were to bring to you the poems just as they are, without any re-arrangement. If I stitch them together it will be more difficult to rearrange them. There are verses pencilled in, and here and there a word altered in pencil. If I were to see you we might decide what to do about these. The first poems and the last few have been arranged, but I am not sure that the ones in the middle of the book were arranged. No doubt there would have been considerable revision.

The collected manuscripts, like the extra manuscripts, fully confirm what Florence Hardy called 'Hardy's artistic inability to rest content with anything that he wrote until he had brought the expression as near to his thought as language would allow'. There is a wide range of revision. Words are crossed through sometimes so heavily that they cannot be read, sometimes so lightly that we can make out what Hardy first wrote, and ponder on the reasons for the alteration. Deletions, additions, substitutions abound, frequently of a punctuation-mark or word, sometimes of a whole line, occasionally of a stanza. I have regarded it as my duty to give the facts, not to interpret them, and to examine the trees with a magnifying glass is not the best way of seeing the forest, but it is clear that the commonest reason for revision is stylistic, and the second commonest the sharpening of meaning. But there are other reasons, such as the removal or insertion of dialect, the need for greater or lesser caution in sexual or biographical references, and Hardy's sensitivity to the comments of reviewers who had criticised words or phrases. The workings are sometimes in pencil, as if Hardy, poring over his manuscripts months, or even years, later could not resist yet another attempt to improve. Unfortunately, many of the pencilled workings have been so well erased that they are unreadable, a matter of particular regret when they are found in the manuscript of a poem as deeply autobiographical as 'The Place on the Map' (263). An example of the interest of such revisions occurs in 'When I Set Out for Lyonnesse' (254). Above lines 2 and 6 of the collected manuscript can still be read in partially erased pencil 'While night was waiting day', a line which it might be argued is more poetic than 'A hundred miles away', but Hardy decided against it.

The reader of the manuscripts is helped by Hardy's neat and clear hand, and there are few difficulties of comprehension. The three most serious arise from his habit of writing certain letters almost identically whether they are upper or lower case, from an occasional confusion between colons and semi-colons, and from the habit of joining together words in such a way that it is not clear whether the joining is intentional or not. Where there is uncertainty, I have normally assumed that the printed version is correct unless there is a clear doubt that it is so. Where there is a little doubt in a reading I have expressed this by means of a question-mark in square brackets. I have regarded it as my duty to give all the uncancelled variants in the manuscripts as fully and precisely as possible. The cancelled material presents more of a problem. There is so much of this in the collected and extra manuscripts that it would be impracticable to present it all, even where it can be deciphered. Here, therefore, personal judgement is necessary, and I have selected those variants which, either for reasons of meaning or style, seem to be of interest or importance. I have assumed that the justification for this book will lie not just in its presentation of what Hardy actually wrote, but also in what it can tell us about Hardy the craftsman.

Another valuable insight is provided by the journal appearances of Hardy's poems. Hardy, as we know from the novels, and more recently from the publication of the first volume of Professor R. L. Purdy and Professor M. Millgate's *The Collected Letters of Thomas Hardy*, was in every way a professional writer, and he did not neglect the opportunity offered by his growing reputation as a poet to place his poems in the leading journals of the time. Journal publication was a useful way of getting his poetry better known, and this was something that Hardy was anxious to do as he regarded himself as more instinctively a poet than a novelist, and the total sales of his poetry in his lifetime were never more than a small part of the sales of his novels. His very first published poem, 'The Fire at Tranter Sweatley's', was printed in *The Gentleman's Magazine* in 1875. In all, just over two hundred poems have been identified as having separate publication in journals, newspapers, private editions, or as contributions to books, before they were printed in the eight books of verse. Some of them had more than one such appearance, and the total number of printings must exceed three hundred. This does not, of course, include the many journal and anthology printings which took place after poems had been published in the eight books, and I have checked these only if there is evidence that Hardy had been textually involved with them. These original printings in journals and the like are another important source of information about Hardy's methods of writing, for many poems were heavily revised before he included them in his own books of verse. This revision may be evidence that some of his writing for journals was done in a hurry, and he was much in demand as a contributor to journals during the poetry-writing period. Certainly, journal publication gave him a further chance of revision, of which he took full advantage. All but a very few of these printings have been checked and their variants recorded. A small number of accompanying typescripts, proofs and off-prints has survived, and wherever possible these have been checked. They have revealed little of interest. One literary curiosity needs to be mentioned here. In 1922, Hardy was asked to make a selection of his poems for a miniature book to be included in the Library of the Royal Dolls' House at Windsor Castle. On checking, I found that, although approved and signed by Hardy, it is written out in a hand not his own, and that the only variants are minor ones of punctuation. Details of such variants as do occur are given by me in the notes identifying the nine poems he chose.

The eight bound-up volumes of manuscripts are neatly balanced by the eight first editions, the basic books of verse, from *Wessex Poems* to *Winter Words*. These and, wherever possible, their first reprints have all been checked and have provided further variants. Hardy's letters to Macmillan frequently refer to corrections. Thus, *Time's Laughingstocks* was published on 3 December 1909, and by the eighteenth of that month Hardy was sending a list of 'such errata as I have discovered' for a reprint which Macmillan were rushing through, and this was followed by yet another correction (in fact, a revision) from him a fortnight later. Occasionally, the collected manuscripts have the first-edition form cancelled, clear evidence that Hardy continued to revise his fair copies after the publication of the first editions. It is worth mentioning, as an indication of how small Hardy's sales of poetry were, that the first printings of the first editions of *Wessex Poems* and *Poems of the Past and the Present* were of a mere 500 copies each (*Tess of the d'Urbervilles* sold 100,000 copies in paperback alone in the year June 1900–June 1901), and even *Winter Words* in 1928 had a first edition of just 5000 copies. The three books which were set up in the United States and had their own first editions there – *Wessex Poems*, *Human Shows* and *Winter Words* – have revealed nothing of textual importance. Professor Purdy in 1954 drew attention to an interesting aspect of the publication of at least one of the first editions. He pointed out that in a review which had appeared in *The Academy* on 23 November 1901 a number of variant readings occurred in the quoted poems, and that this suggested that the reviewer was working from an uncorrected proof copy. The variants found in that review are of a nature which, even allowing for the possibility of transcription errors, make it certain that Professor Purdy's theory is correct, and I have found another review with variant readings which supports his conclusion. There is a need here for further research, but in the meantime we have evidence of some significant revision at proof stage.

Wessex Poems and *Poems of the Past and the Present* were published by Harper, but Macmillan, who had acquired the colonial rights of Hardy's books in 1894, became his main publishers in 1902. In the same year they began the publication of the Uniform Edition of his works in their Three-and-Sixpenny Library series. No doubt for reasons of economy Macmillan published their first editions of Hardy's verse in a format which was identical with that of the Uniform Edition, except for the use of green cloth in place of the Uniform blue. Volumes of verse in the Uniform Edition, then, may be regarded as reprints of the first editions, and it is an interesting insight into Macmillan's publishing methods that after the first-edition printing of *Late Lyrics* in May 1922 there was a reprint in August in green cloth, and one in December in blue cloth. The Uniform Edition is not without textual significance as it provided Hardy with another opportunity for revision. The sales of *Wessex Poems* in the 1898 Harper first edition were so slow that the first reprint is the Macmillan Uniform Edition of 1903, and it was this which provided the first opportunity for correction and revision. It is more difficult to find the early printings in the Uniform Edition than it is to find some of the first editions, but wherever possible I have traced and checked them. The position with the Pocket Edition is very similar. Macmillan began the publication of this in 1906 and, with the same admirable sense of economy, used the plates of the Uniform Edition, which in its turn had used the plates of the Osgood, McIlvaine edition of 1895–7 for the novels, and for *Wessex Poems* and *Poems of the Past and the Present* the Harper plates from the first editions of 1898 and 1901. The Pocket Edition was cheaper than the Uniform Edition, and for at least thirty years, until Macmillan introduced the Cottage Library edition and the Scholar's Library edition in the 1930s, it was the most popular and best-selling of the British editions. But even in this edition the sales of the poetry were never large. Macmillan's records show that between April 1907, when they placed their first printing order for the Pocket Edition of the combined *Wessex Poems and Poems of the Past and the Present*, and July 1921 their total printing order amounted to no more than 11,000 copies. All eight books of verse were published in the Pocket Edition, and I have been able to check most of the first printings. With a few exceptions, which I record, they are identical with their Uniform Edition counterparts. It is worth noting that Macmillan did not embody the Wessex Edition revisions of 1912 in the corresponding volumes in the Pocket Edition until the mid-1920s, even though it was their best-selling edition.

The Wessex Edition provides the single most important revision of the three books of verse which had been published by 1912. *Wessex Poems* was published in one book with *Poems of the Past and the Present* in 1912, *Time's Laughingstocks* (with *The Dynasts*, Part III) in 1913, *Satires of Circumstance* with *Moments of Vision* in one book in 1919, *Late Lyrics and Earlier* (with *The Famous Tragedy of the Queen of Cornwall*) in 1926, and *Human Shows* and

Winter Words in one book in 1931. Hardy revised the early volumes with his usual care, and there are some very interesting variants, a few of which are not found elsewhere, possibly because Hardy had second thoughts about them. I have checked not only all the first printings in this edition, but also the 1920 reprint of *Wessex Poems and Poems of the Past and the Present*, and of *Time's Laughingstocks* in the same year.

What Hardy regarded as the 'de luxe' edition was published in 1919–20. The Mellstock Edition had, in addition to *The Dynasts*, four volumes of verse: *Wessex Poems* and *Poems of the Past and the Present* were in one volume again, as in the Pocket and Wessex Editions, but *Time's Laughingstocks*, *Satires of Circumstance* and *Moments of Vision* had each a volume to itself. It is regrettable that Macmillan never added the remaining three volumes of verse to this limited edition. The pattern of variants in the Mellstock Edition shows that the copy-text was the Wessex Edition, corrected by Hardy to embody revisions he was about to make in the 1920 reprints mentioned above. On 29 January 1920, Hardy wrote to Macmillan:

> In respect of the 7 volumes of verse (31 to 37) in the same edition [i.e., the Mellstock], what do you think about my reading them over? The Clarks are quite excellent printers, but as no human printer, or even one sent from Heaven direct, can be trusted with verse, I don't mind reading them, since, unlike prose, there is so little on each page in poetry that I can soon run through them. On the other hand if the Mellstock edition is one merely for collectors which nobody will read it may not matter. I shall be glad for you to decide.

We know from a further letter to Macmillan, dated 31 January, that it was decided that he should read them:

> As to proofs of the verse-volumes, it is certainly safer that I should read them, and whenever the printers begin to send them . . . I shall be ready for them.

It is clear, therefore, that the proofs of the five books of verse (in four volumes) in the Mellstock Edition were proof-read by Hardy. The amount of revision is small, and one or two variants found only in the Mellstock Edition may be undiscovered printing errors or corrections by Hardy which, through oversight, were not embodied in subsequent editions.

It will be seen that the period 1919–20 was a busy publishing-time for Hardy because it saw not only the publication of the Mellstock Edition, of reprints of the two Wessex Edition volumes containing the first three books of verse, of the Wessex Edition of *Satires of Circumstance and Moments of Vision*, but also, in 1919, the first edition of his *Collected Poems*. Hardy had been thinking for some time of collecting together his poems, and on 22 March 1919 he wrote to Macmillan:

> I also get inquiries for a compact edition of all the poetry only. And I have thought that we might some day carry this out by making a companion volume to the one-volume Dynasts of all the rest of my verse. . . .

Macmillan agreed, and by 15 June he had a proof of the title-page. On 10 October 1919 the *Collected Poems of Thomas Hardy* was published in an edition of 3000 copies. It included all the poems published in the first five books of verse, from *Wessex Poems* to *Moments of Vision*, and it provided Hardy with yet another opportunity for revision, one which went on even while the book was being printed. We know this because an errata-slip was included in some late copies of the first printing, at Hardy's request; and, although in a letter to Macmillan dated 22 November 1919 he refers to 'errata that I and other people have noted in Collected Poems', some of the errata are revisions rather than printing errors. Further editions of *Collected Poems* followed in 1923 (when *Late Lyrics and Earlier*, published in 1922, was added), 1928 (when *Human Shows*, published in 1925, was added), and posthumously in 1930 (when *Winter Words*, published in 1928, was added). Hardy continued to tinker with the text of *Collected Poems* until he died. The changes in text which occur from edition to edition are partly the result of correction necessary because of changes elsewhere. Thus, the note at the end of 'On Stinsford Hill at Midnight' (550) was not present in the first edition of *Late Lyrics* in 1922, or in *Collected Poems* 1923, but Hardy added it to the Wessex Edition when it was published in 1926, and we find it in *Collected Poems* 1928. Other changes in the 1928 edition, which was published two months after Hardy's death, are the result of instructions left by him. The few further changes in the 1930 *Collected Poems* can be traced in part to his work on *Chosen Poems*, the selection of his verse which occupied him during the last few months of his life.

Hardy's first selection of his verse had been published in Macmillan's Golden Treasury series in 1916 with the title *Selected Poems of Thomas Hardy*. It included eighteen poems from *Wessex Poems*, twenty-eight from *Poems of the Past and the Present*, six from *The Dynasts*, twenty-six from *Time's Laughingstocks*, thirty-three from *Satires of Circumstance*, and nine to be published a year later in *Moments of Vision*. Even for this selection he made some revisions. A few of the variants are to be found nowhere else, but most of them were subsequently incorporated in the later Wessex Edition printings and in *Collected Poems*. It was a popular little book – Hardy hoped that it might help to make his poetry better known – and it had been reprinted five times by 1925. In February 1927, Hardy suggested to Macmillan that it should be brought up-to-date by the inclusion of 'a dozen or twenty' poems from his later books. Macmillan agreed, and the enlarged copy of *Selected*

Poems, with some 'corrections', was sent to them on 18 September 1927. On 10 November, only two months before he died, he wrote to Macmillan:

> I am much obliged for the proof of the new edition of 'Selected Poems', and will read them through. . . . I find that some stupid people confuse 'Selected' with 'Collected'. . . . Could this selection be called 'Selections from the Poems of T.H.', 'Select Poems of T.H.' or 'Chosen Poems of T.H.' to make more difference?

Even at the age of eighty-seven Hardy had checked the proofs of a 272-page book within a week. He was always given to understatement, and the inclusion of 'a dozen or twenty' poems meant the omission of eight poems he had included in *Selected Poems*, and the inclusion of a further three poems from his first four books of verse together with eleven from *Moments of Vision*, fifteen from *Late Lyrics*, seventeen from *Human Shows*, two from *The Famous Tragedy of the Queen of Cornwall*, and a further poem from *The Dynasts*. The resulting book, *Chosen Poems*, may be regarded as his last thought on the text of the 161 poems it contains. It tells us, for example, that his last thought on whether, in 'In Time of "The Breaking of Nations"' (500), war's annals should 'fade' or 'cloud' into night was 'cloud'. *Selected Poems* and *Chosen Poems*, which was not published until 1929 and seems, from the fact that it is very difficult to find, to have had very small sales, are two of Hardy's most interesting books of verse, and it is surprising that there has been so little examination of the criteria which Hardy used in making the selections and in arranging them. It is even more surprising that Macmillan, having been provided by Hardy in *Chosen Poems* with such an excellent selection of his verse, replaced it in 1940 with a markedly inferior selection by G. M. Young.

The text which is used in this Variorum Edition is based upon that of *Collected Poems* 1928 and 1930. These two texts are almost identical except for (1) the inclusion in 1930 of a few revisions found in *Chosen Poems*, (2) a small number of corrections in 1930 of obvious errors in 1928, and (3) the correction of print defects. From the beginning *Collected Poems* had suffered from defective printing, and as early 1923 commas were losing their tails and full stops disappearing. The 1930 edition was reprinted so many times from the original 1919, 1923, 1928 and 1930 plates that by 1975 it was in a state best described as 'dirty'. When in that year I was asked to edit a *Complete Poems*, my first task was to get back to the 1928 and 1930 texts and see to what extent they themselves were corrupt. In this I was helped, of course, by the fact that I had been working on a variorum edition for several years. I hesitate to describe the text of *Complete Poems* as a definitive text as I have yet to find a satisfactory definition of 'definitive'. Hardy's copy of the 1923 *Collected*

Poems in the Dorset County Museum contains more than fifty corrections in his hand. Some of these have been embodied in the 1928 edition, but others have been passed over and we may never know whether this was because Hardy had second thoughts or because they were overlooked. A good many other problems of interpretation remain. As the word 'terrestrial' in the poem 'Friends Beyond' (36) was printed as 'terrestial' throughout the four editions of *Collected Poems* without the mistake being noticed, other mistakes of a more serious nature may also have gone unnoticed. For example, I have retained 'brood' in the last line of 'The Pity of It' (498) as this is the reading throughout *Collected Poems*, but it could be an undiscovered misreading of 'breed' which is found in all editions before *Collected Poems*. And must all the variants found in the Wessex and Mellstock Editions but not in *Collected Poems* be regarded as of inferior authority? With problems such as these I am content to present in this Variorum Edition all the information available to me and leave the reader to establish his own definitive text.

Hardy's manuscript revisions in his own copy of the 1923 *Collected Poems*, and his revisions in his copies of *Selected Poems* 1916 and 1917, provide yet another proof, if any were wanted, of his painstaking care for his texts. This care extended to such matters as the insertion and removal of hyphens, the number of stops following a word, and slight adjustments to indentation. In 'A Broken Appointment' (99), as it appeared in *Selected Poems*, he asks that the first and last lines of each stanza should be moved one em left when it is reprinted in *Chosen Poems*, thus confirming his strong visual sense of the poem on the page. His care for the minutiæ of expression is all the more remarkable when it is remembered that the revisions in his 1923 *Collected Poems* were made by a man in his eighties. From this, and from all that has been said earlier, it will be realised that the amount of revision and the number and variety of editions make the textual situation both complex and interesting. This Variorum Edition will have fulfilled its purpose if it leads to further research and an increased understanding of Hardy's writing.

It is necessary to mention here that the economics of book production have led to the use of the *Complete Poems* plates (very slightly corrected and revised for the 1978 reprint) for the basic text used by me. There was no idea that this would happen when *Complete Poems* was published in 1976, and it was decided then to follow the Macmillan house style for reported speech and the capitalisation of titles. Hardy used double quotes for direct speech, and single quotes for speech within speech. *Complete Poems* reversed this pattern. To have two conflicting systems of quotes would have been so confusing that I had to decide that the only possible solution was to change all the quotes to conform with modern practice, and inform the reader that this had happened. The capitalisation issue has been less worrying. I do not myself attach much importance to the capitalisation of Hardy's titles. He seems to have followed the practice of his own time when writing them out in his manuscripts, and discrepancies in capitalisation between the tables of contents and the writing of the titles later in the books seems to show that he himself was not particularly concerned about it. He knew, too, that in almost all the printed editions published in his lifetime every letter of the title would be in capitals. In *Complete Poems* Macmillan followed the modern custom of capitalisation, which is close to Hardy's own, and used capitals only for the initial letters of some of the words in the title. However, in the interests of recording as factually and completely as possible, I have given details of Hardy's capitalisation wherever it differs. Hardy, like all writers, was to some extent in the hands of his printers, and as it is clear that the presentation of the title in the journal appearances of his poems was governed by the practices of the individual journal I have standardised all journal titles of poems. There is some evidence that Hardy saw an introductory dash, or quotes, at the beginning of the line as being outside normal indentation, but that his printers ignored this, and there is often ambiguity as to whether a dash should be inside or outside quotes because of Hardy's habit of sometimes writing the dash immediately below the quotes. I have not recorded American spellings, and Hardy's own spelling idiosyncrasies have been recorded only where it seemed possible that pronunciation might be affected. Thus, I have recorded 'carolings' and 'carollings', but not 'grey' and 'gray'. Obvious printing errors, such as the omission of quotes, and inconsistencies of punctuation, such as the occasional putting of a punctuation-mark outside rather than inside quotes, have been silently passed over. Finally, it must be mentioned that Hardy habitually used the ampersand, and that this has been spelled out in this edition.

Perhaps, after a labour of so many years, I may be allowed to end on a personal note. A variorum edition of the poems of a writer as prolific and assiduous as Hardy is a formidable task, both mentally and physically demanding. In spite of the invaluable help of others, it is essentially a lonely occupation, one in which days of work may reveal not one variant, and one in which the editor has few precedents and little experience. However, as I commit this book to posterity as my tribute, fifty years after his death, to Hardy the Poet, I am deeply aware that I have had the privilege of being associated with a writer who is truly great. My admiration for his creative genius, his integrity, the quality of his feeling, and the professionalism of his approach to his writing has grown with the years and made the labour eminently worthwhile. For me he has triumphantly passed Dr Johnson's test of 'length of duration and continuance of esteem'.

15 April 1978 JAMES GIBSON

Acknowledgements

MY WORK has brought me in touch with very many people and institutions, and I am glad to have this opportunity of expressing my gratitude for the help, the kindness and the courtesy which I have received from almost everyone. I wish to make special mention of the untiring efficiency of the librarians and curators, both at home and in the United States, whom I have visited or with whom I have been in correspondence. Nothing has been too much trouble for them, and I finish my work with a deep sense of admiration for the part they play in the advancement of knowledge.

A number of personal acknowledgements are due: to Prof. Harold Brooks for his scholarly advice on many points; to Prof. Richard Purdy who, although he felt unable to let me see his Hardy poetry manuscripts, has helped me in many other ways; to Mr Roger Peers and the staff of the Dorset County Museum for being so helpful and friendly throughout my frequent visits to them; to Dr Elizabeth de Groot and Mr and Mrs J. Skilling for assistance in checking some individual manuscripts; and to Miss Caroline Hobhouse, Mr Richard Garnett and Mr Edward Leeson of my publishers, whose enthusiasm, energy and vision have made this project possible. And there are others who have helped me in a variety of ways, to whom I would express my appreciation: Prof. J. A. W. Bennett, Mr Edward Black, Prof. Robert Cathcart, Miss Ellen S. Dunlap, Miss Phyllis M. Giles, Dr Robert Gittings, Miss Evelyn Hardy, Prof. Samuel Hynes, Miss K. McIntosh, Mrs Vera Jesty, Mr W. M. King, Mrs Sally Leach, Prof. Tetsuwo Maekawa, Mrs June Moll, Prof. William W. Morgan, Julian and Edith Nangle, Mr V. Rigby, Miss Andrea Rose, Mrs Lola L. Szladits, Miss Marjorie G. Wynne and the Rev. John Yates. I am grateful, too, for the support of the Governors of Christ Church College, who allowed me a sabbatical year, the Master and Fellows of Corpus Christi College, Cambridge, who generously awarded me a Fellow-Commonership, and the Central Research Fund of the University of London.

My acknowledgements for permission to reproduce copyright material are due to the Trustees of the Hardy Estate; Aberdeen University Library; the Birmingham Museums and Art Gallery; the Bodleian Library, Oxford; the Bancroft Library of the University of California at Berkeley; Colby College Library (Special Collections); the Dorset County Museum; the

Syndics of the Fitzwilliam Museum, Cambridge; the Huntington Library, San Marino, California; the Curator of the Keats Memorial House; The Library of Congress (Halsted B. Vander Poel Collection, Manuscript Division); the Master and Fellows of Magdalene College, Cambridge; the New York Public Library (Henry W. and Albert A. Berg Collection, Astor, Lenox and Tilden Foundation); the Pierpont Morgan Library; the Provost and Scholars of The Queen's College, Oxford; the Humanities Research Center of the University of Texas at Austin; the Librarian of the London Borough of Wandsworth; the Beinecke Rare Book and Manuscript Library of Yale University; and the Provost and Fellows of King's College, Cambridge.

Notes for Users of the Variorum

1. There are three kinds of abbreviation:

   (*a*) General to the volume. These are:

   SP = *Selected Poems of Thomas Hardy* 1916
   CP1 = *Collected Poems of Thomas Hardy* 1919
   CP2 = *Collected Poems of Thomas Hardy* 1923
   CP3 = *Collected Poems of Thomas Hardy* 1928
   CP4 = *Collected Poems of Thomas Hardy* 1930
   CP = Found in CP1 – 4
   CHP = *Chosen Poems of Thomas Hardy* 1929

   (*b*) Specific to each of the eight books of verse. Details of these abbreviations will be found as follows:

   (*c*) Specific to a poem. These will be found, where they occur, alongside the poem.

Note. For reasons of economy and clarity 'MS' has been used throughout in preference to the conventional 'MS.'.

2. Where it is necessary to indicate indentation the method used is to number each line of indentation from the left, and then to give the line numbers within each line of indentation. Thus, if it were necessary to give the indentation of poem 18, it would appear as:

1 = ll. 1, 3, 5–8	}	and so throughout
2 = ll. 2, 4, 9		

3. Square brackets in quotes are Hardy's; without quotes the editor's.

THE VARIORUM EDITION OF THE COMPLETE POEMS OF THOMAS HARDY

Domicilium

[T. Hardy's earliest known production in verse] (original written between 1857 and [illegible] this being a copy some years later.)

It faces west, and round the back and sides
High beeches, bending, hang a veil of boughs
And sweep against the roof. Wild honeysucks
Climb on the walls, and seem to sprout a wish
(If we may fancy wish of trees and plants)
To overtop the appletrees hard by.

Red roses, lilacs, variegated box
Are there in plenty, and such hardy flowers
As flourish best untrained. Adjoining these
Are herbs and esculents; and farther still
A field; then cottages with trees, and last
The distant hills and sky.

Behind, the scene is wilder. Heath and furze
Are everything that seems to grow and thrive
Upon the uneven ground. A stunted thorn
Stands here and there indeed; and from a pit
An oak uprises, springing from a seed
Dropped by some bird a hundred years ago.

In days by-gone —
Long gone — my father's mother who is now
Blest with the blest, would take me out to walk.
At such a time I once inquired of her
How looked the spot when first she settled here.
The answer I remember. "Fifty years
Have passed since then, my child, and change has marked
The face of all things. Yonder garden plots
And orchards were uncultivated slopes
O'ergrown with bramble bushes, furze, and thorn:
The road a narrow path shut in by ferns,
Which, almost trees, obscured the passer by.
Our house stood quite alone, and those tall firs
And beeches were not planted. Snakes and efts
Swarmed in the summer days, and nightly bats
Would fly about our bedrooms. Heathcroppers
Lived on the hills, and were our only friends;
So wild it was when first we settled here."

T. H.

1 *Domicilium*

It faces west, and round the back and sides
High beeches, bending, hang a veil of boughs,
And sweep against the roof. Wild honeysucks
Climb on the walls, and seem to sprout a wish
(If we may fancy wish of trees and plants)
To overtop the apple-trees hard by.

Red roses, lilacs, variegated box
Are there in plenty, and such hardy flowers
As flourish best untrained. Adjoining these
Are herbs and esculents; and farther still
A field; then cottages with trees, and last
The distant hills and sky.

Behind, the scene is wilder. Heath and furze
Are everything that seems to grow and thrive
Upon the uneven ground. A stunted thorn
Stands here and there, indeed; and from a pit
An oak uprises, springing from a seed
Dropped by some bird a hundred years ago.

In days bygone –
Long gone – my father's mother, who is now
Blest with the blest, would take me out to walk.
At such a time I once inquired of her
How looked the spot when first she settled here.
The answer I remember. 'Fifty years
Have passed since then, my child, and change has marked
The face of all things. Yonder garden-plots
And orchards were uncultivated slopes
O'ergrown with bramble bushes, furze and thorn:
That road a narrow path shut in by ferns,
Which, almost trees, obscured the passer-by.

Text used here is from *The Early Life of Thomas Hardy* (London, 1928), pp. 4–5 = EL

MANUSCRIPT: In the Dorset County Museum = MS

TYPESCRIPT, ETC.:
It has not been possible to trace the typescript and proof once in the possession of Sir Sydney Cockerell

OTHER PRINTINGS: Privately by Clement Shorter (1916) = CS, and by Florence Hardy (1918) = FH

MS after title: [T. Hardy's [first *del*] earliest known production in verse] (original written between 1857 and 1860 this being a copy some years later.)

CS below title: Thomas Hardy's earliest known production in verse. (Written between 1857 and 1860)

Domicilium
2 boughs,] boughs MS
6 apple-trees] appletrees MS, CS
7 variegated] varigated MS, CS, FH. All add '[sic]'
12–13 No stanza break in MS, CS
13 MS, CS, FH have this line indented right
16 there,] there MS, CS
18–19 No stanza break in MS: page turn in FH
19 bygone] by-gone MS
20 mother,] mother MS
26 garden-plots] garden plots MS, CS
28 furze] furze, MS, FH
29 That] The MS
30 passer-by] passer by MS, CS
30–1 Stanza break in EL, FH: no break in MS: page turn in CS

'Our house stood quite alone, and those tall firs
And beeches were not planted. Snakes and efts
Swarmed in the summer days, and nightly bats
Would fly about our bedrooms. Heathcroppers
Lived on the hills, and were our only friends;
So wild it was when first we settled here.'

Domicilium
31 'Our] Our MS, CS, FH
36 here.'] here. MS
CS adds at end: (Not to be published.)

WESSEX POEMS AND OTHER VERSES

Abbreviations Specific to 'Wessex Poems'

MS = The bound-up volume of manuscripts in the Birmingham City Museum and Art Gallery

WP1 = *Wessex Poems and Other Verses* (London, 1898) and *Wessex Poems and Other Verses* (New York, 1899). Where New York differs from London, WPA is used to identify the New York variant

WP2 = *Wessex Poems and Other Verses* (London, 1903)

WP = Found in both WP1 and WP2

PE = Pocket Edition 1907

UE = Uniform Edition 1911

PUE = Found in both PE and UE

WE1 = Wessex Edition 1912

WE2 = Wessex Edition 1920

WE = Found in both WE1 and WE2

ME = Mellstock Edition 1920

PREFACE

Of the miscellaneous collection of verse that follows, only four pieces have been published, though many were written long ago, and others partly written. In some few cases the verses were turned into prose and printed as such, it having been unanticipated at that time that they might see the light.

Whenever an ancient and legitimate word of the district, for which there was no equivalent in received English, suggested itself as the most natural, nearest, and often only expression of a thought, it has been made use of, on what seemed good grounds.

The pieces are in a large degree dramatic or personative in conception; and this even where they are not obviously so.

The dates attached to some of the poems do not apply to the rough sketches given in illustration,[1] which have been recently made, and, as may be surmised, are inserted for personal and local reasons rather than for their intrinsic qualities.

September 1898 T.H.

[1] The early editions were illustrated by the writer.

Preface
4 such,] such in a novel, WE, ME
4 having . . . unanticipated] it not having been anticipated MS, WE, ME
5 light.] light in their original shape. WE, ME
6 Whenever] Here and there, when WE, ME
6 word . . . district,] word, MS
6 of] still current in WE, ME
7 no equivalent] no close equivalent WE, ME
7–8 itself . . . thought,] itself, WE, ME
9 of . . . grounds.] of. MS
11–12 and . . . The dates] and the dates WE, ME
13 illustration,[1]] illustration, MS, WP, PUE
13–15 made, . . . qualities.] made. MS
T.H.] Not in WE, ME
Footnote not in MS, WP, PUE

2 *The Temporary the All*

(*Sapphics*)

CHANGE and chancefulness in my flowering youthtime,
Set me sun by sun near to one unchosen;
Wrought us fellowlike, and despite divergence,
        Fused us in friendship.

'Cherish him can I while the true one forthcome –
Come the rich fulfiller of my prevision;
Life is roomy yet, and the odds unbounded.'
        So self-communed I.

'Thwart my wistful way did a damsel saunter,
Fair, albeit unformed to be all-eclipsing;
'Maiden meet,' held I, 'till arise my forefelt
        Wonder of women.'

Long a visioned hermitage deep desiring,
Tenements uncouth I was fain to house in:
'Let such lodging be for a breath-while,' thought I,
        'Soon a more seemly.

'Then high handiwork will I make my life-deed,
Truth and Light outshow; but the ripe time pending,
Intermissive aim at the thing sufficeth.'
        Thus I. . . . But lo, me!

Mistress, friend, place, aims to be bettered straightway,
Bettered not has Fate or my hand's achievement;
Sole the showance those of my onward earth-track –
        Never transcended!

EXTRA PRINTINGS:
(1) *Selected Poems of Thomas Hardy* (London, 1916), pp. 45–6 = SP
(2) *Chosen Poems of Thomas Hardy* (London, 1929), pp. 44–5 = CHP

TITLE: (*Sapphics*) Not in MS, WP, PUE, WE1, CP1

Note This was one of nine poems chosen by Hardy For the Library of the Royal Dolls' House at Windsor Castle. The copy there has 'youthtime' (l. 1), 'forth-come' (l. 5), 'Thwart' (l. 9), 'in;' (l. 14), 'Then,' (l. 17) and 'showings' (l. 23)

The Temporary the All
1 flowering] bloothing MS
1 youthtime,] youthtime MS, WE, SP, ME, CHP
3 fellowlike] fellowly MS, WP: fellow-like PUE
3 divergence,] misfitness MS: divergence CP1, 2
4] Friends interknit us. MS: Friends interblent us. WP: Friends interlinked us. PUE
9 'Thwart] Thwart MS, WP, PUE, WE, SP, ME, CP1, 2
10] Fair not fairest, good not best of her feather; MS, WP1
10 albeit] the while WP2, PUE
14] Tenement uncouth did I fain abide in; MS
14 in:] in; MS, WP, PUE, WE, SP, ME, CP1–3
15 lodging] lodgment MS
17 Then] Then, WP, PUE, WE, SP, ME, CP1, 2
17 high handiwork] achievement large MS
18 pending,] pending MS
20 I. . . .] I . . . WP, PUE, WE, SP, ME
20 lo, me!] woe me, MS
21 place] home MS
21 straightway] forthwith MS
22 has . . . achievement] have I by the full in each kind MS
22 achievement] achieving WP, PUE
23] They as tokens sole of my sorry earth-way MS
23 showance] showings WE1, SP, CP1, 3
23 earth-track] earthtrack CP1, 2
24] Stand in their scantness! MS
[N.B. Hardy's copy of SP (1917) in DCM corrects 'Thwart' to ' 'Thwart' (l. 9), 'Then,' to 'Then' (l. 17) and 'showings' to 'showance' (l. 23)]

EXTRA PRINTINGS:
(1) *Selected Poems*, pp. 82–3
(2) *Chosen Poems*, pp. 77–8

3 Amabel

I MARKED her ruined hues,
Her custom-straitened views,
And asked, 'Can there indwell
My Amabel?'

I looked upon her gown,
Once rose, now earthen brown;
The change was like the knell
Of Amabel.

Her step's mechanic ways
Had lost the life of May's;
Her laugh, once sweet in swell,
Spoilt Amabel.

I mused: 'Who sings the strain
I sang ere warmth did wane?
Who thinks its numbers spell
His Amabel?' –

Knowing that, though Love cease,
Love's race shows no decrease;
All find in dorp or dell
An Amabel.

– I felt that I could creep
To some housetop, and weep
That Time the tyrant fell
Ruled Amabel!

I said (the while I sighed
That love like ours had died),
'Fond things I'll no more tell
To Amabel,

Amabel
2] Her faded iris=blues, MS
18 no decrease] undecrease MS, WP, PUE
22 housetop,] housetop SP
22 weep] weep, WP, PUE, WE, ME
26 died),] died) MS
27 Fond] Sweet MS

'But leave her to her fate,
And fling across the gate,
"Till the Last Trump, farewell,
O Amabel!" '

1865

4 *Hap*

IF but some vengeful god would call to me
From up the sky, and laugh: 'Thou suffering thing,
Know that thy sorrow is my ecstasy,
That thy love's loss is my hate's profiting!'

Then would I bear it, clench myself, and die,
Steeled by the sense of ire unmerited;
Half-eased in that a Powerfuller than I
Had willed and meted me the tears I shed.

But not so. How arrives it joy lies slain,
And why unblooms the best hope ever sown?
– Crass Casualty obstructs the sun and rain,
And dicing Time for gladness casts a moan. . . .
These purblind Doomsters had as readily strown
Blisses about my pilgrimage as pain.

1866

EXTRA PRINTING:
Chosen Poems, p. 32

TITLE:
Chance MS

INDENTATION:
1 = ll. 1, 3 } and so throughout
2 = ll. 2, 4 } WPA

5 *In Vision I Roamed*

To ——

IN vision I roamed the flashing Firmament,
So fierce in blazon that the Night waxed wan,
As though with awe at orbs of such ostént;
And as I thought my spirit ranged on and on

TITLE:
'In vision I roamed' MS
To ——] Not in MS

INDENTATION:
1 = ll. 1, 3 } and so throughout
2 = ll. 2, 4 } WPA

Amabel
30 fling] cry MS
31 farewell,] farewell MS
1865] 1866 MS
1865/16 Westbourne Park Villas WE, ME
1866/16 Westbourne Park Villas SP

Hap
5 bear it,] bear, and MS, WP, PUE
6 unmerited;] unmerited, MS
7 Half-eased in] Half-eased, too, MS, WP1
12 gladness] laughter MS
12 moan. . . .] moan. . . . . MS
14 pain.] pain! MS
1866] WE, ME add: W.P.V.

In Vision I Roamed
2 wan,] wan MS
3 awe at orbs] an awed sense MS, WP, PUE
3 ostént] ostent MS, WP, PUE, WE, ME
4–5 Stanza break in all editions

In footless traverse through ghast heights of sky,
To the last chambers of the monstrous Dome,
Where stars the brightest here are lost to the eye:
Then, any spot on our own Earth seemed Home!

And the sick grief that you were far away
Grew pleasant thankfulness that you were near,
Who might have been, set on some foreign Sphere,
Less than a Want to me, as day by day
I lived unware, uncaring all that lay
Locked in that Universe taciturn and drear.

1866

TITLE:
Nature's Indifference Not in MS, WP, PUE:
WP, PUE have below title:
TO ——

INDENTATION:
1 = ll. 1, 4, 5, 8, 9, 11, 14
2 = ll. 2, 3, 6, 7, 10, 12, 13 WPA

6 At a Bridal

Nature's Indifference

WHEN you paced forth, to await maternity,
A dream of other offspring held my mind,
Compounded of us twain as Love designed;
Rare forms, that corporate now will never be!

Should I, too, wed as slave to Mode's decree,
And each thus found apart, of false desire,
A stolid line, whom no high aims will fire
As had fired ours could ever have mingled we;

And, grieved that lives so matched should miscompose,
Each mourn the double waste; and question dare
To the Great Dame whence incarnation flows,
Why those high-purposed children never were:
What will she answer? That she does not care
If the race all such sovereign types unknows.

1866

In Vision I Roamed
5 sky,] sky MS
6 Dome] dome MS
7 are . . . eye] to darkness die MS, WP, PUE
11 foreign Sphere] outstep sphere MS, WP, PUE
12 me,] me MS
14 taciturn and] trackless, distant, WE, ME

At a Bridal
1 await] wait MS, WP, PUE
8 we;] we, MS
11 flows,] flows MS
14] If all such aimed ideals have such a close. MS
1866] ME, WE2 add: 8 Adelphi Terrace.

7 *Postponement*

SNOW-BOUND in woodland, a mournful word,
Dropt now and then from the bill of a bird,
Reached me on wind-wafts; and thus I heard,
Wearily waiting: –

'I planned her a nest in a leafless tree,
But the passers eyed and twitted me,
And said: "How reckless a bird is he,
Cheerily mating!"

'Fear-filled, I stayed me till summer-tide,
In lewth of leaves to throne her bride;
But alas! her love for me waned and died,
Wearily waiting.

'Ah, had I been like some I see,
Born to an evergreen nesting-tree,
None had eyed and twitted me,
Cheerily mating!'

1866

8 *A Confession to a Friend in Trouble*

TITLE:
To a Friend in trouble.
(A confession of selfishness)
MS title *before revision*

INDENTATION:
1 = ll. 1, 3, 5, 8
2 = ll. 2, 4, 6, 7, 9–14 WPA

YOUR troubles shrink not, though I feel them less
Here, far away, than when I tarried near;
I even smile old smiles – with listlessness –
Yet smiles they are, not ghastly mockeries mere.

A thought too strange to house within my brain
Haunting its outer precincts I discern:
– That I will not show zeal again to learn
Your griefs, and, sharing them, renew my pain. . . .

Postponement
3 on . . . thus] from windward; and this MS
8 Cheerily] Dreaming of MS
9 Fear-filled . . . till] Stricken, I stayed till the MS
10 throne] house MS
11 died,] died WE, ME
16 Cheerily] Dreaming of MS

A Confession to a Friend in Trouble
2 tarried] lingered MS
6 precincts] chambers MS
8 *pain. . . .*] pain. . . . . MS
8–9 Stanza break in all editions

It goes, like murky bird or buccaneer
That shapes its lawless figure on the main,
And staunchness tends to banish utterly
The unseemly instinct that had lodgment here;
Yet, comrade old, can bitterer knowledge be
Than that, though banned, such instinct was in me!

1866

EXTRA PRINTINGS:
(1) *Selected Poems*, p. 139
(2) *Chosen Poems*, p. 170

9 *Neutral Tones*

WE stood by a pond that winter day,
And the sun was white, as though chidden of God,
And a few leaves lay on the starving sod;
– They had fallen from an ash, and were gray.

Your eyes on me were as eyes that rove
Over tedious riddles of years ago;
And some words played between us to and fro
On which lost the more by our love.

The smile on your mouth was the deadest thing
Alive enough to have strength to die;
And a grin of bitterness swept thereby
Like an ominous bird a-wing. . . .

Since then, keen lessons that love deceives,
And wrings with wrong, have shaped to me
Your face, and the God-curst sun, and a tree,
And a pond edged with grayish leaves.

1867

She at His Funeral

EXTRA PRINTINGS:
(1) *Selected Poems*, p. 53
(2) *Chosen Poems*, p. 52

TITLE:
In all editions before CP3, except SP, title appeared as:

SHE
AT HIS FUNERAL

MS has: She At his Funeral
SP has: AT HIS FUNERAL

INDENTATION:
1 = ll. 1, 3, 5, 7
2 = ll. 2, 4, 6, 8 WPA

10 *She at His Funeral*

THEY bear him to his resting-place –
In slow procession sweeping by;
I follow at a stranger's space;
His kindred they, his sweetheart I.

A Confession to a Friend in Trouble
11] And each new impulse tends to make outflee MS, WP, PUE, CP1
12 here;] here: MS
13 Yet,] Yet MS
1866] WE, ME add: W.P.V.

Neutral Tones
1 day,] day MS
3 starving] withered MS
3 sod;] sod, WP, PUE, WE, SP, ME
6 of] solved MS, WP, PUE, WE, SP, ME, CP1
7 And some] And WE, SP, ME
7 fro] fro – MS. WP, PUE, WE, SP, ME
8 lost the more] was more wrecked MS *del*
12 a-wing. . . .] a-wing. . . . . . . MS
16 pond] pond, MS
1867] WE, ME add: W.P.V.
SP adds: Westbourne Park Villas

She at His Funeral
4–5 No stanza break

Unchanged my gown of garish dye,
Though sable-sad is their attire;
But they stand round with griefless eye,
Whilst my regret consumes like fire!

187–

11 *Her Initials*

EXTRA PRINTINGS:
(1) *Selected Poems*, p. 30
(2) *Chosen Poems*, p. 30

INDENTATION:
1 = ll. 1, 3, 5, 7
2 = ll. 2, 4, 6, 8 WPA

UPON a poet's page I wrote
Of old two letters of her name;
Part seemed she of the effulgent thought
Whence that high singer's rapture came.
– When now I turn the leaf the same
Immortal light illumes the lay,
But from the letters of her name
The radiance has waned away!

1869

12 *Her Dilemma*

(*In —— Church*)

INDENTATION:
1 = ll. 1, 3 } and so throughout
2 = ll. 2, 4 } WPA

THE two were silent in a sunless church,
Whose mildewed walls, uneven paving-stones,
And wasted carvings passed antique research;
And nothing broke the clock's dull monotones.

Leaning against a wormy poppy-head,
So wan and worn that he could scarcely stand,
– For he was soon to die, – he softly said,
'Tell me you love me!' – holding long her hand.

She would have given a world to breathe 'yes' truly,
So much his life seemed hanging on her mind,
And hence she lied, her heart persuaded throughly
'Twas worth her soul to be a moment kind.

She at His Funeral
8 fire!] fire. MS

Her Initials
2 two letters] the initials MS
2 name;] name, MS
3] For she seemed woven of the thought MS
4–5 Stanza break in WE, SP, ME
6 lay,] lay WPA
7 letters of her] margin-written MS
8 waned] died MS, WP, PUE
8 away!] away. MS, WPA

Her Dilemma
3 carvings] carvings, MS
5 poppy-head] poppyhead MS
7 die,] die MS
8 long] hard MS, WP, PUE
9 yes] Yes MS
11 throughly] throughly, WP1
12–13 Stanza break in all editions

But the sad need thereof, his nearing death,
So mocked humanity that she shamed to prize
A world conditioned thus, or care for breath
Where Nature such dilemmas could devise.

1866

INDENTATION:
1 = ll. 1, 3 } and so throughout
2 = ll. 2, 4 } WPA

13 *Revulsion*

THOUGH I waste watches framing words to fetter
Some unknown spirit to mine in clasp and kiss,
Out of the night there looms a sense 'twere better
To fail obtaining whom one fails to miss.

For winning love we win the risk of losing,
And losing love is as one's life were riven;
It cuts like contumely and keen ill-using
To cede what was superfluously given.

Let me then never feel the fateful thrilling
That devastates the love-worn wooer's frame,
The hot ado of fevered hopes, the chilling
That agonizes disappointed aim!
So may I live no junctive law fulfilling,
And my heart's table bear no woman's name.

1866

TITLE:
She, to him I MS

INDENTATION:
1 = ll. 1, 3 } and so throughout
2 = ll. 2, 4 } WPA

14 *She, to Him I*

WHEN you shall see me in the toils of Time,
My lauded beauties carried off from me,
My eyes no longer stars as in their prime,
My name forgot of Maiden Fair and Free;

When, in your being, heart concedes to mind,
And judgment, though you scarce its process know,
Recalls the excellencies I once enshrined,
And you are irked that they have withered so:

Her Dilemma
16 Nature] nature MS
Note Before revision MS had 'We' for 'The' (l. 1), 'my' for 'her' (ll. 8, 10, 11, 12), 'I' for 'She' (l. 9), and 'I' for 'she' (ll. 11, 14).

Revulsion
2 unknown . . . mine] spirit to mine own MS, WP, PUE
3 night] Night MS
8 superfluously] superfluous when WE, ME
9 never feel] feel no more MS, WP, PUE
13 fulfilling,] fulfilling MS
1866] 186–/16 Westbourne Park Villas. WE, ME

She, to Him I
1 in the toils] lined by tool MS, WP1
5] When alienation comes of heart and mind, MS
5 When,] When WP, PUE
5 being,] being WP, PUE
8–9 Stanza break in all editions

Remembering mine the loss is, not the blame,
That Sportsman Time but rears his brood to kill,
Knowing me in my soul the very same –
One who would die to spare you touch of ill! –
Will you not grant to old affection's claim
The hand of friendship down Life's sunless hill?

1866

15 *She, to Him* II

EXTRA PRINTINGS:
(1) *Selected Poems*, p. 140
(2) *Chosen Poems*, p. 171

TITLE:
She, to him II MS
To Him SP, CHP
II] Not in SP, CHP

INDENTATION:
1 = ll. 1, 3 } and so throughout
2 = ll. 2, 4 } WPA

PERHAPS, long hence, when I have passed away,
Some other's feature, accent, thought like mine,
Will carry you back to what I used to say,
And bring some memory of your love's decline.

Then you may pause awhile and think, 'Poor jade!'
And yield a sigh to me – as ample due,
Not as the tittle of a debt unpaid
To one who could resign her all to you –

And thus reflecting, you will never see
That your thin thought, in two small words conveyed,
Was no such fleeting phantom-thought to me,
But the Whole Life wherein my part was played;
And you amid its fitful masquerade
A Thought – as I in your life seem to be!

1866

16 *She, to Him* III

TITLE:
She, to him III MS

INDENTATION:
1 = ll. 1, 3, 5, 7, 9, 11, 13, 14
2 = ll. 2, 4, 6, 8, 10, 12 WPA

I WILL be faithful to thee; aye, I will!
And Death shall choose me with a wondering eye
That he did not discern and domicile
One his by right ever since that last Good-bye!

She, to Him I
9 mine . . . is,] that with me lies MS, WP, PUE
11 soul] heart MS
12 ill! –] ill; MS

She, to Him II
1 Perhaps,] Perhaps MS
5 awhile] awhile, MS
5 jade] maid MS
6 ample due] gift benign MS, WP1
8 resign . . . you] to you her all resign MS, WP1
14 your . . . be!] yours but seem to be. MS, WP, PUE, WE, SP, ME
Below 1866 in MS: Prosed in 'Desperate Remedies'.
SP adds: Westbourne Park Villas.

She, to Him III
1 will!] will, MS
3 domicile] domicil WE, ME
4 ever since] e'ersince MS
4–5 Stanza break in all editions

I have no care for friends, or kin, or prime
Of manhood who deal gently with me here;
Amid the happy people of my time
Who work their love's fulfilment, I appear

Numb as a vane that cankers on its point,
True to the wind that kissed ere canker came:
Despised by souls of Now, who would disjoint
The mind from memory, making Life all aim,

My old dexterities in witchery gone,
And nothing left for Love to look upon.

1866

TITLE:
She; to him MS

INDENTATION:
1 = ll. 1, 3 ⎫ and so throughout
2 = ll. 2, 4 ⎭ WPA

17 *She, to Him* IV

THIS love puts all humanity from me;
I can but maledict her, pray her dead,
For giving love and getting love of thee –
Feeding a heart that else mine own had fed!

How much I love I know not, life not known,
Save as one unit I would add love by;
But this I know, my being is but thine own –
Fused from its separateness by ecstasy.

And thus I grasp thy amplitudes, of her
Ungrasped, though helped by nigh-regarding eyes;
Canst thou then hate me as an envier
Who see unrecked what I so dearly prize?
Believe me, Lost One, Love is lovelier
The more it shapes its moan in selfish-wise.

1866

She, to Him III
10 came:] came; MS, WP, PUE, WE, ME
12 making] and make MS, WP, PUE
13 in witchery] of hue quite MS, WP, PUE
13 gone,] gone MS

She, to Him IV
2 dead,] dead MS
3 giving love] giving love, MS
6 one] some MS, WP, PUE, WE, ME
1866] WE, ME add: W.P.V.

18 Ditty

(E.L.G.)

BENEATH a knap where flown
Nestlings play,
Within walls of weathered stone,
Far away
From the files of formal houses,
By the bough the firstling browses,
Lives a Sweet: no merchants meet,
No man barters, no man sells
Where she dwells.

Upon that fabric fair
'Here is she!'
Seems written everywhere
Unto me.
But to friends and nodding neighbours,
Fellow-wights in lot and labours,
Who descry the times as I,
No such lucid legend tells
Where she dwells.

Should I lapse to what I was
Ere we met;
(Such will not be, but because
Some forget
Let me feign it) – none would notice
That where she I know by rote is
Spread a strange and withering change,
Like a drying of the wells
Where she dwells.

To feel I might have kissed –
Loved as true –
Otherwhere, nor Mine have missed
My life through,

EXTRA PRINTINGS:
(1) *Selected Poems*, pp. 20–1
(2) *Chosen Poems*, pp. 20–1

INDENTATION:
In MS the last line of each stanza is indented farther right

Ditty
10 that] the MS
15 Fellow-wights] Fellow wights MS, WPA
20] In days by; (by – WPA) MS, WP1
21 will not] cannot WPA
21 will] can MS, WP, PUE
22] Some loves die MS, WP1

Had I never wandered near her,
Is a smart severe – severer
In the thought that she is nought,
Even as I, beyond the dells
        Where she dwells.

And Devotion droops her glance
        To recall
What bond-servants of Chance
        We are all.
I but found her in that, going
On my errant path unknowing,
I did not out-skirt the spot
That no spot on earth excels,
        – Where she dwells!

1870

19 *The Sergeant's Song*

(1803)

WHEN Lawyers strive to heal a breach,
And Parsons practise what they preach;
Then Boney he'll come pouncing down,
And march his men on London town!
        Rollicum-rorum, tol-lol-lorum,
        Rollicum-rorum, tol-lol-lay!

When Justices hold equal scales,
And Rogues are only found in jails;
Then Boney he'll come pouncing down,
And march his men on London town!
        Rollicum-rorum, &c.

When Rich Men find their wealth a curse,
And fill therewith the Poor Man's purse;
Then Boney he'll come pouncing down,
And march his men on London town!
        Rollicum-rorum, &c.

The Sergeant's Song

EXTRA PRINTINGS:

(1) *Good Words* (1880), p. 106, stanzas 1 and 4 only

(2) *The Trumpet-Major* (London, 1880), pp. 77 and 79, stanzas 1 and 4 only

(3) *The Trumpet-Major* (London, 1881), pp. 40–1 = TM2

The following is the text used in the above printings:

(No title or year)

When law'-yers strive' to heal' a breach',
And par'-sons prac'-tise what' they preach',
                (preach'; TM2)
Then lit'-tle Bo'-ney he"ll pounce down',
And march' his men' on Lon'-don town'!
Chorus. –
Rol'-li-cum ro'-rum, tol'-lol-lo'-rum,
Rol'-li-cum ro'-rum, tol'-lol-lay'.

When jus'-ti-ces' hold e'qual scales',
And rogues' are on'-ly found' in jails';
Then lit'-tle Bo'-ney he"ll pounce down',
And march' his men' on Lon'-don town'!

When rich' men find' their wealth' a curse',
And fill' there-with' the poor' man's purse';
Then lit'-tle Bo'-ney he"ll pounce down',
And march' his men' on Lon'-don town'!

When hus'-bands with' their wives' a-gree',
And maids' won't wed' from mod'-es-ty',
Then lit'-tle Bo'-ney he"ll pounce down',
And march' his men' on Lon'-don town'!

Ditty

34 nought,] nought MS
37 Devotion] devotion MS
39 bond-servants] bond servants MS: bondservants WE, SP, ME
44] By the breadth of some few ells MS
44 excels,] excels – WPA
45 – Where] Where MS, WPA
45 dwells!] dwells. MS

The Sergeant's Song

3] Then Little Boney he'll pounce down, (down MS) MS, WP, PUE
6 tol-lol-lay!] tol-lol-lay. MS
9] Then Little Boney he'll pounce down, MS, WP, PUE
14] Then Little Boney he'll pounce down, MS, WP, PUE
15 town!] town. MS

When Husbands with their Wives agree,
And Maids won't wed from modesty;
Then Boney he'll come pouncing down,
And march his men on London town!
Rollicum-rorum, tol-tol-lorum,
Rollicum-rorum, tol-lol-lay!

1878
Published in 'The Trumpet-Major' 1880

20 *Valenciennes*

(1793)

By Corp'l Tullidge, in 'The Trumpet-Major'

IN MEMORY OF S.C. (PENSIONER). DIED 184–

WE trenched, we trumpeted and drummed,
And from our mortars tons of iron hummed
Ath'art the ditch, the month we bombed
The Town o' Valencieën.

'Twas in the June o' Ninety-dree
(The Duke o' Yark our then Commander beën)
The German Legion, Guards, and we
Laid siege to Valencieën.

This was the first time in the war
That French and English spilled each other's gore;
– Few dreamt how far would roll the roar
Begun at Valencieën!

'Twas said that we'd no business there
A-topperèn the French for disagreën;
However, that's not my affair –
We were at Valencieën.

Such snocks and slats, since war began
Never knew raw recruit or veteràn:
Stone-deaf therence went many a man
Who served at Valencieën.

TITLE:
in] *vide* MS: see WP, PUE,
(PENSIONER)] Not in MS
WE, ME add (WESSEX DIALECT)

INDENTATION:
MS shows some irregularity in stanzas 1–5 before settling down to the pattern printed here. In *The Sphere*, 9 Nov 1918, p. 98, the pattern throughout is 1 = ll. 1–3, 2 = l. 4
In ME stanza 1 has 1 = ll. 1–3, 2 = l. 4, with all subsequent stanzas as printed here

The Sergeant's Song
19] Then Little Boney he'll pounce down, MS, WP, PUE

Valenciennes
1 trenched] bugled MS
1 trumpeted] trumpeted, MS
5 Ninety-dree] ninety dree MS [Could be one word]
6 Commander] commander MS
10 spilled] spilt MS
11] – God knows what year will end (still MS) the roar MS, WP1
17 snocks and slats] devillish din MS
19 Stone-deaf] Stone deaf MS
19 went] walked MS

Into the streets, ath'art the sky,
A hundred thousand balls and bombs were fleën;
And harmless townsfolk fell to die
Each hour at Valencieën!

And, sweatèn wi' the bombardiers,
A shell was slent to shards anighst my ears:
– 'Twas nigh the end of hopes and fears
For me at Valencieën!

They bore my wownded frame to camp,
And shut my gapèn skull, and washed en cleän,
And jined en wi' a zilver clamp
Thik night at Valencieën.

'We've fetched en back to quick from dead;
But never more on earth while rose is red
Will drum rouse Corpel!' Doctor said
O' me at Valencieën.

'Twer true. No voice o' friend or foe
Can reach me now, or any livèn beën;
And little have I power to know
Since then at Valencieën!

I never hear the zummer hums
O' bees; and don' know when the cuckoo comes;
But night and day I hear the bombs
We threw at Valencieën. . . .

As for the Duke o' Yark in war,
There may be volk whose judgment o' en is meän;
But this I say – he was not far
From great at Valencieën.

O' wild wet nights, when all seems sad,
My wownds come back, as though new wownds I'd had;
But yet – at times I'm sort o' glad
I fout at Valencieën.

Valenciennes
25 bombardiers,] bombardiers MS
26 slent . . . my] rent to rags anigh mine MS
27 nigh] near MS
37 friend] friend, MS
37 foe] foe, MS
40 Valencieën!] Valencieën. MS
42 don'] don't WPA
46 may be] be some MS, WP, PUE
46 volk] folk MS
47 he] 'a MS, WP, PUE

Well: Heaven wi' its jasper halls
Is now the on'y Town I care to be in. . . .
Good Lord, if Nick should bomb the walls
As we did Valencieën!

1878–1897

21 *San Sebastian*

(*August 1813*)

WITH THOUGHTS OF SERGEANT M—— (PENSIONER), WHO DIED 185–

TITLE:
WITH . . . 185–] In memory of Sergeant M——. Died 184–. MS

'WHY, Sergeant, stray on the Ivel Way,
As though at home there were spectres rife?
From first to last 'twas a proud career!
And your sunny years with a gracious wife
Have brought you a daughter dear.

'I watched her to-day; a more comely maid,
As she danced in her muslin bowed with blue,
Round a Hintock maypole never gayed.'
– 'Aye, aye; I watched her this day, too,
As it happens,' the Sergeant said.

'My daughter is now,' he again began,
'Of just such an age as one I knew
When we of the Line, the Forlorn-hope van,
On an August morning – a chosen few –
Stormed San Sebastian.

'She's a score less three; so about was *she* –
The maiden I wronged in Peninsular days. . . .
You may prate of your prowess in lusty times,
But as years gnaw inward you blink your bays,
And see too well your crimes!

'We'd stormed it at night, by the flapping light
Of burning towers, and the mortar's boom:
We'd topped the breach; but had failed to stay,
For our files were misled by the baffling gloom;
And we said we'd storm by day.

San Sebastian
9 – 'Aye,] ' – Aye; MS
13 Line, the] Line and WP2, PUE: Line – the WE, ME
13 the Forlorn-hope] in the Foot-Guard MS, WP1
17 days. . . .] days. . . . . MS
21 flapping light] vlanker-light WP, PUE
23 topped] scaled MS
23 breach;] breach WPA

'So, out of the trenches, with features set,
On that hot, still morning, in measured pace,
Our column climbed; climbed higher yet,
Passed the fauss'bray, scarp, up the curtain-face,
    And along the parapet.

'From the batteried hornwork the cannoneers
Hove crashing balls of iron fire;
On the shaking gap mount the volunteers
In files, and as they mount expire
    Amid curses, groans, and cheers.

'Five hours did we storm, five hours re-form,
As Death cooled those hot blood pricked on;
Till our cause was helped by a woe within:
They were blown from the summit we'd leapt upon,
    And madly we entered in.

'On end for plunder, 'mid rain and thunder
That burst with the lull of our cannonade,
We vamped the streets in the stifling air –
Our hunger unsoothed, our thirst unstayed –
    And ransacked the buildings there.

'From the shady vaults of their walls of white
We rolled rich puncheons of Spanish grape,
Till at length, with the fire of the wine alight,
I saw at a doorway a fair fresh shape –
    A woman, a sylph, or sprite.

'Afeard she fled, and with heated head
I pursued to the chamber she called her own;
– When might is right no qualms deter,
And having her helpless and alone
    I wreaked my will on her.

'She raised her beseeching eyes to me,
And I heard the words of prayer she sent
In her own soft language. . . . Fatefully
I copied those eyes for my punishment
    In begetting the girl you see!

San Sebastian
26 with] their MS
33 shaking gap] quaking breach MS
36 re-form,] re-form MS
38 within:] within; MS
39 were blown] swerved MS: swayed WP, PUE
41 On end for] Intent on MS
43 vamped] thridded MS
46] 'Down the stony steps of the house-fronts white MS, WP, PUE
51 Afeard] Dismayed MS
55 will] lust MS, WP1
58 language. . . .] language. . . . . . MS
58 Fatefully] Seemingly MS, WP, PUE

'So, to-day I stand with a God-set brand
Like Cain's, when he wandered from kindred's ken. . . .
I served through the war that made Europe free;
I wived me in peace-year. But, hid from men,
I bear that mark on me.

'Maybe we shape our offspring's guise
From fancy, or we know not what,
And that no deep impression dies, –
For the mother of my child is not
The mother of her eyes.

'And I nightly stray on the Ivel Way
As though at home there were spectres rife;
I delight me not in my proud career;
And 'tis coals of fire that a gracious wife
Should have brought me a daughter dear!'

22 *The Stranger's Song*

(*As sung by* Mr Charles Charrington *in the play of 'The Three Wayfarers'*)

O my trade it is the rarest one,
Simple shepherds all –
My trade is a sight to see;
For my customers I tie, and take 'em up on high,
And waft 'em to a far countree!

My tools are but common ones,
Simple shepherds all –
My tools are no sight to see:
A little hempen string, and a post whereon to swing,
Are implements enough for me!

To-morrow is my working day,
Simple shepherds all –
To-morrow is a working day for me:
For the farmer's sheep is slain, and the lad who did it ta'en,
And on his soul may God ha' mer-cy!

Printed in 'The Three Strangers', 1883

EXTRA PRINTINGS:
(1) *Longman's Magazine*, March 1883, pp. 579–81 = LM
(2) *Songs from the Novelists*, ed. W. D. Adams (London, 1885), p. 130 = SN
(3) *Wessex Tales* (London, 1888), pp. 30–4 = WT
(4) *The Three Wayfarers* (New York, 1893), pp. 16–18 = TW1
(5) *The Three Wayfarers* (New York and London, 1930), pp. 17–21 = TW2

TITLE:
No title in LM, WT, TW1, TW2
The Hangman's Song SN

INDENTATION:
There is some variation in the printings. MS and SN are as printed here except that ll. 3 and 5 in each stanza are lined up together.
LM has 1 = l. 4
2 = l. 1
3 = ll. 3, 5
4 = l.2
TW1, TW2 have 1 = l. 4
2 = ll. 1, 3, 5
3 = l. 2

San Sebastian
66–70] This stanza is found only in WE, ME, CP
66 shape] draw WE, ME
66 offspring's] children's WE, ME
67 we know] one knows WE, ME

The Stranger's Song
(*As . . .*)] Not in LM, SN, WT, TW1, TW2
1 O] O, TW2
4 'em] them LM, SN, WT, TW1, TW2
4 high,] high MS
5 countree!] countree. LM, SN
5 'em] them SN, TW1
7 all –] all, LM, WT
8 see:] see; TW1, TW2
9 string,] string TW2
9 swing,] swing TW2
10 me!] me. LM, SN, TW1: me – TW2
11 working day] working-day MS
13 me:] me; TW2
14 ta-en,] ta'en – TW1
15 mer-cy!] merc-y! LM, SN, WT
Note TW1, 2 have l. 5 repeated, with 'Hee-hee!' inserted between as an extra line and some variation in final punctuation

EXTRA PRINTINGS:
(1) *Selected Poems*, pp. 163–6
(2) *Chosen Poems*, pp. 189–92

TITLE:
The (Three *del*) Burghers MS
(17—)] (CASTERBRIDGE: 17—) WE, SP, ME

23 *The Burghers*

(*17—*)

THE sun had wheeled from Grey's to Dammer's Crest,
And still I mused on that Thing imminent:
At length I sought the High-street to the West.

The level flare raked pane and pediment
And my wrecked face, and shaped my nearing friend
Like one of those the Furnace held unshent.

'I've news concerning her,' he said. 'Attend.
They fly to-night at the late moon's first gleam:
Watch with thy steel: two righteous thrusts will end

Her shameless visions and his passioned dream.
I'll watch with thee, to testify thy wrong –
To aid, maybe. – Law consecrates the scheme.'

I started, and we paced the flags along
Till I replied: 'Since it has come to this
I'll do it! But alone. I can be strong.'

Three hours past Curfew, when the Froom's mild hiss
Reigned sole, undulled by whirr of merchandize,
From Pummery-Tout to where the Gibbet is,

I crossed my pleasaunce hard by Glyd'path Rise,
And stood beneath the wall. Eleven strokes went,
And to the door they came, contrariwise,

And met in clasp so close I had but bent
My lifted blade on either to have let
Their two souls loose upon the firmament.

But something held my arm. 'A moment yet
As pray-time ere you wantons die!' I said;
And then they saw me. Swift her gaze was set

The Burghers
2 imminent:] imminent: – SP
4 pediment] pediment, SP
5 wrecked] worn WE, SP, ME
6 of . . . held] who walked the Furnace-fire MS
9 steel:] steel; MS
9 thrusts] strokes MS
10 shameless] lawless MS
12 maybe. –] maybe – WPA
12 consecrates] sanctifies MS
15 it!] it. MS
19 Glyd'path] Glyd Lybbeth MS *del*
23 on either] upon them MS, WP, PUE

With eye and cry of love illimited
Upon her Heart-king. Never upon me
Had she thrown look of love so thoroughsped! . . .

At once she flung her faint form shieldingly
On his, against the vengeance of my vows;
The which o'erruling, her shape shielded he.

Blanked by such love, I stood as in a drowse,
And the slow moon edged from the upland nigh,
My sad thoughts moving thuswise: 'I may house

And I may husband her, yet what am I
But licensed tyrant to this bonded pair?
Says Charity, Do as ye would be done by.' . . .

Hurling my iron to the bushes there,
I bade them stay. And, as if brain and breast
Were passive, they walked with me to the stair.

Inside the house none watched; and on we prest
Before a mirror, in whose gleam I read
Her beauty, his, – and mine own mien unblest;

Till at her room I turned. 'Madam,' I said,
'Have you the wherewithal for this? Pray speak.
Love fills no cupboard. You'll need daily bread.'

'We've nothing, sire,' she lipped; 'and nothing seek.
'Twere base in me to rob my lord unware;
Our hands will earn a pittance week by week.'

And next I saw she had piled her raiment rare
Within the garde-robes, and her household purse,
Her jewels, her least lace of personal wear;

And stood in homespun. Now grown wholly hers,
I handed her the gold, her jewels all,
And him the choicest of her robes diverse.

'I'll take you to the doorway in the wall,
And then adieu,' I told them. 'Friends, withdraw.'
They did so; and she went – beyond recall.

The Burghers
30 thoroughsped! . . .] thoroughsped! . . . . . MS
31 At once] And then MS
36 thuswise] thiswise MS
39 by.' . . .] by.' . . . . . MS
40 Hurling] Flinging MS
40 there,] there MS, WE, SP, ME, CHP
41 And,] And MS
45 his, –] his; MS
45 mine own mien] my own face SP [Hardy wrote this correction on the flyleaf of his copy of WE1 as one to be embodied in the Mellstock and subsequent editions. But his copy of SP corrects to 'mine own mien']
47 speak.] speak; MS
49 she lipped] said she (she, WPA) MS, WP, PUE, WE, SP, ME
52 next] then MS
52 she had] she'd MS, WP, PUE
53 garde-robes] garderobes MS
54 her] and MS, WP, PUE
54 wear;] wear, WE, SP, ME, CHP
55 hers,] hers MS
59 adieu] Adieu MS
59 told] to MS, WP, PUE

And as I paused beneath the arch I saw
Their moonlit figures – slow, as in surprise –
Descend the slope, and vanish on the haw.

' "Fool," some will say,' I thought. – 'But who is wise,
Save God alone, to weigh my reasons why?'
– 'Hast thou struck home?' came with the boughs' night-sighs.

It was my friend. 'I have struck well. They fly,
But carry wounds that none can cicatrize.'
– 'Not mortal?' said he. 'Lingering – worse,' said I.

EXTRA PRINTING:
Hardy used ll. 101–8 in *The Dynasts*, Part Third (London, 1908), III, iv, p. 112; and ll. 117–32 in III, v, pp. 117–18. Scattered lines are found in III, ii. The variants are minor, being mainly changes of tense

24 *Leipzig*

(1813)

SCENE. – *The Master-tradesmen's Parlour at the Old Ship Inn, Casterbridge. Evening.*

'OLD Norbert with the flat blue cap –
A German said to be –
Why let your pipe die on your lap,
Your eyes blink absently?'

– 'Ah! . . . Well, I had thought till my cheek was wet
Of my mother – her voice and mien
When she used to sing and pirouette,
And tap the tambourine

'To the march that yon street-fiddler plies:
She told me 'twas the same
She'd heard from the trumpets, when the Allies
Burst on her home like flame.

'My father was one of the German Hussars,
My mother of Leipzig; but he,
Being quartered here, fetched her at close of the wars,
And a Wessex lad reared me.

The Burghers
63 on] Hardy has corrected his copy of CP2 to read: from
64 thought. –] thought. WP, PUE, WE, SP, ME
68 none] naught MS
69] – 'Mortal?' said he. 'Remorseful – worse,' said I. CP1

Leipzig
SCENE . . . *Evening.*] Scene: Interior of the Old Ship Inn, Casterbridge. Evening. MS
4 eyes] eye MS
4 absently?'] absently?' – MS, WP, PUE, WE, ME
5 Ah! . . .] Ah! . . . . . MS
8 tap] touse MS, WP, PUE
9 plies:] plies; WPA
11 trumpets, when] trumpets of MS
12] When their troops to her city came. MS: Her city overcame. WP, PUE
15 Being] Long MS, WP, PUE
15 quartered] camped ME, WE2. Hardy has written this correction in his copy of WE1 as one to be made in later editions
15 wars,] wars MS

'And as I grew up, again and again
  She'd tell, after trilling that air,
Of her youth, and the battles on Leipzig plain
  And of all that was suffered there! . . .

' – 'Twas a time of alarms. Three Chiefs-at-arms
  Combined them to crush One,
And by numbers' might, for in equal fight
  He stood the matched of none.

'Carl Schwarzenberg was of the plot,
  And Blücher, prompt and prow,
And Jean the Crown-Prince Bernadotte:
  Buonaparte was the foe.

'City and plain had felt his reign
  From the North to the Middle Sea,
And he'd now sat down in the noble town
  Of the King of Saxony.

'October's deep dew its wet gossamer threw
  Upon Leipzig's lawns, leaf-strewn,
Where lately each fair avenue
  Wrought shade for summer noon.

'To westward two dull rivers crept
  Through miles of marsh and slough,
Whereover a streak of whiteness swept –
  The Bridge of Lindenau.

'Hard by, in the City, the One, care-tossed,
  Sat pondering his shrunken power;
And without the walls the hemming host
  Waxed denser every hour.

'He had speech that night on the morrow's designs
  With his chiefs by the bivouac fire,
While the belt of flames from the enemy's lines
  Flared nigher him yet and nigher.

Leipzig
20 there! . . .] there. . . . . . MS
21 Chiefs-at-arms] chiefs at arms MS
25 Schwarzenberg] Schwartzenburg MS, WP1
33–6] October's deep dews sprinkled Leipzig's purlieus/And ramparts of ashlar hewn,/Beneath whose fronts fair avenues/Made eve of afternoon. MS
41 care-tossed] care-crossed MS, WPA
42 Sat pondering] Gloomed over MS, WP, PUE, WE, ME
42 shrunken power] narrowing powers MS
43 hemming] encircling MS
44 every hour] with the hours MS
47 belt] zone MS

'Three rockets then from the girdling trine
Told, "Ready!" As they rose
Their flashes seemed his Judgment-Sign
For bleeding Europe's woes.

' 'Twas seen how the French watch-fires that night
Glowed still and steadily;
And the Three rejoiced, for they read in the sight
That the One disdained to flee....

' – Five hundred guns began the affray
On next day morn at nine;
Such mad and mangling cannon-play
Had never torn human line.

'Around the town three battles beat,
Contracting like a gin;
As nearer marched the million feet
Of columns closing in.

'The first battle nighed on the low Southern side;
The second by the Western way;
The nearing of the third on the North was heard;
– The French held all at bay.

'Against the first band did the Emperor stand;
Against the second stood Ney;
Marmont against the third gave the order-word:
– Thus raged it throughout the day.

'Fifty thousand sturdy souls on those trampled plains and knolls,
Who met the dawn hopefully,
And were lotted their shares in a quarrel not theirs,
Dropt then in their agony.

' "O," the old folks said, "ye Preachers stern!
O so-called Christian time!
When will men's swords to ploughshares turn?
When come the promised prime?" ...

Leipzig
49 rockets] sky-signs MS: sky-lights WP, PUE, CP1
51 flashes] lightnings MS
51 Judgment-Sign] judgment-sign MS
54 steadily;] steadily, MS
55 rejoiced,] rejoiced; MS
56 flee. . . .] flee. . . . . . MS
62 Contracting] Constricting MS
63 As] And MS
63 million] myriad MS
67 heard;] heard: MS, WP, PUE, WE, ME
72 – Thus raged] Thus was MS
73 Fifty thousand sturdy] Sixty thousand harmless MS
73 trampled] girdling MS
75 theirs,] theirs MS
77 Preachers] preachers MS
78 so-called] so called MS
79 swords] spears MS
80 prime?" . . .] prime?" . . . . MS

' – The clash of horse and man which that day began,
Closed not as evening wore;
And the morrow's armies, rear and van,
Still mustered more and more.

'From the City towers the Confederate Powers
Were eyed in glittering lines,
And up from the vast a murmuring passed
As from a wood of pines.

' " 'Tis well to cover a feeble skill
By numbers' might!" scoffed He;
"But give me a third of their strength, I'd fill
Half Hell with their soldiery!"

'All that day raged the war they waged,
And again dumb night held reign,
Save that ever upspread from the dank deathbed
A miles-wide pant of pain.

'Hard had striven brave Ney, the true Bertrand,
Victor, and Augereau,
Bold Poniatowski, and Lauriston,
To stay their overthrow;

'But, as in the dream of one sick to death
There comes a narrowing room
That pens him, body and limbs and breath,
To wait a hideous doom,

'So to Napoleon, in the hush
That held the town and towers
Through these dire nights, a creeping crush
Seemed borne in with the hours.

'One road to the rearward, and but one,
Did fitful Chance allow;
'Twas where the Pleiss' and Elster run –
The Bridge of Lindenau.

Leipzig
81 began,] began MS
83 van,] van MS
86 eyed] marked MS
90 numbers' . . . scoffed] numbers!' scoffèd (scoffed MS) MS, WP, PUE
90 He;] He, MS
91 strength] force (strength *del*) MS
94 again dumb] another hushed MS
95 dank] wide MS: dark WP, PUE
95 deathbed] death-bed MS, WP, PUE, WE, ME
96 A . . . pant] Dull monotones MS
100 overthrow;] overthrow, MS
107 nights,] nights; MS
108 borne in] nearing MS: inborne WP, PUE
109 road . . . rearward] track from the cincture MS
111 run –] run MS

'The nineteenth dawned. Down street and Platz
The wasted French sank back,
Stretching long lines across the Flats
And on the bridgeway track:

'When there surged on the sky an earthen wave,
And stones, and men, as though
Some rebel churchyard crew updrave
Their sepulchres from below.

'To Heaven is blown Bridge Lindenau;
Wrecked regiments reel therefrom;
And rank and file in masses plough
The sullen Elster-Strom.

'A gulf was Lindenau; and dead
Were fifties, hundreds, tens;
And every current rippled red
With Marshal's blood and men's.

'The smart Macdonald swam therein,
And barely won the verge;
Bold Poniatowski plunged him in
Never to re-emerge.

'Then stayed the strife. The remnants wound
Their Rhineward way pell-mell;
And thus did Leipzig City sound
An Empire's passing bell;

'While in cavalcade, with band and blade,
Came Marshals, Princes, Kings;
And the town was theirs. . . . Ay, as simple maid,
My mother saw these things!

'And whenever those notes in the street begin,
I recall her, and that far scene,
And her acting of how the Allies marched in,
And her tap of the tambourine!'

Leipzig
113 Down] By MS
114 wasted] writhing MS
116 bridgeway track:] bridge-way track; MS, WP, PUE, WE, ME
128 Marshal's] marshal's MS
129 therein,] therein MS
135 City] city MS
139 theirs. . . .] theirs. . . . . . MS
141 begin,] begin MS
142 her,] her; MS
144] To the touse of her tambourine!' MS
144 tap] touse WP, PUE
144 of] on WE, ME

25 *The Peasant's Confession*

'Si le maréchal Grouchy avait été rejoint par l'officier que Napoléon lui avait expédié la veille à dix heures du soir, toute question eût disparu. Mais cet officier n'était point parvenu à sa destination, ainsi que le maréchal n'a cessé de l'affirmer toute sa vie, et il faut l'en croire, car autrement il n'aurait eu aucune raison pour hésiter. Cet officier avait-il été pris? avait-il passé à l'ennemi? c'est ce qu'on a toujours ignoré.' – THIERS, *Histoire de l'Empire*. 'Waterloo'.

GOOD Father! . . . It was eve in middle June,
 And war was waged anew
By great Napoleon, who for years had strewn
 Men's bones all Europe through.

Three nights ere this, with columned corps he'd cross'd
 The Sambre at Charleroi,
To move on Brussels, where the English host
 Dallied in Parc and Bois.

The yestertide we'd heard the gloomy gun
 Growl through the long-sunned day
From Quatre-Bras and Ligny; till the dun
 Twilight suppressed the fray;

Albeit therein – as lated tongues bespoke –
 Brunswick's high heart was drained,
And Prussia's Line and Landwehr, though unbroke,
 Stood cornered and constrained.

And at next noon-time Grouchy slowly passed
 With thirty thousand men:
We hoped thenceforth no army, small or vast,
 Would trouble us again.

My hut lay deeply in a vale recessed,
 And never a soul seemed nigh
When, reassured at length, we went to rest –
 My children, wife, and I.

The Peasant's Confession
Histoire de l'Empire] *Histoire du Consulat et de l'Empire* WE, ME
1 Father! . . .] Father! . . . . MS
1 It was] 'Twas an MS, WP, PUE, WE, ME
5 cross'd] crossed MS, WP, PUE, WE, ME
10 Growl] Roar MS
11 the dun] anon MS
12] Silence enwrapt the fray. MS
13–16] Not in MS
19 vast,] vast MS
21 lay] stood MS
23 reassured] re-assured MS

But what was this that broke our humble ease?
What noise, above the rain,
Above the dripping of the poplar trees
That smote along the pane?

– A call of mastery, bidding me arise,
Compelled me to the door,
At which a horseman stood in martial guise –
Splashed – sweating from every pore.

Had I seen Grouchy? Yes? What track took he?
Could I lead thither on? –
Fulfilment would ensure much gold for me,
Perhaps more gifts anon.

'I bear the Emperor's mandate,' then he said,
'Charging the Marshal straight
To strike between the double host ahead
Ere they co-operate,

'Engaging Blücher till the Emperor put
Lord Wellington to flight,
And next the Prussians. This to set afoot
Is my emprise to-night.'

I joined him in the mist; but, pausing, sought
To estimate his say.
Grouchy had made for Wavre; and yet, on thought,
I did not lead that way.

I mused: 'If Grouchy thus and thus be told,
The clash comes sheer hereon;
My farm is stript. While, as for gifts of gold,
Money the French have none.

'Grouchy unwarned, moreo'er, the English win,
And mine is left to me –
They buy, not borrow.' – Hence did I begin
To lead him treacherously.

The Peasant's Confession
29 – A] A MS
31 At which] Whereat MS
32 from] at MS
33 Grouchy?] Grouchy! CP
33 What] Which MS, WP, PUE, WE, ME
34 thither on? –] thenceward on? MS
35 much gold for me] gold pieces three MS, WP, PUE, WE, ME
36 Perhaps] Perchance MS, WP, PUE
49 and . . . told] instructed be MS, WP, PUE
50 clash] crash WE, ME
50 sheer] straight MS
51 gifts of gold] pieces three MS, WP, PUE

And as we edged Joidoigne with cautious view
Dawn pierced the humid air;
And still I easted with him, though I knew
Never marched Grouchy there.

Near Ottignies we passed, across the Dyle
(Lim'lette left far aside),
And thence direct toward Pervez and Noville
Through green grain, till he cried:

'I doubt thy conduct, man! no track is here –
I doubt thy gagèd word!'
Thereat he scowled on me, and prancing near,
He pricked me with his sword.

'Nay, Captain, hold! We skirt, not trace the course
Of Grouchy,' said I then:
'As we go, yonder went he, with his force
Of thirty thousand men.'

– At length noon nighed; when west, from Saint-John's-Mound,
A hoarse artillery boomed,
And from Saint-Lambert's upland, chapel-crowned,
The Prussian squadrons loomed.

Then leaping to the wet wild path we had kept,
'My mission fails!' he cried;
'Too late for Grouchy now to intercept,
For, peasant, you have lied!'

He turned to pistol me. I sprang, and drew
The sabre from his flank,
And 'twixt his nape and shoulder, ere he knew,
I struck, and dead he sank.

I hid him deep in nodding rye and oat –
His shroud green stalks and loam;
His requiem the corn-blade's husky note –
And then I hastened home. . . .

The Peasant's Confession
57] By Joidogne, near to east, as we ondrew, MS, WP, PUE
57 view] view, WE, ME
58 air;] air, MS
59 still I easted] eastward faced I MS, WP, PUE, WE, ME
61 Dyle] Dyle, MS
67 Thereat] Thereon MS
67 on] at MS
67 prancing] pranced me MS, WP, PUE
68 He] And MS, WP, PUE
73 nighed] struck WE, ME
77] Then to the wayless wet gray ground he leapt; MS, WP, PUE
86 loam;] loam: MS
88 home. . . .] home. . . . . . MS

– Two armies writhe in coils of red and blue,
And brass and iron clang
From Goumont, past the front of Waterloo,
To Pap'lotte and Smohain.

The Guard Imperial wavered on the height;
The Emperor's face grew glum;
'I sent,' he said, 'to Grouchy yesternight,
And yet he does not come!'

'Twas then, Good Father, that the French espied,
Streaking the summer land,
The men of Blücher. But the Emperor cried,
'Grouchy is now at hand!'

And meanwhile Vand'leur, Vivian, Maitland, Kempt,
Met d'Erlon, Friant, Ney;
But Grouchy – mis-sent, blamed, yet blame-exempt –
Grouchy was far away.

By even, slain or struck, Michel the strong,
Bold Travers, Dnop, Delord,
Smart Guyot, Reil-le, l'Heriter, Friant,
Scattered that champaign o'er.

Fallen likewise wronged Duhesme, and skilled Lobau
Did that red sunset see;
Colbert, Legros, Blancard! . . . And of the foe
Picton and Ponsonby;

With Gordon, Canning, Blackman, Ompteda,
L'Estrange, Delancey, Packe,
Grose, D'Oyly, Stables, Morice, Howard, Hay,
Von Schwerin, Watzdorf, Boek,

Smith, Phelips, Fuller, Lind, and Battersby,
And hosts of ranksmen round. . . .
Memorials linger yet to speak to thee
Of those that bit the ground!

The Peasant's Confession
91 Goumont,] Goumont MS
91 Waterloo,] Waterloo MS
97 espied,] espied MS
98 land,] land MS
111 Blancard! . . .] Blancard! . . . . MS, WP, PUE, WE, ME
113 Blackman] Reignolds MS
115] Hay, Howard, D'Oyly, Stables, Macara, MS
116 Watzdorf] Lettlow MS
117 Fuller] Cameron MS
118 round. . . .] round. . . . . MS, WP, PUE, WE, ME
119 speak to] witness MS
120 that] who MS

The Guards' last column yielded; dykes of dead
    Lay between vale and ridge,
As, thinned yet closing, faint yet fierce, they sped
    In packs to Genappe Bridge.

Safe was my stock; my capple cow unslain;
    Intact each cock and hen;
But Grouchy far at Wavre all day had lain,
    And thirty thousand men.

O Saints, had I but lost my earing corn
    And saved the cause once prized!
O Saints, why such false witness had I borne
    When late I'd sympathized! . . .

So now, being old, my children eye askance
    My slowly dwindling store,
And crave my mite; till, worn with tarriance,
    I care for life no more.

To Almighty God henceforth I stand confessed,
    And Virgin-Saint Marie;
O Michael, John, and Holy Ones in rest,
    Entreat the Lord for me!

26 *The Alarm*

(*Traditional*)

IN MEMORY OF ONE OF THE WRITER'S FAMILY WHO WAS A VOLUNTEER DURING THE WAR WITH NAPOLEON

    In a ferny byway
    Near the great South-Wessex Highway,
  A homestead raised its breakfast-smoke aloft;
The dew-damps still lay steamless, for the sun had made no skyway,
        And twilight cloaked the croft.

TITLE:
(*Traditional*)] (1804)/*vide* 'The Trumpet-Major' MS: (1803)/*See 'The Trumpet-Major'* WP, PUE

INDENTATION:
MS is variable but the basic pattern is:
Odd-numbered stanzas: 1 = l. 4
2 = l. 3
3 = ll. 2, 5
4 = l. 1
Even-numbered stanzas: 1 = l. 4
2 = l. 3
3 = ll. 1, 2, 5

The Peasant's Confession
124 packs] throngs MS
125 capple] milkwhite MS
130 prized!] prized; MS
132 sympathized! . . .] sympathized! . . . . . MS
137 confessed,] confessed MS
140 Entreat] Intreat MS

The Alarm
2 Highway,] Highway MS
4 skyway] sky-way WP, PUE, WE, ME

It was almost past conceiving
Here, where woodbines hung inweaving,
That quite closely hostile armaments might steer,
Save from seeing in the porchway a fair woman mutely grieving,
And a harnessed Volunteer.

In haste he'd flown there
To his comely wife alone there,
While marching south hard by, to still her fears,
For she soon would be a mother, and few messengers were known there
In these campaigning years.

'Twas time to be Good-bying,
Since the assembly-hour was nighing
In royal George's town at six that morn;
And betwixt its wharves and this retreat were ten good miles of hieing
Ere ring of bugle-horn.

'I've laid in food, Dear,
And broached the spiced and brewed, Dear;
And if our July hope should antedate,
Let the char-wench mount and gallop by the halterpath and wood, Dear,
And fetch assistance straight.

'As for Buonaparte, forget him;
He's not like to land! But let him,
Those strike with aim who strike for wives and sons!
And the war-boats built to float him; 'twere but wanted to upset him
A slat from Nelson's guns!

'But, to assure thee,
And of creeping fears to cure thee,
If he *should* be rumoured anchoring in the Road,
Drive with the nurse to Kingsbere; and let nothing thence allure thee
Till we have him safe-bestowed.

The Alarm
6] 'Twas hard to realize on MS, WP, PUE
7] Hitherside the snug horizon MS
This snug side the mute horizon WP, PUE
8 quite closely] beyond it MS, WP, PUE
9 seeing] this, that MS
9 mutely grieving,] weep (wept MS) with eyes on MS, WP, PUE
10 And a] A MS, WP, PUE
10 Volunteer] volunteer MS
12 there,] there MS
17 Since] For MS
18 royal . . . town] regal Budmouth Town MS
19 its wharves] the port MS
22 spiced and] cask of MS
24] The lad will mount and gallop by the cut through Yalbury Wood, Dear, MS
24 char-wench] chore-wench WE, ME
24 halterpath] halter-path ME: WE has line break
34 with . . . and] under tilt to Weatherb'ry: MS
35 we have] we've MS, WP, PUE

'Now, to turn to marching matters: –
I've my knapsack, firelock, spatters,
Crossbelts, priming-horn, stock, bay'net, blackball, clay,
Pouch, magazine, and flint-box that at every quick-step clatters; –
My heart, Dear; that must stay!'

– With breathings broken
Farewell was kissed unspoken,
And they parted there as morning stroked the panes;
And the Volunteer went on, and turned, and twirled his glove for token,
And took the coastward lanes.

When above He'th Hills he found him,
He saw, on gazing round him,
The Barrow-Beacon burning – burning low,
As if, perhaps, enkindled ever since he'd homeward bound him;
And it meant: Expect the Foe!

Leaving the byway,
He entered on the highway,
Where were cars and chariots, faring fast inland;
'He's anchored, Soldier!' shouted some: 'God save thee, marching thy way,
Th'lt front him on the strand!'

He slowed; he stopped; he paltered
Awhile with self, and faltered,
'Why courting misadventure shoreward roam?
To Molly, surely! Seek the woods with her till times have altered;
Charity favours home.

'Else, my denying
He'd come, she'll read as lying –
Think the Barrow-Beacon must have met my eyes –
That my words were not unwareness, but deceit of her, while vying
In deeds that jeopardize.

The Alarm
36 Now,] Now; MS
38 Crossbelts] Cross-belts MS
38 clay,] clay; MS
39 and] flints, MS, WP, PUE
39 flint-box] flintbox MS
39 clatters; –] clatters; MS, WP, PUE, WE, ME
40 My] . . . My MS: . . . My WP, PUE, WE, ME
43 panes;] panes: MS
44 Volunteer] volunteer MS
44 token,] token; MS
46 him,] him MS
48 The Barrow-Beacon] Rain-Barrow's Beacon MS
49 enkindled] uplighted MS, WP, PUE
52 He . . . on] And following swift MS, WP, PUE
53] Cars and chariots met he, hasting hot inland; MS
Car and chariot met he, faring fast inland; WP, PUE
53 were . . . faring] cars and chariots fared them WE2, ME
53 chariots,] chariots WE1
54 anchored . . . some:] landed, Soldier!' cried the throng. MS
56 He . . . stopped;] Stressed for his Dear, MS
57 faltered,] faltered: MS
62 He'd come,] He would come MS, WP, PUE
62 she'll] may MS
63 Think . . . Beacon] She will think the Beacon MS
63 eyes –] eyes; MS
64 unwareness] my un-wit MS
64 vying] trying MS, WP, PUE
65 In deeds that] My life to MS, WP, PUE

'At home is stocked provision,
And to-night, without suspicion,
We might bear it with us to a covert near;
Such sin, to save a childing wife, would earn it Christ's remission,
Though none forgive it here!'

While he stood thinking,
A little bird, perched drinking
Among the crowfoot tufts the river bore,
Was tangled in their stringy arms and fluttered, almost sinking
Near him, upon the moor.

He stepped in, reached, and seized it,
And, preening, had released it
But that a thought of Holy Writ occurred,
And Signs Divine ere battle, till it seemed him Heaven had pleased it
As guide to send the bird.

'O Lord, direct me! . . .
Doth Duty now expect me
To march a-coast, or guard my weak ones near?
Give this bird a flight according, that I thence learn to elect me
The southward or the rear.'

He loosed his clasp; when, rising,
The bird – as if surmising –
Bore due to southward, crossing by the Froom,
And Durnover Great Field and Fort, the soldier clear advising –
Prompted he deemed by Whom.

Then on he panted
By grim Mai-Don, and slanted
Up the steep Ridge-way, hearkening between whiles;
Till nearing coast and harbour he beheld the shore-line planted
With Foot and Horse for miles.

Mistrusting not the omen,
He gained the beach, where Yeomen,
Militia, Fencibles and Pikemen bold,
With Regulars in thousands, were enmassed to meet the Foemen,
Whose fleet had not yet shoaled.

The Alarm
70 here!] here. MS
71 he stood] thus he, MS, WP, PUE
71 stood] stood, WE, ME
72 perched] quick MS, WP, PUE
73 bore,] bore MS
74 arms] arms, MS, WP, PUE, WE, ME
74 almost] well-nigh MS, WP, PUE
74 sinking] sinking, WP, PUE, WE, ME
75 Near him] Hard by MS
75 moor] Moor MS
79 battle] Battle MS
81 me! . . .] me! . . . . MS, WP, PUE, WE, ME
84 learn] know MS, WP, PUE
85 southward] southward, MS
89 Great Field] Great-Field WP, PUE, WE, ME
90 deemed] knew MS: wist WP, PUE: read WE, ME
91 Then] Then, MS
92 By . . . Don] Through Casterbridge MS
93 between] betwixt MS, WP, PUE, WE, ME
94 Till] Till, MS, WP, PUE, WE, ME
94 harbour] harbour, WP, PUE, WE, ME
96 omen,] omen MS
97 Yeomen,] Yeomen CP
98 Fencibles] Fencibles, MS, WP, PUE, WE, ME

Captain and Colonel,
Sere Generals, Ensigns vernal,
Were there; of neighbour-natives, Michel, Smith,
Meggs, Bingham, Gambier, Cunningham, to face the said nocturnal
Swoop on their land and kith.

But Buonaparte still tarried:
His project had miscarried;
At the last hour, equipped for victory,
The fleet had paused; his subtle combinations had been parried
By British strategy.

Homeward returning
Anon, no beacons burning,
No alarms, the Volunteer, in modest bliss,
Te Deum sang with wife and friends: 'We praise Thee, Lord, discerning
That Thou hast helped in this!'

27 *Her Death and After*

EXTRA PRINTINGS:
(1) *Selected Poems*, pp. 172–7
(2) *Chosen Poems*, pp. 198–203

THE summons was urgent: and forth I went –
By the way of the Western Wall, so drear
On that winter night, and sought a gate,
Where one, by Fate,
Lay dying that I held dear.

And there, as I paused by her tenement,
And the trees shed on me their rime and hoar,
I thought of the man who had left her lone –
Him who made her his own
When I loved her, long before.

The rooms within had the piteous shine
That home-things wear when there's aught amiss;
From the stairway floated the rise and fall
Of an infant's call,
Whose birth had brought her to this.

The Alarm
102 vernal,] vernal MS
103 there;] there, WPA
103 of . . . Michel] among them Stickland, Mitchell MS
104 to . . . said] roused by the hued (said MS) MS, WP, PUE
106 tarried:] tarried, MS: tarried; WP, PUE, WE, ME
110 British] English MS
113 Volunteer] volunteer MS

Her Death and After
1 The . . . urgent:] 'Twas a death-bed summons, MS, WP, PUE
1 urgent:] urgent, WE, SP, ME
1 went –] went MS, WP, PUE, WE, SP, ME
3 gate,] gate – MS, WP, PUE, WE, SP, ME
4 Where one] The home MS, WP, PUE
4 Fate,] Fate MS
5 Lay . . . I] Of one I had long MS, WP, PUE
12 when . . . amiss;] which the housewife miss; (miss: MS) MS, WP
13 rise and] feeble (rise and *del*) MS

Her life was the price she would pay for that whine –
For a child by the man she did not love.
'But let that rest for ever,' I said,
And bent my tread
To the bedchamber above.

She took my hand in her thin white own,
And smiled her thanks – though nigh too weak –
And made them a sign to leave us there,
Then faltered, ere
She could bring herself to speak.

'Just to see you – before I go – he'll condone
Such a natural thing now my time's not much –
When Death is so near it hustles hence
All passioned sense
Between woman and man as such!

'My husband is absent. As heretofore
The City detains him. But, in truth,
He has not been kind. . . . I will speak no blame,
But – the child is lame;
O, I pray she may reach his ruth!

'Forgive past days – I can say no more –
Maybe had we wed you would now repine! . . .
But I treated you ill. I was punished. Farewell!
– Truth shall I tell?
Would the child were yours and mine!

'As a wife I was true. But, such my unease
That, could I insert a deed back in Time,
I'd make her yours, to secure your care;
And the scandal bear,
And the penalty for the crime!'

– When I had left, and the swinging trees
Rang above me, as lauding her candid say,
Another was I. Her words were enough:
Came smooth, came rough,
I felt I could live my day.

Her Death and After
17 love.] love: MS
18 for ever] forever WPA
20 bedchamber] chamber up MS, WP, PUE
23 there,] there; MS, WPA: there WP, PUE
26 Just] 'Twas MS, WP, PUE
26 you –] you MS, WP, PUE, WE, SP, ME
33 kind. . . .] kind. . . . . . MS
37 had . . . would] if we'd wedded you'd MS, WP, PUE, WE, SP, ME
37 repine! . . .] repine! . . . . . MS
41 I was] I've been WE, SP, ME
43 care;] care, MS
45 crime!] crime. MS
46 – When] When MS
49 rough,] rough MS

Next night she died; and her obsequies
In the Field of Tombs where the earthworks frowned
Had her husband's heed. His tendance spent,
I often went
And pondered by her mound.

All that year and the next year whiled,
And I still went thitherward in the gloam;
But the Town forgot her and her nook,
And her husband took
Another Love to his home.

And the rumour flew that the lame lone child
Whom she wished for its safety child of mine,
Was treated ill when offspring came
Of the new-made dame,
And marked a more vigorous line.

A smarter grief within me wrought
Than even at loss of her so dear –
That the being whose soul my soul suffused
Had a child ill-used,
While I dared not interfere!

One eve as I stood at my spot of thought
In the white-stoned Garth, brooding thus her wrong,
Her husband neared; and to shun his nod
By her hallowed sod
I went from the tombs among

To the Cirque of the Gladiators which faced –
That haggard mark of Imperial Rome,
Whose Pagan echoes mock the chime
Of our Christian time
From its hollows of chalk and loam.

The sun's gold touch was scarce displaced
From the vast Arena where men once bled,
When her husband followed; bowed; half-passed
With lip upcast;
Then halting sullenly said:

Her Death and After

52 Tombs . . . frowned] Tombs, by the Via renowned, MS, WP, PUE
62 she] she'd MS
62 mine,] mine MS
64 dame] Dame MS
67 dear –] dear; MS, WP, PUE: dear, WE, SP, ME: dear CP1–3
68 That] Dead MS, WP, PUE
68 suffused] suffused, MS, WP, PUE
69 Had a] Her MS, WP, PUE
70 While . . . not] I helpless to MS, WP, PUE, WE, SP, ME
72 white-stoned] Holy MS
72 Garth . . . wrong] Garth with these brooding glooms WE, SP, ME
73 nod] view MS, WP, PUE, CP1
74] In the hallowed mew MS
74 sod] mew WP, PUE, CP1
75 the tombs among] among the tombs WE, SP, ME
79 time] time: MS, WP, PUE: time; WE1: time – CP1
80] It was void, and I inward clomb. MS, WP, PUE: And I drew to its bank and clomb. WE1, CP1 [but CP1 corrected on errata slip to reading given here]
80 chalk] turf SP [There is a manuscript correction from 'chalk' to 'turf' in Hardy's copy of WE1, which had already been corrected to read 'From its hollows of chalk and loam.']
81] Scarce (had MS, WP1) night the sun's gold touch displaced MS, WP, PUE
81 scarce] just WE, SP, ME
82 once] Corrected to 'had' in Hardy's copy of CP2
82 Arena . . . bled,] Rotund and the neighbouring dead MS, WP, PUE
83 half-passed] half-passed, MS, WP, PUE, WE, SP, ME
85 Then halting] Then, halting, MS, WP, PUE, WE, SP, ME
85 said:] said: – MS

'It is noised that you visit my first wife's tomb.
Now, I gave her an honoured name to bear
While living, when dead. So I've claim to ask
By what right you task
My patience by vigiling there?

'There's decency even in death, I assume;
Preserve it, sir, and keep away;
For the mother of my first-born you
Show mind undue!
– Sir, I've nothing more to say.'

A desperate stroke discerned I then –
God pardon – or pardon not – the lie;
She had sighed that she wished (lest the child should pine
Of slights) 'twere mine,
So I said: 'But the father I.

'That you thought it yours is the way of men;
But I won her troth long ere your day:
You learnt how, in dying, she summoned me?
'Twas in fealty.
– Sir, I've nothing more to say,

'Save that, if you'll hand me my little maid,
I'll take her, and rear her, and spare you toil.
Think it more than a friendly act none can;
I'm a lonely man,
While you've a large pot to boil.

'If not, and you'll put it to ball or blade –
To-night, to-morrow night, anywhen –
I'll meet you here. . . . But think of it,
And in season fit
Let me hear from you again.'

– Well, I went away, hoping; but nought I heard
Of my stroke for the child, till there greeted me
A little voice that one day came
To my window-frame
And babbled innocently:

Her Death and After
86 tomb.] tomb: MS
89] Your right to task SP, ME, WE2 [Hardy has corrected his copy of WE1 to read as WE2]
90 vigiling] darkling WE, SP, ME [Hardy spells it 'vigilling' in MS]
92 sir] Sir MS
93 For the mother] The mother she MS
93 first-born] firstborn, MS
94 mind undue!] zest undue MS
95] In haunting her grave, I say.' MS [The printed form of this line is in erased pencil in MS]
105 – Sir,] Sir; MS
107 toil.] toil; MS
113 here. . . .] here. . . . . MS
116 – Well,] Well: MS
118 that] which MS
120 innocently:] innocently: – MS

'My father who's not my own, sends word
I'm to stay here, sir, where I belong!'
Next a writing came: 'Since the child was the fruit
        Of your lawless suit,
    Pray take her, to right a wrong.'

And I did. And I gave the child my love,
And the child loved me, and estranged us none.
But compunctions loomed; for I'd harmed the dead
        By what I said
    For the good of the living one.

– Yet though, God wot, I am sinner enough,
And unworthy the woman who drew me so,
Perhaps this wrong for her darling's good
        She forgives, or would,
    If only she could know!

28 *The Dance at the Phœnix*

TITLE:
The Dance at The Phoenix MS

To Jenny came a gentle youth
    From inland leazes lone,
His love was fresh as apple-blooth
    By Parrett, Yeo, or Tone.
And duly he entreated her
To be his tender minister,
    And take him for her own.

Now Jenny's life had hardly been
    A life of modesty;
And few in Casterbridge had seen
    More loves of sorts than she
From scarcely sixteen years above;
Among them sundry troopers of
    The King's-Own Cavalry.

Her Death and After
121 father] father, SP
122 sir] Sir MS
122 belong!] belong. MS
124 lawless suit] passions brute MS, WP1
129 I] I'd MS, WP, PUE, WE, SP, ME
131 – Yet] Yet MS

The Dance at the Phœnix
1 Jenny] Nelly MS
2 inland leazes lone,] Wessex leazes lone; MS
2 lone,] lone; WPA
7 take him for] call him aye MS, WP, PUE
8 Now] Fair MS, WP, PUE, WE1
8 Jenny's] Nelly's MS
10–11] At Casterbridge experience keen/
    Of many loves had she MS, WP, PUE

But each with charger, sword, and gun,
Had bluffed the Biscay wave;
And Jenny prized her rural one
For all the love he gave.
She vowed to be, if they were wed,
His honest wife in heart and head
From bride-ale hour to grave.

Wedded they were. Her husband's trust
In Jenny knew no bound,
And Jenny kept her pure and just,
Till even malice found
No sin or sign of ill to be
In one who walked so decently
The duteous helpmate's round.

Two sons were born, and bloomed to men,
And roamed, and were as not:
Alone was Jenny left again
As ere her mind had sought
A solace in domestic joys,
And ere the vanished pair of boys
Were sent to sun her cot.

She numbered near on sixty years,
And passed as elderly,
When, on a day, with flushing fears,
She learnt from shouts of glee,
And shine of swords, and thump of drum,
Her early loves from war had come,
The King's-Own Cavalry.

She turned aside, and bowed her head
Anigh Saint Peter's door;
'Alas for chastened thoughts!' she said;
'I'm faded now, and hoar,
And yet those notes – they thrill me through,
And those gay forms move me anew
As they moved me of yore!' . . .

The Dance at the Phœnix
15 gun,] gun MS
16 bluffed the Biscay] gone across the MS
17 Jenny] Nelly MS
17 rural] gentle MS, WP, PUE, WE, ME
23 Jenny] Nelly MS
24 Jenny] Nelly MS
27 decently] carefully MS
29 born,] born MS
29 bloomed] grew MS
31 Jenny] Nelly MS
35 sun] light MS
36 near on sixty] more than fifty MS
36 on] to WE, ME
38–9 When, in the street, with flush of fears,/ One day discovered she, (she MS) MS, WP, PUE
40 And] From MS, WP, PUE
40 swords,] swords MS, WP, PUE, WE, ME
40 thump] throb MS
40 drum,] drum MS
49 they moved me] in the years MS, WP, PUE: I was moved WE, ME
49 moved me of yore] Corrected to 'did heretofore' in Hardy's copy of CP2
49 yore!' . . .] yore! . . . . . MS

'Twas Christmas, and the Phœnix Inn
Was lit with tapers tall,
For thirty of the trooper men
Had vowed to give a ball
As 'Theirs' had done ('twas handed down)
When lying in the selfsame town
Ere Buonaparté's fall.

That night the throbbing 'Soldier's Joy',
The measured tread and sway
Of 'Fancy-Lad' and 'Maiden Coy',
Reached Jenny as she lay
Beside her spouse; till springtide blood
Seemed scouring through her like a flood
That whisked the years away.

She rose, arrayed, and decked her head
Where the bleached hairs grew thin;
Upon her cap two bows of red
She fixed with hasty pin;
Unheard descending to the street
She trod the flags with tune-led feet,
And stood before the Inn.

Save for the dancers', not a sound
Disturbed the icy air;
No watchman on his midnight round
Or traveller was there;
But over All-Saints', high and bright,
Pulsed to the music Sirius white,
The Wain by Bullstake Square.

She knocked, but found her further stride
Checked by a sergeant tall:
'Gay Granny, whence come you?' he cried;
'This is a private ball.'
– 'No one has more right here than me!
Ere you were born, man,' answered she,
'I knew the regiment all!'

The Dance at the Phœnix
54 'twas] fame WP1
55 selfsame] self-same WPA, WE, ME
60 Jenny] Nelly MS
62 scouring] rushing MS
64 arrayed] and rayed MS, WP, PUE
65] To hide her ringlets thin; (thin: MS) MS, WP1
65 grew] ran WP2, PUE
66 Upon her cap two] She pranked her cap with MS
66 red] red, MS
67] And stuck rosettes therein; MS
68 street] street, WP, PUE, WE, ME
69 tune-led feet] footing fleet MS
74 there;] there: MS
77 by] towards WE, ME
79 sergeant tall] Corrected to 'sergeant's call' in Hardy's copy of CP2
80 cried;] cried, MS

'Take not the lady's visit ill!'
The steward said; 'for see,
We lack sufficient partners still,
So, prithee, let her be!'
They seized and whirled her mid the maze,
And Jenny felt as in the days
Of her immodesty.

Hour chased each hour, and night advanced;
She sped as shod with wings;
Each time and every time she danced –
Reels, jigs, poussettes, and flings:
They cheered her as she soared and swooped,
(She had learnt ere art in dancing drooped
From hops to slothful swings).

The favourite Quick-step 'Speed the Plough' –
(Cross hands, cast off, and wheel) –
'The Triumph', 'Sylph', 'The Row-dow-dow',
Famed 'Major Malley's Reel',
'The Duke of York's', 'The Fairy Dance',
'The Bridge of Lodi' (brought from France),
She beat out, toe and heel.

The 'Fall of Paris' clanged its close,
And Peter's chime went four,
When Jenny, bosom-beating, rose
To seek her silent door.
They tiptoed in escorting her,
Lest stroke of heel or clink of spur
Should break her goodman's snore.

The fire that lately burnt fell slack
When lone at last was she;
Her nine-and-fifty years came back;
She sank upon her knee
Beside the durn, and like a dart
A something arrowed through her heart
In shoots of agony.

The Dance at the Phœnix
86] Upspoke the steward free; (free, MS) MS, WP, PUE
86 for] for, WE, ME
87 We] 'We MS, WP, PUE
88 prithee,] pri'thee MS: prithee WP, PUE, WE, ME
89 mid] 'mid MS, WP, PUE
90 Jenny] Nelly MS
93 wings;] wings WP1 [WPA has: wings;]
95 jigs, poussettes] allemandes MS
96 swooped,] swooped WPA
97 She had] She'd MS, WP, PUE, WE, ME
99–105] Not in MS
106 clanged] trilled MS
107 chime went] Corrected to 'chimed to' in Hardy's copy of CP2
107 went] told MS, WP, PUE
108 Jenny] Nelly MS
108 bosom-beating] bosom-bursting MS
113 lately] late had MS, WP, PUE
114 was] stood MS, WP, PUE
115 nine-and-fifty] five and fifty MS
115 back;] back, MS
117 durn,] durn; MS

Their footsteps died as she leant there,
    Lit by the morning star
Hanging above the moorland, where
    The aged elm-rows are;
As overnight, from Pummery Ridge
To Maembury Ring and Standfast Bridge
    No life stirred, near or far.

Though inner mischief worked amain,
    She reached her husband's side;
Where, toil-weary, as he had lain
    Beneath the patchwork pied
When forthward yestereve she crept,
And as unwitting, still he slept
    Who did in her confide.

A tear sprang as she turned and viewed
    His features free from guile;
She kissed him long, as when, just wooed,
    She chose his domicile.
She felt she would give more than life
To be the single-hearted wife
    That she had been erstwhile. . . .

Time wore to six. Her husband rose
    And struck the steel and stone;
He glanced at Jenny, whose repose
    Seemed deeper than his own.
With dumb dismay, on closer sight,
He gathered sense that in the night,
    Or morn, her soul had flown.

When told that some too mighty strain
    For one so many-yeared
Had burst her bosom's master-vein,
    His doubts remained unstirred.
His Jenny had not left his side
Betwixt the eve and morning-tide:
    – The King's said not a word.

The Dance at the Phœnix
120 there,] there WE, ME
124 As overnight] And, as o'ernight MS, WP, PUE
125 Standfast] Friary MS
128] She crawled to her bed side; MS
131] When with lax longings she had crept WE, ME
131 forthward . . . she] yestereve she'd forthward (thenceward MS) MS, WP, PUE
132 And as unwitting] Therefrom at midnight WE, ME
138 would . . . than] could have given her PUE
138–9] Death neighboured now; yet, more than life,/She craved that she were still the wife MS
Death menaced now; yet less for life/She wished than that she were the wife WP
140 erstwhile. . . .] erstwhile. MS, WP, PUE, WE, ME
143 Jenny] Nelly MS
146 night,] night MS
149 many-yeared] heavy-yeared MS
150 bosom's master-vein] heart's intensest vein MS
152 Jenny] Nelly MS

Well! times are not as times were then,
Nor fair ones half so free;
And truly they were martial men,
The King's-Own Cavalry.
And when they went from Casterbridge
And vanished over Mellstock Ridge,
'Twas saddest morn to see.

29 *The Casterbridge Captains*

TITLE:
A ... L——] In memory of L——, B——, and L——. MS

(*Khyber Pass, 1842*)

A Tradition of J. B. L——, T. G. B——, and J. L——

THREE captains went to Indian wars,
And only one returned:
Their mate of yore, he singly wore
The laurels all had earned.

At home he sought the ancient aisle
Wherein, untrumped of fame,
The three had sat in pupilage,
And each had carved his name.

The names, rough-hewn, of equal size,
Stood on the panel still;
Unequal since. – ' 'Twas theirs to aim,
Mine was it to fulfil!'

– 'Who saves his life shall lose it, friends!'
Outspake the preacher then,
Unweeting he his listener, who
Looked at the names again.

That he had come and they had been stayed
Was but the chance of war:
Another chance, and they had been here,
And he had lain afar.

The Dance at the Phœnix
155 Well!] Well: MS
157 men,] men MS
160 Ridge,] Ridge MS

The Casterbridge Captains
4 laurels] bays that MS
5 sought. . . aisle] entered All-Saints' aisle, MS
13 – 'Who] 'Who MS
14 Outspake] Outspoke MS
17 come] come, MS, WE, ME
17 they had been stayed] they'd been stayed, MS, WP, PUE, WE, ME
18 Was] 'Twas MS, WP, PUE, WE
19 they had been] they'd sat MS, WP, PUE, WE, ME

Yet saw he something in the lives
Of those who had ceased to live
That sphered them with a majesty
Which living failed to give.

Transcendent triumph in return
No longer lit his brain;
Transcendence rayed the distant urn
Where slept the fallen twain.

30 *A Sign-Seeker*

TITLE:
A Sign-seeker MS

INDENTATION:
1 = l. 4
2 = l. 1
3 = ll. 2, 3
} and so throughout MS

I MARK the months in liveries dank and dry,
The noontides many-shaped and hued;
I see the nightfall shades subtrude,
And hear the monotonous hours clang negligently by.

I view the evening bonfires of the sun
On hills where morning rains have hissed;
The eyeless countenance of the mist
Pallidly rising when the summer droughts are done.

I have seen the lightning-blade, the leaping star,
The cauldrons of the sea in storm,
Have felt the earthquake's lifting arm,
And trodden where abysmal fires and snow-cones are.

I learn to prophesy the hid eclipse,
The coming of eccentric orbs;
To mete the dust the sky absorbs,
To weigh the sun, and fix the hour each planet dips.

I witness fellow earth-men surge and strive;
Assemblies meet, and throb, and part;
Death's sudden finger, sorrow's smart;
– All the vast various moils that mean a world alive.

The Casterbridge Captains
22 who had] who'd MS, WP, PUE, WE, ME
23 sphered them with a] rounded them with WP1
23 sphered] marked MS
27 distant] lonely MS
26–8] His heart no longer knew;/Transcendence rayed the distant urn/Above the other two. MS *before revision*
28 fallen] distant MS

A Sign-Seeker
1 months] Months MS
2 noontides] Day-tides MS: day-tides WP1
2 many-shaped] many shaped MS
3] I know the nod of Night subdued, MS
4 hours] Hours MS
5 sun] Sun MS
7 mist] Mist MS
9 lightning-blade] Lightning-blade MS
9 star] Star MS
10 sea] Sea MS
11 earthquake's] Earthquake's MS
12 fires] Fires MS
12 snow-cones] Snow-cones MS
13 eclipse] Eclipse MS
14 orbs] Orbs MS
16 sun] Sun MS
16 planet] Planet MS
19 sudden] soothing MS, WP, PUE
19 sorrow's smart] Sorrow's Dart MS
20 moils] Moils MS

But that I fain would wot of shuns my sense –
Those sights of which old prophets tell,
Those signs the general word so well
As vouchsafed their unheed, denied my long suspense.

In graveyard green, where his pale dust lies pent
To glimpse a phantom parent, friend,
Wearing his smile, and 'Not the end!'
Outbreathing softly: that were blest enlightenment;

Or, if a dead Love's lips, whom dreams reveal
When midnight imps of King Decay
Delve sly to solve me back to clay,
Should leave some print to prove her spirit-kisses real;

Or, when Earth's Frail lie bleeding of her Strong,
If some Recorder, as in Writ,
Near to the weary scene should flit
And drop one plume as pledge that Heaven inscrolls the wrong.

– There are who, rapt to heights of trancelike trust,
These tokens claim to feel and see,
Read radiant hints of times to be –
Of heart to heart returning after dust to dust.

Such scope is granted not to lives like mine . . .
I have lain in dead men's beds, have walked
The tombs of those with whom I had talked,
Called many a gone and goodly one to shape a sign,

And panted for response. But none replies;
No warnings loom, nor whisperings
To open out my limitings,
And Nescience mutely muses: When a man falls he lies.

A Sign-Seeker
23 well] well; MS: well, WP, PUE, WE, ME
24 As vouchsafed] Vouchsafed to MS, WP, PUE, WE, ME
24 long suspense] watchings tense MS, WP1
25 where . . . pent] behind his monument MS, WP, PUE
25 pent] pent, WE, ME
29 dead] lost MS
32 real;] real. MS
36 pledge . . . inscrolls] sign Heaven registers MS
37] There are who, blest with store of stoic trust MS
37 trancelike] trancéd WP, PUE, WE, ME
41 scope] gift MS
41 to . . . mine . . .] my lot (power WP1) in-dign. . . . . . (. . . WP1) MS, WP1
43 I had] I'd MS, WP, PUE

31 *My Cicely*

(17—)

'ALIVE?' – And I leapt in my wonder,
  Was faint of my joyance,
And grasses and grove shone in garments
  Of glory to me.

'She lives, in a plenteous well-being,
  To-day as aforehand;
The dead bore the name – though a rare one –
  The name that bore she.'

She lived . . . I, afar in the city
  Of frenzy-led factions,
Had squandered green years and maturer
  In bowing the knee

To Baals illusive and specious,
  Till chance had there voiced me
That one I loved vainly in nonage
  Had ceased her to be.

The passion the planets had scowled on,
  And change had let dwindle,
Her death-rumour smartly relifted
  To full apogee.

I mounted a steed in the dawning
  With acheful remembrance,
And made for the ancient West Highway
  To far Exonb'ry.

Passing heaths, and the House of Long Sieging,
  I neared the thin steeple
That tops the fair fane of Poore's olden
  Episcopal see;

TITLE:
MS has 'Cicely' written over an erased name which, on the evidence of l. 112, seems likely to have been 'Naomi'
(17—)] Not in MS

My Cicely
2 joyance,] joyance WE1
6 aforehand] aforetime WE, ME
7 though] not MS
8 The name that] That whilom MS
9 lived . . .] lived. . . . . MS
17 on,] on MS
25 heaths] Heaths MS
27 olden] ancient MS

And, changing anew my blown bearer,
  I traversed the downland
Whereon the bleak hill-graves of Chieftains
  Bulge barren of tree;

And still sadly onward I followed
  That Highway the Icen,
Which trails its pale riband down Wessex
  By lynchet and lea.

Along through the Stour-bordered Forum,
  Where Legions had wayfared,
And where the slow river-face glasses
  Its green canopy,

And by Weatherbury Castle, and thencefrom
  Through Casterbridge held I
Still on, to entomb her my mindsight
  Saw stretched pallidly.

No highwayman's trot blew the night-wind
  To me so life-weary,
But only the creak of a gibbet
  Or waggoner's jee.

Triple-ramparted Maidon gloomed grayly
  Above me from southward,
And north the hill-fortress of Eggar,
  And square Pummerie.

The Nine-Pillared Cromlech, the Bride-streams,
  The Axe, and the Otter
I passed, to the gate of the city
  Where Exe scents the sea;

Till, spent, in the graveacre pausing,
  I learnt 'twas not *my* Love
To whom Mother Church had just murmured
  A last lullaby.

My Cicely
29 blown bearer] onbearer MS, WP, PUE
30 traversed] thridded MS
31 hill-graves] hillgraves MS
33 followed] travelled MS
34] That highway Icenian, MS
35 [MS has particularly interesting printer's note: new sig returned to here Oct 16 – 98]
35 riband] ribbon WPA
36 By] O'er MS, WP, PUE
37] By Egdon and Casterbridge bore I, MS
38 Legions] legions MS
39–40] To tomb her I deemed sent to silence/ By will of the Three. MS
39 river-face glasses] river upglasses WP, PUE
41–8] Not in MS
41 thencefrom] therence WP1
42 Casterbridge held I] Casterbridge, bore I, WP
43–4] To tomb her whose light, in my deeming,/Extinguished had He. WP
43 mindsight] vision PUE, WE, ME
47 a gibbet] the gibbets WP, PUE: the gibbet WE, ME
48 waggoner's] waggoners' WP, PUE, WE, ME
53 Bride-streams] Bredy MS
57 pausing,] pausing MS
58 *my*] my MS, WP, PUE

– 'Then, where dwells the Canon's kinswoman,
My friend of aforetime?'
I asked, to disguise my heart-heavings
And new ecstasy.

'She wedded.' – 'Ah!' – 'Wedded beneath her –
She keeps the stage-hostel
Ten miles hence, beside the great Highway –
The famed Lions-Three.

'Her spouse was her lackey – no option
'Twixt wedlock and worse things;
A lapse over-sad for a lady
Of her pedigree!'

I shuddered, said nothing, and wandered
To shades of green laurel:
More ghastly than death were these tidings
Of life's irony!

For, on my ride down I had halted
Awhile at the Lions,
And her – her whose name had once opened
My heart as a key –

I'd looked on, unknowing, and witnessed
Her jests with the tapsters,
Her liquor-fired face, her thick accents
In naming her fee.

'O God, why this seeming derision!'
I cried in my anguish:
'O once Loved, O fair Unforgotten –
That Thing – meant it thee!

'Inurned and at peace, lost but sainted,
Were grief I could compass;
Depraved – 'tis for Christ's poor dependent
A cruel decree!'

My Cicely
61 dwells] is WE, ME
62 aforetime?'] aforetime?' – MS, WP, PUE, WE, ME
63 I . . . disguise] ('Twas hard to repress MS, WP, PUE
63 to disguise] and disguised WE, ME
64 ecstacy.] ecstacy.) MS, WP, PUE
68 Lions-Three] Fleur-de-Lis (Old Holly-Tree *del*) MS
75–6] Too ghastly had grown those first tidings/So brightsome of blee! MS, WP, PUE
76 life's] Life's WE, ME
77] For riding down hither I'd halted WE, ME
77 ride . . . had] ride (track MS) hither, I'd MS, WP, PUE
78 Lions] Hostel (Holly *del*) MS
81 unknowing, and witnessed] unweeting, and noted MS
85 seeming derision] hocus satiric MS, WP
87 O once] O, Once MS
87 fair] Fair MS
88 thee!] thee. MS

I backed on the Highway; but passed not
The hostel. Within there
Too mocking to Love's re-expression
Was Time's repartee!

Uptracking where Legions had wayfared
By cromlechs unstoried,
And lynchets, and sepultured Chieftains,
In self-colloquy,

A feeling stirred in me and strengthened
That *she* was not my Love,
But she of the garth, who lay rapt in
Her long reverie.

And thence till to-day I persuade me
That this was the true one;
That Death stole intact her young dearness
And innocency.

Frail-witted, illuded they call me;
I may be. Far better
To dream than to own the debasement
Of sweet Cicely.

Moreover I rate it unseemly
To hold that kind Heaven
Could work such device – to her ruin
And my misery.

So, lest I disturb my choice vision,
I shun the West Highway,
Even now, when the knaps ring with rhythms
From blackbird and bee;

And feel that with slumber half-conscious
She rests in the church-hay,
Her spirit unsoiled as in youth-time
When lovers were we.

My Cicely
94 hostel] Hostel (Holly *del*) MS
97 wayfared] wayfared, MS, WP, PUE, WE, ME
98 cromlechs] Cromlechs MS
107 Death] Time MS
107 dearness] sweetness MS
108 innocency] innocent 'ee MS
110 Far] 'Tis MS, WP, PUE
112 Cicely] Naomi MS *before revision*
122 church-hay] churchhay MS
123 youth-time] youthtime MS

32 *Her Immortality*

UPON a noon I pilgrimed through
A pasture, mile by mile,
Unto the place where last I saw
My dead Love's living smile.

And sorrowing I lay me down
Upon the heated sod:
It seemed as if my body pressed
The very ground she trod.

I lay, and thought; and in a trance
She came and stood thereby –
The same, even to the marvellous ray
That used to light her eye.

'You draw me, and I come to you,
My faithful one,' she said,
In voice that had the moving tone
It bore ere she was wed.

'Seven years have circled since I died:
Few now remember me;
My husband clasps another bride:
My children's love has she.

'My brethren, sisters, and my friends
Care not to meet my sprite:
Who prized me most I did not know
Till I passed down from sight.'

I said: 'My days are lonely here;
I need thy smile alway:
I'll use this night my ball or blade,
And join thee ere the day.'

Her Immortality
1 pilgrimed] wayfared MS
3 last I] I last MS, WP, PUE
10 thereby] me by MS, WP, PUE
13 you,] you MS
14 said,] said MS
16 It bore] Of days WE, ME
16 ere . . . wed] in maidenhead WP1
16 she was wed] life had sped MS: breath had fled WP2, PUE, CP1
17 'Seven . . . circled] She said: ' 'Tis seven years MS, WP, PUE
19 bride:] bride; MS, WP, PUE, WE, ME
20] My children mothers she. MS, WP1

A tremor stirred her tender lips,
  Which parted to dissuade:
'That cannot be, O friend,' she cried;
  'Think, I am but a Shade!

'A Shade but in its mindful ones
  Has immortality;
By living, me you keep alive,
  By dying you slay me.

'In you resides my single power
  Of sweet continuance here;
On your fidelity I count
  Through many a coming year.'

– I started through me at her plight,
  So suddenly confessed:
Dismissing late distaste for life,
  I craved its bleak unrest.

'I will not die, my One of all! –
  To lengthen out thy days
I'll guard me from minutest harms
  That may invest my ways!'

She smiled and went. Since then she comes
  Oft when her birth-moon climbs,
Or at the seasons' ingresses,
  Or anniversary times;

But grows my grief. When I surcease,
  Through whom alone lives she,
Her spirit ends its living lease,
  Never again to be!

Her Immortality
29 stirred] passed MS
32 Think,] Think; MS
33 Shade] shade MS
35 living . . . keep] living you keep me MS
41 – I] I MS
43 life,] life MS
51 ingresses,] ingresses WP, PUE, WE1
52] Or August's still noon-times; MS
55] Ceases my Love, her words, her ways, MS, WP, PUE: Ceases my Love's terrestrial lease, WE, ME
56 be!] be. MS

33 *The Ivy-Wife*

TITLE:
The Ivy-wife MS

I LONGED to love a full-boughed beech
And be as high as he:
I stretched an arm within his reach,
And signalled unity.
But with his drip he forced a breach,
And tried to poison me.

I gave the grasp of partnership
To one of other race –
A plane: he barked him strip by strip
From upper bough to base;
And me therewith; for gone my grip,
My arms could not enlace.

In new affection next I strove
To coll an ash I saw,
And he in trust received my love;
Till with my soft green claw
I cramped and bound him as I wove . . .
Such was my love: ha-ha!

By this I gained his strength and height
Without his rivalry.
But in my triumph I lost sight
Of afterhaps. Soon he,
Being bark-bound, flagged, snapped, fell outright,
And in his fall felled me!

34 *A Meeting with Despair*

TITLE:
MS has *deleted* below title: (Egdon Heath)

AS evening shaped I found me on a moor
Sight shunned to entertain:
The black lean land, of featureless contour,
Was like a tract in pain.

The Ivy-Wife
3 reach,] reach; MS
11 grip,] grip MS
13 strove] clove MS
14 coll an] a smooth MS
17] I choked him as I wove and wove . . . . MS
22 afterhaps] afterclaps MS
23 bark-bound, flagged] dead, decayed MS

A Meeting with Despair
2] Which sight could scarce sustain: MS, WP, PUE

'This scene, like my own life,' I said, 'is one
    Where many glooms abide;
Toned by its fortune to a deadly dun –
    Lightless on every side.'

I glanced aloft and halted, pleasure-caught
    To see the contrast there:
The ray-lit clouds gleamed glory; and I thought,
    'There's solace everywhere!'

Then bitter self-reproaches as I stood
    I dealt me silently
As one perverse, misrepresenting Good
    In graceless mutiny.

Against the horizon's dim-discernèd wheel
    A form rose, strange of mould:
That he was hideous, hopeless, I could feel
    Rather than could behold.

' 'Tis a dead spot, where even the light lies spent
    To darkness!' croaked the Thing.
'Not if you look aloft!' said I, intent
    On my new reasoning.

'Yea – but await awhile!' he cried. 'Ho-ho! –
    Now look aloft and see!'
I looked. There, too, sat night: Heaven's radiant show
    Had gone that heartened me.

EXTRA PRINTINGS:
(1) *Selected Poems*, pp. 51–2
(2) *Chosen Poems*, pp. 50–1

35 *Unknowing*

WHEN, soul in soul reflected,
We breathed an æthered air,
    When we neglected
    All things elsewhere,
And left the friendly friendless
To keep our love aglow,
    We deemed it endless . . .
    – We did not know!

A Meeting with Despair
11 ray-lit] raylit MS
12 There's] Ah – CP1
15 perverse,] perverse – MS, WP, PUE, WE, ME
21 dead] drear MS
25 Yea . . . await] Yes – should you wait MS
26 Now look] Look now MS, WP, PUE, WE, ME
27 There . . . night:] There too sat night. MS
28] Had gone; and gone had he. MS:
Had gone. Then chuckled he. WP, PUE

Unknowing
7 endless . . .] endless. . . . . MS

When panting passion-goaded,
We planned to hie away,
But, unforeboded,
All the long day
The storm so pierced and pattered
That none could up and go,
Our lives seemed shattered . . .
– We did not know!

When I found you helpless lying,
And you waived my long misprise,
And swore me, dying,
In phantom-guise
To wing to me when grieving,
And touch away my woe,
We kissed, believing . . .
– We did not know!

But though, your powers outreckoning,
You tarry dead and dumb,
Or scorn my beckoning,
And will not come:
And I say, 'Why thus inanely
Brood on her memory so!'
I say it vainly –
I feel and know!

36 Friends Beyond

WILLIAM DEWY, Tranter Reuben, Farmer Ledlow late at plough,
Robert's kin, and John's, and Ned's,
And the Squire, and Lady Susan, lie in Mellstock churchyard now!

'Gone,' I call them, gone for good, that group of local hearts and heads;
Yet at mothy curfew-tide,
And at midnight when the noon-heat breathes it back from walls and leads,

Unknowing
9] When, by mad passion goaded, MS, WP, PUE
12] The livelong day CP1
12–13] The storm-shafts gray
So heavily down-pattered MS, WP, PUE
13 The storm] Wild storms WE, SP, ME: Wild storm CP1
14 up and] thenceward MS: forthward WP, PUE
15 shattered . . .] shattered. . . . . . MS
17 you] you, MS, WP, PUE, WE, SP, ME
18 long] deep MS, WP, PUE
23 believing . . .] believing. . . . . MS
25 outreckoning] out-reckoning SP
26 tarry] hold you MS, WP, PUE
28 come:] come; MS, WP, PUE, WE, SP, ME
29 Why thus inanely] 'Twere mood ungainly MS, WP, PUE
30] To store her memory so:' MS, WP, PUE
30 so!] so: WE, SP, ME
31 vainly –] vainly MS

EXTRA PRINTINGS:
(1) *Selected Poems*, pp. 112–14
(2) *Chosen Poems*, pp. 146–8

INDENTATION:
In MS speakers' names are indicated clear to the left and do not interfere with the normal pattern

Note This was one of nine poems chosen by Hardy for the Library of the Royal Dolls' House at Windsor Castle. The copy there has 'Thus' (l. 31)

They've a way of whispering to me – fellow-wight who yet abide –
In the muted, measured note
Of a ripple under archways, or a lone cave's stillicide:

'We have triumphed: this achievement turns the bane to antidote,
Unsuccesses to success,
Many thought-worn eves and morrows to a morrow free of thought.

'No more need we corn and clothing, feel of old terrestrial stress;
Chill detraction stirs no sigh;
Fear of death has even bygone us: death gave all that we possess.'

W.D. – 'Ye mid burn the old bass-viol that I set such value by.'
Squire. – 'You may hold the manse in fee,
You may wed my spouse, may let my children's memory of me die.'

Lady S. – 'You may have my rich brocades, my laces; take each household key;
Ransack coffer, desk, bureau;
Quiz the few poor treasures hid there, con the letters kept by me.'

Far. – 'Ye mid zell my favourite heifer, ye mid let the charlock grow,
Foul the grinterns, give up thrift.'
Far. Wife. – 'If ye break my best blue china, children, I shan't care or ho.'

All. – 'We've no wish to hear the tidings, how the people's fortunes shift;
What your daily doings are;
Who are wedded, born, divided; if your lives beat slow or swift.

'Curious not the least are we if our intents you make or mar,
If you quire to our old tune,
If the City stage still passes, if the weirs still roar afar.'

– Thus, with very gods' composure, freed those crosses late and soon
Which, in life, the Trine allow
(Why, none witteth), and ignoring all that haps beneath the moon,

William Dewy, Tranter Reuben, Farmer Ledlow late at plough,
Robert's kin, and John's, and Ned's,
And the Squire, and Lady Susan, murmur mildly to me now.

Friends Beyond
12 thought-worn] thoughtworn MS
13 No . . . we] Nought we need of MS
13 feel] know MS
13 terrestrial] terrestial CP
16 old] wold MS, WP, PUE
16 bass-viol] base-viol SP
16 value] vallie MS, WP, PUE
18 may . . . die] my children's memory of me may decry MS, WP, PUE
19 *Lady S.* –] *Lady.* – WP, PUE, WE, SP, ME
22 *Far.* –] *Farmer.* – MS
22 zell] sell MS
24 *Far. Wife.* –] *Wife.* – MS, WP, PUE, WE, SP, ME
24 shan't] sha'n't WPA

37 *To Outer Nature*

TITLE:
To External Nature MS

SHOW thee as I thought thee
When I early sought thee,
  Omen-scouting,
  All undoubting
Love alone had wrought thee –

Wrought thee for my pleasure,
Planned thee as a measure
  For expounding
  And resounding
Glad things that men treasure.

O for but a moment
Of that old endowment –
  Light to gaily
  See thy daily
Iris-hued embowment!

But such re-adorning
Time forbids with scorning –
  Makes me see things
  Cease to be things
They were in my morning.

Fad'st thou, glow-forsaken,
Darkness-overtaken!
  Thy first sweetness,
  Radiance, meetness,
None shall re-awaken.

Why not sempiternal
Thou and I? Our vernal
  Brightness keeping,
  Time outleaping;
Passed the hodiernal!

To Outer Nature
3–4] Sorrow-scouting,
  Never doubting MS
6 my] our MS
15 Iris-hued] Irisèd MS, WP, PUE
16 re-adorning] readorning MS, WPA, WE, ME
22] Darkness overtaken; MS
25 re-awaken] reawaken MS, WPA

EXTRA PRINTINGS:
(1) *Selected Poems*, pp. 37–8
(2) *Chosen Poems*, pp. 38–9

TITLE:
T—— a
At news of her death
(Died 1890 *del*) MS

Thoughts of Ph—a
At news of her death WP1

At News of a Woman's Death SP

38 *Thoughts of Phena*

At News of Her Death

NOT a line of her writing have I,
Not a thread of her hair,
No mark of her late time as dame in her dwelling, whereby
I may picture her there;
And in vain do I urge my unsight
To conceive my lost prize
At her close, whom I knew when her dreams were upbrimming with light,
And with laughter her eyes.

What scenes spread around her last days,
Sad, shining, or dim?
Did her gifts and compassions enray and enarch her sweet ways
With an aureate nimb?
Or did life-light decline from her years,
And mischances control
Her full day-star; unease, or regret, or forebodings, or fears
Disennoble her soul?

Thus I do but the phantom retain
Of the maiden of yore
As my relic; yet haply the best of her – fined in my brain
It may be the more
That no line of her writing have I,
Nor a thread of her hair,
No mark of her late time as dame in her dwelling, whereby
I may picture her there.

March 1890

Thoughts of Phena
3 time . . . dwelling] time, her bower, her lattice MS
4 picture] image MS
7 At] In MS
10–12] Sad, sharp, or serene?/Did the Fates and Affections combine to embow her sweet ways/With an irisèd sheen? MS
13 life-light] lifelight MS
15 day-star] daystar MS
17 phantom] vision MS
23 time . . . dwelling] time, her bower, her lattice MS
24 picture] image MS

39 *Middle-Age Enthusiasms*

EXTRA PRINTING:
Selected Poems, pp. 39–40

TITLE:
Middle-age Enthusiasms MS

To M.H.

WE passed where flag and flower
Signalled a jocund throng;
We said: 'Go to, the hour
Is apt!' – and joined the song;
And, kindling, laughed at life and care,
Although we knew no laugh lay there.

We walked where shy birds stood
Watching us, wonder-dumb;
Their friendship met our mood;
We cried: 'We'll often come:
We'll come morn, noon, eve, everywhen!'
– We doubted we should come again.

We joyed to see strange sheens
Leap from quaint leaves in shade;
A secret light of greens
They'd for their pleasure made.
We said: 'We'll set such sorts as these!'
– We knew with night the wish would cease.

'So sweet the place,' we said,
'Its tacit tales so dear,
Our thoughts, when breath has sped,
Will meet and mingle here!' . . .
'Words!' mused we. 'Passed the mortal door,
Our thoughts will reach this nook no more.'

Middle-Age Enthusiasms
17 set such sorts] plant such growths MS
22 here!' . . .] here!' . . . . MS
24] This nook will know our thoughts no more.' MS

EXTRA PRINTINGS:
(1) *Selected Poems*, pp. 88–9
(2) *Chosen Poems*, pp. 83–4

TITLE:
See] *vide* MS: *From* WE, ME, CP
See 'The Woodlanders'] Not in SP, CHP

40 In a Wood

See 'The Woodlanders'

PALE beech and pine so blue,
Set in one clay,
Bough to bough cannot you
Live out your day?
When the rains skim and skip,
Why mar sweet comradeship,
Blighting with poison-drip
Neighbourly spray?

Heart-halt and spirit-lame,
City-opprest,
Unto this wood I came
As to a nest;
Dreaming that sylvan peace
Offered the harrowed ease –
Nature a soft release
From men's unrest.

But, having entered in,
Great growths and small
Show them to men akin –
Combatants all!
Sycamore shoulders oak,
Bines the slim sapling yoke,
Ivy-spun halters choke
Elms stout and tall.

Touches from ash, O wych,
Sting you like scorn!
You, too, brave hollies, twitch
Sidelong from thorn.
Even the rank poplars bear
Lothly a rival's air,
Cankering in black despair
If overborne.

In a Wood
1 pine so] pine-tree MS, WP, PUE
4 Live] Bide MS, WP, PUE
5 skip,] skip MS
7 poison-drip] poisoned drip MS
13 Dreaming] Deeming MS
14] Offered my soul release – MS
15 release] surcease MS
16 From men's] To man's MS
30 Lothly] Illy MS, WP, PUE, WE1: Poorly SP: [CP1 has 'Illy', but corrected to 'Lothly' on errata slip]
31 black] blank WE, SP, ME, CHP

Since, then, no grace I find
    Taught me of trees,
Turn I back to my kind,
    Worthy as these.
There at least smiles abound,
There discourse trills around,
There, now and then, are found
    Life-loyalties.

1887: 1896

41 *To a Lady*

Offended by a Book of the Writer's

NOW that my page is exiled, – doomed, maybe,
Never to press thy cosy cushions more,
Or wake thy ready Yeas as heretofore,
Or stir thy gentle vows of faith in me:

Knowing thy natural receptivity,
I figure that, as flambeaux banish eve,
My sombre image, warped by insidious heave
Of those less forthright, must lose place in thee.

So be it. I have borne such. Let thy dreams
Of me and mine diminish day by day,
And yield their space to shine of smugger things;
Till I shape to thee but in fitful gleams,
And then in far and feeble visitings,
And then surcease. Truth will be truth alway.

TITLE:
To Lady —— / Offended by something the Author had written MS

42 *To a Motherless Child*

AH, child, thou art but half thy darling mother's;
    Hers couldst thou wholly be,
My light in thee would outglow all in others;
    She would relive to me.

To a Motherless Child

EXTRA PRINTINGS:
(1) *Selected Poems*, p. 96
(2) *Chosen Poems*, p. 91

TITLE:
To an Orphan Child MS, WP, PUE
WP, PUE add: A Whimsy

INDENTATION:
1 = ll. 1, 3 } in both stanzas MS
2 = ll. 5, 7
3 = ll. 2, 4, 6
4 = l. 8

In a Wood
39 then,] then MS

To a Lady
1 is exiled, –] upcloses, MS, WP, PUE: is exiled, WE, ME
5 receptivity,] susceptivity MS
11 yield] cede MS
14 alway.] alway! MS

To a Motherless Child
1 child] Child MS
2 be,] be MS
4–5 No stanza break

But niggard Nature's trick of birth
Bars, lest she overjoy,
Renewal of the loved on earth
Save with alloy.

The Dame has no regard, alas, my maiden,
For love and loss like mine –
No sympathy with mindsight memory-laden;
Only with fickle eyne.
To her mechanic artistry
My dreams are all unknown,
And why I wish that thou couldst be
But One's alone!

43 *Nature's Questioning*

When I look forth at dawning, pool,
Field, flock, and lonely tree,
All seem to gaze at me
Like chastened children sitting silent in a school;

Their faces dulled, constrained, and worn,
As though the master's ways
Through the long teaching days
Had cowed them till their early zest was overborne.

Upon them stirs in lippings mere
(As if once clear in call,
But now scarce breathed at all) –
'We wonder, ever wonder, why we find us here!

'Has some Vast Imbecility,
Mighty to build and blend,
But impotent to tend,
Framed us in jest, and left us now to hazardry?

'Or come we of an Automaton
Unconscious of our pains? . . .
Or are we live remains
Of Godhead dying downwards, brain and eye now gone?

To a Motherless Child
7 loved] Loved MS
11 mindsight] mind-sight WP, PUE, WE, SP, ME
12 eyne.] eyne! MS
16 alone!] alone. MS

Nature's Questioning
3 gaze] look MS, WP1
4 children] children, MS
6 ways] way WE, ME
7 days] day WE, ME
8] Their first terrestrial zest had chilled and overborne. MS, WP, PUE
9 Upon them stirs] And on them stirs, MS, WP, PUE, WE, ME
9 mere] mere – MS: mere, WE, ME
11 all) –] all) MS

'Or is it that some high Plan betides,
As yet not understood,
Of Evil stormed by Good,
We the Forlorn Hope over which Achievement strides?'

Thus things around. No answerer I. . . .
Meanwhile the winds, and rains,
And Earth's old glooms and pains
Are still the same, and Life and Death are neighbours nigh.

44 The Impercipient

(At a Cathedral Service)

TITLE:
The Agnostic MS *before revision*
(*At* . . .)] (Evensong; —— Cathedral) MS

THAT with this bright believing band
I have no claim to be,
That faiths by which my comrades stand
Seem fantasies to me,
And mirage-mists their Shining Land,
Is a strange destiny.

Why thus my soul should be consigned
To infelicity,
Why always I must feel as blind
To sights my brethren see,
Why joys they've found I cannot find,
Abides a mystery.

Since heart of mine knows not that ease
Which they know; since it be
That He who breathes All's Well to these
Breathes no All's-Well to me,
My lack might move their sympathies
And Christian charity!

I am like a gazer who should mark
An inland company
Standing upfingered, with, 'Hark! hark!
The glorious distant sea!'
And feel, 'Alas, 'tis but yon dark
And wind-swept pine to me!'

Nature's Questioning
25 I. . . .] I . . . CP
28 and . . . nigh] and gladdest Life dawns but to die MS:
and gladdest Life Death neighbours nigh WP, PUE:
and Death and glad Life neighbour nigh CP1

The Impercipient
1 with] from MS, WP, PUE
2] An outcast I should be, MS, WP, PUE
5] And mirage-mist their Happy Land, MS
6 strange] drear MS, WP, PUE
7 thus my] my sad MS *before revision*
10] To bliss my neighbours see; MS
11 they've] they have WE, ME
17 lack] loss MS
18 charity!] charity. WE, ME

18–19 MS has extra stanza here:

But ah, they love me not, although
I treat them tenderly,
And while I bear with them they go
To no such length with me,
Because – to match their sight I show
An incapacity.

21 Hark! hark!] Hark; Hark; MS

Yet I would bear my shortcomings
With meet tranquillity,
But for the charge that blessed things
I'd liefer not have be.
O, doth a bird deprived of wings
Go earth-bound wilfully!

. . .

Enough. As yet disquiet clings
About us. Rest shall we.

45 *At an Inn*

EXTRA PRINTINGS:
(1) *Selected Poems*, pp. 34–5
(2) *Chosen Poems*, pp. 35–6

WHEN we as strangers sought
Their catering care,
Veiled smiles bespoke their thought
Of what we were.
They warmed as they opined
Us more than friends –
That we had all resigned
For love's dear ends.

And that swift sympathy
With living love
Which quicks the world – maybe
The spheres above,
Made them our ministers,
Moved them to say,
'Ah, God, that bliss like theirs
Would flush our day!'

And we were left alone
As Love's own pair;
Yet never the love-light shone
Between us there!
But that which chilled the breath
Of afternoon,
And palsied unto death
The pane-fly's tune.

The Impercipient
26 meet tranquillity] equanimity MS *before revision*
28] I'd rather to unbe (not have be *del*). MS
28 not have be] have unbe WP, PUE
29 deprived] beshorn ME, WE2 [Hardy corrected his copy of WE1 to read 'beshorn']
30] Go earthbound wilfully? MS
31 disquiet] confusion MS
32 Rest shall we] We shall see MS

At an Inn
2 catering] sheltering MS
8 love's] Love's MS
15 Ah,] Ah MS
20 there!] there; MS: there, WE, SP, ME

The kiss their zeal foretold,
 And now deemed come,
Came not: within his hold
 Love lingered numb.
Why cast he on our port
 A bloom not ours?
Why shaped us for his sport
 In after-hours?

As we seemed we were not
 That day afar,
And now we seem not what
 We aching are.
O severing sea and land,
 O laws of men,
Ere death, once let us stand
 As we stood then!

46 *The Slow Nature*

(*An Incident of Froom Valley*)

'THY husband – poor, poor Heart! – is dead –
 Dead, out by Moreford Rise;
A bull escaped the barton-shed,
 Gored him, and there he lies!'

– 'Ha, ha – go away! 'Tis a tale, methink,
 Thou joker Kit!' laughed she.
'I've known thee many a year, Kit Twink,
 And ever hast thou fooled me!'

– 'But, Mistress Damon – I can swear
 Thy goodman John is dead!
And soon th'lt hear their feet who bear
 His body to his bed.'

The Slow Nature
4 him,] him; MS
5 – 'Ha] 'Ha MS
9 – 'But,] 'But MS

So unwontedly sad was the merry man's face –
  That face which had long deceived –
That she gazed and gazed; and then could trace
  The truth there; and she believed.

She laid a hand on the dresser-ledge,
  And scanned far Egdon-side;
And stood; and you heard the wind-swept sedge
  And the rippling Froom; till she cried:

'O my chamber's untidied, unmade my bed,
  Though the day has begun to wear!
"What a slovenly hussif!" it will be said,
  When they all go up my stair!'

She disappeared; and the joker stood
  Depressed by his neighbour's doom,
And amazed that a wife struck to widowhood
  Thought first of her unkempt room.

But a fortnight thence she could take no food,
  And she pined in a slow decay;
While Kit soon lost his mournful mood
  And laughed in his ancient way.

1894

47 *In a Eweleaze near Weatherbury*

EXTRA PRINTINGS:
(1) *Selected Poems*, p. 41
(2) *Chosen Poems*, p. 40

TITLE:
In a Eweleaze SP [It seems probable that this was the first title in MS]

THE years have gathered grayly
  Since I danced upon this leaze
With one who kindled gaily
  Love's fitful ecstasies!
But despite the term as teacher,
  I remain what I was then
In each essential feature
  Of the fantasies of men.

Yet I note the little chisel
  Of never-napping Time
Defacing wan and grizzel
  The blazon of my prime.

The Slow Nature
18 scanned] glanced at MS
27 to] in, MS

In a Eweleaze near Weatherbury
1 grayly] grayly, MS
3 gaily] daily MS
3 kindled] here learnt MS *before revision*
5 teacher,] teacher MS, SP
8] And in fervours hid from men. MS *before revision*
9 note] mark MS
10 never-napping] never nodding MS: ever-napping WPA
10 Time] Time, WP, PUE, WE, ME
11 wan] ghast MS, WP, PUE, WE, SP, ME

When at night he thinks me sleeping
    I feel him boring sly
Within my bones, and heaping
    Quaintest pains for by-and-by.

Still, I'd go the world with Beauty,
    I would laugh with her and sing,
I would shun divinest duty
    To resume her worshipping.
But she'd scorn my brave endeavour,
    She would not balm the breeze
By murmuring 'Thine for ever!'
    As she did upon this leaze.

1890

48 *The Bride-Night Fire*

(*A Wessex Tradition*)

THEY had long met o' Zundays – her true love and she –
    And at junketings, maypoles, and flings;
But she bode wi' a thirtover[1] uncle, and he
Swore by noon and by night that her goodman should be
Naibour Sweatley – a wight often weak at the knee
From taking o' sommat more cheerful than tea –
    Who tranted,[2] and moved people's things.

She cried, 'O pray pity me!' Nought would he hear;
    Then with wild rainy eyes she obeyed.
She chid when her Love was for clinking off wi' her:
The pa'son was told, as the season drew near,
To throw over pu'pit the names of the pair
    As fitting one flesh to be made.

The wedding-day dawned and the morning drew on;
    The couple stood bridegroom and bride;
The evening was passed, and when midnight had gone
The feasters horned,[3] 'God save the King,' and anon
    The pair took their homealong[4] ride.

[1] *thirtover*, cross
[2] *tranted*, traded as carrier
[3] *horned*, sang loudly
[4] *homealong*, homeward

In a Eweleaze near Weatherbury
13 sleeping] sleeping, WP, PUE, WE, ME
16 by-and-by] by and by MS, SP
19 divinest] Divinest MS
23 By . . . 'Thine] With 'Love, I'm thine MS
[After this poem MS has: Addenda: WP, PUE have: Additions]

The Bride-Night Fire

EXTRA MANUSCRIPT:
In the Bancroft Library of the University of California at Berkeley = BL [This is in Emma Hardy's hand with corrections by Hardy, and is almost certainly the copy-text for LJ. It is identical with LJ *except* where indicated below by 'BL'. Indentation has not been examined because of the difficulties caused by the drift right of the handwriting]

EXTRA PRINTINGS:
(1) *The Gentleman's Magazine*, Nov 1875, pp. [552]–555 = GM
(2) *Appleton's Journal*, 6 Nov 1875, p. 594 = AJ
(3) *The Art of Thomas Hardy* by Lionel Johnson (London, 1894), pp. lix–lxiv = LJ

TITLE:
The Fire at Tranter Sweatley's MS, GM, AJ, LJ, WP, PUE
The Bride-Night Fire or, The Fire at Tranter Sweatley's WE2, ME [Hardy's copy of CP2 is corrected so]
(*A* . . .)] Not in MS, WP, PUE: A Wessex Ballad GM, AJ, LJ: (Wessex Dialect) WE, ME
LJ adds below title: (Printed, by permission, from the original MS)/[N.B. A bowdlerised version of this ballad appeared in *The Gentleman's Magazine* for November 1875]

The Bride-Night Fire
1 Zundays] Sundays GM, AJ, LJ
1 true love] true-love MS, GM, AJ, LJ
1 love] Love WE, ME
2 maypoles] May-poles AJ
3] But she dwelt wi' a crabbed (crabbèd AJ) old uncle, and he GM, AJ
3 thirtover uncle] crabbed old nuncle LJ
3 uncle] nuncle MS
4 goodman] husband GM, AJ, LJ
5 – a wight] (a man GM, AJ, LJ
5 wight often] gaffer oft MS, WP, PUE
6 tea –] tea), GM, AJ, LJ: tea) BL
8 me!'] me!' – GM, LJ
8 Nought] naught AJ
10 Love] love AJ
10 clinking off] vanishing WE, ME
10 her:] her; AJ: her. WP, PUE
11 pa'son] passon GM, AJ
11 near,] near MS, WP, PUE
12 pu'pit] pulpit GM, AJ, LJ
12 pair] peäir MS, LJ, WP, PUE
13 one] woone LJ
14 dawned] dawned, AJ
14 on;] on: GM, LJ: on, AJ
15 bride;] bride: GM, LJ
17 feasters horned,] folks horned out, (out MS, GM, AJ, LJ) MS, GM, AJ, LJ, WP, PUE
18] The twain homealong (two home-along WP, PUE) gloomily hied. MS, WP, PUE: To their home the pair gloomily hied. GM, AJ, LJ
18 pair] twain WE, ME
18 homealong] home-along WE, ME
There are no footnotes in MS, WP, PUE: Minor variants occur in WE, ME

The lover Tim Tankens mourned heart-sick and leer[1]
  To be thus of his darling deprived:
He roamed in the dark ath'art field, mound, and mere,
And, a'most without knowing it, found himself near
The house of the tranter, and now of his Dear,
  Where the lantern-light showed 'em arrived.

The bride sought her chamber so calm and so pale
  That a Northern had thought her resigned;
But to eyes that had seen her in tidetimes[2] of weal,
Like the white cloud o' smoke, the red battlefield's vail,
  That look spak' of havoc behind.

The bridegroom yet laitered a beaker to drain,
  Then reeled to the linhay[3] for more,
When the candle-snoff kindled some chaff from his grain –
Flames spread, and red vlankers[4] wi' might and wi' main
  Around beams, thatch, and chimley-tun[5] roar.

Young Tim away yond, rafted[6] up by the light,
  Through brimbles and underwood tears,
Till he comes to the orchet, when crooping[7] from sight
In the lewth[8] of a codlin-tree, bivering[9] wi' fright,
Wi' on'y her night-rail to cover her plight,
  His lonesome young Barbree appears.

Her cwold little figure half-naked he views
  Played about by the frolicsome breeze,
Her light-tripping totties,[10] her ten little tooes,
All bare and besprinkled wi' Fall's[11] chilly dews,
While her great gallied[12] eyes through her hair hanging loose
  Shone as stars through a tardle[13] o' trees.

[1] *leer*, empty-stomached
[2] *tidetimes*, holidays
[3] *linhay*, lean-to building
[4] *vlankers*, fire-flakes
[5] *chimley-tun*, chimney-stack
[6] *rafted*, roused
[7] *crooping*, squatting down
[8] *lewth*, shelter
[9] *bivering*, with chattering teeth
[10] *totties*, feet
[11] *Fall*, autumn
[12] *gallied*, frightened
[13] *tardle*, entanglement

The Bride-Night Fire

19 lover Tim Tankens] lover, Sim (Tim LJ) Tankens, GM, AJ, LJ
19 leer] drear MS, GM, AJ, LJ, WP, PUE
20 deprived:] deprived; AJ
21 ath'art] around GM, AJ
23 Dear] dear GM, AJ, LJ
24 lantern-light showed 'em] moving lights showed they'd GM, AJ, LJ
25 chamber] cham'mer MS: chimmer GM, AJ, LJ: cham'er WP, PUE
27 But] But, MS, GM, LJ
27 seen] zeed LJ [BL has 'seen']
27 tidetimes of] seasons o' (of GM, AJ) MS, GM, AJ, LJ
27 tidetimes] tide-times WP, PUE, WE, ME
27 weal,] weal – AJ
28 o'] of GM, AJ
28 battlefield's] battle-field's GM, WE, ME
28 vail,] veil, GM: veil – AJ: vail BL
29 spak'] told GM, AJ
30 laitered] loitered GM, AJ, WE, ME
31 more,] more; GM, AJ, LJ
32 some] the GM, AJ, LJ
32 grain –] grain, AJ
33 spread, and red vlankers] sprout and rush upwards (upward AJ) GM, AJ
33 spread,] spread MS, LJ: sprout BL
33 red vlankers] rush upwards LJ
33 vlankers] vlankers, MS, WP, PUE, WE, ME
33 main] main, MS, GM, AJ, WP, PUE, WE, ME
34 Around] And round MS, GM, AJ, LJ, WP, PUE, WE, ME
35] Young Sim in the distance, (distance AJ) aroused by the light, GM, AJ
35 yond, rafted up] yonder (yander LJ), aroused MS, LJ
35 light,] light MS
36 brimbles] brimble MS, WP, PUE
37 when . . . sight] where (when AJ) slap in his sight, GM, AJ, LJ
37 from sight] there right MS: thereright WP, PUE
38] Beneath a bowed codlin-tree, (codlin-tree AJ) trimbling wi' fright, GM, AJ, LJ
38 codlin-tree] codlin tree WE, ME
38 fright,] fright BL
39] In (Wi' AJ) an old coat she'd found on a scarecrow bedight, GM, AJ: Wi' nought but her shimmy 'tween her and the night, (night BL) LJ
39 cover her plight] screen her from sight MS, WP, PUE
40 lonesome] litsome MS: gentle GM, AJ, LJ
40 Barbree] Barbara GM, AJ
41] Her form in these cold (cold, AJ) mildewed tatters he views, GM, AJ
41 cwold] cold MS, LJ, WE, ME
41 figure] buzzom MS: buzzoms LJ
41 half-naked] half naked LJ
42 breeze,] breeze; GM, AJ, LJ
44 Fall's] fall's AJ: Falls' LJ
45 gallied] frightened GM, AJ, LJ
45 eyes] eyes, AJ, WP, PUE, WE, ME
45 hair hanging] ringlets let MS: ringlets so GM, AJ, LJ
45 loose] loose, AJ, WP, PUE, WE, ME
46 Shone] Sheened MS, LJ, WP, PUE
46 as] like MS, GM, AJ, LJ
46 tardle o'] tangle of GM, AJ: tangle o' LJ

She eyed him; and, as when a weir-hatch is drawn,
  Her tears, penned by terror afore,
With a rushing of sobs in a shower were strawn,
Till her power to pour 'em seemed wasted and gone
  From the heft[1] o' misfortune she bore.

'O Tim, my *own* Tim I must call 'ee – I will!
  All the world has turned round on me so!
Can you help her who loved 'ee, though acting so ill?
Can you pity her misery – feel for her still?
When worse than her body so quivering and chill
  Is her heart in its winter o' woe!

'I think I mid[2] almost ha' borne it,' she said,
  'Had my griefs one by one come to hand;
But O, to be slave to thik husbird,[3] for bread,
And then, upon top o' that, driven to wed,
And then, upon top o' that, burnt out o' bed,
  Is more than my nater can stand!'

Like a lion 'ithin en Tim's spirit outsprung –
(Tim had a great soul when his feelings were wrung) –
  'Feel for 'ee, dear Barbree?' he cried;
And his warm working-jacket then straightway he flung
Round about her, and horsed her by jerks, till she clung
Like a chiel on a gipsy, her figure uphung
  By the sleeves that he tightly had tied.

Over piggeries, and mixens,[4] and apples, and hay,
  They lumpered[5] straight into the night;
And finding ere long where a halter-path[6] lay,
Sighted Tim's house by dawn, on'y seen on their way
By a naibour or two who were up wi' the day,
  But who gathered no clue to the sight.

Then tender Tim Tankens he searched here and there
  For some garment to clothe her fair skin;
But though he had breeches and waistcoats to spare,

[1] *heft*, weight
[2] *mid*, might
[3] *thik husbird*, that rascal
[4] *mixens*, manure-heaps
[5] *lumpered*, stumbled
[6] *halter-path*, bridle-path

The Bride-Night Fire

47 him] en MS, LJ, WP, PUE
48 afore] before GM, AJ
49 With] Wi' GM, AJ, LJ
49 shower] torrent GM, AJ
49 strawn,] strawn AJ
51 o'] of GM, AJ, LJ
52 Tim,] Sim, GM: Sim! AJ
52 Tim] Sim GM: Sim, AJ
53 has] ha' MS, WP, PUE: hev GM, LJ: have AJ
56 When] When, GM
56 chill] chill, GM, LJ
57 o'] of GM, AJ, LJ
58 I . . . ha'] I think I could almost hev (have AJ) GM, AJ, LJ
59 hand;] hand: AJ
60 thik husbird] an uncle GM, AJ, LJ
60 husbird,] husbird MS, WP, PUE, WE, ME
63 nater] natur AJ
64] Tim's soul like a lion 'ithin (within LJ) en outsprung – MS, LJ, WP, PUE: Sim's soul like a lion within him out-sprung (outsprung AJ) – GM, AJ
64 'ithin en] within him WE, ME
65 (Tim] (Sim GM, AJ
65 wrung) –] wrung) MS, GM, LJ
66 Barbree] Barbie GM, AJ
66 cried;] cried: GM, LJ: cried. AJ
67 And] Then GM, AJ, LJ
67 then . . . flung] about her he flung, MS, GM, AJ, LJ, WP, PUE
68] Made a back, horsed her up, (up MS) till behind him she clung: (clung WP, PUE) MS, GM, AJ, LJ, WP, PUE
68 horsed . . . till] bending his back, there WE, ME
69 gipsy,] gipsy MS, GM, AJ, LJ
69 her figure uphung] her round figure hung GM
69 uphung] up-hung LJ
70] As the two sleeves before (afore MS, LJ) him he tied. MS, GM, AJ, LJ
70 he tightly had] around her he WP, PUE
72 lumpered] stumbled, GM, LJ: stumbled AJ
72 night;] night, GM, LJ
73 finding] finding, AJ
73 ere long] bylong MS, WP, PUE: at length (length, AJ) GM, AJ, LJ: erelong WE
73 halter-path] bridle-path GM, AJ, LJ, WE, ME: bridle path BL
73 lay,] lay MS, GM, LJ
74–6] By dawn reached Sim's mother's – who, up with the day,/In round (round, AJ) kindly spectacles glared every way, (way AJ)/To gather some clue (clew AJ) to the sight. GM, AJ
74] By (At WP, PUE) dawn reached Tim's house, on'y (only LJ) zeed (seen WP, PUE: seed BL) on their way MS, LJ, WP, PUE
74 Sighted . . . on'y] Lit on Tim's house at dawn, only WE, ME
75 day,] day; MS, LJ, WP, PUE
76 who] they MS, LJ, WP, PUE
77–82] Then old Mis'ess Tankens she searched here and there/For some closet – though fearing 'twas sin – /Where Barbie could hide, and for clothes she could wear,/A task hard enough with a creature so fair,/Who (Who, AJ) half scrammed to death, sat and cried in a chair/To think what a stoor she was in. GM, AJ
79 But] But, LJ
79 breeches] breeches, LJ
79 waistcoats] weskets LJ
79 spare,] spare MS

He had nothing quite seemly for Barbree to wear,
Who, half shrammed[1] to death, stood and cried on a chair
  At the caddle[2] she found herself in.

There was one thing to do, and that one thing he did,
  He lent her some clothes of his own,
And she took 'em perforce; and while swiftly she slid
Them upon her Tim turned to the winder, as bid,
Thinking, 'O that the picter my duty keeps hid
  To the sight o' my eyes mid[3] be shown!'

In the tallet[4] he stowed her; there huddied[5] she lay,
  Shortening sleeves, legs, and tails to her limbs;
But most o' the time in a mortal bad way,
Well knowing that there'd be the divel to pay
If 'twere found that, instead o' the elements' prey,
  She was living in lodgings at Tim's.

'Where's the tranter?' said men and boys; 'where can he be?'
  'Where's the tranter?' said Barbree alone.
'Where on e'th is the tranter?' said everybod-y:
They sifted the dust of his perished roof-tree,
  And all they could find was a bone.

Then the uncle cried, 'Lord, pray have mercy on me!'
  And in terror began to repent.
But before 'twas complete, and till sure she was free,
Barbree drew up her loft-ladder, tight turned her key –
Tim bringing up breakfast and dinner and tea –
  Till the news of her hiding got vent.

Then followed the custom-kept rout, shout, and flare
Of a skimmity-ride[6] through the naibourhood, ere
  Folk had proof o' wold[7] Sweatley's decay.
Whereupon decent people all stood in a stare,
Saying Tim and his lodger should risk it, and pair:
So he took her to church. An' some laughing lads there
Cried to Tim, 'After Sweatley!' She said, 'I declare
  I stand as a maiden to-day!'

Written 1866; printed 1875

[1] *shrammed*, numbed [2] *caddle*, quandary [3] *mid*, might [4] *tallet*, loft [5] *huddied*, hidden [6] *skimmity-ride*, satirical procession with effigies [7] *wold*, old

The Bride-Night Fire
81 shrammed] scrammed MS, LJ
81 chair] chair, LJ
83–8 Not in GM, AJ
84 some] these LJ
84 clothes] clouts MS, LJ, WP, PUE
85 swiftly] in 'em MS, LJ, WP, PUE
85 slid] slid, WP, PUE
86] Tim turned to the winder, as modesty bid, MS, LJ, WP, PUE
87 hid] hid, LJ
88 mid] might BL
89–91] The loft, up the ladder, seemed safe; and all day/In that hiding she laid her sweet limbs;/But most of the time in a terrible way, GM, AJ
89 huddied] hidied MS: huddled LJ
89 lay,] lay MS, LJ
90 Shortening] Suiting MS, LJ
90 limbs;] limbs, MS, LJ
91 o'] of LJ
91 mortal bad] terrible MS, LJ
92 divel] devil MS, LJ: piper GM, AJ
93 If 'twere] When 'twas GM, AJ: If 'twas LJ
93 o'] of GM, AJ
93 elements'] element's GM, AJ, CP
93 prey,] prey MS
94 Tim's] Sim's GM, AJ
95 boys;] boys, GM, LJ
95 where] Where GM, AJ
95 he] er MS, WP, PUE
96 Barbree] Barbie GM, AJ
96 alone.] alone, LJ: alone; AJ
97 Where on e'th is] Wherever's AJ
97 e'th] earth GM, LJ
97 tranter?] tranter! GM
97 everybod-y:] everybody: GM: everybod-y; AJ
99 bone.] bone! GM, AJ, BL
100 uncle] nuncle MS, LJ
101 terror] sorrow GM, AJ
101 repent.] repent: MS, GM, LJ: repent; AJ, WE, ME
103 Barbree] Barbie GM, AJ
103 key –] key AJ
104] Sim ((Sim AJ) handing in breakfast, and dinner, and tea (tea) AJ) – GM, AJ
105] Till the crabbed (crabbèd AJ) man gied his consent. GM, AJ: Till one morning they packed up, and went. BL
106–13] There was skimmity-riding with rout, shout, and flare, (flare AJ)/In Weatherbury, Stokeham, and Windleton, ere/They had proof of old Sweatley's decay: (decay; AJ)/The Mellstock and Yalbury folk stood in a stare/(The tranter owned houses and garden-ground there),/But little did Sim or his Barbara care, (care – AJ)/For he took her to church the next day. GM, AJ
106–8] There was skimmity-riding wi' rout, shout, and flare,/In Weatherbury, Drouse, and out Egdon way, ere/They had proof of old Sweatley's decay: LJ
106 Then] There MS
107 skimmity-ride] skimmington-ride MS, WP, PUE
108 o' wold] of old MS, WE, ME
108 decay.] decay: MS
109–13] The Mellstock and Yalbury folk stood in a stare/(The tranter had houses and commonage there),/But little did Tim and his Barbaree care,/In the country out west far away. BL
111 An'] And LJ
111 laughing lads] laughing-lads MS
Written . . . 1875] Not in GM, AJ, LJ
1866] 1867 MS
1875] 1874 MS

49 Heiress and Architect

For A. W. Blomfield

SHE sought the Studios, beckoning to her side
An arch-designer, for she planned to build.
He was of wise contrivance, deeply skilled
In every intervolve of high and wide –
    Well fit to be her guide.

        'Whatever it be,'
        Responded he,
With cold, clear voice, and cold, clear view,
'In true accord with prudent fashionings
For such vicissitudes as living brings,
And thwarting not the law of stable things,
        That will I do.'

'Shape me,' she said, 'high halls with tracery
And open ogive-work, that scent and hue
Of buds, and travelling bees, may come in through,
The note of birds, and singings of the sea,
    For these are much to me.'

        'An idle whim!'
        Broke forth from him
Whom nought could warm to gallantries:
'Cede all these buds and birds, the zephyr's call,
And scents, and hues, and things that falter all,
And choose as best the close and surly wall,
        For winters freeze.'

'Then frame,' she cried, 'wide fronts of crystal glass,
That I may show my laughter and my light –
Light like the sun's by day, the stars' by night –
Till rival heart-queens, envying, wail, "Alas,
    Her glory!" as they pass.'

TITLE:
For A. W. Blomfield] To A.W.B. MS
For A.W.B. WP, PUE, WE1

INDENTATION:
In MS ll. 20, 32, 44, 56, are farther right, in line with l. 5

Heiress and Architect
8 cold . . . cold] cold . . . cold MS
8 voice,] voice MS
13 high . . . tracery] a pile of light degree MS
14 And . . . work] With open lattice-work MS
15 through,] through WE1
28 Alas,] Alas MS
29–30 Stanza break in all editions

'O maid misled!'
He sternly said
Whose facile foresight pierced her dire;
'Where shall abide the soul when, sick of glee,
It shrinks, and hides, and prays no eye may see?
Those house them best who house for secrecy,
For you will tire.'

'A little chamber, then, with swan and dove
Ranged thickly, and engrailed with rare device
Of reds and purples, for a Paradise
Wherein my Love may greet me, I my Love,
When he shall know thereof?'

'This, too, is ill,'
He answered still,
The man who swayed her like a shade.
'An hour will come when sight of such sweet nook
Would bring a bitterness too sharp to brook,
When brighter eyes have won away his look;
For you will fade.'

Then said she faintly: 'O, contrive some way –
Some narrow winding turret, quite mine own,
To reach a loft where I may grieve alone!
It is a slight thing; hence do not, I pray,
This last dear fancy slay!'

'Such winding ways
Fit not your days,'
Said he, the man of measuring eye;
'I must even fashion as the rule declares,
To wit: Give space (since life ends unawares)
To hale a coffined corpse adown the stairs;
For you will die.'

1867. 8 Adelphi Terrace

Heiress and Architect
31 said] said, WP, PUE, WE, ME
32 dire;] dire: MS
37 chamber,] chamber MS
49 O,] O MS
52 hence] then MS
55 days,] days MS
57 the] my MS, WP, PUE
58 life] Life MS
8 . . . Terrace] Not in MS, WP, PUE, WE1, CP1

50 The Two Men

TITLE: The World's Verdict
A Morality-rime MS

THERE were two youths of equal age,
Wit, station, strength, and parentage;
They studied at the selfsame schools,
And shaped their thoughts by common rules.

One pondered on the life of man,
His hopes, his ending, and began
To rate the Market's sordid war
As something scarce worth living for.

'I'll brace to higher aims,' said he,
'I'll further Truth and Purity;
Thereby to mend the mortal lot
And sweeten sorrow. Thrive I not,

'Winning their hearts, my kind will give
Enough that I may lowly live,
And house my Love in some dim dell,
For pleasing them and theirs so well.'

Idly attired, with features wan,
In secret swift he laboured on:
Such press of power had brought much gold
Applied to things of meaner mould.

Sometimes he wished his aims had been
To gather gains like other men;
Then thanked his God he'd traced his track
Too far for wish to drag him back.

He looked down from his loft one day
To where his slighted garden lay;
Nettles and hemlock hid each lawn,
And every flower was starved and gone.

He fainted in his heart, whereon
He rose, and sought his plighted one,
Resolved to loose her bond withal,
Lest she should perish in his fall.

The Two Men
2 parentage;] parentage: MS
3 selfsame] self-same WPA, ME
13 hearts,] hearts MS
17 wan,] wan MS
18 on:] on; WPA
24 Too . . . to] So far no wish could MS
25 looked down] lookèd MS, WP, PUE
25 down] out WE, ME

He met her with a careless air,
As though he'd ceased to find her fair,
And said: 'True love is dust to me;
I cannot kiss: I tire of thee!'

(That she might scorn him was he fain,
To put her sooner out of pain;
For angered love breathes quick and dies,
When famished love long-lingering lies.)

Once done, his soul was so betossed,
It found no more the force it lost:
Hope was his only drink and food,
And hope extinct, decay ensued.

And, living long so closely penned,
He had not kept a single friend;
He dwindled thin as phantoms be,
And drooped to death in poverty....

Meantime his schoolmate had gone out
To join the fortune-finding rout;
He liked the winnings of the mart,
But wearied of the working part.

He turned to seek a privy lair,
Neglecting note of garb and hair,
And day by day reclined and thought
How he might live by doing nought.

'I plan a valued scheme,' he said
To some. 'But lend me of your bread,
And when the vast result looms nigh,
In profit you shall stand as I.'

Yet they took counsel to restrain
Their kindness till they saw the gain;
And, since his substance now had run,
He rose to do what might be done.

The Two Men
38 pain;] pain: MS
39 angered] incensed MS, WP, PUE
40 long-lingering] a-lingering MS, WP, PUE: long lingering WE, ME
41 betossed,] betossed MS
44 extinct,] extinct MS
48 poverty....] poverty...... MS: poverty... WP, PUE
49 Meantime] Meanwhile WE, ME
50 rout;] rout, MS
57 scheme,] scheme MS, CP
59 nigh,] nigh MS

He went unto his Love by night,
And said: 'My Love, I faint in fight:
Deserving as thou dost a crown,
My cares shall never drag thee down.'

(He had descried a maid whose line
Would hand her on much corn and wine,
And held her far in worth above
One who could only pray and love.)

But this Fair read him; whence he failed
To do the deed so blithely hailed;
He saw his projects wholly marred,
And gloom and want oppressed him hard;

Till, living to so mean an end,
Whereby he'd lost his every friend,
He perished in the pauper sty
Where his old mate lay dying nigh.

And moralists, reflecting, said,
As 'dust to dust' anon was read
And echoed from each coffin-lid,
'These men were like in all they did.'

1866

51 Lines

Spoken by Miss Ada Rehan *at the Lyceum Theatre, 23 July 1890, at a performance on behalf of Lady Jeune's Holiday Fund for City Children.*

Before we part to alien thoughts and aims,
Permit the one brief word the occasion claims:
– When mumming and grave motives are allied,
Perhaps an Epilogue is justified.

Our under-purpose has, in truth, to-day
Commanded most our musings; least the play:
A purpose futile but for your good-will
Swiftly responsive to the cry of ill:

EXTRA MANUSCRIPTS:

(1) In the Miriam Lutcher Stark Library of the University of Texas = UT

(2) In the possession of Prof. R. L. Purdy. This has not been available for checking.

EXTRA PRINTINGS:

(1) *The Pall Mall Gazette*, 23 July 1890, p. 4, ll. 13–24 and 31–4 only = PMG

(2) *The Pall Mall Budget*, 24 July 1890, p. 960, ll. 13–24 and 31–4 only. Identical with PMG

(3) *Dorset County Chronicle and Somersetshire Gazette*, 31 July 1890, p. 4 = DCC

Note The information given after the title is reworded in UT, PMG, DCC

The Two Men

70 on] down MS

79 the] a MS, WP, PUE

79 sty] sty, MS, WP, PUE

80] His mate the dying pauper nigh. MS, WP, PUE

82 anon was] in burial MS, WP, PUE

83 And] Was MS, WP, PUE

1866] WE, ME add: W.P.V.

Lines

1 aims,] aims UT, DCC

2 brief] frank UT

2 claims:] claims; WPA

3 motives] projects MS, UT, DCC, WP, PUE

3 allied,] allied UT

4] A brief unmasking may be justified. UT

4 Epilogue] epilogue DCC

6 musings;] musings: DCC

7 good-will] good-will, WE, ME

8 Swiftly] Promptly MS, UT, DCC

8 ill:] ill. UT, DCC

8–9 No stanza break

A purpose all too limited! – to aid
Frail human flowerets, sicklied by the shade,
In winning some short spell of upland breeze,
Or strengthening sunlight on the level leas.

Who has not marked, where the full cheek should be,
Incipient lines of lank flaccidity,
Lymphatic pallor where the pink should glow,
And where the throb of transport, pulses low? –
Most tragical of shapes from Pole to Line,
O wondering child, unwitting Time's design,
Why should Man add to Nature's quandary,
And worsen ill by thus immuring thee?
– That races do despite unto their own,
That Might supernal do indeed condone
Wrongs individual for the general ease,
Instance the proof in victims such as these.

Launched into thoroughfares too thronged before,
Mothered by those whose protest is 'No more!'
Vitalized without option: who shall say
That did Life hang on choosing – Yea or Nay –
They had not scorned it with such penalty,
And nothingness implored of Destiny?

And yet behind the horizon smile serene
The down, the cornland, and the stretching green –
Space – the child's heaven: scenes which at least ensure
Some palliative for ill they cannot cure.

Dear friends – now moved by this poor show of ours
To make your own long joy in buds and bowers
For one brief while the joy of infant eyes,
Changing their urban murk to paradise –
You have our thanks! – may your reward include
More than our thanks, far more: their gratitude.

Savile Club, Midnight, July 1890

Lines
11 breeze,] breeze UT, DCC
12 Or] And UT, DCC
13 be,] be UT
14 Incipient] The incipient UT, PMG
15 glow,] glow UT
16 low? –] low? UT
18 child,] child UT
18 unwitting] unweeting UT, PMG, DCC
18 design,] design! – DCC
19 Man] man MS, UT, PMG, DCC: Art WP, PUE, CP1
19 Nature's] nature's UT
19 quandary,] cruelty, MS, UT, DCC: cruelty PMG
20 thee?] thee; DCC
21] If Nature can do despite to her own, UT, PMG, DCC
21 – That] That MS
21 do despite unto] can do despite to MS, WP1
22 That Might] If might UT, PMG, DCC
24] Draw we the proof from instances like these. PMG
24 Instance] Draw we UT
24 in] from UT
24–5 Page break in MS, WP, PUE, WE, ME: no stanza break in UT, DCC
26 is] is, UT, DCC
26 No] no DCC
28 That] That, UT, DCC
28 choosing . . . Nay –] choosing, yea or nay, UT, DCC
29 penalty,] penalty UT
30 Destiny] destiny UT, DCC
33 heaven:] heaven – UT, PMG
34 ill] ills UT, PMG, DCC, WE, ME
37 brief] short UT
37 eyes,] eyes UT
39 thanks! – may] thanks! . . . May UT, DCC
Savile . . . 1890] Not found before WE1

52 *I Look Into My Glass*

I LOOK into my glass,
And view my wasting skin,
And say, 'Would God it came to pass
My heart had shrunk as thin!'

For then, I, undistrest
By hearts grown cold to me,
Could lonely wait my endless rest
With equanimity.

But Time, to make me grieve,
Part steals, lets part abide;
And shakes this fragile frame at eve
With throbbings of noontide.

EXTRA MANUSCRIPT:
In the Bancroft Library of the University of California at Berkeley = BL

EXTRA PRINTINGS:
(1) *Selected Poems*, p. 106
(2) *Chosen Poems*, p. 138

TITLE:
'I look into my Glass' MS

INDENTATION:
1 = l. 3
2 = ll. 1, 2, 4 — and so throughout BL

1 = ll. 1, 3
2 = ll. 2, 4 — and so throughout WPA

I Look Into My Glass
1 glass] Glass BL
6 hearts grown cold] friendships lost MS
10 abide;] abide, MS
12 noontide] noon-tide MS

To an Unborn [Pauper] Child.

"She must go to the Union[house], to have her baby": ~~Casterbridge~~ Petty Sessions.

i.

Breathe not, hid Heart: cease silently,
And though thy birth-hour beckons thee
Sleep the long sleep:
The Doomsters heap
Travails & teens around us here,
And Time-wraiths turn ~~our songsingings~~ [festivity] to fear.

ii.

Hark, how the peoples surge & sigh,
And laughters fail, & greetings die:
Hopes dwindle; yea
Faiths waste away,
Affections & enthusiasms numb;
Thou canst not mend these things if thou dost come.

iii

Had I the ~~cast of all~~ [ear of wombèd] souls
Ere their terrestrial ~~page~~ [chart] unrolls,
And thou wert free
To cease, or be,
Then would I tell thee all I know,
And put it to thee: Wilt thou take life so?

iv

See page 127

POEMS OF THE PAST AND THE PRESENT

Abbreviations Specific to 'Poems of the Past and the Present'

MS = The bound-up volume of manuscripts in the Bodleian Library of the University of Oxford

PPP1 = *Poems of the Past and the Present* (London, 1902)

PPP2 = *Poems of the Past and the Present* (London, 1903)

PPP = Found in both PPP1 and PPP2

PE = Pocket Edition 1907

UE = Uniform Edition 1919

PUE = Found in both PE and UE

WE1 = Wessex Edition 1912

WE2 = Wessex Edition 1920

WE = Found in both WE1 and WE2

ME = Mellstock Edition 1920

PREFACE

HEREWITH I tender my thanks to the editors and proprietors of *The Times*, the *Morning Post*, the *Daily Chronicle*, the *Westminster Gazette*, *Literature*, the *Graphic*, *Cornhill*, *Sphere*, and other papers, for permission to reprint from their pages such of the following pieces of verse as have already been published.

Of the subject-matter of this volume – even that which is in other than narrative form – much is dramatic or impersonative even where not explicitly so. Moreover, that portion which may be regarded as individual comprises a series of feelings and fancies written down in widely differing moods and circumstances, and at various dates. It will probably be found, therefore, to possess little cohesion of thought or harmony of colouring. I do not greatly regret this. Unadjusted impressions have their value, and the road to a true philosophy of life seems to lie in humbly recording diverse readings of its phenomena as they are forced upon us by chance and change.

August 1901 T.H.

Preface

6–7 Of . . . much] As was said of *Wessex Poems*, of the subject-matter of this volume much WE, ME

6 volume . . . which] volume which MS, PPP, PUE

7 form –] form, MS, PPP, PUE

7 impersonative] personative MS

8 Moreover,] And WE, ME

10 dates. It] dates; it WE, ME

12–15] I do not greatly regret this fault, as it may be considered, since the road to a true philosophy of life seems to lie in humbly recording diverse impressions of its meaning as they occur. MS *before revision*

53 V.R. 1819–1901

A Reverie

THE mightiest moments pass uncalendared,
    And when the Absolute
In backward Time pronounced the deedful word
    Whereby all life is stirred:
'Let one be born and throned whose mould shall constitute
The norm of every royal-reckoned attribute,'
    No mortal knew or heard.

But in due days the purposed Life outshone –
    Serene, sagacious, free;
Her waxing seasons bloomed with deeds well done,
    And the world's heart was won . . .
Yet may the deed of hers most bright in eyes to be
Lie hid from ours – as in the All-One's thought lay she –
    Till ripening years have run.

Sunday Night,
27 January 1901

EXTRA PRINTINGS:
(1) *The Times*, 29 Jan 1901, p. 9 = T
(2) *The Passing of Victoria*, ed. J. A. Hammerton (London, 1901), p. 15 = PV

TITLE:
A Reverie] Not in MS, T

INDENTATION:
CP lined up 1 and 3 with 5 and 6. It seems probable that this was an error. All earlier editions, except T, were as printed here. T has 5 and 6 lined up with 1, 3, 8, 10.

Note This was one of nine poems chosen by Hardy for the Library of the Royal Dolls' House at Windsor Castle. The copy there has 'uncalendared' (l. 1) and 'won. . . .' (l. 11)

V.R. 1819–1901
1 The mightiest moments] Moments the mightiest MS, T, PV, PPP, PUE
1 uncalendared,] uncalendared; T, PV
3 In backward Time] In Time agone T, PV
3 pronounced] out gave MS: outgave T, PV, PPP, PUE
3 word] word, T, PV
4 stirred:] stirred; PV
6 royal-reckoned] royal-rated T, PV
8 outshone –] outshone, T, PV
9 free;] free – MS
10 Her . . . bloomed] Its fourscore cycles beamed T, PV
10 Her] – Her PPP, PUE, WE, ME, CP1, 2
11 won . . .] won. . . . PV
Sunday Night,] Not in T, PV
27 . . . *1901*] Not in PV
27] Not in T

WAR POEMS

54 Embarcation

(Southampton Docks: October 1899)

HERE, where Vespasian's legions struck the sands,
And Cerdic with his Saxons entered in,
And Henry's army leapt afloat to win
Convincing triumphs over neighbour lands,

Vaster battalions press for further strands,
To argue in the selfsame bloody mode
Which this late age of thought, and pact, and code,
Still fails to mend. – Now deckward tramp the bands,

Yellow as autumn leaves, alive as spring;
And as each host draws out upon the sea
Beyond which lies the tragical To-be,
None dubious of the cause, none murmuring,

Wives, sisters, parents, wave white hands and smile,
As if they knew not that they weep the while.

EXTRA PRINTINGS:
(1) *The Daily Chronicle*, 25 Oct 1899, p. 6 = DC
(2) *Selected Poems*, p. 187
(3) *Chosen Poems*, p. 241

TITLE:
The Departure DC
Embarkation WE, SP, ME
October 1899] Not in SP

55 Departure

(Southampton Docks: October 1899)

WHILE the far farewell music thins and fails,
And the broad bottoms rip the bearing brine –
All smalling slowly to the gray sea-line –
And each significant red smoke-shaft pales,

Keen sense of severance everywhere prevails,
Which shapes the late long tramp of mounting men
To seeming words that ask and ask again:
'How long, O striving Teutons, Slavs, and Gaels

EXTRA PRINTINGS:
(1) *Selected Poems*, p. 188
(2) *Chosen Poems*, p. 242

TITLE:
October 1899] Not in SP

Embarcation
6 selfsame] self-same PPP, PUE, WE, SP, ME
8 deckward . . . bands] shipped each war-troop stands DC
10 each] the DC
10 sea] sea, DC
11 To-be,] To-be – DC
12 cause] Cause DC
12 murmuring,] murmuring – DC
DC adds: No copyright claimed

Departure
3 sea-line] sea line MS, PPP, PUE, WE, SP, ME
8 striving] ruling WE, SP, ME
8–9 Stanza break in all editions

Must your wroth reasonings trade on lives like these,
That are as puppets in a playing hand? –
When shall the saner softer polities
Whereof we dream, have sway in each proud land
And patriotism, grown Godlike, scorn to stand
Bondslave to realms, but circle earth and seas?'

56 The Colonel's Soliloquy

(*Southampton Docks: October 1899*)

'THE quay recedes. Hurrah! Ahead we go! . . .
It's true I've been accustomed now to home,
And joints get rusty, and one's limbs may grow
More fit to rest than roam.

'But I can stand as yet fair stress and strain;
There's not a little steel beneath the rust;
My years mount somewhat, but here's to't again!
And if I fall, I must.

'God knows that for myself I have scanty care;
Past scrimmages have proved as much to all;
In Eastern lands and South I have had my share
Both of the blade and ball.

'And where those villains ripped me in the flitch
With their old iron in my early time,
I'm apt at change of wind to feel a twitch,
Or at a change of clime.

'And what my mirror shows me in the morning
Has more of blotch and wrinkle than of bloom;
My eyes, too, heretofore all glasses scorning,
Have just a touch of rheum. . . .

'Now sounds "The Girl I've left behind me", – Ah,
The years, the ardours, wakened by that tune!
Time was when, with the crowd's farewell "Hurrah!"
'Twould lift me to the moon.

Departure
9 Must] 'Must WE2, ME
12 sway] play MS, PPP, PUE [CP1 had 'play' but corrected to 'sway' on errata slip]
12 land] land, MS, PPP, PUE, WE, SP, ME

The Colonel's Soliloquy
1 go! . . .] go! . . . . . . MS
9 I have] I've MS, PPP, PUE
11 I have] I've MS, PPP, PUE
20 rheum. . . .] rheum. . . . . MS

'But now it's late to leave behind me one
Who if, poor soul, her man goes underground,
Will not recover as she might have done
In days when hopes abound.

'She's waving from the wharfside, palely grieving,
As down we draw. . . . Her tears make little show,
Yet now she suffers more than at my leaving
Some twenty years ago!

'I pray those left at home will care for her;
I shall come back; I have before; though when
The Girl you leave behind you is a grandmother,
Things may not be as then.'

57 *The Going of the Battery*

Wives' Lament

(*2 November 1899*)

I

O IT was sad enough, weak enough, mad enough –
Light in their loving as soldiers can be –
First to risk choosing them, leave alone losing them
Now, in far battle, beyond the South Sea! . . .

II

– Rain came down drenchingly; but we unblenchingly
Trudged on beside them through mirk and through mire,
They stepping steadily – only too readily! –
Scarce as if stepping brought parting-time nigher.

III

Great guns were gleaming there, living things seeming there,
Cloaked in their tar-cloths, upmouthed to the night;
Wheels wet and yellow from axle to felloe,
Throats blank of sound, but prophetic to sight.

EXTRA PRINTINGS:
(1) *The Graphic*, 11 Nov 1899, p. 662 = G
(2) *The Academy*, 18 Nov 1899, p. [559] = A
(3) *Selected Poems*, pp. 189–90
(4) *Chosen Poems*, pp. 243–4

TITLE:
THE GOING OF THE BATTERY
[November 2, 1899. Late at night, in rain and in darkness, the 73rd Battery, R.F.A., left Dorchester Barracks for the War in South Africa, marching on foot to the railway station, where their guns were already entrained]
Wives' Voices: G, A

WE adds 'Casterbridge' before the date
SP omits '*Wives*' . . . *1899*)'

INDENTATION:
1 = ll. 1, 3 } and so throughout
2 = ll. 2, 4 } G, A

The Colonel's Soliloquy
32 ago!] ago. PPP, PUE, WE, ME
33 her;] her! MS, PPP, PUE, WE, ME
35 grandmother,] grandmother MS

The Going of the Battery
1–4 Not in G, A, SP
4 Sea! . . .] Sea! . . . . MS
5 – Rain] Rain MS, G, A, SP, CHP [Repeatedly in MS Hardy puts opening dashes outside the normal indentation]
9 there, . . . there,] there – . . . there – G, A
10 upmouthed] upnosed G, A
10 night;] night: G, A

IV

Gas-glimmers drearily, blearily, eerily
Lit our pale faces outstretched for one kiss,
While we stood prest to them, with a last quest to them
Not to court perils that honour could miss.

V

Sharp were those sighs of ours, blinded these eyes of ours,
When at last moved away under the arch
All we loved. Aid for them each woman prayed for them,
Treading back slowly the track of their march.

VI

Some one said: 'Nevermore will they come: evermore
Are they now lost to us.' O it was wrong!
Though may be hard their ways, some Hand will guard their ways,
Bear them through safely, in brief time or long.

VII

– Yet, voices haunting us, daunting us, taunting us,
Hint in the night-time when life beats are low
Other and graver things. . . . Hold we to braver things,
Wait we, in trust, what Time's fulness shall show.

58 *At the War Office, London*

(Affixing the Lists of Killed and Wounded: December 1899)

I

LAST year I called this world of gaingivings
The darkest thinkable, and questioned sadly
If my own land could heave its pulse less gladly,
So charged it seemed with circumstance that brings
The tragedy of things.

At the War Office, London

EXTRA MANUSCRIPTS:
In the University of Texas Library. See below.

EXTRA PRINTINGS:
(1) *The Sphere*, 27 Jan 1900, p. 18. This is a facsimile of the MS now in the University of Texas Library = s1
(2) *The Sphere*, 17 Feb 1900, p. 136. A printed version of s1 = s2
(3) *Lest We Forget*, ed. H. B. Elliott (London, 1915), p. 94 = LWF

TITLE:
At the War Office
After a Bloody Battle s1, s2

The War-Shadow LWF

The Going of the Battery
13] Lamplight all drearily blinking and blearily G, A
13 eerily] eerily, MS
17–20 Not in G, A
21 Some one] Someone MS, PPP, PUE, WE, SP, ME
21 said:] said, G, A
21–2 'Nevermore . . . us.'] Italicised in G, A
21 come: evermore] *come! Evermore* G, A
22 us.'] *us!* G: *us!'* A
22 O] O, G, A
23 Though may be] Howsoe'er G, A
23 guard their ways,] guard their ways – G, A
24 safely,] safely – G, A
25 – Yet,] Yet – G, A
26 night-time when life beats are low] night-time, when life-beats are low, G, A
27 things. . . .] things. . . . . MS: things . . . G, PPP, PUE, WE, SP, ME
27 things,] things – G, A
28 we, in trust,] we – in trust – G, A
28 show] know G
Note No stanza numbers in G, A

At the War Office, London
3 gladly,] gladly – s1, s2
4 that brings] whence springs MS, s1, s2, PPP, PUE

II

Yet at that censured time no heart was rent
Or feature blanched of parent, wife, or daughter
By hourly posted sheets of scheduled slaughter;
Death waited Nature's wont; Peace smiled unshent
        From Ind to Occident.

59 A Christmas Ghost-Story

EXTRA PRINTINGS:
(1) *The Westminster Gazette*, 23 Dec 1899, p. 5 = WG
(2) *War against War in South Africa*, 29 Dec 1899, p. 166 = WW

TITLE:
A Christmas Ghost-story MS

SOUTH of the Line, inland from far Durban,
A mouldering soldier lies – your countryman.
Awry and doubled up are his gray bones,
And on the breeze his puzzled phantom moans
Nightly to clear Canopus: 'I would know
By whom and when the All-Earth-gladdening Law
Of Peace, brought in by that Man Crucified,
Was ruled to be inept, and set aside?
And what of logic or of truth appears
In tacking "Anno Domini" to the years?
Near twenty-hundred liveried thus have hied,
But tarries yet the Cause for which He died.'

Christmas-eve 1899

60 Drummer Hodge

EXTRA PRINTINGS:
(1) *Literature*, 25 Nov 1899, p. 513 = L
(2) *Selected Poems*, p. 191
(3) *Chosen Poems*, p. 245

TITLE:
The Dead Drummer MS, L, PPP, PUE
L adds after title: 'One of the Drummers killed was a native of a village near Casterbridge.'

I

THEY throw in Drummer Hodge, to rest
    Uncoffined – just as found:
His landmark is a kopje-crest
    That breaks the veldt around;
And foreign constellations west
    Each night above his mound.

At the War Office, London
7 parent, wife,] parent wife s1
7 daughter] daughter, MS
8 posted] blazoned MS, s1, s2, LWF, PPP, PUE, WE, ME
8 scheduled] listed MS, s1, s2, LWF, PPP, PUE, WE, ME
8 slaughter;] slaughter: s1, s2
9 wont . . . unshent] wont: men came and went s1, s2
10] Abroad, at home, unshent. s1, s2

A Christmas Ghost-Story
2–3] There lies – be he or not your countryman –/A fellow-mortal. Riddled are his bones, WG, WW
4 And on] But 'mid WG, WW
5 Canopus . . . know] Canopus – fain to know WG, WW
6 whom] whom, WG
6 when . . . gladdening] when, the All-Earth-Gladdening WG, WW
7 that Man Crucified] Some-One crucified WG, WW
9–12 Not in WG, WW
11 twenty-hundred] twenty hundred MS
Christmas-eve 1899] December 23. 1899 MS: Not in WG, WW
WG adds: *Not copyright*

Drummer Hodge
2 found:] found. L
3 kopje-crest] Kopje-crest MS, L
4 veldt] Veldt MS, L
4 around;] around: CP1

II

Young Hodge the Drummer never knew –
Fresh from his Wessex home –
The meaning of the broad Karoo,
The Bush, the dusty loam,
And why uprose to nightly view
Strange stars amid the gloam.

III

Yet portion of that unknown plain
Will Hodge for ever be;
His homely Northern breast and brain
Grow to some Southern tree,
And strange-eyed constellations reign
His stars eternally.

61 *A Wife in London*

(*December 1899*)

I

SHE sits in the tawny vapour
That the Thames-side lanes have uprolled,
Behind whose webby fold on fold
Like a waning taper
The street-lamp glimmers cold.

A messenger's knock cracks smartly,
Flashed news is in her hand
Of meaning it dazes to understand
Though shaped so shortly:
He – has fallen – in the far South Land. . . .

TITLE:
MS, PPP, PUE have sectional titles:
I
THE TRAGEDY
II
THE IRONY

Drummer Hodge
16 to some] up a MS, L, PPP, PUE, WE, SP, ME

A Wife in London
2 Thames-side] City MS, PPP, PUE
10 *Land. . . .*] *Land. . . . . .* MS
Note MS shows that the poem was first written in the first-person singular

II

'Tis the morrow; the fog hangs thicker,
The postman nears and goes:
A letter is brought whose lines disclose
By the firelight flicker
His hand, whom the worm now knows:

Fresh – firm – penned in highest feather –
Page-full of his hoped return,
And of home-planned jaunts by brake and burn
In the summer weather,
And of new love that they would learn.

62 *The Souls of the Slain*

EXTRA MANUSCRIPT:
Permission was refused to see the MS in the possession of Mr Frederick B. Adams, Jnr

EXTRA PRINTINGS:
(1) *The Cornhill Magazine*, April 1900, p. [433] = C
(2) *Selected Poems*, pp. 193–8
(3) *Chosen Poems*, pp. 247–52

I

THE thick lids of Night closed upon me
Alone at the Bill
Of the Isle by the Race[1] –
Many-caverned, bald, wrinkled of face –
And with darkness and silence the spirit was on me
To brood and be still.

II

No wind fanned the flats of the ocean,
Or promontory sides,
Or the ooze by the strand,
Or the bent-bearded slope of the land,
Whose base took its rest amid everlong motion
Of criss-crossing tides.

[1] The 'Race' is the turbulent sea-area off the Bill of Portland, where contrary tides meet.

The Souls of the Slain
1 lids] lid C
5 was] came C
9 ooze] spawls C
Note C does not have the footnote about the 'Race', but has the following after the title: NOTE. – The spot indicated in the following poem is the Bill of Portland, which stands, roughly, on a line drawn from South Africa to the middle of the United Kingdom; in other words, the flight of a bird along a 'great circle' of the earth, cutting through South Africa and the British Isles, might land him at Portland Bill. The 'Race' is the turbulent sea-area off the Bill, where contrary tides meet. 'Spawls' are the chips of freestone left by the quarriers.

III

Soon from out of the Southward seemed nearing
A whirr, as of wings
Waved by mighty-vanned flies,
Or by night-moths of measureless size,
And in softness and smoothness well-nigh beyond hearing
Of corporal things.

IV

And they bore to the bluff, and alighted –
A dim-discerned train
Of sprites without mould,
Frameless souls none might touch or might hold –
On the ledge by the turreted lantern, far-sighted
By men of the main.

V

And I heard them say 'Home!' and I knew them
For souls of the felled
On the earth's nether bord
Under Capricorn, whither they'd warred,
And I neared in my awe, and gave heedfulness to them
With breathings inheld.

VI

Then, it seemed, there approached from the northward
A senior soul-flame
Of the like filmy hue:
And he met them and spake: 'Is it you,
O my men?' Said they, 'Aye! We bear homeward and
hearthward
To feast on our fame!'

The Souls of the Slain
13 Soon] Soon, C
16 night-moths] night birds C: MS has both 'night-moths' and 'night-birds' as alternatives
17 well-nigh] wellnigh MS
34 them] them, C
36 feast on] list to MS, C, PPP, PUE

VII

'I've flown there before you,' he said then:
'Your households are well;
But – your kin linger less
On your glory and war-mightiness
Than on dearer things.' – 'Dearer?' cried these from the dead then,
'Of what do they tell?'

VIII

'Some mothers muse sadly, and murmur
Your doings as boys –
Recall the quaint ways
Of your babyhood's innocent days.
Some pray that, ere dying, your faith had grown firmer,
And higher your joys.

IX

'A father broods: "Would I had set him
To some humble trade,
And so slacked his high fire,
And his passionate martial desire;
And told him no stories to woo him and whet him
To this dire crusade!" '

X

'And, General, how hold out our sweethearts,
Sworn loyal as doves?'
– 'Many mourn; many think
It is not unattractive to prink
Them in sables for heroes. Some fickle and fleet hearts
Have found them new loves.'

XI

'And our wives?' quoth another resignedly,
'Dwell they on our deeds?'

The Souls of the Slain
41 dearer . . . Dearer?'] other things.' 'Other?' C
41 things.' –] things.' MS
52 desire;] desire, C
53 And] Had MS, PPP, PUE, WE, SP, ME: And had C
57] 'Many mourn . . . Many think C
57 – 'Many] 'Many MS
59 heroes.] heroes . . . C

– 'Deeds of home; that live yet
Fresh as new – deeds of fondness or fret;
Ancient words that were kindly expressed or unkindly,
These, these have their heeds.'

XII

– 'Alas! then it seems that our glory
Weighs less in their thought
Than our old homely acts,
And the long-ago commonplace facts
Of our lives – held by us as scarce part of our story,
And rated as nought!'

XIII

Then bitterly some: 'Was it wise now
To raise the tomb-door
For such knowledge? Away!'
But the rest: 'Fame we prized till to-day;
Yet that hearts keep us green for old kindness we prize now
A thousand times more!'

XIV

Thus speaking, the trooped apparitions
Began to disband
And resolve them in two:
Those whose record was lovely and true
Bore to northward for home: those of bitter traditions
Again left the land,

XV

And, towering to seaward in legions,
They paused at a spot
Overbending the Race –
That engulphing, ghast, sinister place –
Whither headlong they plunged, to the fathomless regions
Of myriads forgot.

The Souls of the Slain
63 – 'Deeds] 'Deeds MS, C
67 – 'Alas] 'Alas MS, C
69 old] small C
71 story,] story C
75 Away!'] Away!' . . . C
89 plunged,] plunged C

XVI

And the spirits of those who were homing
Passed on, rushingly,
Like the Pentecost Wind;
And the whirr of their wayfaring thinned
And surceased on the sky, and but left in the gloaming
Sea-mutterings and me.

December 1899

EXTRA PRINTINGS:
(1) *The Morning Post*, 30 Nov 1900, p. 5 = MP
(2) *Khaki*, March 1915 = K
(3) Two identical off-prints in the Berg Collection of the New York Public Library = B

TITLE:
Song of the Soldiers' Wives MS, MP, PPP, PUE: Hope-Song of the Soldiers' Sweethearts and Wives K

63 Song of the Soldiers' Wives and Sweethearts

I

AT last! In sight of home again,
Of home again;
No more to range and roam again
As at that bygone time?
No more to go away from us
And stay from us? –
Dawn, hold not long the day from us,
But quicken it to prime!

II

Now all the town shall ring to them,
Shall ring to them,
And we who love them cling to them
And clasp them joyfully;
And cry, 'O much we'll do for you
Anew for you,
Dear Loves! – aye, draw and hew for you,
Come back from oversea.'

The Souls of the Slain
94 thinned] thinned, C

Song of the Soldiers' Wives and Sweethearts
1 At last] Some day K
1 last!] last? MS, MP, B
2 again;] again, MS, MP
3 again] again, MP
7 the] that K
9 Now] Then K
13 O] O, MP
15 Loves! –] Loves; MP
15 you,] you MP
16 oversea.] oversea! MP, B

III

Some told us we should meet no more,
Yea, meet no more! –
Should wait, and wish, but greet no more
Your faces round our fires;
That, in a while, uncharily
And drearily
Men gave their lives – even wearily,
Like those whom living tires.

IV

And now you are nearing home again,
Dears, home again;
No more, may be, to roam again
As at that bygone time,
Which took you far away from us
To stay from us;
Dawn, hold not long the day from us,
But quicken it to prime!

64 *The Sick Battle-God*

TITLE:
The Sick God MS, PPP, PUE

I

In days when men found joy in war,
A God of Battles sped each mortal jar;
The peoples pledged him heart and hand,
From Israel's land to isles afar.

II

His crimson form, with clang and chime,
Flashed on each murk and murderous meeting-time,
And kings invoked, for rape and raid,
His fearsome aid in rune and rhyme.

Song of the Soldiers' Wives and Sweethearts
17–24 Not in K
18 Yea,] Should MS, MP, B, PPP, PUE
18 more! –] more; MS, MP, B, PPP, PUE
20 round] by MP, B
20 fires;] fires: MP
25 And . . . are] O you'll be K
27 may be] maybe MS, K
28 time,] time MS, MP
29 far] all MP
30 us;] us: MP
Note No stanza numbers in MP

The Sick Battle-God
1 found joy in] had joy of MS, PPP, PUE
2 God] god MS
3 hand,] hand MS
6 meeting-time,] meeting-time WE1

III

On bruise and blood-hole, scar and seam,
On blade and bolt, he flung his fulgid beam:
His haloes rayed the very gore,
And corpses wore his glory-gleam.

IV

Often an early King or Queen,
And storied hero onward, caught his sheen;
'Twas glimpsed by Wolfe, by Ney anon,
And Nelson on his blue demesne.

V

But new light spread. That god's gold nimb
And blazon have waned dimmer and more dim;
Even his flushed form begins to fade,
Till but a shade is left of him.

VI

That modern meditation broke
His spell, that penmen's pleadings dealt a stroke,
Say some; and some that crimes too dire
Did much to mire his crimson cloak.

VII

Yea, seeds of crescent sympathy
Were sown by those more excellent than he,
Long known, though long contemned till then –
The gods of men in amity.

VIII

Souls have grown seers, and thought outbrings
The mournful many-sidedness of things
With foes as friends, enfeebling ires
And fury-fires by gaingivings!

The Sick Battle-God
14 caught] knew MS, PPP, PUE
15 anon,] anon – MS
17 spread] shone MS, PPP1
25 crescent] crescive MS, PPP, PUE, WE, ME
30 many-sidedness] manysidedness MS

IX

He rarely gladdens champions now;
They do and dare, but tensely – pale of brow;
And would they fain uplift the arm
Of that weak form they know not how.

X

Yet wars arise, though zest grows cold;
Wherefore, at times, as if in ancient mould
He looms, bepatched with paint and lath;
But never hath he seemed the old!

XI

Let men rejoice, let men deplore,
The lurid Deity of heretofore
Succumbs to one of saner nod;
The Battle-god is god no more.

The Sick Battle-God
33 rarely gladdens] scarce impassions MS, PPP, PUE
34 brow;] brow WE1: brow, WE2, ME
36 weak] faint MS, PPP, PUE
38 times, as if] whiles, as 'twere MS, PPP, PUE
42 lurid Deity] Power predominant MS *before revision*

65 Genoa and the Mediterranean

(*March 1887*)

O EPIC-FAMED, god-haunted Central Sea,
Heave careless of the deep wrong done to thee
When from Torino's track I saw thy face first flash on me.

And multimarbled Genova the Proud,
Gleam all unconscious how, wide-lipped, up-browed,
I first beheld thee clad – not as the Beauty but the Dowd.

Out from a deep-delved way my vision lit
On housebacks pink, green, ochreous – where a slit
Shoreward 'twixt row and row revealed the classic blue through it.

And thereacross waved fishwives' high-hung smocks,
Chrome kerchiefs, scarlet hose, darned underfrocks;
Often since when my dreams of thee, O Queen, that frippery mocks:

Whereat I grieve, Superba! . . . Afterhours
Within Palazzo Doria's orange bowers
Went far to mend these marrings of thy soul-subliming powers.

But, Queen, such squalid undress none should see,
Those dream-endangering eyewounds no more be
Where lovers first behold thy form in pilgrimage to thee.

Genoa and the Mediterranean
4 Genova] Genoa CP1
12 Often since when] Since when too oft MS, PPP, PUE
13 Superba! . . .] Superba! . . . . MS

66 *Shelley's Skylark*

(The neighbourhood of Leghorn: March 1887)

SOMEWHERE afield here something lies
In Earth's oblivious eyeless trust
That moved a poet to prophecies –
A pinch of unseen, unguarded dust:

The dust of the lark that Shelley heard,
And made immortal through times to be; –
Though it only lived like another bird,
And knew not its immortality:

Lived its meek life; then, one day, fell –
A little ball of feather and bone;
And how it perished, when piped farewell,
And where it wastes, are alike unknown.

Maybe it rests in the loam I view,
Maybe it throbs in a myrtle's green,
Maybe it sleeps in the coming hue
Of a grape on the slopes of yon inland scene.

Go find it, faeries, go and find
That tiny pinch of priceless dust,
And bring a casket silver-lined,
And framed of gold that gems encrust;

And we will lay it safe therein,
And consecrate it to endless time;
For it inspired a bard to win
Ecstatic heights in thought and rhyme.

EXTRA MANUSCRIPT:
In the Ashley Library in the British Library = A

EXTRA PRINTINGS:
(1) *Selected Poems*, pp. 99–100
(2) *Chosen Poems*, pp. 94–5

TITLE:
March] March (April *del*) MS

Shelley's Skylark
8 immortality:] immortality. MS, PPP, PUE
22 time;] time, A

EXTRA PRINTING:
The Academy, 23 Nov 1901, p. 476 [quoted in full in a review which seems to have been based on an early proof of PPP1] = A

67 In the Old Theatre, Fiesole

(*April 1887*)

I TRACED the Circus whose gray stones incline
Where Rome and dim Etruria interjoin,
Till came a child who showed an ancient coin
That bore the image of a Constantine.

She lightly passed; nor did she once opine
How, better than all books, she had raised for me
In swift perspective Europe's history
Through the vast years of Cæsar's sceptred line.

For in my distant plot of English loam
'Twas but to delve, and straightway there to find
Coins of like impress. As with one half blind
Whom common simples cure, her act flashed home
In that mute moment to my opened mind
The power, the pride, the reach of perished Rome.

68 Rome: On the Palatine

(*April 1887*)

WE walked where Victor Jove was shrined awhile,
And passed to Livia's rich red mural show,
Whence, thridding cave and Criptoportico,
We gained Caligula's dissolving pile.

And each ranked ruin tended to beguile
The outer sense, and shape itself as though
It wore its marble gleams, its pristine glow
Of scenic frieze and pompous peristyle.

In the Old Theatre, Fiesole
11 impress] gravure PPP1 [MS has 'gravure' written and deleted above 'impress', which has been deleted and then stetted]
14 power . . . reach] world-imprinting power PPP1
14 reach] reach, A

Rome: On the Palatine
4 pile.] pile; MS
7 gleams] hues MS, PPP, PUE
7 gleams, it] gleams in WE, ME
8–9 Stanza break in all editions

When lo, swift hands, on strings nigh overhead,
Began to melodize a waltz by Strauss:
It stirred me as I stood, in Cæsar's house,
Raised the old routs Imperial lyres had led,

And blended pulsing life with lives long done,
Till Time seemed fiction, Past and Present one.

69 Rome
Building a New Street in the Ancient Quarter

(April 1887)

THESE umbered cliffs and gnarls of masonry
Outskeleton Time's central city, Rome;
Whereof each arch, entablature, and dome
Lies bare in all its gaunt anatomy.

And cracking frieze and rotten metope
Express, as though they were an open tome
Top-lined with caustic monitory gnome;
'Dunces, Learn here to spell Humanity!'

And yet within these ruins' very shade
The singing workmen shape and set and join
Their frail new mansion's stuccoed cove and quoin
With no apparent sense that years abrade,
Though each rent wall their feeble works invade
Once shamed all such in power of pier and groin.

TITLE:
Rome. Building a new street in the Ancient quarter/(April, 1887) MS

70 Rome
The Vatican: Sala delle Muse

(1887)

I SAT in the Muses' Hall at the mid of the day,
And it seemed to grow still, and the people to pass away,
And the chiselled shapes to combine in a haze of sun,
Till beside a Carrara column there gleamed forth One.

EXTRA PRINTINGS:
(1) *Selected Poems*, pp. 141–2
(2) *Chosen Poems*, pp. 172–3

She looked not this nor that of those beings divine,
But each and the whole – an essence of all the Nine;
With tentative foot she neared to my halting-place,
A pensive smile on her sweet, small, marvellous face.

'Regarded so long, we render thee sad?' said she.
'Not you,' sighed I, 'but my own inconstancy!
I worship each and each; in the morning one,
And then, alas! another at sink of sun.

'To-day my soul clasps Form; but where is my troth
Of yesternight with Tune: can one cleave to both?'
– 'Be not perturbed,' said she. 'Though apart in fame,
As I and my sisters are one, those, too, are the same.'

– 'But my love goes further – to Story, and Dance, and Hymn,
The lover of all in a sun-sweep is fool to whim –
Is swayed like a river-weed as the ripples run!'
– 'Nay, wooer, thou sway'st not. These are but phases of one;

'And that one is I; and I am projected from thee,
One that out of thy brain and heart thou causest to be –
Extern to thee nothing. Grieve not, nor thyself becall,
Woo where thou wilt; and rejoice thou canst love at all!'

71 Rome
At the Pyramid of Cestius near the Graves of Shelley and Keats

(1887)

EXTRA MANUSCRIPT:
In the Ashley Library in the British Library = A

EXTRA PRINTINGS:
(1) *Selected Poems*, pp. 143–4
(2) *Chosen Poems*, pp. 174–5

TITLE:
Rome. At the Pyramid of Cestius/Near the Graves of Shelley and Keats (April, 1887) MS

WHO, then, was Cestius,
And what is he to me? –
Amid thick thoughts and memories multitudinous
One thought alone brings he.

Rome
The Vatican: Sala delle Muse
5 looked not] was nor MS, PPP, PUE
12 alas!] alas, MS
14 Tune:] Tune; MS
17 – 'But my love goes] 'But my loves go MS
17 love goes] loves go PPP, PUE
19 run!'] run!' – MS
20 – 'Nay] 'Nay MS
20 wooer] wight MS, PPP, PUE, WE1, SP, CP1
24 all!] all. MS

I can recall no word
Of anything he did;
For me he is a man who died and was interred
To leave a pyramid

Whose purpose was exprest
Not with its first design,
Nor till, far down in Time, beside it found their rest
Two countrymen of mine.

Cestius in life, maybe,
Slew, breathed out threatening;
I know not. This I know: in death all silently
He does a finer thing,

In beckoning pilgrim feet
With marble finger high
To where, by shadowy wall and history-haunted street,
Those matchless singers lie. . . .

– Say, then, he lived and died
That stones which bear his name
Should mark, through Time, where two immortal Shades abide;
It is an ample fame.

72 Lausanne
In Gibbon's Old Garden: 11–12 p.m.

27 June 1897

(*The 110th anniversary of the completion of the 'Decline and Fall' at the same hour and place*)

A SPIRIT seems to pass,
Formal in pose, but grave withal and grand:
He contemplates a volume in his hand,
And far lamps fleck him through the thin acacias.

EXTRA PRINTING:
The Later Years of Thomas Hardy (London, 1930), pp. 68–9. Identical with the version printed here

TITLE:
Lausanne
In Gibbon's old Garden: 11–12 p.m. June 27: 1897 MS

Rome
At the Pyramid of Cestius
12 mine.] mine. . . . A
14 threatening;] threatening: A
16 finer] sweeter MS: kindlier PPP, PUE: rarer WE, SP, ME
17 pilgrim feet] pilgrim-feet MS
19 street,] street A
20 lie. . . .] lie. . . . . MS: lie . . . A: lie. SP

Lausanne
2 withal and grand] and grand withal MS, PPP, PUE, CP1
3 volume] writing WE, ME
3 in his hand] stout and tall MS, PPP, PUE, CP1

Anon the book is closed,
With 'It is finished!' And at the alley's end
He turns, and when on me his glances bend
As from the Past comes speech – small, muted, yet composed.

'How fares the Truth now? – Ill?
– Do pens but slily further her advance?
May one not speed her but in phrase askance?
Do scribes aver the Comic to be Reverend still?

'Still rule those minds on earth
At whom sage Milton's wormwood words were hurled:
"*Truth like a bastard comes into the world*
Never without ill-fame to him who gives her birth"?'

73 Zermatt
To the Matterhorn

(June–July 1897)

THIRTY-TWO years since, up against the sun,
Seven shapes, thin atomies to lower sight,
Labouringly leapt and gained thy gabled height,
And four lives paid for what the seven had won.

They were the first by whom the deed was done,
And when I look at thee, my mind takes flight
To that day's tragic feat of manly might,
As though, till then, of history thou hadst none.

Yet ages ere men topped thee, late and soon
Thou didst behold the planets lift and lower;
Saw'st, maybe, Joshua's pausing sun and moon,
And the betokening sky when Cæsar's power
Approached its bloody end; yea, even that Noon
When darkness filled the earth till the ninth hour.

Lausanne
5 book is] leaves are WE, ME
7 when] soon MS, PPP, PUE
7 bend] bend; MS, PPP, PUE
8 As . . . Past] And, as from earth, MS, PPP, PUE
15 *world*] *world,* MS
Note Hardy's copy of WE1 in the DCM has a manuscript note which by means of an asterisk at the end of l. 16 adds the following: "Truth is as impossible to be soiled by an outward touch as is the sunbeam; though this ill-hap wait on her nativity, that she never comes into the world, but like a bastard, to the ignominy of him that brought her forth." The Doctrine and Discipline of Divorce.

Zermatt
10 didst behold] watch'dst (watch'st MS) each night MS, PPP, PUE
11 Saw'st, maybe,] Thou gleam'dst to MS, PPP, PUE
12 the betokening] brav'dst the tokening MS, PPP, PUE
13 end; yea, even] end: yea, saw'st MS, PPP, PUE

74 *The Bridge of Lodi* [1]

(*Spring 1887*)

I

WHEN of tender mind and body,
I was moved by minstrelsy,
And that air 'The Bridge of Lodi'
Brought a strange delight to me.

II

In the battle-breathing jingle
Of its forward-footing tune
I could see the armies mingle,
And the columns crushed and hewn

III

On that far-famed spot by Lodi
Where Napoleon clove his way
To his fame, when like a god he
Bent the nations to his sway.

IV

Hence the tune came capering to me
While I traced the Rhone and Po;
Nor could Milan's Marvel woo me
From the spot englamoured so.

V

And to-day, sunlit and smiling,
Here I stand upon the scene,
With its saffron walls, dun tiling,
And its meads of maiden green,

[1] Pronounce 'Loddy'.

TITLE:
(*Spring 1887*)] (*Visited 23 April, 1887: Battle fought May 10, 1796*) MS

The Bridge of Lodi
1 body,] body MS, PPP, PUE, WE, ME
3 air] strain MS, PPP, PUE
8 crushed] cleft MS, PPP, PUE, CP1
17 sunlit] sun-lit MS
17 smiling,] smiling MS

VI

Even as when the trackway thundered
    With the charge of grenadiers,
And the blood of forty hundred
    Splashed its parapets and piers. . . .

VII

Any ancient crone I'd toady
    Like a lass in young-eyed prime,
Could she tell some tale of Lodi
    At that moving mighty time.

VIII

So, I ask the wives of Lodi
    For traditions of that day;
But, alas! not anybody
    Seems to know of such a fray.

IX

And they heed but transitory
    Marketings in cheese and meat,
Till I judge that Lodi's story
    Is extinct in Lodi's street.

X

Yet while here and there they thrid them
    In their zest to sell and buy,
Let me sit me down amid them
    And behold those thousands die. . . .

XI

– Not a creature cares in Lodi
    How Napoleon swept each arch,
Or where up and downward trod he,
    Or for his outmatching march!

The Bridge of Lodi
24 piers. . . .] piers. . . . . MS
30 day;] day: MS
31 But, alas!] But alas; MS: But alas! PPP, PUE, WE
40 die. . . .] die. . . . . MS
44 outmatching] memorial MS, PPP, PUE
44 march!] March! PPP, PUE, CP1: march. WE, ME

XII

So that wherefore should I be here,
    Watching Adda lip the lea,
When the whole romance to see here
    Is the dream I bring with me?

XIII

And why sing 'The Bridge of Lodi'
    As I sit thereon and swing,
When none shows by smile or nod he
    Guesses why or what I sing? . . .

XIV

Since all Lodi, low and head ones,
    Seem to pass that story by,
It may be the Lodi-bred ones
    Rate it truly, and not I.

XV

Once engrossing Bridge of Lodi,
    Is thy claim to glory gone?
Must I pipe a palinody,
    Or be silent thereupon?

XVI

And if here, from strand to steeple,
    Be no stone to fame the fight,
Must I say the Lodi people
    Are but viewing war aright? . . .

XVII

Nay; I'll sing 'The Bridge of Lodi' –
    That long-loved, romantic thing,
Though none show by smile or nod he
    Guesses why and what I sing!

The Bridge of Lodi
45 here,] here MS
52 sing? . . .] sing? . . . . MS
59 palinody,] palinody MS
64 war] crime MS, PPP, PUE, WE, ME
64 aright? . . .] aright? . . . . MS
66 long-loved] longloved MS [but could be two words]

EXTRA PRINTINGS:
(1) *Selected Poems*, p. 145
(2) *Chosen Poems*, p. 176

75 *On an Invitation to the United States*

I

MY ardours for emprize nigh lost
Since Life has bared its bones to me,
I shrink to seek a modern coast
Whose riper times have yet to be;
Where the new regions claim them free
From that long drip of human tears
Which peoples old in tragedy
Have left upon the centuried years.

II

For, wonning in these ancient lands,
Enchased and lettered as a tomb,
And scored with prints of perished hands,
And chronicled with dates of doom,
Though my own Being bear no bloom
I trace the lives such scenes enshrine,
Give past exemplars present room,
And their experience count as mine.

MISCELLANEOUS POEMS

76 The Mother Mourns

WHEN mid-autumn's moan shook the night-time,
And sedges were horny,
And summer's green wonderwork faltered
On leaze and in lane,

I fared Yell'ham-Firs way, where dimly
Came wheeling around me
Those phantoms obscure and insistent
That shadows unchain.

Till airs from the needle-thicks brought me
A low lamentation,
As though from a tree-god disheartened,
Perplexed, or in pain.

And, heeding, it awed me to gather
That Nature herself there
Was breathing in aëry accents,
With dirge-like refrain,

Weary plaint that Mankind, in these late days,
Had grieved her by holding
Her ancient high fame of perfection
In doubt and disdain. . . .

– 'I had not proposed me a Creature
(She soughed) so excelling
All else of my kingdom in compass
And brightness of brain

'As to read my defects with a god-glance,
Uncover each vestige
Of old inadvertence, annunciate
Each flaw and each stain!

The Mother Mourns
1 mid-autumn's] mid-Autumn's MS
3 summer's] Summer's MS
9 needle-thicks] needle-boughs WE1
11 though from] 'twere of MS, PPP, PUE
15 aëry] aërie MS, PPP, PUE, WE, ME
16 dirge-like] dirgeful MS, PPP, PUE: dirgelike WE, ME
17 days,] days MS
20 disdain. . . .] disdain. . . . . MS
24 brain] brain, MS

'My purpose went not to develop
 Such insight in Earthland;
Such potent appraisements affront me,
 And sadden my reign!

'Why loosened I olden control here
 To mechanize skywards,
Undeeming great scope could outshape in
 A globe of such grain?

'Man's mountings of mindsight I checked not,
 Till range of his vision
Now tops my intent, and finds blemish
 Throughout my domain.

'He holds as inept his own soul-shell –
 My deftest achievement –
Contemns me for fitful inventions
 Ill-timed and inane:

'No more sees my sun as a Sanct-shape,
 My moon as the Night-queen,
My stars as august and sublime ones
 That influences rain:

'Reckons gross and ignoble my teaching,
 Immoral my story,
My love-lights a lure that my species
 May gather and gain.

' "Give me," he has said, "but the matter
 And means the gods lot her,
My brain could evolve a creation
 More seemly, more sane."

– 'If ever a naughtiness seized me
 To woo adulation
From creatures more keen than those crude ones
 That first formed my train –

The Mother Mourns
31 me,] me MS
36 grain?] grain! MS
37 mindsight] mind-sight PPP, PUE, WE, ME
39 Now tops] Has topped MS, PPP, PUE, WE, ME
39 finds] found MS, PPP, PUE
51 lure] lure, MS, PPP, PUE, WE, ME
56 sane.'] sane.' . . . . . . MS
57 – 'If] 'If MS

'If inly a moment I murmured,
"The simple praise sweetly,
But sweetlier the sage" – and did rashly
Man's vision unrein,

'I rue it! . . . His guileless forerunners,
Whose brains I could blandish,
To measure the deeps of my mysteries
Applied them in vain.

'From them my waste aimings and futile
I subtly could cover;
"Every best thing," said they, "to best purpose
Her powers preordain." –

'No more such! . . . My species are dwindling,
My forests grow barren,
My popinjays fail from their tappings,
My larks from their strain.

'My leopardine beauties are rarer,
My tusky ones vanish,
My children have aped mine own slaughters
To quicken my wane.

'Let me grow, then, but mildews and mandrakes,
And slimy distortions,
Let nevermore things good and lovely
To me appertain;

'For Reason is rank in my temples,
And Vision unruly,
And chivalrous laud of my cunning
Is heard not again!'

The Mother Mourns
65 it! . . .] it! . . . . . MS
72 preordain." –] preordain." MS
73 such! . . .] such! . . . . . MS

EXTRA PRINTINGS:
(1) *Selected Poems*, pp. 84–5
(2) *Chosen Poems*, pp. 79–80

TITLE:
'I said to Love' MS

77 *I Said to Love*

I SAID to Love,
'It is not now as in old days
When men adored thee and thy ways
All else above;
Named thee the Boy, the Bright, the One
Who spread a heaven beneath the sun,'
I said to Love.

I said to him,
'We now know more of thee than then;
We were but weak in judgment when,
With hearts abrim,
We clamoured thee that thou would'st please
Inflict on us thine agonies,'
I said to him.

I said to Love,
'Thou art not young, thou art not fair,
No elfin darts, no cherub air,
Nor swan, nor dove
Are thine; but features pitiless,
And iron daggers of distress,'
I said to Love.

'Depart then, Love! . . .
– Man's race shall perish, threatenest thou,
Without thy kindling coupling-vow?
The age to come the man of now
Know nothing of? –
We fear not such a threat from thee;
We are too old in apathy!
Mankind shall cease. – So let it be,'
I said to Love.

I Said to Love
3 ways] ways – CP1
4] Set none above; CP1
6 heaven] Heaven MS
17 elfin] faery MS, PPP, PUE
18 dove] dove, MS
19–20] But features wry and reasonless,/And hidden vials of distress,' MS *before revision*
22 Love! . . .] Love! . . . . . MS
23 – Man's] Man's MS
23 perish . . . thou,] end, dost threaten thou? MS, PPP, PUE
24] Not in MS, PPP, PUE
24 coupling-vow] coupling vow CP1

78 A Commonplace Day

EXTRA PRINTINGS:
(1) *Selected Poems*, pp. 170–1
(2) *Chosen Poems*, pp. 196–7

THE day is turning ghost,
And scuttles from the kalendar in fits and furtively,
To join the anonymous host
Of those that throng oblivion; ceding his place, maybe,
To one of like degree.

I part the fire-gnawed logs,
Rake forth the embers, spoil the busy flames, and lay the ends
Upon the shining dogs;
Further and further from the nooks the twilight's stride extends,
And beamless black impends.

Nothing of tiniest worth
Have I wrought, pondered, planned; no one thing asking blame or praise,
Since the pale corpse-like birth
Of this diurnal unit, bearing blanks in all its rays –
Dullest of dull-hued Days!

Wanly upon the panes
The rain slides, as have slid since morn my colourless thoughts; and yet
Here, while Day's presence wanes,
And over him the sepulchre-lid is slowly lowered and set,
He wakens my regret.

Regret – though nothing dear
That I wot of, was toward in the wide world at his prime,
Or bloomed elsewhere than here,
To die with his decease, and leave a memory sweet, sublime,
Or mark him out in Time. . . .

– Yet, maybe, in some soul,
In some spot undiscerned on sea or land, some impulse rose,
Or some intent upstole
Of that enkindling ardency from whose maturer glows
The world's amendment flows;

A Commonplace Day
15] Flattest of flat-pitched Days. MS *before revision*
15 Days!] Days. MS
17 slides,] slides MS, PPP, PUE
25 Time. . . .] Time. . . . . . MS

But which, benumbed at birth
By momentary chance or wile, has missed its hope to be
Embodied on the earth;
And undervoicings of this loss to man's futurity
May wake regret in me.

79 *At a Lunar Eclipse*

EXTRA PRINTINGS:
(1) *Selected Poems*, p. 146
(2) *Chosen Poems*, p. 177

THY shadow, Earth, from Pole to Central Sea,
Now steals along upon the Moon's meek shine
In even monochrome and curving line
Of imperturbable serenity.

How shall I link such sun-cast symmetry
With the torn troubled form I know as thine,
That profile, placid as a brow divine,
With continents of moil and misery?

And can immense Mortality but throw
So small a shade, and Heaven's high human scheme
Be hemmed within the coasts yon arc implies?

Is such the stellar gauge of earthly show,
Nation at war with nation, brains that teem,
Heroes, and women fairer than the skies?

80 *The Lacking Sense*

INDENTATION:
The indentation of stanza 1 given here is that found in MS, WE, ME. There seems to be no reason except error for the variant found in PPP, PUE, CP, where 1 = ll. 1, 2, 4; 2 = l. 3; and 3 = l. 5

SCENE. – *A sad-coloured landscape, Waddon Vale*

I

'O TIME, whence comes the Mother's moody look amid her labours,
As of one who all unwittingly has wounded where she loves?
Why weaves she not her world-webs to according lutes and tabors,
With nevermore this too remorseful air upon her face,
As of angel fallen from grace?'

At a Lunar Eclipse
13 brains] Brains MS, PPP1

The Lacking Sense
5 grace?'] grace?' – MS

II

– 'Her look is but her story: construe not its symbols keenly:
In her wonderworks yea surely has she wounded where she loves.
The sense of ills misdealt for blisses blanks the mien most queenly,
Self-smitings kill self-joys; and everywhere beneath the sun
Such deeds her hands have done.'

III

– 'And how explains thy Ancient Mind her crimes upon her creatures,
These fallings from her fair beginnings, woundings where she loves,
Into her would-be perfect motions, modes, effects, and features
Admitting cramps, black humours, wan decay, and baleful blights,
Distress into delights?'

IV

– 'Ah! knowest thou not her secret yet, her vainly veiled deficience,
Whence it comes that all unwittingly she wounds the lives she loves?
That sightless are those orbs of hers? – which bar to her omniscience
Brings those fearful unfulfilments, that red ravage through her zones
Whereat all creation groans.

V

'She whispers it in each pathetic strenuous slow endeavour,
When in mothering she unwittingly sets wounds on what she loves;
Yet her primal doom pursues her, faultful, fatal is she ever;
Though so deft and nigh to vision is her facile finger-touch
That the seers marvel much.

The Lacking Sense
7 yea surely] most truly MS, PPP1
11 – 'And] 'And MS
16 – 'Ah! knowest] 'Ah – know'st MS
16 knowest] know'st PPP, PUE, WE, ME
25 much.] much! MS

VI

'Deal, then, her groping skill no scorn, no note of malediction;
Not long on thee will press the hand that hurts the lives it
loves;
And while she plods dead-reckoning on, in darkness of affliction,
Assist her where thy creaturely dependence can or may,
For thou art of her clay.'

81 *To Life*

EXTRA PRINTINGS:
(1) *Selected Poems*, p. 50
(2) *Chosen Poems*, p. 49

O LIFE with the sad seared face,
I weary of seeing thee,
And thy draggled cloak, and thy hobbling pace,
And thy too-forced pleasantry!

I know what thou would'st tell
Of Death, Time, Destiny –
I have known it long, and know, too, well
What it all means for me.

But canst thou not array
Thyself in rare disguise,
And feign like truth, for one mad day,
That Earth is Paradise?

I'll tune me to the mood,
And mumm with thee till eve;
And maybe what as interlude
I feign, I shall believe!

82 *Doom and She*

I

THERE dwells a mighty pair –
Slow, statuesque, intense –
Amid the vague Immense:
None can their chronicle declare,
Nor why they be, nor whence.

The Lacking Sense
26 then,] then MS
28 plods] dares MS, PPP, PUE, CP1
29 can or may] gives thee room MS, PPP1
30 clay] womb MS, PPP1

II

Mother of all things made,
Matchless in artistry,
Unlit with sight is she. –
And though her ever well-obeyed
Vacant of feeling he.

III

The Matron mildly asks –
A throb in every word –
'Our clay-made creatures, lord,
How fare they in their mortal tasks
Upon Earth's bounded bord?

IV

'The fate of those I bear,
Dear lord, pray turn and view,
And notify me true;
Shapings that eyelessly I dare
Maybe I would undo.

V

'Sometimes from lairs of life
Methinks I catch a groan,
Or multitudinous moan,
As though I had schemed a world of strife,
Working by touch alone.'

VI

'World-weaver!' he replies,
'I scan all thy domain;
But since nor joy nor pain
It lies in me to recognize,
Thy questionings are vain.

Doom and She
6 made,] made MS
13 clay-made] clay made MS [could be one word]
22 groan,] groan MS
24 strife,] strife MS
26 World-weaver!] World-weaver, MS
29–30 Doth my clear substance recognize, (recognize MS)/I read thy realms in vain. MS, PPP, PUE, CP1

VII

'World-weaver! what *is* Grief?
And what are Right, and Wrong,
And Feeling, that belong
To creatures all who owe thee fief?
Why is Weak worse than Strong?' . . .

VIII

– Unanswered, curious, meek,
She broods in sad surmise. . . .
– Some say they have heard her sighs
On Alpine height or Polar peak
When the night tempests rise.

EXTRA PRINTINGS:
(1) *The Academy*, 23 Nov 1901, p. 475 [quoted in full in a review which seems to have been based on an early proof of PPP1] = A
(2) *Selected Poems*, pp. 147–8
(3) *Chosen Poems*, pp. 178–9

83 The Problem

SHALL we conceal the Case, or tell it –
We who believe the evidence?
Here and there the watch-towers knell it
With a sullen significance,
Heard of the few who hearken intently and carry an eagerly upstrained sense.

Hearts that are happiest hold not by it;
Better we let, then, the old view reign:
Since there is peace in that, why decry it?
Since there is comfort, why disdain?
Note not the pigment so long as the painting determines humanity's joy and pain.

84 The Subalterns

I

'POOR wanderer,' said the leaden sky,
'I fain would lighten thee,
But there are laws in force on high
Which say it must not be.'

Doom and She
31 World-weaver!] World-weaver, MS
31 Grief?] Grief? – MS
34 fief?] fief? – MS
35 Why . . . worse] What worse is Weak MS, PPP, PUE
35 Strong?' . . .] Strong?' . . . . MS
36 – Unanswered] Unlightened MS: – Unlightened PPP, PUE: – So, baffled CP1
39] On High-Stoy Hill or Pilsdon Peak
On Pilsdon Pen or Lewsdon Peak
MS *before revision*

The Problem
1 Case] truth MS *before revision*
2 evidence?] evidence? – MS
5 hearken . . . upstrained] listen intently with strained and eager and reaching WE, ME
7 let, then,] hence let CP1
7 reign:] reign; MS, PPP, PUE, WE, CP1, ME
8 that] it MS, PPP, PUE, WE, ME [Hardy's copy of CP2 in DCM has 'it?' written in margin]
10] Never the substance but always the seeming determines humanity's joy and pain! MS *before revision*
10 pigment . . . as] pigment, then, in that CP1
10 so long as] the while that MS, PPP, PUE
10 pain.] pain! MS, PPP, PUE, WE, ME

The Subalterns
3 are] be MS, A, PPP, PUE, WE1, [CP1 has 'be' corrected to 'are' by errata slip]

II

– 'I would not freeze thee, shorn one,' cried
  The North, 'knew I but how
To warm my breath, to slack my stride;
  But I am ruled as thou.'

III

– 'To-morrow I attack thee, wight,'
  Said Sickness. 'Yet I swear
I bear thy little ark no spite,
  But am bid enter there.'

IV

– 'Come hither, Son,' I heard Death say;
  'I did not will a grave
Should end thy pilgrimage to-day,
  But I, too, am a slave!'

V

We smiled upon each other then,
  And life to me had less
Of that fell look it wore ere when
  They owned their passiveness.

85 The Sleep-Worker

EXTRA PRINTINGS:
(1) *Selected Poems*, p. 149
(2) *Chosen Poems*, p. 180

TITLE:
The Sleep-worker MS

WHEN wilt thou wake, O Mother, wake and see –
As one who, held in trance, has laboured long
By vacant rote and prepossession strong –
The coils that thou hast wrought unwittingly;

Wherein have place, unrealized by thee,
Fair growths, foul cankers, right enmeshed with wrong,
Strange orchestras of victim-shriek and song,
And curious blends of ache and ecstasy? –

The Subalterns
5 – 'I] 'I A
9 – 'To-morrow] 'To-morrow A
13 – 'Come] 'Come A
16 slave!] slave. MS, A
18 had] wore MS, A, PPP, PUE, CP1, 2
19 Of . . . it] That fell contour MS, A, PPP, PUE
19 look] guise CP1

The Sleep-Worker
3 vacant rote and] automatic MS, PPP1

Should that morn come, and show thy opened eyes
All that Life's palpitating tissues feel,
How wilt thou bear thyself in thy surprise? –

Wilt thou destroy, in one wild shock of shame,
Thy whole high heaving firmamental frame,
Or patiently adjust, amend, and heal?

86 The Bullfinches

BROTHER Bulleys, let us sing
From the dawn till evening! –
For we know not that we go not
When to-day's pale pinions fold
Where they be that sang of old.

When I flew to Blackmoor Vale,
Whence the green-gowned faeries hail,
Roosting near them I could hear them
Speak of queenly Nature's ways,
Means, and moods, – well known to fays.

All we creatures, nigh and far
(Said they there), the Mother's are;
Yet she never shows endeavour
To protect from warrings wild
Bird or beast she calls her child.

Busy in her handsome house
Known as Space, she falls a-drowse;
Yet, in seeming, works on dreaming,
While beneath her groping hands
Fiends make havoc in her bands.

How her hussif'ry succeeds
She unknows or she unheeds,
All things making for Death's taking!
– So the green-gowned faeries say
Living over Blackmoor way.

The Sleep-Worker
9 morn] day WE, SP, ME

The Bullfinches
4 to-day's] the day's MS, PPP, PUE, CP1
5] Unto those who sang of old. (old! MS) MS, PPP, PUE
5 they] those CP1
9 queenly] Mother MS
10 well known] well-known MS
11 creatures,] creatures MS
11 far] far, MS
23 taking!] taking! . . . . MS
24 – So] So MS

Come then, brethren, let us sing,
From the dawn till evening! –
For we know not that we go not
When the day's pale pinions fold
Where those be that sang of old.

87 God-Forgotten

I TOWERED far, and lo! I stood within
The presence of the Lord Most High,
Sent thither by the sons of Earth, to win
Some answer to their cry.

– 'The Earth, sayest thou? The Human race?
By Me created? Sad its lot?
Nay: I have no remembrance of such place:
Such world I fashioned not.' –

– 'O Lord, forgive me when I say
Thou spakest the word that made it all.' –
'The Earth of men – let me bethink me. . . . Yea!
I dimly do recall

'Some tiny sphere I built long back
(Mid millions of such shapes of mine)
So named . . . It perished, surely – not a wrack
Remaining, or a sign?

'It lost my interest from the first,
My aims therefor succeeding ill;
Haply it died of doing as it durst?' –
'Lord, it existeth still.' –

'Dark, then, its life! For not a cry
Of aught it bears do I now hear;
Of its own act the threads were snapt whereby
Its plaints had reached mine ear.

TITLE:
God-forgotten MS

INDENTATION:
That used here is the one found in all editions up to WE2. It seems certain that the irregular ll. 3 and 23 in CP were incorrect. MS has all except stanzas 1 and 2 indented as here. In those two stanzas l. 2 forms a new line of indentation between ll. 1 and 4

The Bullfinches
26 sing,] sing MS
29] When the day's white wings upfold MS *before revision*
29 the day's] to-day's WE, ME
30 Where . . . that] Unto those who MS, PPP, PUE
30 those be] they sleep WE, ME

God-Forgotten
1 lo!] lo, MS
3 Earth] earth MS, PPP, PUE, WE, ME
5 – 'The] 'The MS
5 sayest] say'st MS, PPP, PUE, WE, ME
9 – 'O Lord,] 'O Lord MS
10] Thou spak'st the word, and mad'st it all.' – MS, PPP, PUE
10 word that made] word, and madest CP1
10 that] and WE2, ME
11 men –] men . . . WE, ME
13 built] framed MS, PPP1
13 back] back, MS
15 named . . .] named. . . . . MS

'It used to ask for gifts of good,
Till came its severance, self-entailed,
When sudden silence on that side ensued,
And has till now prevailed.

'All other orbs have kept in touch;
Their voicings reach me speedily:
Thy people took upon them overmuch
In sundering them from me!

'And it is strange – though sad enough –
Earth's race should think that one whose call
Frames, daily, shining spheres of flawless stuff
Must heed their tainted ball!...

'But sayest it is by pangs distraught,
And strife, and silent suffering? –
Sore grieved am I that injury should be wrought
Even on so poor a thing!

'Thou shouldst have learnt that *Not to Mend*
For Me could mean but *Not to Know*:
Hence, Messengers! and straightway put an end
To what men undergo.'...

Homing at dawn, I thought to see
One of the Messengers standing by.
– Oh, childish thought!... Yet often it comes to me
When trouble hovers nigh.

88 The Bedridden Peasant

To an Unknowing God

MUCH wonder I – here long low-laid –
That this dead wall should be
Betwixt the Maker and the made,
Between Thyself and me!

EXTRA PRINTING:
The Academy, 23 Nov 1901, p. 475, stanzas 4–8 only [quoted in a review which seems to have been based on an early proof of PPP1] = A

TITLE:
A Peasant's Philosophy MS *before revision*
Unknowing] CP1 has 'UNKNOWN' corrected on errata slip to 'UNKNOWING'

God-Forgotten
26 severance,] severance MS, PPP, PUE
36 ball!...] ball!.... MS
37 sayest it is] say'st thou 'tis MS, PPP, PUE
39 Sore] Deep MS, PPP, PUE
41 shouldst] should'st MS, PPP, PUE
44 undergo.'...] undergo!'.... MS
47 – Oh,] Oh, MS: – O WE, ME
47 thought!...] hope!.... MS
47 often] oft MS, PPP, PUE: still WE, ME

For, say one puts a child to nurse,
He eyes it now and then
To know if better it is, or worse,
And if it mourn, and when.

But Thou, Lord, giv'st us men our day
In helpless bondage thus
To Time and Chance, and seem'st straightway
To think no more of us!

That some disaster cleft Thy scheme
And tore us wide apart,
So that no cry can cross, I deem;
For Thou art mild of heart,

And wouldst not shape and shut us in
Where voice can not be heard:
Plainly Thou meant'st that we should win
Thy succour by a word.

Might but Thy sense flash down the skies
Like man's from clime to clime,
Thou wouldst not let me agonize
Through my remaining time;

But, seeing how much Thy creatures bear –
Lame, starved, or maimed, or blind –
Wouldst heal the ills with quickest care
Of me and all my kind.

Then, since Thou mak'st not these things be,
But these things dost not know,
I'll praise Thee as were shown to me
The mercies Thou wouldst show!

The Bedridden Peasant
7 it is] 'tis MS, PPP, PUE
9 giv'st us men our] givest men their WE, ME
9 giv'st] givest CP1
12 us!] us. MS
13 scheme] scheme, MS
14 us] it WE, ME
16 mild] broad A
17 wouldst] would'st MS, A, PPP, PUE
19 Plainly] 'Tis plain MS, A, PPP, PUE
19 meant'st that] meantest WE, ME
23 wouldst] would'st MS, A, PPP, PUE
26 starved,] starved A
27 Wouldst] Thou'dst MS, A, PPP, PUE
28 kind.] kind. . . . WE, ME
29] Since, making not these things to be, WE, ME
30 But these things] These things Thou WE, ME
32 wouldst] would'st MS, A, PPP, PUE
32 show!] show. A

89 *By the Earth's Corpse*

I

'O LORD, why grievest Thou? –
Since Life has ceased to be
Upon this globe, now cold
As lunar land and sea,
And humankind, and fowl, and fur
Are gone eternally,
All is the same to Thee as ere
They knew mortality.'

II

'O Time,' replied the Lord,
'Thou readest me ill, I ween;
Were all *the same*, I should not grieve
At that late earthly scene,
Now blestly past – though planned by me
With interest close and keen! –
Nay, nay: things now are *not* the same
As they have earlier been.

III

'Written indelibly
On my eternal mind
Are all the wrongs endured
By Earth's poor patient kind,
Which my too oft unconscious hand
Let enter undesigned.
No god can cancel deeds foredone,
Or thy old coils unwind!

IV

'As when, in Noë's days,
I whelmed the plains with sea,
So at this last, when flesh
And herb but fossils be,

TITLE:
'And it repented the Lord that he had made man' MS *del*, below title

INDENTATION:
Stanzas 1, 3, 4: 1 = ll. 5, 7
2 = ll. 1–4, 6, 8
Stanza 2: 1 = ll. 3, 5, 7
2 = ll. 1, 2, 4, 6, 8 MS

By the Earth's Corpse
5 humankind, and fowl,] humankind and fowl MS
10 readest] read'st MS, PPP, PUE, WE, ME

And, all extinct, their piteous dust
    Revolves obliviously,
That I made Earth, and life, and man,
    It still repenteth me!'

90 Mute Opinion

EXTRA PRINTING:
The Academy, 23 Nov 1901, p. 476 [quoted in full in a review which seems to have been based on an early proof of PPP1] = A

I

I TRAVERSED a dominion
Whose spokesmen spake out strong
Their purpose and opinion
Through pulpit, press, and song.
I scarce had means to note there
A large-eyed few, and dumb,
Who thought not as those thought there
That stirred the heat and hum.

II

When, grown a Shade, beholding
That land in lifetime trode,
To learn if its unfolding
Fulfilled its clamoured code,
I saw, in web unbroken,
Its history outwrought
Not as the loud had spoken,
But as the mute had thought.

91 To an Unborn Pauper Child

EXTRA PRINTINGS:
(1) *The Academy*, 23 Nov 1901, p. 475, stanzas 3–5 only, and printed in order 3, 5, 4 [quoted in a review which seems to have been based on an early proof of PPP1] = A
(2) *Selected Poems*, pp. 102–3
(3) *Chosen Poems*, pp. 134–5

TITLE:
To an Unborn Child MS *before revision*
To an Unborn Pauper-Child MS
'She must go to the Union-house to have her baby.' (Casterbridge *del*) *Petty Sessions*. MS below title

I

BREATHE not, hid Heart: cease silently,
And though thy birth-hour beckons thee,
    Sleep the long sleep:
    The Doomsters heap
Travails and teens around us here,
And Time-wraiths turn our songsingings to fear.

Mute Opinion
2 spake] spoke A
5 scarce had means] almost failed WE, ME
9 When, grown] When as WE1: When, as WE2, ME
15 Had] has MS, A
16 mute] dumb MS, A

To an Unborn Pauper Child
2 thee,] thee MS
3 sleep:] sleep; [?] MS

II

Hark, how the peoples surge and sigh,
And laughters fail, and greetings die:
    Hopes dwindle; yea,
    Faiths waste away,
Affections and enthusiasms numb;
Thou canst not mend these things if thou dost come.

III

Had I the ear of wombèd souls
Ere their terrestrial chart unrolls,
    And thou wert free
    To cease, or be,
Then would I tell thee all I know,
And put it to thee: Wilt thou take Life so?

IV

Vain vow! No hint of mine may hence
To theeward fly: to thy locked sense
    Explain none can
    Life's pending plan:
Thou wilt thy ignorant entry make
Though skies spout fire and blood and nations quake.

V

Fain would I, dear, find some shut plot
Of earth's wide wold for thee, where not
    One tear, one qualm,
    Should break the calm.
But I am weak as thou and bare;
No man can change the common lot to rare.

VI

Must come and bide. And such are we –
Unreasoning, sanguine, visionary –
    That I can hope
    Health, love, friends, scope
In full for thee; can dream thou'lt find
Joys seldom yet attained by humankind!

To an Unborn Pauper Child
8 die:] die; MS
9 yea,] yea MS
11 numb;] numb, MS
13 ear of wombèd] circuit of all A
22 pending] dismal MS, A
26 wold] world A
30 change . . . rare.] move the stony gods to spare! A
30 rare.] rare! MS
32 sanguine] fatuous MS *before revision*
35 thou'lt] thou wilt CP1–3 [Hardy's copy of SP (1917) has been corrected to 'thou wilt', and his copy of CP2 to 'thou 'ilt']
36 seldom] MS has 'seldom' replaced by 'never' and then reinstated

92 *To Flowers from Italy in Winter*

TITLE:
To Flowers from Italy in winter MS

SUNNED in the South, and here to-day;
– If all organic things
Be sentient, Flowers, as some men say,
What are your ponderings?

How can you stay, nor vanish quite
From this bleak spot of thorn,
And birch, and fir, and frozen white
Expanse of the forlorn?

Frail luckless exiles hither brought!
Your dust will not regain
Old sunny haunts of Classic thought
When you shall waste and wane;

But mix with alien earth, be lit
With frigid Boreal flame,
And not a sign remain in it
To tell man whence you came.

93 *On a Fine Morning*

I

WHENCE comes Solace? – Not from seeing
What is doing, suffering, being,
Not from noting Life's conditions,
Nor from heeding Time's monitions;
But in cleaving to the Dream,
And in gazing at the gleam
Whereby gray things golden seem.

II

Thus do I this heyday, holding
Shadows but as lights unfolding,

To Flowers from Italy in Winter
16 man] men MS, PPP, PUE, WE, ME
16 came.] came! MS

As no specious show this moment
With its iris-hued embowment;
    But as nothing other than
    Part of a benignant plan;
    Proof that earth was made for man.

February 1899

94 To Lizbie Browne

EXTRA PRINTINGS:
(1) *Selected Poems*, pp. 23–5
(2) *Chosen Poems*, pp. 23–5

I

DEAR Lizbie Browne,
Where are you now?
In sun, in rain? –
Or is your brow
Past joy, past pain,
Dear Lizbie Browne?

II

Sweet Lizbie Browne,
How you could smile,
How you could sing! –
How archly wile
In glance-giving,
Sweet Lizbie Browne!

III

And, Lizbie Browne,
Who else had hair
Bay-red as yours,
Or flesh so fair
Bred out of doors,
Sweet Lizbie Browne?

On a Fine Morning
11 iris-hued] irisèd MS, PPP, PUE: iridized WE1: iriséd WE2, ME [Hardy's copy of WE1 has been corrected to 'iriséd']

To Lizbie Browne
7 Browne,] Browne MS, PPP, PUE, WE, ME, CP1–3
10 archly] Hardy's copy of CP2 has in margin '?weave a'
11 glance-giving] glancegiving MS [could be two words]

IV

When, Lizbie Browne,
You had just begun
To be endeared
By stealth to one,
You disappeared
My Lizbie Browne!

V

Ay, Lizbie Browne,
So swift your life,
And mine so slow,
You were a wife
Ere I could show
Love, Lizbie Browne.

VI

Still, Lizbie Browne,
You won, they said,
The best of men
When you were wed. . . .
Where went you then,
O Lizbie Browne?

VII

Dear Lizbie Browne,
I should have thought,
'Girls ripen fast,'
And coaxed and caught
You ere you passed,
Dear Lizbie Browne!

VIII

But, Lizbie Browne,
I let you slip;
Shaped not a sign;
Touched never your lip
With lip of mine,
Lost Lizbie Browne!

To Lizbie Browne
23 disappeared] disappeared, MS, WE2, ME
32 said,] said WE1
34 wed. . . .] wed. SP

IX

So, Lizbie Browne,
When on a day
Men speak of me
As not, you'll say,
'And who was he?' –
Yes, Lizbie Browne!

95 *Song of Hope*

O SWEET To-morrow! –
After to-day
There will away
This sense of sorrow.
Then let us borrow
Hope, for a gleaming
Soon will be streaming,
Dimmed by no gray –
No gray!

While the winds wing us
Sighs from The Gone,
Nearer to dawn
Minute-beats bring us;
When there will sing us
Larks, of a glory
Waiting our story
Further anon –
Anon!

Doff the black token,
Don the red shoon,
Right and retune
Viol-strings broken:
Null the words spoken
In speeches of rueing,
The night cloud is hueing,
To-morrow shines soon –
Shines soon!

EXTRA PRINTINGS:
(1) *Selected Poems*, pp. 12–13
(2) *Chosen Poems*, pp. 12–13

TITLE:

Young Hope
(Song)
MS *before revision*

Note This was one of nine poems chosen by Hardy for the Library of the Royal Dolls' House at Windsor Castle. The copy there has 'streaming' (l. 7) and 'Viol strings' (l. 22)

Song of Hope
15 Larks,] Larks MS, PPP, PUE
22 broken:] broken; MS, PPP, PUE, WE, SP, ME, CHP

96 *The Well-Beloved*

I WENT by star and planet shine
 Towards the dear one's home
At Kingsbere, there to make her mine
 When the next sun upclomb.

I edged the ancient hill and wood
 Beside the Ikling Way,
Nigh where the Pagan temple stood
 In the world's earlier day.

And as I quick and quicker walked
 On gravel and on green,
I sang to sky, and tree, or talked
 Of her I called my queen.

– 'O faultless is her dainty form,
 And luminous her mind;
She is the God-created norm
 Of perfect womankind!'

A shape whereon one star-blink gleamed
 Slid softly by my side,
A woman's; and her motion seemed
 The motion of my bride.

And yet methought she'd drawn erstwhile
 Out from the ancient leaze,
Where once were pile and peristyle
 For men's idolatries.

– 'O maiden lithe and lone, what may
 Thy name and lineage be
Who so resemblest by this ray
 My darling? – Art thou she?'

The Shape: 'Thy bride remains within
 Her father's grange and grove.'
– 'Thou speakest rightly,' I broke in,
 'Thou art not she I love.'

The Well-Beloved
1 went] wayed MS, PPP, PUE
2] Towards my Dear's abode WE, ME
3 Kingsbere] Jordon WE, ME
4 sun upclomb] noon-tide glowed WE, ME [Hardy's copy of CP2 has been corrected to the variants given here and in ll. 2 and 3]
7 Nigh] Near WE, ME
11 sky,] sky WE, ME
18 Slid] Glode MS, PPP, PUE, CP1
18 softly] smoothly (softly *del*) MS
18 by] to WE, ME
21 erstwhile] the while WE, ME
22 Out from] Adown MS, PPP, PUE, WE, ME
24 men's] Love's CP1
26 be] be, MS, PPP, PUE, WE, ME
29 Shape] shape MS

– 'Nay: though thy bride remains inside
 Her father's walls,' said she,
'The one most dear is with thee here,
 For thou dost love but me.'

Then I: 'But she, my only choice,
 Is now at Kingsbere Grove?'
Again her soft mysterious voice:
 'I am thy only Love.'

Thus still she vouched, and still I said,
 'O sprite, that cannot be!' . . .
It was as if my bosom bled,
 So much she troubled me.

The sprite resumed: 'Thou hast transferred
 To her dull form awhile
My beauty, fame, and deed, and word,
 My gestures and my smile.

'O fatuous man, this truth infer,
 Brides are not what they seem;
Thou lovest what thou dreamest her;
 I am thy very dream!'

– 'O then,' I answered miserably,
 Speaking as scarce I knew,
'My loved one, I must wed with thee
 If what thou sayest be true!'

She, proudly, thinning in the gloom:
 'Though, since troth-plight began,
I have ever stood as bride to groom,
 I wed no mortal man!'

Thereat she vanished by the lane
 Adjoining Kingsbere town,
Near where, men say, once stood the Fane
 To Venus, on the Down.

The Well-Beloved
36 me.'] me.' – MS
38 Kingsbere] Jordon WE, ME
42 be!' . . .] be!' . . . . . MS
56 sayest] say'st MS, PPP, PUE, WE, ME
59 I have] I've MS, PPP, PUE, WE, ME
60 man!] man. MS
61 lane] Cross MS, PPP, PUE
62–4] That, entering Kingsbere town,/The two long lanes form, near the fosse/Below the faneless Down. MS, PPP, PUE
62 Kingsbere] Budmouth WE, ME

– When I arrived and met my bride
    Her look was pinched and thin,
As if her soul had shrunk and died,
    And left a waste within.

97 Her Reproach

CON the dead page as 'twere live love: press on!
Cold wisdom's words will ease thy track for thee;
Aye, go; cast off sweet ways, and leave me wan
To biting blasts that are intent on me.

But if thy object Fame's far summits be,
Whose inclines many a skeleton overlies
That missed both dream and substance, stop and see
How absence wears these cheeks and dims these eyes!

It surely is far sweeter and more wise
To water love, than toil to leave anon
A name whose glory-gleam will but advise
Invidious minds to eclipse it with their own,

And over which the kindliest will but stay
A moment; musing, 'He, too, had his day!'

Westbourne Park Villas, 1867

98 The Inconsistent

I SAY, 'She was as good as fair!'
    When standing by her mound;
'Such passing sweetness,' I declare,
    'No longer treads the ground.'
I say, 'What living Love can catch
    Her bloom and bonhomie,
And what in recent maidens match
    Her olden warmth to me!'

The Well-Beloved
65 bride] bride, PPP, PUE, WE, ME

Her Reproach
1 love:] love; MS
1 on!] on. CP1–3
6 overlies] o'erlies MS, PPP, PUE
7 stop] stop, MS
10 love,] love WE, ME
12 eclipse] quench MS, PPP, PUE: dull CP1
14 moment;] moment, MS, PPP, PUE, WE, ME
14 musing,] musing WE1
Westbourne] 16 Westbourne WE, ME

The Inconsistent
1 fair!] fair, MS, PPP, PUE, WE, ME
7 recent] newer MS, PPP, PUE: later WE, ME
8–9 Stanza break in all editions

– There stands within yon vestry-nook
    Where bonded lovers sign,
Her name upon a faded book
    With one that is not mine.
To him she breathed the tender vow
    She once had breathed to me,
But yet I say, 'O Love, even now
    Would I had died for thee!'

EXTRA PRINTINGS:
(1) *Selected Poems*, p. 36
(2) *Chosen Poems*, p. 37

INDENTATION:
Hardy has corrected his copy of SP (1917) so that ll. 1, 8, 9, 16 are moved left. The effect there is to place the 'Y' of 'You' in l. 1 over the 'T' of 'Time'

99 A Broken Appointment

        YOU did not come,
And marching Time drew on, and wore me numb. –
Yet less for loss of your dear presence there
Than that I thus found lacking in your make
That high compassion which can overbear
Reluctance for pure lovingkindness' sake
Grieved I, when, as the hope-hour stroked its sum,
        You did not come.

        You love not me,
And love alone can lend you loyalty;
– I know and knew it. But, unto the store
Of human deeds divine in all but name,
Was it not worth a little hour or more
To add yet this: Once you, a woman, came
To soothe a time-torn man; even though it be
        You love not me?

TITLE:
'Between us now' MS

100 Between Us Now

BETWEEN us now and here –
    Two thrown together
Who are not wont to wear
    Life's flushest feather –

The Inconsistent
15 Love] love PPP, PUE

A Broken Appointment
2 on,] on WE, SP, ME
6 Reluctance] Averseness MS *before revision*
6 lovingkindness'] loving-kindness' SP
7 sum,] sum MS
10 lend you] move your MS *before revision*
14 Once] Once, MS, PPP, PUE, WE, SP, ME
15 time-torn] soul-sad MS *before revision*

Who see the scenes slide past,
The daytimes dimming fast,
Let there be truth at last,
    Even if despair.

So thoroughly and long
    Have you now known me,
So real in faith and strong
    Have I now shown me,
That nothing needs disguise
Further in any wise,
Or asks or justifies
    A guarded tongue.

Face unto face, then, say,
    Eyes my own meeting,
Is your heart far away,
    Or with mine beating?
When false things are brought low,
And swift things have grown slow,
Feigning like froth shall go,
    Faith be for aye.

101 *How Great My Grief*

EXTRA PRINTINGS:
(1) *Selected Poems*, p. 33
(2) *Chosen Poems*, p. 34

TITLE:
'How Great my Grief' MS
MS has either an earlier title or sub-title *deleted*:
His Love brings little Pleasure

(*Triolet*)

How great my grief, my joys how few,
    Since first it was my fate to know thee!
– Have the slow years not brought to view
How great my grief, my joys how few,
Nor memory shaped old times anew,
    Nor loving-kindness helped to show thee
How great my grief, my joys how few,
    Since first it was my fate to know thee?

Between Us Now
18 my] mine MS, PPP, PUE, WE, CP1, ME

How Great My Grief
1 few,] few MS
2 thee!] thee! – MS
3 – Have] Have MS
6 loving-kindness] lovingkindness MS
7 few,] few MS

EXTRA PRINTINGS:
(1) *Selected Poems*, pp. 97–8
(2) *Chosen Poems*, pp. 92–3

TITLE:
'I need not go' MS

102 *I Need Not Go*

I NEED not go
Through sleet and snow
To where I know
She waits for me;
She will tarry me there
Till I find it fair,
And have time to spare
From company.

When I've overgot
The world somewhat,
When things cost not
Such stress and strain,
Is soon enough
By cypress sough
To tell my Love
I am come again.

And if some day,
When none cries nay,
I still delay
To seek her side,
(Though ample measure
Of fitting leisure
Await my pleasure)
She will not chide.

What – not upbraid me
That I delayed me,
Nor ask what stayed me
So long? Ah, no! –
New cares may claim me,
New loves inflame me,
She will not blame me,
But suffer it so.

I Need Not Go
4 me;] me: MS
5 tarry] wait MS, PPP, PUE, CP1
11 cost] wear MS, PPP1
16 I am] I'm MS
17 day,] day MS
20 side,] side MS
32] But let me go. MS *before revision*

103 *The Coquette, and After*

(*Triolets*)

I

FOR long the cruel wish I knew
That your free heart should ache for me
While mine should bear no ache for you;
For long – the cruel wish! – I knew
How men can feel, and craved to view
My triumph – fated not to be
For long! . . . The cruel wish I knew
That your free heart should ache for me!

II

At last one pays the penalty –
The woman – women always do.
My farce, I found, was tragedy
At last! – One pays the penalty
With interest when one, fancy-free,
Learns love, learns shame. . . . Of sinners two
At last *one* pays the penalty –
The woman – women always do!

104 *A Spot*

EXTRA PRINTINGS:
(1) *Selected Poems*, p. 42
(2) *Chosen Poems*, p. 41

In years defaced and lost,
Two sat here, transport-tossed,
Lit by a living love
The wilted world knew nothing of:
Scared momently
By gaingivings,
Then hoping things
That could not be. . . .

The Coquette, and After
2 me] me, MS, PPP, PE, WE, ME
4 For] For, MS, PPP, PUE, WE, ME
7 long! . . .] long! . . . . . MS
14 shame. . . .] shame. . . . . MS

A Spot
8 be. . . .] be. MS, PPP, PUE

Of love and us no trace
Abides upon the place;
The sun and shadows wheel,
Season and season sereward steal;
Foul days and fair
Here, too, prevail,
And gust and gale
As everywhere.

But lonely shepherd souls
Who bask amid these knolls
May catch a faery sound
On sleepy noontides from the ground:
'O not again
Till Earth outwears
Shall love like theirs
Suffuse this glen!'

105 *Long Plighted*

Is it worth while, dear, now,
To call for bells, and sally forth arrayed
For marriage-rites – discussed, descried, delayed
So many years?

Is it worth while, dear, now,
To stir desire for old fond purposings,
By feints that Time still serves for dallyings,
Though quittance nears?

Is it worth while, dear, when
The day being so far spent, so low the sun,
The undone thing will soon be as the done,
And smiles as tears?

Is it worth while, dear, when
Our cheeks are worn, our early brown is gray;
When, meet or part we, none says yea or nay,
Or heeds, or cares?

A Spot
12 sereward] sere-ward WE, SP, ME
22 Earth] earth ME

Long Plighted
3 descried] decried MS, PPP, PUE, WE, ME
6 purposings,] purposings MS

Is it worth while, dear, since
We still can climb old Yell'ham's wooded mounds
Together, as each season steals its rounds
And disappears?

Is it worth while, dear, since
As mates in Mellstock churchyard we can lie,
Till the last crash of all things low and high
Shall end the spheres?

106 The Widow Betrothed

TITLE:
The Widow MS, PPP, PUE

I PASSED the lodge and avenue
To her fair tenement,
And sunset on her window-panes
Reflected our intent.

The creeper on the gable nigh
Was fired to more than red,
And when I came to halt thereby
'Bright as my joy!' I said.

Of late days it had been her aim
To meet me in the hall;
Now at my footsteps no one came,
And no one to my call.

Again I knocked, and tardily
An inner tread was heard,
And I was shown her presence then
With a mere answering word.

She met me, and but barely took
My proffered warm embrace;
Preoccupation weighed her look,
And hardened her sweet face.

'To-morrow – could you – would you call?
Abridge your present stay?
My child is ill – my one, my all! –
And can't be left to-day.'

Long Plighted
22 lie,] lie MS

The Widow Betrothed
1–2] By Mellstock Lodge and Avenue/Towards her door I went, MS, PPP, PUE
6 red,] red PPP2, PUE
7 thereby] thereby, MS, PPP1
14 tread] step MS, PPP, PUE
16 a mere] scarce an MS, PPP, PUE
22 Abridge] Make brief MS, PPP, PUE: Shorten WE, ME
24 to-day.] to-day! MS

And then she turns, and gives commands
   As I were out of sound,
Or were no more to her and hers
   Than any neighbour round. . . .

– As maid I loved her; but one came
   And pleased, and coaxed, and wooed,
And when in time he wedded her
   I deemed her gone for good.

He won, I lost her; and my loss
   I bore I know not how;
But I do think I suffered then
   Less wretchedness than now.

For Time, in taking him, unclosed
   An unexpected door
Of bliss for me, which grew to seem
   Far surer than before.

Yet in my haste I overlooked
   When secondly I sued
That then, as not at first, she had learnt
   The call of motherhood. . . .

Her word is steadfast, and I know
   How firmly pledged are we:
But a new love-claim shares her since
   She smiled as maid on me!

EXTRA PRINTINGS:
(1) In the short story, 'A Changed Man', in *The Sphere*, 21 April 1900, p. 420 = S
(2) In *A Changed Man* (London, 1913), p. 8 = CM

INDENTATION:
1 = ll. 1, 3 } and so throughout
2 = ll. 2, 4 }   S, CM

107 *At a Hasty Wedding*

(*Triolet*)

IF hours be years the twain are blest,
For now they solace swift desire
By bonds of every bond the best,
If hours be years. The twain are blest
Do eastern stars slope never west,
Nor pallid ashes follow fire:
If hours be years the twain are blest,
For now they solace swift desire.

The Widow Betrothed
29 loved] wooed MS, PPP, PUE
30] And coaxed her heart away, MS, PPP, PUE
30 wooed,] wooed. CP
32 good] aye MS, PPP, PUE
34 know] knew MS
37 unclosed] had oped MS, PPP, PUE
40 before.] before. . . . . MS: before. . . . PPP, PUE, WE1, ME: before . . . WE2
41–4 Not in MS, PPP, PUE
46 How firmly pledged] That plighted firm MS, PPP, PUE
46 How] That WE, ME
47] But she has caught new love-calls since MS, PPP, PUE
48 me!] me. WE, ME

At a Hasty Wedding
3] By lifelong ties that tether zest S, CM
5 stars] suns S, CM
6 fire:] fire. S, CM
7 blest,] blest S, CM

108 The Dream-Follower

A DREAM of mine flew over the mead
To the halls where my old Love reigns;
And it drew me on to follow its lead:
And I stood at her window-panes;

And I saw but a thing of flesh and bone
Speeding on to its cleft in the clay;
And my dream was scared, and expired on a moan,
And I whitely hastened away.

EXTRA PRINTINGS:
(1) *Selected Poems*, p. 92
(2) *Chosen Poems*, p. 87

109 His Immortality

I

I SAW a dead man's finer part
Shining within each faithful heart
Of those bereft. Then said I: 'This must be
His immortality.'

II

I looked there as the seasons wore,
And still his soul continuously bore
A life in theirs. But less its shine excelled
Than when I first beheld.

III

His fellow-yearsmen passed, and then
In later hearts I looked for him again;
And found him – shrunk, alas! into a thin
And spectral mannikin.

IV

Lastly I ask – now old and chill –
If aught of him remain unperished still;
And find, in me alone, a feeble spark,
Dying amid the dark.

February 1899

EXTRA PRINTING:
The Academy, 23 Nov 1901, p. 476 [quoted in full in a review which seems to have been based on an early proof of PPP1] = A

INDENTATION:
1 = l. 3
2 = ll. 1, 2
3 = l. 4 MS, A in stanza 1 only

The Dream-Follower
4 window-panes;] window-panes: MS

His Immortality
5 as . . . wore] on a later day A
6 continuously bore] outshaped, as when in clay, A
6 bore] upbore MS, PPP, PUE
7 A] Its MS, A, PPP, PUE
9 fellow-yearsmen] fellow-yearsman A
11 alas!] alas, MS
13 old] aged A
February 1899] Not in A

TITLE:
The To-be-Forgotten MS
MS has the following *deleted* below the title:

(In Stourcastle churchyard)

In All Saint's[?] Churchyard Casterbridge

'Neither have they any more a reward, for the memory of them is forgotten.'

110 *The To-Be-Forgotten*

I

I HEARD a small sad sound,
And stood awhile among the tombs around:
'Wherefore, old friends,' said I, 'are you distrest,
Now, screened from life's unrest?'

II

– 'O not at being here;
But that our future second death is near;
When, with the living, memory of us numbs,
And blank oblivion comes!

III

'These, our sped ancestry,
Lie here embraced by deeper death than we;
Nor shape nor thought of theirs can you descry
With keenest backward eye.

IV

'They count as quite forgot;
They are as men who have existed not;
Theirs is a loss past loss of fitful breath;
It is the second death.

V

'We here, as yet, each day
Are blest with dear recall; as yet, can say
We hold in some soul loved continuance
Of shape and voice and glance.

VI

'But what has been will be –
First memory, then oblivion's swallowing sea;
Like men foregone, shall we merge into those
Whose story no one knows.

The To-Be-Forgotten
2 among] amid MS, PPP, PUE
3 you] ye MS, PPP, PUE
4 unrest?'] unrest?' – MS
6 near] drear MS, PPP, PUE
9] 'Those who our grandsires be MS, PPP, PUE, WE, ME
11 can you] canst thou MS, PPP, PUE
13 count] bide MS, PPP, PUE
18 yet,] yet WE, ME
18 can say] alway MS, PPP, PUE
19 We . . . soul] In some soul hold a MS, PPP, PUE
22 swallowing] turbid MS, PPP, PUE
23 foregone,] foregone WE, ME
23 shall . . . into] we join us unto MS, PPP1

VII

'For which of us could hope
To show in life that world-awakening scope
Granted the few whose memory none lets die,
But all men magnify?

VIII

'We were but Fortune's sport;
Things true, things lovely, things of good report
We neither shunned nor sought . . . We see our bourne,
And seeing it we mourn.'

111 *Wives in the Sere*

EXTRA MANUSCRIPT:
In the Bancroft Library of the University of California at Berkeley = BL

EXTRA PRINTINGS:
(1) *The Tatler*, 31 July 1901, p. 216 = T
(2) *Selected Poems*, p. 101
(3) *Chosen Poems*, p. 96

I

NEVER a careworn wife but shows,
If a joy suffuse her,
Something beautiful to those
Patient to peruse her,
Some one charm the world unknows
Precious to a muser,
Haply what, ere years were foes,
Moved her mate to choose her.

II

But, be it a hint of rose
That an instant hues her,
Or some early light or pose
Wherewith thought renews her –
Seen by him at full, ere woes
Practised to abuse her –
Sparely comes it, swiftly goes,
Time again subdues her.

The To-Be-Forgotten
31 sought . . .] sought. . . . . MS
MS has a date *deleted* at the end of the poem. It looks as if 'Feb. 9. 1889' has been changed to 'Feb. 9. 1899'.

Wives in the Sere
4 her,] her – BL, T
5 unknows] unknows, MS, BL, T, SP, CHP
6 muser,] muser; BL, T

EXTRA PRINTING:
The May Book, ed. Mrs Aria (London, 1901), pp. 62–3 = MB

112 The Superseded

I

As newer comers crowd the fore,
We drop behind.
– We who have laboured long and sore
Times out of mind,
And keen are yet, must not regret
To drop behind.

II

Yet there are some of us who grieve
To go behind;
Staunch, strenuous souls who scarce believe
Their fires declined,
And know none spares, remembers, cares
Who go behind.

III

'Tis not that we have unforetold
The drop behind;
We feel the new must oust the old
In every kind;
But yet we think, must we, must *we*,
Too, drop behind?

113 An August Midnight

I

A SHADED lamp and a waving blind,
And the beat of a clock from a distant floor:
On this scene enter – winged, horned, and spined –
A longlegs, a moth, and a dumbledore;
While 'mid my page there idly stands
A sleepy fly, that rubs its hands . . .

The Superseded
1 fore,] fore MS, MB
2 behind.] behind. . . . . MS: behind . . . MB
3 – We] We MS, MB
7 some of us] of us some MS, MB, PPP, PUE
11 spares] cares MS, MB, PPP, PUE
11 cares] spares MS, MB, PPP, PUE
13 'Tis] Tis WE2
16 kind;] kind, MS, MB
17 yet] yet, MB

An August Midnight
1 lamp] lamp, MS
5 'mid] mid MS, WE, ME
6 hands . . .] hands. . . . . MS

II

Thus meet we five, in this still place,
At this point of time, at this point in space.
– My guests besmear my new-penned line,
Or bang at the lamp and fall supine.
'God's humblest, they!' I muse. Yet why?
They know Earth-secrets that know not I.

Max Gate, 1899

114 *The Caged Thrush Freed and Home Again*

TITLE:
The Caged Thrush freed and home again MS

(*Villanelle*)

'MEN know but little more than we,
Who count us least of things terrene,
How happy days are made to be!

'Of such strange tidings what think ye,
O birds in brown that peck and preen?
Men know but little more than we!

'When I was borne from yonder tree
In bonds to them, I hoped to glean
How happy days are made to be,

'And want and wailing turned to glee;
Alas, despite their mighty mien
Men know but little more than we!

'They cannot change the Frost's decree,
They cannot keep the skies serene;
How happy days are made to be

'Eludes great Man's sagacity
No less than ours, O tribes in treen!
Men know but little more than we
How happy days are made to be.'

An August Midnight
9 – My] My MS
9 besmear] parade MS, PPP, PUE, WE, ME
9 line] ink MS, PPP, PUE
10 lamp . . . supine] lamp-glass, whirl, and sink MS, PPP, PUE
10 lamp] lamp, WE, ME
10 fall] sink WE, ME
11 muse.] muse. – MS
12 Earth-secrets] earth-secrets (life-secrets *del*) MS

The Caged Thrush Freed and Home Again
4 ye,] ye MS
11 Alas,] Alas! MS
13 Frost's] frost's WE, ME

115 *Birds at Winter Nightfall*

(*Triolet*)

AROUND the house the flakes fly faster,
And all the berries now are gone
From holly and cotonea-aster
Around the house. The flakes fly! – faster
Shutting indoors that crumb-outcaster
We used to see upon the lawn
Around the house. The flakes fly faster,
And all the berries now are gone!

Max Gate

TITLE:
The Puzzled Game-birds MS
The Battue WE, ME

116 *The Puzzled Game-Birds*

(*Triolet*)

THEY are not those who used to feed us
When we were young – they cannot be –
These shapes that now bereave and bleed us?
They are not those who used to feed us,
For did we then cry, they would heed us.
– If hearts can house such treachery
They are not those who used to feed us
When we were young – they cannot be!

INDENTATION:
MS makes it clear that the birds' names were to be clear to the left of the one rank of indentation, as printed here but not in earlier editions

117 *Winter in Durnover Field*

SCENE. – *A wide stretch of fallow ground recently sown with wheat, and frozen to iron hardness. Three large birds walking about thereon, and wistfully eyeing the surface. Wind keen from north-east: sky a dull grey.*

(*Triolet*)

Rook. – Throughout the field I find no grain;
The cruel frost encrusts the cornland!

Birds at Winter Nightfall
3 cotonea-aster] cotoneaster MS, PPP, PUE, WE, CP1, ME
Note Hardy's copy of WE1 in DCM has '1900' added to *Max Gate*

The Puzzled Game-Birds
4 us,] us, – MS, PPP, PUE, WE, ME
5] For would they not fair terms concede us? MS, PPP, PUE, WE, ME

Starling. – Aye: patient pecking now is vain
Throughout the field, I find . . .
Rook. – No grain!
Pigeon. – Nor will be, comrade, till it rain,
Or genial thawings loose the lorn land
Throughout the field.
Rook. – I find no grain:
The cruel frost encrusts the cornland!

118 *The Last Chrysanthemum*

WHY should this flower delay so long
To show its tremulous plumes?
Now is the time of plaintive robin-song,
When flowers are in their tombs.

Through the slow summer, when the sun
Called to each frond and whorl
That all he could for flowers was being done,
Why did it not uncurl?

It must have felt that fervid call
Although it took no heed,
Waking but now, when leaves like corpses fall,
And saps all retrocede.

Too late its beauty, lonely thing,
The season's shine is spent,
Nothing remains for it but shivering
In tempests turbulent.

Had it a reason for delay,
Dreaming in witlessness
That for a bloom so delicately gay
Winter would stay its stress?

– I talk as if the thing were born
With sense to work its mind;
Yet it is but one mask of many worn
By the Great Face behind.

Winter in Durnover Field
4 find . . .] find. . . . MS
5 be,] be MS

The Last Chrysanthemum
20 stress?] stress? . . . . . MS
21 – I] I MS
22 mind;] mind, MS

EXTRA MANUSCRIPT:
Permission has been refused to see the MS in the possession of Mr Frederick B. Adams, Jnr.

EXTRA PRINTINGS:
(1) *The Graphic*, 29 Dec 1900, p. 956 = G
(2) *Selected Poems*, pp. 43–4
(3) *Chosen Poems*, pp. 42–3

TITLE:
By the Century's Deathbed G

Note This was one of nine poems chosen by Hardy for the Library of the Royal Dolls' House at Windsor Castle. The copy there has 'carollings' (l. 25)

119 *The Darkling Thrush*

I LEANT upon a coppice gate
When Frost was spectre-gray,
And Winter's dregs made desolate
The weakening eye of day.
The tangled bine-stems scored the sky
Like strings of broken lyres,
And all mankind that haunted nigh
Had sought their household fires.

The land's sharp features seemed to be
The Century's corpse outleant,
His crypt the cloudy canopy,
The wind his death-lament.
The ancient pulse of germ and birth
Was shrunken hard and dry,
And every spirit upon earth
Seemed fervourless as I.

At once a voice arose among
The bleak twigs overhead
In a full-hearted evensong
Of joy illimited;
An aged thrush, frail, gaunt, and small,
In blast-beruffled plume,
Had chosen thus to fling his soul
Upon the growing gloom.

So little cause for carolings
Of such ecstatic sound
Was written on terrestrial things
Afar or nigh around,
That I could think there trembled through
His happy good-night air
Some blessed Hope, whereof he knew
And I was unaware.

31 December 1900

The Darkling Thrush
1 coppice] paddock G
2 Frost was] shades were G
6 of] from MS, G, PPP, PUE, CP1
13 birth] birth, G
14 shrunken hard] shrunken, hard, G
17 arose] outburst MS, G, PPP, PUE
20 illimited;] illimited. G
21 gaunt] thin G
25 carolings] carollings MS, G, PPP, PUE, SP, WE, CP1, 2: [Hardy's copy of SP (1917), corrected for CHP, has been amended to 'carolings']
30 good-night] goodnight MS
31 blessed] Blessed G
31 December 1900] The Century's End, (1899 *del*) 1900 MS: December 1900 PPP, PUE, WE, SP, ME, CP1–3
Note Stanzas are numbered in G

120 *The Comet at Yell'ham*

I

It bends far over Yell'ham Plain,
And we, from Yell'ham Height,
Stand and regard its fiery train,
So soon to swim from sight.

II

It will return long years hence, when
As now its strange swift shine
Will fall on Yell'ham; but not then
On that sweet form of thine.

TITLE:
The Comet at Yalbury (Yalbury, MS) or Yell'ham MS, PPP, PUE, WE, CP1, ME ['or Yell'ham' looks like a late addition to MS]

121 *Mad Judy*

When the hamlet hailed a birth
Judy used to cry:
When she heard our christening mirth
She would kneel and sigh.
She was crazed, we knew, and we
Humoured her infirmity.

When the daughters and the sons
Gathered them to wed,
And we like-intending ones
Danced till dawn was red,
She would rock and mutter, 'More
Comers to this stony shore!'

When old Headsman Death laid hands
On a babe or twain,
She would feast, and by her brands
Sing her songs again.
What she liked we let her do,
Judy was insane, we knew.

The Comet at Yell'ham
8] On face of mine or thine. WE, ME

Mad Judy
3 christening mirth] christening-mirth MS
6 infirmity] aberrancy MS, PPP1

TITLE:
WE2, ME add: (OVERHEARD)

122 *A Wasted Illness*

THROUGH vaults of pain,
Enribbed and wrought with groins of ghastliness,
I passed, and garish spectres moved my brain
To dire distress.

And hammerings,
And quakes, and shoots, and stifling hotness, blent
With webby waxing things and waning things
As on I went.

'Where lies the end
To this foul way?' I asked with weakening breath.
Thereon ahead I saw a door extend –
The door to Death.

It loomed more clear:
'At last!' I cried. 'The all-delivering door!'
And then, I knew not how, it grew less near
Than theretofore.

And back slid I
Along the galleries by which I came,
And tediously the day returned, and sky,
And life – the same.

And all was well:
Old circumstance resumed its former show,
And on my head the dews of comfort fell
As ere my woe.

I roam anew,
Scarce conscious of my late distress. . . . And yet
Those backward steps to strength I cannot view
Without regret.

For that dire train
Of waxing shapes and waning, passed before,
And those grim chambers, must be ranged again
To reach that door.

A Wasted Illness
12 Death] death MS, PPP, PUE
26 distress. . . .] distress . . . MS
27 to strength] through pain MS, PPP, PUE
31 chambers] aisles MS, PPP, PUE
31 ranged] traversed MS, PPP, PUE

123 A Man

(In Memory of H. of M.)

I

IN Casterbridge there stood a noble pile,
Wrought with pilaster, bay, and balustrade
In tactful times when shrewd Eliza swayed. –
On burgher, squire, and clown
It smiled the long street down for near a mile.

II

But evil days beset that domicile;
The stately beauties of its roof and wall
Passed into sordid hands. Condemned to fall
Were cornice, quoin, and cove,
And all that art had wove in antique style.

III

Among the hired dismantlers entered there
One till the moment of his task untold.
When charged therewith he gazed, and answered bold:
'Be needy I or no,
I will not help lay low a house so fair!

IV

'Hunger is hard. But since the terms be such –
No wage, or labour stained with the disgrace
Of wrecking what our age cannot replace
To save its tasteless soul –
I'll do without your dole. Life is not much!'

V

Dismissed with sneers he backed his tools and went,
And wandered workless; for it seemed unwise
To close with one who dared to criticize
And carp on points of taste:
Rude men should work where placed, and be content.

A Man
2 balustrade] balustrade, MS
5 mile.] mile PPP2, PUE
6 domicile;] domicile, MS
12 untold.] untold; MS
13 When] Being MS
21 backed] Some late reprints of CP4 have 'packed'. An interesting error
21 went,] went WE, ME
25] To work where they were placed rude men were meant. MS, PPP, PUE, WE, ME

VI

Years whiled. He aged, sank, sickened; and was not:
And it was said, 'A man intractable
And curst is gone.' None sighed to hear his knell,
None sought his churchyard-place;
His name, his rugged face, were soon forgot.

VII

The stones of that fair hall lie far and wide,
And but a few recall its ancient mould;
Yet when I pass the spot I long to hold
As truth what fancy saith:
'His protest lives where deathless things abide!'

124 The Dame of Athelhall

TITLE:
The Return of Athelhall *The Academy*, 23 Nov 1901 [Mentioned in a review which seems to have been based on an early proof of PPP1]

I

'DEAR! Shall I see thy face,' she said,
'In one brief hour?
And away with thee from a loveless bed
To a far-off sun, to a vine-wrapt bower,
And be thine own unseparated,
And challenge the world's white glower?'

II

She quickened her feet, and met him where
They had predesigned:
And they clasped, and mounted, and cleft the air
Upon whirling wheels; till the will to bind
Her life with his made the moments there
Efface the years behind.

III

Miles slid, and the port uprose to view
As they sped on;
When slipping its bond the bracelet flew
From her fondled arm. Replaced anon,
Its cameo of the abjured one drew
Her musings thereupon.

A Man
26 whiled] wore MS
26 sickened;] sickened, MS, PPP, PUE, WE, ME

The Dame of Athelhall
1 Dear] Soul MS, PPP, PUE
8 predesigned:] predesigned; MS
13 port . . . view] sight of the port upgrew MS, PPP, PUE
13 uprose to] appeared in WE, ME

IV

The gaud with his image once had been
A gift from him:
And so it was that its carving keen
Refurbished memories wearing dim,
Which set in her soul a twinge of teen,
And a tear on her lashes' brim.

V

'I may not go!' she at length outspake,
'Thoughts call me back –
I would still lose all for your dear, true sake;
My heart is thine, friend! But my track
Home, home to Athelhall I must take
To hinder household wrack!'

VI

He was wroth. And they parted, weak and wan;
And he left the shore;
His ship diminished, was low, was gone;
And she heard in the waves as the daytide wore,
And read in the leer of the sun that shone,
That they parted for evermore.

VII

She homed as she came, at the dip of eve
On Athel Coomb
Regaining the Hall she had sworn to leave.
The house was soundless as a tomb,
And she stole to her chamber, there to grieve
Lone, kneeling, in the gloom.

VIII

From the lawn without rose her husband's voice
To one his friend:
'Another her Love, another my choice,
Her going is good. Our conditions mend;
In a change of mates we shall both rejoice;
I hoped that it thus might end!

The Dame of Athelhall
23 twinge] throe MS, PPP, PUE
25 outspake] upspake MS, PPP, PUE, WE, ME
27 dear, true] dear dear MS: dear, dear PPP, PUE, WE, ME
29 Home. . . I] I home to Athelhall MS, PPP, PUE
29 Home,] Home – WE, ME
31 He . . . And] He appealed. But MS, PPP, PUE
39 leave.] leave. . . . . MS: leave . . . PPP, PUE
41 stole to] entered MS, PPP, PUE

IX

'A quick divorce; she will make him hers,
    And I wed mine.
So Time rights all things in long, long years –
Or rather she, by her bold design!
I admire a woman no balk deters:
    She has blessed my life, in fine.

X

'I shall build new rooms for my new true bride,
    Let the bygone be:
By now, no doubt, she has crossed the tide
With the man to her mind. Far happier she
In some warm vineland by his side
    Than ever she was with me.'

125 *The Seasons of Her Year*

TITLE:
The Seasons of her Year MS
The Pathetic Fallacy MS *deleted* below title. This may have been a first title or a sub-title

I

WINTER is white on turf and tree,
    And birds are fled;
But summer songsters pipe to me,
    And petals spread,
For what I dreamt of secretly
    His lips have said!

II

O 'tis a fine May morn, they say,
    And blooms have blown;
But wild and wintry is my day,
    My song-birds moan;
For he who vowed leaves me to pay
    Alone – alone!

The Dame of Athelhall
49 quick] due WE, ME
51 long,] long MS

The Seasons of Her Year
10 song-birds] birds make MS, PPP, PUE, CP1: songbirds WE, ME

126 The Milkmaid

UNDER a daisied bank
There stands a rich red ruminating cow,
And hard against her flank
A cotton-hooded milkmaid bends her brow.

The flowery river-ooze
Upheaves and falls; the milk purrs in the pail;
Few pilgrims but would choose
The peace of such a life in such a vale.

The maid breathes words – to vent,
It seems, her sense of Nature's scenery,
Of whose life, sentiment,
And essence, very part itself is she.

She bends a glance of pain,
And, at a moment, lets escape a tear;
Is it that passing train,
Whose alien whirr offends her country ear? –

Nay! Phyllis does not dwell
On visual and familiar things like these;
What moves her is the spell
Of inner themes and inner poetries:

Could but by Sunday morn
Her gay new gown come, meads might dry to dun,
Trains shriek till ears were torn,
If Fred would not prefer that Other One.

127 The Levelled Churchyard

TITLE:
(W——e Minster) MS *deleted* below title

'O PASSENGER, pray list and catch
Our sighs and piteous groans,
Half stifled in this jumbled patch
Of wrenched memorial stones!

The Milkmaid
6 Upheaves] Uplifts WE, ME
10 Nature's] nature's MS
13 bends] throws WE, ME: Hardy's copy of CP2 has 'bends' underlined with 'throws' written in margin, and '["bends" just above]' written below
18 visual] neighbouring MS
20 inner . . . inner] other . . . other MS
21 but by] she next MS
22 Her . . . come,] Sport silk attire, the MS

'We late-lamented, resting here,
Are mixed to human jam,
And each to each exclaims in fear,
"I know not which I am!"

'The wicked people have annexed
The verses on the good;
A roaring drunkard sports the text
Teetotal Tommy should!

'Where we are huddled none can trace,
And if our names remain,
They pave some path or porch or place
Where we have never lain!

'Here's not a modest maiden elf
But dreads the final Trumpet,
Lest half of her should rise herself,
And half some sturdy strumpet!

'From restorations of Thy fane,
From smoothings of Thy sward,
From zealous Churchmen's pick and plane
Deliver us O Lord! Amen!'

1882

128 *The Ruined Maid*

'O 'MELIA, my dear, this does everything crown!
Who could have supposed I should meet you in Town?
And whence such fair garments, such prosperi-ty?' –
'O didn't you know I'd been ruined?' said she.

– 'You left us in tatters, without shoes or socks,
Tired of digging potatoes, and spudding up docks;
And now you've gay bracelets and bright feathers three!' –
'Yes: that's how we dress when we're ruined,' said she.

The Levelled Churchyard
14 remain,] remain MS
15 porch or] p—ing MS, PPP, PUE, CP1 [CP1 corrected to 'porch or' on errata slip]
17 Here's] There's MS, PPP, PUE
20 sturdy] local MS, PPP, PUE, CP1
21 Thy] In MS it seems probable that Hardy has changed the upper-case 'T' to a lower-case
23 plane] plane, MS, PPP1
24 us] us, WE
24 Amen!] Amen. MS
1882] About 1882 MS

The Ruined Maid
1 O 'Melia] O, Melia MS
1 crown!] crown! – MS
2 Town?] Town! MS
4 O] O, MS

– 'At home in the barton you said "thee" and "thou",
And "thik oon", and "theäs oon", and "t'other"; but now
Your talking quite fits 'ee for high compa-ny!' –
'Some polish is gained with one's ruin,' said she.

– 'Your hands were like paws then, your face blue and bleak
But now I'm bewitched by your delicate cheek,
And your little gloves fit as on any la-dy!' –
'We never do work when we're ruined,' said she.

– 'You used to call home-life a hag-ridden dream,
And you'd sigh, and you'd sock; but at present you seem
To know not of megrims or melancho-ly!' –
'True. One's pretty lively when ruined,' said she.

– 'I wish I had feathers, a fine sweeping gown,
And a delicate face, and could strut about Town!' –
'My dear – a raw country girl, such as you be,
Cannot quite expect that. You ain't ruined,' said she.

Westbourne Park Villas, 1866

129 The Respectable Burgher

On 'The Higher Criticism'

SINCE Reverend Doctors now declare
That clerks and people must prepare
To doubt if Adam ever were;
To hold the flood a local scare;
To argue, though the stolid stare,
That everything had happened ere
The prophets to its happening sware;
That David was no giant-slayer,
Nor one to call a God-obeyer
In certain details we could spare,
But rather was a debonair
Shrewd bandit, skilled as banjo-player:

The Ruined Maid
12 Some] A WE, ME
13 bleak] bleak, MS, PPP, PUE, WE, ME
17 – 'You] 'You MS
20 One's . . . ruined] There's an advantage in ruin MS, PPP, PUE
21 – 'I] 'I MS
23 My dear – a] Ah – no! – A MS
24 Cannot quite expect] Isn't equal to MS, PPP, PUE
1866] 1866 (1867 *del*) MS

The Respectable Burgher
4 flood] Flood MS
8 giant-slayer] Giant-slayer MS

That Solomon sang the fleshly Fair,
And gave the Church no thought whate'er,
That Esther with her royal wear,
And Mordecai, the son of Jair,
And Joshua's triumphs, Job's despair,
And Balaam's ass's bitter blare;
Nebuchadnezzar's furnace-flare,
And Daniel and the den affair,
And other stories rich and rare,
Were writ to make old doctrine wear
Something of a romantic air:
That the Nain widow's only heir,
And Lazarus with cadaverous glare
(As done in oils by Piombo's care)
Did not return from Sheol's lair:
That Jael set a fiendish snare,
That Pontius Pilate acted square,
That never a sword cut Malchus' ear;
And (but for shame I must forbear)
That —— —— did not reappear! . . .
– Since thus they hint, nor turn a hair,
All churchgoing will I forswear,
And sit on Sundays in my chair,
And read that moderate man Voltaire.

130 *Architectural Masks*

I

THERE is a house with ivied walls,
And mullioned windows worn and old,
And the long dwellers in those halls
Have souls that know but sordid calls,
And daily dote on gold.

The Respectable Burgher
14 whate'er,] whate'er; MS, PPP, PUE, WE, ME
16 Mordecai,] Mordecai MS
30 Malchus'] Malchu's MS
31 And] And – MS
32 That —— ——] That —— WE, ME
32 reappear! . . .] reappear! . . . . MS
32–3 Between these two lines in MS written in pencil and probably in Hardy's hand is found: [white line]
33 – Since] Since MS

Architectural Masks
1 walls,] walls MS
2 old,] old: MS
5 dote on] dream of PPP1

II

In blazing brick and plated show
Not far away a 'villa' gleams,
And here a family few may know,
With book and pencil, viol and bow,
Lead inner lives of dreams.

III

The philosophic passers say,
'See that old mansion mossed and fair,
Poetic souls therein are they:
And O that gaudy box! Away,
You vulgar people there.'

131 *The Tenant-for-Life*

THE sun said, watching my watering-pot:
'Some morn you'll pass away;
These flowers and plants I parch up hot –
Who'll water them that day?

'Those banks and beds whose shape your eye
Has planned in line so true,
New hands will change, unreasoning why
Such shape seemed best to you.

'Within your house will strangers sit,
And wonder how first it came;
They'll talk of their schemes for improving it,
And will not mention your name.

'They'll care not how, or when, or at what
You sighed, laughed, suffered here,
Though you feel more in an hour of the spot
Than they will feel in a year.

Architectural Masks
6 show] show, WE2
8 know,] know MS
12 fair,] fair; MS
14 Away,] Away MS

'As I look on at you here, now,
Shall I look on at these;
But as to our old times, avow
No knowledge – hold my peace!...

'O friend, it matters not, I say;
Bethink ye, I have shined
On nobler ones than you, and they
Are dead men out of mind!'

132 *The King's Experiment*

It was a wet wan hour in spring,
And Nature met King Doom beside a lane,
Wherein Hodge tramped, all blithely balladiing
The Mother's smiling reign.

'Why warbles he that skies are fair
And coombs alight,' she cried, 'and fallows gay,
When I have placed no sunshine in the air
Or glow on earth to-day?'

' 'Tis in the comedy of things
That such should be,' returned the one of Doom;
'Charge now the scene with brightest blazonings,
And he shall call them gloom.'

She gave the word: the sunbeams broke,
All Froomside shone, the hedgebirds raised a strain;
And later Hodge, upon the midday stroke,
Returned along the lane,

Low murmuring: 'O this bitter scene,
And thrice accurst horizon hung with gloom!
How deadly like this sky, these fields, these treen,
To trappings of the tomb!'

The Beldame then: 'The fool and blind!
Such mad perverseness who may apprehend?' –
'Nay; there's no madness in it; thou shalt find
Thy law there,' said her friend.

The Tenant-for-Life
24 mind!] mind. MS

The King's Experiment
2 beside a lane] by Long-ash Lane MS *before revision*
3 tramped] trudged MS, PPP, PUE, CP1
10 Doom;] Doom, MS
13 sunbeams broke] sun outbroke MS, PPP, PUE, WE, ME
14 Froomside] Blackmoor MS *before revision*
14 strain] song MS, PPP, PUE, CP1
15 And later] And, later, MS
15 stroke,] stroke MS
16 along the lane] the lane along MS, PPP, PUE, CP1

'When Hodge went forth 'twas to his Love,
To make her, ere this eve, his wedded prize,
And Earth, despite the heaviness above,
    Was bright as Paradise.

'But I sent on my messenger,
With cunning arrows poisonous and keen,
To take forthwith her laughing life from her,
    And dull her little een,

'And white her cheek, and still her breath,
Ere her too buoyant Hodge had reached her side;
So, when he came, he clasped her but in death,
    And never as his bride.

'And there's the humour, as I said;
Thy dreary dawn he saw as gleaming gold,
And in thy glistening green and radiant red
    Funereal gloom and cold.'

133 *The Tree*

An Old Man's Story

I

ITS roots are bristling in the air
Like some mad Earth-god's spiny hair;
The loud south-wester's swell and yell
Smote it at midnight, and it fell.
    Thus ends the tree
    Where Some One sat with me.

II

Its boughs, which none but darers trod,
A child may step on from the sod,
And twigs that earliest met the dawn
Are lit the last upon the lawn.
    Cart off the tree
    Beneath whose trunk sat we!

INDENTATION:
MS, at stanza 7 and subsequently, indents l. 5 of each stanza farther right

The King's Experiment
29 messenger,] messenger MS
30 keen,] keen MS
34 Ere her too] Hardy's copy of WE1 is corrected to 'Before her'

The Tree
3 south-wester's] Southwester's MS
6 Some One] Someone MS

III

Yes, there we sat: she cooed content,
And bats ringed round, and daylight went;
The gnarl, our seat, is wrenched and sunk,
Prone that queer pocket in the trunk
    Where lay the key
    To her pale mystery.

IV

'Years back, within this pocket-hole
I found, my Love, a hurried scrawl
Meant not for me,' at length said I;
'I glanced thereat, and let it lie:
    The words were three –
    "*Beloved, I agree.*"

V

'Who placed it here; to what request
It gave assent, I never guessed.
Some prayer of some hot heart, no doubt,
To some coy maiden hereabout,
    Just as, maybe,
    With you, Sweet Heart, and me.'

VI

She waited, till with quickened breath
She spoke, as one who banisheth
Reserves that lovecraft heeds so well,
To ease some mighty wish to tell:
    ' 'Twas I,' said she,
    'Who wrote thus clinchingly.

VII

'My lover's wife – aye, wife – knew nought
Of what we felt, and bore, and thought. . . .
He'd said: "*I wed with thee or die:*
She stands between, 'tis true. But why?
    Do thou agree,
    And – she shall cease to be."

The Tree
14 went;] went, WE2 [Very probably print deterioration]
19–21] I said to her: 'I found a scrawl,/ My Love, within this pocket hole/Years back, not meant to meet my eye; WE, ME
37 aye, wife –] aye, wife! – MS, PPP, PUE, WE, ME
38 thought. . . .] thought. . . . . MS
39 '*I*] *I* MS
39 *die:*] *die;* MS
42 *be.*'] *be.* MS

VIII

'How I held back, how love supreme
Involved me madly in his scheme
Why should I say? . . . I wrote assent
(You found it hid) to his intent. . . .
She – *died*. . . . But he
Came not to wed with me.

IX

'O shrink not, Love! – Had these eyes seen
But once thine own, such had not been!
But we were strangers. . . . Thus the plot
Cleared passion's path. – Why came he not
To wed with me? . . .
He wived the gibbet-tree.'

X

– Under that oak of heretofore
Sat Sweetheart mine with me no more:
By many a Fiord, and Strom, and Fleuve
Have I since wandered. . . . Soon, for love,
Distraught went she –
'Twas said for love of me.

134 Her Late Husband

(*King's Hintock, 182–*)

'NO – not where I shall make my own;
But dig his grave just by
The woman's with the initialed stone –
As near as he can lie –
After whose death he seemed to ail,
Though none considered why.

TITLE:
King's Hintock] King's-Hintock PPP, PUE, WE, ME

The Tree
45 say? . . .] say? . . . . MS
46 intent. . . .] intent. . . . . MS
53 me? . . .] me? . . . . MS
55 – Under] Under MS
58 wandered. . . .] wandered. . . . . MS

Her Late Husband
3 stone –] stone, MS
4 lie –] lie, MS

'And when I also claim a nook,
And your feet tread me in,
Bestow me, in my maiden name,
Among my kith and kin,
That strangers gazing may not dream
I did a husband win.'

'Widow, your wish shall be obeyed:
Though, thought I, certainly
You'd lay him where your folk are laid,
And your grave, too, will be,
As custom hath it; you to right,
And on the left hand he.'

'Aye, sexton; such the Hintock rule,
And none has said it nay;
But now you find a native here
Eschews that ancient way . . .
And it may be, some Christmas night,
When angels walk, they'll say:

' "O strange interment! Civilized lands
Afford few types thereof;
Here is a man who takes his rest
Beside his very Love,
Beside the one who was his wife
In our sight up above!" '

EXTRA PRINTINGS:
(1) *Selected Poems*, p. 49
(2) *Chosen Poems*, p. 48

TITLE:
The Self-unseeing MS

135 *The Self-Unseeing*

HERE is the ancient floor,
Footworn and hollowed and thin,
Here was the former door
Where the dead feet walked in.

She sat here in her chair,
Smiling into the fire;
He who played stood there,
Bowing it higher and higher.

Her Late Husband
7 nook,] nook MS
9 in my maiden] under my old MS, PPP, PUE
13 obeyed:] obeyed; MS, PPP, PUE, WE, ME
14 Though, thought I,] Though I thought MS
19 sexton] Sexton MS
21 you find] it haps MS, PPP, PUE
22 way . . .] way. . . . . MS
30] By our laws up above!" ' MS *before revision*

Childlike, I danced in a dream;
Blessings emblazoned that day;
Everything glowed with a gleam;
Yet we were looking away!

136 *In Tenebris I*

'Percussus sum sicut fœnum, et aruit cor meum.' – Ps. CI

WINTERTIME nighs;
But my bereavement-pain
It cannot bring again:
Twice no one dies.

Flower-petals flee;
But, since it once hath been,
No more that severing scene
Can harrow me.

Birds faint in dread:
I shall not lose old strength
In the lone frost's black length:
Strength long since fled!

Leaves freeze to dun;
But friends can not turn cold
This season as of old
For him with none.

Tempests may scath;
But love can not make smart
Again this year his heart
Who no heart hath.

Black is night's cope;
But death will not appal
One who, past doubtings all,
Waits in unhope.

TITLE:
MS has 'De Profundis' first, and then 'In Tenebris'. Both have been crossed through, but 'De Profundis' has been stetted

De Profundis
I PPP, PUE

The Self-Unseeing
9 Childlike,] Childlike MS

In Tenebris I
23 all,] all MS

EXTRA PRINTINGS:
(1) *Selected Poems*, pp. 180–1
(2) *Chosen Poems*, pp. 234–5

TITLE:
MS has 'De Profundis' first, and then 'In Tenebris'. Both have been crossed through, but 'De Profundis' has been stetted

De Profundis
II PPP, PUE

Note Before the present Latin quotation MS had the following *deleted*: "Quare fremuerunt gentes, et populi meditati sunt inania?" Ps. II.

137 *In Tenebris* II

Considerabam ad dexteram, et videbam; et non erat qui cognosceret me. . . . non est qui requirat animam meam.' – Ps. CXLI

WHEN the clouds' swoln bosoms echo back the shouts of the many and strong
That things are all as they best may be, save a few to be right ere long,
And my eyes have not the vision in them to discern what to these is so clear,
The blot seems straightway in me alone; one better he were not here.

The stout upstanders say, All's well with us: ruers have nought to rue!
And what the potent say so oft, can it fail to be somewhat true?
Breezily go they, breezily come; their dust smokes around their career,
Till I think I am one born out of due time, who has no calling here.

Their dawns bring lusty joys, it seems; their evenings all that is sweet;
Our times are blessed times, they cry: Life shapes it as is most meet,
And nothing is much the matter; there are many smiles to a tear;
Then what is the matter is I, I say. Why should such an one be here? . . .

Let him in whose ears the low-voiced Best is killed by the clash of the First,
Who holds that if way to the Better there be, it exacts a full look at the Worst,
Who feels that delight is a delicate growth cramped by crookedness, custom, and fear,
Get him up and be gone as one shaped awry; he disturbs the order here.

1895–96

In Tenebris II
3 what to these is] demonstration MS, PPP1
4 here.] here! MS
5 say] chime WE, SP, ME
6 say so oft] so often say WE, SP, ME
7 dust . . . career] fame stretches far and near MS *before revision*
8 time,] time MS
9 evenings all that is] eves exultance MS, PPP, PUE, CP1
12 Why . . . here? . . .] Good God, why should I be here! . . . . MS *before revision*
12 here? . . .] here! . . . . MS: here? WE2, ME
13 in] to MS, PPP, PUE, CP1
13 is killed] seems stilled MS, PPP, PUE, CP1
16 here.] here! MS
Note Before revision to MS the last stanza had begun 'Maybe all to whose ears . . .' and ended (l. 16) 'Should up and be gone as men shaped awry, or as weird ghosts wandering here!', with 'hold' in l. 14 and 'feel' in l. 15

138 In Tenebris III

'Heu mihi, quia incolatus meus prolongatus est! Habitavi cum habitantibus Cedar. Multum incola fuit anima mea.' – Ps. CXIX

THERE have been times when I well might have passed and the ending have come –
Points in my path when the dark might have stolen on me, artless, unrueing –
Ere I had learnt that the world was a welter of futile doing:
Such had been times when I well might have passed, and the ending have come!

Say, on the noon when the half-sunny hours told that April was nigh,
And I upgathered and cast forth the snow from the crocus-border,
Fashioned and furbished the soil into a summer-seeming order,
Glowing in gladsome faith that I quickened the year thereby.

Or on that loneliest of eves when afar and benighted we stood,
She who upheld me and I, in the midmost of Egdon together,
Confident I in her watching and ward through the blackening heather,
Deeming her matchless in might and with measureless scope endued.

Or on that winter-wild night when, reclined by the chimney-nook quoin,
Slowly a drowse overgat me, the smallest and feeblest of folk there,
Weak from my baptism of pain; when at times and anon I awoke there –
Heard of a world wheeling on, with no listing or longing to join.

Even then! while unweeting that vision could vex or that knowledge could numb,
That sweets to the mouth in the belly are bitter, and tart, and untoward,
Then, on some dim-coloured scene should my briefly raised curtain have lowered,
Then might the Voice that is law have said 'Cease!' and the ending have come.

1896

TITLE:
MS has 'De Profundis' first, and then 'In Tenebris'. Both have been crossed through, but 'De Profundis' has been stetted

De Profundis III PPP, PUE

In Tenebris III
13 winter-wild] winterwild MS [but could be two words]

TITLE:
MS shows that 'Nisi Dominus Frustra' was considered as a title or part-title

139 The Church-Builder

I

THE church flings forth a battled shade
Over the moon-blanched sward;
The church; my gift; whereto I paid
My all in hand and hoard;
Lavished my gains
With stintless pains
To glorify the Lord.

II

I squared the broad foundations in
Of ashlared masonry;
I moulded mullions thick and thin,
Hewed fillet and ogee:
I circleted
Each sculptured head
With nimb and canopy.

III

I called in many a craftsmaster
To fix emblazoned glass,
To figure Cross and Sepulchre
On dossal, boss, and brass.
My gold all spent,
My jewels went
To gem the cups of Mass.

IV

I borrowed deep to carve the screen
And raise the ivoried Rood;
I parted with my small demesne
To make my owings good.
Heir-looms unpriced
I sacrificed,
Until debt-free I stood.

The Church-Builder
1 flings forth] projects WE, ME
2 moon-blanched] moon-lit WE, ME
4 hoard;] hoard: MS, PPP, PUE, WE, ME
8 in] in, WE, ME
9 Of] Set WE, ME
11 ogee:] ogee. MS
27 sacrificed,] sacrificed MS

V

So closed the task. 'Deathless the Creed
Here substanced!' said my soul:
'I heard me bidden to this deed,
And straight obeyed the call.
Illume this fane,
That not in vain
I build it, Lord of all!'

VI

But, as it chanced me, then and there
Did dire misfortunes burst;
My home went waste for lack of care,
My sons rebelled and curst;
Till I confessed
That aims the best
Were looking like the worst.

VII

Enkindled by my votive work
No burning faith I find;
The deeper thinkers sneer and smirk,
And give my toil no mind;
From nod and wink
I read they think
That I am fool and blind.

VIII

My gift to God seems futile, quite;
The world moves as erstwhile;
And powerful Wrong on feeble Right
Tramples in olden style.
My faith burns down,
I see no crown;
But Cares, and Griefs, and Guile.

The Church-Builder
52 Wrong] wrong MS, PPP, PUE
52 Right] right MS, PPP, PUE

IX

So now, the remedy? Yea, this:
I gently swing the door
Here, of my fane – no soul to wis –
And cross the patterned floor
To the rood-screen
That stands between
The nave and inner chore.

X

The rich red windows dim the moon,
But little light need I;
I mount the prie-dieu, lately hewn
From woods of rarest dye;
Then from below
My garment, so,
I draw this cord, and tie

XI

One end thereof around the beam
Midway 'twixt Cross and truss:
I noose the nethermost extreme,
And in ten seconds thus
I journey hence –
To that land whence
No rumour reaches us.

XII

Well: Here at morn they'll light on one
Dangling in mockery
Of what he spent his substance on
Blindly and uselessly! . . .
'He might,' they'll say,
'Have built, some way,
A cheaper gallows-tree!'

The Church-Builder
65 I;] I: MS
78 morn] dawn WE, ME
81 uselessly! . . .] uselessly! . . . . . MS

140 The Lost Pyx

A Mediæval Legend [1]

SOME say the spot is banned: that the pillar Cross-and-Hand
  Attests to a deed of hell;
But of else than of bale is the mystic tale
  That ancient Vale-folk tell.

Ere Cernel's Abbey ceased hereabout there dwelt a priest,
  (In later life sub-prior
Of the brotherhood there, whose bones are now bare
  In the field that was Cernel choir).

One night in his cell at the foot of yon dell
  The priest heard a frequent cry:
'Go, father, in haste to the cot on the waste,
  And shrive a man waiting to die.'

Said the priest in a shout to the caller without,
  'The night howls, the tree-trunks bow;
One may barely by day track so rugged a way,
  And can I then do so now?'

No further word from the dark was heard,
  And the priest moved never a limb;
And he slept and dreamed; till a Visage seemed
  To frown from Heaven at him.

In a sweat he arose; and the storm shrieked shrill,
  And smote as in savage joy;
While High-Stoy trees twanged to Bubb-Down Hill,
  And Bubb-Down to High-Stoy.

[1] On a lonely table-land above the Vale of Blackmore, between High-Stoy and Bubb-Down hills, and commanding in clear weather views that extend from the English to the Bristol Channel, stands a pillar, apparently mediæval, called Cross-and-Hand, or Christ-in-Hand. One tradition of its origin is mentioned in *Tess of the d'Urbervilles*; another, more detailed, preserves the story here given.

The Lost Pyx
1 banned:] banned; MS, UT, S, PPP, PUE, WE, ME
1 pillar] pillar, UT
4 Vale-folk] Valefolk UT, S
5 priest,] priest ME
6 (In] In UT, S
8 choir).] choir.) MS: Choir. UT, S
11 father] Father S
11 waste,] waste MS, UT, S
19 dreamed;] dreamed, UT
20 Heaven] heaven UT
24 to High-Stoy] Hill to Stoy WE1
commanding . . . views] commanding views UT, S
One . . . detailed,] Among other stories of its origin a local tradition MS, UT, S, PPP, PUE
story] one MS, UT, S, PPP, PUE

EXTRA MANUSCRIPT:
Permission was refused to see the MS in the possession of Mr Frederick B. Adams, Jnr

PROOFS:
In the Miriam Lutcher Stark Library of the University of Texas = UT

EXTRA PRINTING:
The Sphere, 22 Dec 1900, p. 330 = S

TITLE:
A Mediæval Legend] Not in S

There seemed not a holy thing in hail,
Nor shape of light or love,
From the Abbey north of Blackmore Vale
To the Abbey south thereof.

Yet he plodded thence through the dark immense,
And with many a stumbling stride
Through copse and briar climbed nigh and nigher
To the cot and the sick man's side.

When he would have unslung the Vessels uphung
To his arm in the steep ascent,
He made loud moan: the Pyx was gone
Of the Blessed Sacrament.

Then in dolorous dread he beat his head:
'No earthly prize or pelf
Is the thing I've lost in tempest tossed,
But the Body of Christ Himself!'

He thought of the Visage his dream revealed,
And turned towards whence he came,
Hands groping the ground along foot-track and field,
And head in a heat of shame.

Till here on the hill, betwixt vill and vill,
He noted a clear straight ray
Stretching down from the sky to a spot hard by,
Which shone with the light of day.

And gathered around the illumined ground
Were common beasts and rare,
All kneeling at gaze, and in pause profound
Attent on an object there.

'Twas the Pyx, unharmed 'mid the circling rows
Of Blackmore's hairy throng,
Whereof were oxen, sheep, and does,
And hares from the brakes among;

The Lost Pyx
27 Abbey] abbey UT
28 Abbey] abbey UT
33 uphung] hung WE, ME
35 moan:] moan; UT, S
37 dolorous] dolour and UT, S
37 head:] head, UT
40 Body] body UT
41 Visage] visage UT
45 Till] And UT, S
45 hill,] hill MS, UT, S
45 vill,] vill MS, UT, S
47 by,] by MS
52 Attent] Intent UT
52 on] to S
53 'mid] mid MS, UT, S, WE, ME
56 among;] among, MS

And badgers grey, and conies keen,
    And squirrels of the tree,
And many a member seldom seen
    Of Nature's family.

The ireful winds that scoured and swept
    Through coppice, clump, and dell,
Within that holy circle slept
    Calm as in hermit's cell.

Then the priest bent likewise to the sod
    And thanked the Lord of Love,
And Blessed Mary, Mother of God,
    And all the saints above.

And turning straight with his priceless freight,
    He reached the dying one,
Whose passing sprite had been stayed for the rite
    Without which bliss hath none.

And when by grace the priest won place,
    And served the Abbey well,
He reared this stone to mark where shone
    That midnight miracle.

141 *Tess's Lament*

TITLE: Her Lament MS *before revision*

I

I WOULD that folk forgot me quite,
                Forgot me quite!
I would that I could shrink from sight,
    And no more see the sun.
Would it were time to say farewell,
To claim my nook, to need my knell,
Time for them all to stand and tell
    Of my day's work as done.

The Lost Pyx
64 hermit's] hermits' MS
67 Mary,] Mary MS
68 saints] Saints S
69 freight,] freight MS, UT, S
74 Abbey] abbey UT

Tess's Lament
1 I] O MS
3 I] O MS
8 Of] O' WE, ME

II

Ah! dairy where I lived so long,
I lived so long;
Where I would rise up staunch and strong,
And lie down hopefully.
'Twas there within the chimney-seat
He watched me to the clock's slow beat –
Loved me, and learnt to call me Sweet,
And whispered words to me.

III

And now he's gone; and now he's gone; . . .
And now he's gone!
The flowers we potted perhaps are thrown
To rot upon the farm.
And where we had our supper-fire
May now grow nettle, dock, and briar,
And all the place be mould and mire
So cozy once and warm.

IV

And it was I who did it all,
Who did it all;
'Twas I who made the blow to fall
On him who thought no guile.
Well, it is finished – past, and he
Has left me to my misery,
And I must take my Cross on me
For wronging him awhile.

V

How gay we looked that day we wed,
That day we wed!
'May joy be with ye!' they all said
A-standing by the durn.
I wonder what they say o'us now,
And if they know my lot; and how
She feels who milks my favourite cow,
And takes my place at churn!

Tess's Lament
11 staunch] stanch MS, PPP, PUE
14 clock's slow beat] slow clock-beat MS
15 Sweet] sweet MS, PPP, PUE
17 gone; . . .] gone; . . . . . MS
19 perhaps] p'rhaps MS, PPP, PUE, WE, ME
29 Well,] Well; MS
35 they all] all o'm MS, PPP, PUE, WE, ME
36 A-standing] A standing PPP, PUE, WE, ME
37 o'us] o's MS, PPP, PUE, WE, ME

VI

It wears me out to think of it,
To think of it;
I cannot bear my fate as writ,
I'd have my life unbe;
Would turn my memory to a blot,
Make every relic of me rot,
My doings be as they were not,
And gone all trace of me!

142 *The Supplanter*

A Tale

TITLE:
At the Cemetery Lodge MS *before revision*
A Tale] Not in WE, ME

I

HE bends his travel-tarnished feet
To where she wastes in clay:
From day-dawn until eve he fares
Along the wintry way;
From day-dawn until eve he bears
A wreath of blooms and bay.

II

'Are these the gravestone shapes that meet
My forward-straining view?
Or forms that cross a window-blind
In circle, knot, and queue:
Gay forms, that cross and whirl and wind
To music throbbing through?' –

III

'The Keeper of the Field of Tombs
Dwells by its gateway-pier;
He celebrates with feast and dance
His daughter's twentieth year:
He celebrates with wine of France
The birthday of his dear.' –

Tess's Lament
48] And what they've brought to me! MS, PPP, PUE
48 gone all] leave no WE, ME

The Supplanter
3 day-dawn until eve] dawn till eventide WE, ME
5 day-dawn until eve] dawn till eventide WE, ME
5 he bears] repairs MS, PPP, PUE, CP1
6] Unto (Towards CP1) her mound to pray. MS, PPP, PUE, CP1
18 dear.' –] dear.' MS

IV

'The gates are shut when evening glooms:
Lay down your wreath, sad wight;
To-morrow is a time more fit
For placing flowers aright:
The morning is the time for it;
Come, wake with us to-night!' –

V

He drops his wreath, and enters in,
And sits, and shares their cheer. –
'I fain would foot with you, young man,
Before all others here;
I fain would foot it for a span
With such a cavalier!'

VI

She coaxes, clasps, nor fails to win
His first-unwilling hand:
The merry music strikes its staves,
The dancers quickly band;
And with the Damsel of the Graves
He duly takes his stand.

VII

'You dance divinely, stranger swain,
Such grace I've never known.
O longer stay! Breathe not adieu
And leave me here alone!
O longer stay: to her be true
Whose heart is all your own!' –

VIII

'I mark a phantom through the pane,
That beckons in despair,
Its mouth all drawn with heavy moan –
Her to whom once I sware!' –
'Nay; 'tis the lately carven stone
Of some strange girl laid there!' –

The Supplanter
25] He downs his wreath when entered in, WE, ME
25 drops] grounds MS, PPP, PUE
26 cheer. –] cheer. MS
28 here;] here WE1: here, WE2, ME
35 Damsel] damsel MS, PPP, PUE, WE, ME
35 Graves] graves MS, PPP, PUE, WE, ME
42 own!' –] own!' MS
45 all . . . heavy] drawn down as by a WE, ME

IX

'I see white flowers upon the floor
        Betrodden to a clot;
My wreath were they?' – 'Nay; love me much,
        Swear you'll forget me not!
'Twas but a wreath! Full many such
        Are brought here and forgot.'

. . .

X

The watches of the night grow hoar,
        He wakens with the sun;
'Now could I kill thee here!' he says,
        'For winning me from one
Who ever in her living days
        Was pure as cloistered nun!'

XI

She cowers; and, rising, roves he then
        Afar for many a mile,
For evermore to be apart
        From her who could beguile
His senses by her burning heart,
        And win his love awhile.

XII

A year beholds him wend again
        To her who wastes in clay;
From day-dawn until eve he fares
        Along the wintry way,
From day-dawn until eve repairs
        Towards her mound to pray.

The Supplanter
53 wreath!] wreath. MS
54 forgot.'] forgot.' . . . WE, ME
54–5 No dots in WE, ME
56 wakens with] rises ere MS, PPP, PUE
61] She cowers, and he takes his track MS, PPP, PUE: Out from her arms he takes his track WE, ME
66 awhile.] awhile. . . . WE, ME
67] A year: and he is travelling back MS, PPP, PUE, WE, ME
68 her] one WE, ME
69 day-dawn until eve] dawn till eventide WE, ME
71–2] From dawn till eventide he bears/A wreath of blooms and bay. WE, ME
72 Towards] Unto MS, PPP, PUE

XIII

And there he sets him to fulfil
His frustrate first intent:
And lay upon her bed, at last,
The offering earlier meant:
When, on his stooping figure, ghast
And haggard eyes are bent.

XIV

'O surely for a little while
You can be kind to me.
For do you love her, do you hate,
She knows not – cares not she:
Only the living feel the weight
Of loveless misery!

XV

'I own my sin; I've paid its cost,
Being outcast, shamed, and bare:
I give you daily my whole heart,
Your child my tender care,
I pour you prayers; this life apart
Is more than I can bear!'

XVI

He turns – unpitying, passion-tossed;
'I know you not!' he cries,
'Nor know your child. I knew this maid,
But she's in Paradise!'
And he has vanished in the shade
From her beseeching eyes.

The Supplanter
80 me.] me! MS, PPP, PUE, WE, ME
85 sin] fault MS
88 child] babe MS, PPP, PUE, CP1
89 this life apart] and aye to part MS, PPP, PUE, CP1
91] He turns remorseless – passion-tossed: MS: He turns – remorseless, passion-tossed: PPP1
91 passion-tossed;] passion-tossed, CP1
95–6] And swiftly in the winter shade/He breaks from her and flies. MS, PPP, PUE, CP1

IMITATIONS, ETC.

143 *Sapphic Fragment*

'Thou shalt be – Nothing.' – OMAR KHAYYÁM
'Tombless, with no remembrance.' – W. SHAKESPEARE

DEAD shalt thou lie; and nought
Be told of thee or thought,
For thou hast plucked not of the Muses' tree:
And even in Hades' halls
Amidst thy fellow-thralls
No friendly shade thy shade shall company!

144 *Catullus: XXXI*

(*After passing Sirmione, April 1887*)

SIRMIO, thou dearest dear of strands
That Neptune strokes in lake and sea,
With what high joy from stranger lands
Doth thy old friend set foot on thee!
Yea, barely seems it true to me
That no Bithynia holds me now,
But calmly and assuringly
Around me stretchest homely Thou.

Is there a scene more sweet than when
Our clinging cares are undercast,
And, worn by alien moils and men,
The long untrodden sill repassed,
We press the pined for couch at last,
And find a full repayment there?
Then hail, sweet Sirmio; thou that wast,
And art, mine own unrivalled Fair!

TITLE:
MS lacks the quotations from Omar Khayyám and Shakespeare, but has the following quotation *deleted*: ' "Neither have they any more a reward, for the memory of them is forgotten." Eccles. IX. 5.'
Khayyám] Khayyam WE2, CP4, ME

Sapphic Fragment
5 fellow-thralls] fellow thralls MS
6 thy shade shall] shall keep thee WE, ME

Catullus: XXXI
13 pined for] kindly PPP1: pined-for WE, ME [It is not clear on whose authority the hyphen is restored in some reprints of CP4]

145 *After Schiller*

KNIGHT, a true sister-love
This heart retains;
Ask me no other love,
That way lie pains!

Calm must I view thee come,
Calm see thee go;
Tale-telling tears of thine
I must not know!

TITLE:
MS reads:
Song. (After *del*) From Heine
(Die Heimkehr *del*)

146 *Song from Heine*

I SCANNED her picture, dreaming,
Till each dear line and hue
Was imaged, to my seeming,
As if it lived anew.

Her lips began to borrow
Their former wondrous smile;
Her fair eyes, faint with sorrow,
Grew sparkling as erstwhile.

Such tears as often ran not
Ran then, my love, for thee;
And O, believe I cannot
That thou art lost to me!

TITLE:
MS reads:
(After *del*) From Victor Hugo

INDENTATION:
1 = ll. 1–4, 6–9
2 = ll. 5, 10 MS

147 *From Victor Hugo*

CHILD, were I king, I'd yield my royal rule,
My chariot, sceptre, vassal-service due,
My crown, my porphyry-basined waters cool,
My fleets, whereto the sea is but a pool,
For a glance from you!

After Schiller
1 sister-love] sister love MS [could be one word]

Song from Heine
1 picture,] picture PPP, PUE, WE1, CP1
1 dreaming,] dreaming; MS
10 love] Love MS
11 O,] O – MS
11 cannot] can not MS
12 art] are PPP, PUE

From Victor Hugo
3 porphyry-basined] porphyry basined MS
5–6 Stanza break in all editions

Love, were I God, the earth and its heaving airs,
        Angels, the demons abject under me,
Vast chaos with its teeming womby lairs,
Time, space, all would I give – aye, upper spheres,
        For a kiss from thee!

148 Cardinal Bembo's Epitaph on Raphael

HERE's one in whom Nature feared – faint at such vying –
Eclipse while he lived, and decease at his dying.

From Victor Hugo
9 space,] space, – MS

MS has 'Conclusion' *deleted* below 'Retrospect'

EXTRA PRINTINGS:
(1) *Selected Poems*, pp. 182–3
(2) *Chosen Poems*, pp. 236–7

RETROSPECT

149 *I Have Lived with Shades*

I

I HAVE lived with Shades so long,
And talked to them so oft,
Since forth from cot and croft
I went mankind among,
        That sometimes they
        In their dim style
        Will pause awhile
        To hear my say;

II

And take me by the hand,
And lead me through their rooms
In the To-be, where Dooms
Half-wove and shapeless stand:
        And show from there
        The dwindled dust
        And rot and rust
        Of things that were.

III

'Now turn,' they said to me
One day: 'Look whence we came,
And signify his name
Who gazes thence at thee.' –
        – 'Nor name nor race
        Know I, or can,'
        I said, 'Of man
        So commonplace.

I Have Lived with Shades
1 Shades] shades MS, PPP, PUE
2–4] So long have talked to them,/Since from the forest's hem/I sped to street and throng, WE, SP, ME
12 stand:] stand; MS
17 they said] spake they MS, PPP, PUE, CP1

IV

'He moves me not at all;
I note no ray or jot
Of rareness in his lot,
Or star exceptional.
        Into the dim
        Dead throngs around
        He'll sink, nor sound
        Be left of him.'

V

'Yet,' said they, 'his frail speech,
Hath accents pitched like thine –
Thy mould and his define
A likeness each to each –
        But go! Deep pain
        Alas, would be
        His name to thee,
        And told in vain!'

2 February 1899

150 *Memory and I*

'O MEMORY, where is now my youth,
Who used to say that life was truth?'

'I saw him in a crumbled cot
   Beneath a tottering tree;
That he as phantom lingers there
   Is only known to me.'

'O Memory, where is now my joy,
Who lived with me in sweet employ?'

'I saw him in gaunt gardens lone,
   Where laughter used to be;
That he as phantom wanders there
   Is known to none but me.'

I Have Lived with Shades
37 pain] pain, WE2, ME

Memory and I
1 youth] Youth WE, ME
7 joy] Joy WE, ME
9 in . . . lone] on a lonely lawn WE, ME
9 gaunt] gray MS

'O Memory, where is now my hope,
Who charged with deeds my skill and scope?'

'I saw her in a tomb of tomes,
Where dreams are wont to be;
That she as spectre haunteth there
Is only known to me.'

'O Memory, where is now my faith,
One time a champion, now a wraith?'

'I saw her in a ravaged aisle,
Bowed down on bended knee;
That her poor ghost outflickers there
Is known to none but me.'

'O Memory, where is now my love,
That rayed me as a god above?'

'I saw her in an ageing shape
Where beauty used to be;
That her fond phantom lingers there
Is only known to me.'

151 'ΑΓΝΩΣΤΩΙ ΘΕΩΙ

TITLE:
MS has title:
'ΑΓΝΩΣΤΩι ΘΕΩι.
This was followed in all editions until *Complete Poems*

LONG have I framed weak phantasies of Thee,
O Willer masked and dumb!
Who makest Life become, –
As though by labouring all-unknowingly,
Like one whom reveries numb.

How much of consciousness informs Thy will,
Thy biddings, as if blind,
Of death-inducing kind,
Nought shows to us ephemeral ones who fill
But moments in Thy mind.

Memory and I
13 hope] Hope WE, ME
19 faith] Faith WE, ME
22 Bowed down] Sunken MS
25 love] Love WE, ME
27 her in] him by MS, PPP, PUE [Both 'hope' and 'faith' were masculine in ll. 15 and 21 of MS *before revision*]
29 her] his MS, PPP, PUE

'ΑΓΝΩΣΤΩΙ ΘΕΩΙ
4] By labouring all unknowingly, maybe, MS, PPP1

Perhaps Thy ancient rote-restricted ways
Thy ripening rule transcends;
That listless effort tends
To grow percipient with advance of days,
And with percipience mends.

For, in unwonted purlieus, far and nigh,
At whiles or short or long,
May be discerned a wrong
Dying as of self-slaughter; whereat I
Would raise my voice in song.

’ΑΓΝΩΣΤΩΙ ΘΕΩΙ
11 Perhaps] Haply MS, PPP1
11 rote-restricted] tentative, slow MS: automatic PPP1
20 Would] Do PPP1

Reminiscences of a Dancing Man.

by Thomas Hardy.

I

Who now remembers Almack's balls —
Willis's sometime named —
In those two smooth-floored upper halls
For faded ones so famed?
Where as we trod to trilling sound
The fancied phantoms stood around,
Or joined us in the maze,
Of the powdered Dears from Georgian years,
Whose dust lay in sightless sealed-up biers;
The fairest of former days.

II.

Who now remembers gay Cremorne
And all its jaunty jills,
And those wild whirling figures born
Of Jullien's grand quadrilles?
With hats on head & morning coats
There footed to his prancing notes
Our partner-girls & we;
And the gas-jets winked, & the lustres clinked,
And the platform throbbed as with arms enlinked
We moved to the minstrelsy.

See page 216

Who

TIME'S LAUGHINGSTOCKS AND OTHER VERSES

Abbreviations Specific to 'Time's Laughingstocks'

MS = The bound-up volume of manuscripts in the Fitzwilliam Museum at Cambridge
TL1 = *Time's Laughingstocks* (London, 1909)
TL2 = *Time's Laughingstocks* (London, 1910)
TL = Found in both TL1 and TL2
WE1 = Wessex Edition 1913
WE2 = Wessex Edition 1920
WE = Found in both WE1 and WE2
PE = Pocket Edition 1919
ME = Mellstock Edition 1920

PREFACE

IN collecting the following poems I have to thank the editors and proprietors of the periodicals in which certain of them have appeared for permission to reclaim them.

Now that the miscellany is brought together, some lack of concord in pieces written at widely severed dates, and in contrasting moods and circumstances, will be obvious enough. This I cannot help, but the sense of disconnection, particularly in respect of those lyrics penned in the first person, will be immaterial when it is borne in mind that they are to be regarded, in the main, as dramatic monologues by different characters.

As a whole they will, I hope, take the reader forward, even if not far, rather than backward. I should add that some lines in the early-dated poems have been rewritten, though they have been left substantially unchanged.

September 1909 T.H.

Preface

1 poems] poems to form a volume, (volume MS) MS, TL, WE, PE

2 certain] some MS

4–8 together, . . . immaterial] together a lack of harmony will be apparent in the pieces. This I cannot help, and perhaps any sense of discontinuity therefrom, particularly in respect of those lyrics penned in the first person, will be accepted MS

11–12 forward, . . . backward] forward rather than backward, even if not far. MS

12–13 early-dated] earlier MS, TL1

13–14 though . . . unchanged] though their meaning has not been changed MS *before revision*

152 *The Revisitation*

EXTRA PRINTING:
The Fortnightly Review, 1 Aug 1904, pp. [193]–197 = FR

TITLE:

Time's Laughingstocks
A Summer Romance FR

As I lay awake at night-time
In an ancient country barrack known to ancient cannoneers,
And recalled the hopes that heralded each seeming brave and bright time
Of my primal purple years,

Much it haunted me that, nigh there,
I had borne my bitterest loss – when One who went, came not again;
In a joyless hour of discord, in a joyless-hued July there –
A July just such as then.

And as thus I brooded longer,
With my faint eyes on the feeble square of wan-lit window frame,
A quick conviction sprung within me, grew, and grew yet stronger
That the month-night was the same,

Too, as that which saw her leave me
On the rugged ridge of Waterstone, the peewits plaining round;
And a lapsing twenty years had ruled that – as it were to grieve me –
I should near the once-loved ground.

Though but now a war-worn stranger
Chance had quartered here, I rose up and descended to the yard.
All was soundless, save the troopers' horses tossing at the manger,
And the sentry keeping guard.

Through the gateway I betook me
Down the High Street and beyond the lamps, across the battered bridge,
Till the country darkness clasped me and the friendly shine forsook me,
And I bore towards the Ridge,

With a dim unowned emotion
Saying softly: 'Small my reason, now at midnight, to be here. . . .
Yet a sleepless swain of fifty with a brief romantic notion
May retrace a track so dear.'

The Revisitation
6 went,] went MS, FR
6 again;] again, MS, FR
8 just] there MS, FR
10 wan-lit window frame] wansome window-frame MS, FR
11 stronger] stronger, MS, FR, TL, WE, PE, ME, CP1, 2
12 month-night] night, too, FR
12 same,] same; FR
13 Too] Ay FR
14 round;] round. . . . MS, FR
18 rose up] clothed me MS, FR
19 soundless,] soundless FR
21 me] me, FR
22 High Street] High-street MS
26 here. . . .] here. . . . . MS: here! . . . FR

Thus I walked with thoughts half-uttered
Up the lane I knew so well, the grey, gaunt, lonely Lane of Slyre;
And at whiles behind me, far at sea, a sullen thunder muttered
As I mounted high and higher.

Till, the upper roadway quitting,
I adventured on the open drouthy downland thinly grassed,
While the spry white scuts of conies flashed before me, earthward flitting,
And an arid wind went past.

Round about me bulged the barrows
As before, in antique silence – immemorial funeral piles –
Where the sleek herds trampled daily the remains of flint-tipt arrows
Mid the thyme and chamomiles;

And the Sarsen stone there, dateless,
On whose breast we had sat and told the zephyrs many a tender vow,
Held the heat of yester sun, as sank thereon one fated mateless
From those far fond hours till now.

Maybe flustered by my presence
Rose the peewits, just as all those years back, wailing soft and loud,
And revealing their pale pinions like a fitful phosphorescence
Up against the cope of cloud,

Where their dolesome exclamations
Seemed the voicings of the self-same throats I had heard when life was green,
Though since that day uncounted frail forgotten generations
Of their kind had flecked the scene. –

And so, living long and longer
In a past that lived no more, my eyes discerned there, suddenly,
That a figure broke the skyline – first in vague contour, then stronger,
And was crossing near to me.

Some long-missed familiar gesture,
Something wonted, struck me in the figure's pause to list and heed,
Till I fancied from its handling of its loosely wrapping vesture
That it might be She indeed.

The Revisitation
30 grey, gaunt, lonely] grey gaunt lonesome MS
30 grey] long FR
30 lonely] lonesome FR
33 Till,] Till MS, FR
36 an arid] a sultry FR
42 On . . . had] Where of old we'd FR
44 fond] fair FR
50 self-same] selfsame MS
55 skyline] sky-line FR

'Twas not reasonless: below there
In the vale, had been her home; the nook might hold her even yet,
And the downlands were her father's fief; she still might come and go there; –
So I rose, and said, 'Agnette!'

With a little leap, half-frightened,
She withdrew some steps; then letting intuition smother fear
In a place so long-accustomed, and as one whom thought enlightened,
She replied: 'What – *that* voice? – here!'

'Yes, Agnette! – And did the occasion
Of our marching hither make you think I *might* walk where we two –'
'O, I often come,' she murmured with a moment's coy evasion,
'('Tis not far), – and – think of you.'

Then I took her hand, and led her
To the ancient people's stone whereon I had sat. There now sat we;
And together talked, until the first reluctant shyness fled her,
And she spoke confidingly.

'It is *just* as ere we parted!'
Said she, brimming high with joy. – 'And when, then, came you here, and why?'
'– Dear, I could not sleep for thinking of our trystings when twin-hearted.'
She responded, 'Nor could I.

'There are few things I would rather
Than be wandering at this spirit-hour – lone-lived, my kindred dead –
On this wold of well-known feature I inherit from my father:
Night or day, I have no dread. . . .

'O I wonder, wonder whether
Any heartstring bore a signal-thrill between us twain or no? –
Some such influence can, at times, they say, draw severed souls together.'
I said, 'Dear, we'll dream it so.'

The Revisitation
70 two –] two – – FR
71 murmured] murmured, FR
79 – Dear] – – Dear FR
84 dread. . . .] dread. . . . . MS
85 O] O, FR
86 bore] sent FR

Each one's hand the other's grasping,
And a mutual forgiveness won, we sank to silent thought,
A large content in us that seemed our rended lives reclasping,
And contracting years to nought.

Till I, maybe overweary
From the lateness, and a wayfaring so full of strain and stress
For one no longer buoyant, to a peak so steep and eery,
Sank to slow unconsciousness. . . .

How long I slept I knew not,
But the brief warm summer night had slid when, to my swift surprise,
A red upedging sun, of glory chambered mortals view not,
Was blazing on my eyes,

From the Milton Woods to Dole-Hill
All the spacious landscape lighting, and around about my feet
Flinging tall thin tapering shadows from the meanest mound and mole-hill,
And on trails the ewes had beat.

She was sitting still beside me,
Dozing likewise; and I turned to her, to take her hanging hand;
When, the more regarding, that which like a spectre shook and tried me
In her image then I scanned;

That which Time's transforming chisel
Had been tooling night and day for twenty years, and tooled too well,
In its rendering of crease where curve was, where was raven, grizzle –
Pits, where peonies once did dwell.

She had wakened, and perceiving
(I surmise) my sigh and shock, my quite involuntary dismay,
Up she started, and – her wasted figure all throughout it heaving –
Said, 'Ah, yes: I am *thus* by day!

'Can you really wince and wonder
That the sunlight should reveal you such a thing of skin and bone,
As if unaware a Death's-head must of need lie not far under
Flesh whose years out-count your own?

The Revisitation
95 steep] still FR
99 of] in MS, FR
106 Dozing] Sleeping MS
107 spectre] phantom FR
108 image then I] shape I straightway FR
111 grizzle] grizzel MS, FR
112 Pits] White FR
112 peonies] roses MS, FR
114 quite] vague FR
120 Flesh] One FR, TL, PE

'Yes: that movement was a warning
Of the worth of man's devotion! – Yes, Sir, I am *old*,' said she,
'And the thing which should increase love turns it quickly into scorning –
And your new-won heart from me!'

Then she went, ere I could call her,
With the too proud temper ruling that had parted us before,
And I saw her form descend the slopes, and smaller grow and smaller,
Till I caught its course no more. . . .

True; I might have dogged her downward;
– But it *may* be (though I know not) that this trick on us of Time
Disconcerted and confused me. – Soon I bent my footsteps townward,
Like to one who had watched a crime.

Well I knew my native weakness,
Well I know it still. I cherished her reproach like physic-wine,
For I saw in that emaciate shape of bitterness and bleakness
A nobler soul than mine.

Did I not return, then, ever? –
Did we meet again? – mend all? – Alas, what greyhead perseveres! –
Soon I got the Route elsewhither. – Since that hour I have seen her never:
Love is lame at fifty years.

153 *A Trampwoman's Tragedy*

(*182–*)

I

FROM Wynyard's Gap the livelong day,
The livelong day,
We beat afoot the northward way
We had travelled times before.
The sun-blaze burning on our backs,
Our shoulders sticking to our packs,
By fosseway, fields, and turnpike tracks
We skirted sad Sedge-Moor.

A Trampwoman's Tragedy

EXTRA MANUSCRIPT:
The manuscript used for the printing of NAR (see below) was in the Bliss Collection. Its present whereabouts are unknown. It has not been checked

PROOF:
In the Berg Collection of the New York Public Library = B

EXTRA PRINTINGS:
(1) *The North American Review*, Nov 1903, pp. [775]–778 = NAR
(2) Privately by Florence Hardy (1917) = FH
(3) *Chosen Poems*, pp. 204–9

TITLE:
The Tramp's Tragedy B *before revision*
(*182–*)] (1827) MS: (The incidents on which this tale is based occurred in 1827.) B, NAR

The Revisitation
121 Yes:] Yes; FR
122 Sir] sir FR
124 me!'] me!' . . . . FR
128 caught its course] noted it MS, FR
128 more. . . .] more. . . . . . MS: more. – FR
129 dogged] tracked FR
129 downward;] downward. MS, FR
132 watched] seen FR
134 Well] And FR
139 never:] never. MS, FR
Note MS has 'Thomas Hardy' deleted at end and seems to have been the one used for printing FR

A Trampwoman's Tragedy
1 Wynyard's Gap] Wynyard's-Gap MS
2 day,] day MS

II

Full twenty miles we jaunted on,
We jaunted on, –
My fancy-man, and jeering John,
And Mother Lee, and I.
And, as the sun drew down to west,
We climbed the toilsome Poldon crest,
And saw, of landskip sights the best,
The inn that beamed thereby.

III

For months we had padded side by side,
Ay, side by side
Through the Great Forest, Blackmoor wide,
And where the Parret ran.
We'd faced the gusts on Mendip ridge,
Had crossed the Yeo unhelped by bridge,
Been stung by every Marshwood midge,
I and my fancy-man.

IV

Lone inns we loved, my man and I,
My man and I;
'King's Stag', 'Windwhistle' high and dry,
'The Horse' on Hintock Green,
The cosy house at Wynyard's Gap,
'The Hut' renowned on Bredy Knap,
And many another wayside tap
Where folk might sit unseen.

V

Now as we trudged – O deadly day,
O deadly day! –
I teased my fancy-man in play
And wanton idleness.
I walked alongside jeering John,
I laid his hand my waist upon;
I would not bend my glances on
My lover's dark distress.

A Trampwoman's Tragedy
10 on, –] on, MS, B, NAR
14 toilsome] parching B, NAR
16 beamed] stood B, NAR
18] All side by side, (side B, TL1) MS, B, NAR, TL1
18 Ay,] Close TL2, FH, PE
25 I,] I MS
26 I;] I, MS, NAR
27 'King's Stag', 'Windwhistle'] King's-Stag, Windwhistle MS, B, NAR
28 'The Horse'] The 'Horse' B, NAR
30 'The Hut'] The 'Hut' B, NAR
30 renowned] for rest WE2
30 Bredy] Bredy's B, NAR
30 Knap,] Knap MS
37 alongside] along side TL1
37 John,] John MS

VI

Thus Poldon top at last we won,
At last we won,
And gained the inn at sink of sun
Far-famed as 'Marshal's Elm'.
Beneath us figured tor and lea,
From Mendip to the western sea –
I doubt if finer sight there be
Within this royal realm.

VII

Inside the settle all a-row –
All four a-row
We sat, I next to John, to show
That he had wooed and won.
And then he took me on his knee,
And swore it was his turn to be
My favoured mate, and Mother Lee
Passed to my former one.

VIII

Then in a voice I had never heard,
I had never heard,
My only Love to me: 'One word,
My lady, if you please!
Whose is the child you are like to bear? –
His? After all my months o' care?'
God knows 'twas not! But, O despair!
I nodded – still to tease.

IX

Then up he sprung, and with his knife –
And with his knife
He let out jeering Johnny's life,
Yes; there, at set of sun.
The slant ray through the window nigh
Gilded John's blood and glazing eye,
Ere scarcely Mother Lee and I
Knew that the deed was done.

A Trampwoman's Tragedy
44 'Marshal's Elm'] Marshal's Elm MS, B, NAR
46 western] Western MS, B, NAR
49 a-row] arow MS, B, NAR
50] Ay, all arow (a-row TL, PE) – MS, B, NAR, TL, PE
55 mate] man MS, B, NAR
57 I had] I'd B, NAR
58 I had] I'd B, NAR
59 word,] word MS
60 lady] Lady MS, B, NAR: doxy TL1
61 bear? –] bear? MS, B, NAR
67 life,] life; MS, NAR
68 set] sink B, NAR
70 eye,] eye MS

X

The taverns tell the gloomy tale,
The gloomy tale,
How that at Ivel-chester jail
My Love, my sweetheart swung;
Though stained till now by no misdeed
Save one horse ta'en in time o' need;
(Blue Jimmy stole right many a steed
Ere his last fling he flung.)

XI

Thereaft I walked the world alone,
Alone, alone!
On his death-day I gave my groan
And dropt his dead-born child.
'Twas nigh the jail, beneath a tree,
None tending me; for Mother Lee
Had died at Glaston, leaving me
Unfriended on the wild.

XII

And in the night as I lay weak,
As I lay weak,
The leaves a-falling on my cheek,
The red moon low declined –
The ghost of him I'd die to kiss
Rose up and said: 'Ah, tell me this!
Was the child mine, or was it his?
Speak, that I rest may find!'

XIII

O doubt not but I told him then,
I told him then,
That I had kept me from all men
Since we joined lips and swore.

A Trampwoman's Tragedy
73 tale,] tale MS
76] My man, my lover, (lover B) swung; B, NAR
91 cheek,] cheek MS
94 up] up, NAR
94 Ah,] O MS, B, NAR
97 O] O, NAR

Whereat he smiled, and thinned away
As the wind stirred to call up day ...
– 'Tis past! And here alone I stray
        Haunting the Western Moor.

NOTES. – 'Windwhistle' (Stanza IV). The highness and dryness of Windwhistle Inn was impressed upon the writer two or three years ago, when, after climbing on a hot afternoon to the beautiful spot near which it stands and entering the inn for tea, he was informed by the landlady that none could be had, unless he would fetch water from a valley half a mile off, the house containing not a drop, owing to its situation. However, a tantalizing row of full barrels behind her back testified to a wetness of a certain sort, which was not at that time desired.

'Marshal's Elm' (Stanza VI), so picturesquely situated, is no longer an inn, though the house, or part of it, still remains. It used to exhibit a fine old swinging sign.

'Blue Jimmy' (Stanza X) was a notorious horse-stealer of Wessex in those days, who appropriated more than a hundred horses before he was caught, among others one belonging to a neighbour of the writer's grandfather. He was hanged at the now demolished Ivel-chester or Ilchester jail above mentioned – that building formerly of so many sinister associations in the minds of the local peasantry, and the continual haunt of fever, which at last led to its condemnation. Its site is now an innocent-looking green meadow.

April 1902

154 *The Two Rosalinds*

I

THE dubious daylight ended,
And I walked the Town alone, unminding whither bound and why,
As from each gaunt street and gaping square a mist of light ascended
    And dispersed upon the sky.

II

Files of evanescent faces
Passed each other without heeding, in their travail, teen, or joy,
Some in void unvisioned listlessness inwrought with pallid traces
    Of keen penury's annoy.

EXTRA MANUSCRIPT:
Permission was refused to see the MS in the possession of Mr Frederick B. Adams, Jnr

EXTRA PRINTINGS:
(1) *Collier's* (New York), 20 March 1909, p. 24 = C
(2) *The English Review*, April 1909, pp. 1–3 = ER

Note In ER 'The Two Rosalinds' was followed by 'Reminiscences of a Dancing Man', and the two poems were given the collective title 'London Nights'

A Trampwoman's Tragedy
102 day . . .] day. . . . . . MS
103 here alone I stray] lonely here I stay MS: I alone now stay B, NAR
NOTES. The only important variants are the omission of 'It . . . sign.' in B, NAR; of 'among . . . grandfather.' in MS, B, NAR, TL, PE; and of 'and . . . condemnation.' in MS, B, NAR. Hardy's copy of CP2 adds the following note at the end of para. 2: "King's Stag" (stanza iv) was an inn down to 1829, and I know not how much later.

The Two Rosalinds
2 unminding] unweeting C
2 Town] town C
6 Passed . . . heeding,] Passed, unheeding one another C
6 teen,] teen MS

III

Nebulous flames in crystal cages
Leered as if with discontent at city movement, murk, and grime,
And as waiting some procession of great ghosts from bygone ages
To exalt the ignoble time.

IV

In a colonnade high-lighted,
By a thoroughfare where stern utilitarian traffic dinned,
On a red and white emblazonment of players and parts, I sighted
The name of 'Rosalind',

V

And her famous mates of 'Arden',
Who observed no stricter customs than 'the seasons' difference' bade,
Who lived with running brooks for books in Nature's wildwood garden,
And called idleness their trade. . . .

VI

Now the poster stirred an ember
Still remaining from my ardours of some forty years before,
When the self-same portal on an eve it thrilled me to remember
A like announcement bore;

VII

And expectantly I had entered,
And had first beheld in human mould a Rosalind woo and plead,
On whose transcendent figuring my speedy soul had centred
As it had been she indeed. . . .

VIII

So; all other plans discarding,
I resolved on entrance, bent on seeing what I once had seen,
And approached the gangway of my earlier knowledge, disregarding
The tract of time between.

The Two Rosalinds
10 Leered] Gleamed MS, ER, TL, PE
10 with] in C
10 murk] mulch C
13 colonnade] colonnade, C
17 'Arden',] 'Arden' ER
18 seasons'] season's C, ER
18 bade,] bade MS
19 Nature's] nature's C
20 trade. . . .] trade. . . . . MS
22 before,] before C, ER
23 self-same] selfsame MS, ER, TL, PE, WE, ME
28 indeed. . . .] indeed. . . . . MS
29 So;] So, C
29 discarding,] discarding MS, ER
30 I . . . entrance] I now turned me inward C
31 approached the gangway] pursued the pathway C
32 tract] expanse MS, C, ER, TL, PE

IX

'The words, sir?' cried a creature
Hovering mid the shine and shade as 'twixt the live world and the tomb;
But the well-known numbers needed not for me a text or teacher
To revive and re-illume.

X

Then the play. . . . But how unfitted
Was *this* Rosalind! – a mammet quite to me, in memories nurst,
And with chilling disappointment soon I sought the street I had quitted,
To re-ponder on the first.

XI

The hag still hawked, – I met her
Just without the colonnade. 'So you don't like her, sir?' said she.
'Ah – *I* was once that Rosalind! – I acted her – none better –
Yes – in eighteen sixty-three.

XII

'Thus I won Orlando to me
In my then triumphant days when I had charm and maidenhood,
Now some forty years ago. – I used to say, *Come woo me, woo me!'*
And she struck the attitude.

XIII

It was when I had gone there nightly;
And the voice – though raucous now – was yet the old one. – Clear as noon
My Rosalind was here. . . . Thereon the band withinside lightly
Beat up a merry tune.

155 *A Sunday Morning Tragedy*

(circa 186–)

I BORE a daughter flower-fair,
In Pydel Vale, alas for me;
I joyed to mother one so rare,
But dead and gone I now would be.

EXTRA MANUSCRIPT:
In the Henry E. Huntington Library = HL

EXTRA PRINTING:
The English Review, Dec 1908, pp. 1–4 = ER

TITLE:
(*circa 186–*)] (*circa* 1860) MS, ER: (186–) HL

The Two Rosalinds
34 mid] 'twixt MS, C, ER, TL, PE
34 'twixt] mid MS, C, ER, TL, PE
36 re-illume] reillume C
37 Then the play. . . .] In I went. . . . (went. . . . . MS) MS, TL, PE: I passed in. . . . C: I was in . . . ER
39 quitted,] quitted MS, C, ER
40 re-ponder] reponder C, ER
41 hawked, –] hawked – C
42 said] cried MS, C, ER
43 Ah – *I*] Ah, well – I C
44 eighteen sixty-three.] eighteen-sixty-three! C
44 sixty-three.] sixty-three! MS, ER
45 Thus. . . Orlando] This is how I won him C
46 then] once C, ER
47 say,] say: C
47 *Come*] *Come*, C
47 *Come . . . me!*] Not italicised in MS
47 *me!'*] *me!'* – C
49 It was when] 'Twas the year C
51 My . . . Thereon] This was my Rosalind . . . . As interlude C
51 here. . . .] here. . . . . MS
51 Thereon . . . withinside] The band within, as int'ract ER

A Sunday Morning Tragedy
2 In Pydel Vale] Yea, flower-fair MS, HL, ER

Men looked and loved her as she grew,
And she was won, alas for me;
She told me nothing, but I knew,
And saw that sorrow was to be.

I knew that one had made her thrall,
A thrall to him, alas for me;
And then, at last, she told me all,
And wondered what her end would be.

She owned that she had loved too well,
Had loved too well, unhappy she,
And bore a secret time would tell,
Though in her shroud she'd sooner be.

I plodded to her sweetheart's door
In Pydel Vale, alas for me:
I pleaded with him, pleaded sore,
To save her from her misery.

He frowned, and swore he could not wed,
Seven times he swore it could not be;
'Poverty's worse than shame,' he said,
Till all my hope went out of me.

'I've packed my traps to sail the main' –
Roughly he spake, alas did he –
'Wessex beholds me not again,
'Tis worse than any jail would be!'

– There was a shepherd whom I knew,
A subtle man, alas for me:
I sought him all the pastures through,
Though better I had ceased to be.

I traced him by his lantern light,
And gave him hint, alas for me,
Of how she found her in the plight
That is so scorned in Christendie.

A Sunday Morning Tragedy
6 me;] me: HL
8 be.] be: HL, ER
15 time] Time HL
16 shroud she'd sooner] grave she'd gladlier HL
17 door] door, MS, HL, ER
18 In Pydel Vale] Went to his door MS, HL, ER
18 me:] me. HL, ER
25 main' –] main,' HL, ER
26 he –] he. HL, ER
27 Wessex] This spot HL
29 – There] There HL
36 in] by HL, ER

'Is there an herb. . . ?' I asked. 'Or none?'
Yes, thus I asked him desperately.
' – There is,' he said; 'a certain one. . . .'
Would he had sworn that none knew he!

'To-morrow I will walk your way,'
He hinted low, alas for me. –
Fieldwards I gazed throughout next day;
Now fields I never more would see!

The sunset-shine, as curfew strook,
As curfew strook beyond the lea,
Lit his white smock and gleaming crook,
While slowly he drew near to me.

He pulled from underneath his smock
The herb I sought, my curse to be –
'At times I use it in my flock,'
He said, and hope waxed strong in me.

' 'Tis meant to balk ill-motherings' –
(Ill-motherings! Why should they be?) –
'If not, would God have sent such things?'
So spoke the shepherd unto me.

That night I watched the poppling brew,
With bended back and hand on knee:
I stirred it till the dawnlight grew,
And the wind whiffled wailfully.

'This scandal shall be slain,' said I,
'That lours upon her innocency:
I'll give all whispering tongues the lie;' –
But worse than whispers was to be.

'Here's physic for untimely fruit,'
I said to her, alas for me,
Early that morn in fond salute;
And in my grave I now would be.

A Sunday Morning Tragedy
39 – There] There HL, ER
39 one. . . .] one. . . . . HL
40 that none knew he!] naught (none HL) such to be. (be! MS, TL1) MS, HL, ER, TL1
41 way,] way MS
45 sunset-shine] sunset shine MS, HL, ER
47 crook,] crook MS, HL, ER
50 sought,] sought – HL
57 brew,] brew – HL
58] Watched it all night determinedly: HL
59 dawnlight] dawn-light HL, ER
59 grew,] grew; HL
60] Would it had never gleamed on me! HL
60 And] While ER
63 lie;' –] lie'; HL, ER
64 was] were HL

– Next Sunday came, with sweet church chimes
In Pydel Vale, alas for me:
I went into her room betimes;
No more may such a Sunday be!

'Mother, instead of rescue nigh,'
She faintly breathed, alas for me,
'I feel as I were like to die,
And underground soon, soon should be.'

From church that noon the people walked
In twos and threes, alas for me,
Showed their new raiment – smiled and talked,
Though sackcloth-clad I longed to be.

Came to my door her lover's friends,
And cheerly cried, alas for me,
'Right glad are we he makes amends,
For never a sweeter bride can be.'

My mouth dried, as 'twere scorched within,
Dried at their words, alas for me:
More and more neighbours crowded in,
(O why should mothers ever be!)

'Ha-ha! Such well-kept news!' laughed they,
Yes – so they laughed, alas for me.
'Whose banns were called in church to-day?' –
Christ, how I wished my soul could flee!

'Where is she? O the stealthy miss,'
Still bantered they, alas for me,
'To keep a wedding close as this. . . .'
Ay, Fortune worked thus wantonly!

'But you are pale – you did not know?'
They archly asked, alas for me,
I stammered, 'Yes – some days – ago,'
While coffined clay I wished to be.

A Sunday Morning Tragedy
69 chimes] chimes; MS, ER: chimes, TL, WE, PE, ME
70 In Pydel Vale] Next Sunday came MS, HL, ER, WE, ME
70 me:] me; HL
71 betimes;] betimes, HL
72] And the wind whiffled wearily. HL
79 raiment –] raiment, – HL, ER
90 me.] me: MS, HL, ER
92 my . . . flee!] I could un-be! – HL, ER
93 miss,] miss! HL
94 Still] So HL
95 this. . . .'] this.' . . . . HL
96 Ay] Yes HL
96 wantonly!] wantonly. HL
98 me,] me. MS, HL, ER
99 days –] days HL

' 'Twas done to please her, we surmise?'
(They spoke quite lightly in their glee)
'Done by him as a fond surprise?'
I thought their words would madden me.

Her lover entered. 'Where's my bird? –
My bird – my flower – my picotee?
First time of asking, soon the third!'
Ah, in my grave I well may be.

To me he whispered: 'Since your call – '
So spoke he then, alas for me –
'I've felt for her, and righted all.'
– I think of it to agony.

'She's faint to-day – tired – nothing more— '
Thus did I lie, alas for me....
I called her at her chamber door
As one who scarce had strength to be.

No voice replied. I went within –
O women! scourged the worst are we....
I shrieked. The others hastened in
And saw the stroke there dealt on me.

There she lay – silent, breathless, dead,
Stone dead she lay – wronged, sinless she! –
Ghost-white the cheeks once rosy-red:
Death had took her. Death took not me.

I kissed her colding face and hair,
I kissed her corpse – the bride to be! –
My punishment I cannot bear,
But pray God *not* to pity me.

January 1904

A Sunday Morning Tragedy
101 her,] her HL, ER
101 surmise?'] surmise?' – ER
102 (They] They HL, ER
102 glee)] glee, HL, ER
103 Done] – Done HL, ER
107 asking,] asking – HL
107 third!'] third!' – HL
109 call – '] call' – MS, HL, ER
110 me –] me, HL, ER
113 more – '] more' – MS, HL, ER
114 me. . . .] me. . . . . HL
115 chamber door] chamber-door HL, ER
117 within –] within, – MS, HL, ER
118 we. . . .] we. . . . . MS, HL
119 in] in. HL
120 on] to HL: at ER
121 dead,] dead – MS, HL, ER
122 Stone dead she lay] In Pydel Vale TL, PE
123 rosy-red] rosy red HL, ER
124 her.] her: MS, HL, ER

EXTRA PRINTINGS:
(1) *The New Quarterly*, Jan 1909, p. 124 = NQ
(2) *Selected Poems*, p. 77
(3) *Chosen Poems*, p. 72

156 *The House of Hospitalities*

HERE we broached the Christmas barrel,
Pushed up the charred log-ends;
Here we sang the Christmas carol,
And called in friends.

Time has tired me since we met here
When the folk now dead were young,
Since the viands were outset here
And quaint songs sung.

And the worm has bored the viol
That used to lead the tune,
Rust eaten out the dial
That struck night's noon.

Now no Christmas brings in neighbours,
And the New Year comes unlit;
Where we sang the mole now labours,
And spiders knit.

Yet at midnight if here walking,
When the moon sheets wall and tree,
I see forms of old time talking,
Who smile on me.

Note In WE, ME placed after 'The Farm-Woman's Winter'

157 *Bereft*

IN the black winter morning
No light will be struck near my eyes
While the clock in the stairway is warning
For five, when he used to rise.
Leave the door unbarred,
The clock unwound,
Make my lone bed hard –
Would 'twere underground!

The House of Hospitalities
2] And up-piled the billet-ends; NQ
3 carol] Carol NQ
5 here] here, NQ
6 young,] young, – MS: young – NQ
7 here] here, NQ
8 sung.] sung MS
11 Rust eaten] Rust has eaten [There is no authority for this variant which is found in some reprints of CP4]
17 here walking,] I walk here NQ
17 walking,] walking MS
19] Forms outshape and seem to talk here, NQ
20 Who] And NQ

Bereft
6 unwound,] Print deterioration resulted in the disappearance of the comma in CP4

When the summer dawns clearly,
And the appletree-tops seem alight,
Who will undraw the curtain and cheerly
Call out that the morning is bright?

When I tarry at market
No form will cross Durnover Lea
In the gathering darkness, to hark at
Grey's Bridge for the pit-pat o' me.

When the supper crock's steaming,
And the time is the time of his tread,
I shall sit by the fire and wait dreaming
In a silence as of the dead.
Leave the door unbarred,
The clock unwound,
Make my lone bed hard –
Would 'twere underground!

1901

158 *John and Jane*

I

HE sees the world as a boisterous place
Where all things bear a laughing face,
And humorous scenes go hourly on,
Does John.

II

They find the world a pleasant place
Where all is ecstasy and grace,
Where a light has risen that cannot wane,
Do John and Jane.

III

They see as a palace their cottage-place,
Containing a pearl of the human race,
A hero, maybe, hereafter styled,
Do John and Jane with a baby-child.

Bereft
16 o'] of MS

John and Jane
7 wane,] wane MS
9 cottage-place,] cottage-place MS
11 hero, maybe,] hero maybe MS
11 styled,] styled MS

IV

They rate the world as a gruesome place,
Where fair looks fade to a skull's grimace, –
As a pilgrimage they would fain get done –
Do John and Jane with their worthless son.

159 The Curate's Kindness

A Workhouse Irony

INDENTATION:
1 = l. 3
2 = ll. 1, 4
3 = l. 2
and so throughout MS

I

I THOUGHT they'd be strangers aroun' me,
But she's to be there!
Let me jump out o' waggon and go back and drown me
At Pummery or Ten-Hatches Weir.

II

I thought: 'Well, I've come to the Union –
The workhouse at last –
After honest hard work all the week, and Communion
O' Zundays, these fifty years past.

III

' 'Tis hard; but,' I thought, 'never mind it:
There's gain in the end:
And when I get used to the place I shall find it
A home, and may find there a friend.

IV

'Life there will be better than t'other,
For peace is assured.
The men in one wing and their wives in another
Is strictly the rule of the Board.'

John and Jane
13 place,] place MS
14 grimace, –] grimace, MS
15 done –] done MS

The Curate's Kindness
1 me,] me MS
4 Ten-Hatches] Ten-Hatches' MS

V

Just then one young Pa'son arriving
        Steps up out of breath
To the side o' the waggon wherein we were driving
        To Union; and calls out and saith:

VI

'Old folks, that harsh order is altered,
        Be not sick of heart!
The Guardians they poohed and they pished and they paltered
        When urged not to keep you apart.

VII

' "It is wrong," I maintained, "to divide them,
        Near forty years wed."
"Very well, sir. We promise, then, they shall abide them
        In one wing together," they said.'

VIII

Then I sank – knew 'twas quite a foredone thing
        That misery should be
To the end! . . . To get freed of her there was the one thing
        Had made the change welcome to me.

IX

To go there was ending but badly;
        'Twas shame and 'twas pain;
'But anyhow,' thought I, 'thereby I shall gladly
        Get free of this forty years' chain.'

X

I thought they'd be strangers aroun' me,
        But she's to be there!
Let me jump out o' waggon and go back and drown me
        At Pummery or Ten-Hatches Weir.

The Curate's Kindness
17 one] our MS, WE, ME [Hardy's copy of CP2 in DCM has been corrected to 'our']
26 wed.'] wed.' – MS
27 sir] Sir MS
31 end! . . .] end! . . . . . MS
37 me,] me MS
39 waggon] waggon, MS

160 *The Flirt's Tragedy*

(*17—*)

HERE alone by the logs in my chamber,
Deserted, decrepit –
Spent flames limning ghosts on the wainscot
Of friends I once knew –

My drama and hers begins weirdly
Its dumb re-enactment,
Each scene, sigh, and circumstance passing
In spectral review.

– Wealth was mine beyond wish when I met her –
The pride of the lowland –
Embowered in Tintinhull Valley
By laurel and yew;

And love lit my soul, notwithstanding
My features' ill favour,
Too obvious beside her perfections
Of line and of hue.

But it pleased her to play on my passion,
And whet me to pleadings
That won from her mirthful negations
And scornings undue.

Then I fled her disdains and derisions
To cities of pleasure,
And made me the crony of idlers
In every purlieu.

Of those who lent ear to my story,
A needy Adonis
Gave hint how to grizzle her garden
From roses to rue,

The Flirt's Tragedy
1 chamber,] chamber – MS
4 knew –] knew, MS
13 notwithstanding] though misgiving MS
17 passion,] passion WE
24 purlieu.] purlieu, CP1–3 [certainly an undetected error in CP1–3]
25 story,] story MS

Could his price but be paid for so purging
My scorner of scornings:
Thus tempted, the lust to avenge me
Germed inly and grew.

I clothed him in sumptuous apparel,
Consigned to him coursers,
Meet equipage, liveried attendants
In full retinue.

So dowered, with letters of credit
He wayfared to England,
And spied out the manor she goddessed,
And handy thereto,

Set to hire him a tenantless mansion
As coign-stone of vantage
For testing what gross adulation
Of beauty could do.

He laboured through mornings and evens,
On new moons and sabbaths,
By wiles to enmesh her attention
In park, path, and pew;

And having afar played upon her,
Advanced his lines nearer,
And boldly outleaping conventions,
Bent briskly to woo.

His gay godlike face, his rare seeming
Anon worked to win her,
And later, at noontides and night-tides
They held rendezvous.

His tarriance full spent, he departed
And met me in Venice,
And lines from her told that my jilter
Was stooping to sue.

The Flirt's Tragedy
31 avenge me] retaliate MS, TL, WE1, PE
32 inly] in me MS, TL, WE1, PE
40 And] And, WE, ME
40 thereto,] thereto MS
49 her,] her MS
51 conventions,] conventions MS
55 night-tides] nighttides MS
57 spent,] spent MS

Not long could be further concealment,
She pled to him humbly:
'By our love and our sin, O protect me;
I fly unto you!'

A mighty remorse overgat me,
I heard her low anguish,
And there in the gloom of the *calle*
My steel ran him through.

A swift push engulphed his hot carrion
Within the canal there –
That still street of waters dividing
The city in two.

– I wandered awhile all unable
To smother my torment,
My brain racked by yells as from Tophet
Of Satan's whole crew.

A month of unrest brought me hovering
At home in her precincts,
To whose hiding-hole local story
Afforded a clue.

Exposed, and expelled by her people,
Afar off in London
I found her alone, in a sombre
And soul-stifling mew.

Still burning to make reparation
I pleaded to wive her,
And father her child, and thus faintly
My mischief undo.

She yielded, and spells of calm weather
Succeeded the tempest;
And one sprung of him stood as scion
Of my bone and thew. . . .

The Flirt's Tragedy
61 concealment,] concealment MS
69 push] thrust MS, TL, PE
92 thew. . . .] thew. . . . . MS

But Time unveils sorrows and secrets,
And so it befell now:
By inches the curtain was twitched at,
And slowly undrew.

As we lay, she and I, in the night-time,
We heard the boy moaning:
'O misery mine! My false father
Has murdered my true!'

She gasped: yea, she heard; understood it.
Next day the child fled us;
And nevermore sighted was even
A print of his shoe.

Thenceforward she shunned me, and languished;
Till one day the park-pool
Embraced her fair form, and extinguished
Her eyes' living blue.

– So; ask not what blast may account for
This aspect of pallor,
These bones that just prison within them
Life's poor residue;

But pass by, and leave unregarded
A Cain to his suffering,
For vengeance too dark on the woman
Whose lover he slew.

161 *The Rejected Member's Wife*

WE shall see her no more
On the balcony,
Smiling, while hurt, at the roar
As of surging sea
From the stormy sturdy band
Who have doomed her lord's cause,
Though she waves her little hand
As it were applause.

EXTRA MANUSCRIPT:
In the Miriam Lutcher Stark Library of the University of Texas = UT

EXTRA PRINTING:
The Spectator, 27 Jan 1906, p. 146 = S

TITLE:
The Rejected One's Wife UT
The Ejected Member's Wife S

Note In WE, ME placed after 'Geographical Knowledge'

The Flirt's Tragedy
112 residue;] residue, MS

The Rejected Member's Wife
2 the] that UT, S
3 Smiling,] Smiling UT, S
3 hurt,] hurt UT, S
5 the] our UT, S

Here will be candidates yet,
            And candidates' wives,
Fervid with zeal to set
            Their ideals on our lives:
Here will come market-men
            On the market-days,
Here will clash now and then
            More such party assays.

And the balcony will fill
            When such times are renewed,
And the throng in the street will thrill
            With to-day's mettled mood;
But she will no more stand
            In the sunshine there,
With that wave of her white-gloved hand,
            And that chestnut hair.

January 1906

162 *The Farm-Woman's Winter*

EXTRA MANUSCRIPT:
In the Bancroft Library of the University of California at Berkeley = BL

EXTRA PRINTING:
The Pall Mall Magazine, Jan 1905, p. 1 = PM

INDENTATION:
PM has all lines indented equally

I

If seasons all were summers,
   And leaves would never fall,
And hopping casement-comers
   Were foodless not at all,
And fragile folk might be here
   That white winds bid depart;
Then one I used to see here
   Would warm my wasted heart!

II

One frail, who, bravely tilling
   Long hours in gripping gusts,
Was mastered by their chilling,
   And now his ploughshare rusts.

The Rejected Member's Wife
10 wives,] wives UT, S
11 zeal] zest UT, S
12 lives:] lives; UT, S
16] More party-assays. UT, S
20 mood;] mood; – UT, S
23 white-gloved hand,] white gloved hand MS
23 hand,] hand UT, S
January 1906] Not in UT, S

The Farm-Woman's Winter
1 all were] were all PM
6 depart;] depart, BL
8 heart!] heart. PM
11 chilling,] chilling; BL, PM

So savage winter catches
  The breath of limber things,
And what I love he snatches,
  And what I love not, brings.

163 Autumn in King's Hintock Park

HERE by the baring bough
  Raking up leaves,
Often I ponder how
  Springtime deceives, –
I, an old woman now,
  Raking up leaves.

Here in the avenue
  Raking up leaves,
Lords' ladies pass in view,
  Until one heaves
Sighs at life's russet hue,
  Raking up leaves!

Just as my shape you see
  Raking up leaves,
I saw, when fresh and free,
  Those memory weaves
Into grey ghosts by me,
  Raking up leaves.

Yet, Dear, though one may sigh,
  Raking up leaves,
New leaves will dance on high –
  Earth never grieves! –
Will not, when missed am I
  Raking up leaves.

1901

EXTRA MANUSCRIPTS:
(1) Was in the possession of the Ilchester Family. Unchecked as present whereabouts are unknown
(2) In the Bancroft Library of the University of California at Berkeley = BL

EXTRA PRINTING:
Daily Mail Books' Supplement, 17 Nov 1906, p. 1 = DM

TITLE:
Autumn in the Park MS, TL
Autumn in my Lord's Park BL, DM
Hardy's copy of CP2 adds '[Melbury]' between 'Hintock' and 'Park'

Note In WE, ME this poem is placed after 'She Hears the Storm' in the sequence: 'The Flirt's Tragedy', 'The Farm-Woman's Winter', 'Bereft', 'She Hears the Storm', 'Autumn in King's Hintock Park', and 'Shut Out That Moon'

The Farm-Woman's Winter
15 snatches,] snatches MS, TL1

Autumn in King's Hintock Park
1 bough] bough, DM
4 Springtime]Spring-time BL
4 deceives, –] deceives, BL, DM
7 avenue] avenue, DM
8 leaves,] leaves MS, BL
9] Ladies and lords I view, BL, DM
10 Until one] Till a sigh BL, DM
11 Sighs at] At my BL, DM
11 hue,] hue MS, BL, DM
12 leaves!] leaves. MS, BL, DM
13 shape] form BL, DM
15 fresh] fair MS, BL, DM
16 memory] Memory DM
17 by] for DM
17 me,] me MS, BL
19 sigh,] sigh MS, BL
22 grieves! –] grieves! BL, DM
23 Will] – Will BL, DM
23 I] I, DM
1901] Not in BL, DM

EXTRA PRINTINGS:
(1) *Selected Poems*, p. 78
(2) *Chosen Poems*, p. 73

TITLE:
'Shut Out That Moon' SP

164 *Shut Out That Moon*

CLOSE up the casement, draw the blind,
    Shut out that stealing moon,
She wears too much the guise she wore
    Before our lutes were strewn
With years-deep dust, and names we read
    On a white stone were hewn.

Step not forth on the dew-dashed lawn
    To view the Lady's Chair,
Immense Orion's glittering form,
    The Less and Greater Bear:
Stay in; to such sights we were drawn
    When faded ones were fair.

Brush not the bough for midnight scents
    That come forth lingeringly,
And wake the same sweet sentiments
    They breathed to you and me
When living seemed a laugh, and love
    All it was said to be.

Within the common lamp-lit room
    Prison my eyes and thought;
Let dingy details crudely loom,
    Mechanic speech be wrought:
Too fragrant was Life's early bloom,
    Too tart the fruit it brought!

1904

Reminiscences of a Dancing Man

EXTRA MANUSCRIPT:
At the University of Yale = Y

EXTRA PRINTINGS:
(1) *Collier's*, 27 March 1909, p. 23 = C
(2) *The English Review*, April 1909, pp. 4–5 = ER
(3) *Selected Poems*, pp. 86–7
(4) *Chosen Poems*, pp. 81–2

TITLE:
In ER this poem followed 'The Two Rosalinds' and the two poems were given the collective title 'London Nights'

INDENTATION:
1 = ll. 8, 9
2 = ll. 1, 3, 5, 6
3 = ll. 2, 4, 7, 10
} and so throughout Y, ER

165 *Reminiscences of a Dancing Man*

I

WHO now remembers Almack's balls –
    Willis's sometime named –
In those two smooth-floored upper halls
    For faded ones so famed?

Shut Out That Moon
2 stealing] sad-shaped MS, TL1
3 wears] bears WE2, ME
3 guise] look SP
7 forth] out MS, TL, PE, CP1–3
10 Less] small MS: Small TL1
10 Greater] greater MS
22 wrought:] wrought; MS

Reminiscences of a Dancing Man
2 sometime] sometimes C

Where as we trod to trilling sound
The fancied phantoms stood around,
    Or joined us in the maze,
Of the powdered Dears from Georgian years,
Whose dust lay in sightless sealed-up biers,
    The fairest of former days.

II

Who now remembers gay Cremorne,
    And all its jaunty jills,
And those wild whirling figures born
    Of Jullien's grand quadrilles?
With hats on head and morning coats
There footed to his prancing notes
    Our partner-girls and we;
And the gas-jets winked, and the lustres clinked,
And the platform throbbed as with arms enlinked
    We moved to the minstrelsy.

III

Who now recalls those crowded rooms
    Of old yclept 'The Argyle',
Where to the deep Drum-polka's booms
    We hopped in standard style?
Whither have danced those damsels now!
Is Death the partner who doth moue
    Their wormy chaps and bare?
Do their spectres spin like sparks within
The smoky halls of the Prince of Sin
    To a thunderous Jullien air?

166 The Dead Man Walking

THEY hail me as one living,
    But don't they know
That I have died of late years,
    Untombed although?

EXTRA PRINTINGS:
(1) *Selected Poems*, pp. 104–5
(2) *Chosen Poems*, pp. 136–7

TITLE:
The Dead man walking MS

Reminiscences of a Dancing Man
9 sightless] eighteen C
9 biers,] biers; Y, C, ER
11 Cremorne,] Cremorne Y, C, ER
16 There] Then C
19 enlinked] enlinked, C
22 Argyle] Argyll MS, Y, C, TL, WE1, PE
24 hopped] swung TL, PE
24 standard] boisterous MS, Y, C, ER
26 moue] mowe Y: mow C
Y, C add at end: 1895

I am but a shape that stands here,
A pulseless mould,
A pale past picture, screening
Ashes gone cold.

Not at a minute's warning,
Not in a loud hour,
For me ceased Time's enchantments
In hall and bower.

There was no tragic transit,
No catch of breath,
When silent seasons inched me
On to this death. . . .

– A Troubadour-youth I rambled
With Life for lyre,
The beats of being raging
In me like fire.

But when I practised eyeing
The goal of men,
It iced me, and I perished
A little then.

When passed my friend, my kinsfolk,
Through the Last Door,
And left me standing bleakly,
I died yet more;

And when my Love's heart kindled
In hate of me,
Wherefore I knew not, died I
One more degree.

And if when I died fully
I cannot say,
And changed into the corpse-thing
I am to-day;

The Dead Man Walking
10 Not] Nor MS
10 hour,] hour MS
14 No] Nor MS
16 On to this] Onward to MS
25 kinsfolk,] kinsfolk TL, WE, SP, PE, ME, CHP
36 to-day;] to-day, MS, CHP, CP4

Yet is it that, though whiling
The time somehow
In walking, talking, smiling,
I live not now.

The Dead Man Walking
MS adds: 1896

MORE LOVE LYRICS] Love Poems of Past Days (Years *del*) MS: LOVE LYRICS TL, PE

MORE LOVE LYRICS

167 1967

In five-score summers! All new eyes,
New minds, new modes, new fools, new wise;
New woes to weep, new joys to prize;

With nothing left of me and you
In that live century's vivid view
Beyond a pinch of dust or two;

A century which, if not sublime,
Will show, I doubt not, at its prime,
A scope above this blinkered time.

– Yet what to me how far above?
For I would only ask thereof
That thy worm should be my worm, Love!

16 Westbourne Park Villas, 1867

168 Her Definition

I lingered through the night to break of day,
Nor once did sleep extend a wing to me,
Intently busied with a vast array
Of epithets that should outfigure thee.

Full-featured terms – all fitless – hastened by,
And this sole speech remained: 'That maiden mine!' –
Debarred from due description then did I
Perceive the indefinite phrase could yet define.

As common chests encasing wares of price
Are borne with tenderness through halls of state,
For what they cover, so the poor device
Of homely wording I could tolerate,
Knowing its unadornment held as freight
The sweetest image outside Paradise.

W.P.V., Summer: 1866

1967
Westbourne Park] W.P. TL, PE

Her Definition
1 day,] day MS
5 Full-featured] Full-feathered MS
10 state,] state WE, ME
11 For . . . cover] Their core their warrant MS, TL, PE
W.P.V.] Westbourne Park Villas MS

169 *The Division*

RAIN on the windows, creaking doors,
With blasts that besom the green,
And I am here, and you are there,
And a hundred miles between!

O were it but the weather, Dear,
O were it but the miles
That summed up all our severance,
There might be room for smiles.

But that thwart thing betwixt us twain,
Which nothing cleaves or clears,
Is more than distance, Dear, or rain,
And longer than the years!

1893

EXTRA MANUSCRIPT:
In possession of Professor R. L. Purdy. This has not been available for checking.

EXTRA PRINTINGS:
(1) Stanzas 2 and 3 in *Second Fiddle* by Florence Henniker (London, 1912), p. 259 = SF
(2) *Selected Poems*, p. 28
(3) *Chosen Poems*, p. 28

170 *On the Departure Platform*

WE kissed at the barrier; and passing through
She left me, and moment by moment got
Smaller and smaller, until to my view
She was but a spot;

A wee white spot of muslin fluff
That down the diminishing platform bore
Through hustling crowds of gentle and rough
To the carriage door.

Under the lamplight's fitful glowers,
Behind dark groups from far and near,
Whose interests were apart from ours,
She would disappear,

Then show again, till I ceased to see
That flexible form, that nebulous white;
And she who was more than my life to me
Had vanished quite. . . .

EXTRA MANUSCRIPT:
Permission was refused to see the MS in the possession of Mr Frederick B. Adams, Jnr

EXTRA PRINTINGS:
(1) *Selected Poems*, pp. 8–9
(2) *Chosen Poems*, pp. 8–9

The Division
1–4 Not in SF
2 blasts] gusts MS
2 green,] green; MS
5 O] 'O! SF
5 Dear,] Dear; SF
6 O] O! SF
7 summed up all our] make our sum of MS, TL, SF, PE
7 summed] made WE1
8 smiles.] smiles! SF
9 But] 'But SF
9 thwart thing] dark cloud MS
9 twain,] twain SF, WE2 [MS has 'still' *deleted* in front of 'twain']
10] Which hides, yet reappears, TL, SF, PE
10 cleaves] cloaks MS
12 years!] years!' SF
1893] Not in MS, TL, SF, WE1, SP, PE: 189– WE2, ME, CP1–3 [Hardy's copy of SP in DCM adds '189–'. His copy of CP2 has been corrected to '1893']

On the Departure Platform
4 spot;] spot, – MS
10 near,] near WE, SP, ME
15 my life] them all MS
16 quite. . . .] quite. . . . . MS

We have penned new plans since that fair fond day,
And in season she will appear again –
Perhaps in the same soft white array –
But never as then!

– 'And why, young man, must eternally fly
A joy you'll repeat, if you love her well?'
– O friend, nought happens twice thus; why,
I cannot tell!

171 *In a Cathedral City*

EXTRA PRINTINGS:
(1) *Selected Poems*, p. 10
(2) *Chosen Poems*, p. 10

THESE people have not heard your name;
No loungers in this placid place
Have helped to bruit your beauty's fame.

The grey Cathedral, towards whose face
Bend eyes untold, has met not yours;
Your shade has never swept its base,

Your form has never darked its doors,
Nor have your faultless feet once thrown
A pensive pit-pat on its floors.

Along the street to maids well known
Blithe lovers hum their tender airs,
But in your praise voice not a tone. . . .

– Since nought bespeaks you here, or bears,
As I, your imprint through and through,
Here might I rest, till my heart shares
The spot's unconsciousness of you!

Salisbury

172 *I Say, 'I'll Seek Her*

EXTRA PRINTINGS:
(1) *Selected Poems*, p. 11
(2) *Chosen Poems*, p. 11

TITLE:
'I say I'll seek her' MS [The comma and quote were missing from all editions until *Complete Poems* when they were introduced in keeping with the first line]

I SAY, 'I'll seek her side
Ere hindrance interposes;'
But eve in midnight closes,
And here I still abide.

On the Departure Platform
17 penned] shaped MS
21 fly] die MS
23 why,] why MS

In a Cathedral City
2 placid] quiet MS
3 bruit] spread MS
10 maids well] maidens WE, SP, ME
16 you!] you. MS

I Say, 'I'll Seek Her
2 hindrance] peril MS, TL, PE

When darkness wears I see
        Her sad eyes in a vision;
        They ask, 'What indecision
Detains you, Love, from me? –

'The creaking hinge is oiled,
        I have unbarred the backway,
        But you tread not the trackway;
And shall the thing be spoiled?

'Far cockcrows echo shrill,
        The shadows are abating,
        And I am waiting, waiting;
But O, you tarry still!'

173 Her Father

TITLE:
Her father MS

I MET her, as we had privily planned,
Where passing feet beat busily:
She whispered: 'Father is at hand!
        He wished to walk with me.'

His presence as he joined us there
Banished our words of warmth away;
We felt, with cloudings of despair,
        What Love must lose that day.

Her crimson lips remained unkissed,
Our fingers kept no tender hold,
His lack of feeling made the tryst
        Embarrassed, stiff, and cold.

A cynic ghost then rose and said,
'But is his love for her so small
That, nigh to yours, it may be read
        As of no worth at all?

'You love her for her pink and white;
But what when their fresh splendours close?
His love will last her in despite
        Of Time, and wrack, and foes.'

Weymouth

I Say, 'I'll Seek Her
6 sad] great MS, TL, WE, SP, PE
6 vision;] vision: MS
11 trackway;] trackway CP4 [probably print deterioration]

Her Father
16 worth] count MS, TL, PE
MS has '1869' *deleted* at end

174 At Waking

WHEN night was lifting,
And dawn had crept under its shade,
Amid cold clouds drifting
Dead-white as a corpse outlaid,
With a sudden scare
I seemed to behold
My Love in bare
Hard lines unfold.

Yea, in a moment,
An insight that would not die
Killed her old endowment
Of charm that had capped all nigh,
Which vanished to none
Like the gilt of a cloud,
And showed her but one
Of the common crowd.

She seemed but a sample
Of earth's poor average kind,
Lit up by no ample
Enrichments of mien or mind.
I covered my eyes
As to cover the thought,
And unrecognize
What the morn had taught.

O vision appalling
When the one believed-in thing
Is seen falling, falling,
With all to which hope can cling.
Off: it is not true;
For it cannot be
That the prize I drew
Is a blank to me!

Weymouth, 1869

At Waking
1 lifting,] lifting MS
4 Dead-white] Dead white MS
10] Those words she had written awry MS *before revision*
12] And gifts that had cheaped all nigh, MS *before revision*

175 Four Footprints

HERE are the tracks upon the sand
Where stood last evening she and I –
Pressed heart to heart and hand to hand;
The morning sun has baked them dry.

I kissed her wet face – wet with rain,
For arid grief had burnt up tears,
While reached us as in sleeping pain
The distant gurgling of the weirs.

'I have married him – yes; feel that ring;
'Tis a week ago that he put it on. . . .
A dutiful daughter does this thing,
And resignation succeeds anon!

'But that I body and soul was yours
Ere he'd possession, he'll never know.
He's a confident man. "The husband scores,"
He says, "in the long run" . . . Now, Dear, go!'

I went. And to-day I pass the spot;
It is only a smart the more to endure;
And she whom I held is as though she were not,
For they have resumed their honeymoon tour.

176 In the Vaulted Way

TITLE:
In the Crypted Way MS, TL, PE

IN the vaulted way, where the passage turned
To the shadowy corner that none could see,
You paused for our parting, – plaintively;
Though overnight had come words that burned
My fond frail happiness out of me.

And then I kissed you, – despite my thought
That our spell must end when reflection came
On what you had deemed me, whose one long aim
Had been to serve you; that what I sought
Lay not in a heart that could breathe such blame.

Four Footprints
16 run" . . .] run" . . . . . MS
18 smart] pang MS, TL, PE
19 not,] not: MS
20 For they] The pair MS

In the Vaulted Way
1 vaulted] crypted MS, TL, PE
3] You lingered, to part from me, – wistfully; MS
3 for our parting] to part from me TL, WE1, PE, CP1

But yet I kissed you; whereon you again
As of old kissed me. Why, why was it so?
Do you cleave to me after that light-tongued blow?
If you scorned me at eventide, how love then?
The thing is dark, Dear. I do not know.

177 *In the Mind's Eye*

THAT was once her casement,
  And the taper nigh,
Shining from within there,
  Beckoned, 'Here am I!'

Now, as then, I see her
  Moving at the pane;
Ah; 'tis but her phantom
  Borne within my brain! –

Foremost in my vision
  Everywhere goes she;
Change dissolves the landscapes,
  She abides with me.

Shape so sweet and shy, Dear,
  Who can say thee nay?
Never once do I, Dear,
  Wish thy ghost away.

EXTRA PRINTINGS:
(1) *Selected Poems*, p. 81
(2) *Chosen Poems*, p. 76

TITLE:
The Phantom MS, TL, WE, PE, CP1–3
The Face in the Mind's Eye SP
[Hardy's copy of WE1 has note 'Better = In the mind's eye'. His CP2 has note 'Alter title "The Phantom" to "In the Mind's Eye" as in Selections . . .']

Note In MS 'Looking Back' (928) is written between 'In the Crypted Way' and 'The Phantom'

178 *The End of the Episode*

INDULGE no more may we
In this sweet-bitter pastime:
The love-light shines the last time
Between you, Dear, and me.

In the Vaulted Way
13 light-tongued] hot-tongued MS
MS adds '1870'

In the Mind's Eye
3 there,] there MS, TL, WE, PE, ME, CP1–3 [The comma in Hardy's copy of SP (1917) has been deleted, and then stetted. A note inserted on a sheet of paper says 'We think that the comma should stand unless the one in l. 2 is also deleted.']
14 nay?] nay! MS

The End of the Episode
4 Dear] Sweet TL, WE1, PE, CP1

There shall remain no trace
Of what so closely tied us,
And blank as ere love eyed us
Will be our meeting-place.

The flowers and thymy air,
Will they now miss our coming?
The dumbles thin their humming
To find we haunt not there?

Though fervent was our vow,
Though ruddily ran our pleasure,
Bliss has fulfilled its measure,
And sees its sentence now.

Ache deep; but make no moans:
Smile out; but stilly suffer:
The paths of love are rougher
Than thoroughfares of stones.

179 *The Sigh*

LITTLE head against my shoulder,
Shy at first, then somewhat bolder,
And up-eyed;
Till she, with a timid quaver,
Yielded to the kiss I gave her;
But, she sighed.

That there mingled with her feeling
Some sad thought she was concealing
It implied.
– Not that she had ceased to love me,
None on earth she set above me;
But she sighed.

She could not disguise a passion,
Dread, or doubt, in weakest fashion
If she tried:

The End of the Episode
8 meeting-place] trysting-place MS
16 sentence] ending MS

Nothing seemed to hold us sundered,
Hearts were victors; so I wondered
Why she sighed.

Afterwards I knew her throughly,
And she loved me staunchly, truly,
Till she died;
But she never made confession
Why, at that first sweet concession,
She had sighed.

It was in our May, remember;
And though now I near November,
And abide
Till my appointed change, unfretting,
Sometimes I sit half regretting
That she sighed.

TITLE:
'In the night she came' MS

180 *In the Night She Came*

I TOLD her when I left one day
That whatsoever weight of care
Might strain our love, Time's mere assault
Would work no changes there.
And in the night she came to me,
Toothless, and wan, and old,
With leaden concaves round her eyes,
And wrinkles manifold.

I tremblingly exclaimed to her,
'O wherefore do you ghost me thus!
I have said that dull defacing Time
Will bring no dreads to us.'
'And is that true of *you*?' she cried
In voice of troubled tune.
I faltered: 'Well . . . I did not think
You would test me quite so soon!'

In the Night She Came
11 dull] mere MS
15 Well . . .] Well. . . . MS

She vanished with a curious smile,
Which told me, plainlier than by word,
That my staunch pledge could scarce beguile
The fear she had averred.
Her doubts then wrought their shape in me,
And when next day I paid
My due caress, we seemed to be
Divided by some shade.

181 The Conformers

YES; we'll wed, my little fay,
And you shall write you mine,
And in a villa chastely gray
We'll house, and sleep, and dine.
But those night-screened, divine,
Stolen trysts of heretofore,
We of choice ecstasies and fine
Shall know no more.

The formal faced cohue
Will then no more upbraid
With smiting smiles and whisperings two
Who have thrown less loves in shade.
We shall no more evade
The searching light of the sun,
Our game of passion will be played,
Our dreaming done.

We shall not go in stealth
To rendezvous unknown,
But friends will ask me of your health,
And you about my own.
When we abide alone,
No leapings each to each,
But syllables in frigid tone
Of household speech.

The Conformers
1 fay,] fay WE2
5 night-screened, divine,] night-screened divine MS
6] Stolen dalliances of yore, MS
9 formal faced] Some late reprints of CP4 have 'formal-faced'
21 alone,] alone MS

Note On the verso of f. 53 of MS Hardy has written, and then crossed through:

The Conformers
Yes, we'll wed, my little fay/And you shall write you mine,/ And in a cot of brown or gray/We'll house, and sleep, and dine./But those night-screened divine

When down to dust we glide
Men will not say askance,
As now: 'How all the country side
Rings with their mad romance!'
But as they graveward glance
Remark: 'In them we lose
A worthy pair, who helped advance
Sound parish views.'

182 *The Dawn after the Dance*

HERE is your parents' dwelling with its curtained windows telling
Of no thought of us within it or of our arrival here;
Their slumbers have been normal after one day more of formal
Matrimonial commonplace and household life's mechanic gear.

I would be candid willingly, but dawn draws on so chillingly
As to render further cheerlessness intolerable now,
So I will not stand endeavouring to declare a day for severing,
But will clasp you just as always – just the olden love avow.

Through serene and surly weather we have walked the ways together,
And this long night's dance this year's end eve now finishes the spell;
Yet we dreamt us but beginning a sweet sempiternal spinning
Of a cord we have spun to breaking – too intemperately, too well.

Yes; last night we danced I know, Dear, as we did that year ago, Dear,
When a new strange bond between our days was formed, and felt, and heard;
Would that dancing were the worst thing from the latest to the first thing
That the faded year can charge us with; but what avails a word!

That which makes man's love the lighter and the woman's burn no brighter
Came to pass with us inevitably while slipped the shortening year....
And there stands your father's dwelling with its blind bleak windows telling
That the vows of man and maid are frail as filmy gossamere.

Weymouth, 1869

The Dawn after the Dance
5 I would be candid] Be candid would I MS, TL, PE
10 this year's end eve] This phrase is found like this in MS and all editions up to CP4, except WE and ME where it became 'this year's-end eve'. In CP4 it became 'this-year's end eve'. I can find no authority for this change
13 Dear . . . Dear] dear . . . dear MS
14 heard;] heard: MS
17 lighter] lighter, MS
17 burn no] love the MS *before revision*
17 brighter] brighter, MS
18 year. . . .] year. . . . . MS
19 blind] blank MS, TL1
19 bleak] blear MS
20 frail . . . gossamere] flimsy, frail, and insincere MS, TL1
20 as filmy gossamere] and fitful mouthings mere TL2, PE

Note In Vere H. Collins's *Talks with Thomas Hardy at Max Gate 1920–1922* (London, 1928), in reply to the question, 'What is "that which makes man's love the lighter and the woman's burn no brighter"?', Hardy replied, 'I suppose when they got intimate . . . I think perhaps I originally wrote "*the* brighter".'

183 *The Sun on the Letter*

TITLE:
A Discord MS *before revision*

I DREW the letter out, while gleamed
The sloping sun from under a roof
Of cloud whose verge rose visibly.

The burning ball flung rays that seemed
Stretched like a warp without a woof
Across the levels of the lea

To where I stood, and where they beamed
As brightly on the page of proof
That she had shown her false to me

As if it had shown her true – had teemed
With passionate thought for my behoof
Expressed with their own ardency!

184 *The Night of the Dance*

EXTRA PRINTINGS:
(1) *Selected Poems*, p. 22
(2) *Chosen Poems*, p. 22

THE cold moon hangs to the sky by its horn,
    And centres its gaze on me;
The stars, like eyes in reverie,
Their westering as for a while forborne,
    Quiz downward curiously.

Old Robert draws the backbrand in,
    The green logs steam and spit;
The half-awakened sparrows flit
From the riddled thatch; and owls begin
    To whoo from the gable-slit.

Yes; far and nigh things seem to know
    Sweet scenes are impending here;
That all is prepared; that the hour is near
For welcomes, fellowships, and flow
    Of sally, song, and cheer;

The Sun on the Letter
4 burning] red round MS
10 it] she MS, TL, PE
10 – had] and MS

The Night of the Dance
1 horn,] horn MS
3 in reverie] that idle be MS, TL, PE
6 draws] drags MS: hauls WE, SP, ME

That spigots are pulled and viols strung;
That soon will arise the sound
Of measures trod to tunes renowned;
That She will return in Love's low tongue
My vows as we wheel around.

185 Misconception

I BUSIED myself to find a sure
Snug hermitage
That should preserve my Love secure
From the world's rage;
Where no unseemly saturnals,
Or strident traffic-roars,
Or hum of intervolved cabals
Should echo at her doors.

I laboured that the diurnal spin
Of vanities
Should not contrive to suck her in
By dark degrees,
And cunningly operate to blur
Sweet teachings I had begun;
And then I went full-heart to her
To expound the glad deeds done.

She looked at me, and said thereto
With a pitying smile,
'And *this* is what has busied you
So long a while?
O poor exhausted one, I see
You have worn you old and thin
For naught! Those moils you fear for me
I find most pleasure in!'

Misconception
16 deeds] deed MS
19 *this*] this MS
22 thin] bare MS
23–4] For naught! Fear you those things for me?/For little else I care!' MS
24] My nature revels in!' WE, ME

186 *The Voice of the Thorn*

I

When the thorn on the down
Quivers naked and cold,
And the mid-aged and old
Pace the path there to town,
In these words dry and drear
It seems to them sighing:
'O winter is trying
To sojourners here!'

II

When it stands fully tressed
On a hot summer day,
And the ewes there astray
Find its shade a sweet rest,
By the breath of the breeze
It inquires of each farer:
'Who would not be sharer
Of shadow with these?'

III

But by day or by night,
And in winter or summer,
Should I be the comer
Along that lone height,
In its voicing to me
Only one speech is spoken:
'Here once was nigh broken
A heart, and by thee.'

The Voice of the Thorn
24 thee.] thee! MS

TITLE:
From her in the country MS

187 From Her in the Country

I THOUGHT and thought of thy crass clanging town
To folly, till convinced such dreams were ill,
I held my heart in bond, and tethered down
Fancy to where I was, by force of will.

I said: How beautiful are these flowers, this wood,
One little bud is far more sweet to me
Than all man's urban shows; and then I stood
Urging new zest for bird, and bush, and tree;

And strove to feel my nature brought it forth
Of instinct, or no rural maid was I;
But it was vain; for I could not see worth
Enough around to charm a midge or fly,

And mused again on city din and sin,
Longing to madness I might move therein!

16 W.P.V., 1866

188 Her Confession

AS some bland soul, to whom a debtor says
'I'll now repay the amount I owe to you,'
In inward gladness feigns forgetfulness
That such a payment ever was his due

(His long thought notwithstanding), so did I
At our last meeting waive your proffered kiss
With quick divergent talk of scenery nigh,
By such suspension to enhance my bliss.

And as his looks in consternation fall
When, gathering that the debt is lightly deemed,
The debtor makes as not to pay at all,
So faltered I, when your intention seemed

Converted by my false uneagerness
To putting off for ever the caress.

W.P.V., 1865–67

From Her in the Country
8 zest . . . bush] interest in bird, bush MS
14] Longing still more that I might be therein! MS
W.P.V.] Westbourne Park Villas MS

Her Confession
1 soul,] soul (MS
2 amount] sum MS
2 you,'] you,') MS
12 faltered] also MS
W.P.V.] Westbourne Park Villas MS

189 *To an Impersonator of Rosalind*

TITLE:
To an impersonator of Rosalind MS

DID he who drew her in the years ago –
Till now conceived creator of her grace –
With telescopic sight high natures know,
Discern remote in Time's untravelled space

Your soft sweet mien, your gestures, as do we,
And with a copyist's hand but set them down,
Glowing yet more to dream our ecstasy
When his Original should be forthshown?

For, kindled by that animated eye,
Whereto all fairnesses about thee brim,
And by thy tender tones, what wight can fly
The wild conviction welling up in him

That he at length beholds woo, parley, plead,
The 'very, very Rosalind' indeed!

8 Adelphi Terrace, 21 April 1867

190 *To an Actress*

I READ your name when you were strange to me,
Where it stood blazoned bold with many more;
I passed it vacantly, and did not see
Any great glory in the shape it wore.

O cruelty, the insight barred me then!
Why did I not possess me with its sound,
And in its cadence catch and catch again
Your nature's essence floating therearound?

Could *that* man be this I, unknowing you,
When now the knowing you is all of me,
And the old world of then is now a new,
And purpose no more what it used to be –
A thing of formal journeywork, but due
To springs that then were sealed up utterly?

1867

To an Impersonator of Rosalind
3 telescopic sight high] that far prescience highest MS
13 plead,] plead WE, ME
8 Adelphi Terrace] Not in MS (which has 'W.P.V.' *deleted*), TL, PE, WE1

To an Actress
14 then . . . up] were a sealed source MS, TL, PE
MS has *deleted* at end: Westbourne Park Villas

TITLE:
The minute before meeting MS

191 *The Minute before Meeting*

THE grey gaunt days dividing us in twain
Seemed hopeless hills my strength must faint to climb,
But they are gone; and now I would detain
The few clock-beats that part us; rein back Time,

And live in close expectance never closed
In change for far expectance closed at last,
So harshly has expectance been imposed
On my long need while these slow blank months passed.

And knowing that what is now about to be
Will all *have been* in O, so short a space!
I read beyond it my despondency
When more dividing months shall take its place,
Thereby denying to this hour of grace
A full-up measure of felicity.

1871

EXTRA PRINTINGS:
(1) *Selected Poems*, pp. 90–1
(2) *Chosen Poems*, pp. 85–6

TITLE:
He abjures Love MS

192 *He Abjures Love*

AT last I put off love,
For twice ten years
The daysman of my thought,
And hope, and doing;
Being ashamed thereof,
And faint of fears
And desolations, wrought
In his pursuing,

Since first in youthtime those
Disquietings
That heart-enslavement brings
To hale and hoary,

Became my housefellows,
  And, fool and blind,
I turned from kith and kind
  To give him glory.

I was as children be
  Who have no care;
I did not shrink or sigh,
  I did not sicken;
But lo, Love beckoned me,
  And I was bare,
And poor, and starved, and dry,
  And fever-stricken.

Too many times ablaze
  With fatuous fires,
Enkindled by his wiles
  To new embraces,
Did I, by wilful ways
  And baseless ires,
Return the anxious smiles
  Of friendly faces.

No more will now rate I
  The common rare,
The midnight drizzle dew,
  The gray hour golden,
The wind a yearning cry,
  The faulty fair,
Things dreamt, of comelier hue
  Than things beholden!...

– I speak as one who plumbs
  Life's dim profound,
One who at length can sound
  Clear views and certain.
But – after love what comes?
  A scene that lours,
A few sad vacant hours,
  And then, the Curtain.

1883

He Abjures Love
19 shrink] think MS, TL, WE1, SP, PE
26 fatuous] sudden MS
37 wind a yearning] creak a jealous TL, PE
37 yearning] jealous MS
38] The day a care, MS: The speech a snare, TL, PE
39] Things dreamt of as more fair MS
40 beholden! . . .] beholden! . . . . MS
42 profound,] profound – MS
43 can sound] has found MS
44 Clear] Vast MS
48 then,] then MS
48 Curtain] curtain MS

A SET OF COUNTRY SONGS

193 Let Me Enjoy

(MINOR KEY)

I

LET me enjoy the earth no less
Because the all-enacting Might
That fashioned forth its loveliness
Had other aims than my delight

II

About my path there flits a Fair,
Who throws me not a word or sign;
I'll charm me with her ignoring air,
And laud the lips not meant for mine.

III

From manuscripts of moving song
Inspired by scenes and dreams unknown
I'll pour out raptures that belong
To others, as they were my own.

IV

And some day hence, toward Paradise
And all its blest – if such should be –
I will lift glad, afar-off eyes,
Though it contain no place for me.

EXTRA PRINTINGS:
(1) *The Cornhill Magazine*, April 1909, p. [433] = C
(2) *Putnam's Magazine* (New York), April 1909, p. 60 = P
(3) *Selected Poems*, p. 26
(4) *Chosen Poems*, p. 26

TITLE:
Let me enjoy MS
'Let Me Enjoy' SP
(MINOR KEY)] Not in SP, CHP, CP4 [Hardy's corrected copy of SP (1917) has the manuscript note, 'Possibly these words are not required here when the poem is detached from "A Set of Country Songs".']

INDENTATION:
1 = ll. 1, 3 } and so throughout P
2 = ll. 2, 4 }

Note This was one of nine poems chosen by Hardy for the Library of the Royal Dolls' House at Windsor Castle

Let Me Enjoy
1 earth] Earth MS, C, P
5 Fair,] Fair C, P
7] I will find charm in her uncare, (loth air, C, P) MS, C, P, TL, PE
8 the] those MS, C, P, TL, PE
9 moving song] rapturous strain MS
9 moving] tender C, P
10 dreams] souls MS, C, P, TL, CP1, 2
10 unknown] unknown, MS, C, P, TL, WE, ME, CP1–3, PE [Hardy's copy of SP in DCM has the comma inserted, then deleted, with the note, 'Omit in Collected Edn & C']
11 raptures that belong] songs that appertain MS
13] Perhaps some day, toward Paradise MS, TL, PE
13 toward] towards TL, PE, CP3, 4
15 will] shall MS, TL, PE
15 lift] cast C, P

At Casterbridge Fair

194 I. The Ballad-Singer

SING, Ballad-singer, raise a hearty tune;
Make me forget that there was ever a one
I walked with in the meek light of the moon
When the day's work was done.

Rhyme, Ballad-rhymer, start a country song;
Make me forget that she whom I loved well
Swore she would love me dearly, love me long,
Then – what I cannot tell!

Sing, Ballad-singer, from your little book;
Make me forget those heart-breaks, achings, fears;
Make me forget her name, her sweet sweet look –
Make me forget her tears.

EXTRA PRINTINGS:
(1) *The Cornhill Magazine*, April 1902, p. [433] = C
(2) *Selected Poems*, p. 27
(3) *Chosen Poems*, p. 27

TITLE:
C has title 'At Casterbridge Fair', not *The Ballad-Singer*

195 II. Former Beauties

THESE market-dames, mid-aged, with lips thin-drawn,
And tissues sere,
Are they the ones we loved in years agone,
And courted here?

Are these the muslined pink young things to whom
We vowed and swore
In nooks on summer Sundays by the Froom,
Or Budmouth shore?

Do they remember those gay tunes we trod
Clasped on the green;
Aye; trod till moonlight set on the beaten sod
A satin sheen?

The Ballad-Singer
1 tune;] tune! C
5 song;] song! C
7 long,] long; C
8 tell!] tell. C
9 book;] book! C
10 heart-breaks] heartbreaks C
11 her sweet] her sweet, C, SP
11 look –] look; C
1901 *del* MS at end

They must forget, forget! They cannot know
    What once they were,
Or memory would transfigure them, and show
    Them always fair.

TITLE:
After the Club-dance MS

196 *III. After the Club-Dance*

BLACK'ON frowns east on Maidon,
    And westward to the sea,
But on neither is his frown laden
    With scorn, as his frown on me!

At dawn my heart grew heavy,
    I could not sip the wine,
I left the jocund bevy
    And that young man o' mine.

The roadside elms pass by me, –
    Why do I sink with shame
When the birds a-perch there eye me?
    They, too, have done the same!

EXTRA PRINTING:
The Venture, ed. Laurence Housman and W. Somerset Maugham (London, 1903), p. 10 = V

TITLE:
The market-girl MS
The Market Girl
(Country Song) V

197 *IV. The Market-Girl*

NOBODY took any notice of her as she stood on the causey kerb,
All eager to sell her honey and apples and bunches of garden herb;
And if she had offered to give her wares and herself with them too that day,
I doubt if a soul would have cared to take a bargain so choice away.

But chancing to trace her sunburnt grace that morning as I passed nigh,
I went and I said 'Poor maidy dear! – and will none of the people buy?'
And so it began; and soon we knew what the end of it all must be,
And I found that though no others had bid, a prize had been won by me.

After the Club-Dance
1 Maidon,] Maidon MS
4 as] like MS, TL, PE
5 heavy,] heavy MS
8] Full o' this fault o' mine. MS

The Market-Girl
1 causey kerb] causey-kerb V
2 All eager] A-trying MS, V, TL, PE
2 apples] apples, V
3 wares] wares, V
3 too] too, V
6 said] said, MS, V, WE, ME
6 maidy dear! – and] maidy, dear! And V
6 of] o' V

198 V. *The Inquiry*

TITLE:
The inquiry MS

AND are ye one of Hermitage –
Of Hermitage, by Ivel Road,
And do ye know, in Hermitage
A thatch-roofed house where sengreens grow?
And does John Waywood live there still –
He of the name that there abode
When father hurdled on the hill
Some fifteen years ago?

Does he now speak o' Patty Beech,
The Patty Beech he used to – see,
Or ask at all if Patty Beech
Is known or heard of out this way?
– Ask ever if she's living yet,
And where her present home may be,
And how she bears life's fag and fret
After so long a day?

In years agone at Hermitage
This faded face was counted fair,
None fairer; and at Hermitage
We swore to wed when he should thrive.
But never a chance had he or I,
And waiting made his wish outwear,
And Time, that dooms man's love to die,
Preserves a maid's alive.

199 VI. *A Wife Waits*

TITLE:
Waiting MS

WILL's at the dance in the Club-room below,
Where the tall liquor-cups foam;
I on the pavement up here by the Bow,
Wait, wait, to steady him home.

The Inquiry
3 Hermitage] Hermitage, MS

Will and his partner are treading a tune,
        Loving companions they be;
Willy, before we were married in June,
        Said he loved no one but me;

Said he would let his old pleasures all go
        Ever to live with his Dear.
Will's at the dance in the Club-room below,
        Shivering I wait for him here.

NOTE. – 'The Bow' (line 3). The old name for the curved corner by the cross-streets in the middle of Casterbridge.

200 VII. *After the Fair*

INDENTATION:
1 = ll. 1, 3, 5
2 = l. 6
3 = ll. 2, 4
} and so throughout MS, TL, WE, PE

THE singers are gone from the Cornmarket-place
        With their broadsheets of rhymes,
The street rings no longer in treble and bass
        With their skits on the times,
And the Cross, lately thronged, is a dim naked space
        That but echoes the stammering chimes.

From Clock-corner steps, as each quarter ding-dongs,
        Away the folk roam
By the 'Hart' and Grey's Bridge into byways and 'drongs',
        Or across the ridged loam;
The younger ones shrilling the lately heard songs,
        The old saying, 'Would we were home.'

The shy-seeming maiden so mute in the fair
        Now rattles and talks,
And that one who looked the most swaggering there
        Grows sad as she walks,
And she who seemed eaten by cankering care
        In statuesque sturdiness stalks.

And midnight clears High Street of all but the ghosts
        Of its buried burghees,
From the latest far back to those old Roman hosts
        Whose remains one yet sees,

A Wife Waits
7 Willy,] Willy MS, TL, WE, ME
7 June,] June MS
8 me;] me. MS
10 live] be MS
NOTE] MS, TL, PE add: It is not now so inscribed, and the spot has to be designated by a circumlocution, to the inconvenience of market-men in their appointments.

After the Fair
1 Cornmarket-place] cornmarket-place MS
19 High Street] High-street MS

Who loved, laughed, and fought, hailed their friends, drank their toasts
    At their meeting-times here, just as these!

1902

NOTE. – 'The chimes' (line 6) will be listened for in vain here at midnight now, having been abolished some years ago.

201 *The Dark-Eyed Gentleman*

TITLE: The Dark-eyed Gentleman MS

I

I PITCHED my day's leazings in Crimmercrock Lane,
To tie up my garter and jog on again,
When a dear dark-eyed gentleman passed there and said,
In a way that made all o' me colour rose-red,
        'What do I see –
        O pretty knee!'
And he came and he tied up my garter for me.

II

'Twixt sunset and moonrise it was, I can mind:
Ah, 'tis easy to lose what we nevermore find! –
Of the dear stranger's home, of his name, I knew nought,
But I soon knew his nature and all that it brought.
        Then bitterly
        Sobbed I that he
Should ever have tied up my garter for me!

III

Yet now I've beside me a fine lissom lad,
And my slip's nigh forgot, and my days are not sad;
My own dearest joy is he, comrade, and friend,
He it is who safe-guards me, on him I depend;
        No sorrow brings he,
        And thankful I be
That his daddy once tied up my garter for me!

NOTE. – 'Leazings' (line 1), bundle of gleaned corn.

After the Fair
NOTE] Not in MS

The Dark-Eyed Gentleman
1 leazings] leaze-nitch MS [A note is added that a 'leaze-nitch' is a bundle of gleaned corn]
1 Lane,] Lane MS
4 rose-red] up red MS
12 bitterly] bitter-ly MS
18 depend;] depend. MS

202 *To Carrey Clavel*

YOU turn your back, you turn your back,
And never your face to me,
Alone you take your homeward track,
And scorn my company.

What will you do when Charley's seen
Dewbeating down this way?
– You'll turn your back as now, you mean?
Nay, Carrey Clavel, nay!

You'll see none's looking; put your lip
Up like a tulip, so;
And he will coll you, bend, and sip:
Yes, Carrey, yes; I know!

203 *The Orphaned Old Maid*

I WANTED to marry, but father said, 'No –
'Tis weakness in women to give themselves so;
If you care for your freedom you'll listen to me,
Make a spouse in your pocket, and let the men be.'

I spake on't again and again: father cried,
'Why – if you go husbanding, where shall I bide?
For never a home's for me elsewhere than here!'
And I yielded; for father had ever been dear.

But now father's gone, and I feel growing old,
And I'm lonely and poor in this house on the wold,
And my sweetheart that was found a partner elsewhere,
And nobody flings me a thought or a care.

204 *The Spring Call*

DOWN Wessex way, when spring's a-shine,
The blackbird's 'pret-ty de-urr!'
In Wessex accents marked as mine
Is heard afar and near.

The Spring Call

EXTRA PRINTINGS:
(1) *The Cornhill Magazine*, May 1906, p. 596 = C
(2) *The Society of Dorset Men in London Year-Book*, 1914–15, p. [2] = DYB

TITLE:
Down Wessex Way DYB

INDENTATION:
1 = ll. 1, 2, 3 } Stanzas 1 and 6 only of WE
2 = l. 4

The Spring Call
2 pret-ty] purr-ty C
3 mine] mine, C
4 near] ne-ar MS

He flutes it strong, as if in song
No R's of feebler tone
Than his appear in 'pretty dear',
Have blackbirds ever known.

Yet they pipe 'prattie deerh!' I glean,
Beneath a Scottish sky,
And 'pehty de-aw!' amid the treen
Of Middlesex or nigh.

While some folk say – perhaps in play –
Who know the Irish isle,
'Tis 'purrity dare!' in treeland there
When songsters would beguile.

Well: I'll say what the listening birds
Say, hearing 'pret-ty de-urr!' –
However strangers sound such words,
That's how we sound them here.

Yes, in this clime at pairing time,
As soon as eyes can see her
At dawn of day, the proper way
To call is 'pret-ty de-urr!'

205 *Julie-Jane*

SING; how 'a would sing!
How 'a would raise the tune
When we rode in the waggon from harvesting
By the light o' the moon!

Dance; how 'a would dance!
If a fiddlestring did but sound
She would hold out her coats, give a slanting glance,
And go round and round.

Laugh; how 'a would laugh!
Her peony lips would part
As if none such a place for a lover to quaff
At the deeps of a heart.

The Spring Call
7 pretty dear',] purr-ty de-urr!' C
7 dear',] dear' MS
9 prattie] prittie C, DYB
11 de-aw] deaw C
12 nigh.] nigh: DYB
18 pret-ty] purr-ty C
18 de-urr!' –] de-urr!' DYB
19 However] "However C
20 them here] 'em *he-urr* C
21 Yes] "Yes C
21 pairing time,] pairing-time C
22 her] her, C
23 At dawn of] At eve or C
24 pret-ty de-urr!'] purr-ty de-urr!' " C

Julie, O girl of joy,
Soon, soon that lover he came.
Ah, yes; and gave thee a baby-boy,
But never his name. . . .

– Tolling for her, as you guess;
And the baby too. . . . 'Tis well.
You knew her in maidhood likewise? – Yes,
That's her burial bell.

'I suppose,' with a laugh, she said,
'I should blush that I'm not a wife;
But how can it matter, so soon to be dead,
What one does in life!'

When we sat making the mourning
By her death-bed side, said she,
'Dears, how can you keep from your lovers, adorning
In honour of me!'

Bubbling and brightsome eyed!
But now – O never again.
She chose her bearers before she died
From her fancy-men.

NOTE. – It is, or was, a common custom in Wessex, and probably other country places, to prepare the mourning beside the death-bed, the dying person sometimes assisting, who also selects his or her bearers on such occasions.

'Coats' (line 7), old name for petticoats.

EXTRA PRINTINGS:
(1) *Selected Poems*, pp. 54–5
(2) *The Society of Dorset Men in London Year-Book*, 1922, pp. 3–4 = DYB

TITLE:
News for her mother MS

206 News for Her Mother

I

ONE mile more is
Where your door is,
Mother mine! –
Harvest's coming,
Mills are strumming,
Apples fine,
And the cider made to-year will be as wine.

Julie-Jane
18 too. . . .] too. . . . . MS
21 laugh,] laugh WE, ME

News for Her Mother
2 is,] is MS, TL, WE, SP, PE, ME
7 made] wrung DYB

II

Yet, not viewing
What's a-doing
Here around
Is it thrills me,
And so fills me
That I bound
Like a ball or leaf or lamb along the ground.

III

Tremble not now
At your lot now,
Silly soul!
Hosts have sped them
Quick to wed them,
Great and small,
Since the first two sighing half-hearts made a whole.

IV

Yet I wonder,
Will it sunder
Her from me?
Will she guess that
I said 'Yes,' – that
His I'd be,
Ere I thought she might not see him as I see!

V

Old brown gable,
Granary, stable,
Here you are!
O my mother,
Can another
Ever bar
Mine from thy heart, make thy nearness seem afar?

News for Her Mother
16 now,] now MS, TL, WE, SP, PE, ME

EXTRA PRINTING:
Chosen Poems, p. 53

207 *The Fiddler*

THE fiddler knows what's brewing
 To the lilt of his lyric wiles:
The fiddler knows what rueing
 Will come of this night's smiles!

He sees couples join them for dancing,
 And afterwards joining for life,
He sees them pay high for their prancing
 By a welter of wedded strife.

He twangs: 'Music hails from the devil,
 Though vaunted to come from heaven,
For it makes people do at a revel
 What multiplies sins by seven.

'There's many a heart now mangled,
 And waiting its time to go,
Whose tendrils were first entangled
 By my sweet viol and bow!'

208 *The Husband's View*

'CAN anything avail
Beldame, for my hid grief? –
Listen: I'll tell the tale,
It may bring faint relief! –

'I came where I was not known,
In hope to flee my sin;
And walking forth alone
A young man said, "Good e'en."

'In gentle voice and true
He asked to marry me;
"You only – only you
Fulfil my dream!" said he.

The Fiddler
2 wiles:] wiles, MS
10 heaven,] heaven CHP

The Husband's View
2 my hid] hidden WE, ME
3 tale,] tale MS
5 known,] known MS
8 e'en.] e'en, CP

'We married o' Monday morn,
In the month of hay and flowers;
My cares were nigh forsworn,
And perfect love was ours.

'But ere the days are long
Untimely fruit will show;
My Love keeps up his song,
Undreaming it is so.

'And I awake in the night,
And think of months gone by,
And of that cause of flight
Hidden from my Love's eye.

'Discovery borders near,
And then! . . . But something stirred? –
My husband – he is here!
Heaven – has he overheard?' –

'Yes; I have heard, sweet Nan;
I have known it all the time.
I am not a particular man;
Misfortunes are no crime:

'And what with our serious need
Of sons for soldiering,
That accident, indeed,
To maids, is a useful thing!'

209 *Rose-Ann*

WHY didn't you say you was promised, Rose-Ann?
  Why didn't you name it to me,
Ere ever you tempted me hither, Rose-Ann,
  So often, so wearifully?

O why did you let me be near 'ee, Rose-Ann,
  Talking things about wedlock so free,
And never by nod or by whisper, Rose-Ann,
  Give a hint that it wasn't to be?

The Husband's View
24 Hidden] Concealed WE, ME
26 then! . . .] then! . . . . MS
28 Heaven] God MS
34 sons] youths MS, TL, PE
36 maids] girls MS
36 thing!] thing. MS
33–6] 'And what with our want of men/For ships and soldiering,/That accident, now and then/To girls, is a useful thing.' MS *before revision*

Rose-Ann
1 Rose-Ann?] Rose-Ann, WE, ME [CP1 and 4 have the question-mark: CP2 and 3 lack it. This must be the result of print deterioration, put right in CP4]

Down home I was raising a flock of stock ewes,
    Cocks and hens, and wee chickens by scores,
And lavendered linen all ready to use,
    A-dreaming that they would be yours.

Mother said: 'She's a sport-making maiden, my son;'
    And a pretty sharp quarrel had we;
O why do you prove by this wrong you have done
    That I saw not what mother could see?

Never once did you say you was promised, Rose-Ann,
    Never once did I dream it to be;
And it cuts to the heart to be treated, Rose-Ann,
    As you in your scorning treat me!

EXTRA PRINTING:
The Graphic, Christmas Number 1903, p. 17 = G
Note The two-line stanzas are not italicised in MS

210 The Homecoming

Gruffly growled the wind on Toller downland broad and bare,
And lonesome was the house, and dark; and few came there.

'Now don't ye rub your eyes so red; we're home and have no cares;
Here's a skimmer-cake for supper, peckled onions, and some pears;
I've got a little keg o' summat strong, too, under stairs:
– What, slight your husband's victuals? Other brides can tackle theirs!'

The wind of winter mooed and mouthed their chimney like a horn,
And round the house and past the house 'twas leafless and lorn.

'But my dear and tender poppet, then, how came ye to agree
In Ivel church this morning? Sure, there-right you married me!'
– 'Hoo-hoo! – I don't know – I forgot how strange and far 'twould be,
An' I wish I was at home again with dear daddee!'

Gruffly growled the wind on Toller downland broad and bare,
And lonesome was the house and dark; and few came there.

'I didn't think such furniture as this was all you'd own,
And great black beams for ceiling, and a floor o' wretched stone,
And nasty pewter platters, horrid forks of steel and bone,
And a monstrous crock in chimney. 'Twas to me quite unbeknown!'

Rose-Ann
17 Rose-Ann,] Rose-Ann WE

The Homecoming
1 *downland*] *Downland* G
1 *broad*] *bleak* G
2 *house,*] *house* G
3 home] home, MS, G
3 have] hae G
4 skimmer-cake] skimmercake G
5 summat] sommat MS, G
6 tackle] welcome G
7 *mooed*] *mooed,* G
8 *the house 'twas*] *it all was* G
9 But] But, G
10 Ivel church] Ivell Church G
10 there-right] thereright MS
11 – 'Hoo-hoo] ' – Hoo-hoo G
11 don't know] don' know! G
11 strange] dark G
13 *downland*] *Downland* G
13 *broad*] *bleak* G
15 didn't . . . this] didn' think this ugly furniture G
16 wretched] chilly G
17 of] o' G
18 unbeknown!] unbeknown? G

Rattle rattle went the door; down flapped a cloud of smoke,
As shifting north the wicked wind assayed a smarter stroke.

'Now sit ye by the fire, poppet; put yourself at ease:
And keep your little thumb out of your mouth, dear, please!
And I'll sing to 'ee a pretty song of lovely flowers and bees,
And happy lovers taking walks within a grove o' trees.'

Gruffly growled the wind on Toller Down, so bleak and bare,
And lonesome was the house, and dark; and few came there.

'Now, don't ye gnaw your handkercher; 'twill hurt your little tongue,
And if you do feel spitish, 'tis because ye are over young;
But you'll be getting older, like us all, ere very long,
And you'll see me as I am – a man who never did 'ee wrong.'

Straight from Whit'sheet Hill to Benvill Lane the blusters pass,
Hitting hedges, milestones, handposts, trees, and tufts of grass.

'Well, had I only known, my dear, that this was how you'd be,
I'd have married her of riper years that was so fond of me.
But since I can't, I've half a mind to run away to sea,
And leave 'ee to go barefoot to your d—d daddee!'

Up one wall and down the other – past each window-pane –
Prance the gusts, and then away down Crimmercrock's long lane.

'I – I – don't know what to say to't, since your wife I've vowed to be;
And as 'tis done, I s'pose here I must bide – poor me!
Aye – as you are ki-ki-kind, I'll try to live along with 'ee,
Although I'd fain have stayed at home with dear daddee!'

Gruffly growled the wind on Toller Down, so bleak and bare,
And lonesome was the house and dark; and few came there.

'That's right, my Heart! And though on haunted Toller Down we be,
And the wind swears things in chimley, we'll to supper merrily!
So don't ye tap your shoe so pettish-like; but smile at me,
And ye'll soon forget to sock and sigh for dear daddee!'

December 1901

The Homecoming
19 *Rattle*] *Rattle*, G
19 *flapped*] *flopped* G
20 *As shifting north*] *As, shifting north*, G
20 *assayed*] *essayed* G
21–38 These lines are re-arranged in G as follows: 21–4 = G 27–30: 25–6 = G 31–2: 27–30 = G 33–6: 31–2 = G 37–8: 33–6 = G 21–4: 37–8 = G 25–6
21 yourself at ease:] yerself at ease, G
22 dear] Dear G
25 *Down*,] Down MS
25 *Down, so*] *Downland* G
26 *house*,] *house* G
27 Now, don't ye gnaw] Now don't ye bite G
30 am – a man] am, Dear – one G
30 wrong.] wrong!
33 Well,] Well; G
33 only] on'y MS, G, TL, WE, PE, ME
33 dear] Dear G
34 of . . . of] o' . . . o' G
36 d—d] dear G
37 *other* –] *other*, G
37 *window-pane* –] *window-pane*, G
39 your wife I've vowed] I've vowed your wife G
40 And] And, G
41 Aye . . . ki-ki-kind,] Aye, as you're ki-ki-kind G
43 *Down*,] Down MS
43 *Down, so*] *Downland* G
47 pettish-like;] pettish-like, G
48 sock] sob G
December 1901] Not in G

PIECES OCCASIONAL AND VARIOUS

PIECES . . .] MS shows that Hardy's first thought was 'Miscellaneous Verses', and then 'Miscellaneous Pieces'. Both were deleted

EXTRA PRINTINGS:
(1) *The Saturday Review*, 8 Sept 1906, p. 293 = SR
(2) *Selected Poems*, p. 128
(3) *The Early Life of Thomas Hardy* by Florence Emily Hardy (London, 1928), p. 17 = EL
(4) *Chosen Poems*, p. 162

TITLE:
A Church romance MS
Mellstock] Not in MS, SR, TL, PE
1835] 1836 EL

211 A Church Romance

(Mellstock: circa 1835)

SHE turned in the high pew, until her sight
Swept the west gallery, and caught its row
Of music-men with viol, book, and bow
Against the sinking sad tower-window light.

She turned again; and in her pride's despite
One strenuous viol's inspirer seemed to throw
A message from his string to her below,
Which said: 'I claim thee as my own forthright!'

Thus their hearts' bond began, in due time signed.
And long years thence, when Age had scared Romance,
At some old attitude of his or glance
That gallery-scene would break upon her mind,
With him as minstrel, ardent, young, and trim,
Bowing 'New Sabbath' or 'Mount Ephraim'.

EXTRA PRINTING:
The Graphic, Christmas Number 1902, p. 5 = G

INDENTATION:
1 = ll. 1, 3 } and so throughout
2 = ll. 2, 4 } G

212 The Rash Bride

An Experience of the Mellstock Quire

I

WE Christmas-carolled down the Vale, and up the Vale, and round the Vale,
We played and sang that night as we were yearly wont to do –
A carol in a minor key, a carol in the major D,
Then at each house: 'Good wishes: many Christmas joys to you!'

A Church Romance
1 She . . . pew] In the high pew she turned SR
3 viol, book,] viol book SR
4 sinking] sinking, EL
8 said:] said, SR
9 hearts'] heart's SR
9 signed.] signed, WE, SP, ME, EL
12–13 SR has stanza break
13 minstrel,] minstrel – SR
13 trim,] trim – SR

The Rash Bride
1 down] up G
1 and up] across G
1 round the Vale,] down the Vale; G
3 D,] D – G
4 Then] Then, G
4 house:] house, G
Note No stanza numbers in G

II

Next, to the widow's John and I and all the rest drew on. And I
Discerned that John could hardly hold the tongue of him for joy.
The widow was a sweet young thing whom John was bent on marry-
ing,
And quiring at her casement seemed romantic to the boy.

III

'She'll make reply, I trust,' said he, 'to our salute? She must!' said he,
'And then I will accost her gently – much to her surprise! –
For knowing not I am with you here, when I speak up and call her dear
A tenderness will fill her voice, a bashfulness her eyes.'

IV

So, by her window-square we stood; ay, with our lanterns there we
stood,
And he along with us, – not singing, waiting for a sign;
And when we'd quired her carols three a light was lit and out looked
she,
A shawl about her bedgown, and her colour red as wine.

V

And sweetly then she bowed her thanks, and smiled, and spoke aloud
her thanks;
When lo, behind her back there, in the room, a man appeared.
I knew him – one from Woolcomb way – Giles Swetman – honest as
the day,
But eager, hasty; and I felt that some strange trouble neared.

VI

'How comes he there? . . . Suppose,' said we, 'she's wed of late! Who
knows?' said we.
– 'She married yester-morning – only mother yet has known
The secret o't!' shrilled one small boy. 'But now I've told, let's wish
'em joy!'
A heavy fall aroused us: John had gone down like a stone.

The Rash Bride
5] Next to the widow's – John, and I, and Michael, and the rest. And I G
5 Next,] Next MS
6 joy.] joy: G
7 whom] who G
7 bent] nigh G
9 reply, I trust,'] reply,' at last G
9 salute?] salute. G
9 must!] must, MS, G
9 he,] he. ME
10 surprise! –] surprise! G
11 For] For, G
11 I am] I'm G
11 dear] Dear, G
13 So] – So G
13 window-square] darkened house G
14 us, . . . sign;] us – not singing – watching for a sign! G
15 three] three, G
16 bedgown,] bedgown G
17 bowed] spoke G
17 smiled, . . . aloud] bowed her thanks, and smiled G
18 back there] shoulder G
19 Woolcomb] Ivel G
21 there . . . late!] there?' at length said we. 'She wed?' said we. G
21 there? . . .] there? . . . . . MS
21 wed . . . Who] wed! said we. 'Who MS, TL, WE1, PE, CP1
22 yester-morning – only] yester morning! Only G
23 o't!] o't, G
23 shrilled] quoth MS, G, TL, WE1, PE
24 A] – A G
24 us:] us. G

VII

We rushed to him and caught him round, and lifted him, and brought him round,
When, hearing something wrong had happened, oped the window she:
'Has one of you fallen ill?' she asked, 'by these night labours over-tasked?'
None answered. That she'd done poor John a cruel turn felt we.

VIII

Till up spoke Michael: 'Fie, young dame! You've broke your promise, sly young dame,
By forming this new tie, young dame, and jilting John so true,
Who trudged to-night to sing to 'ee because he thought he'd bring to 'ee
Good wishes as your coming spouse. May ye such trifling rue!'

IX

Her man had said no word at all; but being behind had heard it all,
And now cried: 'Neighbours, on my soul I knew not 'twas like this!'
And then to her: 'If I had known you'd had in tow not me alone,
No wife should you have been of mine. It is a dear bought bliss!'

X

She changed death-white, and heaved a cry: we'd never heard so grieved a cry
As came from her at this from him: heartbroken quite seemed she;
And suddenly, as we looked on, she turned, and rushed; and she was gone,
Whither, her husband, following after, knew not; nor knew we.

XI

We searched till dawn about the house; within the house, without the house,
We searched among the laurel boughs that grew beneath the wall,
And then among the crocks and things, and stores for winter junketings,
In linhay, loft, and dairy; but we found her not at all.

The Rash Bride
25] We raised him, brought some life to him; and steadied him and spoke to him, G
26 she:] she. G
27 asked,] asked; G
28 None] – None G
28 turn] turn, G
29] Till up spoke Michael Mail: 'Young dame, you've wronged a loving heart, young dame, G
30 forming . . . tie] wedding this new man G
31 trudged] came
33 Her] – Her G
33 all . . . behind] all, but, being behind, G
33 all,] all: G
34 on my soul] scourge it all; G
35 had in tow] promised him – G
35 alone,] alone MS: alone – G
36 mine.] mine! G
36 dear bought] dear-bought G
37 She changed] – She grew G
37 cry: we'd] cry. We'd G
38 him:] him; G
39 And] And, G
39 rushed;] rushed, G
39 gone,] gone; G
40 Whither,] Whither MS: Where to, G
40 nor knew] nor did G
41] We searched till dawn – around the house, behind the house, and in the house; G
41 without the house,] without the house. ME
43 junketings,] junketings; G
44 dairy; but] outhouse. But G

XII

Then John rushed in: 'O friends,' he said, 'hear this, this, this!' and bends his head:
'I've – searched round by the – *well*, and find the cover open wide!
I am fearful that – I can't say what. . . . Bring lanterns, and some cords to knot.'
We did so, and we went and stood the deep dark hole beside.

XIII

And then they, ropes in hand, and I – ay, John, and all the band, and I
Let down a lantern to the depths – some hundred feet and more;
It glimmered like a fog-dimmed star; and there, beside its light, afar,
White drapery floated, and we knew the meaning that it bore.

XIV

The rest is naught. . . . We buried her o' Sunday. Neighbours carried her;
And Swetman – he who'd married her – now miserablest of men,
Walked mourning first; and then walked John; just quivering, but composed anon;
And we the quire formed round the grave, as was the custom then.

XV

Our old bass player, as I recall – his white hair blown – but why recall! –
His viol upstrapped, bent figure – doomed to follow her full soon –
Stood bowing, pale and tremulous; and next to him the rest of us. . . .
We sang the Ninetieth Psalm to her – set to Saint Stephen's tune.

213 *The Dead Quire*

I

BESIDE the Mead of Memories,
Where Church-way mounts to Moaning Hill,
The sad man sighed his phantasies:
He seems to sigh them still.

The Rash Bride
45] Then John rushed in. 'O, Will!' he said. 'Hear this,' he said, 'Ay, *this!*' he said. G
46 the – *well*,] the *well;* G
47 I am] I'm G
47 what. . . .] what. . . . . MS: what. – G
48 so,] so; G
48 went] went; G
48 hole] well G
49] And then in silence they and I – ay, John, and all the quire and I – G
49 I] I – MS
50 more;] more. MS, G
51 its light,] the light G
52 floated,] floated; G
53 Sunday. Neighbours] Sunday; neighbours G
53 her;] her: G
55 anon;] anon: G
56 formed round] drew nigh G
57 as . . . recall! –] I well can mind, his white hair fluttering, I can mind, G
58–60] His viol unstrapped – ay, sixty years ago it will be soon! . . ./ Stood bowing 'twixt the grave and wall; and next to him stood I, and all. . . ./The ninetieth Psalm we sung to her – set to St. Stephen's tune. G
60 Saint Stephen's] 'Saint Stephen's' WE2, ME [Hardy's copy of WE1 is corrected thus]

EXTRA PRINTINGS:
(1) *The Graphic*, Christmas Number 1901, p. 16 = G
(2) *Selected Poems*, pp. 155–60
(3) *Chosen Poems*, pp. 183–8

INDENTATION:
1 = ll. 1, 3 } and so throughout
2 = ll. 2, 4 } G

The Dead Quire
2 Church-way] Church-Way G
2 Hill,] Hill WE2
3 sad] meek TL, PE
3 sighed his phantasies:] spoke his phantasies G
4 sigh] speak G

II

' 'Twas the Birth-tide Eve, and the hamleteers
Made merry with ancient Mellstock zest,
But the Mellstock quire of former years
Had entered into rest.

III

'Old Dewy lay by the gaunt yew tree,
And Reuben and Michael a pace behind,
And Bowman with his family
By the wall that the ivies bind.

IV

'The singers had followed one by one,
Treble, and tenor, and thorough-bass;
And the worm that wasteth had begun
To mine their mouldering place.

V

'For two-score years, ere Christ-day light,
Mellstock had throbbed to strains from these;
But now there echoed on the night
No Christmas harmonies.

VI

'Three meadows off, at a dormered inn,
The youth had gathered in high carouse,
And, ranged on settles, some therein
Had drunk them to a drowse.

VII

'Loud, lively, reckless, some had grown,
Each dandling on his jigging knee
Eliza, Dolly, Nance, or Joan –
Livers in levity.

The Dead Quire
5 Birth-tide] Birthtide G
6 zest,] zest; MS, G
7 quire] Quire G
9 gaunt] great G
10 behind,] behind. SP
14] Treble and tenor and thorough-bass, G
15 worm] Worm G
16 mouldering place] mouldering-place G
17 years . . . light,] years ere Christday-light G
18 Mellstock had] Had Mellstock G
18 these;] these, MS, G
21 off,] off MS
25 reckless,] reckless G
27] Eliza, Betsy, Nancy, Joan, G
27 or] and MS

VIII

'The taper flames and hearthfire shine
Grew smoke-hazed to a lurid light,
And songs on subjects not divine
Were warbled forth that night.

IX

'Yet many were sons and grandsons here
Of those who, on such eves gone by,
At that still hour had throated clear
Their anthems to the sky.

X

'The clock belled midnight; and ere long
One shouted, "Now 'tis Christmas morn;
Here's to our women old and young,
And to John Barleycorn!"

XI

They drink the toast and shout again:
The pewter-ware rings back the boom,
And for a breath-while follows then
A silence in the room.

XII

'When nigh without, as in old days,
The ancient quire of voice and string
Seemed singing words of prayer and praise
As they had used to sing:

XIII

'*While shepherds watch'd their flocks by night*, –
Thus swells the long familiar sound
In many a quaint symphonic flight –
To, *Glory shone around.*

The Dead Quire
29–30] 'The taper-flame and chimney-shine/Grew hazed with smoke and lurid light; G
31 not] scarce G
33 many] some G
35 throated] voiced out G
37 The . . . midnight] Midnight resounded G
38 shouted,] shouted G
38 morn;] morn! G
39 women] women, G
41] 'They drink it; and they shout again; G
41 toast] toast, MS, TL, WE, SP, ME
41 again:] again; MS, G: again WE2
42 pewter-ware] dresser-ware G
42 boom,] boom MS: boom; G
43 And for a breath-while] And, for a breath-while, G
43 breath-while] breathwhile MS
46 quire] Quire G
48 sing:] sing. MS, G, TL, WE, SP, PE, ME
49 *night*, –] *night* – G
50 long] once G
51 flight –] flight MS, G, SP, CHP
52 To,] To MS

XIV

'The sons defined their fathers' tones,
The widow his whom she had wed,
And others in the minor moans
The viols of the dead.

XV

'Something supernal has the sound
As verse by verse the strain proceeds,
And stilly staring on the ground
Each roysterer holds and heeds.

XVI

'Towards its chorded closing bar
Plaintively, thinly, waned the hymn,
Yet lingered, like the notes afar
Of banded seraphim.

XVII

'With brows abashed, and reverent tread,
The hearkeners sought the tavern door:
But nothing, save wan moonlight, spread
The empty highway o'er.

XVIII

'While on their hearing fixed and tense
The aerial music seemed to sink,
As it were gently moving thence
Along the river brink.

XIX

'Then did the Quick pursue the Dead
By crystal Froom that crinkles there;
And still the viewless quire ahead
Voiced the old holy air.

The Dead Quire
53 defined] discerned G
53 tones,] tones MS
58 strain proceeds,] quire proceeds MS: Quire proceeds; G
60 holds] lists G
62 hymn,] hymn. G
64 seraphim] Seraphim G
65 abashed,] abashed G
65 tread,] tread G
66 hearkeners] listeners G
66 door:] door; MS: door, G
70 aerial] æthereal G
74 crystal] flowery G
74 crinkles] meanders G
75 quire] Quire G
76 Voiced] Tuned G

XX

'By Bank-walk wicket, brightly bleached,
It passed, and 'twixt the hedges twain,
Dogged by the living; till it reached
The bottom of Church Lane.

XXI

'There, at the turning, it was heard
Drawing to where the churchyard lay:
But when they followed thitherward
It smalled, and died away.

XXII

'Each headstone of the quire, each mound,
Confronted them beneath the moon;
But no more floated therearound
That ancient Birth-night tune.

XXIII

'There Dewy lay by the gaunt yew tree,
There Reuben and Michael, a pace behind,
And Bowman with his family
By the wall that the ivies bind. . . .

XXIV

'As from a dream each sobered son
Awoke, and musing reached his door:
'Twas said that of them all, not one
Sat in a tavern more.'

XXV

– The sad man ceased; and ceased to heed
His listener, and crossed the leaze
From Moaning Hill towards the mead –
The Mead of Memories.

1897

The Dead Quire
77–80 Not in MS, G
81–2] 'Till, where the cascade's cry is heard,/The music took the churchyard side; G
81 There] Till MS
82 lay:] lay; MS
84] It paused, and there it died. G
85 headstone] gravestone MS, G, TL, PE
85 quire] Quire G
85 mound,] mound G
87 therearound] there around G
88 Birth-night] Bethlehem G
89–92 Not in G
90 behind,] behind WE2
91 And] There MS
92 bind. . . .] bind. . . . . . MS
94 and musing] and, musing, G
94 door:] door: – MS: door G
95 all,] all G
96 more.] more. . . . G
97 – The] The G
97 sad] meek TL, PE
98 listener,] listener; G
1897] Not in G

214 The Christening

WHOSE child is this they bring
Into the aisle? –
At so superb a thing
The congregation smile
And turn their heads awhile.

Its eyes are blue and bright,
Its cheeks like rose;
Its simple robes unite
Whitest of calicoes
With lawn, and satin bows.

A pride in the human race
At this paragon
Of mortals, lights each face
While the old rite goes on;
But ah, they are shocked anon.

What girl is she who peeps
From the gallery stair,
Smiles palely, redly weeps,
With feverish furtive air
As though not fitly there?

'I am the baby's mother;
This gem of the race
The decent fain would smother,
And for my deep disgrace
I am bidden to leave the place.'

'Where is the baby's father?' –
'In the woods afar.
He says there is none he'd rather
Meet under moon or star
Than me, of all that are.

The Christening
14 on;] on, MS
15] And they ask its name anon. MS
15 ah] lo TL, PE
26 the] your MS

'To clasp me in lovelike weather,
    Wish fixing when,
He says: To be together
At will, just now and then,
Makes him the blest of men;

'But chained and doomed for life
    To slovening
As vulgar man and wife,
He says, is another thing:
Yea: sweet Love's sepulchring!'

1904

215 *A Dream Question*

TITLE:
A Dream-Question (An Inquiry *del*) MS
MS title is followed by: ' "Thy footsteps are not known" – Ps LXXVII.19.' The quotation from Micah is not in MS

'It shall be dark unto you, that ye shall not divine.' – MICAH, III 6

I ASKED the Lord: 'Sire, is this true
Which hosts of theologians hold,
That when we creatures censure you
For shaping griefs and ails untold
(Deeming them punishments undue)
You rage, as Moses wrote of old?

When we exclaim: "Beneficent
He is not, for he orders pain,
Or, if so, not omnipotent:
To a mere child the thing is plain!"
Those who profess to represent
You, cry out: "Impious and profane!" '

He: 'Save me from my friends, who deem
That I care what my creatures say!
Mouth as you list: sneer, rail, blaspheme,
O manikin, the livelong day,
Not one grief-groan or pleasure-gleam
Will you increase or take away.

The Christening
31 clasp] see MS
31 weather,] weather MS
40 sepulchring!] sepulchring. MS

A Dream Question
4] For scheming griefs and pains untold MS *before revision*

'Why things are thus, whoso derides,
May well remain my secret still. . . .
A fourth dimension, say the guides,
To matter is conceivable.
Think some such mystery resides
Within the ethic of my will.'

216 *By the Barrows*

NOT far from Mellstock – so tradition saith –
Where barrows, bulging as they bosoms were
Of Multimammia stretched supinely there,
Catch night and noon the tempest's wanton breath,

A battle, desperate doubtless unto death,
Was one time fought. The outlook, lone and bare,
The towering hawk and passing raven share,
And all the upland round is called 'The He'th'.

Here once a woman, in our modern age,
Fought singlehandedly to shield a child –
One not her own – from a man's senseless rage.
And to my mind no patriots' bones there piled
So consecrate the silence as her deed
Of stoic and devoted self-unheed.

TITLE:
A wife and another MS

217 *A Wife and Another*

'WAR ends, and he's returning
Early; yea,
The evening next to-morrow's!' –
– This I say
To her, whom I suspiciously survey,

Holding my husband's letter
To her view. –
She glanced at it but lightly,
And I knew
That one from him that day had reached her too.

A Dream Question
20 still. . . .] still. . . . . MS

By the Barrows
2 as . . . were] like the paps in air MS *before revision*
5 death,] death MS
12–14] And to my mind no clash of warriors wild/To save their land, outvalues what did she/In self-forgetting stoical bravery. MS *before revision*

A Wife and Another
2 yea,] yea MS

There was no time for scruple;
Secretly
I filched her missive, conned it,
Learnt that he
Would lodge with her ere he came home to me.

To reach the port before her,
And, unscanned,
There wait to intercept them
Soon I planned:
That, in her stead, *I* might before him stand.

So purposed, so effected;
At the inn
Assigned, I found her hidden: –
O that sin
Should bear what she bore when I entered in!

Her heavy lids grew laden
With despairs,
Her lips made soundless movements
Unawares,
While I peered at the chamber hired as theirs.

And as beside its doorway,
Deadly hued,
One inside, one withoutside
We two stood,
He came – my husband – as she knew he would.

No pleasurable triumph
Was that sight!
The ghastly disappointment
Broke them quite.
What love was theirs, to move them with such might!

'Madam, forgive me!' said she,
Sorrow bent,
'A child – I soon shall bear him. . . .
Yes – I meant
To tell you – that he won me ere he went.'

A Wife and Another
14 he] she MS, TL, PE
15 lodge] tryst MS, TL, PE
15 her] him MS, TL, PE
19 planned:] planned, MS
31 doorway,] doorway MS
32 hued,] hued MS
41 she,] she MS
45 won] knew MS, TL, PE

Then, as it were, within me
Something snapped,
As if my soul had largened:
Conscience-capped,
I saw myself the snarer – them the trapped.

'My hate dies, and I promise,
Grace-beguiled,'
I said, 'to care for you, be
Reconciled;
And cherish, and take interest in the child.'

Without more words I pressed him
Through the door
Within which she stood, powerless
To say more,
And closed it on them, and downstairward bore.

'He joins his wife – my sister,'
I, below,
Remarked in going – lightly –
Even as though
All had come right, and we had arranged it so....

As I, my road retracing,
Left them free,
The night alone embracing
Childless me,
I held I had not stirred God wrothfully.

EXTRA PRINTINGS:
(1) *Selected Poems*, p. 129
(2) *Chosen Poems*, p. 163

218 The Roman Road

THE Roman Road runs straight and bare
As the pale parting-line in hair
Across the heath. And thoughtful men
Contrast its days of Now and Then,
And delve, and measure, and compare;

A Wife and Another
47 snapped,] snapped MS
49] Conscience-capped MS
65 so. . . .] so. . . . . MS
70 stirred] moved TL, PE

The Roman Road
5–6 Stanza break in all editions

Visioning on the vacant air
Helmed legionaries, who proudly rear
The Eagle, as they pace again
The Roman Road.

But no tall brass-helmed legionnaire
Haunts it for me. Uprises there
A mother's form upon my ken,
Guiding my infant steps, as when
We walked that ancient thoroughfare,
The Roman Road.

219 *The Vampirine Fair*

TITLE:
The Fair Vampire MS

GILBERT had sailed to India's shore,
And I was all alone:
My lord came in at my open door
And said, 'O fairest one!'

He leant upon the slant bureau,
And sighed, 'I am sick for thee!'
'My Lord,' said I, 'pray speak not so,
Since wedded wife I be.'

Leaning upon the slant bureau,
Bitter his next words came:
'So much I know; and likewise know
My love burns on the same!

'But since you thrust my love away,
And since it knows no cure,
I must live out as best I may
The ache that I endure.'

When Michaelmas browned the nether Coomb,
And Wingreen Hill above,
And made the hollyhocks rags of bloom,
My lord grew ill of love.

The Roman Road
14 thoroughfare,] thoroughfare MS

The Vampirine Fair
2 alone:] alone; MS
9 bureau,] bureau MS
19 bloom,] bloom MS

My lord grew ill with love for me;
    Gilbert was far from port;
And – so it was – that time did see
    Me housed at Manor Court.

About the bowers of Manor Court
    The primrose pushed its head
When, on a day at last, report
    Arrived of him I had wed.

'Gilbert, my Lord, is homeward bound,
    His sloop is drawing near,
What shall I do when I am found
    Not in his house but here?'

'O I will heal the injuries
    I've done to him and thee.
I'll give him means to live at ease
    Afar from Shastonb'ry.'

When Gilbert came we both took thought:
    'Since comfort and good cheer,'
Said he, 'so readily are bought,
    He's welcome to thee, Dear.'

So when my lord flung liberally
    His gold in Gilbert's hands,
I coaxed and got my brothers three
    Made stewards of his lands.

And then I coaxed him to install
    My other kith and kin,
With aim to benefit them all
    Before his love ran thin.

And next I craved to be possessed
    Of plate and jewels rare.
He groaned: 'You give me, Love, no rest,
    Take all the law will spare!'

The Vampirine Fair
26] The leaves were reaching red MS
29 Lord] lord MS
37 thought:] thought; MS
39 so] So TL, PE, WE1, CP1–3
41 So] So, MS
49 possessed] possest MS
51 me, Love,] me Love MS

And so in course of years my wealth
Became a goodly hoard,
My steward brethren, too, by stealth
Had each a fortune stored.

Thereafter in the gloom he'd walk,
And by and by began
To say aloud in absent talk,
'I am a ruined man! –

'I hardly could have thought,' he said,
'When first I looked on thee,
That one so soft, so rosy red,
Could thus have beggared me!'

Seeing his fair estates in pawn,
And him in such decline,
I knew that his domain had gone
To lift up me and mine.

Next month upon a Sunday morn
A gunshot sounded nigh:
By his own hand my lordly born
Had doomed himself to die.

'Live, my dear Lord, and much of thine
Shall be restored to thee!'
He smiled, and said 'twixt word and sign,
'Alas – that cannot be!'

And while I searched his cabinet
For letters, keys, or will,
'Twas touching that his gaze was set
With love upon me still.

And when I burnt each document
Before his dying eyes,
'Twas sweet that he did not resent
My fear of compromise.

The Vampirine Fair
73 Lord] lord MS

The steeple-cock gleamed golden when
I watched his spirit go:
And I became repentant then
That I had wrecked him so.

Three weeks at least had come and gone,
With many a saddened word,
Before I wrote to Gilbert on
The stroke that so had stirred.

And having worn a mournful gown,
I joined, in decent while,
My husband at a dashing town
To live in dashing style.

Yet though I now enjoy my fling,
And dine and dance and drive,
I'd give my prettiest emerald ring
To see my lord alive.

And when the meet on hunting-days
Is near his churchyard home,
I leave my bantering beaux to place
A flower upon his tomb;

And sometimes say: 'Perhaps too late
The saints in Heaven deplore
That tender time when, moved by Fate,
He darked my cottage door.'

220 *The Reminder*

WHILE I watch the Christmas blaze
Paint the room with ruddy rays,
Something makes my vision glide
To the frosty scene outside.

There, to reach a rotting berry,
Toils a thrush, – constrained to very
Dregs of food by sharp distress,
Taking such with thankfulness.

The Vampirine Fair
92] Events that had occurred. MS, TL, PE: The crash that had occurred. WE1
97 fling,] fling MS
98 drive,] drive MS
104 tomb;] tomb. MS
107 time] day MS

The Reminder
5 berry,] berry MS

Why, O starving bird, when I
One day's joy would justify,
And put misery out of view,
Do you make me notice you!

221 *The Rambler*

I DO not see the hills around,
Nor mark the tints the copses wear;
I do not note the grassy ground
And constellated daisies there.

I hear not the contralto note
Of cuckoos hid on either hand,
The whirr that shakes the nighthawk's throat
When eve's brown awning hoods the land.

Some say each songster, tree, and mead –
All eloquent of love divine –
Receives their constant careful heed:
Such keen appraisement is not mine.

The tones around me that I hear,
The aspects, meanings, shapes I see,
Are those far back ones missed when near,
And now perceived too late by me!

222 *Night in the Old Home*

EXTRA PRINTINGS:
(1) *Selected Poems*, pp. 134–5
(2) *Chosen Poems*, pp. 168–9

TITLE:
Night in the old home MS

WHEN the wasting embers redden the chimney-breast,
And Life's bare pathway looms like a desert track to me,
And from hall and parlour the living have gone to their rest,
My perished people who housed them here come back to me.

They come and seat them around in their mouldy places,
Now and then bending towards me a glance of wistfulness,
A strange upbraiding smile upon all their faces,
And in the bearing of each a passive tristfulness.

The Reminder
10] Fain to-day would shun a sigh, MS, TL, PE

The Rambler
15 those . . . ones] far back ones I MS
15 far back] removed WE, ME
16 me!] me. MS, WE, ME

Night in the Old Home
4 My perished] The bygone MS
7 upbraiding] pale tearful MS

'Do you uphold me, lingering and languishing here,
A.pale late plant of your once strong stock?' I say to them;
'A thinker of crooked thoughts upon Life in the sere,
And on That which consigns men to night after showing the day to them?'

' – O let be the Wherefore! We fevered our years not thus:
Take of Life what it grants, without question!' they answer me seemingly.
'Enjoy, suffer, wait: spread the table here freely like us,
And, satisfied, placid, unfretting, watch Time away beamingly!'

EXTRA PRINTINGS:
(1) *Selected Poems*, pp. 132–3
(2) *Chosen Poems*, pp. 166–7

TITLE:
After the last breath MS
(*J.H. . . .*)] Not in MS, TL, PE

223 *After the Last Breath*

(*J.H. 1813–1904*)

THERE'S no more to be done, or feared, or hoped;
None now need watch, speak low, and list, and tire;
No irksome crease outsmoothed, no pillow sloped
Does she require.

Blankly we gaze. We are free to go or stay;
Our morrow's anxious plans have missed their aim;
Whether we leave to-night or wait till day
Counts as the same.

The lettered vessels of medicaments
Seem asking wherefore we have set them here;
Each palliative its silly face presents
As useless gear.

And yet we feel that something savours well;
We note a numb relief withheld before;
Our well-beloved is prisoner in the cell
Of Time no more.

We see by littles now the deft achievement
Whereby she has escaped the Wrongers all,
In view of which our momentary bereavement
Outshapes but small.

1904

Night in the Old Home
10 pale] poor MS
12 which] Which MS
13 – O] O MS
16 beamingly!] beamingly. MS

After the Last Breath
2 watch] wait MS
2 list] watch MS
5 stay;] stay, MS
6 aim;] aim, MS
1904] 190– MS

224 In Childbed

In the middle of the night
Mother's spirit came and spoke to me,
Looking weariful and white –
As 'twere untimely news she broke to me.

'O my daughter, joyed are you
To own the weetless child you mother there;
"Men may search the wide world through,"
You think, "nor find so fair another there!"

'Dear, this midnight time unwombs
Thousands just as rare and beautiful;
Thousands whom High Heaven foredooms
To be as bright, as good, as dutiful.

'Source of ecstatic hopes and fears
And innocent maternal vanity,
Your fond exploit but shapes for tears
New thoroughfares in sad humanity.

'Yet as you dream, so dreamt I
When Life stretched forth its morning ray to me;
Other views for by and by!' . . . .
Such strange things did mother say to me.

225 The Pine Planters

(Marty South's Reverie)

I

We work here together
In blast and breeze;
He fills the earth in,
I hold the trees.

EXTRA PRINTINGS:
(1) *The Cornhill Magazine*, June 1903, pp. [721]–722, Part II only = C
(2) *Selected Poems*, pp. 161–2, Part II only

TITLE:
The Pine-Planters C, SP
(*Marty* . . .)] (*The man fills in the earth; the sad-faced woman holds the tree upright, and meditates*). C: (In *The Woodlanders*) SP

In Childbed
11 High] high MS
19 by and by!' . . . .] by-and-by!' . . . . MS

The Pine Planters
2 blast and] Winter's MS, TL, PE

He does not notice
 That what I do
Keeps me from moving
 And chills me through.

He has seen one fairer
 I feel by his eye,
Which skims me as though
 I were not by.

And since she passed here
 He scarce has known
But that the woodland
 Holds him alone.

I have worked here with him
 Since morning shine,
He busy with his thoughts
 And I with mine.

I have helped him so many,
 So many days,
But never win any
 Small word of praise!

Shall I not sigh to him
 That I work on
Glad to be nigh to him
 Though hope is gone?

Nay, though he never
 Knew love like mine,
I'll bear it ever
 And make no sign!

II

From the bundle at hand here
 I take each tree,
And set it to stand, here
 Always to be;

The Pine Planters
21 many,] many MS
29 Nay, though] Nay. Though MS
32 sign!] sign. MS
33] From the unwound bundle C
34 I] We C
35–6] And set it up/Where it has to be; C
35 stand,] stand MS

When, in a second,
    As if from fear
Of Life unreckoned
    Beginning here,
It starts a sighing
    Through day and night,
Though while there lying
    'Twas voiceless quite.

It will sigh in the morning,
    Will sigh at noon,
At the winter's warning,
    In wafts of June;
Grieving that never
    Kind Fate decreed
It should for ever
    Remain a seed,
And shun the welter
    Of things without,
Unneeding shelter
    From storm and drought.

Thus, all unknowing
    For whom or what
We set it growing
    In this bleak spot,
It still will grieve here
    Throughout its time,
Unable to leave here,
    Or change its clime;
Or tell the story
    Of us to-day
When, halt and hoary,
    We pass away.

The Pine Planters
37 second] moment C
39 unreckoned] in earnest C
43 there] down MS, TL, WE1, PE
43 there lying] downlying C
51 should] could MS
51 should for] could not C, TL1
52 seed,] seed MS
63 here,] here C
68 We pass] We've passed C
Note The three stanzas printed in SP are numbered

EXTRA PRINTINGS:
(1) *The Monthly Review*, June 1902, p. [163] = MR
(2) *Selected Poems*, p. 136

226 The Dear

I PLODDED to Fairmile Hill-top, where
A maiden one fain would guard
From every hazard and every care
Advanced on the roadside sward.

I wondered how succeeding suns
Would shape her wayfarings,
And wished some Power might take such ones
Under Its warding wings.

The busy breeze came up the hill
And smartened her cheek to red,
And frizzled her hair to a haze. With a will
'Good-morning, my Dear!' I said.

She glanced from me to the far-off gray,
And, with proud severity,
'Good-morning to you – though I may say
I am not *your* Dear,' quoth she:

'For I am the Dear of one not here –
One far from his native land!' –
And she passed me by; and I did not try
To make her understand.

1901

EXTRA PRINTINGS:
(1) *The Tatler*, 2 Dec 1903, p. 342 = T
(2) *Harper's Weekly* (New York), Christmas Number 1903, p. 35 = H
(3) *Selected Poems*, pp. 137–8

TITLE:
Remembrance H
(*M.H . . .*)] Not in H

227 One We Knew

(*M.H. 1772–1857*)

SHE told how they used to form for the country dances –
'The Triumph', 'The New-rigged Ship' –
To the light of the guttering wax in the panelled manses,
And in cots to the blink of a dip.

The Dear
5–8 Not in MR
8 Its] its SP
8 warding] shielding
9 hill] hill, MR
11] And hazed her hair. Commiserate still, SP
11 haze.] haze. – MR
11 will] will, MR
12 Good-morning] Good morning MS, MR
14 severity,] severity: MR
15 Good-morning] Good morning MS, MR
1901] Not in MR

One We Knew
1 country dances] country-dances T
2 New-rigged] New Rigged H

She spoke of the wild 'poussetting' and 'allemanding'
    On carpet, on oak, and on sod;
And the two long rows of ladies and gentlemen standing,
    And the figures the couples trod.

She showed us the spot where the maypole was yearly planted,
    And where the bandsmen stood
While breeched and kerchiefed partners whirled, and panted
    To choose each other for good.

She told of that far-back day when they learnt astounded
    Of the death of the King of France:
Of the Terror; and then of Bonaparte's unbounded
    Ambition and arrogance.

Of how his threats woke warlike preparations
    Along the southern strand,
And how each night brought tremors and trepidations
    Lest morning should see him land.

She said she had often heard the gibbet creaking
    As it swayed in the lightning flash,
Had caught from the neighbouring town a small child's shrieking
    At the cart-tail under the lash. . . .

With cap-framed face and long gaze into the embers –
    We seated around her knees –
She would dwell on such dead themes, not as one who remembers,
    But rather as one who sees.

She seemed one left behind of a band gone distant
    So far that no tongue could hail:
Past things retold were to her as things existent,
    Things present but as a tale.

20 May 1902

228 *She Hears the Storm*

THERE was a time in former years –
    While my roof-tree was his –
When I should have been distressed by fears
    At such a night as this!

EXTRA PRINTINGS:
(1) *Selected Poems*, p. 131
(2) *Chosen Poems*, p. 165

TITLE:
The Widow's Thought MS

Note In WE, ME this poem is placed earlier in the book between 'Bereft' and 'Autumn in King's Hintock Park'

One We Knew
6] On carpet on oak and on green; H
8] And the couples that tripped between. H
9 maypole] May-pole H
10 stood] stood, T, H
11 kerchiefed partners] kerchiefed-partners H
11 whirled,] whirled MS
13 far-back] distant T, H
14 France:] France, T: France; H
15 Terror;] Terror, T
16 arrogance.] arrogance: T
18 southern] Southern H
19 tremors] terrors MS, T, H
20 morning] morn H
22 lightning flash] lightning-flash T
23 neighbouring town] neighbour borough T: distant borough H
24 lash. . . .] lash. . . . . . MS
25 face] face, H
25 embers –] embers, T
26 knees –] knees, T
30 hail:] hail; T
20 May 1902] Not in T, H
Note T has numbered stanzas

She Hears the Storm
4 this!] this. MS, TL, PE

I should have murmured anxiously,
    'The pricking rain strikes cold;
His road is bare of hedge or tree,
    And he is getting old.'

But now the fitful chimney-roar,
    The drone of Thorncombe trees,
The Froom in flood upon the moor,
    The mud of Mellstock Leaze,

The candle slanting sooty wick'd,
    The thuds upon the thatch,
The eaves-drops on the window flicked,
    The clacking garden-hatch,

And what they mean to wayfarers,
    I scarcely heed or mind;
He has won that storm-tight roof of hers
    Which Earth grants all her kind.

229 *A Wet Night*

I PACE along, the rain-shafts riddling me,
Mile after mile out by the moorland way,
And up the hill, and through the ewe-leaze gray
Into the lane, and round the corner tree;

Where, as my clothing clams me, mire-bestarred,
And the enfeebled light dies out of day,
Leaving the liquid shades to reign, I say,
'This is a hardship to be calendared!'

Yet sires of mine now perished and forgot,
When worse beset, ere roads were shapen here,
And night and storm were foes indeed to fear,
Times numberless have trudged across this spot
In sturdy muteness on their strenuous lot,
And taking all such toils as trifles mere.

She Hears the Storm

13 sooty wick'd] At some time after 1930 a hyphen was inserted in reprints of CP4. This is not found in any earlier editions and is of dubious authority

19–20] He has reached the roof well-known as hers/That Earth provides her kind. MS

A Wet Night

4 tree;] tree, MS

13] Making no plaint of their less kindly lot, MS *before revision*

230 *Before Life and After*

TITLE:
Before Life and after MS

A TIME there was – as one may guess
And as, indeed, earth's testimonies tell –
Before the birth of consciousness,
When all went well.

None suffered sickness, love, or loss,
None knew regret, starved hope, or heart-burnings;
None cared whatever crash or cross
Brought wrack to things.

If something ceased, no tongue bewailed,
If something winced and waned, no heart was wrung;
If brightness dimmed, and dark prevailed,
No sense was stung.

But the disease of feeling germed,
And primal rightness took the tinct of wrong;
Ere nescience shall be reaffirmed
How long, how long?

231 *New Year's Eve*

EXTRA MANUSCRIPT:
In the Miriam Lutcher Stark Library of the University of Texas = UT

EXTRA PRINTING:
The Fortnightly Review, Jan 1907, pp. [1]–2 = FR

'I HAVE finished another year,' said God,
'In grey, green, white, and brown;
I have strewn the leaf upon the sod,
Sealed up the worm within the clod,
And let the last sun down.'

'And what's the good of it?' I said,
'What reasons made you call
From formless void this earth we tread,
When nine-and-ninety can be read
Why nought should be at all?

Before Life and After
1 guess] guess, MS
2 earth's] Earth's MS
6 heart-burnings] heartburnings MS
13 feeling germed] thought engermed MS *before revision*
14 wrong;] wrong. – MS

New Year's Eve
4 clod,] clod UT
6 said,] said. TL, WE, PE, ME
7 you] You UT, FR
8 we] I UT, FR

'Yea, Sire; why shaped you us, "who in
This tabernacle groan" –
If ever a joy be found herein,
Such joy no man had wished to win
If he had never known!'

Then he: 'My labours – logicless –
You may explain; not I:
Sense-sealed I have wrought, without a guess
That I evolved a Consciousness
To ask for reasons why.

'Strange that ephemeral creatures who
By my own ordering are,
Should see the shortness of my view,
Use ethic tests I never knew,
Or made provision for!'

He sank to raptness as of yore,
And opening New Year's Day
Wove it by rote as theretofore,
And went on working evermore
In his unweeting way.

1906

TITLE:
His Education MS, TL, PE

232 God's Education

I SAW him steal the light away
That haunted in her eye:
It went so gently none could say
More than that it was there one day
And missing by-and-by.

I watched her longer, and he stole
Her lily tincts and rose;
All her young sprightliness of soul
Next fell beneath his cold control,
And disappeared like those.

New Year's Eve
11 you] You FR
11 "who in] who "in WE, ME
12 groan"] groan?" MS: groan"? UT, FR
13 herein,] herein UT
16 he] He UT, FR
16 labours – logicless –] labours logicless UT, FR
20 why.] why! UT, FR
21 Strange] Strange, UT, FR
26 yore,] yore: UT
30 his] His UT, FR
1906] Not in MS, UT, FR

I asked: 'Why do you serve her so?
    Do you, for some glad day,
Hoard these her sweets – ?' He said, 'O no,
They charm not me; I bid Time throw
    Them carelessly away.'

Said I: 'We call that cruelty –
    We, your poor mortal kind.'
He mused. 'The thought is new to me.
Forsooth, though I men's master be,
    Theirs is the teaching mind!'

233 *To Sincerity*

O SWEET sincerity! –
Where modern methods be
What scope for thine and thee?

Life may be sad past saying,
Its greens for ever graying,
Its faiths to dust decaying;

And youth may have foreknown it,
And riper seasons shown it,
But custom cries: 'Disown it:

'Say ye rejoice, though grieving,
Believe, while unbelieving,
Behold, without perceiving!'

– Yet, would men look at true things,
And unilluded view things,
And count to bear undue things,

The real might mend the seeming,
Facts better their foredeeming,
And Life its disesteeming.

February 1899

God's Education
11 so?] so, TL, PE
13 sweets – ?'] sweets?' – MS
14 me;] me. MS
15] Each promptly to decay.' MS, TL, PE
19 be,] be MS, TL, PE

To Sincerity
1 sincerity] Sincerity MS
6 decaying;] decaying, MS
8 it,] it; MS
9 cries:] cries, MS
10 rejoice,] rejoice MS
11 Believe,] Believe MS

234 *Panthera*

(For other forms of this legend – first met with in the second century – see Origen contra Celsum; the Talmud; Sepher Toldoth Jeschu; quoted fragments of lost Apocryphal gospels; Strauss, Haeckel; etc.)

YEA, as I sit here, crutched, and cricked, and bent,
I think of Panthera, who underwent
Much from insidious aches in his decline;
But his aches were not radical like mine;
They were the twinges of old wounds – the feel
Of the hand he had lost, shorn by barbarian steel,
Which came back, so he said, at a change in the air,
Fingers and all, as if it still were there.
My pains are otherwise: upclosing cramps
And stiffened tendons from this country's damps,
Where Panthera was never commandant. –
The Fates sent him by way of the Levant.

He had been blithe in his young manhood's time,
And as centurion carried well his prime.
In Ethiop, Araby, climes fair and fell,
He had seen service and had borne him well.
Nought shook him then: he was serene as brave;
Yet later knew some shocks, and would grow grave
When pondering them; shocks less of corporal kind
Than phantom-like, that disarranged his mind;
And it was in the way of warning me
(By much his junior) against levity
That he recounted them; and one in chief
Panthera loved to set in bold relief.

This was a tragedy of his Eastern days,
Personal in touch – though I have sometimes thought
That touch a possible delusion – wrought
Of half-conviction carried to a craze –
His mind at last being stressed by ails and age: –
Yet his good faith thereon I well could wage.

Panthera
see] *vide* MS
Sepher Toldoth Jeschu] Toldoth Jeshu MS
gospels] writings MS, TL
Strauss,] Strauss; MS, TL, WE, ME
1 crutched,] crutched MS
1 cricked,] cricked MS
7 air,] air WE, ME
13 This line is not indented in MS
15 Araby,] Araby – MS
15 fell,] fell – MS
24–5 No stanza break in MS, but l. 25 is indented
25 This] It MS
30–1 Stanza break in all editions

I had said it long had been a wish with me
That I might leave a scion – some small tree
As channel for my sap, if not my name –
Ay, offspring even of no legitimate claim,
In whose advance I secretly could joy.
Thereat he warmed.
'Cancel such wishes, boy!
A son may be a comfort or a curse,
A seer, a doer, a coward, a fool; yea, worse –
A criminal. . . . That I could testify!' . . .
'Panthera has no guilty son!' cried I
All unbelieving. 'Friend, you do not know,'
He darkly dropt: 'True, I've none now to show,
For *the law took him*. Ay, in sooth, Jove shaped it so!'

'This noon is not unlike,' he again began,
'The noon these pricking memories print on me –
Yea, that day, when the sun grew copper-red,
And I served in Judæa. . . . 'Twas a date
Of rest for arms. The *Pax Romana* ruled,
To the chagrin of frontier legionaries!
Palestine was annexed – though sullen yet, –
I, being in age some two-score years and ten,
And having the garrison in Jerusalem
Part in my hands as acting officer
Under the Governor. A tedious time
I found it, of routine, amid a folk
Restless, contentless, and irascible. –
Quelling some riot, sentrying court and hall,
Sending men forth on public meeting-days
To maintain order, were my duties there.

'Then came a morn in spring, and the cheerful sun
Whitened the city and the hills around,
And every mountain-road that clambered them,
Tincturing the greyness of the olives warm,
And the rank cacti round the valley's sides.
The day was one whereon death-penalties
Were put in force, and here and there were set

Panthera
39 criminal. . . .] criminal. . . . . MS
39 That] *That* WE, ME
39 testify!' . . .] testify!' . . . . MS
43 Ay . . . it] Ay; in sooth Jove ordered MS
43 In MS, WE, ME this line is indented farther left, and the stanza-break space in MS is doubled
44 again] then MS
46 Yea, that] A past MS, TL, PE
47 Judæa. . . .] Judæa. . . . . MS
48 *Pax Romana*] Pax Romana MS
52 And Having] Having MS
53–4] Part under my command. A tedious time MS, TL, PE

The soldiery for order, as I said,
Since one of the condemned had raised some heat,
And crowds surged passionately to see him slain.
I, mounted on a Cappadocian horse,
With some half-company of auxiliaries,
Had captained the procession through the streets
When it came streaming from the judgment-hall
After the verdicts of the Governor.
It drew to the great gate of the northern way
That bears towards Damascus; and to a knoll
Upon the common, just beyond the walls –
Whence could be swept a wide horizon round
Over the housetops to the remotest heights.
Here was the public execution-ground
For city crimes, called then and doubtless now
Golgotha, Kranion, or Calvaria.

'The usual dooms were duly meted out;
Some three or four were stript, transfixed, and nailed,
And no great stir occurred. A day of wont
It was to me, so far, and would have slid
Clean from my memory at its squalid close
But for an incident that followed these.

'Among the tag-rag rabble of either sex
That hung around the wretches as they writhed,
Till thrust back by our spears, one held my eye –
A weeping woman, whose strained countenance,
Sharpened against a looming livid cloud,
Was mocked by the crude rays of afternoon –
The mother of one of those who suffered there
I had heard her called when spoken roughly to
By my ranged men for pressing forward so.
It stole upon me hers was a face I knew;
Yet when, or how, I had known it, for a while
Eluded me. And then at once it came.

'Some thirty years or more before that noon
I was sub-captain of a company

Panthera
74 verdicts] sentence MS
78 swept] seen MS, TL, PE
82 Kranion] Cranion MS, TL, WE1, PE, CP1
83 dooms . . . meted] sentences were acted MS
84 stript] roped MS, TL, PE
93 looming livid cloud,] rising cliff of cloud MS

Drawn from the legion of Calabria,
That marched up from Judæa north to Tyre.
We had pierced the old flat country of Jezreel,
The great Esdraelon Plain and fighting-floor
Of Jew with Canaanite, and with the host
Of Pharaoh-Necho, king of Egypt, met
While crossing there to strike the Assyrian pride.
We left behind Gilboa; passed by Nain;
Till bulging Tabor rose, embossed to the top
With arbute, terebinth, and locust growths.

'Encumbering me were sundry sick, so fallen
Through drinking from a swamp beside the way;
But we pressed on, till, bearing over a ridge,
We dipt into a world of pleasantness –
A vale, the fairest I had gazed upon –
Which lapped a village on its furthest slopes
Called Nazareth, brimmed round by uplands nigh.
In the midst thereof a fountain bubbled, where,
Lime-dry from marching, our glad halt we made
To rest our sick ones, and refresh us all.

'Here a day onward, towards the eventide,
Our men were piping to a Pyrrhic dance
Trod by their comrades, when the young women came
To fill their pitchers, as their custom was.
I proffered help to one – a slim girl, coy
Even as a fawn, meek, and as innocent.
Her long blue gown, the string of silver coins
That hung down by her banded beautiful hair,
Symboled in full immaculate modesty.

'Well, I was young, and hot, and readily stirred
To quick desire. 'Twas tedious timing out
The convalescence of the soldiery;
And I beguiled the long and empty days
By blissful yieldance to her sweet allure,
Who had no arts, but what out-arted all,
The tremulous tender charm of trustfulness.

Panthera
103 Not in MS
105 pierced] crossed MS, TL1
112–13 No stanza space in MS, but l. 113 is indented
122–3 No stanza break in MS, but l. 123 is indented
131–2 No stanza break in MS, but l. 132 is indented
136 allure,] allure MS

We met, and met, and under the winking stars
That passed which peoples earth – true union, yea,
To the pure eye of her simplicity.

'Meanwhile the sick found health; and we pricked on.
I made her no rash promise of return,
As some do use; I was sincere in that;
I said we sundered never to meet again –
And yet I spoke untruth unknowingly! –
For meet again we did. Now, guess you aught?
The weeping mother on Calvaria
Was she I had known – albeit that time and tears
Had wasted rudely her once flowerlike form,
And her soft eyes, now swollen with sorrowing.

'Though I betrayed some qualms, she marked me not;
And I was scarce of mood to comrade her
And close the silence of so wide a time
To claim a malefactor as my son –
(For so I guessed him). And inquiry made
Brought rumour how at Nazareth long before
An old man wedded her for pity's sake
On finding she had grown pregnant, none knew how,
Cared for her child, and loved her till he died.

'Well; there it ended; save that then I learnt
That he – the man whose ardent blood was mine –
Had waked sedition long among the Jews,
And hurled insulting parlance at their god,
Whose temple bulked upon the adjoining hill,
Vowing that he would raze it, that himself
Was god as great as he whom they adored,
And by descent, moreover, was their king;
With sundry other incitements to misrule.

'The impalements done, and done the soldiers' game
Of raffling for the clothes, a legionary,
Longinus, pierced the young man with his lance
At signs from me, moved by his agonies
Through naysaying the drug they had offered him.

Panthera

140 true union] a marriage MS, TL, PE

141–2 No stanza break in MS, but l. 142 is indented

142 pricked] marched MS, TL, PE

149 time] grief MS, TL1

169–70 No stanza break in MS, but l. 170 is indented

170–1] 'The impalements duly done, a legionary, MS, TL, PE

173–5] To silence him. And when he had breathed his last MS

173 agonies] agonies. TL, PE

174 Not in TL, PE

It brought the end. And when he had breathed his last
The woman went. I saw her never again. . . .
Now glares my moody meaning on you, friend? –
That when you talk of offspring as sheer joy
So trustingly, you blink contingencies.
Fors Fortuna! He who goes fathering
Gives frightful hostages to hazardry!'

Thus Panthera's tale. 'Twas one he seldom told,
But yet it got abroad. He would unfold,
At other times, a story of less gloom,
Though his was not a heart where jests had room.
He would regret discovery of the truth
Was made too late to influence to ruth
The Procurator who had condemned his son –
Or rather him so deemed. For there was none
To prove that Panthera erred not: and indeed,
When vagueness of identity I would plead,
Panther himself would sometimes own as much –
Yet lothly. But, assuming fact was such,
That the said woman did not recognize
Her lover's face, is matter for surprise.
However, there's his tale, fantasy or otherwise.

Thereafter shone not men of Panthera's kind:
The indolent heads at home were ill-inclined
To press campaigning that would hoist the star
Of their lieutenants valorous afar.
Jealousies kept him irked abroad, controlled
And stinted by an Empire no more bold.
Yet in some actions southward he had share –
In Mauretania and Numidia; there
With eagle eye, and sword and steed and spur,
Quelling uprisings promptly. Some small stir
In Parthia next engaged him, until maimed,
As I have said; and cynic Time proclaimed
His noble spirit broken. What a waste
Of such a Roman! – one in youth-time graced
With indescribable charm, so I have heard,

Panthera
176 again. . . .] again. . . . . MS
177 friend? –] friend? MS
181–2 The stanza break space is doubled in MS
188 condemned] deathed MS
193 lothly. But,] seldom. But MS
193 fact] it MS, TL
193 such,] such; MS
196 Indented left in MS, WE, ME
196–7 The stanza-break space is increased in MS

Yea, magnetism impossible to word
When faltering as I saw him. What a fame,
O Son of Saturn, had adorned his name,
Might the Three so have urged Thee! – Hour by hour
His own disorders hampered Panthera's power
To brood upon the fate of those he had known,
Even of that one he always called his own –
Either in morbid dream or memory. . . .
He died at no great age, untroublously,
An exit rare for ardent soldiers such as he.

EXTRA MANUSCRIPT:
In the Berg Collection of the New York Public Library = B

EXTRA PRINTING:
Wayfarer's Love, ed. Duchess of Sutherland (London, 1904), p. 16 = WL

TITLE:
Life's Opportunity B, WL

235 *The Unborn*

I ROSE at night, and visited
The Cave of the Unborn:
And crowding shapes surrounded me
For tidings of the life to be,
Who long had prayed the silent Head
To haste its advent morn.

Their eyes were lit with artless trust,
Hope thrilled their every tone;
'A scene the loveliest, is it not?
A pure delight, a beauty-spot
Where all is gentle, true and just,
And darkness is unknown?'

My heart was anguished for their sake,
I could not frame a word;
And they descried my sunken face,
And seemed to read therein, and trace
The news that pity would not break,
Nor truth leave unaverred.

And as I silently retired
I turned and watched them still,
And they came helter-skelter out,

Panthera
212 Yea,] And MS, TL1
214 Saturn,] Saturn MS
218 that] Hardy's copy of CP2 has been corrected to 'the'
219 memory. . . .] memory. . . . . MS
221 Indented left in MS, WE, ME

The Unborn
4 be,] be – B, WL
5] Long having prayed the Eternal Head B
5 Who long had prayed] Long having prayed WL
6 haste] speed B, WL
11 true] true, WL
14 word;] word, B
16 therein,] therein B, WL
17 pity] Pity B
18 truth] Truth B
19–24] A voice like Ocean's heard (caught WL) afar/Broke (Rolled WL) forth on them and me: – /'For Lovingkindness Life (life WL) supplies/A scope superber than the skies./ So ask no more. Life's gladdening star (gladdening-star WL)/In Lovingkindness see.' B, WL

Driven forward like a rabble rout
Into the world they had so desired,
By the all-immanent Will.

1905

236 The Man He Killed

'HAD he and I but met
By some old ancient inn,
We should have sat us down to wet
Right many a nipperkin!

'But ranged as infantry,
And staring face to face,
I shot at him as he at me,
And killed him in his place.

'I shot him dead because –
Because he was my foe,
Just so: my foe of course he was;
That's clear enough; although

'He thought he'd 'list, perhaps,
Off-hand like – just as I –
Was out of work – had sold his traps –
No other reason why.

'Yes; quaint and curious war is!
You shoot a fellow down
You'd treat if met where any bar is,
Or help to half-a-crown.'

1902

EXTRA MANUSCRIPT:
In the Berg Collection of the New York Public Library = B

EXTRA PRINTINGS:
(1) *Harper's Weekly* (New York), 8 Nov 1902, p. 1649 = H
(2) *The Sphere*, 22 Nov 1902, p. 173a = S
(3) *Selected Poems*, p. 192
(4) *Chosen Poems*, p. 246

TITLE:
The Man he Killed MS
B, H, S have after title: SCENE: The settle of the Fox ('The Fox' B) Inn, Stagfoot Lane. CHARACTERS: The speaker (a returned soldier), and his friends, natives of the hamlet.

INDENTATION:
1 = ll. 1, 3 } and so throughout
2 = ll. 2, 4 } H, S

237 Geographical Knowledge

(A Memory of Christiana C——)

WHERE Blackmoor was, the road that led
To Bath, she could not show,
Nor point the sky that overspread
Towns ten miles off or so.

EXTRA PRINTING:
The Outlook, 1 April 1905, p. 454 = O

TITLE:
(*A* . . .)] Not in O
A] In MS

The Unborn
23 world] life MS
23 desired,] desired MS, TL, WE, PE, ME
24 all-immanent] great nescient MS
1905] Not in MS, B, WL, TL, WE, PE, CP1, ME

The Man He Killed
No quotes in H
2 inn,] inn S
4 nipperkin!] nipperkin. MS, H, S
7 him] him, H, S
9 dead] dead, H, S
11 Just so:] You see; B, H, S
13 perhaps,] perhaps MS
18 You] – You B
19 You'd treat if met] That you would treat B
1902] Not in MS, B, H, S
Note Stanzas are numbered in B, H, S

Geographical Knowledge
1 was] lay O
3 point] tell O
4 ten] twelve O

But that Calcutta stood this way,
    Cape Horn there figured fell,
That here was Boston, here Bombay,
    She could declare full well.

Less known to her the track athwart
    Froom Mead or Yell'ham Wood
Than how to make some Austral port
    In seas of surly mood.

She saw the glint of Guinea's shore
    Behind the plum-tree nigh,
Heard old unruly Biscay's roar
    In the weir's purl hard by. . . .

'My son's a sailor, and he knows
    All seas and many lands,
And when he's home he points and shows
    Each country where it stands.

'He's now just there – by Gib's high rock –
    And when he gets, you see,
To Portsmouth here, behind the clock,
    Then he'll come back to me!'

238 *One Ralph Blossom Soliloquizes*

TITLE:
One Ralph Blossom soliloquizes MS

('It being deposed that vij women who were mayds before he knew them have been brought upon the towne [rates?] by the fornicacions of one Ralph Blossom, Mr. Maior inquired why he should not contribute xiv pence weekly toward their mayntenance. But it being shewn that the sayd R.B. was dying of a purple feaver, no order was made.' – *Budmouth Borough Minutes: 16—*)

WHEN I am in hell or some such place,
A-groaning over my sorry case,
What will those seven women say to me
Who, when I coaxed them, answered 'Aye' to me?

Geographical Knowledge
6 Cape] That O
7 Bombay,] Bombay WE2
10 Mead] mead MS: Mead, O
10 Wood] Wood, O
16 In . . . purl] Amid the weirs' O
16 by. . . .] by. . . . . . MS

O has extra stanza between ll. 16–17:

At last came explanation why/Her mind should be so clear/On distant scenes, and blank wellnigh/On places that were near.

17 My] – My O

'I did not understand your sign!'
Will be the words of Caroline;
While Jane will cry, 'If I'd had proof of you,
I should have learnt to hold aloof of you!'

'I won't reproach: it was to be!'
Will dryly murmur Cicely;
And Rosa: 'I feel no hostility,
For I must own I lent facility.'

Lizzy says: 'Sharp was my regret,
And sometimes it is now! But yet
I joy that, though it brought notoriousness,
I knew Love once and all its gloriousness!'

Says Patience: 'Why are we apart?
Small harm did you, my poor Sweet Heart!
A manchild born, now tall and beautiful,
Was worth the ache of days undutiful.'

And Anne cries: 'O the time was fair,
So wherefore should you burn down there?
There is a deed under the sun, my Love,
And that was ours. What's done is done, my Love.
These trumpets here in Heaven are dumb to me
With you away. Dear, come, O come to me!'

239 *The Noble Lady's Tale*

(*circa 1790*)

I

'WE moved with pensive paces,
    I and he,
And bent our faded faces
    Wistfully,
For something troubled him, and troubled me.

EXTRA PRINTINGS:
(1) *Harper's Weekly* (New York), 18 Feb 1905, p. 234 = H
(2) *The Cornhill Magazine*, March 1905, pp. 307–12 = C

TITLE:
The Noble Lady's Story H

One Ralph Blossom Soliloquizes
7 cry] say MS
18 Heart!] Heart WE1: Heart, WE2: Heart. ME
23 There] – There WE, ME

'The lanthorn feebly lightened
Our grey hall,
Where ancient brands had brightened
Hearth and wall,
And shapes long vanished whither vanish all.

' "O why, Love, nightly, daily,"
I had said,
"Dost sigh, and smile so palely,
As if shed
Were all Life's blossoms, all its dear things dead?"

' "Since silence sets thee grieving,"
He replied,
"And I abhor deceiving
One so tried,
Why, Love, I'll speak, ere time us twain divide."

'He held me, I remember,
Just as when
Our life was June – (September
It was then);
And we walked on, until he spoke again:

' "Susie, an Irish mummer,
Loud-acclaimed
Through the gay London summer,
Was I; named
A master in my art, who would be famed.

' "But lo, there beamed before me
Lady Su;
God's altar-vow she swore me
When none knew,
And for her sake I bade the sock adieu.

' "My Lord your father's pardon
Thus I won:
He let his heart unharden
Towards his son,
And honourably condoned what we had done;

The Noble Lady's Tale
23 (September] September H, C
24] Though 'twas then; H, C
28 summer,] summer H, C
29 I;] I; – H, C
32 Su;] Su: H, C
37 won:] won; MS, H, C, TL, WE, ME

'"But said – recall you, dearest? –
As for Su,
I'd see her – ay, though nearest
Me unto –
Sooner entombed than in a stage purlieu!

'"Just so. – And here he housed us,
In this nook,
Where Love like balm has drowsed us:
Robin, rook,
Our chief familiars, next to string and book.

'"Our days here, peace-enshrouded,
Followed strange
The old stage-joyance, crowded,
Rich in range;
But never did my soul desire a change,

'"Till now, when far uncertain
Lips of yore
Call, call me to the curtain,
There once more,
But *once*, to tread the boards I trod before.

'"A night – the last and single
Ere I die –
To face the lights, to mingle
As did I
Once in the game, and rivet every eye!"

'Such was his wish. He feared it,
Feared it though
Rare memories so endeared it.
I, also,
Feared it still more; its outcome who could know?

'"Alas, my Love," said I then,
"Since it be
A wish so mastering, why, then,
E'en go ye! –
Despite your pledge to father and to me . . ."

The Noble Lady's Tale
44] *Now to you* – MS, H, C
56 when] the H, C
57 Lips] Voice H, C
58 Call, call] Calls – calls H, C
58 curtain,] curtain; H, C
70 more;] more: MS, H, C
70 know?] know! MS, H, C
73 then,] then H, C
75 me . . .'] me' . . . . MS: me. . . .' H: me.' . . . C

‘ ’Twas fixed; no more was spoken
Thereupon;
Our silences were broken
Only on
The petty items of his needs while gone.

‘Farewell he bade me, pleading
That it meant
So little, thus conceding
To his bent;
And then, as one constrained to go, he went.

‘Thwart thoughts I let deride me,
As, ’twere vain
To hope him back beside me
Ever again:
Could one plunge make a waxing passion wane?

‘I thought, “Some wild stage-woman,
Honour-wrecked . . .”
But no: it was inhuman
To suspect;
Though little cheer could my lone heart affect!

II

‘Yet came it, to my gladness,
That, as vowed,
He did return. – But sadness
Swiftly cowed
The joy with which my greeting was endowed.

‘Some woe was there. Estrangement
Marked his mind.
Each welcome-warm arrangement
I had designed
Touched him no more than deeds of careless kind.

The Noble Lady's Tale
92 Honour-wrecked . . .’] Honour-wrecked . . . . .’ MS Honour-wrecked. . . .’ C
95 affect!] affect. MS, H, C
98 return. –] return. H, C

' "I – *failed*!" escaped him glumly.
" – I went on
In my old part. But dumbly –
Memory gone –
Advancing, I sank sick; my vision drawn

' "To something drear, distressing
As the knell
Of all hopes worth possessing!"...
– What befell
Seemed linked with me, but how I could not tell.

'Hours passed; till I implored him,
As he knew
How faith and frankness toward him
Ruled me through,
To say what ill I had done, and could undo.

' "*Faith – frankness*. Ah! Heaven save such!"
Murmured he,
"They are wedded wealth! *I* gave such
Liberally,
But you, Dear, not. For you suspected me."

'I was about beseeching
In hurt haste
More meaning, when he, reaching
To my waist,
Led me to pace the hall as once we paced.

' "I never meant to draw you
To own all,"
Declared he, "But – I *saw* you –
By the wall,
Half-hid. And that was why I failed withal!"

' "Where? when?" said I – "Why, nigh me,
At the play
That night. That you should spy me,
Doubt my fay,
And follow, furtive, took my heart away!"

The Noble Lady's Tale
113 possessing!" . . .] possessing!" . . . . . MS
128 he,] he MS, H, C
129 waist,] waist MS, H, C
133 he,] he. H, C
136 I –] I. H, C

'That I had never been there,
But had gone
To my locked room – unseen there,
Curtains drawn,
Long days abiding – told I, wonder-wan.

' "Nay, 'twas your form and vesture,
Cloak and gown,
Your hooded features – gesture
Half in frown,
That faced me, pale," he urged, "that night in town.

' "And when, outside, I handed
To her chair
(As courtesy demanded
Of me there)
The leading lady, you peeped from the stair."

'Straight pleaded I: "Forsooth, Love,
Had I gone,
I must have been in truth, Love,
Mad to don
Such well-known raiment." But he still went on

'That he was not mistaken
Nor misled. –
I felt like one forsaken,
Wished me dead,
That he could think thus of the wife he had wed!

'His going seemed to waste him
Like a curse,
To wreck what once had graced him;
And, averse
To my approach, he mused, and moped, and worse.

'Till, what no words effected
Thought achieved:
It was my wraith – projected,
He conceived,
Thither, by my tense brain at home aggrieved.

The Noble Lady's Tale
151–5 Not in H, C
158 been] been, MS, H, C
165 wed!] wed. MS, H, C
166–70 Not in H, C
166 His] That MS, TL, PE
168 To wreck what] Spoil all that MS, TL, PE
171 Till,] Well: H, C
172 achieved:] achieved. H, C
173 *It was my*] It was my H, C
173 projected,] projected H, C
174] (He conceived) H, C
175 Thither,] Thither H, C

'Thereon his credence centred
Till he died;
And, no more tempted, entered
Sanctified,
The little vault with room for one beside.'

III

Thus far the lady's story. –
Now she, too,
Reclines within that hoary
Last dark mew
In Mellstock Quire with him she loved so true.

A yellowing marble, placed there
Tablet-wise,
And two joined hearts enchased there
Meet the eyes;
And reading their twin names we moralize:

Did she, we wonder, follow
Jealously?
And were those protests hollow? –
Or saw he
Some semblant dame? Or can wraiths really be?

Were it she went, her honour,
All may hold,
Pressed truth at last upon her
Till she told –
(Him only – others as these lines unfold).

Riddle death-sealed for ever,
Let it rest! . . .
One's heart could blame her never
If one guessed
That go she did. She knew her actor best.

The Noble Lady's Tale
178 entered] entered – WE, ME
179 Sanctified,] Sanctified – WE, ME
181 story. –] story. H, C
185 Quire] Quire, MS, H, C
193] Was her denial hollow? (hollow? – MS, TL, PE) MS, H, C, TL, PE
201 for ever] forever H
202 rest! . . .] rest! . . . . MS: rest . . . H, C

240 Unrealized

EXTRA PRINTING:
The Queen's Christmas Carol (London, 1905), p. 58 = Q

TITLE:
Orphaned
A Point of View Q

DOWN comes the winter rain –
Spoils my hat and bow –
Runs into the poll of me;
But mother won't know.

We've been out and caught a cold,
Knee-deep in snow;
Such a lucky thing it is
That mother won't know!

Rosy lost herself last night –
Couldn't tell where to go.
Yes – it rather frightened her,
But mother didn't know.

Somebody made Willy drunk
At the Christmas show:
O 'twas fun! It's well for him
That mother won't know!

Howsoever wild we are,
Late at school or slow,
Mother won't be cross with us,
Mother won't know.

How we cried the day she died!
Neighbours whispering low . . .
But we now do what we will –
Mother won't know.

241 Wagtail and Baby

EXTRA PRINTING:
The Albany Review, April 1907, p. 34 = AR

TITLE:
AR has below title:
An Incident of Civilization

A BABY watched a ford, whereto
A wagtail came for drinking;
A blaring bull went wading through,
The wagtail showed no shrinking.

Unrealized
1 rain –] rain, Q
2 bow –] bow, Q
3 of me;] o' me – Q
4 know.] know! Q
5–6] We played and caught a cold/Knee deep in snow: Q
5 cold,] cold MS
8 know!] know. Q
9] Rosy, she got lost one night – Q
12 know.] know! Q
14 show:] show; MS: show. Q
15 O] Oh, Q
16 won't know!] didn't know. Q
18 school] school, Q
19 Mother won't be] Mother's never Q
19 us,] us – Q
20 won't] don't Q
21–2] 'Cause she's dead. The neighbours say/'Tis our ruin. No! MS
21 died!] died; Q: died, WE, ME
22–5] All the folk said, 'Oh,/It's those children's ruin!' – Still,/We may now do what we will – /Mother won't know. TL, PE [with extra line]
22] How we miss her. . . . Though Q
22 low . . .] low! . . . WE
23 But we] We may MS, Q
23 will –] will, Q
24 know.] know! Q, ME

Wagtail and Baby
3 through,] through MS: through: AR: through; WE, ME

A stallion splashed his way across,
    The birdie nearly sinking;
He gave his plumes a twitch and toss,
    And held his own unblinking.

Next saw the baby round the spot
    A mongrel slowly slinking;
The wagtail gazed, but faltered not
    In dip and sip and prinking.

A perfect gentleman then neared;
    The wagtail, in a winking,
With terror rose and disappeared;
    The baby fell a-thinking.

242 *Aberdeen*

(*April: 1905*)

And wisdom and knowledge shall be the stability of thy times.' –
ISAIAH, XXXIII 6

I LOOKED and thought, 'All is too gray and cold
To wake my place-enthusiasms of old!'
Till a voice passed: 'Behind that granite mien
Lurks the imposing beauty of a Queen.'
I looked anew; and saw the radiant form
Of Her who soothes in stress, who steers in storm,
On the grave influence of whose eyes sublime
Men count for the stability of the time.

EXTRA MANUSCRIPT:
In Aberdeen University Library = AU

EXTRA PRINTING:
Alma Mater (Aberdeen University Magazine), Quatercentenary Number, Sept 1906, p. 11. [Identical with AU]

243 *George Meredith*

(*1828–1909*)

FORTY years back, when much had place
That since has perished out of mind,
I heard that voice and saw that face.

EXTRA PRINTINGS:
(1) *The Times*, 22 May 1909, p. 11 = T
(2) *Selected Poems*, p. 123
(3) *Chosen Poems*, p. 157

TITLE:
G.M.
1828–1909 MS, T, TL, PE

Wagtail and Baby
6 sinking;] sinking: AR
8 own] own, AR
13 neared;] neared: AR
15] Rose terrified, and disappeared . . . AR
15 disappeared;] disappeared. MS

Aberdeen
1 looked] looked; AU
1 All] She MS, AU
2 my place-enthusiasms] the warm enthusiasms AU
6 soothes] stays AU
6 steers in storm,] guides in storm; AU

He spoke as one afoot will wind
A morning horn ere men awake;
His note was trenchant, turning kind.

He was of those whose wit can shake
And riddle to the very core
The counterfeits that Time will break....

Of late, when we two met once more,
The luminous countenance and rare
Shone just as forty years before.

So that, when now all tongues declare
His shape unseen by his green hill,
I scarce believe he sits not there.

No matter. Further and further still
Through the world's vaporous vitiate air
His words wing on – as live words will.

May 1909

EXTRA PRINTINGS:
(1) *Selected Poems*, p. 29
(2) *Chosen Poems*, p. 29

TITLE:
Yell'ham-Wood's story MS

244 *Yell'ham-Wood's Story*

COOMB-FIRTREES say that Life is a moan,
  And Clyffe-hill Clump says 'Yea!'
But Yell'ham says a thing of its own:
    It's not 'Gray, gray
    Is Life alway!'
    That Yell'ham says,
  Nor that Life is for ends unknown.

It says that Life would signify
  A thwarted purposing:
That we come to live, and are called to die.
    Yes, that's the thing
    In fall, in spring,
    That Yell'ham says: –
  'Life offers – to deny!'

1902

George Meredith
6 turning] smart, but MS, T
7 wit] words T
9 counterfeits] falsities T
14 His shape] He is T
18 live] strong T
May 1909] Not in T

Yell'ham Wood's Story
2 Clyffe-hill] Dudd-hill MS
3 says a thing] Wood says things MS

245 *A Young Man's Epigram on Existence*

TITLE:
Epigram on Existence MS

Note In MS placed between 'Aberdeen' and 'G.M.'

A SENSELESS school, where we must give
Our lives that we may learn to live!
A dolt is he who memorizes
Lessons that leave no time for prizes.

16 W.P.V., 1866

Beeny Cliff

(March 1870 – March 1913)

I.

O the opal and the sapphire of that wandering western sea,
And the woman riding high above with bright hair flapping free –
The woman whom I loved so, and who loyally loved me.

II.

The ~~white mews~~ puffins plained below us, and the waves seemed far away
In a nether sky, engrossed in saying their endless babbling say,
As we laughed lightheartedly aloft on that clear-sunned March day.

III

A little cloud then cloaked us, and there flew an irised rain,
And the Atlantic dyed its levels with a dull-misfeatured stain,
And then the sun burst out ~~anew~~ again, and purples prinked the main.

IV.

– Still in all its chasmal beauty bulks old Beeny to the sky.
And shall she and I not go there once again now March is nigh,
And the sweet things said in that March say anew there by and by?

V.

~~Nay, though~~ What if still in chasmal beauty looms that wild weird western shore!
The woman now is – elsewhere – whom the ambling pony bore,
And nor knows nor cares for Beeny, and will see it nevermore.

See page 350

SATIRES OF CIRCUMSTANCE
LYRICS AND REVERIES

Abbreviations Specific to 'Satires of Circumstance'

MS = The bound-up volume of manuscripts in the Dorset County Museum
SC1 = *Satires of Circumstance* 1914
SC2 = *Satires of Circumstance* 1915
SC = Found in both SC1 and SC2
WE = Wessex Edition 1919
PE = Pocket Edition 1919
ME = Mellstock Edition 1920

LYRICS AND REVERIES

EXTRA PRINTINGS:
(1) *Selected Poems*, pp. 115–18
(2) *Chosen Poems*, pp. 149–52

246 *In Front of the Landscape*

PLUNGING and labouring on in a tide of visions,
        Dolorous and dear,
Forward I pushed my way as amid waste waters
        Stretching around,
Through whose eddies there glimmered the customed landscape
        Yonder and near

Blotted to feeble mist. And the coomb and the upland
        Coppice-crowned,
Ancient chalk-pit, milestone, rills in the grass-flat
        Stroked by the light,
Seemed but a ghost-like gauze, and no substantial
        Meadow or mound.

What were the infinite spectacles featuring foremost
        Under my sight,
Hindering me to discern my paced advancement
        Lengthening to miles;
What were the re-creations killing the daytime
        As by the night?

O they were speechful faces, gazing insistent,
        Some as with smiles,
Some as with slow-born tears that brinily trundled
        Over the wrecked
Cheeks that were fair in their flush-time, ash now with anguish,
        Harrowed by wiles.

Yes, I could see them, feel them, hear them, address them –
        Halo-bedecked –
And, alas, onwards, shaken by fierce unreason,
        Rigid in hate,
Smitten by years-long wryness born of misprision,
        Dreaded, suspect.

In Front of the Landscape
2 Dolorous and] Bitterly (Corpse-like, yet *del*) MS
6 near] near, SC, PE
7 mist. And] mist; and MS
8] Foliage-crowned, MS, SC, SP, PE
11 ghost-like] ghostlike MS
13 featuring] bulking MS, SC, SP, PE
15 advancement] advancement, SP, CHP
19 insistent,] insistent – MS

Then there would breast me shining sights, sweet seasons
Further in date;
Instruments of strings with the tenderest passion
Vibrant, beside
Lamps long extinguished, robes, cheeks, eyes with the earth's crust
Now corporate.

Also there rose a headland of hoary aspect
Gnawed by the tide,
Frilled by the nimb of the morning as two friends stood there
Guilelessly glad –
Wherefore they knew not – touched by the fringe of an ecstasy
Scantly descried.

Later images too did the day unfurl me,
Shadowed and sad,
Clay cadavers of those who had shared in the dramas,
Laid now at ease,
Passions all spent, chiefest the one of the broad brow
Sepulture-clad.

So did beset me scenes, miscalled of the bygone,
Over the leaze,
Past the clump, and down to where lay the beheld ones;
– Yea, as the rhyme
Sung by the sea-swell, so in their pleading dumbness
Captured me these.

For, their lost revisiting manifestations
In their live time
Much had I slighted, caring not for their purport,
Seeing behind
Things more coveted, reckoned the better worth calling
Sweet, sad, sublime.

Thus do they now show hourly before the intenser
Stare of the mind
As they were ghosts avenging their slights by my bypast
Body-borne eyes,
Show, too, with fuller translation than rested upon them
As living kind.

In Front of the Landscape
36 corporate.] corporate! MS
49 scenes,] scenes MS, SC, PE
56 live] own MS, SC, SP, PE

Hence wag the tongues of the passing people, saying
    In their surmise,
'Ah – whose is this dull form that perambulates, seeing nought
    Round him that looms
Whithersoever his footsteps turn in his farings,
    Save a few tombs?'

247 *Channel Firing*

EXTRA PRINTING:
The Fortnightly Review, May 1914, pp. [769]–770 = FR

THAT night your great guns, unawares,
Shook all our coffins as we lay,
And broke the chancel window-squares,
We thought it was the Judgment-day

And sat upright. While drearisome
Arose the howl of wakened hounds:
The mouse let fall the altar-crumb,
The worms drew back into the mounds,

The glebe cow drooled. Till God called, 'No;
It's gunnery practice out at sea
Just as before you went below;
The world is as it used to be:

'All nations striving strong to make
Red war yet redder. Mad as hatters
They do no more for Christés sake
Than you who are helpless in such matters.

'That this is not the judgment-hour
For some of them's a blessed thing,
For if it were they'd have to scour
Hell's floor for so much threatening....

'Ha, ha. It will be warmer when
I blow the trumpet (if indeed
I ever do; for you are men,
And rest eternal sorely need).'

Channel Firing
4 Judgment-day] Judgment-day, FR
7 altar-crumb,] altar-crumb; FR
8 worms] worm FR
8 mounds,] mounds; FR
13 striving strong] trying how MS, FR
14 hatters] hatters, FR
15 Christés] Christ his MS, FR
20 threatening. . . .] threatening. FR
21 ha] no FR
22 if indeed] if, indeed, FR
24 need).'] need.)' MS

So down we lay again. 'I wonder,
Will the world ever saner be,'
Said one, 'than when He sent us under
In our indifferent century!'

And many a skeleton shook his head.
'Instead of preaching forty year,'
My neighbour Parson Thirdly said,
'I wish I had stuck to pipes and beer.'

Again the guns disturbed the hour,
Roaring their readiness to avenge,
As far inland as Stourton Tower,
And Camelot, and starlit Stonehenge.

April 1914

248 *The Convergence of the Twain*

(Lines on the loss of the 'Titanic')

I

In a solitude of the sea
Deep from human vanity,
And the Pride of Life that planned her, stilly couches she.

II

Steel chambers, late the pyres
Of her salamandrine fires,
Cold currents thrid, and turn to rhythmic tidal lyres.

III

Over the mirrors meant
To glass the opulent
The sea-worm crawls – grotesque, slimed, dumb, indifferent.

EXTRA MANUSCRIPT:
In the Bancroft Library of the University of California at Berkeley, marked 'Replica of Original MS' = BL

PROOFS:
(1) There is a first proof of M in the Yale University Library = Y
(2) There are three sets of proofs in the Berg Collection of the New York Public Library. The third (= B) is a revision which incorporates the manuscript changes of the other two, which are identical

EXTRA PRINTINGS:
(1) The Souvenir Programme of the 'Dramatic and Operatic Matinée in Aid of the "Titanic" Disaster Fund' at Covent Garden, 14 May 1912, pp. [2]–[3] = TF
(2) *The Fortnightly Review*, June 1912, pp. [981]–982 = FR
(3) A limited printing of ten copies by Macmillan, dated 1912 = M
(4) *Selected Poems*, pp. 119–21
(5) *Chosen Poems*, pp. 153–5

TITLE:
(*Lines* . . .)] [Improvised on the loss of "The Titanic"] TF

Channel Firing
35 inland] in land FR
April 1914] Not in FR

The Convergence of the Twain
1] In the solitudes of the sea, TF
1 sea] sea, BL, Y, B, FR, M
4 Steel chambers, late] In retorts that were TF
5 fires,] fires MS, BL, Y, B, TF, FR, M
6 Cold . . . to] The cold, calm currents strike their TF
6 turn] tune BL, B, M
6 rhythmic] rhymic Y
7 mirrors] mirrors, BL
8 glass the] flash forms TF
8 opulent] opulent, BL
9 crawls . . . indifferent] creeps – grotesque, unweeting, mean, content TF

IV

Jewels in joy designed
To ravish the sensuous mind
Lie lightless, all their sparkles bleared and black and blind.

V

Dim moon-eyed fishes near
Gaze at the gilded gear
And query: 'What does this vaingloriousness down here?' ...

VI

Well: while was fashioning
This creature of cleaving wing,
The Immanent Will that stirs and urges everything

VII

Prepared a sinister mate
For her – so gaily great –
A Shape of Ice, for the time far and dissociate.

VIII

And as the smart ship grew
In stature, grace, and hue,
In shadowy silent distance grew the Iceberg too.

IX

Alien they seemed to be:
No mortal eye could see
The intimate welding of their later history,

X

Or sign that they were bent
By paths coincident
On being anon twin halves of one august event,

XI

Till the Spinner of the Years
Said 'Now!' And each one hears,
And consummation comes, and jars two hemispheres.

The Convergence of the Twain
12 sparkles] flashes BL
13–15 Not in TF
13 moon-eyed] moon-eyen Y
14] The daintily gilded gear, Y, FR
14 gear] gear, B, M
15] Gaze querying: 'What does all this sumptuousness down here?' Y, FR
15 this . . . here?' . . .] all this sumptuousness down here?' B, M
15 here?' . . .] here?' . . . . MS, BL
16 Well:] For, TF
17 creature of cleaving] ship of swiftest BL, Y, B, TF, FR, M
18 everything] everything. TF: everything, Y, B, FR, M
19 mate] Mate BL, Y, B, TF, FR, M
20 her – so] her so TF
23 grace,] grace FR
27 The . . . of] How closely welded was TF
28–9] And so coincident/In course as to be meant TF
30 On being] To form TF
30 event,] event; Y, B, TF, FR, M: event: BL
31 Spinner] Mover TF
32 And each one] The which each Y, TF, FR
32 hears,] hears MS, BL
33 jars] clouds TF
BL, B, M have at end: *April* 24, 1912
TF has at end: *April*, 1912

EXTRA PRINTINGS:
(1) *Selected Poems*, pp. 47–8
(2) *Chosen Poems*, pp. 46–7

249 *The Ghost of the Past*

WE two kept house, the Past and I,
The Past and I;
Through all my tasks it hovered nigh,
Leaving me never alone.
It was a spectral housekeeping
Where fell no jarring tone,
As strange, as still a housekeeping
As ever has been known.

As daily I went up the stair
And down the stair,
I did not mind the Bygone there –
The Present once to me;
Its moving meek companionship
I wished might ever be,
There was in that companionship
Something of ecstasy.

It dwelt with me just as it was,
Just as it was
When first its prospects gave me pause
In wayward wanderings,
Before the years had torn old troths
As they tear all sweet things,
Before gaunt griefs had torn old troths
And dulled old rapturings.

And then its form began to fade,
Began to fade,
Its gentle echoes faintlier played
At eves upon my ear
Than when the autumn's look embrowned
The lonely chambers here,
When autumn's settling shades embrowned
Nooks that it haunted near.

The Ghost of the Past
2 I;] I, MS
3 Through all my tasks] I tended while MS, SC, PE
9 stair] stair, MS, SC1
19 prospects] visions (a figure *del*) MS
20 wayward] western MS *before revision*
23 torn] wrecked SP
29 look] eye MS
30 chambers] parlours MS
31 When] The MS, SC, SP, PE

And so with time my vision less,
    Yea, less and less
Makes of that Past my housemistress,
    It dwindles in my eye;
It looms a far-off skeleton
    And not a comrade nigh,
A fitful far-off skeleton
    Dimming as days draw by.

250 *After the Visit*

(*To F.E.D.*)

    COME again to the place
Where your presence was as a leaf that skims
Down a drouthy way whose ascent bedims
    The bloom on the farer's face.

    Come again, with the feet
That were light on the green as a thistledown ball,
And those mute ministrations to one and to all
    Beyond a man's saying sweet.

    Until then the faint scent
Of the bordering flowers swam unheeded away,
And I marked not the charm in the changes of day
    As the cloud-colours came and went.

    Through the dark corridors
Your walk was so soundless I did not know
Your form from a phantom's of long ago
    Said to pass on the ancient floors,

    Till you drew from the shade,
And I saw the large luminous living eyes
Regard me in fixed inquiring-wise
    As those of a soul that weighed,

EXTRA MANUSCRIPT:
In possession of Professor R. L. Purdy. This has not been available for checking

EXTRA PRINTINGS:
(1) *The Spectator*, 13 Aug 1910, p. 242 = S
(2) *Selected Poems*, pp. 3–4
(3) *Chosen Poems*, pp. 3–4

TITLE:
(*To F.E.D.*)] Not in MS, S

The Ghost of the Past
33 my vision] the chambers MS
35 Makes of] Retain MS
36 It dwindles] Its mien smalls MS
39 fitful far-off] flitting fitful SP

After the Visit
2 leaf] waft S
6 green] lawn S
7 all] all, S
8 a man's] the tongue's S
12 cloud-colours] cloud-shadows S
13 dark] dusk S
16 pass] glide S
18 large] great S
19 inquiring-wise] inquiring-wise, S
20 As] Even as S
20 weighed,] weighed S

Scarce consciously,
The eternal question of what Life was,
And why we were there, and by whose strange laws
That which mattered most could not be.

251 To Meet, or Otherwise

EXTRA MANUSCRIPTS:
(1) In the Dorset County Museum = DCM
(2) In Yale University Library = Y

EXTRA PRINTINGS:
(1) *The Sphere*, 20 Dec 1913, p. 316 = S
(2) *Selected Poems*, pp. 5–6
(3) *Chosen Poems*, pp. 5–6

TITLE:
To Meet, or Not MS *before revision*
To Meet or Otherwise DCM, Y, S

INDENTATION:
1 = ll. 1, 3, 5, 7 } and so throughout
2 = ll. 2, 4, 6 } DCM

WHETHER to sally and see thee, girl of my dreams,
Or whether to stay
And see thee not! How vast the difference seems
Of Yea from Nay
Just now. Yet this same sun will slant its beams
At no far day
On our two mounds, and then what will the difference weigh!

Yet I will see thee, maiden dear, and make
The most I can
Of what remains to us amid this brake
Cimmerian
Through which we grope, and from whose thorns we ache,
While still we scan
Round our frail faltering progress for some path or plan.

By briefest meeting something sure is won;
It will have been:
Nor God nor Demon can undo the done,
Unsight the seen,
Make muted music be as unbegun,
Though things terrene
Groan in their bondage till oblivion supervene.

So, to the one long-sweeping symphony
From times remote
Till now, of human tenderness, shall we
Supply one note,
Small and untraced, yet that will ever be
Somewhere afloat
Amid the spheres, as part of sick Life's antidote.

After the Visit
21 consciously,] consciously S
23 by whose] what sad S
24] Made us crave that which could not be! S

To Meet, or Otherwise
1 sally] sail S
1 girl] child MS *before revision*
5 will] shall S
7 weigh!] weigh? S
8 maiden] phantom MS *before revision*
16 been:] been; Y
17 God] god S
17 Demon] Daemon MS, SC, PE: dæmon S
21] Remain as now they are until oblivion supervene. MS *before revision*
26 untraced,] untraced; S
Note Stanzas are numbered in S

252 The Difference

EXTRA PRINTINGS:
(1) *Selected Poems*, p. 7
(2) *Chosen Poems*, p. 7

I

SINKING down by the gate I discern the thin moon,
And a blackbird tries over old airs in the pine,
But the moon is a sorry one, sad the bird's tune,
For this spot is unknown to that Heartmate of mine.

II

Did my Heartmate but haunt here at times such as now,
The song would be joyous and cheerful the moon;
But she will see never this gate, path, or bough,
Nor I find a joy in the scene or the tune.

253 The Sun on the Bookcase

EXTRA PRINTINGS:
(1) *Selected Poems*, p. 16
(2) *Chosen Poems*, p. 16

TITLE:
1870] Not in MS, SC, SP, PE: 1872 *del* MS

(*Student's Love-Song: 1870*)

ONCE more the cauldron of the sun
Smears the bookcase with winy red,
And here my page is, and there my bed,
And the apple-tree shadows travel along.
Soon their intangible track will be run,
    And dusk grow strong
    And they have fled.

Yes: now the boiling ball is gone,
And I have wasted another day. . . .
But wasted – *wasted*, do I say?
Is it a waste to have imaged one
Beyond the hills there, who, anon,
    My great deeds done,
    Will be mine alway?

The Sun on the Bookcase
4 apple-tree] appletree MS
7 have] be MS, SC, SP, PE
8 gone,] gone. SP
9 day. . . .] day. . . . . MS
10 *wasted*,] wasted MS
12 who] whom SC1
13 deeds] deed MS
13 done,] done MS, SC, WE, PE, CP1–3 [Hardy's copy of SP (1917), corrected for CHP, has the comma deleted, but on an inserted sheet of paper, not in Hardy's hand, is: 'We think that the comma in the last line but one should be retained, as it completes the parenthesis.']

EXTRA MANUSCRIPT:
In possession of Mr Frederick B. Adams, Jnr = A [Checked from the facsimile in Sotheby's catalogue, 30 Oct 1956]

EXTRA PRINTINGS:
(1) *Selected Poems*, p. 17
(2) *Chosen Poems*, p. 17

TITLE:
'When I set out for Lyonnesse' MS
(*1870*)] Not in MS, A, SC, SP, PE

Note This was one of nine poems chosen by Hardy for the Library of the Royal Dolls' House at Windsor Castle

254 *When I Set Out for Lyonnesse*

(1870)

WHEN I set out for Lyonnesse,
A hundred miles away,
The rime was on the spray,
And starlight lit my lonesomeness
When I set out for Lyonnesse
A hundred miles away.

What would bechance at Lyonnesse
While I should sojourn there
No prophet durst declare,
Nor did the wisest wizard guess
What would bechance at Lyonnesse
While I should sojourn there.

When I came back from Lyonnesse
With magic in my eyes,
All marked with mute surmise
My radiance rare and fathomless,
When I came back from Lyonnesse
With magic in my eyes!

TITLE:
1893] Not in MS, SC, PE

255 *A Thunderstorm in Town*

(A Reminiscence: 1893)

SHE wore a new 'terra-cotta' dress,
And we stayed, because of the pelting storm,
Within the hansom's dry recess,
Though the horse had stopped; yea, motionless
We sat on, snug and warm.

When I Set Out for Lyonnesse
2 and 6] While night was waiting day MS *written in pencil and then erased*
14 eyes,] eyes A
15–16] None managed to surmise/What meant my godlike gloriousness, MS, SC, PE
16 fathomless,] fathomless A
18 eyes!] eyes. MS, A, SC, WE, PE, CP1, ME

A Thunderstorm in Town
2 storm,] storm MS
5–6 Stanza break in all editions

Then the downpour ceased, to my sharp sad pain,
And the glass that had screened our forms before
Flew up, and out she sprang to her door:
I should have kissed her if the rain
    Had lasted a minute more.

256 The Torn Letter

EXTRA PRINTING:
The English Review, Dec 1910, pp. 1–2 = ER

I

I TORE your letter into strips
    No bigger than the airy feathers
    That ducks preen out in changing weathers
Upon the shifting ripple-tips.

II

In darkness on my bed alone
    I seemed to see you in a vision,
    And hear you say: 'Why this derision
Of one drawn to you, though unknown?'

III

Yes, eve's quick mood had run its course,
    The night had cooled my hasty madness;
    I suffered a regretful sadness
Which deepened into real remorse.

IV

I thought what pensive patient days
    A soul must know of grain so tender,
    How much of good must grace the sender
Of such sweet words in such bright phrase.

V

Uprising then, as things unpriced
    I sought each fragment, patched and mended;
    The midnight whitened ere I had ended
And gathered words I had sacrificed.

A Thunderstorm in Town
6 sharp sad pain] lasting pain MS
6 pain,] pain CP2–4 [but some evidence of print deterioration]

The Torn Letter
2 airy] tiny ER
5 In darkness] Thereafter ER
9 Yes] Yea MS, ER
13 pensive] pensive, ER
14 tender,] tender; ER
19 whitened] faded ER

VI

But some, alas, of those I threw
    Were past my search, destroyed for ever:
    They were your name and place; and never
Did I regain those clues to you.

VII

I learnt I had missed, by rash unheed,
    My track; that, so the Will decided,
    In life, death, we should be divided,
And at the sense I ached indeed.

VIII

That ache for you, born long ago,
    Throbs on: I never could outgrow it.
    What a revenge, did you but know it!
But that, thank God, you do not know.

257 *Beyond the Last Lamp*

(Near Tooting Common)

I

WHILE rain, with eve in partnership,
Descended darkly, drip, drip, drip,
Beyond the last lone lamp I passed
    Walking slowly, whispering sadly,
    Two linked loiterers, wan, downcast:
Some heavy thought constrained each face,
And blinded them to time and place.

II

The pair seemed lovers, yet absorbed
In mental scenes no longer orbed
By love's young rays. Each countenance

EXTRA MANUSCRIPT:
In the Miriam Lutcher Library of the University of Texas = UT

EXTRA PRINTINGS:
(1) *Harper's Monthly Magazine* (New York), Dec 1911, p. [92] = H
(2) *Selected Poems*, pp. 150–1
(3) *Chosen Poems*, pp. 181–2

TITLE:
Beyond the last Lamp (Night in a Suburb *del*) MS
Night in a Suburb UT, H

INDENTATION:
1 = ll. 1, 2, 3, 5, 6, 7 } and so throughout H
2 = l. 4

The Torn Letter
21 threw] threw, ER
25 I learnt I had] And having ER
26–7] My first, last, only means to know you,/It dawned on me I must forgo you, ER
29 born] got ER
30 Throbs on:] Comes back; ER
30 on:] on; MS, SC, PE
31 revenge,] revenge ER
32] But that you will not, cannot know. ER

Beyond the Last Lamp
5 downcast:] downcast; UT, H
7 blinded them] made them blank UT, H
10 rays] light UT, H
Note H has no stanza numbers

As it slowly, as it sadly
Caught the lamplight's yellow glance,
Held in suspense a misery
At things which had been or might be.

III

When I retrod that watery way
Some hours beyond the droop of day,
Still I found pacing there the twain
Just as slowly, just as sadly,
Heedless of the night and rain.
One could but wonder who they were
And what wild woe detained them there.

IV

Though thirty years of blur and blot
Have slid since I beheld that spot,
And saw in curious converse there
Moving slowly, moving sadly
That mysterious tragic pair,
Its olden look may linger on –
All but the couple; they have gone.

V

Whither? Who knows, indeed. . . . And yet
To me, when nights are weird and wet,
Without those comrades there at tryst
Creeping slowly, creeping sadly,
That lone lane does not exist.
There they seem brooding on their pain,
And will, while such a lane remain.

258 *The Face at the Casement*

EXTRA PRINTING:
Selected Poems, pp. 152–4

If ever joy leave
An abiding sting of sorrow,
So befell it on the morrow
Of that May eve. . . .

Beyond the Last Lamp
12 glance,] glance MS, SC, PE
14 had . . . be] might, or might not, be UT, H
16 droop] death UT, H
20 were] were, UT, H, WE, CP1–3, ME
23 slid] flown UT, H
25 sadly] sadly, UT, H
29 indeed. . . .] indeed. . . . . MS: indeed! . . . . . UT: indeed! . . . H
34 There] Still MS, UT, H
UT has at end: Sept: 1911

The Face at the Casement
4 May eve. . . .] June eve. . . . . MS

The travelled sun dropped
To the north-west, low and lower,
The pony's trot grew slower,
Until we stopped.

'This cosy house just by
I must call at for a minute,
A sick man lies within it
Who soon will die.

'He wished to – marry me,
So I am bound, when I drive near him,
To inquire, if but to cheer him,
How he may be.'

A message was sent in,
And wordlessly we waited,
Till some one came and stated
The bulletin.

And that the sufferer said,
For her call no words could thank her;
As his angel he must rank her
Till life's spark fled.

Slowly we drove away,
When I turned my head, although not
Called to: why I turned I know not
Even to this day:

And lo, there in my view
Pressed against an upper lattice
Was a white face, gazing at us
As we withdrew.

And well did I divine
It to be the man's there dying,
Who but lately had been sighing
For her pledged mine.

The Face at the Casement
6 north-west] north west MS
8 Until] And then MS, SC, PE
13 to –] to MS, SC, SP, PE
21 said,] said MS
25 drove] moved MS
27 Called . . . turned] Called; and why I did MS: Called; why I so (so I SC2, PE) turned SC, PE
27 to:] to; SP
28 day:] day. MS, SC, SP, PE
30 an upper] a bedroom MS
34 It] That MS

Then I deigned a deed of hell;
It was done before I knew it;
What devil made me do it
I cannot tell!

Yes, while he gazed above,
I put my arm about her
That he might see, nor doubt her
My plighted Love.

The pale face vanished quick,
As if blasted, from the casement,
And my shame and self-abasement
Began their prick.

And they prick on, ceaselessly,
For that stab in Love's fierce fashion
Which, unfired by lover's passion,
Was foreign to me.

She smiled at my caress,
But why came the soft embowment
Of her shoulder at that moment
She did not guess.

Long long years has he lain
In thy garth, O sad Saint Cleather:
What tears there, bared to weather,
Will cleanse that stain!

Love is long-suffering, brave,
Sweet, prompt, precious as a jewel;
But jealousy is cruel,
Cruel as the grave!

The Face at the Casement
49 ceaselessly,] ceaselessly MS
59 bared to] in what MS
61 long-suffering] long suffering MS
63 jealousy] O, too, Love MS, SC, SP, WE, PE, CP1, ME
64 grave!] grave. MS, SC, SP, WE, PE, CP1, ME

EXTRA PRINTINGS:
(1) *Selected Poems*, p. 56
(2) *Chosen Poems*, p. 54

259 *Lost Love*

I PLAY my sweet old airs –
The airs he knew
When our love was true –
But he does not balk
His determined walk,
And passes up the stairs.

I sing my songs once more,
And presently hear
His footstep near
As if it would stay;
But he goes his way,
And shuts a distant door.

So I wait for another morn,
And another night
In this soul-sick blight;
And I wonder much
As I sit, why such
A woman as I was born!

EXTRA PRINTINGS:
(1) *Poetry and Drama*, Dec 1913, pp. 395–6 = PD
(2) *Selected Poems*, p. 76
(3) *Chosen Poems*, p. 71

TITLE:
'My Spirit will not haunt the Mound' MS

260 *My Spirit Will Not Haunt the Mound*

MY spirit will not haunt the mound
Above my breast,
But travel, memory-possessed,
To where my tremulous being found
Life largest, best.

My phantom-footed shape will go
When nightfall grays
Hither and thither along the ways
I and another used to know
In backward days.

Lost Love
8–9] And his step I hear/In the passage near MS *before revision*
13 morn,] morn MS, SC, SP, WE, PE, ME

My Spirit Will Not Haunt the Mound
2] Wherein I rest, PD

And there you'll find me, if a jot
You still should care
For me, and for my curious air;
If otherwise, then I shall not,
For you, be there.

261 Wessex Heights

(1896)

THERE are some heights in Wessex, shaped as if by a kindly hand
For thinking, dreaming, dying on, and at crises when I stand,
Say, on Ingpen Beacon eastward, or on Wylls-Neck westwardly,
I seem where I was before my birth, and after death may be.

In the lowlands I have no comrade, not even the lone man's friend –
Her who suffereth long and is kind; accepts what he is too weak to mend:
Down there they are dubious and askance; there nobody thinks as I,
But mind-chains do not clank where one's next neighbour is the sky.

In the towns I am tracked by phantoms having weird detective ways –
Shadows of beings who fellowed with myself of earlier days:
They hang about at places, and they say harsh heavy things –
Men with a wintry sneer, and women with tart disparagings.

Down there I seem to be false to myself, my simple self that was,
And is not now, and I see him watching, wondering what crass cause
Can have merged him into such a strange continuator as this,
Who yet has something in common with himself, my chrysalis.

I cannot go to the great grey Plain; there's a figure against the moon,
Nobody sees it but I, and it makes my breast beat out of tune;
I cannot go to the tall-spired town, being barred by the forms now passed
For everybody but me, in whose long vision they stand there fast.

EXTRA PRINTINGS:
(1) *Selected Poems*, pp. 93–5
(2) *Chosen Poems*, pp. 88–90

Note The heading 'Lyrics and Reveries' is *deleted* in MS just above 'Wessex Heights'

My Spirit Will Not Haunt the Mound
11 find] see PD
13 me,] me PD
13 curious] creepy PD

Wessex Heights
10 with myself] with the myself MS
12 wintry] frigid MS, SC, SP, PE
17 great] Great MS

There's a ghost at Yell'ham Bottom chiding loud at the fall of the night,
There's a ghost in Froom-side Vale, thin-lipped and vague, in a shroud of white,
There is one in the railway train whenever I do not want it near,
I see its profile against the pane, saying what I would not hear.

As for one rare fair woman, I am now but a thought of hers,
I enter her mind and another thought succeeds me that she prefers;
Yet my love for her in its fulness she herself even did not know;
Well, time cures hearts of tenderness, and now I can let her go.

So I am found on Ingpen Beacon, or on Wylls-Neck to the west,
Or else on homely Bulbarrow, or little Pilsdon Crest,
Where men have never cared to haunt, nor women have walked with me,
And ghosts then keep their distance; and I know some liberty.

EXTRA PRINTINGS:
(1) *Selected Poems*, pp. 178–9
(2) *Chosen Poems*, pp. 232–3

262 *In Death Divided*

I

I SHALL rot here, with those whom in their day
You never knew,
And alien ones who, ere they chilled to clay,
Met not my view,
Will in your distant grave-place ever neighbour you.

II

No shade of pinnacle or tree or tower,
While earth endures,
Will fall on my mound and within the hour
Steal on to yours;
One robin never haunt our two green covertures.

III

Some organ may resound on Sunday noons
By where you lie,
Some other thrill the panes with other tunes
Where moulder I;
No selfsame chords compose our common lullaby.

Wessex Heights
22 Vale,] Vale – MS
22 thin-lipped] thin lipped MS, SC, WE, PE, CP1–3
23 railway train] railway-train MS, SC, SP, WE, PE, ME, CHP
23 it near] her there MS *before revision*
28 time] God MS *before revision*
MS has 'December, 1896' *deleted* at end

In Death Divided
6 tower,] tower MS
7 endures,] endures MS
15 selfsame] self-same ME

IV

The simply-cut memorial at my head
Perhaps may take
A rustic form, and that above your bed
A stately make;
No linking symbol show thereon for our tale's sake.

V

And in the monotonous moils of strained, hard-run
Humanity,
The eternal tie which binds us twain in one
No eye will see
Stretching across the miles that sever you from me.

189–

263 *The Place on the Map*

EXTRA PRINTING:
The English Review, Sept 1913, pp. 161–2 = ER

TITLE:
ER has sub-title:
A Poor Schoolmaster's Story

I

I LOOK upon the map that hangs by me –
Its shires and towns and rivers lined in varnished artistry –
And I mark a jutting height
Coloured purple, with a margin of blue sea.

II

– 'Twas a day of latter summer, hot and dry;
Ay, even the waves seemed drying as we walked on, she and I,
By this spot where, calmly quite,
She unfolded what would happen by and by.

III

This hanging map depicts the coast and place,
And re-creates therewith our unforeboded troublous case
All distinctly to my sight,
And her tension, and the aspect of her face.

In Death Divided
16 simply-cut] simply graved MS
18 rustic] Gothic MS, SC, PE
19] Be Greek in make; SC, PE
19 stately] classic MS
189–] Not in MS, SC, SP, WE, PE, CP1–3, ME

The Place on the Map
2 artistry –] artistry, MS, ER
6 walked] rode MS *before revision*
8 unfolded] informed me MS, ER, SC, WE, PE, ME
9 place,] place MS
10 re-creates] adumbrates too MS, ER, SC1: resuscitates SC2, PE
10 unforeboded] unexpected MS, ER, SC, PE

IV

Weeks and weeks we had loved beneath that blazing blue,
Which had lost the art of raining, as her eyes to-day had too,
While she told what, as by sleight,
Shot our firmament with rays of ruddy hue.

V

For the wonder and the wormwood of the whole
Was that what in realms of reason would have joyed our double soul
Wore a torrid tragic light
Under order-keeping's rigorous control.

VI

So, the map revives her words, the spot, the time,
And the thing we found we had to face before the next year's prime;
The charted coast stares bright,
And its episode comes back in pantomime.

264 The Schreckhorn

(With thoughts of Leslie Stephen)
(June 1897)

ALOOF, as if a thing of mood and whim;
Now that its spare and desolate figure gleams
Upon my nearing vision, less it seems
A looming Alp-height than a guise of him
Who scaled its horn with ventured life and limb,
Drawn on by vague imaginings, maybe,
Of semblance to his personality
In its quaint glooms, keen lights, and rugged trim.

At his last change, when Life's dull coils unwind,
Will he, in old love, hitherward escape,
And the eternal essence of his mind
Enter this silent adamantine shape,
And his low voicing haunt its slipping snows
When dawn that calls the climber dyes them rose?

EXTRA PRINTINGS:
(1) *The Life and Letters of Leslie Stephen* by F. W. Maitland (London, 1906), p. 278 = LS
(2) *Selected Poems*, p. 122
(3) *Chosen Poems*, p. 156

Note 'Where the Picnic Was' is placed between 'The Place on the Map' and 'The Schreckhorn' in MS, SC, PE

The Place on the Map
13 blazing] beaming MS, ER
13 blue,] blue MS
14 her eyes to-day] of late her eyes ER
14 to-day] of late MS, SC1
20 order-keeping's rigorous] superstition's hideous ER
20 rigorous] merciless MS
21 time,] time MS
22 prime;] prime: MS, ER

The Schreckhorn
1 whim;] whim, LS
9 At] – At LS

265 *A Singer Asleep*

(*Algernon Charles Swinburne, 1837–1909*)

I

IN this fair niche above the unslumbering sea,
That sentrys up and down all night, all day,
From cove to promontory, from ness to bay,
The Fates have fitly bidden that he should be
Pillowed eternally.

II

– It was as though a garland of red roses
Had fallen about the hood of some smug nun
When irresponsibly dropped as from the sun,
In fulth of numbers freaked with musical closes,
Upon Victoria's formal middle time
His leaves of rhythm and rhyme.

III

O that far morning of a summer day
When, down a terraced street whose pavements lay
Glassing the sunshine into my bent eyes,
I walked and read with a quick glad surprise
New words, in classic guise, –

IV

The passionate pages of his earlier years,
Fraught with hot sighs, sad laughters, kisses, tears;
Fresh-fluted notes, yet from a minstrel who
Blew them not naïvely, but as one who knew
Full well why thus he blew.

EXTRA MANUSCRIPTS:
(1) In Newnes Public Library (Borough of Wandsworth) = NPL
(2) In the British Library (Ashley Library) = A
(3) It has not been possible to trace the MS once in the possession of C. H. St John Hornby.

EXTRA PRINTINGS:
(1) *The English Review*, April 1910, pp. 1–3 = ER
(2) *Selected Poems*, pp. 124–6
(3) *Chosen Poems*, pp. 158–60

TITLE:
(*Algernon* . . .)] (A.C.S. 1837–1909) NPL, ER

A South Coast Nocturne NPL *before revision*

A Singer Asleep
8 sun,] sun NPL, ER
9 closes,] closes NPL, ER
10 time] time, ER
16 words,] words A
18 tears;] tears; – NPL, ER

V

I still can hear the brabble and the roar
At those thy tunes, O still one, now passed through
That fitful fire of tongues then entered new!
Their power is spent like spindrift on this shore;
        Thine swells yet more and more.

VI

– His singing-mistress verily was no other
Than she the Lesbian, she the music-mother
Of all the tribe that feel in melodies;
Who leapt, love-anguished, from the Leucadian steep
Into the rambling world-encircling deep
        Which hides her where none sees.

VII

And one can hold in thought that nightly here
His phantom may draw down to the water's brim,
And hers come up to meet it, as a dim
Lone shine upon the heaving hydrosphere,
And mariners wonder as they traverse near,
        Unknowing of her and him.

VIII

One dreams him sighing to her spectral form:
'O teacher, where lies hid thy burning line;
Where are those songs, O poetess divine
Whose very orts are love incarnadine?'
And her smile back: 'Disciple true and warm,
        Sufficient now are thine.' . . .

IX

So here, beneath the waking constellations,
Where the waves peal their everlasting strains,
And their dull subterrene reverberations
Shake him when storms make mountains of their plains –

A Singer Asleep
27 – His] His NPL
31 world-encircling] world encircling MS
37 wonder] wonder, AL
41 divine] divine, NPL, ER
42 orts] arts SC, SP, PE
44 thine.' . . .] thine.' . . . . MS, NPL: thine . . .' ER

Him once their peer in sad improvisations,
And deft as wind to cleave their frothy manes –
I leave him, while the daylight gleam declines
Upon the capes and chines.

Bonchurch, 1910

266 *A Plaint to Man*

TITLE:
The Plaint of a Puppet MS, *before revision*

WHEN you slowly emerged from the den of Time,
And gained percipience as you grew,
And fleshed you fair out of shapeless slime,

Wherefore, O Man, did there come to you
The unhappy need of creating me –
A form like your own – for praying to?

My virtue, power, utility,
Within my maker must all abide,
Since none in myself can ever be,

One thin as a phasm on a lantern-slide
Shown forth in the dark upon some dim sheet,
And by none but its showman vivified.

'Such a forced device,' you may say, 'is meet
For easing a loaded heart at whiles:
Man needs to conceive of a mercy-seat

Somewhere above the gloomy aisles
Of this wailful world, or he could not bear
The irk no local hope beguiles.'

– But since I was framed in your first despair
The doing without me has had no play
In the minds of men when shadows scare;

And now that I dwindle day by day
Beneath the deicide eyes of seers
In a light that will not let me stay,

A Singer Asleep
Bonchurch, 1910] Not in NPL, ER

A Plaint to Man
10 phasm] shape MS, SC, PE
15 mercy-seat] mercy seat MS [Could be one word]

And to-morrow the whole of me disappears,
The truth should be told, and the fact be faced
That had best been faced in earlier years:

The fact of life with dependence placed
On the human heart's resource alone,
In brotherhood bonded close and graced

With loving-kindness fully blown,
And visioned help unsought, unknown.

1909–10

267 *God's Funeral*

EXTRA MANUSCRIPT:
Permission was refused to see the MS in the possession of Mr Frederick B. Adams, Jnr

EXTRA PRINTING:
The Fortnightly Review, 1 March 1912, pp. [397]–399 = FR

TITLE:
FR has sub-title:
An Allegorical Conception
Of the present state of Theology

I

I SAW a slowly-stepping train –
Lined on the brows, scoop-eyed and bent and hoar –
Following in files across a twilit plain
A strange and mystic form the foremost bore.

II

And by contagious throbs of thought
Or latent knowledge that within me lay
And had already stirred me, I was wrought
To consciousness of sorrow even as they.

III

The fore-borne shape, to my blurred eyes,
At first seemed man-like, and anon to change
To an amorphous cloud of marvellous size,
At times endowed with wings of glorious range.

IV

And this phantasmal variousness
Ever possessed it as they drew along:
Yet throughout all it symboled none the less
Potency vast and loving-kindness strong.

A Plaint to Man
31 loving-kindness] lovingkindness MS

God's Funeral
1 slowly-stepping] slowly stepping MS, FR
2 scoop-eyed and bent] scoop-eyed, and bent, FR
5 thought] thought, FR
14 along:] along; FR
16 vast] vast, FR
16 loving-kindness] lovingkindness MS, FR

V

Almost before I knew I bent
Towards the moving columns without a word;
They, growing in bulk and numbers as they went,
Struck out sick thoughts that could be overheard: –

VI

'O man-projected Figure, of late
Imaged as we, thy knell who shall survive?
Whence came it we were tempted to create
One whom we can no longer keep alive?

VII

'Framing him jealous, fierce, at first,
We gave him justice as the ages rolled,
Will to bless those by circumstance accurst,
And longsuffering, and mercies manifold.

VIII

'And, tricked by our own early dream
And need of solace, we grew self-deceived,
Our making soon our maker did we deem,
And what we had imagined we believed.

IX

'Till, in Time's stayless stealthy swing,
Uncompromising rude reality
Mangled the Monarch of our fashioning,
Who quavered, sank; and now has ceased to be.

X

'So, toward our myth's oblivion,
Darkling, and languid-lipped, we creep and grope
Sadlier than those who wept in Babylon,
Whose Zion was a still abiding hope.

God's Funeral
18 columns] columns, FR
22 survive?] survive! FR
36 quavered,] quavering FR
37 toward] towards FR
38] Darkling and languid-lipped we creep and grope, FR
38 grope] grope, MS
39 who] that FR

XI

'How sweet it was in years far hied
To start the wheels of day with trustful prayer,
To lie down liegely at the eventide
And feel a blest assurance he was there!

XII

'And who or what shall fill his place?
Whither will wanderers turn distracted eyes
For some fixed star to stimulate their pace
Towards the goal of their enterprise?' . . .

XIII

Some in the background then I saw,
Sweet women, youths, men, all incredulous,
Who chimed: 'This is a counterfeit of straw,
This requiem mockery! Still he lives to us!'

XIV

I could not buoy their faith: and yet
Many I had known: with all I sympathized;
And though struck speechless, I did not forget
That what was mourned for, I, too, long had prized.

XV

Still, how to bear such loss I deemed
The insistent question for each animate mind,
And gazing, to my growing sight there seemed
A pale yet positive gleam low down behind,

XVI

Whereof, to lift the general night,
A certain few who stood aloof had said,
'See you upon the horizon that small light –
Swelling somewhat?' Each mourner shook his head.

God's Funeral
48 enterprise?' . . .] enterprise?' . . . . MS
51] Who chimed as one: 'This figure is of straw, MS, FR, SC, PE
53 buoy] prop MS, FR, SC, PE
53 faith:] faith; FR
54 known:] known; FR
56 for,] for FR
56 long] once MS, FR, SC, WE, PE, ME
64 head.] head CP4 [print deterioration?]

XVII

And they composed a crowd of whom
Some were right good, and many nigh the best. . . .
Thus dazed and puzzled 'twixt the gleam and gloom
Mechanically I followed with the rest.

1908–10

268 Spectres that Grieve

EXTRA PRINTING:
The Saturday Review, 3 Jan 1914, p. 16 = SR

TITLE:
The Plaint of Certain Spectres SR

'IT is not death that harrows us,' they lipped,
'The soundless cell is in itself relief,
For life is an unfenced flower, benumbed and nipped
At unawares, and at its best but brief.'

The speakers, sundry phantoms of the gone,
Had risen like filmy flames of phosphor dye,
As if the palest of sheet lightnings shone
From the sward near me, as from a nether sky.

And much surprised was I that, spent and dead,
They should not, like the many, be at rest,
But stray as apparitions; hence I said,
'Why, having slipped life, hark you back distressed?'

'We are among the few death sets not free,
The hurt, misrepresented names, who come
At each year's brink, and cry to History
To do them justice, or go past them dumb.

'We are stript of rights; our shames lie unredressed,
Our deeds in full anatomy are not shown,
Our words in morsels merely are expressed
On the scriptured page, our motives blurred, unknown.'

Then all these shaken slighted visitants sped
Into the vague, and left me musing there
On fames that well might instance what they had said,
Until the New-Year's dawn strode up the air.

God's Funeral
1908–10] Not in FR

Spectres that Grieve
5 the] men SR
7 sheet lightnings] sheet-lightnings SR
21 slighted] ill-vouched MS: ill-writ SR

EXTRA PRINTING:
The Saturday Review, 27 Sept 1913, p. 396 = SR

TITLE:
'Ah, Are you digging on my grave?' MS

269 *Ah, Are You Digging on My Grave?*

'AH, are you digging on my grave,
    My loved one? – planting rue?'
– 'No: yesterday he went to wed
One of the brightest wealth has bred.
"It cannot hurt her now," he said,
    "That I should not be true." '

'Then who is digging on my grave?
    My nearest dearest kin?'
– 'Ah, no: they sit and think, "What use!
What good will planting flowers produce?
No tendance of her mound can loose
    Her spirit from Death's gin." '

'But some one digs upon my grave?
    My enemy? – prodding sly?'
– 'Nay: when she heard you had passed the Gate
That shuts on all flesh soon or late,
She thought you no more worth her hate,
    And cares not where you lie.'

'Then, who is digging on my grave?
    Say – since I have not guessed!'
– 'O it is I, my mistress dear,
Your little dog, who still lives near,
And much I hope my movements here
    Have not disturbed your rest?'

'Ah, yes! *You* dig upon my grave. . . .
    Why flashed it not on me
That one true heart was left behind!
What feeling do we ever find
To equal among human kind
    A dog's fidelity!'

Ah, Are You Digging on My Grave?
1 grave,] grave MS, SC, WE, PE, CP1–3
2 loved] beloved CP1 [Corrected to 'loved' on errata slip]
4] One in the prime of lustihead. SR
9 – 'Ah] ' – Ah MS, SR
9 no:] no; MS, SR, SC, WE, PE, ME
10 What good] To what SR
10 produce] conduce SR
15 – 'Nay] 'Nay SR
16 flesh] flesh, SR
21 – 'O] ' – O MS, SR
29 human kind] human-kind SR

'Mistress, I dug upon your grave
To bury a bone, in case
I should be hungry near this spot
When passing on my daily trot.
I am sorry, but I quite forgot
It was your resting-place.'

270 Self-Unconscious

TITLE:
Self-unconscious MS

Note
In MS, SC, PE the 'Satires of Circumstance/In Fifteen Glimpses' are found between 'Ah, Are You Digging on My Grave?' and 'Self-Unconscious'

ALONG the way
He walked that day,
Watching shapes that reveries limn,
And seldom he
Had eyes to see
The moment that encompassed him.

Bright yellowhammers
Made mirthful clamours,
And billed long straws with a bustling air,
And bearing their load
Flew up the road
That he followed, alone, without interest there.

From bank to ground
And over and round
They sidled along the adjoining hedge;
Sometimes to the gutter
Their yellow flutter
Would dip from the nearest slatestone ledge.

The smooth sea-line
With a metal shine,
And flashes of white, and a sail thereon,
He would also descry
With a half-wrapt eye
Between the projects he mused upon.

Ah, Are You Digging on My Grave?
35 I quite] I had quite SR

Self-Unconscious
6] The life that lay in front of him. MS
19 sea-line] sea-line, MS
20 shine,] shine MS

Yes, round him were these
Earth's artistries,
But specious plans that came to his call
Did most engage
His pilgrimage,
While himself he did not see at all.

Dead now as sherds
Are the yellow birds,
And all that mattered has passed away;
Yet God, the Elf,
Now shows him that self
As he was, and should have been shown, that day.

O it would have been good
Could he then have stood
At a clear-eyed distance, and conned the whole,
But now such vision
Is mere derision,
Nor soothes his body nor saves his soul.

Not much, some may
Incline to say,
To see therein, had it all been seen.
Nay! he is aware
A thing was there
That loomed with an immortal mien.

Near Bossiney

271 *The Discovery*

I WANDERED to a crude coast
Like a ghost;
Upon the hills I saw fires –
Funeral pyres
Seemingly – and heard breaking
Waves like distant cannonades that set the land shaking.

Self-Unconscious
32 birds,] birds MS
34 Elf] elf MS
39 clear-eyed] focussed MS, SC, PE
45 therein] in him MS, SC1
Near Bossiney] Not in MS, SC, WE, PE, CP1

The Discovery
5 Seemingly] Seeming MS
5 and] and I MS
6–7 Stanza break in all editions

And so I never once guessed
  A Love-nest,
Bowered and candle-lit, lay
  In my way,
Till I found a hid hollow,
Where I burst on her my heart could not but follow.

272 *Tolerance*

'It is a foolish thing,' said I,
'To bear with such, and pass it by;
Yet so I do, I know not why!'

And at each cross I would surmise
That if I had willed not in that wise
I might have spared me many sighs.

But now the only happiness
In looking back that I possess –
Whose lack would leave me comfortless –

Is to remember I refrained
From masteries I might have gained,
And for my tolerance was disdained;

For see, a tomb. And if it were
I had bent and broke, I should not dare
To linger in the shadows there.

273 *Before and after Summer*

EXTRA PRINTINGS:
(1) *The New Weekly*, 4 April 1914, p. 77 = NW
(2) *Selected Poems*, p. 14
(3) *Chosen Poems*, p. 14

INDENTATION:
ll. 4, 6, 14, 16 in NW are indented right

I

Looking forward to the spring
One puts up with anything.
On this February day
Though the winds leap down the street
Wintry scourgings seem but play, .
And these later shafts of sleet

Tolerance
4 cross] clash MS, SC, PE
5 willed . . . wise] acted otherwise MS, SC, PE
6 spared] saved MS, SC, PE
14 bent] wrenched MS

Before and after Summer
1 spring] Spring MS, NW
3 day] day, SC, SP, PE
4 street] street, NW, SC, PE
5 play,] play; NW

– Sharper pointed than the first –
And these later snows – the worst –
Are as a half-transparent blind
Riddled by rays from sun behind.

II

Shadows of the October pine
Reach into this room of mine:
On the pine there swings a bird;
He is shadowed with the tree.
Mutely perched he bills no word;
Blank as I am even is he.
For those happy suns are past,
Fore-discerned in winter last.
When went by their pleasure, then?
I, alas, perceived not when.

274 *At Day-Close in November*

TITLE:
At Day-close in November (Autumn Evening *del*) MS

THE ten hours' light is abating,
    And a late bird wings across,
Where the pines, like waltzers waiting,
    Give their black heads a toss.

Beech leaves, that yellow the noon-time,
    Float past like specks in the eye;
I set every tree in my June time,
    And now they obscure the sky.

And the children who ramble through here
    Conceive that there never has been
A time when no tall trees grew here,
    That none will in time be seen.

Before and after Summer
7 Sharper pointed] sharper-pointed MS, NW
9 as] not in NW
9 a] not in MS
9 blind] panes MS: pane NW
10] Giving on a bright domain. NW
10 sun behind] gay champaigns MS
12 mine:] mine; NW
13 swings] stands MS, NW, SC, PE
17 past,] past MS, NW
NW has at end: Written in 1910. Now first published.

At Day-Close in November
2 wings] flies MS, SC, PE
12] A time when none will be seen. MS, SC, PE, CP1 [But CP1 corrected on errata slip to later version]

275 *The Year's Awakening*

EXTRA PRINTINGS:
(1) *The New Weekly*, 21 March 1914, p. 9 = NW
(2) *The Society of Dorset Men in London Year-Book*, 1914–15 = DYB

How do you know that the pilgrim track
Along the belting zodiac
Swept by the sun in his seeming rounds
Is traced by now to the Fishes' bounds
And into the Ram, when weeks of cloud
Have wrapt the sky in a clammy shroud,
And never as yet a tinct of spring
Has shown in the Earth's apparelling;
O vespering bird, how do you know,
How do you know?

How do you know, deep underground,
Hid in your bed from sight and sound,
Without a turn in temperature,
With weather life can scarce endure,
That light has won a fraction's strength,
And day put on some moments' length,
Whereof in merest rote will come,
Weeks hence, mild airs that do not numb;
O crocus root, how do you know,
How do you know?

February 1910

276 *Under the Waterfall*

TITLE:
MS has 'The Lost Glass', written in pencil and erased, near title

'WHENEVER I plunge my arm, like this,
In a basin of water, I never miss
The sweet sharp sense of a fugitive day
Fetched back from its thickening shroud of gray.
Hence the only prime
And real love-rhyme
That I know by heart,
And that leaves no smart,

The Year's Awakening
5 Ram,] Ram DYB
7–8 Not in NW
13 turn] change NW
17–18 Not in NW
February 1910] Not in DYB
NW has at end: Written in 1910. Now first published.

Under the Waterfall
2 basin] bason MS
8 No stanza break

Is the purl of a little valley fall
About three spans wide and two spans tall
Over a table of solid rock,
And into a scoop of the self-same block;
The purl of a runlet that never ceases
In stir of kingdoms, in wars, in peaces;
With a hollow boiling voice it speaks
And has spoken since hills were turfless peaks.'

'And why gives this the only prime
Idea to you of a real love-rhyme?
And why does plunging your arm in a bowl
Full of spring water, bring throbs to your soul?'

'Well, under the fall, in a crease of the stone,
Though where precisely none ever has known,
Jammed darkly, nothing to show how prized,
And by now with its smoothness opalized,
            Is a drinking-glass:
            For, down that pass
            My lover and I
            Walked under a sky
Of blue with a leaf-wove awning of green,
In the burn of August, to paint the scene,
And we placed our basket of fruit and wine
By the runlet's rim, where we sat to dine;
And when we had drunk from the glass together,
Arched by the oak-copse from the weather,
I held the vessel to rinse in the fall,
Where it slipped, and sank, and was past recall,
Though we stooped and plumbed the little abyss
With long bared arms. There the glass still is.
And, as said, if I thrust my arm below
Cold water in basin or bowl, a throe
From the past awakens a sense of that time,
And the glass we used, and the cascade's rhyme.
The basin seems the pool, and its edge
The hard smooth face of the brook-side ledge,

Under the Waterfall
12 self-same] selfsame MS
29] Of spotless blue leaf-veiled with green, MS
34 oak-copse] oak-scrub MS
40 basin] bason MS
42 we] both MS, SC, PE
43 basin] bason MS
44 brook-side] brookside MS

And the leafy pattern of china-ware
The hanging plants that were bathing there.

'By night, by day, when it shines or lours,
There lies intact that chalice of ours,
And its presence adds to the rhyme of love
Persistently sung by the fall above.
No lip has touched it since his and mine
In turns therefrom sipped lovers' wine.'

Under the Waterfall
46 were bathing] bordered MS
47 night,] night MS
48 chalice] glass MS *before revision*

EXTRA PRINTINGS:
(1) *Selected Poems*, pp. 59–60
(2) *Chosen Poems*, pp. 55–6

Note In MS, SC, PE 'The Spell of the Rose' and 'St Launce's Revisited' are found between 'Under the Waterfall' and 'The Going'

POEMS OF 1912–13

Veteris vestigia flammae

277 The Going

WHY did you give no hint that night
That quickly after the morrow's dawn,
And calmly, as if indifferent quite,
You would close your term here, up and be gone
        Where I could not follow
        With wing of swallow
To gain one glimpse of you ever anon!

        Never to bid good-bye,
        Or lip me the softest call,
Or utter a wish for a word, while I
Saw morning harden upon the wall,
        Unmoved, unknowing
        That your great going
Had place that moment, and altered all.

Why do you make me leave the house
And think for a breath it is you I see
At the end of the alley of bending boughs
Where so often at dusk you used to be;
        Till in darkening dankness
        The yawning blankness
Of the perspective sickens me!

        You were she who abode
        By those red-veined rocks far West,
You were the swan-necked one who rode
Along the beetling Beeny Crest,
        And, reining nigh me,
        Would muse and eye me,
While Life unrolled us its very best.

The Going
3 quite,] quite MS
9 lip] give MS, SC, SP, PE
11 wall,] wall MS
16 a . . . is] an instant it's MS
19 darkening] creeping MS
26 me,] me MS

Why, then, latterly did we not speak,
Did we not think of those days long dead,
And ere your vanishing strive to seek
That time's renewal? We might have said,
  'In this bright spring weather
  We'll visit together
Those places that once we visited.'

  Well, well! All's past amend,
  Unchangeable. It must go.
I seem but a dead man held on end
To sink down soon. . . . O you could not know
  That such swift fleeing
  No soul foreseeing –
Not even I – would undo me so!

December 1912

278 *Your Last Drive*

TITLE:
Your last Drive MS

HERE by the moorway you returned,
And saw the borough lights ahead
That lit your face – all undiscerned
To be in a week the face of the dead,
And you told of the charm of that haloed view
That never again would beam on you.

And on your left you passed the spot
Where eight days later you were to lie,
And be spoken of as one who was not;
Beholding it with a heedless eye
As alien from you, though under its tree
You soon would halt everlastingly.

I drove not with you. . . . Yet had I sat
At your side that eve I should not have seen
That the countenance I was glancing at
Had a last-time look in the flickering sheen,
Nor have read the writing upon your face,
'I go hence soon to my resting-place;

The Going
33 this bright] the next MS
38 seem but] am now MS
39 soon. . . .] soon. . . . . MS

Your Last Drive
10 heedless] cursory MS, SC, PE
13 you. . . .] you. . . . . MS

'You may miss me then. But I shall not know
How many times you visit me there,
Or what your thoughts are, or if you go
There never at all. And I shall not care.
Should you censure me I shall take no heed,
And even your praises no more shall need.'

True: never you'll know. And you will not mind.
But shall I then slight you because of such?
Dear ghost, in the past did you ever find
The thought 'What profit,' move me much?
Yet abides the fact, indeed, the same, –
You are past love, praise, indifference, blame.

December 1912

279 *The Walk*

You did not walk with me
Of late to the hill-top tree
By the gated ways,
As in earlier days;
You were weak and lame,
So you never came,
And I went alone, and I did not mind,
Not thinking of you as left behind.

I walked up there to-day
Just in the former way;
Surveyed around
The familiar ground
By myself again:
What difference, then?
Only that underlying sense
Of the look of a room on returning thence.

Your Last Drive
23 heed,] heed MS, SC, WE, PE, CP1
24 no more shall] I shall not MS, SC, PE
28] Me one whom consequence influenced much? MS, SC1 [This line has been crossed through in MS, replaced by the later version, which has then also been crossed through while the first version has been stetted]
28 Both SC2 and PE have 'profit?" ' for 'profit," ' and 'much' for 'much?', indicating that PE was set up from SC2
29] Yet the fact indeed remains the same, MS, SC, PE

The Walk
2 hill-top] hill top MS
3–4] As in earlier days,/By the gated ways: MS
10 way;] way: SC, PE

280 Rain on a Grave

TITLE:
Rain on her Grave MS *before revision*

CLOUDS spout upon her
Their waters amain
In ruthless disdain, –
Her who but lately
Had shivered with pain
As at touch of dishonour
If there had lit on her
So coldly, so straightly
Such arrows of rain:

One who to shelter
Her delicate head
Would quicken and quicken
Each tentative tread
If drops chanced to pelt her
That summertime spills
In dust-paven rills
When thunder-clouds thicken
And birds close their bills.

Would that I lay there
And she were housed here!
Or better, together
Were folded away there
Exposed to one weather
We both, – who would stray there
When sunny the day there,
Or evening was clear
At the prime of the year.

Soon will be growing
Green blades from her mound,
And daisies be showing
Like stars on the ground,
Till she form part of them –
Ay – the sweet heart of them,

Rain on a Grave
9 rain:] rain. MS, SC, PE
10 One] She MS, SC, PE
22 there] there – MS
23 weather] weather, MS
24 both,] both MS

Loved beyond measure
With a child's pleasure
 All her life's round.

31 Jan. 1913

EXTRA PRINTINGS:
(1) *Selected Poems*, pp. 61–2
(2) *Chosen Poems*, pp. 57–8

TITLE:
'I found her out there' MS

281 *I Found Her Out There*

I FOUND her out there
On a slope few see,
That falls westwardly
To the salt-edged air,
Where the ocean breaks
On the purple strand,
And the hurricane shakes
The solid land.

I brought her here,
And have laid her to rest
In a noiseless nest
No sea beats near.
She will never be stirred
In her loamy cell
By the waves long heard
And loved so well.

So she does not sleep
By those haunted heights
The Atlantic smites
And the blind gales sweep,
Whence she often would gaze
At Dundagel's famed head,
While the dipping blaze
Dyed her face fire-red;

And would sigh at the tale
Of sunk Lyonnesse,
As a wind-tugged tress
Flapped her cheek like a flail;

I Found Her Out There
4 salt-edged] sharp-edged SC1
22 famed] far MS, SC, SP, PE
22 head,] head MS
27 As] While SC1

Or listen at whiles
With a thought-bound brow
To the murmuring miles
She is far from now.

Yet her shade, maybe,
Will creep underground
Till it catch the sound
Of that western sea
As it swells and sobs
Where she once domiciled,
And joy in its throbs
With the heart of a child.

282 *Without Ceremony*

EXTRA PRINTING:
Selected Poems, p. 63

It was your way, my dear,
To vanish without a word
When callers, friends, or kin
Had left, and I hastened in
To rejoin you, as I inferred.

And when you'd a mind to career
Off anywhere – say to town –
You were all on a sudden gone
Before I had thought thereon,
Or noticed your trunks were down.

So, now that you disappear
For ever in that swift style,
Your meaning seems to me
Just as it used to be:
'Good-bye is not worth while!'

I Found Her Out There
34 creep] glide SC1
39 joy] joys CP1 [Corrected to 'joy' on errata slip]
SP adds at end: *December* 1912

Without Ceremony
2 vanish] be gone (have retired MS *del*) MS, SC, SP, PE
15 while!] while. MS

283 *Lament*

How she would have loved
A party to-day! –
Bright-hatted and gloved,
With table and tray
And chairs on the lawn
Her smiles would have shone
With welcomings. . . . But
She is shut, she is shut
    From friendship's spell
    In the jailing shell
    Of her tiny cell.

Or she would have reigned
At a dinner to-night
With ardours unfeigned,
And a generous delight;
All in her abode
She'd have freely bestowed
On her guests. . . . But alas,
She is shut under grass
    Where no cups flow,
    Powerless to know
    That it might be so.

And she would have sought
With a child's eager glance
The shy snowdrops brought
By the new year's advance,
And peered in the rime
Of Candlemas-time
For crocuses . . . chanced
It that she were not tranced
    From sights she loved best;
    Wholly possessed
    By an infinite rest!

Lament
7 welcomings. . . .] welcomings. . . . . MS
11 tiny] clodded MS *before revision*
14 unfeigned,] unfeigned MS
19] She is shut, she is shut MS *before revision*
29 crocuses . . .] crocuses. . . . . MS
29 chanced] But MS *before revision*
30] She is shut, she is shut MS *before revision*

And we are here staying
Amid these stale things,
Who care not for gaying,
And those junketings
That used so to joy her,
And never to cloy her
As us they cloy! . . . But
She is shut, she is shut
From the cheer of them, dead
To all done and said
In her yew-arched bed.

284 *The Haunter*

He does not think that I haunt here nightly:
How shall I let him know
That whither his fancy sets him wandering
I, too, alertly go? –
Hover and hover a few feet from him
Just as I used to do,
But cannot answer the words he lifts me –
Only listen thereto!

When I could answer he did not say them:
When I could let him know
How I would like to join in his journeys
Seldom he wished to go.
Now that he goes and wants me with him
More than he used to do,
Never he sees my faithful phantom
Though he speaks thereto.

Yes, I companion him to places
Only dreamers know,
Where the shy hares print long paces,
Where the night rooks go;

Lament
35 things,] things MS, SC, PE
40 As us they cloy] By frequency MS *before revision*
40 cloy! . . .] cloy! . . . . . MS
44 her] a MS, SC, PE
44 yew-arched] yew-testered (-screened *del*) MS

The Haunter
7 the words he lifts] his words addressed MS, SC, PE
17 companion] accompany MS, SC, PE
19 print long paces] show their faces MS, SC1
19 print] limp SC2, PE

Into old aisles where the past is all to him,
Close as his shade can do,
Always lacking the power to call to him,
Near as I reach thereto!

What a good haunter I am, O tell him!
Quickly make him know
If he but sigh since my loss befell him
Straight to his side I go.
Tell him a faithful one is doing
All that love can do
Still that his path may be worth pursuing,
And to bring peace thereto.

EXTRA PRINTINGS:
(1) *Selected Poems*, p. 64
(2) *Chosen Poems*, p. 59

285 *The Voice*

WOMAN much missed, how you call to me, call to me,
Saying that now you are not as you were
When you had changed from the one who was all to me,
But as at first, when our day was fair.

Can it be you that I hear? Let me view you, then,
Standing as when I drew near to the town
Where you would wait for me: yes, as I knew you then,
Even to the original air-blue gown!

Or is it only the breeze, in its listlessness
Travelling across the wet mead to me here,
You being ever dissolved to wan wistlessness,
Heard no more again far or near?

Thus I; faltering forward,
Leaves around me falling,
Wind oozing thin through the thorn from norward,
And the woman calling.

December 1912

The Haunter
25 him!] him, MS, SC, PE
29–32] And if it be that at night I am stronger,/Little harm day can do; (Go, too, by day I do: SC1)/Please, then, keep him in gloom no longer,/Even ghosts tend thereto! MS, SC1

The Voice
1 Woman much missed] O woman weird MS
5 you,] you MS
6] Standing attent as I came to the town MS *before revision*
7 would wait for] long waited MS *before revision*
8 air-blue] hat and MS
11 dissolved to wan wistlessness] consigned to existlessness MS, SC, SP, PE
11 wan wistlessness] existlessness WE, CP1, ME
13 I;] I, MS
15 norward,] norward MS, SC, SP, PE
December 1912] Not in MS

286 His Visitor

I COME across from Mellstock while the moon wastes weaker
To behold where I lived with you for twenty years and more:
I shall go in the gray, at the passing of the mail-train,
And need no setting open of the long familiar door
        As before.

The change I notice in my once own quarters!
A formal-fashioned border where the daisies used to be,
The rooms new painted, and the pictures altered,
And other cups and saucers, and no cosy nook for tea
        As with me.

I discern the dim faces of the sleep-wrapt servants;
They are not those who tended me through feeble hours and strong,
But strangers quite, who never knew my rule here,
Who never saw me painting, never heard my softling song
        Float along.

So I don't want to linger in this re-decked dwelling,
I feel too uneasy at the contrasts I behold,
And I make again for Mellstock to return here never,
And rejoin the roomy silence, and the mute and manifold
        Souls of old.

1913

287 A Circular

As 'legal representative'
I read a missive not my own,
On new designs the senders give
        For clothes, in tints as shown.

Here figure blouses, gowns for tea,
And presentation-trains of state,
Charming ball-dresses, millinery,
        Warranted up to date.

His Visitor
6 own] old MS
7 formal-fashioned] brilliant budded MS, SC, WE, PE, CP1, ME
19 and the mute and] where repose the MS

A Circular
2 own,] own MS

And this gay-pictured, spring-time shout
Of Fashion, hails what lady proud?
Her who before last year ebbed out
    Was costumed in a shroud.

EXTRA PRINTING:
Selected Poems, pp. 65–6

TITLE:
A (The *del*) Dream indeed? MS [Workings erased around the title in MS show that 'The Fancy' was considered as a title]

288 A Dream or No

WHY go to Saint-Juliot? What's Juliot to me?
    Some strange necromancy
    But charmed me to fancy
That much of my life claims the spot as its key.

Yes. I have had dreams of that place in the West,
    And a maiden abiding
    Thereat as in hiding;
Fair-eyed and white-shouldered, broad-browed and brown-tressed.

And of how, coastward bound on a night long ago,
    There lonely I found her,
    The sea-birds around her,
And other than nigh things uncaring to know.

So sweet her life there (in my thought has it seemed)
    That quickly she drew me
    To take her unto me,
And lodge her long years with me. Such have I dreamed.

But nought of that maid from Saint-Juliot I see;
    Can she ever have been here,
    And shed her life's sheen here,
The woman I thought a long housemate with me?

Does there even a place like Saint-Juliot exist?
    Or a Vallency Valley
    With stream and leafed alley,
Or Beeny, or Bos with its flounce flinging mist?

February 1913

A Circular
9 spring-time] spring-like MS
11 ebbed] was MS, SC, PE
12 costumed] folded MS

A Dream or No
1 go to Saint-Juliot] journey to Juliot MS
2–3] I've been (I was SC2, PE) but made fancy/ By some necromancy MS, SC, PE
8 brown-tressed.] Hardy's copy of CP2 has been corrected to 'brown-tressed,'
16 lodge her] tarry MS
16 me] her MS
19 here,] here? MS
21 exist] abide MS *before revision*
22 Vallency] Valency WE, ME
24 flounce flinging mist] thunderous tide MS *before revision*
February] Not in MS
[MS shows that Hardy had considered for l. 21:
Is Saint-Juliot a place anywhere in the world?
and for l. 24:
Or Beeny, or Bos with its tides skyward hurled?]

Note In setting WE from SC2 the printer asked Hardy whether 'Vallency' (l. 22) was to be spelled 'Valency' as in poem 290. His reply read: 'No: the two spellings are because of two pronunciations, which the metres require. The river is called either way indifferently.'

289 *After a Journey*

EXTRA PRINTINGS:
(1) *Selected Poems*, pp. 67–8
(2) *Chosen Poems*, pp. 60–1

TITLE:
After a journey MS

HERETO I come to view a voiceless ghost;
Whither, O whither will its whim now draw me?
Up the cliff, down, till I'm lonely, lost,
And the unseen waters' ejaculations awe me.
Where you will next be there's no knowing,
Facing round about me everywhere,
With your nut-coloured hair,
And gray eyes, and rose-flush coming and going.

Yes: I have re-entered your olden haunts at last;
Through the years, through the dead scenes I have tracked you;
What have you now found to say of our past –
Scanned across the dark space wherein I have lacked you?
Summer gave us sweets, but autumn wrought division?
Things were not lastly as firstly well
With us twain, you tell?
But all's closed now, despite Time's derision.

I see what you are doing: you are leading me on
To the spots we knew when we haunted here together,
The waterfall, above which the mist-bow shone
At the then fair hour in the then fair weather,
And the cave just under, with a voice still so hollow
That it seems to call out to me from forty years ago,
When you were all aglow,
And not the thin ghost that I now frailly follow!

Ignorant of what there is flitting here to see,
The waked birds preen and the seals flop lazily;
Soon you will have, Dear, to vanish from me,
For the stars close their shutters and the dawn whitens hazily.
Trust me, I mind not, though Life lours,
The bringing me here; nay, bring me here again!
I am just the same as when
Our days were a joy, and our paths through flowers.

Pentargan Bay

After a Journey
1 view a voiceless] interview a MS, SC, SP, PE
2 Whither,] Whither MS
4 ejaculations] soliloquies MS, SC1
8 rose-flush] rose flush MS
12 Scanned] Viewed MS, SC, SP, PE
16 closed] soothed MS
25 see,] see MS
26 lazily;] lazily, MS, SC, SP, WE, PE, CP1–3, CHP
29 me,] me MS
29 lours] lowers MS
30 bringing me] bringing of me SC1

TITLE:
A Death-Day recalled MS

290 *A Death-Day Recalled*

BEENY did not quiver,
  Juliot grew not gray,
Thin Vallency's river
  Held its wonted way.
Bos seemed not to utter
  Dimmest note of dirge,
Targan mouth a mutter
  To its creamy surge.

Yet though these, unheeding,
  Listless, passed the hour
Of her spirit's speeding,
  She had, in her flower,
Sought and loved the places –
  Much and often pined
For their lonely faces
  When in towns confined.

Why did not Vallency
  In his purl deplore
One whose haunts were whence he
  Drew his limpid store?
Why did Bos not thunder,
  Targan apprehend
Body and Breath were sunder
  Of their former friend?

EXTRA PRINTINGS:
(1) *Selected Poems*, pp. 69–70
(2) *Chosen Poems*, pp. 62–3

291 *Beeny Cliff*

March 1870–March 1913

I

O THE opal and the sapphire of that wandering western sea,
And the woman riding high above with bright hair flapping free –
The woman whom I loved so, and who loyally loved me.

A Death-Day Recalled
3 Vallency's] Valency's MS, SC, WE, PE, ME, CP1–3
6 Dimmest] Narrowest MS
17 Vallency] Valency MS, SC, WE, PE, ME, CP1–3
23 Body and Breath] Soul and flesh MS *before revision*
23 Breath] breath MS, SC, WE, PE

Note For Hardy's spelling of 'Vallency' (ll. 3 and 17), see note to poem 288. It is clear from his instructions to the printer that he wanted 'Valency' here, and that the change to 'Vallency' in CP4 was external interference with his text

II

The pale mews plained below us, and the waves seemed far away
In a nether sky, engrossed in saying their ceaseless babbling say,
As we laughed light-heartedly aloft on that clear-sunned March day.

III

A little cloud then cloaked us, and there flew an irised rain,
And the Atlantic dyed its levels with a dull misfeatured stain,
And then the sun burst out again, and purples prinked the main.

IV

– Still in all its chasmal beauty bulks old Beeny to the sky,
And shall she and I not go there once again now March is nigh,
And the sweet things said in that March say anew there by and by?

V

What if still in chasmal beauty looms that wild weird western shore,
The woman now is – elsewhere – whom the ambling pony bore,
And nor knows nor cares for Beeny, and will laugh there nevermore.

292 *At Castle Boterel*

EXTRA PRINTINGS:
(1) *Selected Poems*, pp. 71–2
(2) *Chosen Poems*, pp. 64–5

As I drive to the junction of lane and highway,
   And the drizzle bedrenches the waggonette,
I look behind at the fading byway,
   And see on its slope, now glistening wet,
      Distinctly yet

Myself and a girlish form benighted
   In dry March weather. We climb the road
Beside a chaise. We had just alighted
   To ease the sturdy pony's load
      When he sighed and slowed.

What we did as we climbed, and what we talked of
   Matters not much, nor to what it led, –
Something that life will not be balked of
   Without rude reason till hope is dead,
      And feeling fled.

Beeny Cliff
4 pale mews] puffins MS
5 ceaseless] endless MS
6 light-heartedly] lightheartedly MS
13 What if] Nay. Though SC1
13 shore,] shore! MS
15 laugh there] see it MS, SC, SP, PE

At Castle Boterel
14 rude reason] sare [sic] pressure MS
15 feeling] Hardy in MS has tried and rejected 'spirit' and 'fancy'

It filled but a minute. But was there ever
  A time of such quality, since or before,
In that hill's story? To one mind never,
  Though it has been climbed, foot-swift, foot-sore,
    By thousands more.

Primaeval rocks form the road's steep border,
  And much have they faced there, first and last,
Of the transitory in Earth's long order;
  But what they record in colour and cast
    Is – that we two passed.

And to me, though Time's unflinching rigour,
  In mindless rote, has ruled from sight
The substance now, one phantom figure
  Remains on the slope, as when that night
    Saw us alight.

I look and see it there, shrinking, shrinking,
  I look back at it amid the rain
For the very last time; for my sand is sinking,
  And I shall traverse old love's domain
    Never again.

March 1913

EXTRA MANUSCRIPT:
The MS given by Hardy to the Plymouth Free Public Library in 1923 is said by the Librarian to have been destroyed by bombing during the Second World War

293 Places

NOBODY says: Ah, that is the place
Where chanced, in the hollow of years ago,
What none of the Three Towns cared to know –
The birth of a little girl of grace –
The sweetest the house saw, first or last;
    Yet it was so
    On that day long past.

Nobody thinks: There, there she lay
In a room by the Hoe, like the bud of a flower,
And listened, just after the bedtime hour,
To the stammering chimes that used to play

At Castle Boterel
19 foot-swift, foot-sore,] Hardy in MS has tried and rejected 'of late and yore,' and 'in sun, rain, hoar,']
Boscastle: Cornwall MS *del* at end

Places
10 hour,] hour MS

The quaint Old Hundred-and-Thirteenth tune
In Saint Andrew's tower
Night, morn, and noon.

Nobody calls to mind that here
Upon Boterel Hill, where the waggoners skid,
With cheeks whose airy flush outbid
Fresh fruit in bloom, and free of fear,
She cantered down, as if she must fall
(Though she never did),
To the charm of all.

Nay: one there is to whom these things,
That nobody else's mind calls back,
Have a savour that scenes in being lack,
And a presence more than the actual brings;
To whom to-day is beneaped and stale,
And its urgent clack
But a vapid tale.

Plymouth, March 1913

294 *The Phantom Horsewoman*

EXTRA PRINTINGS:
(1) *Selected Poems*, pp. 73–4
(2) *Chosen Poems*, pp. 66–7

I

QUEER are the ways of a man I know:
He comes and stands
In a careworn craze,
And looks at the sands
And the seaward haze
With moveless hands
And face and gaze,
Then turns to go . . .
And what does he see when he gazes so?

Places
16 waggoners] carters MS, SC, PE
19 fall] fall, MS
20 did),] did) MS
22 things,] things MS
23 back,] back MS
26 stale,] stale MS

The Phantom Horsewoman
4 sands] sands, MS
5 haze] haze, MS, SC, WE, PE, ME
8 go . . .] go. . . . . MS

II

They say he sees as an instant thing
More clear than to-day,
A sweet soft scene
That was once in play
By that briny green;
Yes, notes alway
Warm, real, and keen,
What his back years bring –
A phantom of his own figuring.

III

Of this vision of his they might say more:
Not only there
Does he see this sight,
But everywhere
In his brain – day, night,
As if on the air
It were drawn rose bright –
Yea, far from that shore
Does he carry this vision of heretofore:

IV

A ghost-girl-rider. And though, toil-tried,
He withers daily,
Time touches her not,
But she still rides gaily
In his rapt thought
On that shagged and shaly
Atlantic spot,
And as when first eyed
Draws rein and sings to the swing of the tide.

1913

The Phantom Horsewoman
13 was once] once was MS, SC, SP, WE, PE, ME, CP1–3 [Hardy's copy of CP2 has been corrected to 'was once']
25 rose bright] rose-bright MS, SP, CHP, CP4 [Hardy's copy of SP (1917) in DCM is corrected to 'rose bright', but this seems to have been overlooked in setting up CHP and correcting CP4]
27 heretofore:] heretofore; MS
28 toil-tried,] toil-tried MS
1913] Not in MS, SC, PE

295 *The Spell of the Rose*

Note In MS, SC, PE this poem is placed earlier in the book, after 'Under the Waterfall'

'I MEAN to build a hall anon,
And shape two turrets there,
And a broad newelled stair,
And a cool well for crystal water;
Yes; I will build a hall anon,
Plant roses love shall feed upon,
And apple-trees and pear.'

He set to build the manor-hall,
And shaped the turrets there,
And the broad newelled stair,
And the cool well for crystal water;
He built for me that manor-hall,
And planted many trees withal,
But no rose anywhere.

And as he planted never a rose
That bears the flower of love,
Though other flowers throve
Some heart-bane moved our souls to sever
Since he had planted never a rose;
And misconceits raised horrid shows,
And agonies came thereof.

'I'll mend these miseries,' then said I,
And so, at dead of night,
I went and, screened from sight,
That nought should keep our souls in severance,
I set a rose-bush. 'This,' said I,
'May end divisions dire and wry,
And long-drawn days of blight.'

But I was called from earth – yea, called
Before my rose-bush grew;
And would that now I knew

The Spell of the Rose
7 apple-trees] appletrees MS: apple trees SC, WE, PE, ME
11 water;] water: MS
18 Some heart-bane] A frost-wind MS, SC, PE
25 severance,] severance MS
26 rose-bush] rosebush MS
29] But – I was called; yea, ghosted – called MS
30 rose-bush] rosebush MS

What feels he of the tree I planted,
And whether, after I was called
To be a ghost, he, as of old,
Gave me his heart anew!

Perhaps now blooms that queen of trees
I set but saw not grow,
And he, beside its glow –
Eyes couched of the mis-vision that blurred me –
Ay, there beside that queen of trees
He sees me as I was, though sees
Too late to tell me so!

296 St Launce's Revisited

TITLE:
At St. Launce's MS *before revision*

Note In MS, SC, PE this poem is placed earlier in the book, after 'The Spell of the Rose' and before 'The Going'

SLIP back, Time!
Yet again I am nearing
Castle and keep, uprearing
Gray, as in my prime.

At the inn
Smiling nigh, why is it
Not as on my visit
When hope and I were twin?

Groom and jade
Whom I found here, moulder;
Strange the tavern-holder,
Strange the tap-maid.

Here I hired
Horse and man for bearing
Me on my wayfaring
To the door desired.

Evening gloomed
As I journeyed forward
To the faces shoreward,
Till their dwelling loomed.

The Spell of the Rose
34 ghost,] ghost MS
38 glow –] glow, MS
39 mis-vision] misvision MS
1913 MS *del* at end

St Launce's Revisited
6 nigh] close MS, SC, PE
16 door] goal MS

If again
Towards the Atlantic sea there
I should speed, they'd be there
Surely now as then?...

Why waste thought,
When I know them vanished
Under earth; yea, banished
Ever into nought!

297 *Where the Picnic Was*

WHERE we made the fire
In the summer time
Of branch and briar
On the hill to the sea,
I slowly climb
Through winter mire,
And scan and trace
The forsaken place
Quite readily.

Now a cold wind blows,
And the grass is gray,
But the spot still shows
As a burnt circle – aye,
And stick-ends, charred,
Still strew the sward
Whereon I stand,
Last relic of the band
Who came that day!

Yes, I am here
Just as last year,
And the sea breathes brine
From its strange straight line
Up hither, the same
As when we four came.

EXTRA PRINTINGS:
(1) *Selected Poems*, pp. 57–8
(2) *Chosen Poems*, pp. 68–9

TITLE:
Where the Picnic was MS
Note In MS, SC, PE this poem is placed after 'The Place on the Map'

St Launce's Revisited
24 then?...] then?.... MS
28 nought!] nought. MS, SC, PE
1913 MS *del* at end

Where the Picnic Was
1 fire] fire, SC, PE
2 summer time] summer-time SP
2 time] time, SC, PE
4 sea,] sea MS, SC, SP, PE
6 mire,] mire MS
13 aye] ay MS
24–5 No stanza break

– But two have wandered far
From this grassy rise
Into urban roar
Where no picnics are,
And one – has shut her eyes
For evermore

MISCELLANEOUS PIECES

298 The Wistful Lady

'LOVE, while you were away there came to me –
        From whence I cannot tell –
A plaintive lady pale and passionless,
Who laid her eyes upon me critically,
And weighed me with a wearing wistfulness,
        As if she knew me well.'

'I saw no lady of that wistful sort
        As I came riding home.
Perhaps she was some dame the Fates constrain
By memories sadder than she can support,
Or by unhappy vacancy of brain,
        To leave her roof and roam?'

'Ah, but she knew me. And before this time
        I have seen her, lending ear
To my light outdoor words, and pondering each,
Her frail white finger swayed in pantomime,
As if she fain would close with me in speech,
        And yet would not come near.

'And once I saw her beckoning with her hand
        As I came into sight
At an upper window. And I at last went out;
But when I reached where she had seemed to stand,
And wandered up and down and searched about,
        I found she had vanished quite.'

Then thought I how my dead Love used to say,
        With a small smile, when she
Was waning wan, that she would hover round
And show herself after her passing day
To any newer Love I might have found,
        But show her not to me.

The Wistful Lady
4 laid] bent MS, SC, PE
4 critically,] critically MS
15 and] and, MS [But there is doubt whether Hardy meant the comma to survive revision]
17 speech,] speech MS
22 stand,] stand WE, ME

299 *The Woman in the Rye*

'Why do you stand in the dripping rye,
Cold-lipped, unconscious, wet to the knee,
When there are firesides near?' said I.
'I told him I wished him dead,' said she.

'Yea, cried it in my haste to one
Whom I had loved, whom I well loved still;
And die he did. And I hate the sun,
And stand here lonely, aching, chill;

'Stand waiting, waiting under skies
That blow reproach, the while I see
The rooks sheer off to where he lies
Wrapt in a peace withheld from me!'

300 *The Cheval-Glass*

Why do you harbour that great cheval-glass
        Filling up your narrow room?
        You never preen or plume
Or look in a week at your full-length figure –
        Picture of bachelor gloom!

'Well, when I dwelt in ancient England,
        Renting the valley farm,
        Thoughtless of all heart-harm,
I used to gaze at the parson's daughter,
        A creature of nameless charm.

'Thither there came a lover and won her,
        Carried her off from my view.
        O it was then I knew
Misery of a cast undreamt of –
        More than, indeed, my due!

The Woman in the Rye
12 me!] me. MS, SC, PE

The Cheval-Glass
3 plume] plume, MS, SC, WE, PE, ME

'Then far rumours of her ill-usage
Came, like a chilling breath
When a man languisheth;
Followed by news that her mind lost balance,
And, in a space, of her death.

'Soon sank her father; and next was the auction –
Everything to be sold:
Mid things new and old
Stood this glass in her former chamber,
Long in her use, I was told.

'Well, I awaited the sale and bought it. . . .
There by my bed it stands,
And as the dawn expands
Often I see her pale-faced form there
Brushing her hair's bright bands.

'There, too, at pallid midnight moments
Quick she will come to my call,
Smile from the frame withal
Ponderingly, as she used to regard me
Passing her father's wall.

'So that it was for its revelations
I brought it oversea,
And drag it about with me. . . .
Anon I shall break it and bury its fragments
Where my grave is to be.'

301 *The Re-Enactment*

TITLE:
The Re-enactment MS

BETWEEN the folding sea-downs,
In the gloom
Of a wailful wintry nightfall,
When the boom
Of the ocean, like a hammering in a hollow tomb,

The Cheval-Glass
21] 'Vanished her husband; and came the auction; MS *before revision*
21 auction –] auction; MS
33–4] Look in my face withal/With her great eyes as, times out of counting, MS *before revision*
38 me. . . .] me. . . . . MS

The Re-Enactment
5 tomb,] tomb MS

Throbbed up the copse-clothed valley
From the shore
To the chamber where I darkled,
Sunk and sore
With gray ponderings why my Loved one had not come before

To salute me in the dwelling
That of late
I had hired to waste a while in –
Dim of date,
Quaint, and remote – wherein I now expectant sate;

On the solitude, unsignalled,
Broke a man
Who, in air as if at home there,
Seemed to scan
Every fire-flecked nook of the apartment span by span.

A stranger's and no lover's
Eyes were these,
Eyes of a man who measures
What he sees
But vaguely, as if wrapt in filmy phantasies.

Yea, his bearing was so absent
As he stood,
It bespoke a chord so plaintive
In his mood,
That soon I judged he would not wrong my quietude.

'Ah – the supper is just ready!'
Then he said,
'And the years'-long-binned Madeira
Flashes red!'
(There was no wine, no food, no supper-table spread.)

'You will forgive my coming,
Lady fair?
I see you as at that time
Rising there,
The self-same curious querying in your eyes and air.

The Re-Enactment
13 waste a while] while a space MS
14 Dim] Vague MS, SC, PE
16 unsignalled,] unsignalled MS
20 span.] Through print deterioration the stop disappeared in CP3 and was mistakenly replaced by a comma in CP4
31 ready!] ready, MS, SC, WE, PE, ME
33 years'-long-binned] years'-long binned MS, SC, PE
40 self-same] selfsame MS
40 air] hair SC1 [Hardy's copy of SC1 has been corrected to 'air']

'Yet no. How so? You wear not
The same gown,
Your locks show woful difference,
Are not brown:
What, is it not as when I hither came from town?

'And the place. . . . But you seem other –
Can it be?
What's this that Time is doing
Unto me?
You dwell here, unknown woman? . . . Whereabouts, then, is she?

'And the house-things are much shifted. –
Put them where
They stood on this night's fellow;
Shift her chair:
Here was the couch: and the piano should be there.'

I indulged him, verily nerve-strained
Being alone,
And I moved the things as bidden,
One by one,
And feigned to push the old piano where he had shown.

'Aha – now I can see her!
Stand aside:
Don't thrust her from the table
Where, meek-eyed,
She makes attempt with matron-manners to preside.

'She serves me: now she rises,
Goes to play. . . .
But you obstruct her, fill her
With dismay,
And all-embarrassed, scared, she vanishes away!'

And, as 'twere useless longer
To persist,
He sighed, and sought the entry
Ere I wist,
And retreated, disappearing soundless in the mist.

The Re-Enactment
70 all-embarrassed] embarrassed MS, SC, WE, PE, CP1 [CP1 corrected on errata slip to 'all embarrassed']: all embarrassed ME
70 away!] away. MS

That here some mighty passion
Once had burned,
Which still the walls enghosted,
I discerned,
And that by its strong spell mine might be overturned.

I sat depressed; till, later,
My Love came;
But something in the chamber
Dimmed our flame, –
An emanation, making our due words fall tame,

As if the intenser drama
Shown me there
Of what the walls had witnessed
Filled the air,
And left no room for later passion anywhere.

So came it that our fervours
Did quite fail
Of future consummation –
Being made quail
By the weird witchery of the parlour's hidden tale,

Which I, as years passed, faintly
Learnt to trace, –
One of sad love, born full-winged
In that place
Where the predestined sorrowers first stood face to face.

And as that month of winter
Circles round,
And the evening of the date-day
Grows embrowned,
I am conscious of those presences, and sit spellbound.

There, often – lone, forsaken –
Queries breed
Within me; whether a phantom
Had my heed
On that strange night, or was it some wrecked heart indeed?

The Re-Enactment
105 presences,] presences MS
105 spellbound] spell-bound MS

302 Her Secret

TITLE:
The jealous husband MS *before revision*

THAT love's dull smart distressed my heart
He shrewdly learnt to see,
But that I was in love with a dead man
Never suspected he.

He searched for the trace of a pictured face,
He watched each missive come,
And a sheet that seemed like a love-line
Wrought his look lurid and numb.

He dogged my feet to the city street,
He followed me to the sea,
But not to the nigh, still churchyard
Did he dream of following me!

303 She Charged Me

TITLE:
'She Charged me' MS

SHE charged me with having said this and that
To another woman long years before,
In the very parlour where we sat, –

Sat on a night when the endless pour
Of rain on the roof and the road below
Bent the spring of the spirit more and more. . . .

– So charged she me; and the Cupid's bow
Of her mouth was hard, and her eyes, and her face,
And her white forefinger lifted slow.

Had she done it gently, or shown a trace
That not too curiously would she view
A folly flown ere her reign had place,

A kiss might have closed it. But I knew
From the fall of each word, and the pause between,
That the curtain would drop upon us two
Ere long, in our play of slave and queen.

Her Secret
7 sheet] note MS, SC, PE
8] Made him look frozen and glum. MS, SC, PE
11 nigh, still] neighbouring MS, SC, PE
12 me!] me. MS, SC, WE, PE, ME

She Charged Me
2 before,] before MS
6 more. . . .] more. . . . . MS
12 flown] passed MS, SC, PE
12 place,] place MS
13 closed] ended MS, SC, PE

304 *The Newcomer's Wife*

HE paused on the sill of a door ajar
That screened a lively liquor-bar,
For the name had reached him through the door
Of her he had married the week before.

'We called her the Hack of the Parade;
But she was discreet in the games she played;
If slightly worn, she's pretty yet,
And gossips, after all, forget:

'And he knows nothing of her past;
I am glad the girl's in luck at last;
Such ones, though stale to native eyes,
Newcomers snatch at as a prize.'

'Yes, being a stranger he sees her blent
Of all that's fresh and innocent,
Nor dreams how many a love-campaign
She had enjoyed before his reign!'

That night there was the splash of a fall
Over the slimy harbour-wall:
They searched, and at the deepest place
Found him with crabs upon his face.

305 *A Conversation at Dawn*

HE lay awake, with a harassed air,
And she, in her cloud of loose lank hair,
        Seemed trouble-tried
As the dawn drew in on their faces there.

The chamber looked far over the sea
From a white hotel on a white-stoned quay,
        And stepping a stride
He parted the window-drapery.

The Newcomer's Wife
8] And after all, folk soon forget. MS *before revision*
8 forget:] forget. MS, SC, PE

A Conversation at Dawn
2 hair,] hair MS

Above the level horizon spread
The sunrise, firing them foot to head
From its smouldering lair,
And painting their pillows with dyes of red.

'What strange disquiets have stirred you, dear,
This dragging night, with starts in fear
Of me, as it were,
Or of something evil hovering near?'

'My husband, can I have fear of you?
What should one fear from a man whom few,
Or none, had matched
In that late long spell of delays undue!'

He watched her eyes in the heaving sun:
'Then what has kept, O reticent one,
Those lids unlatched –
Anything promised I've not yet done?'

'O it's not a broken promise of yours
(For what quite lightly your lip assures
The due time brings)
That has troubled my sleep, and no waking cures!' . . .

'I have shaped my will; 'tis at hand,' said he;
'I subscribe it to-day, that no risk there be
In the hap of things
Of my leaving you menaced by poverty.'

'That a boon provision I'm safe to get,
Signed, sealed by my lord as it were a debt,
I cannot doubt,
Or ever this peering sun be set.'

'But you flung my arms away from your side,
And faced the wall. No month-old bride
Ere the tour be out
In an air so loth can be justified?

A Conversation at Dawn
25 yours] yours, MS
33 get,] get MS
34 debt,] debt MS

'Ah – had you a male friend once loved well,
Upon whose suit disaster fell
  And frustrance swift?
Honest you are, and may care to tell.'

She lay impassive, and nothing broke
The stillness other than, stroke by stroke,
  The lazy lift
Of the tide below them; till she spoke:

'I once had a friend – a Love, if you will –
Whose wife forsook him, and sank until
  She was made a thrall
In a prison-cell for a deed of ill. . . .

'He remained alone; and we met – to love,
But barring legitimate joy thereof
  Stood a doorless wall,
Though we prized each other all else above.

'And this was why, though I'd touched my prime,
I put off suitors from time to time –
  Yourself with the rest –
Till friends, who approved you, called it crime,

'And when misgivings weighed on me
In my lover's absence, hurriedly,
  And much distrest,
I took you. . . . Ah, that such could be! . . .

'Now, saw you when crossing from yonder shore
At yesternoon, that the packet bore
  On a white-wreathed bier
A coffined body towards the fore?

'Well, while you stood at the other end,
The loungers talked, and I couldn't but lend
  A listening ear,
For they named the dead. 'Twas the wife of my friend.

A Conversation at Dawn
64 you. . . .] you. . . . . MS
64 Ah,] Ah MS
64 be! . . .] be! . . . . MS
70 couldn't] could MS, SC, PE

'He was there, but did not note me, veiled,
Yet I saw that a joy, as of one unjailed,
Now shone in his gaze;
He knew not his hope of me just had failed!

'They had brought her home: she was born in this isle;
And he will return to his domicile,
And pass his days
Alone, and not as he dreamt erstwhile!'

' – So you've lost a sprucer spouse than I!'
She held her peace, as if fain deny
She would indeed
For his pleasure's sake, but could lip no lie.

'One far less formal and plain and slow!'
She let the laconic assertion go
As if of need
She held the conviction that it was so.

'Regard me as his he always should,
He had said, and wed me he vowed he would
In his prime or sere
Most verily do, if ever he could;

'And this fulfilment is now his aim,
For a letter, addressed in my maiden name,
Has dogged me here,
Reminding me faithfully of his claim;

'And it started a hope like a lightning-streak
That I might go to him – say for a week –
And afford you right
To put me away, and your vows unspeak.

'To be sure you have said, as of dim intent,
That marriage is a plain event
Of black and white,
Without any ghost of sentiment,

A Conversation at Dawn
92 could;] could. MS, SC, PE
95 here,] here MS
96 claim;] claim. MS, SC, PE

102–4] That marriage is a sacrament/Nor depth nor height/Nor any creature can circumvent, MS *before revision*

'And my heart has quailed. – But deny it true
That you will never this lock undo!
No God intends
To thwart the yearning He's father to!'

The husband hemmed, then blandly bowed
In the light of the angry morning cloud.
'So my idyll ends,
And a drama opens!' he mused aloud;

And his features froze. 'You may take it as true
That I will never this lock undo
For so depraved
A passion as that which kindles you!'

Said she: 'I am sorry you see it so;
I had hoped you might have let me go,
And thus been saved
The pain of learning there's more to know.'

'More? What may that be? Gad, I think
You have told me enough to make me blink!
Yet if more remain
Then own it to me. I will not shrink!'

'Well, it is this. As we could not see
That a legal marriage would ever be,
To end our pain
We united ourselves informally;

'And vowed at a chancel-altar nigh,
With book and ring, a lifelong tie;
A contract vain
To the world, but real to Him on High.'

'And you became as his wife?' – 'I did.' –
He stood as stiff as a caryatid,
And said, 'Indeed! . . .
No matter. You're mine, whatever you've hid!'

A Conversation at Dawn
108 He's] he's MS
109 hemmed] thought MS: sneered SC1
116 you!] you. MS, SC, PE
126 would] could MS, SC, PE
134 caryatid,] caryatid MS

'But is it right! When I only gave
My hand to you in a sweat to save,
Through desperate need
(As I thought), my fame, for I was not brave!'

'To save your fame? Your meaning is dim,
For nobody knew of your altar-whim?'
'I mean – I feared
There might be fruit of my tie with him;

'And to cloak it by marriage I'm not the first,
Though, maybe, morally most accurst
Through your unpeered
And strict uprightness. That's the worst!

'While yesterday his worn contours
Convinced me that love like his endures,
And that my troth-plight
Had been his, in fact, and not truly yours.'

'So, my lady, you raise the veil by degrees. . . .
I own this last is enough to freeze
The warmest wight!
Now hear the other side, if you please:

'I did say once, though without intent,
That marriage is a plain event
Of black and white,
Whatever may be its sentiment:

'I'll act accordingly, none the less
That you soiled the contract in time of stress,
Thereto induced
By the feared results of your wantonness.

'But the thing is over, and no one knows,
And it's nought to the future what you disclose.
That you'll be loosed
For such an episode, don't suppose!

A Conversation at Dawn
139 need] need, MS
140 thought),] thought) MS
156 please:] please. MS
157 intent,] intent MS
160 sentiment:] sentiment. MS, SC, PE
168 suppose!] suppose. MS

'No: I'll not free you. And if it appear
There was too good ground for your first fear
From your amorous tricks,
I'll father the child. Yes, by God, my dear!

'Even should you fly to his arms, I'll damn
Opinion, and fetch you; treat as sham
Your mutinous kicks,
And whip you home. That's the sort I am!'

She whitened. 'Enough. . . . Since you disapprove
I'll yield in silence, and never move
Till my last pulse ticks
A footstep from the domestic groove.'

'Then swear it,' he said, 'and your king uncrown.'
He drew her forth in her long white gown,
And she knelt and swore.
'Good. Now you may go and again lie down.

'Since you've played these pranks and given no sign,
You shall crave this man of yours; pine and pine
With sighings sore,
'Till I've starved your love for him; nailed you mine!

'I'm a practical man, and want no tears;
You've made a fool of me, it appears;
That you don't again
Is a lesson I'll teach you in future years.'

She answered not, lying listlessly
With her dark dry eyes on the coppery sea,
That now and then
Flung its lazy flounce at the neighbouring quay.

1910

A Conversation at Dawn
172 dear!] dear. MS, SC, WE, PE, ME
177 Enough. . . .] Enough. . . . . MS
180–1 MS has following *deleted* stanza here:

'For really I never knew till now/What a hero my lord was. Nothing can bow/Or bend or lower/A soul so cool! Yes, I'll keep my vow.'

181 it,] it MS
188 mine!] mine. MS, SC, PE
193 lying] but lay MS, SC, PE
196 lazy] MS could be 'hazy'
1910] Autumn: 1910 MS

306 A King's Soliloquy

TITLE:
The King's Soliloquy MS *before revision*
On . . . Funeral] Not in MS

On the Night of His Funeral

FROM the slow march and muffled drum,
And crowds distrest,
And book and bell, at length I have come
To my full rest.

A ten years' rule beneath the sun
Is wound up here,
And what I have done, what left undone,
Figures out clear.

Yet in the estimate of such
It grieves me more
That I by some was loved so much
Than that I bore,

From others, judgment of that hue
Which over-hope
Breeds from a theoretic view
Of regal scope.

For kingly opportunities
Right many have sighed;
How best to bear its devilries
Those learn who have tried!

I have eaten the fat and drunk the sweet,
Lived the life out
From the first greeting glad drum-beat
To the last shout.

What pleasure earth affords to kings
I have enjoyed
Through its long vivid pulse-stirrings
Even till it cloyed.

A King's Soliloquy
1 drum,] drum SC2, WE, PE
12 bore,] bore MS
13 others,] others MS

What days of drudgery, nights of stress
        Can cark a throne,
Even one maintained in peacefulness,
        I too have known.

And so, I think, could I step back
        To life again,
I should prefer the average track
        Of average men,

Since, as with them, what kingship would
        It cannot do,
Nor to first thoughts however good
        Hold itself true.

Something binds hard the royal hand,
        As all that be,
And it is That has shaped, has planned
        My acts and me.

May 1910

EXTRA PRINTINGS:
(1) *Selected Poems*, pp. 167–9
(2) *Chosen Poems*, pp. 193–5

307 *The Coronation*

AT Westminster, hid from the light of day,
Many who once had shone as monarchs lay.

Edward the Pious, and two Edwards more,
The second Richard, Henrys three or four;

That is to say, those who were called the Third,
Fifth, Seventh, and Eighth (the much self-widowered);

And James the Scot, and near him Charles the Second,
And, too, the second George could there be reckoned.

Of women, Mary and Queen Elizabeth,
And Anne, all silent in a musing death;

And William's Mary, and Mary, Queen of Scots,
And consort-queens whose names oblivion blots;

And several more whose chronicle one sees
Adorning ancient royal pedigrees.

A King's Soliloquy
29 drudgery,] strain, what MS, SCl
42] Necessity, MS *before revision*

The Coronation
6 self-widowered);] self-widowered) MS: self-widowered), SC, SP, WE, PE, ME
11 Mary, Queen] Mary Queen MS

– Now, as they drowsed on, freed from Life's old thrall,
And heedless, save of things exceptional,

Said one: 'What means this throbbing thudding sound
That reaches to us here from overground;

'A sound of chisels, augers, planes, and saws,
Infringing all ecclesiastic laws?

'And these tons-weight of timber on us pressed,
Unfelt here since we entered into rest?

'Surely, at least to us, being corpses royal,
A meet repose is owing by the loyal?'

' – Perhaps a scaffold!' Mary Stuart sighed,
'If such still be. It was that way I died.'

' – Ods! Far more like,' said he the many-wived,
'That for a wedding 'tis this work's contrived.

'Ha-ha! I never would bow down to Rimmon,
But I had a rare time with those six women!'

'Not all at once?' gasped he who loved confession.
'Nay, nay!' said Hal. 'That would have been transgression.'

'– They build a catafalque here, black and tall,
Perhaps,' mused Richard, 'for some funeral?'

And Anne chimed in: 'Ah, yes: it may be so!'
'Nay!' squeaked Eliza. 'Little you seem to know –

'Clearly 'tis for some crowning here in state,
As they crowned us at our long bygone date;

'Though we'd no such a power of carpentry,
But let the ancient architecture be;

'If I were up there where the parsons sit,
In one of my gold robes, I'd see to it!'

'But you are not,' Charles chuckled. 'You are here,
And never will know the sun again, my dear!'

The Coronation
23 Surely,] Surely MS
27 ' – Ods! Far more like] ' – No, no! . . . . Maybe MS
27 Ods] Od's SP
28 That] 'Tis MS
28 'tis] that MS
32 Nay, nay!] O no! MS

'Yea,' whispered those whom no one had addressed;
'With slow, sad march, amid a folk distressed,
We were brought here, to take our dusty rest.

'And here, alas, in darkness laid below,
We'll wait and listen, and endure the show....
Clamour dogs kingship; afterwards not so!'

1911

308 Aquae Sulis

THE chimes called midnight, just at interlune,
And the daytime parle on the Roman investigations
Was shut to silence, save for the husky tune
The bubbling waters played near the excavations.

And a warm air came up from underground,
And the flutter of a filmy shape unsepulchred,
That collected itself, and waited, and looked around:
Nothing was seen, but utterances could be heard:

Those of the Goddess whose shrine was beneath the pile
Of the God with the baldachined altar overhead:
'And what did you win by raising this nave and aisle
Close on the site of the temple I tenanted?

'The notes of your organ have thrilled down out of view
To the earth-clogged wrecks of my edifice many a year,
Though stately and shining once – ay, long ere you
Had set up crucifix and candle here.

'Your priests have trampled the dust of mine without rueing,
Despising the joys of man whom I so much loved,
Though my springs boil on by your Gothic arcades and pewing,
And sculptures crude.... Would Jove they could be removed!'

'Repress, O lady proud, your traditional ires;
You know not by what a frail thread we equally hang;
It is said we are images both – twitched by people's desires;
And that I, as you, fail like a song men yesterday sang!'

The Coronation
46 slow,] slow MS
49 wait] wait, SP
50] Loudly doth kingship come, and softly go!' MS *before revision*

Aquae Sulis
2 parle on] talk of MS, SC, PE
3 shut to] checked by MS, SC, PE
6 the flutter] a flutter (motion MS), as MS, SC, WE, PE, CP1–3
9 Goddess] goddess MS, SC, WE, PE, CP1, ME
11 win] get MS, SC, PE
15 stately] erect MS
19 arcades] arch MS
21 Repress] – Repress MS, SC, WE, PE, ME
21 ires;] ires, MS
24] And (And that SC1) I, like you, fail as a song that men time agone sang!' MS, SC1
24 as] like SC2, WE, PE, CP1
24 like] as SC2, WE, PE, CP1

'What – a Jumping-jack you, and myself but a poor Jumping-jill,
Now worm-eaten, times agone twitched at Humanity's bid?
O I cannot endure it! – But, chance to us whatso there will,
Let us kiss and be friends! Come, agree you?' – None heard if he did. . . .

And the olden dark hid the cavities late laid bare,
And all was suspended and soundless as before,
Except for a gossamery noise fading off in the air,
And the boiling voice of the waters' medicinal pour.

Bath

309 Seventy-Four and Twenty

TITLE:
Seventy four and Twenty MS

HERE goes a man of seventy-four,
Who sees not what life means for him,
And here another in years a score
Who reads its very figure and trim.

The one who shall walk to-day with me
Is not the youth who gazes far,
But the breezy sire who cannot see
What Earth's ingrained conditions are.

310 The Elopement

'A WOMAN never agreed to it!' said my knowing friend to me.
'That one thing she'd refuse to do for Solomon's mines in fee:
No woman ever will make herself look older than she is.'
I did not answer; but I thought, 'You err there, ancient Quiz.'

It took a rare one, true, to do it; for she was surely rare –
As rare a soul at that sweet time of her life as she was fair,
And urging heart-heaves, too, were strong, for ours was a passionate case,
Yea, passionate enough to lead to freaking with that young face.

Aquae Sulis
25–8 Not in MS, SC, PE, which have a line of dots here
28 Come,] Come – WE, ME

Seventy-Four and Twenty
1 seventy-four] seventy four MS
6 far,] far MS
7 sire] wight MS, SC, PE
8 are.] are MS
MS has extra stanza:

For I am sick of thinking
On whither things tend,
And will foster hoodwinking
Henceforth to the end.

The Elopement
3 she is] her years MS *before revision*
4 ancient Quiz] it appears MS *before revision*
6 fair,] fair. MS, SC, WE, PE, ME
7 heart-heaves] motives MS, SC, PE

I have told no one about it, should perhaps make few believe,
But I think it over now that life looms dull and years bereave,
How blank we stood at our bright wits' end, two blown barks in distress,
How self-regard in her was slain by her large tenderness.

I said: 'The only chance for us in a crisis of this kind
Is going it thorough!' – 'Yes,' she calmly breathed. 'Well, I don't mind.'
And we blanched her dark locks ruthlessly: set wrinkles on her brow;
Ay – she was a right rare woman then, whatever she may be now.

That night we heard a coach drive up, and questions asked below.
'A gent with an elderly wife, sir,' was returned from the bureau.
And the wheels went rattling on, and free at last from public ken
We washed all off in her chamber and restored her youth again.

How many years ago it was! Some fifty can it be
Since that adventure held us, and she played old wife to me?
But in time convention won her, as it wins all women at last,
And now she is rich and respectable, and time has buried the past.

TITLE:
'I rose up as my Custom is' MS

311 *I Rose Up as My Custom Is*

I ROSE up as my custom is
   On the eve of All-Souls' day,
And left my grave for an hour or so
To call on those I used to know
   Before I passed away.

I visited my former Love
   As she lay by her husband's side;
I asked her if life pleased her, now
She was rid of a poet wrung in brow,
   And crazed with the ills he eyed;

Who used to drag her here and there
   Wherever his fancies led,
And point out pale phantasmal things,
And talk of vain vague purposings
   That she discredited.

The Elopement
9 it,] it; MS
10 bereave,] bereave MS
11 blown] frail MS, SC, PE
13 said:] said, MS
21 fifty] forty MS

I Rose Up as My Custom Is
2 All-Souls'] MS shows that 'New Year's' and 'Midsummer' were considered and rejected
9 brow,] brow MS

She was quite civil, and replied,
'Old comrade, is that you?
Well, on the whole, I like my life. –
I know I swore I'd be no wife,
But what was I to do?

'You see, of all men for my sex
A poet is the worst;
Women are practical, and they
Crave the wherewith to pay their way,
And slake their social thirst.

'You were a poet – quite the ideal
That we all love awhile:
But look at this man snoring here –
He's no romantic chanticleer,
Yet keeps me in good style.

'He makes no quest into my thoughts,
But a poet wants to know
What one has felt from earliest days,
Why one thought not in other ways,
And one's Loves of long ago.'

Her words benumbed my fond faint ghost;
The nightmares neighed from their stalls,
The vampires screeched, the harpies flew,
And under the dim dawn I withdrew
To Death's inviolate halls.

312 *A Week*

On Monday night I closed my door,
And thought you were not as heretofore,
And little cared if we met no more.

I seemed on Tuesday night to trace
Something beyond mere commonplace
In your ideas, and heart, and face.

I Rose Up as My Custom Is
36 faint] frail MS, SC, PE
40] To where no sunlight falls. MS *before revision* [As alternatives to 'sunlight' Hardy tried 'dawnlight', 'glimmer', 'daybreak', 'lightshine']

On Wednesday I did not opine
Your life would ever be one with mine,
Though if it were we should well combine.

On Thursday noon I liked you well,
And fondly felt that we must dwell
Not far apart, whatever befell.

On Friday it was with a thrill
In gazing towards your distant vill
I owned you were my dear one still.

I saw you wholly to my mind
On Saturday – even one who shrined
All that was best of womankind.

As wing-clipt sea-gull for the sea
On Sunday night I longed for thee,
Without whom life were waste to me!

TITLE:
Had you Wept MS

313 Had You Wept

HAD you wept; had you but neared me with a hazed uncertain ray,
Dewy as the face of the dawn, in your large and luminous eye,
Then would have come back all the joys the tidings had slain that day,
And a new beginning, a fresh fair heaven, have smoothed the things awry.
But you were less feebly human, and no passionate need for clinging
Possessed your soul to overthrow reserve when I came near;
Ay, though you suffer as much as I from storms the hours are bringing
Upon your heart and mine, I never see you shed a tear.

The deep strong woman is weakest, the weak one is the strong;
The weapon of all weapons best for winning, you have not used;
Have you never been able, or would you not, through the evil times and long?
Has not the gift been given you, or such gift have you refused?
When I bade me not absolve you on that evening or the morrow,
Why did you not make war on me with those who weep like rain?
You felt too much, so gained no balm for all your torrid sorrow,
And hence our deep division, and our dark undying pain.

A Week
12 whatever] whatso (whatever *del*) MS

Had You Wept
1 hazed] frail MS, SC, PE
2 dawn,] dawn MS

314 *Bereft, She Thinks She Dreams*

TITLE:
She thinks she dreams MS

I DREAM that the dearest I ever knew
  Has died and been entombed.
I am sure it's a dream that cannot be true,
  But I am so overgloomed
By its persistence, that I would gladly
  Have quick death take me,
Rather than longer think thus sadly;
    So wake me, wake me!

It has lasted days, but minute and hour
  I expect to get aroused
And find him as usual in the bower
  Where we so happily housed.
Yet stays this nightmare too appalling,
  And like a web shakes me,
And piteously I keep on calling,
    And no one wakes me!

315 *In the British Museum*

'WHAT do you see in that time-touched stone,
    When nothing is there
But ashen blankness, although you give it
    A rigid stare?

'You look not quite as if you saw,
    But as if you heard,
Parting your lips, and treading softly
    As mouse or bird.

'It is only the base of a pillar, they'll tell you,
    That came to us
From a far old hill men used to name
    Areopagus.'

Bereft, She Thinks She Dreams
3 That] than MS [Hardy seldom makes this kind of copying error]
7 sadly] sady MS [But here's another!]
8 me!] me. MS
15 calling,] calling MS

In the British Museum
1 time-touched] As alternatives in MS Hardy tried 'time-eaten' and 'time-hardened'
9 only] Not in MS
11 a far old] an old MS

13 – 'I know no art, and I only view
14 A stone from a wall,
15 But I am thinking that stone has echoed
16 The voice of Paul;

17 'Paul as he stood and preached beside it
18 Facing the crowd,
19 A small gaunt figure with wasted features,
20 Calling out loud

21 'Words that in all their intimate accents
22 Patterned upon
23 That marble front, and were wide reflected,
24 And then were gone.

25 'I'm a labouring man, and know but little,
26 Or nothing at all;
27 But I can't help thinking that stone once echoed
28 The voice of Paul.'

316 *In the Servants' Quarters*

TITLE:
Humour in the servants' quarters MS *before revision*

1 'MAN, you too, aren't you, one of these rough followers of the criminal?
2 All hanging hereabout to gather how he's going to bear
3 Examination in the hall.' She flung disdainful glances on
4 The shabby figure standing at the fire with others there,
5 Who warmed them by its flare.

6 'No indeed, my skipping maiden: I know nothing of the trial here,
7 Or criminal, if so he be. – I chanced to come this way,
8 And the fire shone out into the dawn, and morning airs are cold now;
9 I, too, was drawn in part by charms I see before me play,
10 That I see not every day.'

11 'Ha, ha!' then laughed the constables who also stood to warm themselves,
12 The while another maiden scrutinized his features hard,

In the British Museum
16 Paul;] Paul, MS, SC, PE, CP1–3: Paul. WE
19 features,] features MS
23 wide] far MS, SC, PE

As the blaze threw into contrast every line and knot that wrinkled them,
Exclaiming, 'Why, last night when he was brought in by the guard,
You were with him in the yard!'

'Nay, nay, you teasing wench, I say! You know you speak mistakenly.
Cannot a tired pedestrian who has legged it long and far
Here on his way from northern parts, engrossed in humble marketings,
Come in and rest awhile, although judicial doings are
Afoot by morning star?'

'O, come, come!' laughed the constables. 'Why, man, you speak the dialect
He uses in his answers; you can hear him up the stairs.
So own it. We sha'n't hurt ye. There he's speaking now! His syllables
Are those you sound yourself when you are talking unawares,
As this pretty girl declares.'

'And you shudder when his chain clinks!' she rejoined. 'O yes, I noticed it.
And you winced, too, when those cuffs they gave him echoed to us here.
They'll soon be coming down, and you may then have to defend yourself
Unless you hold your tongue, or go away and keep you clear
When he's led to judgment near!'

'No! I'll be damned in hell if I know anything about the man!
No single thing about him more than everybody knows!
Must not I even warm my hands but I am charged with blasphemies?' . . .
– His face convulses as the morning cock that moment crows,
And he droops, and turns, and goes.

317 *The Obliterate Tomb*

'MORE than half my life long
Did they weigh me falsely, to my bitter wrong,
But they all have shrunk away into the silence
Like a lost song.

In the Servants' Quarters
17 legged . . . far] footed it afar (travelled from afar MS *del*) MS, SC, WE, PE
17 far] far – ME
23 sha'n't] shan't MS
23 now!] now. MS
30 near!] near. MS
35 droops] stops MS, SC, PE

'And the day has dawned and come
For forgiveness, when the past may hold it dumb
On the once reverberate words of hatred uttered
Half in delirium. . . .

'With folded lips and hands
They lie and wait what next the Will commands,
And doubtless think, if think they can: "Let discord
Sink with Life's sands!"

'By these late years their names,
Their virtues, their hereditary claims,
May be as near defacement at their grave-place
As are their fames.'

– Such thoughts bechanced to seize
A traveller's mind – a man of memories –
As he set foot within the western city
Where had died these

Who in their lifetime deemed
Him their chief enemy – one whose brain had schemed
To get their dingy greatness deeplier dingied
And disesteemed.

So, sojourning in their town,
He mused on them and on their once renown,
And said, 'I'll seek their resting-place to-morrow
Ere I lie down,

'And end, lest I forget,
Those ires of many years that I regret,
Renew their names, that men may see some liegeness
Is left them yet.'

Duly next night he went
And sought the church he had known them to frequent,
And wandered, lantern-bearing, in the precincts,
Where they lay pent,

The Obliterate Tomb
11 can: "Let] can, Let MS
12 sands!"] sands. MS
17 – Such] Such MS
25 town,] town MS
27 resting-place] restingplace MS [Possibly two words]
33 night] day MS, SC, PE
35] And wandered in the precincts, set on eying MS, SC, PE

Till by remembrance led
He stood at length beside their slighted bed,
Above which, truly, scarce a line or letter
Could now be read.

'Thus years obliterate
Their graven worth, their chronicle, their date!
At once I'll garnish and revive the record
Of their past state,

'That still the sage may say
In pensive progress here where they decay,
"This stone records a luminous line whose talents
Told in their day." '

While dreaming thus he turned,
For a form shadowed where they lay inurned,
And he beheld a stranger in foreign vesture,
And tropic-burned.

'Sir, I am right pleased to view
That ancestors of mine should interest you,
For I have fared of purpose here to find them. . . .
They are time-worn, true,

'But that's a fault, at most,
Carvers can cure. On the Pacific coast
I have vowed for long that relics of my forbears
I'd trace ere lost,

'And hitherward I come,
Before this same old Time shall strike me numb,
To carry it out.' – 'Strange, this is!' said the other;
'What mind shall plumb

'Coincident design!
Though these my father's enemies were and mine,
I nourished a like purpose – to restore them
Each letter and line.'

The Obliterate Tomb
40 read.] read, WE
49 dreaming] speaking MS, SC, PE
55 fared] come MS, SC, PE
55 find] trace MS, SC, PE
55 them. . . .] them. . . . . MS
57 fault, at most,] fault at most MS
58 Carvers can] Which cash will MS
58 Carvers] Sculptors SC, PE

'Such magnanimity
Is now not needed, sir; for you will see
That since I am here, a thing like this is, plainly,
Best done by me.'

The other bowed, and left,
Crestfallen in sentiment, as one bereft
Of some fair object he had been moved to cherish,
By hands more deft.

And as he slept that night
The phantoms of the ensepulchred stood upright
Before him, trembling that he had set him seeking
Their charnel-site.

And, as unknowing his ruth,
Asked as with terrors founded not on truth
Why he should want them. 'Ha,' they hollowly hackered,
'You come, forsooth,

'By stealth to obliterate
Our graven worth, our chronicle, our date,
That our descendant may not gild the record
Of our past state,

'And that no sage may say
In pensive progress near where we decay:
"This stone records a luminous line whose talents
Told in their day." '

Upon the morrow he went,
And to that town and churchyard never bent
His ageing footsteps till, some twelvemonths onward,
An accident

Once more detained him there;
And, stirred by hauntings, he must needs repair
To where the tomb was. Lo, it stood still wasting
In no man's care.

The Obliterate Tomb
80 charnel-site.] charnel-site MS
93 went,] went MS, SC, PE
95 till,] till MS
95 onward,] onward MS
97 there;] there MS
100–1 MS, SC, PE have two extra stanzas here:

'The travelled man you met/The last time,' said the sexton, 'has not yet/Appeared again, though wealth he had in plenty./Can (– Can SC, PE) he forget?

'The architect was hired/And came here on smart summons as desired,/But never the descendant came to tell him/What he required.'

And so the tomb remained
Untouched, untended, crumbling, weather-stained,
And though the one-time foe was fain to right it
He still refrained.

'I'll set about it when
I am sure he'll come no more. Best wait till then.'
But so it was that never the kinsman entered
That city again.

Till doubts grew keen
If it had chanced not that the figure seen
Shaped but in dream on that dim doubtful midnight:
Such things had been. . . .

So, the well-meaner died
While waiting tremulously unsatisfied
That no return of the family's foreign scion
Would still betide.

And many years slid by,
And active church-restorers cast their eye
Upon the ancient garth and hoary building
The tomb stood nigh.

And when they had scraped each wall,
Pulled out the stately pews, and smartened all,
'It will be well,' declared the spruce church-warden,
'To overhaul

'And broaden this path where shown;
Nothing prevents it but an old tombstone
Pertaining to a family forgotten,
Of deeds unknown.

'Their names can scarce be read;
Depend on't, all who care for them are dead.'
So went the tomb, whose shards were as path-paving
Distributed.

The Obliterate Tomb
107 kinsman] stranger MS, SC, WE, PE, ME
109–12 Not in MS, SC, PE
110 figure] kinsman WE, ME
113 So,] And MS, SC, PE
123 church-warden] churchwarden MS, WE
129 read;] read, MS, SC, WE, PE, CP1–3

Over it and about
Men's footsteps beat, and wind and waterspout,
Until the names, aforetime gnawed by weathers,
Were quite worn out.

So that no sage can say
In pensive progress near where they decay,
'This stone records a luminous line whose talents
Told in their day.'

EXTRA PRINTINGS:
(1) *Selected Poems*, pp. 79–80
(2) *Chosen Poems*, pp. 74–5

TITLE:
'Regret not me' MS

318 Regret Not Me

REGRET not me;
Beneath the sunny tree
I lie uncaring, slumbering peacefully.

Swift as the light
I flew my faery flight;
Ecstatically I moved, and feared no night.

I did not know
That heydays fade and go,
But deemed that what was would be always so.

I skipped at morn
Between the yellowing corn,
Thinking it good and glorious to be born.

I ran at eves
Among the piled-up sheaves,
Dreaming, 'I grieve not, therefore nothing grieves.'

Now soon will come
The apple, pear, and plum,
And hinds will sing, and autumn insects hum.

Again you will fare
To cider-makings rare,
And junketings; but I shall not be there.

Regret Not Me
1 me;] me, MS
12 good and glorious] joy and jubilance MS *before revision*
14 piled-up sheaves,] piled up sheaves MS
17 plum,] plum SC, PE
20 cider-makings] cidermakings MS

Yet gaily sing
Until the pewter ring
Those songs we sang when we went gipsying.

And lightly dance
Some triple-timed romance
In coupled figures, and forget mischance;

And mourn not me
Beneath the yellowing tree;
For I shall mind not, slumbering peacefully.

319 The Recalcitrants

LET us off and search, and find a place
Where yours and mine can be natural lives,
Where no one comes who dissects and dives
And proclaims that ours is a curious case,
Which its touch of romance can scarcely grace.

You would think it strange at first, but then
Everything has been strange in its time.
When some one said on a day of the prime
He would bow to no brazen god again
He doubtless dazed the mass of men.

None will see in us a pair whose claims
To righteous judgment we care not making;
Who have doubted if breath be worth the taking,
And have no respect for the current fames
Whence the savour has flown while abide the names.

We have found us already shunned, disdained,
And for re-acceptance have not once striven;
Whatever offence our course has given
The brunt thereof we have long sustained.
Well, let us away, scorned, unexplained.

Regret Not Me
24 gipsying.] gipsying! SP

The Recalcitrants
5 Which] That MS, SC, WE, PE, ME
11 see in us] recognize us as MS, SC, WE, PE, CP1, ME

PROOF:
In Yale University Library: identical with N

EXTRA PRINTING:
The Nation, 18 Oct 1913, p. 140 = N

TITLE:
(Moving House, Michaelmas.) N as sub-title

320 *Starlings on the Roof*

'NO smoke spreads out of this chimney-pot,
The people who lived here have left the spot,
And others are coming who knew them not.

'If you listen anon, with an ear intent,
The voices, you'll find, will be different
From the well-known ones of those who went.'

'Why did they go? Their tones so bland
Were quite familiar to our band;
The comers we shall not understand.'

'They look for a new life, rich and strange;
They do not know that, let them range
Wherever they may, they will get no change.

'They will drag their house-gear ever so far
In their search for a home no miseries mar;
They will find that as they were they are,

'That every hearth has a ghost, alack,
And can be but the scene of a bivouac
Till they move their last – no care to pack!'

TITLE:
The Moon looks in MS

321 *The Moon Looks In*

I

I HAVE risen again,
And awhile survey
By my chilly ray
Through your window-pane
Your upturned face,
As you think, 'Ah – she
Now dreams of me
In her distant place!'

Starlings on the Roof
2 spot,] spot MS
9 The] Fresh N
10 rich and] strenuous, N
12 change.] change; N
13 house-gear] furniture N
14 mar;] mar: N
16 alack,] alack! N
18] For a fitful (painful N) halt till the time to pack!' MS, N
18 their last] perforce SC, PE, CP1
18 care] time SC, PE, CP1

II

I pierce her blind
In her far-off home:
She fixes a comb,
And says in her mind,
'I start in an hour;
Whom shall I meet?
Won't the men be sweet,
And the women sour!'

322 *The Sweet Hussy*

In his early days he was quite surprised
When she told him she was compromised
By meetings and lingerings at his whim,
And thinking not of herself but him;
While she lifted orbs aggrieved and round
That scandal should so soon abound,
(As she had raised them to nine or ten
Of antecedent nice young men):
And in remorse he thought with a sigh,
How good she is, and how bad am I! –
It was years before he understood
That she was the wicked one – he the good.

323 *The Telegram*

EXTRA PRINTING:
Harper's Monthly Magazine (New York), Dec 1913, p. [103] = H

'O he's suffering – maybe dying – and I not there to aid,
And smooth his bed and whisper to him! Can I nohow go?
Only the nurse's brief twelve words thus hurriedly conveyed,
  As by stealth, to let me know.

'He was the best and brightest! – candour shone upon his brow,
And I shall never meet again a soldier such as he,
And I loved him ere I knew it, and perhaps he's sinking now,
  Far, far removed from me!'

The Moon Looks In
10 far-off] far off MS
15 sweet,] sweet MS

The Sweet Hussy
2 him] me MS
3 meetings] trysts MS
8 men):] men); MS
Note Textual emendation to MS shows that Hardy wrote this poem first in the third person, changed it to the first person, and then reverted to the third person; 'me' in l. 2 is a survival from the second state.

The Telegram
1 O he's] He's H
3 conveyed,] conveyed H
6 soldier such] man so high MS, H
8–9 H has a row of dots between these two lines

– The yachts ride mute at anchor and the fulling moon is fair,
And the giddy folk are strutting up and down the smooth parade,
And in her wild distraction she seems not to be aware
That she lives no more a maid,

But has vowed and wived herself to one who blessed the ground she trod
To and from his scene of ministry, and thought her history known
In its last particular to him – aye, almost as to God,
And believed her quite his own.

So rapt her mind's far-off regard she droops as in a swoon,
And a movement of aversion mars her recent spousal grace,
And in silence we two sit here in our waning honeymoon
At this idle watering-place. . . .

What now I see before me is a long lane overhung
With lovelessness, and stretching from the present to the grave.
And I would I were away from this, with friends I knew when young,
Ere a woman held me slave.

324 *The Moth-Signal*

(*On Egdon Heath*)

'WHAT are you still, still thinking,'
He asked in vague surmise,
'That you stare at the wick unblinking
With those deep lost luminous eyes?'

'O, I see a poor moth burning
In the candle flame,' said she,
'Its wings and legs are turning
To a cinder rapidly.'

'Moths fly in from the heather,'
He said, 'now the days decline.'
'I know,' said she. 'The weather,
I hope, will at last be fine.

The Telegram
9 – The] The H
13 one who] me who have MS, H
13 trod] trod, MS, H
14 To . . . ministry,] One who wooed her single heartedly (single-heartedly H) MS, H
17 rapt . . . regard] great her absentmindedness (absent-mindedness H) MS, H, SC, PE
20 watering-place. . . .] wateringplace. . . . . . MS [possibly two words]: watering-place. H
22 grave.] grave, H
24 held] called H
(Published 1913) MS at end

The Moth-Signal
1 still,] still MS
4 deep] great MS, SC, PE
6 candle flame] candle-flame MS, SC, PE, WE, ME

'I think,' she added lightly,
   'I'll look out at the door.
The ring the moon wears nightly
   May be visible now no more.'

She rose, and, little heeding,
   Her life-mate then went on
With his mute and museful reading
   In the annals of ages gone.

Outside the house a figure
   Came from the tumulus near,
And speedily waxed bigger,
   And clasped and called her Dear.

'I saw the pale-winged token
   You sent through the crack,' sighed she.
'That moth is burnt and broken
   With which you lured out me.

'And were I as the moth is
   It might be better far
For one whose marriage troth is
   Shattered as potsherds are!'

Then grinned the Ancient Briton
   From the tumulus treed with pine:
'So, hearts are thwartly smitten
   In these days as in mine!'

325 Seen by the Waits

THROUGH snowy woods and shady
   We went to play a tune
To the lonely manor-lady
   By the light of the Christmas moon.

We violed till, upward glancing
   To where a mirror leaned,
It showed her airily dancing,
   Deeming her movements screened;

The Moth-Signal
18 life-mate] husband MS, SC, PE
19 mute and museful] attentive MS, SC, PE
19 and] Not in WE, CP1, ME
36 mine!] mine. MS

Seen by the Waits
7 It showed] We saw MS, SC, PE
8 screened;] screened. MS

Dancing alone in the room there,
Thin-draped in her robe of night;
Her postures, glassed in the gloom there,
Were a strange phantasmal sight.

She had learnt (we heard when homing)
That her roving spouse was dead:
Why she had danced in the gloaming
We thought, but never said.

TITLE:
A Rencounter MS *before revision*

326 *The Two Soldiers*

JUST at the corner of the wall
We met – yes, he and I –
Who had not faced in camp or hall
Since we bade home good-bye,
And what once happened came back – all –
Out of those years gone by;

And that strange woman whom we knew
And loved – long dead and gone,
Whose poor half-perished residue,
Tombless and trod, lay yon,
But at this moment to our view
Rose like a phantom wan!

And in his fixed face I could see,
Lit by a lurid shine,
The drama re-enact which she
Had dyed incarnadine
For us, and more. And doubtless he
Beheld it too in mine.

A start, as at one slightly known;
And with an indifferent air
We passed, without a sign being shown
That, as it real were,
A memory-acted scene had thrown
Its tragic shadow there.

Seen by the Waits
14 dead:] dead; MS, SC, WE, PE, ME

The Two Soldiers
4 good-bye] goodbye MS
6 by;] by. MS, SC, WE, PE, CP1–3
10 yon,] yon! MS, SC, WE, PE, CP1–3
12 wan!] wan. MS, SC, WE, PE, CP1–3
19 known;] known, MS, SC, PE

327 The Death of Regret

I OPENED my shutter at sunrise,
And looked at the hill hard by,
And I heartily grieved for the comrade
Who wandered up there to die.

I let in the morn on the morrow,
And failed not to think of him then,
As he trod up that rise in the twilight,
And never came down again.

I undid the shutter a week thence,
But not until after I'd turned
Did I call back his last departure
By the upland there discerned.

Uncovering the casement long later,
I bent to my toil till the gray,
When I said to myself, 'Ah – what ails me,
To forget him all the day!'

As daily I flung back the shutter
In the same blank bald routine,
He scarcely once rose to remembrance
Through a month of my facing the scene.

And ah, seldom now do I ponder
At the window as heretofore
On the long valued one who died yonder,
And wastes by the sycamore.

328 In the Days of Crinoline

A PLAIN tilt-bonnet on her head
She took the path across the leaze.
– Her spouse the vicar, gardening, said,
'Too dowdy that, for coquetries,
So I can hoe at ease.'

TITLE:
The Vicar's Young wife MS *before revision*

In the Days of Crinoline
3 – Her] Her MS
3] Her husband gardening, looked and said,
MS *before revision*

But when she had passed into the heath,
And gained the wood beyond the flat,
She raised her skirts, and from beneath
Unpinned and drew as from a sheath
An ostrich-feathered hat.

And where the hat had hung she now
Concealed and pinned the dowdy hood,
And set the hat upon her brow,
And thus emerging from the wood
Tripped on in jaunty mood.

The sun was low and crimson-faced
As two came that way from the town,
And plunged into the wood untraced....
When severally therefrom they paced
The sun had quite gone down.

The hat and feather disappeared,
The dowdy hood again was donned,
And in the gloom the fair one neared
Her home and husband dour, who conned
Calmly his blue-eyed blonde.

'To-day,' he said, 'you have shown good sense,
A dress so modest and so meek
Should always deck your goings hence
Alone.' And as a recompense
He kissed her on the cheek.

EXTRA MANUSCRIPT:
It has not been possible to trace the MS once in the possession of Prof. J. N. Mavrogordato

329 The Roman Gravemounds

BY Rome's dim relics there walks a man,
Eyes bent; and he carries a basket and spade;
I guess what impels him to scrape and scan;
Yea, his dreams of that Empire long decayed.

EXTRA PRINTING:
The English Review, Dec 1911, p. 1 = ER

TITLE:
Among the Roman Gravemounds ER

INDENTATION:
1 = ll. 1, 3 } and so throughout
2 = ll. 2, 4 } ER

In the Days of Crinoline
19] When flushed therefrom alone she paced MS *before revision*
19 severally] separately MS, SC, PE
July 1911 MS *del* at end

The Roman Gravemounds
1 man,] man MS
2 and] Not in ER
3 scan;] scan – ER
4 Yea, his] His ER

'Vast was Rome,' he must muse, 'in the world's regard,
Vast it looms there still, vast it ever will be;'
And he stoops as to dig and unmine some shard
Left by those who are held in such memory.

But no; in his basket, see, he has brought
A little white furred thing, stiff of limb,
Whose life never won from the world a thought;
It is this, and not Rome, that is moving him.

And to make it a grave he has come to the spot,
And he delves in the ancient dead's long home;
Their fames, their achievements, the man knows not;
The furred thing is all to him – nothing Rome!

'Here say you that Cæsar's warriors lie? –
But my little white cat was my only friend!
Could she but live, might the record die
Of Cæsar, his legions, his aims, his end!'

Well, Rome's long rule here is oft and again
A theme for the sages of history,
And the small furred life was worth no one's pen;
Yet its mourner's mood has a charm for me.

November 1910

330 The Workbox

'SEE, here's the workbox, little wife,
   That I made of polished oak.'
He was a joiner, of village life;
   She came of borough folk.

He holds the present up to her
   As with a smile she nears
And answers to the profferer,
   ''Twill last all my sewing years!'

The Roman Gravemounds
5 regard,] regard; ER
6 still,] still; ER
9 But] But, ER
16 him –] him, ER
16 Rome!] Rome. ER
20 end!'] end!' . . . ER
23 pen;] pen, ER
24 mood has a charm] view is the view ER
November 1910] Not in ER

'I warrant it will. And longer too.
  'Tis a scantling that I got
Off poor John Wayward's coffin, who
  Died of they knew not what.

'The shingled pattern that seems to cease
  Against your box's rim
Continues right on in the piece
  That's underground with him.

'And while I worked it made me think
  Of timber's varied doom;
One inch where people eat and drink,
  The next inch in a tomb.

'But why do you look so white, my dear,
  And turn aside your face?
You knew not that good lad, I fear,
  Though he came from your native place?'

'How could I know that good young man,
  Though he came from my native town,
When he must have left far earlier than
  I was a woman grown?'

'Ah, no. I should have understood!
  It shocked you that I gave
To you one end of a piece of wood
  Whose other is in a grave?'

'Don't, dear, despise my intellect,
  Mere accidental things
Of that sort never have effect
  On my imaginings.'

Yet still her lips were limp and wan,
  Her face still held aside,
As if she had known not only John,
  But known of what he died.

The Workbox
11 John] Hugh MS *before revision*
12] Came from your native spot. MS *before revision*
16 him.] him MS
26–8] Or sorrow that he died,/When it all happened earlier than/I reached this countryside?' MS *before revision*
27 far] there MS, SC, PE
28 grown?'] grown.' – MS
29 Ah,] Ah WE, ME
33 intellect,] intellect. MS

331 The Sacrilege

EXTRA PRINTING:
The Fortnightly Review, 1 Nov 1911, pp. [773]–777 = FR

A Ballad-Tragedy

(*Circa 182–*)

PART I

'I HAVE a Love I love too well
Where Dunkery frowns on Exon Moor;
I have a Love I love too well,
        To whom, ere she was mine,
"Such is my love for you," I said,
"That you shall have to hood your head
A silken kerchief crimson-red,
        Wove finest of the fine."

'And since this Love, for one mad moon,
On Exon Wild by Dunkery Tor,
Since this my Love for one mad moon
        Did clasp me as her king,
I snatched a silk-piece red and rare
From off a stall at Priddy Fair,
For handkerchief to hood her hair
        When we went gallanting.

'Full soon the four weeks neared their end
Where Dunkery frowns on Exon Moor;
And when the four weeks neared their end,
        And their swift sweets outwore,
I said, "What shall I do to own
Those beauties bright as tulips blown,
And keep you here with me alone
        As mine for evermore?"

'And as she drowsed within my van
On Exon Wild by Dunkery Tor –
And as she drowsed within my van,
        And dawning turned to day,

The Sacrilege
20 outwore,] outwore WE
27 van,] van WE, ME

She heavily raised her sloe-black eyes
And murmured back in softest wise,
"One more thing, and the charms you prize
Are yours henceforth for aye.

' "And swear I will I'll never go
While Dunkery frowns on Exon Moor
To meet the Cornish Wrestler Joe
For dance and dallyings,
If you'll to yon cathedral shrine,
And finger from the chest divine
Treasure to buy me ear-drops fine,
And richly jewelled rings."

'I said: "I am one who has gathered gear
From Marlbury Downs to Dunkery Tor,
Who has gathered gear for many a year
From mansion, mart and fair;
But at God's house I've stayed my hand,
Hearing within me some command –
Curbed by a law not of the land
From doing damage there!"

'Whereat she pouts, this Love of mine,
As Dunkery pouts to Exon Moor,
And still she pouts, this Love of mine,
So cityward I go.
But ere I start to do the thing,
And speed my soul's imperilling
For one who is my ravishing
And all the joy I know,

'I come to lay this charge on thee –
On Exon Wild by Dunkery Tor –
I come to lay this charge on thee
With solemn speech and sign:
Should things go ill, and my life pay
For botchery in this rash assay,
You are to take hers likewise – yea,
The month the law takes mine.

The Sacrilege

29 sloe-black] Mistakenly printed as 'sloe-back' CP

30 wise,] wise: FR

35 Wrestler] wrestler MS

36 dallyings,] dallyings. SC, WE, PE, ME, CP [I have preferred the comma as it is found in FR; it could be a comma in MS, and the sense requires a comma]

44 mart] mart, FR

44 fair;] fair: FR

48 there!] there. MS, FR, SC, PE

49 pouts,] pouts – FR

49 mine,] mine – FR

50 pouts to] frowns on MS, FR, SC, PE, CP1

51 pouts,] pouts – FR

51 mine,] mine – FR

53 But] But, FR

'For should my rival, Wrestler Joe,
Where Dunkery frowns on Exon Moor –
My reckless rival, Wrestler Joe,
My Love's bedwinner be,
My rafted spirit would not rest,
But wander weary and distrest
Throughout the world in wild protest:
The thought nigh maddens me!'

Part II

Thus did he speak – this brother of mine –
On Exon Wild by Dunkery Tor,
Born at my birth of mother of mine,
And forthwith went his way
To dare the deed some coming night....
I kept the watch with shaking sight,
The moon at moments breaking bright,
At others glooming gray.

For three full days I heard no sound
Where Dunkery frowns on Exon Moor,
I heard no sound at all around
Whether his fay prevailed,
Or one more foul the master were,
Till some afoot did tidings bear
How that, for all his practised care,
He had been caught and jailed.

They had heard a crash when twelve had chimed
By Mendip east of Dunkery Tor,
When twelve had chimed and moonlight climbed;
They watched, and he was tracked
By arch and aisle and saint and knight
Of sculptured stonework sheeted white
In the cathedral's ghostly light,
And captured in the act.

The Sacrilege
68 bedwinner] possessor MS, FR, SC, PE, CP1 [CP1 corrected to 'bedwinner' on errata slip]
69 rafted] tortured MS, FR, SC, PE, CP1 [CP1 corrected to 'rafted' on errata slip]
74 Tor,] Tor – FR
78 I] – I FR
79 bright,] bright FR
83] For three full days I heard no sound FR
85 more foul] malign MS, FR, SC, PE, CP1 [CP1 corrected to 'more foul' on errata slip]
85 were,] were MS: were; FR
86 afoot] a-foot FR
86 bear] bear, MS
89–96 Not in FR
89 twelve had] midnight MS
91 twelve had] midnight MS

Yes; for this Love he loved too well
Where Dunkery sights the Severn shore,
All for this Love he loved too well
He burst the holy bars,
Seized golden vessels from the chest
To buy her ornaments of the best,
At her ill-witchery's request
And lure of eyes like stars. . . .

When blustering March confused the sky
In Toneborough Town by Exon Moor,
When blustering March confused the sky
They stretched him; and he died.
Down in the crowd where I, to see
The end of him, stood silently,
With a set face he lipped to me –
'Remember.' 'Ay!' I cried.

By night and day I shadowed her
From Toneborough Deane to Dunkery Tor,
I shadowed her asleep, astir,
And yet I could not bear –
Till Wrestler Joe anon began
To figure as her chosen man,
And took her to his shining van –
To doom a form so fair!

He made it handsome for her sake –
And Dunkery smiled to Exon Moor –
He made it handsome for her sake,
Painting it out and in;
And on the door of apple-green
A bright brass knocker soon was seen,
And window-curtains white and clean
For her to sit within.

And all could see she clave to him
As cleaves a cloud to Dunkery Tor,
Yea, all could see she clave to him,
And every day I said,

The Sacrilege
98] On Exon Wild by Dunkery Tor – FR
101 golden] silver FR
102 best,] best MS, FR
103 ill-witchery's] ill witchery's MS, FR
104 stars. . . .] stars. . . . . MS
106 Moor,] Moor; MS, FR
108 him;] him: FR
115] By night and day I shadowed her; FR
126 bright] gay FR
130 Tor,] Tor – FR
131 him,] him; FR

'A pity it seems to part those two
That hourly grow to love more true:
Yet she's the wanton woman who
Sent one to swing till dead!'

That blew to blazing all my hate,
While Dunkery frowned on Exon Moor,
And when the river swelled, her fate
Came to her pitilessly. . . .
I dogged her, crying: 'Across that plank
They use as bridge to reach yon bank
A coat and hat lie limp and dank;
Your goodman's, can they be?'

She paled, and went, I close behind –
And Exon frowned to Dunkery Tor,
She went, and I came up behind
And tipped the plank that bore
Her, fleetly flitting across to eye
What such might bode. She slid awry;
And from the current came a cry,
A gurgle; and no more.

How that befell no mortal knew
From Marlbury Downs to Exon Moor;
No mortal knew that deed undue
But he who schemed the crime,
Which night still covers. . . . But in dream
Those ropes of hair upon the stream
He sees, and he will hear that scream
Until his judgment-time.

332 The Abbey Mason

Inventor of the 'Perpendicular' Style of Gothic Architecture

(*With Memories of John Hicks, Architect*)

THE new-vamped Abbey shaped apace
In the fourteenth century of grace;

EXTRA MANUSCRIPT:
In the Pierpont Morgan Library = PM

EXTRA PRINTING:
Harper's Monthly Magazine (New York), Dec 1912, pp. [21–5] = H

TITLE:
(*With . . .*)] Not in MS, PM, H, SC, PE

The Sacrilege
134 grow] seem FR
134 true:] true; FR
136 swing till dead] his death-bed FR
137 hate,] hate FR
140 pitilessly. . . .] pitilessly. . . . . MS: pitilessly . . . , FR
143 dank;] dank: FR
144 goodman's,] goodman's FR
149 Her,] Her MS, FR
155] How that befel no mortal knew FR
157 covers. . . .] covers. . . . . MS: covers! . . . FR

The Abbey Mason
1 new-vamped] new-schemed H
2 grace;] grace. PM

(The church which, at an after date,
Acquired cathedral rank and state.)

Panel and circumscribing wall
Of latest feature, trim and tall,

Rose roundabout the Norman core
In prouder pose than theretofore,

Encasing magically the old
With parpend ashlars manifold.

The trowels rang out, and tracery
Appeared where blanks had used to be.

Men toiled for pleasure more than pay,
And all went smoothly day by day,

Till, in due course, the transept part
Engrossed the master-mason's art.

– Home-coming thence he tossed and turned
Throughout the night till the new sun burned.

'What fearful visions have inspired
These gaingivings?' his wife inquired;

'As if your tools were in your hand
You have hammered, fitted, muttered, planned;

'You have thumped as you were working hard:
I might have found me bruised and scarred.

'What then's amiss? What eating care
Looms nigh, whereof I am unaware?'

He answered not, but churchward went,
Viewing his draughts with discontent;

And fumbled there the livelong day
Till, hollow-eyed, he came away.

– 'Twas said, 'The master-mason's ill!'
And all the abbey works stood still.

The Abbey Mason
3 after date,] after-date PM: after-date, H
9 old] old, PM, H
16 art.] art. . . . PM
17 – Home-coming] – Homecoming MS: Homecoming PM
20 inquired;] inquired: PM
25 amiss?] amiss. MS, SC, WE, PE
28 discontent;] discontent, H
29 fumbled] fumbling PM, H
29 livelong] live-long H
30 Till,] Till PM
31 – 'Twas] 'Twas PM
32 abbey] Abbey PM

Quoth Abbot Wygmore: 'Why, O why
Distress yourself? You'll surely die!'

The mason answered, trouble-torn,
'This long-vogued style is quite outworn!

'The upper archmould nohow serves
To meet the lower tracery curves:

'The ogees bend too far away
To give the flexures interplay.

'This it is causes my distress. . . .
So it will ever be unless

'New forms be found to supersede
The circle when occasions need.

'To carry it out I have tried and toiled,
And now perforce must own me foiled!

'Jeerers will say: "Here was a man
Who could not end what he began!" '

– So passed that day, the next, the next;
The abbot scanned the task, perplexed;

The townsmen mustered all their wit
To fathom how to compass it,

But no raw artistries availed
Where practice in the craft had failed. . . .

– One night he tossed, all open-eyed,
And early left his helpmeet's side.

Scattering the rushes of the floor
He wandered from the chamber door

And sought the sizing pile, whereon
Struck dimly a cadaverous dawn

Through freezing rain, that drenched the board
Of diagram-lines he last had scored –

The Abbey Mason
33 O] oh, H
37 archmould] arch-mould PM, H
40 flexures] flextures H
41 distress. . . .] distress. . . . . MS: distress; PM
42 be] be, PM, H
46 perforce] I needs H
46 foiled!] foiled. H
49 – So] So PM
50 abbot] Abbot PM
54 failed. . . .] failed. PM
57 of] on PM
57 floor] floor, H
58 chamber door] chamber-door PM
61 freezing rain,] rain PM, H
61 board] diagram-board PM, H
62 diagram-lines] tentative lines PM, H

Chalked phantasies in vain begot
To knife the architectural knot –

In front of which he dully stood,
Regarding them in hopeless mood.

He closelier looked; then looked again:
The chalk-scratched draught-board faced the rain,

Whose icicled drops deformed the lines
Innumerous of his lame designs,

So that they streamed in small white threads
From the upper segments to the heads

Of arcs below, uniting them
Each by a stalactitic stem.

– At once, with eyes that struck out sparks,
He adds accessory cusping-marks,

Then laughs aloud. The thing was done
So long assayed from sun to sun. . . .

– Now in his joy he grew aware
Of one behind him standing there,

And, turning, saw the abbot, who
The weather's whim was watching too.

Onward to Prime the abbot went,
Tacit upon the incident.

– Men now discerned as days revolved
The ogive riddle had been solved;

Templates were cut, fresh lines were chalked
Where lines had been defaced and balked,

And the work swelled and mounted higher,
Achievement distancing desire;

Here jambs with transoms fixed between,
Where never the like before had been –

The Abbey Mason
67 again:] again MS: again; H
68 chalk-scratched] huge black PM
69 icicled drops] drops had so PM, H
70 designs,] designs MS, PM, H
71 So that they] That they had PM, H
75 – At] At PM
78 So long] That he had PM
78 assayed] essayed PM, H
78 sun. . . .] sun. . . . . MS, PM
79 Now] Now, PM, H
79 joy] joy, PM, H
81 And, turning,] And turning PM
81 abbot] Abbot PM
83 abbot went,] Abbot went PM
84 incident.] incident. . . . . PM: incident. . . . H
89 higher,] higher PM
91 between,] between H

There little mullions thinly sawn
Where meeting circles once were drawn.

'We knew,' men said, 'the thing would go
After his craft-wit got aglow,

'And, once fulfilled what he has designed,
We'll honour him and his great mind!'

When matters stood thus poised awhile,
And all surroundings shed a smile,

The master-mason on an eve
Homed to his wife and seemed to grieve. . . .

– 'The abbot spoke to me to-day;
He hangs about the works alway.

'He knows the source as well as I
Of the new style men magnify.

'He said: "You pride yourself too much
On your creation. Is it such?

' "Surely the hand of God it is
That conjured so, and only His! –

' "Disclosing by the frost and rain
Forms your invention chased in vain;

' "Hence the devices deemed so great
You copied, and did not create."

'I feel the abbot's words are just,
And that all thanks renounce I must.

'Can a man welcome praise and pelf
For hatching art that hatched itself? . . .

'So, I shall own the deft design
Is Heaven's outshaping, and not mine.'

'What!' said she. 'Praise your works ensure
To throw away, and quite obscure

The Abbey Mason
97 designed,] designed PM
98 him and his great] such a magic PM, H
98 mind!] mind. PM
99 awhile,] awhile PM
100 smile,] smile PM
101 master-mason] master-mason, PM
101 eve] eve, PM
102 wife] wife, PM, H
102 grieve. . . .] grieve . . . MS, H, SC, PE
103 – 'The] ' – The H
103 abbot] Abbot PM
103 to-day;] to-day: MS, PM, H, SC, WE, PE, ME
106 men] folk PM
110 His! –] his! – MS, PM: His! H
111 frost and] wash of PM, H
115 I] – I H
115 abbot's] Abbot's PM
116 must.] must! H
118 itself? . . .] itself? . . . . MS: itself? – PM
120 mine.'] mine.' – PM, H
121 she. 'Praise] she, 'Praise PM: she, 'praise H
121 ensure] insure H

'Your beaming and beneficent star?
Better you leave things as they are!

'Why, think awhile. Had not your zest
In your loved craft curtailed your rest –

'Had you not gone there ere the day
The sun had melted all away!'

– But, though his good wife argued so,
The mason let the people know

That not unaided sprang the thought
Whereby the glorious fane was wrought,

But that by frost when dawn was dim
The method was disclosed to him.

'Yet,' said the townspeople thereat,
' 'Tis your own doing, even with that!'

But he – chafed, childlike, in extremes –
The temperament of men of dreams –

Aloofly scrupled to admit
That he did aught but borrow it,

And diffidently made request
That with the abbot all should rest.

– As none could doubt the abbot's word,
Or question what the church averred,

The mason was at length believed
Of no more count than he conceived,

And soon began to lose the fame
That late had gathered round his name....

– Time passed, and like a living thing
The pile went on embodying,

And workmen died, and young ones grew,
And the old mason sank from view

The Abbey Mason
127 day] day, PM, H
128] The rain had scoured the lines away!' PM, H
129 But,] But MS, PM, H
129 so,] so MS, PM
133 frost] rain MS: storm, PM: storm H
133 dim] dim, PM
142 abbot] Abbot PM
142 rest.] rest. – PM
143 – As] As PM
143 abbot's! Abbot's PM
144 church] Church MS, PM, H
148 name. . . .] name. . . . . PM
152 view] view, PM: view; H

And Abbots Wygmore and Staunton went
And Horton sped the embellishment.

But not till years had far progressed
Chanced it that, one day, much impressed,

Standing within the well-graced aisle,
He asked who first conceived the style;

And some decrepit sage detailed
How, when invention nought availed,

The cloud-cast waters in their whim
Came down, and gave the hint to him

Who struck each arc, and made each mould;
And how the abbot would not hold

As sole begetter him who applied
Forms the Almighty sent as guide;

And how the master lost renown,
And wore in death no artist's crown.

– Then Horton, who in inner thought
Had more perceptions than he taught,

Replied: 'Nay; art can but transmute;
Invention is not absolute;

'Things fail to spring from nought at call,
And art-beginnings most of all.

'He did but what all artists do,
Wait upon Nature for his cue.'

– 'Had you been here to tell them so,
Lord Abbot, sixty years ago,

'The mason, now long underground,
Doubtless a different fate had found.

'He passed into oblivion dim,
And none knew what became of him!

The Abbey Mason
153 went] went, PM, H
154 embellishment.] embellishment. – PM
156 impressed,] impressed H
157 well-graced] screen-graced H
164 abbot] Abbot PM
176 Nature] nature PM, H
176 cue.'] cue.' – PM
177 – 'Had] ' – Had H
177 so,] so MS, SC, WE, PE
180 found.] found. . . . H
181 dim,] dim MS
182 him!] him. H

'His name? 'Twas of some common kind
And now has faded out of mind.'

The abbot: 'It shall not be hid!
I'll trace it.' . . . But he never did.

– When longer yet dank death had wormed
The brain wherein the style had germed

From Gloucester church it flew afar –
The style called Perpendicular. –

To Winton and to Westminster
It ranged, and grew still beautifuller:

From Solway Frith to Dover Strand
Its fascinations starred the land,

Not only on cathedral walls
But upon courts and castle halls,

Till every edifice in the isle
Was patterned to no other style,

And till, long having played its part
The curtain fell on Gothic art.

– Well: when in Wessex on your rounds,
Take a brief step beyond its bounds,

And enter Gloucester: seek the quoin
Where choir and transept interjoin,

And, gazing at the forms there flung
Against the sky by one unsung –

The ogee arches transom-topped,
The tracery-stalks by spandrels stopped,

Petrified lacework – lightly lined
On ancient massiveness behind –

Muse that some minds so modest be
As to renounce fame's fairest fee,

The Abbey Mason
183 kind] kind, PM, H
184 now has] now it has H
184 mind.'] mind.' . . . . MS, PM: mind.' . . . H
185 Abbot] abbot MS, H
186 it.' . . .] it.' MS, H: it.' – PM
186 did.] did. – PM: did. . . . H
188 germed] germed, PM, H
189 church] Church PM, H
189 flew] spread PM
190 Perpendicular. –] 'Perpendicular'. – PM: 'Perpendicular' – H
192 beautifuller:] beautifuller; PM, H
193 Frith] Firth H
193 Strand] strand MS
195 walls] walls, H
196 castle halls] castle-halls PM
199 part] part, PM, H, SC, WE, PE, ME
200 art.] art. . . . . PM: art. . . . H
201 rounds,] rounds MS, PM
205 there flung] so famed, H
205 flung] flung – PM
206] Charmed from the stone (rock PM) by one unnamed (unsung PM) – PM, H
207 ogee arches] ogee arches, PM
207 transom-topped,] transom-topped – H
208 tracery-stalks] tracery stalks PM
208 stopped,] stopped – H
209 lacework –] lacework, PM: lace-work – H
212 fee,] fee PM, H

(Like him who crystallized on this spot
His visionings, but lies forgot,

And many a mediaeval one
Whose symmetries salute the sun)

While others boom a baseless claim,
And upon nothing rear a name.

333 The Jubilee of a Magazine

EXTRA PRINTING:
The Cornhill Magazine, Jan 1910, pp. 6–7 = C

TITLE:
'The Cornhill's' Jubilee MS *before revision*
An Impromptu to the Editor C
(*To . . .*) MS *del*: Not in C

(*To the Editor*)

YES; your up-dated modern page –
All flower-fresh, as it appears –
Can claim a time-tried lineage,

That reaches backward fifty years
(Which, if but short for sleepy squires,
Is much in magazines' careers).

– Here, on your cover, never tires
The sower, reaper, thresher, while
As through the seasons of our sires

Each wills to work in ancient style
With seedlip, sickle, share and flail,
Though modes have since moved many a mile!

The steel-roped plough now rips the vale,
With cog and tooth the sheaves are won,
Wired wheels drum out the wheat like hail;

But if we ask, what has been done
To unify the mortal lot
Since your bright leaves first saw the sun,

Beyond mechanic furtherance – what
Advance can rightness, candour, claim?
Truth bends abashed, and answers not.

The Abbey Mason
216 sun)] sun), H
217 boom] blow PM
217 claim,] claim MS
218 upon] out of H
218 rear] carve H
At end PM adds: December: 1911 –

The Jubilee of a Magazine
2 flower-fresh,] fancy-fresh C
3 lineage,] lineage MS, C
4 years] years, C
6 much] long C
6 careers).] careers.) MS, C
8 while] while, C
9 through] in C
9 sires] sires, C
11 share] share, C
15 Wired . . . out] And wire-work hurls C
18 sun,] sun – C

Despite your volumes' gentle aim
To straighten visions wry and wrong,
Events jar onward much the same!

– Had custom tended to prolong,
As on your golden page engrained,
Old processes of blade and prong,

And best invention been retained
For high crusades to lessen tears
Throughout the race, the world had gained! . . .
But too much, this, for fifty years.

334 *The Satin Shoes*

EXTRA PRINTING:
Harper's Monthly Magazine (New York), Jan 1910, pp. [165]–167 = H

TITLE:
A Quiet Tragedy H as sub-title

'If ever I walk to church to wed,
    As other maidens use,
And face the gathered eyes,' she said,
    'I'll go in satin shoes!'

She was as fair as early day
    Shining on meads unmown,
And her sweet syllables seemed to play
    Like flute-notes softly blown.

The time arrived when it was meet
    That she should be a bride;
The satin shoes were on her feet,
    Her father was at her side.

They stood within the dairy door,
    And gazed across the green;
The church loomed on the distant moor,
    But rain was thick between.

'The grass-path hardly can be stepped,
    The lane is like a pool!' –
Her dream is shown to be inept,
    Her wish they overrule.

The Jubilee of a Magazine
22 volumes'] volume's ME
23 wrong,] wrong MS
23–4] To lift the mists, let truth be seen,/Pragmatic wiles go on the same, C
24–5 C has extra stanza here:

Though I admit that there have been/Large conquests of the wry and wrong/Effected by your magazine.

28 best] men's C
30 gained! . . .] gained! . . . . MS
31 But] But – C

The Satin Shoes
1 to church to wed,] forth to wed H
5 She] (She H
8 blown.] blown.) H
12 was] Not in H
16 rain was thick] rain-streams fell H
17] 'The grass will drench, even lightly stepped, H
18 lane] road H

'To go forth shod in satin soft
  A coach would be required!'
For thickest boots the shoes were doffed –
  Those shoes her soul desired. . . .

All day the bride, as overborne,
  Was seen to brood apart,
And that the shoes had not been worn
  Sat heavy on her heart.

From her wrecked dream, as months flew on,
  Her thought seemed not to range.
'What ails the wife,' they said anon,
  'That she should be so strange?' . . .

Ah – what coach comes with furtive glide –
  A coach of closed-up kind?
It comes to fetch the last year's bride,
  Who wanders in her mind.

She strove with them, and fearfully ran
  Stairward with one low scream:
'Nay – coax her,' said the madhouse man,
  'With some old household theme.'

'If you will go, dear, you must fain
  Put on those shoes – the pair
Meant for your marriage, which the rain
  Forbade you then to wear.'

She clapped her hands, flushed joyous hues;
  'O yes – I'll up and ride
If I am to wear my satin shoes
  And be a proper bride!'

Out then her little foot held she,
  As to depart with speed;
The madhouse man smiled pleasantly
  To see the wile succeed.

The Satin Shoes
23 thickest boots the] boots the satin H
24 desired. . . .] desired. . . . . MS: desired. H
25 overborne] one down borne H
31 wife,] wife? MS, H, SC, PE
32 strange?' . . .] strange?' . . . . . MS
33 Ah] 'Ah H
34 closed-up] closed up MS
34 kind?] kind?' H
35 It] 'It H
36 mind.] mind.' H
45 hues;] hues: H

She turned to him when all was done,
And gave him her thin hand,
Exclaiming like an enraptured one,
'This time it will be grand!'

She mounted with a face elate,
Shut was the carriage door;
They drove her to the madhouse gate,
And she was seen no more. . . .

Yet she was fair as early day
Shining on meads unmown,
And her sweet syllables seemed to play
Like flute-notes softly blown.

EXTRA PRINTINGS:
(1) *Selected Poems*, p. 107
(2) *Chosen Poems*, p. 139

TITLE:
Exeunt omnes (Epilogue *del*) MS [It is possible that 'Epilogue' was not a tentative title for this poem, but a tentative title for the final section of the book]

335 *Exeunt Omnes*

I

EVERYBODY else, then, going,
And I still left where the fair was? . . .
Much have I seen of neighbour loungers
Making a lusty showing,
Each now past all knowing.

II

There is an air of blankness
In the street and the littered spaces;
Thoroughfare, steeple, bridge and highway
Wizen themselves to lankness;
Kennels dribble dankness.

III

Folk all fade. And whither,
As I wait alone where the fair was?
Into the clammy and numbing night-fog
Whence they entered hither.
Soon one more goes thither!

2 June 1913

The Satin Shoes
55 an enraptured] a raptured H

Exeunt Omnes
2 was? . . .] was? . . . . MS
4 lusty showing] brave outshowing MS
15] Soon do I follow thither! (thither. MS) MS, SC, WE, PE, CP1
15 thither!] thither. SP, CHP

336 A Poet

Attentive eyes, fantastic heed,
Assessing minds, he does not need,
Nor urgent writs to sup or dine,
Nor pledges in the rosy wine.

For loud acclaim he does not care
By the august or rich or fair,
Nor for smart pilgrims from afar,
Curious on where his hauntings are.

But soon or later, when you hear
That he has doffed this wrinkled gear,
Some evening, at the first star-ray,
Come to his graveside, pause and say:

'Whatever his message – glad or grim –
Two bright-souled women clave to him;'
Stand and say that while day decays;
It will be word enough of praise.

July 1914

EXTRA PRINTINGS:
(1) *Selected Poems*, p. 184
(2) *Chosen Poems*, p. 238

TITLE:
The Poet MS *before revision*

Note MS has '[The End]' deleted after this poem. It is followed by a copy of 'Song of the Soldiers' cut from *The Times Literary Supplement* and pasted in. The page is headed 'Postscript' in Hardy's handwriting, and the title 'Men who march away' has been written in above 'Song of the Soldiers'. The copy has been corrected in several places. (See p. 538.) 'Men Who March Away' was published as the final poem in SC, PE, under the heading 'Postscript'

A Poet
4 rosy] roseate MS, SC, PE
12 pause] pause, SP
13–16] 'Whatever the message his to tell,/Two thoughtful (spotless *del* MS: bright-souled SC2, PE) women loved him well.'/Stand and say that amid the dim:/It will be praise enough for him. MS, SC, PE
15 decays;] decays, SP

The 'Satires of Circumstance' first appeared as a sequence of twelve poems in *The Fortnightly Review*, April 1911, pp. [579]–583. Hardy subsequently increased the sequence to fifteen poems by adding 'In the Study', 'At the Draper's', 'On the Death-Bed' and 'In the Moonlight', and omitting 'On the Doorstep' (see p. 944), the title of which was given to a poem in *Moments of Vision* (see p. 525). The Dorchester MS gives the text of all sixteen 'Satires', but that of 'On the Doorstep' has been cancelled. Numbers I–VII in the sequence have kept the same numbers throughout, but there has been some renumbering thereafter. In MS, SC, PE the fifteen poems are printed between 'Ah, Are You Digging on My Grave?' and 'Self-Unconscious'

SATIRES OF CIRCUMSTANCE IN FIFTEEN GLIMPSES

(*First published April 1911*)

EXTRA PRINTING:
The Fortnightly Review, 1 April 1911, p. [579]
= FR

337 I. At Tea

THE kettle descants in a cosy drone,
And the young wife looks in her husband's face,
And then at her guest's, and shows in her own
Her sense that she fills an envied place;
And the visiting lady is all abloom,
And says there was never so sweet a room.

And the happy young housewife does not know
That the woman beside her was first his choice,
Till the fates ordained it could not be so. . . .
Betraying nothing in look or voice
The guest sits smiling and sips her tea,
And he throws her a stray glance yearningly.

EXTRA PRINTING:
The Fortnightly Review, 1 April 1911, p. [579]
= FR

338 II. In Church

'AND now to God the Father,' he ends,
And his voice thrills up to the topmost tiles:
Each listener chokes as he bows and bends,
And emotion pervades the crowded aisles.
Then the preacher glides to the vestry-door,
And shuts it, and thinks he is seen no more.

The door swings softly ajar meanwhile,
And a pupil of his in the Bible class,
Who adores him as one without gloss or guile,

At Tea
8 first his] his first MS, FR [But in MS there is a pencilled transposition to 'first his']
9 so. . . .] so. . . . . MS

In Church
1 he ends] ends he FR
3 and bends] his knee FR
5 to the vestry-door] through the vestry door FR
8 pupil] lover FR
8 his] his, FR
9 Not in FR

Sees her idol stand with a satisfied smile
And re-enact at the vestry-glass
Each pulpit gesture in deft dumb-show
That had moved the congregation so.

339 III. *By Her Aunt's Grave*

EXTRA PRINTING:
The Fortnightly Review, 1 April 1911, p. 580 = FR

TITLE:
By her aunt's grave MS

'SIXPENCE a week,' says the girl to her lover,
'Aunt used to bring me, for she could confide
In me alone, she vowed. 'Twas to cover
The cost of her headstone when she died.
And that was a year ago last June;
I've not yet fixed it. But I must soon.'

'And where is the money now, my dear?'
'O, snug in my purse . . . Aunt was *so* slow
In saving it – eighty weeks, or near.' . . .
'Let's spend it,' he hints. 'For she won't know
There's a dance to-night at the Load of Hay.'
She passively nods. And they go that way.

340 IV. *In the Room of the Bride-Elect*

EXTRA PRINTING:
The Fortnightly Review, 1 April 1911, p. 580 = FR

TITLE:
In the Room of the Bride-elect MS

'WOULD it had been the man of our wish!'
Sighs her mother. To whom with vehemence she
In the wedding-dress – the wife to be –
'Then why were you so mollyish
As not to insist on him for me!'
The mother, amazed: 'Why, dearest one,
Because you pleaded for this or none!'

'But Father and you should have stood out strong!
Since then, to my cost, I have lived to find
That you were right and that I was wrong;
This man is a dolt to the one declined. . . .
Ah! – here he comes with his button-hole rose.
Good God – I must marry him I suppose!'

In Church
10 smile] smile, FR
11 vestry-glass] vestry glass FR

By Her Aunt's Grave
6 fixed it. But] put it here. FR
7 now, my dear?'] now?' asks he. FR
9 weeks, or near.' . . .] weeks!' says she. . . . FR
9 near.' . . .] near.' . . . . MS

In the Room of the Bride-Elect
2 she] she: FR
3 Not in FR
6 mother,] mother FR
11 declined. . . .] declined. FR
12–13 Ah! – here he comes. Well – it's ('tis FR) too late now,/And I must marry him anyhow!' MS, FR

EXTRA PRINTING:
The Fortnightly Review, 1 April 1911, pp. 580–1
= FR

TITLE:
At a watering-place MS

341 V. *At a Watering-Place*

THEY sit and smoke on the esplanade,
The man and his friend, and regard the bay
Where the far chalk cliffs, to the left displayed,
Smile sallowly in the decline of day.
And saunterers pass with laugh and jest –
A handsome couple among the rest.

'That smart proud pair,' says the man to his friend,
'Are to marry next week. . . . How little he thinks
That dozens of days and nights on end
I have stroked her neck, unhooked the links
Of her sleeve to get at her upper arm. . . .
Well, bliss is in ignorance: what's the harm!'

EXTRA PRINTING:
The Fortnightly Review, 1 April 1911, p. 581
= FR

342 VI. *In the Cemetery*

'YOU see those mothers squabbling there?'
Remarks the man of the cemetery.
'One says in tears, "*'Tis mine lies here!*"
Another, "*Nay, mine, you Pharisee!*"
Another, "*How dare you move my flowers*
And put your own on this grave of ours!"
But all their children were laid therein
At different times, like sprats in a tin.

'And then the main drain had to cross,
And we moved the lot some nights ago,
And packed them away in the general foss
With hundreds more. But their folks don't know,
And as well cry over a new-laid drain
As anything else, to ease your pain!'

At a Watering-Place
4 Smile sallowly] Glow ochreous FR
5 jest –] jest, FR
8 week. . . .] week. . . . . MS
11 arm. . . .] arm. . . . . MS

In the Cemetery
5–6 Not in FR
8 times] hours FR
12 know,] know. FR

343 VII. Outside the Window

EXTRA PRINTING:
The Fortnightly Review, 1 April 1911, p. 581 = FR

'My stick!' he says, and turns in the lane
To the house just left, whence a vixen voice
Comes out with the firelight through the pane,
And he sees within that the girl of his choice
Stands rating her mother with eyes aglare
For something said while he was there.

'At last I behold her soul undraped!'
Thinks the man who had loved her more than himself;
'My God! – 'tis but narrowly I have escaped. –
My precious porcelain proves it delf.'
His face has reddened like one ashamed,
And he steals off, leaving his stick unclaimed.

344 VIII. In the Study

He enters, and mute on the edge of a chair
Sits a thin-faced lady, a stranger there,
A type of decayed gentility;
And by some small signs he well can guess
That she comes to him almost breakfastless.

'I have called – I hope I do not err –
I am looking for a purchaser
Of some score volumes of the works
Of eminent divines I own, –
Left by my father – though it irks
My patience to offer them.' And she smiles
As if necessity were unknown;
'But the truth of it is that oftenwhiles
I have wished, as I am fond of art,
To make my rooms a little smart,
And these old books are so in the way.'

Outside the Window
2 vixen voice] vixen-voice FR
9 escaped. –] escaped. FR

In the Study
4–5] And by some small signs he seems to see/That as yet no breakfast has tasted she. MS *before revision*
15 smart,] smart.' SC, PE
16 Not in SC, PE [A late addition to MS]
16 so] much MS
16–17 No stanza break

And lightly still she laughs to him,
As if to sell were a mere gay whim,
And that, to be frank, Life were indeed
To her not vinegar and gall,
But fresh and honey-like; and Need
No household skeleton at all.

EXTRA PRINTING:
The Fortnightly Review, 1 April 1911, p. 582
= FR

TITLE:
At the Altar-rail MS
IX] VIII FR

345 *IX. At the Altar-Rail*

'My bride is not coming, alas!' says the groom,
And the telegram shakes in his hand. 'I own
It was hurried! We met at a dancing-room
When I went to the Cattle-Show alone,
And then, next night, where the Fountain leaps,
And the Street of the Quarter-Circle sweeps.

'Ay, she won me to ask her to be my wife –
'Twas foolish perhaps! – to forsake the ways
Of the flaring town for a farmer's life.
She agreed. And we fixed it. Now she says:
"*It's sweet of you, dear, to prepare me a nest,*
But a swift, short, gay life suits me best.
What I really am you have never gleaned;
I had eaten the apple ere you were weaned." '

EXTRA PRINTING:
The Fortnightly Review, 1 April 1911, p. 582
= FR

TITLE:
X] IX FR

346 *X. In the Nuptial Chamber*

'O that mastering tune!' And up in the bed
Like a lace-robed phantom springs the bride;
'And why?' asks the man she had that day wed,
With a start, as the band plays on outside.
'It's the townsfolk's cheery compliment
Because of our marriage, my Innocent.'

At the Altar-Rail
7 Ay,] Ay – FR
7 wife –] wife. MS, FR
8 foolish] foolish, FR
13 *gleaned;*] *gleaned,* FR

In the Nuptial Chamber
1 mastering] soul-stabbing FR
1 tune!] tune? SC, PE, CP1
3 wed,] wed MS, FR
5 townsfolk's] townsfolks' MS, FR, SC, WE, PE, ME
6–7 Stanza break in all editions

'O but you don't know! 'Tis the passionate air
To which my old Love waltzed with me,
And I swore as we spun that none should share
My home, my kisses, till death, save he!
And he dominates me and thrills me through,
And it's he I embrace while embracing you!'

347 XI. *In the Restaurant*

EXTRA PRINTING:
The Fortnightly Review, 1 April 1911, p. 583 = FR

'BUT hear. If you stay, and the child be born,
It will pass as your husband's with the rest,
While, if we fly, the teeth of scorn
Will be gleaming at us from east to west;
And the child will come as a life despised;
I feel an elopement is ill-advised!'

'O you realize not what it is, my dear,
To a woman! Daily and hourly alarms
Lest the truth should out. How can I stay here
And nightly take him into my arms!
Come to the child no name or fame,
Let us go, and face it, and bear the shame.'

348 XII. *At the Draper's*

EXTRA PRINTING:
The Saturday Review, 16 May 1914, p. 634 = SR

TITLE:
How He Looked in at the Draper's SR
XII] Not in SR

'I STOOD at the back of the shop, my dear,
    But you did not perceive me.
Well, when they deliver what you were shown
    I shall know nothing of it, believe me!'

And he coughed and coughed as she paled and said,
    'O, I didn't see you come in there –
Why couldn't you speak?' – 'Well, I didn't. I left
    That you should not notice I'd been there.

'You were viewing some lovely things. "*Soon required*
    For a widow, of latest fashion;"
And I knew 'twould upset you to meet the man
    Who had to be cold and ashen

In the Restaurant
5 life] thing FR
6 ill-advised!] ill-advised. FR
8 hourly] nightly FR
9 here,] here CP4 [I have re-introduced the comma as copies of CP3 show the comma breaking up]
10 nightly] smile and FR: at his will MS *before revision*]
11 fame,] fame MS, FR
12 Let us] Hardy's copy of CP2 has been corrected to read 'Let's'

At the Draper's
1 stood] was SR
3 shown] shown, SR
4 know nothing of] not know SR
6 O,] Why – SR
7 speak?' –] speak?' SR
9 things.] robes. MS: robes; SR
10 *latest*] *next month's* SR
10 *fashion*;] *fashion*. MS
11 upset you] be awkward SR

'And screwed in a box before they could dress you
"In the last new note in mourning,"
As they defined it. So, not to distress you,
I left you to your adorning.'

TITLE:
On (From At *del*) the Death-bed MS

349 XIII. On the Death-Bed

'I'LL tell – being past all praying for –
Then promptly die. . . . He was out at the war,
And got some scent of the intimacy
That was under way between her and me;
And he stole back home, and appeared like a ghost
One night, at the very time almost
That I reached her house. Well, I shot him dead,
And secretly buried him. Nothing was said.

'The news of the battle came next day;
He was scheduled missing. I hurried away,
Got out there, visited the field,
And sent home word that a search revealed
He was one of the slain; though, lying alone
And stript, his body had not been known.

'But she suspected. I lost her love,
Yea, my hope of earth, and of Heaven above;
And my time's now come, and I'll pay the score,
Though it be burning for evermore.'

EXTRA PRINTING:
The Fortnightly Review, 1 April 1911, p. 583
= FR

TITLE:
XIV] XII FR

350 XIV. Over the Coffin

THEY stand confronting, the coffin between,
His wife of old, and his wife of late,
And the dead man whose they both had been
Seems listening aloof, as to things past date.
– 'I have called,' says the first. 'Do you marvel or not?'
'In truth,' says the second, 'I do – somewhat.'

At the Draper's
13 they] you SR
14 *in*] *of* SR
15 they] you SR
16 adorning.] adorning! SR

On the Death-Bed
2 die. . . .] die. . . . . . MS
Note The poem is not in quotes in MS

Over the Coffin
5 – 'I] 'I FR
6–7 Stanza break in all editions

'Well, there was a word to be said by me! . . .
I divorced that man because of you –
It seemed I must do it, boundenly;
But now I am older, and tell you true,
For life is little, and dead lies he;
I would I had let alone you two!
And both of us, scorning parochial ways,
Had lived like the wives in the patriarchs' days.'

351 XV. *In the Moonlight*

EXTRA PRINTINGS:
(1) *Selected Poems*, p. 127
(2) *Chosen Poems*, p. 161

'O LONELY workman, standing there
In a dream, why do you stare and stare
At her grave, as no other grave there were?

'If your great gaunt eyes so importune
Her soul by the shine of this corpse-cold moon
Maybe you'll raise her phantom soon!'

'Why, fool, it is what I would rather see
Than all the living folk there be;
But alas, there is no such joy for me!'

'Ah – she was one you loved, no doubt,
Through good and evil, through rain and drought,
And when she passed, all your sun went out?'

'Nay: she was the woman I did not love,
Whom all the others were ranked above,
Whom during her life I thought nothing of.'

Over the Coffin
7 me! . . .] me! . . . . MS

In the Moonlight
4 great gaunt] hopeless SP
MS adds at end: 1910

On Stourcastle Foot-bridge

~~(1877.)~~

Reticulations creep upon the slack stream's face
When the wind skims irritably past,
The current clucks smartly into each hollow place
That years of flood have scrabbled in the pier's sodden base;
The ~~water~~ floating lily leaves rot fast.

On a roof stand the swallows equidistantly in rows,
Till they arrow off & drop like stones
Among the eyot-withies at whose roots the river flows;
And beneath the roof is she who in ~~a~~ the dark world shows
~~[illegible]~~ as a lamp-light when midnight moans.

See page 484

MOMENTS OF VISION AND MISCELLANEOUS VERSES

Abbreviations Specific to 'Moments of Vision'

MS = The bound-up volume of manuscripts in the Old Library of Magdalene College, Cambridge

MV1 = *Moments of Vision* 1917

MV2 = *Moments of Vision* 1919

MV = Found in both MV1 and MV2

WE = Wessex Edition 1919

PE = Pocket Edition 1919

ME = Mellstock Edition 1920

352 *Moments of Vision*

EXTRA MANUSCRIPT:
In the Miriam Lutcher Stark Library of the University of Texas = UT

THAT mirror
Which makes of men a transparency,
Who holds that mirror
And bids us such a breast-bare spectacle see
Of you and me?

That mirror
Whose magic penetrates like a dart,
Who lifts that mirror
And throws our mind back on us, and our heart,
Until we start?

That mirror
Works well in these night hours of ache;
Why in that mirror
Are tincts we never see ourselves once take
When the world is awake?

That mirror
Can test each mortal when unaware;
Yea, that strange mirror
May catch his last thoughts, whole life foul or fair,
Glassing it – where?

353 *The Voice of Things*

FORTY Augusts – aye, and several more – ago,
When I paced the headlands loosed from dull employ,
The waves huzza'd like a multitude below
In the sway of an all-including joy
Without cloy.

Blankly I walked there a double decade after,
When thwarts had flung their toils in front of me,
And I heard the waters wagging in a long ironic laughter
At the lot of men, and all the vapoury
Things that be.

Moments of Vision
4 breast-bare] shudderful MS: breast-bared UT, MV, WE, PE, CP1, ME
14 tincts] tints MS
15 the world is] men are UT [Written above 'the world' which has been crossed through and then stetted, so that UT offers two readings]
20 Glassing] Reflecting MS, UT, MV1, PE

The Voice of Things
1 Augusts] years MS, MV1, PE
2 loosed] free MS
3 below] below, MS, MV, WE, PE, CP1
7 toils] shapes MS

Wheeling change has set me again standing where
 Once I heard the waves huzza at Lammas-tide;
But they supplicate now – like a congregation there
 Who murmur the Confession – I outside,
  Prayer denied.

TITLE:
'Why be at pains?' MS

354 *Why Be at Pains?*

(*Wooer's Song*)

WHY be at pains that I should know
 You sought not me?
Do breezes, then, make features glow
 So rosily?
Come, the lit port is at our back,
 And the tumbling sea;
Elsewhere the lampless uphill track
 To uncertainty!

O should not we two waifs join hands?
 I am alone,
You would enrich me more than lands
 By being my own.
Yet, though this facile moment flies,
 Close is your tone,
And ere to-morrow's dewfall dries
 I plough the unknown.

TITLE:
'We sat at the window' MS

355 *We Sat at the Window*

(*Bournemouth, 1875*)

WE sat at the window looking out,
And the rain came down like silken strings
That Swithin's day. Each gutter and spout

Why Be at Pains?
16 plough] seek MS

Babbled unchecked in the busy way
Of witless things:
Nothing to read, nothing to see
Seemed in that room for her and me
On Swithin's day.

We were irked by the scene, by our own selves; yes,
For I did not know, nor did she infer
How much there was to read and guess
By her in me, and to see and crown
By me in her.
Wasted were two souls in their prime,
And great was the waste, that July time
When the rain came down.

356 Afternoon Service at Mellstock

(*Circa 1850*)

On afternoons of drowsy calm
We stood in the panelled pew,
Singing one-voiced a Tate-and-Brady psalm
To the tune of 'Cambridge New'.

We watched the elms, we watched the rooks,
The clouds upon the breeze,
Between the whiles of glancing at our books,
And swaying like the trees.

So mindless were those outpourings! –
Though I am not aware
That I have gained by subtle thought on things
Since we stood psalming there.

We Sat at the Window
9] Yes; we were irked at its nothingness, MS *before revision*
9 our own selves] each other MS

Afternoon Service at Mellstock
3 one-voiced] full-voiced MS, MV1
6 breeze,] breeze MS

TITLE:
At the Wicket-gate MS

357 *At the Wicket-Gate*

THERE floated the sounds of church-chiming,
 But no one was nigh,
Till there came, as a break in the loneness,
 Her father, she, I.
And we slowly moved on to the wicket,
 And downlooking stood,
Till anon people passed, and amid them
 We parted for good.

Greater, wiser, may part there than we three
 Who parted there then,
But never will Fates colder-featured
 Hold sway there again.
Of the churchgoers through the still meadows
 No single one knew
What a play was played under their eyes there
 As thence we withdrew.

358 *In a Museum*

I

HERE'S the mould of a musical bird long passed from light,
Which over the earth before man came was winging;
There's a contralto voice I heard last night,
That lodges in me still with its sweet singing.

II

Such a dream is Time that the coo of this ancient bird
Has perished not, but is blent, or will be blending
Mid visionless wilds of space with the voice that I heard,
In the full-fugued song of the universe unending.

Exeter

At the Wicket-Gate
1 floated] echoed MS, MV1, PE
5 on] up MS, MV1, PE
11 Fates] fates MS
12 Hold sway] Be sealed MS: Nod nay MV1

In a Museum
4 lodges] lingers MS
7 visionless] fathomless MS
8 full-fugued] general MS

359 *Apostrophe to an Old Psalm Tune*

TITLE:
Apostrophe to an old Psalm Tune MS

I MET you first – ah, when did I first meet you?
When I was full of wonder, and innocent,
Standing meek-eyed with those of choric bent,
While dimming day grew dimmer
In the pulpit-glimmer.

Much riper in years I met you – in a temple
Where summer sunset streamed upon our shapes,
And you spread over me like a gauze that drapes,
And flapped from floor to rafters,
Sweet as angels' laughters.

But you had been stripped of some of your old vesture
By Monk, or another. Now you wore no frill,
And at first you startled me. But I knew you still,
Though I missed the minim's waver,
And the dotted quaver.

I grew accustomed to you thus. And you hailed me
Through one who evoked you often. Then at last
Your raiser was borne off, and I mourned you had passed
From my life with your late outsetter;
Till I said, ' 'Tis better!'

But you waylaid me. I rose and went as a ghost goes,
And said, eyes-full: 'I'll never hear it again!
It is overmuch for scathed and memoried men
When sitting among strange people
Under their steeple.'

Now, a new stirrer of tones calls you up before me
And wakes your speech, as she of Endor did
(When sought by Saul who, in disguises hid,
Fell down on the earth to hear it)
Samuel's spirit.

Apostrophe to an Old Psalm Tune
3 of choric bent] whose voices blent MS
5 pulpit-glimmer] candle-glimmer MS, MV1, PE
14 minim's] crotchet's MS
26 me] me, MS
27 did] did, MS

So, your quired oracles beat till they make me tremble
As I discern your mien in the old attire,
Here in these turmoiled years of belligerent fire
Living still on – and onward, maybe,
Till Doom's great day be!

Sunday, 13 August 1916

EXTRA PRINTINGS:
(1) *Selected Poems*, pp. 18–19 [The poem's first printing]
(2) *Chosen Poems*, pp. 18–19

360 At the Word 'Farewell'

SHE looked like a bird from a cloud
On the clammy lawn,
Moving alone, bare-browed
In the dim of dawn.
The candles alight in the room
For my parting meal
Made all things withoutdoors loom
Strange, ghostly, unreal.

The hour itself was a ghost,
And it seemed to me then
As of chances the chance furthermost
I should see her again.
I beheld not where all was so fleet
That a Plan of the past
Which had ruled us from birthtime to meet
Was in working at last:

No prelude did I there perceive
To a drama at all,
Or foreshadow what fortune might weave
From beginnings so small;
But I rose as if quicked by a spur
I was bound to obey,
And stepped through the casement to her
Still alone in the gray.

At the Word 'Farewell'
2 clammy] sloping MS *before revision*
3 bare-browed] bare-browed, SP
4 dawn.] dawn, MS, MV, WE, PE, CP1
16] Was accomplished at last. MS, SP, MV1, PE
20 small;] small. SP

'I am leaving you. . . . Farewell!' I said,
As I followed her on
By an alley bare boughs overspread;
'I soon must be gone!'
Even then the scale might have been turned
Against love by a feather,
– But crimson one cheek of hers burned
When we came in together.

361 *First Sight of Her and After*

EXTRA PRINTINGS:
(1) *Selected Poems*, p. 15 [The poem's first printing]
(2) *Chosen Poems*, p. 15

TITLE:
The Return from First Beholding Her SP
The Day of First Sight MS, MV1, PE

A DAY is drawing to its fall
I had not dreamed to see;
The first of many to enthrall
My spirit, will it be?
Or is this eve the end of all
Such new delight for me?

I journey home: the pattern grows
Of moonshades on the way:
'Soon the first quarter, I suppose,'
Sky-glancing travellers say;
I realize that it, for those,
Has been a common day.

362 *The Rival*

I DETERMINED to find out whose it was –
The portrait he looked at so, and sighed;
Bitterly have I rued my meanness
And wept for it since he died!

I searched his desk when he was away,
And there was the likeness – yes, my own!
Taken when I was the season's fairest,
And time-lines all unknown.

At the Word 'Farewell'
25 Farewell!] Farewell, MS
25 said,] said MS, SP, CP4 [The loss of the comma in CP4 is almost certainly the result of print deterioration]
27 overspread;] overspread: SP
1913 MS *del* at end

First Sight of Her and After
8 moonshades] moon-shades SP
10 say;] say. MS, SP

The Rival
7 fairest] beauty MS, MV1, PE
8 time-lines] crows' feet MS

I smiled at my image, and put it back,
And he went on cherishing it, until
I was chafed that he loved not the me then living,
But that past woman still.

Well, such was my jealousy at last,
I destroyed that face of the former me;
Could you ever have dreamed the heart of woman
Would work so foolishly!

363 Heredity

I AM the family face;
Flesh perishes, I live on,
Projecting trait and trace
Through time to times anon,
And leaping from place to place
Over oblivion.

The years-heired feature that can
In curve and voice and eye
Despise the human span
Of durance – that is I;
The eternal thing in man,
That heeds no call to die.

TITLE:
'You were the sort that men forget' MS

364 You Were the Sort that Men Forget

YOU were the sort that men forget;
Though I – not yet! –
Perhaps not ever. Your slighted weakness
Adds to the strength of my regret!

You'd not the art – you never had
For good or bad –
To make men see how sweet your meaning,
Which, visible, had charmed them glad.

The Rival
15 dreamed . . . of] believed a MS, MV1, PE
16 work] act MS, MV1, PE

Heredity
7 years-heired] family MS, MV1, PE

You Were the Sort that Men Forget
5 You'd] You had MS, MV1, PE
7 meaning] meanings MS

You would, by words inept let fall,
Offend them all,
Even if they saw your warm devotion
Would hold your life's blood at their call.

You lacked the eye to understand
Those friends offhand
Whose mode was crude, though whose dim purport
Outpriced the courtesies of the bland.

I am now the only being who
Remembers you
It may be. What a waste that Nature
Grudged soul so dear the art its due!

365 *She, I, and They*

I WAS sitting,
She was knitting,
And the portraits of our fore-folk hung around;
When there struck on us a sigh;
'Ah – what is that?' said I:
'Was it not you?' said she. 'A sigh did sound.'

I had not breathed it,
Nor the night-wind heaved it,
And how it came to us we could not guess;
And we looked up at each face
Framed and glazed there in its place,
Still hearkening; but thenceforth was silentness.

Half in dreaming,
'Then its meaning,'
Said we, 'must be surely this; that they repine
That we should be the last
Of stocks once unsurpassed,
And unable to keep up their sturdy line.'

1916

You Were the Sort that Men Forget
9 fall,] fall MS
13 eye] art MS, MV1: grasp PE
15 purport] meaning MS, MV1
16 Outpriced] Surpassed MS, MV1, PE

She, I, and They
7 breathed] heaved MS
8 night-wind heaved] night wind breathed MS: hearth-smoke wreathed MV1, PE
1916] August 1. 1916 MS

EXTRA PRINTING:
Chosen Poems, pp. 222–3

366 Near Lanivet, 1872

THERE was a stunted handpost just on the crest,
Only a few feet high:
She was tired, and we stopped in the twilight-time for her rest,
At the crossways close thereby.

She leant back, being so weary, against its stem,
And laid her arms on its own,
Each open palm stretched out to each end of them,
Her sad face sideways thrown.

Her white-clothed form at this dim-lit cease of day
Made her look as one crucified
In my gaze at her from the midst of the dusty way,
And hurriedly 'Don't,' I cried.

I do not think she heard. Loosing thence she said,
As she stepped forth ready to go,
'I am rested now. – Something strange came into my head;
I wish I had not leant so!'

And wordless we moved onward down from the hill
In the west cloud's murked obscure,
And looking back we could see the handpost still
In the solitude of the moor.

'It struck her too,' I thought, for as if afraid
She heavily breathed as we trailed;
Till she said, 'I did not think how 'twould look in the shade,
When I leant there like one nailed.'

I, lightly: 'There's nothing in it. For *you*, anyhow!'
– 'O I know there is not,' said she . . .
'Yet I wonder . . . If no one is bodily crucified now,
In spirit one may be!'

And we dragged on and on, while we seemed to see
In the running of Time's far glass
Her crucified, as she had wondered if she might be
Some day. – Alas, alas!

Near Lanivet, 1872
3 rest,] rest MS
4 close thereby] it stood by MS, MV1
7] With open hands stretched out to the end of them; MS
7 palm] hand MV1, PE
8 sad] wan MS
9 cease] end MS, MV1
23 shade,] shade MS
26 she . . .] she. . . . . MS: she . . MV2, PE
27 wonder . . .] wonder. . . . . MS
From an old note MS *del* at end

367 *Joys of Memory*

EXTRA PRINTING:
(1) *Chosen Poems*, p. 100

WHEN the spring comes round, and a certain day
Looks out from the brume by the eastern copsetrees
And says, Remember,
I begin again, as if it were new,
A day of like date I once lived through,
Whiling it hour by hour away;
So shall I do till my December,
When spring comes round.

I take my holiday then and my rest
Away from the dun life here about me,
Old hours re-greeting
With the quiet sense that bring they must
Such throbs as at first, till I house with dust,
And in the numbness my heartsome zest
For things that were, be past repeating
When spring comes round.

368 To the Moon

EXTRA PRINTING:
Chosen Poems, pp. 101–2

TITLE:
Questions MS *deleted* before title

'WHAT have you looked at, Moon,
In your time,
Now long past your prime?'
'O, I have looked at, often looked at
Sweet, sublime,
Sore things, shudderful, night and noon
In my time.'

'What have you mused on, Moon,
In your day,
So aloof, so far away?'
'O, I have mused on, often mused on
Growth, decay,
Nations alive, dead, mad, aswoon,
In my day!'

Joys of Memory
2 brume] cloud MS
2 copsetrees] copsetrees, MS
5 A day of like] The life of that MS, MV1
13 house with] sink to MS
14 numbness] silence MS

To the Moon
4] 'O, I have looked at, looked at, looked at MS *before revision*
6 Sore] Small MS
11] 'O, I have mused on, mused on, mused on MS *before revision*

'Have you much wondered, Moon,
On your rounds,
Self-wrapt, beyond Earth's bounds?'
'Yea, I have wondered, often wondered
At the sounds
Reaching me of the human tune
On my rounds.'

'What do you think of it, Moon,
As you go?
Is Life much, or no?'
'O, I think of it, often think of it
As a show
God ought surely to shut up soon,
As I go.'

369 Copying Architecture in an Old Minster

(*Wimborne*)

HOW smartly the quarters of the hour march by
That the jack-o'-clock never forgets;
Ding-dong; and before I have traced a cusp's eye,
Or got the true twist of the ogee over,
A double ding-dong ricochetts.

Just so did he clang here before I came,
And so will he clang when I'm gone
Through the Minster's cavernous hollows – the same
Tale of hours never more to be will he deliver
To the speechless midnight and dawn!

I grow to conceive it a call to ghosts,
Whose mould lies below and around.
Yes; the next 'Come, come,' draws them out from their posts,
And they gather, and one shade appears, and another,
As the eve-damps creep from the ground.

To the Moon
18] 'Yea, I have wondered, wondered, wondered MS *before revision*
25] 'O, I think of it, think of it, think of it MS *before revision*
27 God] That MS *before revision*
27 ought] means MV1, PE

Copying Architecture in an Old Minster
10 dawn!] dawn. MS, MV1, PE
13 posts,] posts. WE

See – a Courtenay stands by his quatre-foiled tomb,
And a Duke and his Duchess near;
And one Sir Edmund in columned gloom,
And a Saxon king by the presbytery chamber;
And shapes unknown in the rear.

Maybe they have met for a parle on some plan
To better ail-stricken mankind;
I catch their cheepings, though thinner than
The overhead creak of a passager's pinion
When leaving land behind.

Or perhaps they speak to the yet unborn,
And caution them not to come
To a world so ancient and trouble-torn,
Of foiled intents, vain lovingkindness,
And ardours chilled and numb.

They waste to fog as I stir and stand,
And move from the arched recess,
And pick up the drawing that slipped from my hand,
And feel for the pencil I dropped in the cranny
In a moment's forgetfulness.

370 To Shakespeare

After Three Hundred Years

BRIGHT baffling Soul, least capturable of themes,
Thou, who display'dst a life of commonplace,
Leaving no intimate word or personal trace
Of high design outside the artistry
Of thy penned dreams,
Still shalt remain at heart unread eternally.

Through human orbits thy discourse to-day,
Despite thy formal pilgrimage, throbs on
In harmonies that cow Oblivion,

To Shakespeare

EXTRA MANUSCRIPTS:
In the Ashley Library of the British Library = A
It has not been possible to trace the autographed fair copy transcribed by Hardy for Sir Sydney Cockerell on the flyleaf of a facsimile of Shakespeare's First Folio (London, 1910)

EXTRA PRINTINGS:
(1) *A Book of Homage to Shakespeare*, ed. Israel Gollancz (London, 1916), pp. [1]–2 = HS
(2) *The Fortnightly Review*, 1 June 1916, pp. [927]–928 = FR
(3) Privately printed by Florence Hardy, Aug 1916 = FH

Note It has not been possible to trace the typescript and proofs once in the possession of Sir Sydney Cockerell. There is a typed copy at Stourhead House, Wilts, sent by Florence Hardy to Lady Hoare. It contains no unique variants

Copying Architecture in an Old Minster
16 quatre-foiled] quatrefoiled MS, WE, ME [MV, PE have line breaks]
17 near;] near, MS
24 passager's] puffin's MS

To Shakespeare
1 Bright] Bright, FR, FH

And, like the wind, with all-uncared effect
Maintain a sway
Not fore-desired, in tracks unchosen and unchecked.

And yet, at thy last breath, with mindless note
The borough clocks but samely tongued the hour,
The Avon just as always glassed the tower,
Thy age was published on thy passing-bell
But in due rote
With other dwellers' deaths accorded a like knell.

And at the strokes some townsman (met, maybe,
And thereon queried by some squire's good dame
Driving in shopward) may have given thy name,
With, 'Yes, a worthy man and well-to-do;
Though, as for me,
I knew him but by just a neighbour's nod, 'tis true.

'I' faith, few knew him much here, save by word,
He having elsewhere led his busier life;
Though to be sure he left with us his wife.'
– 'Ah, one of the tradesmen's sons, I now recall. . . .
Witty, I've heard. . . .
We did not know him. . . . Well, good-day. Death comes to all.'

So, like a strange bright bird we sometimes find
To mingle with the barn-door brood awhile,
Then vanish from their homely domicile –
Into man's poesy, we wot not whence,
Flew thy strange mind,
Lodged there a radiant guest, and sped for ever thence.

1916

EXTRA PRINTINGS:
(1) *The Spectator*, 19 Aug 1916, p. 212 = S
(2) Privately printed by Florence Hardy, Oct 1916 = FH

TITLE:
'When I weekly knew' MS, FH
In Time of Slaughter S

Note It has not been possible to trace the typescript and proof once in the possession of Sir Sydney Cockerell

371 *Quid Hic Agis?*

I

When I weekly knew
An ancient pew,
And murmured there
The forms of prayer

To Shakespeare
14 but samely] in sameness MS, MV1, PE: as usual A, HS, FR, FH
15 just . . . the] idled past the garth and HS
15 tower,] tower; MS
17 rote] rote, FH
18 dwellers' deaths] men's that year HS: native men's A, FR, FH
25 word,] word A
31 So,] So – HS, FR, FH
31 bright bird we sometimes] bright-pinioned bird we HS, FR, FH
34 wot] weet HS
34 whence,] whence MS
1916] February 14. 1916 MS, A, HS, FR, FH

Quid Hic Agis?
4 prayer] prayer, S, FH

And thanks and praise
In the ancient ways,
And heard read out
During August drought
That chapter from Kings
Harvest-time brings;
– How the prophet, broken
By griefs unspoken,
Went heavily away
To fast and to pray,
And, while waiting to die,
The Lord passed by,
And a whirlwind and fire
Drew nigher and nigher,
And a small voice anon
Bade him up and be gone, –
I did not apprehend
As I sat to the end
And watched for her smile
Across the sunned aisle,
That this tale of a seer
Which came once a year
Might, when sands were heaping,
Be like a sweat creeping,
Or in any degree
Bear on her or on me!

II

When later, by chance
Of circumstance,
It befel me to read
On a hot afternoon
At the lectern there
The selfsame words
As the lesson decreed,
To the gathered few
From the hamlets near –
Folk of flocks and herds

Quid Hic Agis?
5 thanks] thanks, s, FH
5 praise] praise, s
10 Harvest-time] The Trinity-time s
11 – How] How s, FH
15 And,] And s
15 die,] die s
16 by,] by; s
17 a] Not in s
17 and] of FH
20 gone, –] gone, s, FH
21 apprehend] apprehend, s, FH
22 end] end, s
23 her] a s
24 sunned aisle] south-aisle s
24 sunned] south MS, FH
25 tale] theme MV2, WE, PE, CP1, ME
30 or on] and s
30 me!] me. MS, S, FH, MV1, PE
31–40 When later I stood/By the chancel-rood/On a hot afternoon,/And read the same words/To the gathered few – /Those of flocks and herds s
36–7] The lesson decreed,/In the selfsame words, FH

Sitting half aswoon,
Who listened thereto
As women and men
Not overmuch
Concerned at such –
So, like them then,
I did not see
What drought might be
With me, with her,
As the Kalendar
Moved on, and Time
Devoured our prime.

III

But now, at last,
When our glory has passed,
And there is no smile
From her in the aisle,
But where it once shone
A marble, men say,
With her name thereon
Is discerned to-day;
And spiritless
In the wilderness
I shrink from sight
And desire the night,
(Though, as in old wise,
I might still arise,
Go forth, and stand
And prophesy in the land),
I feel the shake
Of wind and earthquake,
And consuming fire
Nigher and nigher,
And the voice catch clear,
'What doest thou here?'

The Spectator: 1916. During the War

Quid Hic Agis?
44] Detached – even then S
45–6 Not in S
48 drought might] drought there might S
54 glory] sun MS, S, FH
55–60 Not in S
64 night,] night S, FH
73 clear,] clear: S
The . . . War] Not in MS, S
During the War] Not in MV, WE, PE, CP1, ME
FH has '1916' only

372 *On a Midsummer Eve*

EXTRA PRINTINGS:
(1) *Selected Poems*, p. 75 [The poem's first printing]
(2) *Chosen Poems*, p. 70

I IDLY cut a parsley stalk,
And blew therein towards the moon;
I had not thought what ghosts would walk
With shivering footsteps to my tune.

I went, and knelt, and scooped my hand
As if to drink, into the brook,
And a faint figure seemed to stand
Above me, with the bygone look.

I lipped rough rhymes of chance, not choice,
I thought not what my words might be;
There came into my ear a voice
That turned a tenderer verse for me.

373 *Timing Her*

EXTRA PRINTING:
Chosen Poems, pp. 103–5

(*Written to an old folk-tune*)

LALAGE'S coming:
Where is she now, O?
Turning to bow, O,
And smile, is she,
Just at parting,
Parting, parting,
As she is starting
To come to me?

Where is she now, O,
Now, and now, O,
Shadowing a bough, O,
Of hedge or tree
As she is rushing,
Rushing, rushing,
Gossamers brushing
To come to me?

On a Midsummer Eve
1 stalk,] stalk SP

Timing Her
10 and] O, MS, MV1, PE
15] Gossamer-brushing MS

Lalage's coming;
Where is she now, O;
Climbing the brow, O,
Of hills I see?
Yes, she is nearing,
Nearing, nearing,
Weather unfearing
To come to me.

Near is she now, O,
Now, and now, O;
Milk the rich cow, O,
Forward the tea;
Shake the down bed for her,
Linen sheets spread for her,
Drape round the head for her
Coming to me.

Lalage's coming,
She's nearer now, O,
End anyhow, O,
To-day's husbandry!
Would a gilt chair were mine,
Slippers of vair were mine,
Brushes for hair were mine
Of ivory!

What will she think, O,
She who's so comely,
Viewing how homely
A sort are we!
Nothing resplendent,
No prompt attendant,
Not one dependent
Pertaining to me!

Lalage's coming;
Where is she now, O?
Fain I'd avow, O,
Full honestly

Timing Her
26 and] O, MS, MV1, PE

34 She's nearer] Nearer is she MS, MV, WE, PE, CP1: Nearer is ME

Nought here's enough for her,
All is too rough for her,
Even my love for her
Poor in degree.

She's nearer now, O,
Still nearer now, O,
She 'tis, I vow, O,
Passing the lea.
Rush down to meet her there,
Call out and greet her there,
Never a sweeter there
Crossed to me!

Lalage's come; aye,
Come is she now, O! . . .
Does Heaven allow, O,
A meeting to be?
Yes, she is here now,
Here now, here now,
Nothing to fear now,
Here's Lalage!

374 Before Knowledge

WHEN I walked roseless tracks and wide,
Ere dawned your date for meeting me,
O why did you not cry Halloo
Across the stretch between, and say:

'We move, while years as yet divide,
On closing lines which – though it be
You know me not nor I know you –
Will intersect and join some day!'

Then well I had borne
Each scraping thorn;
But the winters froze,
And grew no rose;

Timing Her
57 She's nearer] Nearer is she MS, MV, WE, PE, CP1
58 Still nearer] Now, O, MS, MV1, PE: Now, and MV2, WE, CP1
59 'tis,] it is MS, MV, WE, PE, ME, CP1–3 [Hardy's copy of CP2 has been corrected to ' 'tis,']
66 O! . . .] O! . . . . MS

Before Knowledge
5 while years] though miles MS *before revision*
12–13 No stanza break

No bridge bestrode
The gap at all;
No shape you showed,
And I heard no call!

EXTRA PRINTING:
Chosen Poems, p. 125

375 The Blinded Bird

So zestfully canst thou sing?
And all this indignity,
With God's consent, on thee!
Blinded ere yet a-wing
By the red-hot needle thou,
I stand and wonder how
So zestfully thou canst sing!

Resenting not such wrong,
Thy grievous pain forgot,
Eternal dark thy lot,
Groping thy whole life long,
After that stab of fire;
Enjailed in pitiless wire;
Resenting not such wrong!

Who hath charity? This bird.
Who suffereth long and is kind,
Is not provoked, though blind
And alive ensepulchred?
Who hopeth, endureth all things?
Who thinketh no evil, but sings?
Who is divine? This bird.

TITLE:
'The Wind blew Words' MS

376 The Wind Blew Words

The wind blew words along the skies,
    And these it blew to me
Through the wide dusk: 'Lift up your eyes,

Before Knowledge
13 bridge] bond MS

The Blinded Bird
11 long,] long WE, ME

Behold this troubled tree,
Complaining as it sways and plies;
It is a limb of thee.

'Yea, too, the creatures sheltering round –
Dumb figures, wild and tame,
Yea, too, thy fellows who abound –
Either of speech the same
Or far and strange – black, dwarfed, and browned,
They are stuff of thy own frame.'

I moved on in a surging awe
Of inarticulateness
At the pathetic Me I saw
In all his huge distress,
Making self-slaughter of the law
To kill, break, or suppress.

377 *The Faded Face*

How was this I did not see
Such a look as here was shown
Ere its womanhood had blown
Past its first felicity? –
That I did not know you young,
Faded Face,
Know you young!

Why did Time so ill bestead
That I heard no voice of yours
Hail from out the curved contours
Of those lips when rosy red;
Weeted not the songs they sung,
Faded Face,
Songs they sung!

The Wind Blew Words
4 troubled] writhing MS
18 break] bind MS, MV1

The Faded Face
10 out] 'twixt MS
12 Weeted] Listed MS, MV, WE, PE, CP1, ME

By these blanchings, blooms of old,
And the relics of your voice –
Leavings rare of rich and choice
From your early tone and mould –
Let me mourn, – aye, sorrow-wrung,
    Faded Face,
        Sorrow-wrung!

378 The Riddle

I

STRETCHING eyes west
Over the sea,
Wind foul or fair,
Always stood she
Prospect-impressed;
Solely out there
Did her gaze rest,
Never elsewhere
Seemed charm to be.

II

Always eyes east
Ponders she now –
As in devotion –
Hills of blank brow
Where no waves plough.
Never the least
Room for emotion
Drawn from the ocean
Does she allow.

The Faded Face
15] By your picture as of old, MS
19 mourn] die MS
19 sorrow-wrung] overwrung MS, MV, WE, PE, ME
21] Overwrung! MS, MV, WE, PE, ME

The Riddle
11] She ponders now MS
11 now –] now, MV1, PE
12 devotion –] devotion MS: devotion, MV1, PE

379 The Duel

EXTRA PRINTING:
Chosen Poems, pp. 210–11

'I AM here to time, you see;
The glade is well-screened – eh? – against alarm;
Fit place to vindicate by my arm
The honour of my spotless wife,
Who scorns your libel upon her life
In boasting intimacy!

' "All hush-offerings you'll spurn,
My husband. Two must come; one only go,"
She said. "That he'll be you I know;
To faith like ours Heaven will be just,
And I shall abide in fullest trust
Your speedy glad return." '

'Good. Here am also I;
And we'll proceed without more waste of words
To warm your cockpit. Of the swords
Take you your choice. I shall thereby
Feel that on me no blame can lie,
Whatever Fate accords.'

So stripped they there, and fought,
And the swords clicked and scraped, and the onsets sped;
Till the husband fell; and his shirt was red
With streams from his heart's hot cistern. Nought
Could save him now; and the other, wrought
Maybe to pity, said:

'Why did you urge on this?
Your wife assured you; and 't had better been
That you had let things pass, serene
In confidence of long-tried bliss,
Holding there could be nought amiss
In what my words might mean.'

Then, seeing nor ruth nor rage
Could move his foeman more – now Death's deaf thrall –
He wiped his steel, and, with a call
Like turtledove to dove, swift broke
Into the copse, where under an oak
His horse cropt, held by a page.

'All's over, Sweet,' he cried
To the wife, thus guised; for the young page was she.
' 'Tis as we hoped and said 't would be.
He never guessed. . . . We mount and ride
To where our love can reign uneyed.
He's clay, and we are free.'

TITLE:
At Lodgings in London MS *before revision*

380 At Mayfair Lodgings

How could I be aware,
The opposite window eyeing
As I lay listless there,
That through its blinds was dying
One I had rated rare
Before I had set me sighing
For another more fair?

Had the house-front been glass,
My vision unobscuring,
Could aught have come to pass
More happiness-insuring
To her, loved as a lass
When spouseless, all-alluring?
I reckon not, alas!

So, the square window stood,
Steadily night-long shining
In my close neighbourhood,
Who looked forth undivining
That soon would go for good
One there in pain reclining,
Unpardoned, unadieu'd.

The Duel
38 guised;] guised: WE, ME
42 clay,] dust MS, MV1, PE

At Mayfair Lodgings
3 lay] sat MS
4 was] lay MS
10] Could I have brought to pass MS *before revision*

Silently screened from view
Her tragedy was ending
That need not have come due
Had she been less unbending.
How near, near were we two
At that last vital rending, –
And neither of us knew!

381 To My Father's Violin

TITLE:
To my Father's Fiddle MS *before revision*

DOES he want you down there
In the Nether Glooms where
The hours may be a dragging load upon him,
As he hears the axle grind
Round and round
Of the great world, in the blind
Still profound
Of the night-time? He might liven at the sound
Of your string, revealing you had not forgone him.

In the gallery west the nave,
But a few yards from his grave,
Did you, tucked beneath his chin, to his bowing
Guide the homely harmony
Of the quire
Who for long years strenuously –
Son and sire –
Caught the strains that at his fingering low or higher
From your four thin threads and eff-holes came outflowing.

And, too, what merry tunes
He would bow at nights or noons
That chanced to find him bent to lute a measure,
When he made you speak his heart
As in dream,
Without book or music-chart,
On some theme
Elusive as a jack-o'-lanthorn's gleam,
And the psalm of duty shelved for trill of pleasure.

To My Father's Violin
15 Who] Which MS
19–27 Not in MS

Well, you cannot, alas,
The barrier overpass
That screens him in those Mournful Meads hereunder,
Where no fiddling can be heard
In the glades
Of silentness, no bird
Thrills the shades;
Where no viol is touched for songs or serenades,
No bowing wakes a congregation's wonder.

He must do without you now,
Stir you no more anyhow
To yearning concords taught you in your glory;
While, your strings a tangled wreck,
Once smart drawn,
Ten worm-wounds in your neck,
Purflings wan
With dust-hoar, here alone I sadly con
Your present dumbness, shape your olden story.

1916

382 The Statue of Liberty

THIS statue of Liberty, busy man,
Here erect in the city square,
I have watched while your scrubbings, this early morning,
Strangely wistful,
And half tristful,
Have turned her from foul to fair;

With your bucket of water, and mop, and brush,
Bringing her out of the grime
That has smeared her during the smokes of winter
With such glumness
In her dumbness,
And aged her before her time.

To My Father's Violin
30 those] the MS
41 smart drawn] tight-drawn MS
42 worm-wounds] worm-holes MS, MV1
44 dust-hoar] dust-films MS

The Statue of Liberty
6 fair;] fair, MS

You have washed her down with motherly care –
Head, shoulders, arm, and foot,
To the very hem of the robes that drape her –
All expertly
And alertly,
Till a long stream, black with soot,

Flows over the pavement to the road,
And her shape looms pure as snow:
I read you are hired by the City guardians –
May be yearly,
Or once merely –
To treat the statues so?

'Oh, I'm not hired by the Councilmen
To cleanse the statues here.
I do this one as a self-willed duty,
Not as paid to,
Or at all made to,
But because the doing is dear.'

Ah, then I hail you brother and friend!
Liberty's knight divine.
What you have done would have been my doing,
Yea, most verily,
Well, and thoroughly,
Had but your courage been mine!

'Oh I care not for Liberty's mould,
Liberty charms not me;
What's Freedom but an idler's vision,
Vain, pernicious,
Often vicious,
Of things that cannot be!

'Memory it is that brings me to this –
Of a daughter – my one sweet own.
She grew a famous carver's model,
One of the fairest
And of the rarest: –
She sat for the figure as shown.

The Statue of Liberty
15 hem] skirt MS
47 rarest:] rarest; MS
48–9 MS has the following *deleted* stanza:

'Alas for her calling. It suited her not;/She learnt ways sinister/And – died – And tendance of this her image/With some gladness,/Though in sadness/I give for love of her.'

'But alas, she died in this distant place
Before I was warned to betake
Myself to her side! . . . And in love of my darling,
In love of the fame of her,
And the good name of her,
I do this for her sake.'

Answer I gave not. Of that form
The carver was I at his side;
His child, my model, held so saintly,
Grand in feature,
Gross in nature,
In the dens of vice had died.

383 The Background and the Figure

(Lover's Ditty)

I THINK of the slope where the rabbits fed,
Of the periwinks' rockwork lair,
Of the fuchsias ringing their bells of red –
And the something else seen there.

Between the blooms where the sod basked bright,
By the bobbing fuchsia trees,
Was another and yet more eyesome sight –
The sight that richened these.

I shall seek those beauties in the spring,
When the days are fit and fair,
But only as foils to the one more thing
That also will flower there!

384 The Change

OUT of the past there rises a week –
Who shall read the years O! –
Out of the past there rises a week
Enringed with a purple zone.

The Background and the Figure
7 yet more eyesome] culminating MS, MV1, PE
8 richened] gloried MS
12 there!] there. MS, MV1, PE

Out of the past there rises a week
When thoughts were strung too thick to speak,
And the magic of its lineaments remains with me alone.

In that week there was heard a singing –
Who shall spell the years, the years! –
In that week there was heard a singing,
And the white owl wondered why.
In that week, yea, a voice was ringing,
And forth from the casement were candles flinging
Radiance that fell on the deodar and lit up the path thereby.

Could that song have a mocking note? –
Who shall unroll the years O! –
Could that song have a mocking note
To the white owl's sense as it fell?
Could that song have a mocking note
As it trilled out warm from the singer's throat,
And who was the mocker and who the mocked when two felt all was well?

In a tedious trampling crowd yet later –
Who shall bare the years, the years! –
In a tedious trampling crowd yet later,
When silvery singings were dumb;
In a crowd uncaring what time might fate her,
Mid murks of night I stood to await her,
And the twanging of iron wheels gave out the signal that she was come.

She said with a travel-tired smile –
Who shall lift the years O! –
She said with a travel-tired smile,
Half scared by scene so strange;
She said, outworn by mile on mile,
The blurred lamps wanning her face the while,
'O Love, I am here; I am with you!' . . . Ah, that there should have come a change!

The Change
9 years, the years] years O MS, MV1, PE
12] In that week there was heard a singing, MS, MV1, PE
14 deodar] fuchsia-trees MS
22 crowd yet] crowd, far MS, MV1, PE
23 years, the years] years O MS, MV1, PE
24 crowd yet] crowd, far MS, MV1, PE
26] In a tedious trampling crowd, far later, MS, MV1, PE
27 Mid murks of] In the filmy MS: In the murky MV1, PE
33] She said with a travel-tired smile, MS, MV1
34 blurred] fogged MS
35 you!' . . .] you!' . . . . . MS

O the doom by someone spoken –
  Who shall unseal the years, the years! –
O the doom that gave no token,
  When nothing of bale saw we:
O the doom by someone spoken,
O the heart by someone broken,
The heart whose sweet reverberances are all time leaves to me.

Jan.–Feb. 1913

385 Sitting on the Bridge

(*Echo of an old song*)

  SITTING on the bridge
  Past the barracks, town and ridge,
At once the spirit seized us
To sing a song that pleased us –
As 'The Fifth' were much in rumour;
It was 'Whilst I'm in the humour,
  Take me, Paddy, will you now?'
  And a lancer soon drew nigh,
  And his Royal Irish eye
  Said, 'Willing, faith, am I,
O, to take you anyhow, dears,
  To take you anyhow.'

  But, lo! – dad walking by,
  Cried, 'What, you lightheels! Fie!
  Is this the way you roam
  And mock the sunset gleam?'
  And he marched us straightway home,
Though we said, 'We are only, daddy,
Singing, "Will you take me, Paddy?" '
  – Well, we never saw from then,
  If we sang there anywhen,
  The soldier dear again,
Except at night in dream-time,
  Except at night in dream.

The Change
37 years, the years] years O MS, MV1, PE
38 that gave no token,] by someone spoken MS, MV1
39 we:] we! MS

Sitting on the Bridge
2 Past the barracks,] Between the MS
5 As . . . were] A song then MS
8 lancer soon] soldier MS: lancer MV1, PE
9–10] And the corner of his eye/Said 'Willing quite am I, MS
13–14] But Daddy, walking by,/Cried: 'What you light girls! Fie! MS
19 Paddy?" '] Paddy?" ' – MS
20 – Well,] Well MS
20 then,] then MV2, PE

Perhaps that soldier's fighting
  In a land that's far away,
Or he may be idly plighting
  Some foreign hussy gay;
Or perhaps his bones are whiting
  In the wind to their decay! . . .
  Ah! – does he mind him how
  The girls he saw that day
On the bridge, were sitting singing
At the time of curfew-ringing,
'Take me, Paddy; will you now, dear?
  Paddy, will you now?'

Grey's Bridge

386 The Young Churchwarden

TITLE: At an Evening Service
August 14. 1870
MS *deleted*

WHEN he lit the candles there,
And the light fell on his hand,
And it trembled as he scanned
Her and me, his vanquished air
Hinted that his dream was done,
And I saw he had begun
    To understand.

When Love's viol was unstrung,
Sore I wished the hand that shook
Had been mine that shared her book
While that evening hymn was sung,
His the victor's, as he lit
Candles where he had bidden us sit
    With vanquished look.

Now her dust lies listless there,
His afar from tending hand,
What avails the victory scanned?
Does he smile from upper air:
'Ah, my friend, your dream is done;
And 'tis *you* who have begun
    To understand!'

Sitting on the Bridge
27 idly] lightly MS
30 the wind to their] a graveless MS, MV1, PE
36 Paddy,] Paddy MS
Grey's Bridge] Not in MS

The Young Churchwarden
3–4] And it trembled as I scanned/Book and him whose vanquished air
MS *before revision*
4 me,] me MS
15 Now] Now, MS
16 hand,] hand; MS

TITLE:
'I travel as a phantom now' MS

387 *I Travel as a Phantom Now*

I TRAVEL as a phantom now,
For people do not wish to see
In flesh and blood so bare a bough
As Nature makes of me.

And thus I visit bodiless
Strange gloomy households often at odds,
And wonder if Man's consciousness
Was a mistake of God's.

And next I meet you, and I pause,
And think that if mistake it were,
As some have said, O then it was
One that I well can bear!

1915

TITLE:
Lines/To a movement (Minuet *del*) in Mozart's E-flat Symphony MS

388 *Lines*

To a Movement in Mozart's E-Flat Symphony

SHOW me again the time
When in the Junetide's prime
We flew by meads and mountains northerly! –
Yea, to such freshness, fairness, fulness, fineness, freeness,
Love lures life on.

Show me again the day
When from the sandy bay
We looked together upon the pestered sea! –
Yea, to such surging, swaying, sighing, swelling, shrinking,
Love lures life on.

Show me again the hour
When by the pinnacled tower
We eyed each other and feared futurity! –
Yea, to such bodings, broodings, beatings, blanchings, blessings,
Love lures life on.

I Travel as a Phantom Now
4 of] Not in MS
6 gloomy] MS gives as undeleted alternative 'various'

Lines
4 to] with MS
8 pestered] capricious (burnished *del*) MS
9 to] with MS
14 to] with MS

Show me again just this:
The moment of that kiss
Away from the prancing folk, by the strawberry-tree! –
Yea, to such rashness, ratheness, rareness, ripeness, richness,
Love lures life on.

Begun November 1898

389 In the Seventies

TITLE:
'In the Seventies' MS

'Qui deridetur ab amico suo sicut ego.' – JOB

IN the seventies I was bearing in my breast,
Penned tight,
Certain starry thoughts that threw a magic light
On the worktimes and the soundless hours of rest
In the seventies; aye, I bore them in my breast
Penned tight.

In the seventies when my neighbours – even my friend –
Saw me pass,
Heads were shaken, and I heard the words, 'Alas,
For his onward years and name unless he mend!'
In the seventies, when my neighbours and my friend
Saw me pass.

In the seventies those who met me did not know
Of the vision
That immuned me from the chillings of misprision
And the damps that choked my goings to and fro
In the seventies; yea, those nodders did not know
Of the vision.

In the seventies nought could darken or destroy it,
Locked in me,
Though as delicate as lamp-worm's lucency;
Neither mist nor murk could weaken or alloy it
In the seventies! – could not darken or destroy it,
Locked in me.

Lines
19 to] with MS
19 rashness] Hardy's copy of CP2 has been corrected to place 'rashness' after 'richness'
Begun . . . 1898] Not in MS

In the Seventies
21 lamp-worm's lucency] eve-worm's radiancy MS
22] Neither moth nor rust could tarnish or alloy it MS *before revision*

INDENTATION:
There has been some slight variation in this complex pattern: l. 10 stood by itself in a unique indentation between ll. 9 and 11 in all printed editions, but on the strength of MS has been lined up with l. 9; l. 27 was in the second line of indentation in MS and all editions until CP1 when it was moved into the third line.

390 The Pedigree

I

I BENT in the deep of night
Over a pedigree the chronicler gave
As mine; and as I bent there, half-unrobed,
The uncurtained panes of my window-square let in the watery light
Of the moon in its old age:
And green-rheumed clouds were hurrying past where mute and cold it globed
Like a drifting dolphin's eye seen through a lapping wave.

II

So, scanning my sire-sown tree,
And the hieroglyphs of this spouse tied to that,
With offspring mapped below in lineage,
Till the tangles troubled me,
The branches seemed to twist into a seared and cynic face
Which winked and tokened towards the window like a Mage
Enchanting me to gaze again thereat.

III

It was a mirror now,
And in it a long perspective I could trace
Of my begetters, dwindling backward each past each
All with the kindred look,
Whose names had since been inked down in their place
On the recorder's book,
Generation and generation of my mien, and build, and brow.

IV

And then did I divine
That every heave and coil and move I made
Within my brain, and in my mood and speech,
Was in the glass portrayed
As long forestalled by their so making it;
The first of them, the primest fuglemen of my line,
Being fogged in far antiqueness past surmise and reason's reach.

The Pedigree
1 in] at MS
6 green-rheumed] greenish MS
7 drifting] dying MS, MV1, PE
7 dolphin's] fish's MS
18 kindred] family MS, MV1, PE
19 since been] long stood MS
26 it;] it: MV2, PE

V

Said I then, sunk in tone,
'I am merest mimicker and counterfeit! –
Though thinking, *I am I,*
And what I do I do myself alone.'
– The cynic twist of the page thereat unknnit
Back to its normal figure, having wrought its purport wry,
The Mage's mirror left the window-square,
And the stained moon and drift retook their places there.

1916

391 His Heart

A Woman's Dream

At midnight, in the room where he lay dead
Whom in his life I had never clearly read,
I thought if I could peer into that citadel
His heart, I should at last know full and well

What hereto had been known to him alone,
Despite our long sit-out of years foreflown,
'And if,' I said, 'I do this for his memory's sake,
It would not wound him, even if he could wake.'

So I bent over him. He seemed to smile
With a calm confidence the whole long while
That I, withdrawing his heart, held it and, bit by bit,
Perused the unguessed things found written on it.

It was inscribed like a terrestrial sphere
With quaint vermiculations close and clear –
His graving. Had I known, would I have risked the stroke
Its reading brought, and my own heart nigh broke!

Yes, there at last, eyes opened, did I see
His whole sincere symmetric history;
There were his truth, his simple singlemindedness,
Strained, maybe, by time's storms, but there no less.

The Pedigree
30 I am] I'm MS
30 merest mimicker] mere continuator MS, MV1, PE
36 And . . . drift] And moon and drifting cloud MS

There were the daily deeds from sun to sun
In blindness, but good faith, that he had done;
There were regrets, at instances wherein he swerved
(As he conceived) from cherishings I had deserved.

There were old hours all figured down as bliss –
Those spent with me – (how little had I thought this!)
There those when, at my absence, whether he slept or waked,
(Though I knew not 'twas so!) his spirit ached.

There that when we were severed, how day dulled
Till time joined us anew, was chronicled:
And arguments and battlings in defence of me
That heart recorded clearly and ruddily.

I put it back, and left him as he lay
While pierced the morning pink and then the gray
Into each dreary room and corridor around,
Where I shall wait, but his step will not sound.

TITLE:
Where They lived MS

392 *Where They Lived*

DISHEVELLED leaves creep down
Upon that bank to-day,
Some green, some yellow, and some pale brown;
The wet bents bob and sway;
The once warm slippery turf is sodden
Where we laughingly sat or lay.

The summerhouse is gone,
Leaving a weedy space;
The bushes that veiled it once have grown
Gaunt trees that interlace,
Through whose lank limbs I see too clearly
The nakedness of the place.

His Heart
23 he swerved] he had swerved MS
36 wait . . . step] wait a step that MS

Where They Lived
1 creep] come MS, MV1, PE
8 space;] space, MS
11 lank limbs] flayed fingers MS, MV1, PE

And where were hills of blue,
Blind drifts of vapour blow,
And the names of former dwellers few,
If any, people know,
And instead of a voice that called, 'Come in, Dears,'
Time calls, 'Pass below!'

393 The Occultation

WHEN the cloud shut down on the morning shine,
And darkened the sun,
I said, 'So ended that joy of mine
Years back begun.'

But day continued its lustrous roll
In upper air;
And did my late irradiate soul
Live on somewhere?

394 Life Laughs Onward

RAMBLING I looked for an old abode
Where, years back, one had lived I knew;
Its site a dwelling duly showed,
But it was new.

I went where, not so long ago,
The sod had riven two breasts asunder;
Daisies throve gaily there, as though
No grave were under.

I walked along a terrace where
Loud children gambolled in the sun;
The figure that had once sat there
Was missed by none.

Where They Lived
13 blue,] blue MS
March (Oct.) 1913 MS *del* at end

The Occultation
5 its lustrous roll] on to its goal MS

Life Laughs Onward
2 Where, years back,] Where years back MS

Life laughed and moved on unsubdued,
I saw that Old succumbed to Young:
'Twas well. My too regretful mood
    Died on my tongue.

395 *The Peace-Offering*

It was but a little thing,
Yet I knew it meant to me
Ease from what had given a sting
To the very birdsinging
    Latterly.

But I would not welcome it;
And for all I then declined
O the regrettings infinite
When the night-processions flit
    Through the mind!

396 *Something Tapped*

EXTRA PRINTING:
Chosen Poems, p. 118

TITLE:
'Something Tapped' MS

Something tapped on the pane of my room
  When there was never a trace
Of wind or rain, and I saw in the gloom
  My weary Belovéd's face.

'O I am tired of waiting,' she said,
  'Night, morn, noon, afternoon;
So cold it is in my lonely bed,
  And I thought you would join me soon!'

I rose and neared the window-glass,
  But vanished thence had she:
Only a pallid moth, alas,
  Tapped at the pane for me.

August 1913

The Peace-Offering
6 it;] it, MS
10 the] my MS

Something Tapped
August] Not in MS

397 The Wound

I CLIMBED to the crest,
And, fog-festooned,
The sun lay west
Like a crimson wound:

Like that wound of mine
Of which none knew,
For I'd given no sign
That it pierced me through.

EXTRA PRINTINGS:
(1) *The Sphere*, 27 May 1916, p. 190. There are no variants
(2) *Selected Poems*, p. 31
(3) *Chosen Poems*, p. 31

INDENTATION:
All lines have the same indentation in SP

398 A Merrymaking in Question

'I WILL get a new string for my fiddle,
And call to the neighbours to come,
And partners shall dance down the middle
Until the old pewter-wares hum:
And we'll sip the mead, cyder, and rum!'

From the night came the oddest of answers:
A hollow wind, like a bassoon,
And headstones all ranged up as dancers,
And cypresses droning a croon,
And gurgoyles that mouthed to the tune.

EXTRA PRINTINGS:
(1) *The Sphere*, 27 May 1916, p. 74 = S
(2) *Selected Poems*, p. 32
(3) *Chosen Poems*, p. 33

TITLE:
A merrymaking in Question MS

INDENTATION:
1 = ll. 1, 3, 5 } in both stanzas
2 = ll. 2, 4 } SP

399 I Said and Sang Her Excellence

(*Fickle Lover's Song*)

I SAID and sang her excellence:
They called it laud undue.
(Have your way, my heart, O!)
Yet what was homage far above
The plain deserts of my olden Love
Proved verity of my new.

TITLE:
'I said and sang her Excellence' MS

A Merrymaking in Question
4 hum:] hum; S, SP
10] And crossbones that clicked to the tune. S
10 mouthed] gushed SP

'She moves a sylph in picture-land,
  Where nothing frosts the air:'
    (Have your way, my heart, O!)
'To all winged pipers overhead
She is known by shape and song,' I said,
  Conscious of licence there.

I sang of her in a dim old hall
  Dream-built too fancifully,
    (Have your way, my heart, O!)
But lo, the ripe months chanced to lead
My feet to such a hall indeed,
  Where stood the very She.

Strange, startling, was it then to learn
  I had glanced down unborn time,
    (Have your way, my heart, O!)
And prophesied, whereby I knew
That which the years had planned to do
  In warranty of my rhyme.

By Rushy-Pond

TITLE:
A January night MS

400 *A January Night*

(1879)

THE rain smites more and more,
The east wind snarls and sneezes;
Through the joints of the quivering door
  The water wheezes.

The tip of each ivy-shoot
Writhes on its neighbour's face;
There is some hid dread afoot
  That we cannot trace.

Is it the spirit astray
Of the man at the house below
Whose coffin they took in to-day?
  We do not know.

I Said and Sang Her Excellence
7 picture-land,] picture-land MS
19 startling,] startling MS
Rushy-Pond] Rushy Pond MS

A January Night
1 smites] beats MS
5 tip] point MS, MV1, PE

401 *A Kiss*

By a wall the stranger now calls his,
Was born of old a particular kiss,
Without forethought in its genesis;
Which in a trice took wing on the air.
And where that spot is nothing shows:
    There ivy calmly grows,
    And no one knows
    What a birth was there!

That kiss is gone where none can tell –
Not even those who felt its spell:
It cannot have died; that know we well.
Somewhere it pursues its flight,
One of a long procession of sounds
    Travelling aethereal rounds
    Far from earth's bounds
    In the infinite.

402 *The Announcement*

TITLE:
(January 1879) MS *del* below title

INDENTATION:
1 = ll. 1, 3
2 = l. 2
3 = l. 4
} and so throughout MS, MV, WE, PE, ME

They came, the brothers, and took two chairs
    In their usual quiet way;
And for a time we did not think
    They had much to say.

And they began and talked awhile
    Of ordinary things,
Till spread that silence in the room
    A pent thought brings.

And then they said: 'The end has come.
    Yes: it has come at last.'
And we looked down, and knew that day
    A spirit had passed.

A Kiss
1] By the wall where now the stranger is MS
8 there!] there. MS, MV1, PE

The Announcement
8 A] Which a MS, MV1

403 The Oxen

CHRISTMAS EVE, and twelve of the clock.
  'Now they are all on their knees,'
An elder said as we sat in a flock
  By the embers in hearthside ease.

We pictured the meek mild creatures where
  They dwelt in their strawy pen,
Nor did it occur to one of us there
  To doubt they were kneeling then.

So fair a fancy few would weave
  In these years! Yet, I feel,
If someone said on Christmas Eve,
  'Come; see the oxen kneel

'In the lonely barton by yonder coomb
  Our childhood used to know,'
I should go with him in the gloom,
  Hoping it might be so.

1915

EXTRA MANUSCRIPT:

A separate MS was sold at the Red Cross Sale at Christie's, 26 April 1916. Its present whereabouts are unknown. It has been checked from the facsimile in the Folsom Sale Catalogue (New York, American Art Association Galleries), 6 Dec 1932, p. 39 = RCS

EXTRA PRINTINGS:

(1) *The Times*, 24 Dec 1915, p. 7 = T
(2) In pamphlet for 'private circulation only' printed by E. Williams, bookseller, 37 New Town Road, Hove, 28 Dec 1915 = EW
(3) *Selected Poems*, p. 130
(4) *Chosen Poems*, p. 164

Note This was one of nine poems chosen by Hardy for the Library of the Royal Dolls' House at Windsor Castle. The copy there has 'some one' (l. 11)

404 The Tresses

  'WHEN the air was damp
It made my curls hang slack
As they kissed my neck and back
While I footed the salt-aired track
    I loved to tramp.

  'When it was dry
They would roll up crisp and tight
As I went on in the light
Of the sun, which my own sprite
    Seemed to outvie.

The Oxen
9 would weave] believe T, EW
10 years!] years. RCS
11 someone] some one SP, CHP
11 Eve,] Eve T, EW, RCS
12 kneel] kneel, CP3
15 gloom,] gloom MS
1915] Not in MS, T, EW, SP, MV1, PE, RCS
T adds: (*No Copyright reserved.*)

The Tresses
4 I footed] footing MS

'Now I am old;
And have not one gay curl
As I had when a girl
For dampness to unfurl
Or sun uphold!'

405 *The Photograph*

THE flame crept up the portrait line by line
As it lay on the coals in the silence of night's profound,
And over the arm's incline,
And along the marge of the silkwork superfine,
And gnawed at the delicate bosom's defenceless round.

Then I vented a cry of hurt, and averted my eyes;
The spectacle was one that I could not bear,
To my deep and sad surprise;
But, compelled to heed, I again looked furtivewise
Till the flame had eaten her breasts, and mouth, and hair.

'Thank God, she is out of it now!' I said at last,
In a great relief of heart when the thing was done
That had set my soul aghast,
And nothing was left of the picture unsheathed from the past
But the ashen ghost of the card it had figured on.

She was a woman long hid amid packs of years,
She might have been living or dead; she was lost to my sight,
And the deed that had nigh drawn tears
Was done in a casual clearance of life's arrears;
But I felt as if I had put her to death that night! . . .

. . .

– Well; she knew nothing thereof did she survive,
And suffered nothing if numbered among the dead;
Yet – yet – if on earth alive
Did she feel a smart, and with vague strange anguish strive?
If in heaven, did she smile at me sadly and shake her head?

The Photograph
4 marge] edge MS, MV1, PE
6 eyes;] eyes, MS, MV1, PE
9 furtivewise] furtive-wise MS
20 night! . . .] night. . . . . MS

TITLE:
On a heath MS

406 *On a Heath*

I COULD hear a gown-skirt rustling
Before I could see her shape,
Rustling through the heather
That wove the common's drape,
On that evening of dark weather
When I hearkened, lips agape.

And the town-shine in the distance
Did but baffle here the sight,
And then a voice flew forward:
'Dear, is't you? I fear the night!'
And the herons flapped to norward
In the firs upon my right.

There was another looming
Whose life we did not see;
There was one stilly blooming
Full nigh to where walked we;
There was a shade entombing
All that was bright of me.

407 *An Anniversary*

IT was at the very date to which we have come,
In the month of the matching name,
When, at a like minute, the sun had upswum,
Its couch-time at night being the same.
And the same path stretched here that people now follow,
And the same stile crossed their way,
And beyond the same green hillock and hollow
The same horizon lay;
And the same man pilgrims now hereby who pilgrimed here that day.

On a Heath
4 wove] formed MS, MV1, PE
9 flew] came MS, MV1, PE
10 Dear, is't you] Are you there MS, MV1, PE
14 life] build MS, MV1, PE
15 one stilly] a flower MS
15 stilly] meekly MV1, PE
16] In close propinquity; MS, MV1, PE

An Anniversary
4 couch-time] bed-time MS
6 stile] stiles MS
9 pilgrims] passes MS, MV1, PE
9 hereby] thereby MS
9 pilgrimed here] passed thereby MS: passed hereby MV1, PE
9–10 Stanza break in all editions

Let so much be said of the date-day's sameness;
But the tree that neighbours the track,
And stoops liked a pedlar afflicted with lameness,
Knew of no sogged wound or wind-crack.
And the joints of that wall were not enshrouded
With mosses of many tones,
And the garth up afar was not overcrowded
With a multitude of white stones,
And the man's eyes then were not so sunk that you saw the
socket-bones.

Kingston-Maurward Ewelease

408 *By the Runic Stone*

(*Two who became a story*)

TITLE:
'By the Runic Stone' MS
(*Two . . .*)] Not in MS, MV1, PE

BY the Runic Stone
They sat, where the grass sloped down,
And chattered, he white-hatted, she in brown,
Pink-faced, breeze-blown.

Rapt there alone
In the transport of talking so
In such a place, there was nothing to let them know
What hours had flown.

And the die thrown
By them heedlessly there, the dent
It was to cut in their encompassment,
Were, too, unknown.

It might have strown
Their zest with qualms to see,
As in a glass, Time toss their history
From zone to zone!

An Anniversary
13 Knew of no sogged] Had no waterlogged MS, MV1, PE
13 wind-crack] windcrack WE, ME [Word split between two lines in all earlier editions]
14 joints] stones MS, MV, WE, PE, CP1
14 that] the MS
16 up afar] on the hill MS
Kingston-Maurward Ewelease] Not in MS

By the Runic Stone
6 transport] newness MS, MV1, PE

409 *The Pink Frock*

'O MY pretty pink frock,
I sha'n't be able to wear it!
Why is he dying just now?
  I hardly can bear it!

'He might have contrived to live on;
But they say there's no hope whatever:
And must I shut myself up,
  And go out never?

'O my pretty pink frock?
Puff-sleeved and accordion-pleated!
He might have passed in July,
  And not so cheated!'

TITLE:
In a Churchyard MS *before revision*

410 *Transformations*

PORTION of this yew
Is a man my grandsire knew,
Bosomed here at its foot:
This branch may be his wife,
A ruddy human life
Now turned to a green shoot.

These grasses must be made
Of her who often prayed,
Last century, for repose;
And the fair girl long ago
Whom I often tried to know
May be entering this rose.

So, they are not underground,
But as nerves and veins abound
In the growths of upper air,
And they feel the sun and rain,
And the energy again
That made them what they were!

The Pink Frock
2 sha'n't] shan't MS
9 frock?] frock, MS, MV, WE, PE, ME
12] And me uncheated!' MV1
12 not so] none been MS: me not PE

Transformations
4 may be] maybe MS, MV1, PE
4 wife,] wife, – MS
11 often] vainly ME
14 nerves] films MS

411 *In Her Precincts*

HER house looked cold from the foggy lea,
And the square of each window a dull black blur
    Where showed no stir:
Yes, her gloom within at the lack of me
Seemed matching mine at the lack of her.

The black squares grew to be squares of light
As the eveshade swathed the house and lawn,
    And viols gave tone;
There was glee within. And I found that night
The gloom of severance mine alone.

Kingston-Maurward Park

412 *The Last Signal*

(11 Oct. 1886)

A Memory of William Barnes

SILENTLY I footed by an uphill road
That led from my abode to a spot yew-boughed;
Yellowly the sun sloped low down to westward,
    And dark was the east with cloud.

Then, amid the shadow of that livid sad east,
Where the light was least, and a gate stood wide,
Something flashed the fire of the sun that was facing it,
    Like a brief blaze on that side.

Looking hard and harder I knew what it meant –
The sudden shine sent from the livid east scene;
It meant the west mirrored by the coffin of my friend there,
    Turning to the road from his green,

To take his last journey forth – he who in his prime
Trudged so many a time from that gate athwart the land!
Thus a farewell to me he signalled on his grave-way,
    As with a wave of his hand.

Winterborne-Came Path

TITLE:
A Memory of] In memoriam MS

In Her Precincts
7] As dusk increased round the house MS
Kingston-Maurward Park] Not in MS

The Last Signal
5 amid] below MS, MV, WE, PE, ME, CP1
7 Something . . . fire] Flashed a reflection MS, MV1
7 Something flashed] Flashed back MV2, WE, PE, CP1
11 It meant] 'Twas MS
11 west] sun MV1, PE
Winterborne-Came Path] Not in MS

EXTRA MANUSCRIPT:
In the Dorset County Museum, reproduced in facsimile in *The Strand Magazine*, Oct 1924, p. 341 = DCM

413 The House of Silence

'THAT is a quiet place –
That house in the trees with the shady lawn.'
' – If, child, you knew what there goes on
You would not call it a quiet place.
Why, a phantom abides there, the last of its race,
And a brain spins there till dawn.'

'But I see nobody there, –
Nobody moves about the green,
Or wanders the heavy trees between.'
' – Ah, that's because you do not bear
The visioning powers of souls who dare
To pierce the material screen.

'Morning, noon, and night,
Mid those funereal shades that seem
The uncanny scenery of a dream,
Figures dance to a mind with sight,
And music and laughter like floods of light
Make all the precincts gleam.

'It is a poet's bower,
Through which there pass, in fleet arrays,
Long teams of all the years and days,
Of joys and sorrows, of earth and heaven,
That meet mankind in its ages seven,
An aion in an hour.'

EXTRA PRINTING:
Chosen Poems, pp. 119–20

414 Great Things

SWEET cyder is a great thing,
A great thing to me,
Spinning down to Weymouth town
By Ridgway thirstily,

The House of Silence
10–12] ' – Ah, that's because you are not aware/Of the eyes of souls who inhabit there where/Wondrous things have been. DCM *before revision*
17 light] light, DCM
20 fleet] long MS, DCM
21 Long teams] Processions MS, DCM
23 its] his MS, DCM, MV1, PE
23 seven,] seven – DCM

Great Things
3 Spinning] Vamping MS
3 Weymouth] Budmouth MS

And maid and mistress summoning
  Who tend the hostelry:
O cyder is a great thing,
  A great thing to me!

The dance it is a great thing,
  A great thing to me,
With candles lit and partners fit
  For night-long revelry;
And going home when day-dawning
  Peeps pale upon the lea:
O dancing is a great thing,
  A great thing to me!

Love is, yea, a great thing,
  A great thing to me,
When, having drawn across the lawn
  In darkness silently,
A figure flits like one a-wing
  Out from the nearest tree:
O love is, yes, a great thing,
  A great thing to me!

Will these be always great things,
  Great things to me? . . .
Let it befall that One will call,
  'Soul, I have need of thee:'
What then? Joy-jaunts, impassioned flings,
  Love, and its ecstasy,
Will always have been great things,
  Great things to me!

415 *The Chimes*

THAT morning when I trod the town
The twitching chimes of long renown
    Played out to me

Great Things
9 thing,] thing MS
12 revelry;] revelry. MS
24 A great] Aye, greatest MV2, WE, CP1
26 Great] Greatest MV2, WE, CP1
26 me? . . .] me? MS
27 Let] Will MS
28 thee:'] thee'? . . . MS
29 flings,] flings WE
32 Great] Greatest MV2, WE, CP1

The Chimes
1 when I trod] I walked up MS, MV1

The sweet Sicilian sailors' tune,
And I knew not if late or soon
My day would be:

A day of sunshine beryl-bright
And windless; yea, think as I might,
I could not say,
Even to within years' measure, when
One would be at my side who then
Was far away.

When hard utilitarian times
Had stilled the sweet Saint-Peter's chimes
I learnt to see
That bale may spring where blisses are,
And one desired might be afar
Though near to me.

INDENTATION:
There was some variation in stanza 2 in MV, PE and CP, but here it has been brought into line with stanza 1 on the pattern of MS, WE, ME

416 The Figure in the Scene

It pleased her to step in front and sit
Where the cragged slope was green,
While I stood back that I might pencil it
With her amid the scene;
Till it gloomed and rained;
But I kept on, despite the drifting wet
That fell and stained
My draught, leaving for curious quizzings yet
The blots engrained.

And thus I drew her there alone,
Seated amid the gauze
Of moisture, hooded, only her outline shown,
With rainfall marked across.
– Soon passed our stay;
Yet her rainy form is the Genius still of the spot,
Immutable, yea,
Though the place now knows her no more, and has known her not
Ever since that day.

From an old note

The Chimes
6 be:] be; MS

The Figure in the Scene
4 scene;] scene. MS, MV1, PE
5] And then it rained; MS
13 rainfall] rain-lines MS, MV1
14 – Soon] Soon MS
16 Immutable] MS has *deleted* 'There permanent', 'Inseparable' and 'As pictured'

417 *Why Did I Sketch*

TITLE:
'Why did I sketch' MS

WHY did I sketch an upland green,
And put the figure in
Of one on the spot with me? –
For now that one has ceased to be seen
The picture waxes akin
To a wordless irony.

If you go drawing on down or cliff
Let no soft curves intrude
Of a woman's silhouette,
But show the escarpments stark and stiff
As in utter solitude;
So shall you half forget.

Let me sooner pass from sight of the sky
Than again on a thoughtless day
Limn, laugh, and sing, and rhyme
With a woman sitting near, whom I
Paint in for love, and who may
Be called hence in my time!

From an old note

418 *Conjecture*

IF there were in my kalendar
No Emma, Florence, Mary,
What would be my existence now –
A hermit's? – wanderer's weary? –
How should I live, and how
Near would be death, or far?

Could it have been that other eyes
Might have uplit my highway?

Why Did I Sketch
15 Limn] Sketch MS, MV1, PE
MS has at end in erased pencil: 1913

That fond, sad, retrospective sight
Would catch from this dim byway
Prized figures different quite
From those that now arise?

With how strange aspect would there creep
The dawn, the night, the daytime,
If memory were not what it is
In song-time, toil, or pray-time. –
O were it else than this,
I'd pass to pulseless sleep!

419 *The Blow*

THAT no man schemed it is my hope –
Yea, that it fell by will and scope
Of That Which some enthrone,
And for whose meaning myriads grope.

For I would not that of my kind
There should, of his unbiassed mind,
Have been one known
Who such a stroke could have designed;

Since it would augur works and ways
Below the lowest that man assays
To have hurled that stone
Into the sunshine of our days!

And if it prove that no man did,
And that the Inscrutable, the Hid,
Was cause alone
Of this foul crash our lives amid,

I'll go in due time, and forget
In some deep graveyard's oubliette
The thing whereof I groan,
And cease from troubling; thankful yet

Conjecture
11 Prized] Past MS
13 creep] come MS
16 toil, or pray-time.] say, or pray-time! MS
17–18] Well, were it not as this,/I'd have me dead and dumb. MS

Time's finger should have stretched to show
No aimful author's was the blow
    That swept us prone,
But the Immanent Doer's That doth not know,

Which in some age unguessed of us
May lift Its blinding incubus,
    And see, and own:
'It grieves me I did thus and thus!'

420 Love the Monopolist

(*Young Lover's Reverie*)

THE train draws forth from the station-yard,
    And with it carries me.
I rise, and stretch out, and regard
    The platform left, and see
An airy slim blue form there standing,
    And know that it is she.

While with strained vision I watch on,
    The figure turns round quite
To greet friends gaily; then is gone. . . .
    The import may be slight,
But why remained she not hard gazing
    Till I was out of sight?

'O do not chat with others there,'
    I brood. 'They are not I.
O strain your thoughts as if they were
    Gold bands between us; eye
All neighbour scenes as so much blankness
    Till I again am by!

'A troubled soughing in the breeze
    And the sky overhead
Let yourself feel; and shadeful trees,
    Ripe corn, and apples red,
Read as things barren and distasteful
    While we are separated!

TITLE:
Love the monopolist MS

The Blow
24 Doer's] Doer MS
24 doth] does MS, MV1, PE

Love the Monopolist
14 brood] feel MS
22 apples] poppies MS

'When I come back uncloak your gloom,
    And let in lovely day;
Then the long dark as of the tomb
    Can well be thrust away
With sweet things I shall have to practise,
    And you will have to say!'

Begun 1871: finished —

TITLE:
At Middle-Hill Gate in February MS *before revision*

421 *At Middle-Field Gate in February*

THE bars are thick with drops that show
    As they gather themselves from the fog
Like silver buttons ranged in a row,
And as evenly spaced as if measured, although
    They fall at the feeblest jog.

They load the leafless hedge hard by,
    And the blades of last year's grass,
While the fallow ploughland turned up nigh
In raw rolls, clammy and clogging lie –
    Too clogging for feet to pass.

How dry it was on a far-back day
    When straws hung the hedge and around,
When amid the sheaves in amorous play
In curtained bonnets and light array
    Bloomed a bevy now underground!

Bockhampton Lane

EXTRA PRINTING:
The Aberdeen University Review, Feb 1916, p. 7 = AU

TITLE:
The Youth who carried a Light MS

422 *The Youth Who Carried a Light*

I SAW him pass as the new day dawned,
    Murmuring some musical phrase;
Horses were drinking and floundering in the pond,
    And the tired stars thinned their gaze;
Yet these were not the spectacles at all that he conned,
    But an inner one, giving out rays.

Love the Monopolist
25 gloom,] gloom. CP2–4

At Middle-Field Gate in February
3 ranged] set MS, MV1, PE
4 evenly] equally MS, MV1, PE
8 fallow ploughland] arable ridges MS, MV1, PE
9 raw rolls] brown lines MS, MV1, PE
12 hung] draped MS
15 Bloomed] Moved MS, MV1, PE
Bockhampton Lane] Not in MS

The Youth Who Carried a Light
1 dawned,] dawned MS
2 phrase;] phrase, AU

Such was the thing in his eye, walking there,
The very and visible thing,
A close light, displacing the gray of the morning air,
And the tokens that the dark was taking wing;
And was it not the radiance of a purpose rare
That might ripe to its accomplishing?

What became of that light? I wonder still its fate!
Was it quenched ere its full apogee?
Did it struggle frail and frailer to a beam emaciate?
Did it thrive till matured in verity?
Or did it travel on, to be a new young dreamer's freight,
And thence on infinitely?

1915

423 *The Head above the Fog*

TITLE:
The Head above the fog MS

SOMETHING do I see
Above the fog that sheets the mead,
A figure like to life indeed,
Moving along with spectre-speed,
Seen by none but me.

O the vision keen! –
Tripping along to me for love
As in the flesh it used to move,
Only its hat and plume above
The evening fog-fleece seen.

In the day-fall wan,
When nighted birds break off their song,
Mere ghostly head it skims along,
Just as it did when warm and strong,
Body seeming gone.

Such it is I see
Above the fog that sheets the mead –
Yea, that which once could breathe and plead! –
Skimming along with spectre-speed
To a last tryst with me.

The Youth Who Carried a Light
8 very] real AU
14 ere] at MS, AU, MV1, PE
14 full] very MS, AU, MV1, PE
17 on,] on AU
1915] Not in MS, AU

The Head above the Fog
6 keen! –] keen, MS, MV1, PE
10 evening] filmy MS, MV1, PE
10 fog-fleece] fog-layer MS

TITLE:
Overlooking the Stour
(1877) MS *before revision*

424 *Overlooking the River Stour*

THE swallows flew in the curves of an eight
Above the river-gleam
In the wet June's last beam:
Like little crossbows animate
The swallows flew in the curves of an eight
Above the river-gleam.

Planing up shavings of crystal spray
A moor-hen darted out
From the bank thereabout,
And through the stream-shine ripped his way;
Planing up shavings of crystal spray
A moor-hen darted out.

Closed were the kingcups; and the mead
Dripped in monotonous green,
Though the day's morning sheen
Had shown it golden and honeybee'd;
Closed were the kingcups; and the mead
Dripped in monotonous green.

And never I turned my head, alack,
While these things met my gaze
Through the pane's drop-drenched glaze,
To see the more behind my back. . . .
O never I turned, but let, alack,
These less things hold my gaze!

425 *The Musical Box*

LIFELONG to be
Seemed the fair colour of the time;
That there was standing shadowed near
A spirit who sang to the gentle chime
Of the self-struck notes, I did not hear,
I did not see.

Overlooking the River Stour
1 curves] shape MS
5 curves] shape MS
7 of crystal] made of MS, MV1, PE
8 moor-hen] moorhen MS
11 of crystal] made of MS, MV1, PE
12 moor-hen] moorhen MS
Note A review in *The Nation*, 22 Dec 1917, possibly based on an uncorrected proof copy of MV, has the following variants: l. 4 animate, l. 7 spray, l. 10 her way; l. 11 spray,

Thus did it sing
To the mindless lyre that played indoors
As she came to listen for me without:
'O value what the nonce outpours –
This best of life – that shines about
Your welcoming!'

I had slowed along
After the torrid hours were done,
Though still the posts and walls and road
Flung back their sense of the hot-faced sun,
And had walked by Stourside Mill, where broad
Stream-lilies throng.

And I descried
The dusky house that stood apart,
And her, white-muslined, waiting there
In the porch with high-expectant heart,
While still the thin mechanic air
Went on inside.

At whiles would flit
Swart bats, whose wings, be-webbed and tanned,
Whirred like the wheels of ancient clocks:
She laughed a hailing as she scanned
Me in the gloom, the tuneful box
Intoning it.

Lifelong to be
I thought it. That there watched hard by
A spirit who sang to the indoor tune,
'O make the most of what is nigh!'
I did not hear in my dull soul-swoon –
I did not see.

The Musical Box
17 Stourside Mill] way of the mill MS
27 wheels] fly MS, MV1, PE
33 tune,] tune MS
Note Erased pencil workings show that Hardy considered repeating the last two syllables of l. 2 of each stanza as the beginning of l. 3

426 *On Sturminster Foot-Bridge*

TITLE:
On Stourcastle Foot-bridge MS
(1877) MS *del*
(*Onomatopœic*)] Not in MS, MV, WE, PE, CP1, ME

(*Onomatopœic*)

RETICULATIONS creep upon the slack stream's face
When the wind skims irritably past,
The current clucks smartly into each hollow place
That years of flood have scrabbled in the pier's sodden base;
The floating-lily leaves rot fast.

On a roof stand the swallows ranged in wistful waiting rows,
Till they arrow off and drop like stones
Among the eyot-withies at whose foot the river flows:
And beneath the roof is she who in the dark world shows
As a lattice-gleam when midnight moans.

427 *Royal Sponsors*

'THE king and the queen will stand to the child;
'Twill be handed down in song;
And it's no more than their deserving,
With my lord so faithful at Court so long,
And so staunch and strong.

'O never before was known such a thing!
'Twill be a grand time for all;
And the beef will be a whole-roast bullock,
And the servants will have a feast in the hall,
And the ladies a ball.

'While from Jordan's stream by a traveller,
In a flagon of silver wrought,
And by caravan, stage-coach, wain, and waggon
A precious trickle has been brought,
Clear as when caught.'

On Sturminster Foot-Bridge
6 ranged . . . waiting] equidistantly in MS, MV1
8 foot] roots MS, MV1, PE
8 flows:] flows; MS, MV, WE, PE, ME
10 lattice-gleam] lamp-light MS

Royal Sponsors
3 deserving,] deserving MS
4 Court] court MS
8 whole-roast] whole-roasted MS, MV1, PE

The morning came. To the park of the peer
    The royal couple bore;
And the font was filled with the Jordan water,
And the household awaited their guests before
        The carpeted door.

But when they went to the silk-lined cot
    The child was found to have died.
'What's now to be done? We can disappoint not
The king and queen!' the family cried
        With eyes spread wide.

'Even now they approach the chestnut-drive!
    The service must be read.'
'Well, since we can't christen the child alive,
By God we shall have to christen him dead!'
        The marquis said.

Thus, breath-forsaken, a corpse was taken
    To the private chapel – yea –
And the king knew not, nor the queen, God wot,
That they answered for one returned to clay
        At the font that day.

428 Old Furniture

TITLE:
Old furniture MS

I KNOW not how it may be with others
    Who sit amid relics of householdry
That date from the days of their mothers' mothers,
    But well I know how it is with me
        Continually.

I see the hands of the generations
    That owned each shiny familiar thing
In play on its knobs and indentations,
    And with its ancient fashioning
        Still dallying:

Royal Sponsors
24 queen!] queen? MS
26 chestnut-drive!] chestnut-drive! – MS
33 not,] not MS

Old Furniture
1 I know not] I don't know MS

Hands behind hands, growing paler and paler,
As in a mirror a candle-flame
Shows images of itself, each frailer
As it recedes, though the eye may frame
Its shape the same.

On the clock's dull dial a foggy finger,
Moving to set the minutes right
With tentative touches that lift and linger
In the wont of a moth on a summer night,
Creeps to my sight.

On this old viol, too, fingers are dancing –
As whilom – just over the strings by the nut,
The tip of a bow receding, advancing
In airy quivers, as if it would cut
The plaintive gut.

And I see a face by that box for tinder,
Glowing forth in fits from the dark,
And fading again, as the linten cinder
Kindles to red at the flinty spark,
Or goes out stark.

Well, well. It is best to be up and doing,
The world has no use for one to-day
Who eyes things thus – no aim pursuing!
He should not continue in this stay,
But sink away.

TITLE:
The Thought in Two Moods MS *before revision*

429 A Thought in Two Moods

I SAW it – pink and white – revealed
Upon the white and green;
The white and green was a daisied field,
The pink and white Ethleen.

And as I looked it seemed in kind
That difference they had none;
The two fair bodiments combined
As varied miens of one.

Old Furniture
16 finger,] finger MS
19 wont] way MS
19 night,] night MS
20 to] on MS, MV1, PE
22 As whilom] My father's MS [MS has 'As whilom' in erased pencil]
23 a] his MS
25 plaintive] plaining MS
26–30] From each curled eff-hole the ghosts of ditties/Incanted there by his skill in his prime/Quaver in whispers the pangs and pities/They once could language, and in their time/Would daily chime. MS

A Thought in Two Moods
4 Ethleen] my queen MS
7 bodiments] spectacles MS
8 varied miens] corporate parts MS

A sense that, in some mouldering year,
As one they both would lie,
Made me move quickly on to her
To pass the pale thought by.

She laughed and said: 'Out there, to me,
You looked so weather-browned,
And brown in clothes, you seemed to be
Made of the dusty ground!'

430 *The Last Performance*

TITLE:
The Last performance MS

'I AM playing my oldest tunes,' declared she,
'All the old tunes I know, –
Those I learnt ever so long ago.'
– Why she should think just then she'd play them
Silence cloaks like snow.

When I returned from the town at nightfall
Notes continued to pour
As when I had left two hours before:
'It's the very last time,' she said in closing;
'From now I play no more.'

A few morns onward found her fading,
And, as her life outflew,
I thought of her playing her tunes right through;
And I felt she had known of what was coming,
And wondered how she knew.

1912

431 *You on the Tower*

TITLE:
'You on the Tower' MS

I

'YOU on the tower of my factory –
What do you see up there?
Do you see Enjoyment with wide wings
Advancing to reach me here?'
– 'Yea; I see Enjoyment with wide wings
Advancing to reach you here.'

A Thought in Two Moods
10] To one they would be wrought, MS
12] To kill the pallid thought. MS
16 ground!] ground. MS

The Last Performance
11 fading] dying MS
13 tunes right] repertory MS
From old notes MS *del* at end

You on the Tower
5 Yea;] Yea – MS

II

'Good. Soon I'll come and ask you
To tell me again thereon. . . .
Well, what is he doing now? Hoi, there!'
– 'He still is flying on.'
'Ah, waiting till I have full-finished.
Good. Tell me again anon. . . .

III

'Hoi, Watchman! I'm here. When comes he?
Between my sweats I am chill.'
– 'Oh, you there, working still?
Why, surely he reached you a time back,
And took you miles from your mill?
He duly came in his winging,
And now he has passed out of view.
How can it be that you missed him?
He brushed you by as he flew.'

432 *The Interloper*

TITLE:
One who ought not to be there MS *del* [This could be either an earlier title or a rejected sub-title]
'And . . . home'] Not in MS, MV, WE, PE, CP1, ME

'And I saw the figure and visage of Madness seeking for a home'

THERE are three folk driving in a quaint old chaise,
And the cliff-side track looks green and fair;
I view them talking in quiet glee
As they drop down towards the puffins' lair
By the roughest of ways;
But another with the three rides on, I see,
Whom I like not to be there!

No: it's not anybody you think of. Next
A dwelling appears by a slow sweet stream
Where two sit happy and half in the dark:
They read, helped out by a frail-wick'd gleam,
Some rhythmic text;
But one sits with them whom they don't mark,
One I'm wishing could not be there.

You on the Tower
8 thereon. . . .] thereon. . . . . MS
11 Ah,] Ah – MS
12 anon. . . .] anon. . . . . MS
15 working] asking MS, MV1, PE

The Interloper
3 view] see MS
7 Whom I like] One who ought MS *before revision*
7 there!] there. MS
11 frail-wick'd gleam] candle-gleam MS

No: not whom you knew and name. And now
I discern gay diners in a mansion-place,
And the guests dropping wit – pert, prim, or choice,
And the hostess's tender and laughing face,
    And the host's bland brow;
But I cannot help hearing a hollow voice,
    And I'd fain not hear it there.

No: it's not from the stranger you met once. Ah,
Yet a goodlier scene than that succeeds;
People on a lawn – quite a crowd of them. Yes,
And they chatter and ramble as fancy leads;
    And they say, 'Hurrah!'
To a blithe speech made; save one, mirthless,
    Who ought not to be there.

Nay: it's not the pale Form your imagings raise,
That waits on us all at a destined time,
It is not the Fourth Figure the Furnace showed;
O that it were such a shape sublime
    In these latter days!
It is that under which best lives corrode;
    Would, would it could not be there!

433 Logs on the Hearth

A Memory of a Sister

TITLE:
A . . . Sister] Not in MS, MV1, PE

THE fire advances along the log
    Of the tree we felled,
Which bloomed and bore striped apples by the peck
Till its last hour of bearing knelled.

The fork that first my hand would reach
    And then my foot
In climbings upward inch by inch, lies now
Sawn, sapless, darkening with soot.

The Interloper
15 not whom] it's not one MS
22 stranger] person MS
27 mirthless] shadowless MS, MV1, PE: unwatched MV2
29 Nay:] No; MS
29 Form] form MS
31 Fourth Figure] gaunt shape MS *before revision*

Logs on the Hearth
2 felled,] felled MS, MV1, PE
Note In MS, MV1, PE all stanzas have five lines: l. 3 in each stanza is 'That time O! – ' ('Ah, the time O! – ' MS *before revision*). Indentation of this extra line is to the right of l. 2

Where the bark chars is where, one year,
    It was pruned, and bled –
Then overgrew the wound. But now, at last,
  Its growings all have stagnated.

  My fellow-climber rises dim
    From her chilly grave –
Just as she was, her foot near mine on the bending limb,
  Laughing, her young brown hand awave.

December 1915

434 The Sunshade

AH – it's the skeleton of a lady's sunshade,
  Here at my feet in the hard rock's chink,
  Merely a naked sheaf of wires! –
  Twenty years have gone with their livers and diers
  Since it was silked in its white or pink.

Noonshine riddles the ribs of the sunshade,
  No more a screen from the weakest ray;
  Nothing to tell us the hue of its dyes,
  Nothing but rusty bones as it lies
  In its coffin of stone, unseen till to-day.

Where is the woman who carried that sunshade
  Up and down this seaside place? –
  Little thumb standing against its stem,
  Thoughts perhaps bent on a love-stratagem,
  Softening yet more the already soft face!

Is the fair woman who carried that sunshade
  A skeleton just as her property is,
  Laid in the chink that none may scan?
  And does she regret – if regret dust can –
  The vain things thought when she flourished this?

Swanage Cliffs

The Sunshade
12] Where is the hand that held it in place? – MS *before revision*
13 stem,] stem – MS
14 love-stratagem,] love-stratagem – MS
15 face!] face? MS
16 the fair] not the MS, MV1, PE
Swanage Cliffs] Swanage MS

435 *The Ageing House*

WHEN the walls were red
That now are seen
To be overspread
With a mouldy green,
A fresh fair head
Would often lean
From the sunny casement
And scan the scene,
While blithely spoke the wind to the little sycamore tree.

But storms have raged
Those walls about,
And the head has aged
That once looked out;
And zest is suaged
And trust grows doubt,
And slow effacement
Is rife throughout,
While fiercely girds the wind at the long-limbed sycamore tree!

436 *The Caged Goldfinch*

WITHIN a churchyard, on a recent grave,
I saw a little cage
That jailed a goldfinch. All was silence save
Its hops from stage to stage.

There was inquiry in its wistful eye,
And once it tried to sing;
Of him or her who placed it there, and why,
No one knew anything.

The Ageing House
9 to] in MS
9 little] Not in MS, MV1
14 suaged] suaged, ME
15 grows] is MS, MV, PE
17 Is rife] Proceeds MS, MV1, PE
17 throughout,] throughout MS
18 long-limbed] Not in MS, MV1
18 tree!] tree. MS

The Caged Goldfinch
3 jailed] prisoned MS
MS, MV1 have third stanza as follows:

> But (True, MV1) a woman was found drowned the day ensuing,/And some at times averred/The grave to be her false one's, who when wooing/Gave her the bird.

TITLE:
At Madame Tussaud's and later MS *before revision*

437 *At Madame Tussaud's in Victorian Years*

'THAT same first fiddler who leads the orchéstra to-night
  Here fiddled four decades of years ago;
He bears the same babe-like smile of self-centred delight,
Same trinket on watch-chain, same ring on the hand with the bow.

'But his face, if regarded, is woefully wanner, and drier,
  And his once dark beard has grown straggling and gray;
Yet a blissful existence he seems to have led with his lyre,
In a trance of his own, where no wearing or tearing had sway.

'Mid these wax figures, who nothing can do, it may seem
  That to do but a little thing counts a great deal;
To be watched by kings, councillors, queens, may be flattering
    to him –
With their glass eyes longing they too could wake notes that
    appeal.'

. . .

Ah, but he played staunchly – that fiddler – whoever he was,
  With the innocent heart and the soul-touching string:
May he find the Fair Haven! For did he not smile with good
    cause?
Yes; gamuts that graced forty years'-flight were not a small thing!

438 *The Ballet*

THEY crush together – a rustling heap of flesh –
Of more than flesh, a heap of souls; and then
    They part, enmesh,
  And crush together again,
Like the pink petals of a too sanguine rose
  Frightened shut just when it blows.

Though all alike in their tinsel livery,
And indistinguishable at a sweeping glance,
    They muster, maybe,
  As lives wide in irrelevance;

At Madame Tussaud's in Victorian Years
2 four . . . years] a quarter of a century MS
3 bears] wears MS
5] 'But to come to the flesh. It is wanner, more plough-shared, and drier, MS
6 straggling and gray] whited and stray MS
7 led] had MS, MV1
12] As if they wished *they* could make notes that sigh, wail, and appeal.' MS
12 they too] that they MV1, PE
13 staunchly] well MS
16 Yes . . . were] Yea; what he gave forth forty seasons was MS

The Ballet
5 too] Not in MS
10] London, America, France; MS *before revision*

A world of her own has each one underneath,
Detached as a sword from its sheath.

Daughters, wives, mistresses; honest or false, sold, bought;
Hearts of all sizes; gay, fond, gushing, or penned,
Various in thought
Of lover, rival, friend;
Links in a one-pulsed chain, all showing one smile,
Yet severed so many a mile!

439 *The Five Students*

THE sparrow dips in his wheel-rut bath,
The sun grows passionate-eyed,
And boils the dew to smoke by the paddock-path;
As strenuously we stride, –
Five of us; dark He, fair He, dark She, fair She, I,
All beating by.

The air is shaken, the high-road hot,
Shadowless swoons the day,
The greens are sobered and cattle at rest; but not
We on our urgent way, –
Four of us; fair She, dark She, fair He, I, are there,
But one – elsewhere.

Autumn moulds the hard fruit mellow,
And forward still we press
Through moors, briar-meshed plantations, clay-pits yellow,
As in the spring hours – yes,
Three of us; fair He, fair She, I, as heretofore,
But – fallen one more.

The leaf drops: earthworms draw it in
At night-time noiselessly,
The fingers of birch and beech are skeleton-thin,
And yet on the beat are we, –
Two of us; fair She, I. But no more left to go
The track we know.

The Ballet
17 a one-pulsed] one serpentine MS
17 one-pulsed] one-impulsed MV1, PE

The Five Students
3 smoke] fumes MS
9 sobered] darkened MS, MV1, PE
17 us;] us: MS, MV, WE, PE, ME

Icicles tag the church-aisle leads,
The flag-rope gibbers hoarse,
The home-bound foot-folk wrap their snow-flaked heads,
Yet I still stalk the course –
One of us. . . . Dark and fair He, dark and fair She, gone:
The rest – anon.

440 *The Wind's Prophecy*

I TRAVEL on by barren farms,
And gulls glint out like silver flecks
Against a cloud that speaks of wrecks,
And bellies down with black alarms.
I say: 'Thus from my lady's arms
I go; those arms I love the best!'
The wind replies from dip and rise,
'Nay; toward her arms thou journeyest.'

A distant verge morosely gray
Appears, while clots of flying foam
Break from its muddy monochrome,
And a light blinks up far away.
I sigh: 'My eyes now as all day
Behold her ebon loops of hair!'
Like bursting bonds the wind responds,
'Nay, wait for tresses flashing fair!'

From tides the lofty coastlands screen
Come smitings like the slam of doors,
Or hammerings on hollow floors,
As the swell cleaves through caves unseen.
Say I: 'Though broad this wild terrene,
Her city home is matched of none!'
From the hoarse skies the wind replies:
'Thou shouldst have said her sea-bord one.'

The all-prevailing clouds exclude
The one quick timorous transient star;
The waves outside where breakers are
Huzza like a mad multitude.

The Five Students
28 course] course, MS, MV, WE, PE, ME
30] Somewhither yon. (The rest – anon. *del*) MS
MS has two further stanzas, described as '[Omitted from first edition]', as follows:

And what do they say in that yon Pale Land/Who trod the track with me,/If there they dwell, and watch, and understand?/They murmur, it may be,/'All of us – how we strode, as still does that lean thrall/For nought at all!'

The Years may add: 'Peace; know ye not,/Life's ashy track hence eying,/That though gilt Vanity called your eyes somewhat,/And ye were torn in trying,/All of you, while you panted, saw aureola'd far/Heaven's central star?'

The Wind's Prophecy
2 glint] shine MS
7 dip] vale MS
14 loops] locks MS
17 coastlands] coastlines WE, ME
18 smitings] noises MS
20 cleaves through] dives up MS
21 wild terrene] royal mesne MS
23 hoarse] loud MS
23 replies:] replies; MS

'Where the sun ups it, mist-imbued,'
I cry, 'there reigns the star for me!'
The wind outshrieks from points and peaks:
'Here, westward, where it downs, mean ye!'

Yonder the headland, vulturine,
Snores like old Skrymer in his sleep,
And every chasm and every steep
Blackens as wakes each pharos-shine.
'I roam, but one is safely mine,'
I say. 'God grant she stay my own!'
Low laughs the wind as if it grinned:
'Thy Love is one thou'st not yet known.'

Rewritten from an old copy

441 *During Wind and Rain*

THEY sing their dearest songs –
He, she, all of them – yea,
Treble and tenor and bass,
 And one to play;
With the candles mooning each face. . . .
 Ah, no; the years O!
How the sick leaves reel down in throngs!

They clear the creeping moss –
Elders and juniors – aye,
Making the pathways neat
 And the garden gay;
And they build a shady seat. . . .
 Ah, no; the years, the years;
See, the white storm-birds wing across!

They are blithely breakfasting all –
Men and maidens – yea,
Under the summer tree,
 With a glimpse of the bay,
While pet fowl come to the knee. . . .
 Ah, no; the years O!
And the rotten rose is ript from the wall.

The Wind's Prophecy
29 ups it,] rises MS
30 reigns] shines MS
32 downs] sets MS
32 ye!] ye. MS
34 old Skrymer] a giant MS, MV1
36 pharos-shine] lighthouse-shine MS
37 roam] stray MS *before revision*
37 mine,] mine! MS
Rewritten . . . copy] From old notes MS *before revision*

During Wind and Rain
2 yea,] yea MS
7 sick leaves reel] sickened leaves drop MS *before revision*
9 aye] yea MS, MV1, PE
13 the years, the years;] the years O! MS, MV1, PE
14 white] webbed white MS, MV, WE, PE, CP1, ME
14 across!] across. MS, MV, WE, PE, CP1, ME
19 fowl] birds MS, MV1, PE
21] And the wind-whipt creeper lets go the wall. MS *before revision*

They change to a high new house,
He, she, all of them – aye,
Clocks and carpets and chairs
    On the lawn all day,
And brightest things that are theirs. . . .
    Ah, no; the years, the years;
Down their carved names the rain-drop ploughs.

TITLE:
He prefers the earthly MS

442 *He Prefers Her Earthly*

THIS after-sunset is a sight for seeing,
Cliff-heads of craggy cloud surrounding it.
  – And dwell you in that glory-show?
You may; for there are strange strange things in being,
    Stranger than I know.

Yet if that chasm of splendour claim your presence
Which glows between the ash cloud and the dun,
  How changed must be your mortal mould!
Changed to a firmament-riding earthless essence
    From what you were of old:

All too unlike the fond and fragile creature
Then known to me. . . . Well, shall I say it plain?
  I would not have you thus and there,
But still would grieve on, missing you, still feature
    You as the one you were.

443 *The Dolls*

'WHENEVER you dress me dolls, mammy,
    Why do you dress them so,
And make them gallant soldiers,
    When never a one I know;
And not as gentle ladies
    With frills and frocks and curls,
As people dress the dollies
    Of other little girls?'

During Wind and Rain
23 aye] yea MS, MV1, PE
26 theirs. . . .] theirs. . . . . MS
27 the years, the years;] the years O! MS, MV1, PE
28] On their chiselled names the lichen grows. MS *before revision*
28 carved] chiselled MS, MV, WE, PE, CP1, ME

He Prefers Her Earthly
12 me. . . .] me. . . . . MS

The Dolls
4 know;] know, MS
8–9 Stanza break in all editions

Ah – why did she not answer: –
        'Because your mammy's heed
Is always gallant soldiers,
        As well may be, indeed.
One of them was your daddy,
        His name I must not tell;
He's not the dad who lives here,
        But one I love too well.'

444 *Molly Gone*

TITLE:
Molly gone MS

No more summer for Molly and me;
    There is snow on the tree,
And the blackbirds plump large as the rooks are, almost,
    And the water is hard
Where they used to dip bills at the dawn ere her figure was lost
    To these coasts, now my prison close-barred.

No more planting by Molly and me
    Where the beds used to be
Of sweet-william; no training the clambering rose
    By the framework of fir
Now bowering the pathway, whereon it swings gaily and blows
    As if calling commendment from her.

No more jauntings by Molly and me
    To the town by the sea,
Or along over Whitesheet to Wynyard's green Gap,
    Catching Montacute Crest
To the right against Sedgmoor, and Corton-Hill's far-distant cap,
    And Pilsdon and Lewsdon to west.

No more singing by Molly to me
    In the evenings when she
Was in mood and in voice, and the candles were lit,
    And past the porch-quoin
The rays would spring out on the laurels; and dumbledores hit
    On the pane, as if wishing to join.

Molly Gone
1 me;] me, MS
2 tree,] tree MS
3 plump] seem MS
5 at] in MS
6 my] a MS

Where, then, is Molly, who's no more with me?
– As I stand on this lea,
Thinking thus, there's a many-flamed star in the air,
That tosses a sign
That her glance is regarding its face from her home, so that there
Her eyes may have meetings with mine.

445 *A Backward Spring*

THE trees are afraid to put forth buds,
And there is timidity in the grass;
The plots lie gray where gouged by spuds,
And whether next week will pass
Free of sly sour winds is the fret of each bush
Of barberry waiting to bloom.

Yet the snowdrop's face betrays no gloom,
And the primrose pants in its heedless push,
Though the myrtle asks if it's worth the fight
This year with frost and rime
To venture one more time
On delicate leaves and buttons of white
From the selfsame bough as at last year's prime,
And never to ruminate on or remember
What happened to it in mid-December.

April 1917

446 *Looking Across*

I

IT is dark in the sky,
And silence is where
Our laughs rang high;
And recall do I
That One is out there.

Molly Gone
27 many-flamed] many-rayed MS, MV1, PE
28 tosses] twinkles MS: flickers MV1, PE

A Backward Spring
3 gouged] broken MS, MV1, PE
12 buttons] buds MS, MV1, PE

Looking Across
3] We said Good-bye; MS, MV1

II

The dawn is not nigh,
And the trees are bare,
And the waterways sigh
That a year has drawn by,
And Two are out there.

III

The wind drops to die
Like the phantom of Care
Too frail for a cry,
And heart brings to eye
That Three are out there.

IV

This Life runs dry
That once ran rare
And rosy in dye,
And fleet the days fly,
And Four are out there.

V

Tired, tired am I
Of this earthly air,
And my wraith asks: Why,
Since these calm lie,
Are not Five out there?

December 1915

447 *At a Seaside Town in 1869*

TITLE:
At a Seaside Town, 1869 MS

(*Young Lover's Reverie*)

I WENT and stood outside myself,
 Spelled the dark sky
 And ship-lights nigh,
And grumbling winds that passed thereby.

Looking Across
9 drawn] gone MS
14] And it's in my mind's eye MS, MV1, PE
19 fleet] quick MS
23 asks:] asks; MS
24 calm lie] have passed by MS, MV1, PE
24 calm] calmly MV2, WE, CP1

Then next inside myself I looked,
    And there, above
    All, shone my Love,
That nothing matched the image of.

Beyond myself again I ranged;
    And saw the free
    Life by the sea,
And folk indifferent to me.

O 'twas a charm to draw within
    Thereafter, where
    But she was; care
For one thing only, her hid there!

But so it chanced, without myself
    I had to look,
    And then I took
More heed of what I had long forsook:

The boats, the sands, the esplanade,
    The laughing crowd;
    Light-hearted, loud
Greetings from some not ill-endowed;

The evening sunlit cliffs, the talk,
    Hailings and halts,
    The keen sea-salts,
The band, the Morgenblätter Waltz.

Still, when at night I drew inside
    Forward she came,
    Sad, but the same
As when I first had known her name.

Then rose a time when, as by force,
    Outwardly wooed
    By contacts crude,
Her image in abeyance stood. . . .

At a Seaside Town in 1869
9 ranged] went MS
13 draw] go MS
20 forsook:] forsook. MS, MV, PE
24 ill-endowed;] ill-endowed: MS, MV1, PE
28 Waltz] waltz MS
33 force,] force MS

At last I said; This outside life
Shall not endure;
I'll seek the pure
Thought-world, and bask in her allure.

Myself again I crept within,
Scanned with keen care
The temple where
She'd shone, but could not find her there.

I sought and sought. But O her soul
Has not since thrown
Upon my own
One beam! Yea, she is gone, is gone.

From an old note

448 The Glimpse

SHE sped through the door
And, following in haste,
And stirred to the core,
I entered hot-faced;
But I could not find her,
No sign was behind her.
'Where is she?' I said:
– 'Who?' they asked that sat there;
'Not a soul's come in sight.'
– 'A maid with red hair.'
– 'Ah.' They paled. 'She is dead.
People see her at night,
But you are the first
On whom she has burst
In the keen common light.'

It was ages ago,
When I was quite strong:
I have waited since, – O,
I have waited so long!

At a Seaside Town in 1869
37 said;] said: MS, MV, WE, PE, ME
41 crept] went MS
48 beam!] beam. MS

The Glimpse
11 dead.] dead. . . . MS, MV1, PE

– Yea, I set me to own
The house, where now lone
I dwell in void rooms
Booming hollow as tombs!
But I never come near her,
Though nightly I hear her.
And my cheek has grown thin
And my hair has grown gray
With this waiting therein;
But she still keeps away!

449 *The Pedestrian*

An Incident of 1883

'SIR, will you let me give you a ride?
Nox venit, and the heath is wide.'
– My phaeton-lantern shone on one
Young, fair, even fresh,
But burdened with flesh:
A leathern satchel at his side,
His breathings short, his coat undone.

'Twas as if his corpulent figure slopped
With the shake of his walking when he stopped,
And, though the night's pinch grew acute,
He wore but a thin
Wind-thridded suit,
Yet well-shaped shoes for walking in,
Artistic beaver, cane gold-topped.

'Alas, my friend,' he said with a smile,
'I am daily bound to foot ten mile –
Wet, dry, or dark – before I rest.
Six months to live
My doctors give
Me as my prospect here, at best,
Unless I vamp my sturdiest!'

The Glimpse
Note ll. 20–5 seem to be a later addition to MS

The Pedestrian
2 *Nox venit*, and] The night gets dense, MS, MV1
5 flesh:] flesh; MS
12 Wind-thridded] Alpaca MS
14 beaver] garments MS, MV1
16 foot] walk MS

His voice was that of a man refined,
A man, one well could feel, of mind,
Quite winning in its musical ease;
    But in mould maligned
    By some disease;
And I asked again. But he shook his head;
Then, as if more were due, he said: –

'A student was I – of Schopenhauer,
Kant, Hegel, – and the fountained bower
Of the Muses, too, knew my regard:
    But ah – I fear me
    The grave gapes near me! . . .
Would I could this gross sheath discard,
And rise an ethereal shape, unmarred!'

How I remember him! – his short breath,
His aspect, marked for early death,
As he dropped into the night for ever;
    One caught in his prime
    Of high endeavour;
From all philosophies soon to sever
Through an unconscienced trick of Time!

450 Who's in the Next Room?

TITLE:
'Who's in the Next Room?' MS

'WHO's in the next room? – who?
    I seemed to see
Somebody in the dawning passing through,
    Unknown to me.'
'Nay: you saw nought. He passed invisibly.'

'Who's in the next room? – who?
    I seem to hear
Somebody muttering firm in a language new
    That chills the ear.'
'No: you catch not his tongue who has entered there.'

The Pedestrian
24 ease;] ease, MS
25 mould] form MS
28 Then] And MS
28 he] then MS
30 fountained] rosier MS

'Who's in the next room? – who?
I seem to feel
His breath like a clammy draught, as if it drew
From the Polar Wheel.'
'No: none who breathes at all does the door conceal.'

'Who's in the next room? – who?
A figure wan
With a message to one in there of something due?
Shall I know him anon?'
'Yea he; and he brought such; and you'll know him anon.

451 *At a Country Fair*

AT a bygone Western country fair
I saw a giant led by a dwarf
With a red string like a long thin scarf;
How much he was the stronger there
The giant seemed unaware.

And then I saw that the giant was blind,
And the dwarf a shrewd-eyed little thing;
The giant, mild, timid, obeyed the string
As if he had no independent mind,
Or will of any kind.

Wherever the dwarf decided to go
At his heels the other trotted meekly,
(Perhaps – I know not – reproaching weakly)
Like one Fate bade that it must be so,
Whether he wished or no.

Various sights in various climes
I have seen, and more I may see yet,
But that sight never shall I forget,
And have thought it the sorriest of pantomimes,
If once, a hundred times!

At a Country Fair
19 pantomimes,] pantomimes. MV1, PE
20 times!] times. MS

452 *The Memorial Brass: 186–*

INDENTATION:
In MS l. 1 of each stanza originally had its own line of indentation between that of ll. 3, 5 and 2, 4. Subsequently, l. 1 of stanzas 1 and 3 has been moved right to line up with ll. 2, 4

'WHY do you weep there, O sweet lady,
Why do you weep before that brass? –
(I'm a mere student sketching the mediaeval)
Is some late death lined there, alas? –
Your father's? . . . Well, all pay the debt that paid he!'

'Young man, O must I tell! – My husband's! And under
His name I set mine, and my *death*! –
Its date left vacant till my heirs should fill it,
Stating me faithful till my last breath.'
– 'Madam, that you are a widow wakes my wonder!'

'O wait! For last month I – remarried!
And now I fear 'twas a deed amiss.
We've just come home. And I am sick and saddened
At what the new one will say to this;
And will he think – think that I should have tarried?

'I may add, surely, – with no wish to harm him –
That he's a temper – yes, I fear!
And when he comes to church next Sunday morning,
And sees that written . . . O dear, O dear!'
– 'Madam, I swear your beauty will disarm him!'

453 *Her Love-Birds*

TITLE:
Her (The *del*) Love-birds MS

WHEN I looked up at my love-birds
That Sunday afternoon,
There was in their tiny tune
A dying fetch like broken words,
When I looked up at my love-birds
That Sunday afternoon.

The Memorial Brass: 186–
3 student] architect MS *before revision*
4 Is] – Is MS
7 *death*!] *death* MS
8 it,] it MS
9] As his grieved widow's, at my last breath.' MS
9 faithful] his MV1, PE
11 remarried] re-married MS
14] At what he'll say when he sees this; MS, MV1, PE
16 add,] add WE, ME
17 That he's] He has MS, MV1, PE
19 written . . .] written. . . . MS

Her Love-Birds
4 fetch] fall MS

When he, too, scanned the love-birds
 On entering there that day,
 'Twas as if he had nought to say
Of his long journey citywards,
When he, too, scanned the love-birds,
 On entering there that day.

And billed and billed the love-birds,
 As 'twere in fond despair
 At the stress of silence where
Had once been tones in tenor thirds,
And billed and billed the love-birds
 As 'twere in fond despair.

O, his speech that chilled the love-birds,
 And smote like death on me,
 As I learnt what was to be,
And knew my life was broke in sherds!
O, his speech that chilled the love-birds,
 And smote like death on me!

EXTRA PRINTINGS:
(1) *Selected Poems*, p. 111 [The poem's first printing]
(2) *Chosen Poems*, p. 145

454 *Paying Calls*

I WENT by footpath and by stile
 Beyond where bustle ends,
Strayed here a mile and there a mile
 And called upon some friends.

On certain ones I had not seen
 For years past did I call,
And then on others who had been
 The oldest friends of all.

It was the time of midsummer
 When they had used to roam;
But now, though tempting was the air,
 I found them all at home.

Her Love-Birds
11 love-birds,] love-birds MS
13 love-birds,] love-birds MS
20 me,] me! MS
22 sherds!] sherds. MS

Paying Calls
3 there a mile] there a mile, SP, WE, ME

I spoke to one and other of them
By mound and stone and tree
Of things we had done ere days were dim,
But they spoke not to me.

455 *The Upper Birch-Leaves*

TITLE:
The Upper Leaves MS

INDENTATION:
l. 24 in MS is indented right

WARM yellowy-green
In the blue serene,
How they skip and sway
On this autumn day!
They cannot know
What has happened below, –
That their boughs down there
Are already quite bare,
That their own will be
When a week has passed, –
For they jig as in glee
To this very last.

But no; there lies
At times in their tune
A note that cries
What at first I fear
I did not hear:
'O we remember
At each wind's hollo –
Though life holds yet –
We go hence soon,
For 'tis November;
– But that you follow
You may forget!'

456 *It Never Looks Like Summer*

TITLE:
'It never looks like Summer' MS

'IT never looks like summer here
On Beeny by the sea.'
But though she saw its looks as drear,
Summer it seemed to me.

Paying Calls
14 mound] path MS, MV1, PE

The Upper Birch-Leaves
2 serene] bright sheen MS
11 jig] trill MS
23 you] *you* MS, MV, WE, PE, ME

It Never Looks Like Summer
3 she . . . as] to her its look was MS, MV1, PE
4–5 Stanza break in all editions

It never looks like summer now
    Whatever weather's there;
But ah, it cannot anyhow,
    On Beeny or elsewhere!

Boscastle
8 March 1913

457 *Everything Comes*

'THE house is bleak and cold
    Built so new for me!
All the winds upon the wold
    Search it through for me;
No screening trees abound,
And the curious eyes around,
    Keep on view for me.'

'My Love, I am planting trees
    As a screen for you
Both from winds, and eyes that tease
    And peer in for you.
Only wait till they have grown,
No such bower will be known
    As I mean for you.'

'Then I will bear it, Love,
    And will wait,' she said.
– So, with years, there grew a grove.
    'Skill how great!' she said.
'As you wished, Dear?' – 'Yes, I see!
But – I'm dying; and for me
    'Tis too late,' she said.

458 *The Man with a Past*

THERE was merry-making
When the first dart fell
As a heralding, –

It Never Looks Like Summer
7 ah,] then MS, MV1
8 elsewhere!] elsewhere. MS
MS has 'Saturday' *deleted* between 'Boscastle' and date

Everything Comes
3 All the] All MS
6 around,] around MS, MV, WE, PE, ME
19] 'As you wished?' – 'It is, I see! MS
21 too late] *too late* MS

The Man with a Past
1 merry-making] merrymaking MS

Till grinned the fully bared thing,
And froze like a spell –
Like a spell.

Innocent was she,
Innocent was I,
Too simple we!
Before us we did not see,
Nearing, aught wry –
Aught wry!

I can tell it not now,
It was long ago;
And such things cow;
But that is why and how
Two lives were so –
Were so.

Yes, the years matured,
And the blows were three
That time ensured
On her, which she dumbly endured;
And one on me –
One on me.

459 *He Fears His Good Fortune*

THERE was a glorious time
At an epoch of my prime;
Mornings beryl-bespread,
And evenings golden-red;
Nothing gray:
And in my heart I said,
'However this chanced to be,
It is too full for me,
Too rare, too rapturous, rash,
Its spell must close with a crash
Some day!'

EXTRA MANUSCRIPT:
Present whereabouts unknown. Checked from a facsimile, marked '[First rough Draft?]', in Hodgson's Sale Catalogue, 23 Feb 1961 = H

TITLE:
He fears his Good Fortune MS
He fears his good-fortune H

The Man with a Past
4 bared] seen MS
24 me.] me! MS

He Fears His Good Fortune
4 golden-red] gold and red MS, H
5 gray:] gray; H
7 'However] However H
11 day!'] day! H
11–12 Stanza break in all editions

The radiance went on
Anon and yet anon,
And sweetness fell around
Like manna on the ground.
'I've no claim,'
Said I, 'to be thus crowned:
I am not worthy this: –
Must it not go amiss? –
Well . . . let the end foreseen
Come duly! – I am serene.'
– And it came.

460 *He Wonders About Himself*

No use hoping, or feeling vext,
Tugged by a force above or under
Like some fantocine, much I wonder
What I shall find me doing next!

Shall I be rushing where bright eyes be?
Shall I be suffering sorrows seven?
Shall I be watching the stars of heaven,
Thinking one of them looks like thee?

Part is mine of the general Will,
Cannot my share in the sum of sources
Bend a digit the poise of forces,
And a fair desire fulfil?

Nov. 1893

461 *Jubilate*

TITLE:
Pencil erasions around MS title indicate that 'The Merry Underground Dancing Party' was considered as an alternative

'THE very last time I ever was here,' he said,
'I saw much less of the quick than I saw of the dead.'
– He was a man I had met with somewhere before,
But how or when I now could recall no more.

He Fears His Good Fortune
16 'I've] I've H
16 claim,'] claim, H
17 'to] to H
20 Well . . .] Well. . . . H
21 serene.'] serene. H
Before revision ll. 16–22 in H read:
I exclaim/O why does such abound?/And am I worthy this?/Must it not go amiss? –/The end I have foreseen;/Let it come; I am serene. . . ./Well – it came.

He Wonders About Himself
3 fantocine] automaton MS *before revision*
10–11] Cannot my share in the sum of forces/Bend a hairsbreadth creature-courses, MS [Next to these lines in MS Hardy has written 'Incorrectly printed in some Editions'. His copy of CP2 has been corrected to read: Cannot my share in the sume of forces/Bend a digit creature courses,]
12 fair] fain MS

'The hazy mazy moonlight at one in the morning
Spread out as a sea across the frozen snow,
Glazed to live sparkles like the great breastplate adorning
The priest of the Temple, with Urim and Thummim aglow.

'The yew-tree arms, glued hard to the stiff stark air,
Hung still in the village sky as theatre-scenes
When I came by the churchyard wall, and halted there
At a shut-in sound of fiddles and tambourines.

'And as I stood hearkening, dulcimers, hautboys, and shawms,
And violoncellos, and a three-stringed double-bass,
Joined in, and were intermixed with a singing of psalms;
And I looked over at the dead men's dwelling-place.

'Through the shine of the slippery snow I now could see,
As it were through a crystal roof, a great company
Of the dead minueting in stately step underground
To the tune of the instruments I had before heard sound.

'It was "Eden New", and dancing they sang in a chore,
"We are out of it all! – yea, in Little-Ease cramped no more!"
And their shrouded figures pacing with joy I could see
As you see the stage from the gallery. And they had no heed of me.

'And I lifted my head quite dazed from the churchyard wall
And I doubted not that it warned I should soon have my call.
But—' . . . Then in the ashes he emptied the dregs of his cup,
And onward he went, and the darkness swallowed him up.

462 He Revisits His First School

TITLE:
He revisits his first school MS

I SHOULD not have shown in the flesh,
I ought to have gone as a ghost;
It was awkward, unseemly almost,
Standing solidly there as when fresh,
Pink, tiny, crisp-curled,
My pinions yet furled
From the winds of the world.

Jubilate
7 breastplate] breast-plate ME
11 the churchyard wall,] Mellstock Ridge MS *before revision*
12 tambourines.] tambourines, MS
18 crystal] glass MS
18 a great] quite a great MS
19 minueting . . . step] allemanding without shoes MS
21 Eden] Wilton MS
22 yea . . . cramped] we can suffer on earth MS
23 pacing] whirling MS
26] That for weeks thereafter marked my chin with a gall. . . . MS
27 But –] Yes. MS

He Revisits His First School
1 shown] gone MS

After waiting so many a year
To wait longer, and go as a sprite
From the tomb at the mid of some night
Was the right, radiant way to appear;
    Not as one wanzing weak
    From life's roar and reek,
    His rest still to seek:

Yea, beglimpsed through the quaint quarried glass
Of green moonlight, by me greener made,
When they'd cry, perhaps, 'There sits his shade
In his olden haunt – just as he was
    When in Walkingame he
    Conned the grand Rule-of-Three
    With the bent of a bee.'

But to show in the afternoon sun,
With an aspect of hollow-eyed care,
When none wished to see me come there,
Was a garish thing, better undone.
    Yes; wrong was the way;
    But yet, let me say,
    I may right it – some day.

463 *I Thought, My Heart*

EXTRA MANUSCRIPT:
In the Dorset County Museum = DCM

TITLE:
'I thought, my Heart' MS. DCM

Note A third stanza was written by Hardy on the verso of f. 141 of MS. A pencilled note after stanza 2 says: [A third verse, as overleaf, was not printed]. It was subsequently printed, with the first two stanzas, in *Pages from the Works of Thomas Hardy*, ed. Ruth Head (London, 1922), p. 171 = RH. It is described there as: (Unpublished third verse, specially communicated for this Selection)

I THOUGHT, my Heart, that you had healed
Of those sore smartings of the past,
And that the summers had oversealed
    All mark of them at last.
But closely scanning in the night
I saw them standing crimson-bright
        Just as she made them:
        Nothing could fade them;
        Yea, I can swear
        That there they were –
        They still were there!

He Revisits His First School
12 wanzing] growing MS
14 seek:] seek. MS
15 beglimpsed] in gleams MS
21] Assiduously.' MS
22 show] go MS
28 it – some] it some MS

I Thought, My Heart
3 summers] Summers DCM
7 them:] them; DCM
10 were –] were, DCM
11 there!] there. MS
11–12 Stanza break in all editions

Then the Vision of her who cut them came,
And looking over my shoulder said,
'I am sure you deal me all the blame
For those sharp smarts and red;
But meet me, dearest, to-morrow night,
In the churchyard at the moon's half-height,
And so strange a kiss
Shall be mine, I wis,
That you'll cease to know
If the wounds you show
Be there or no!'

464 *Fragment*

EXTRA PRINTING:
Chosen Poems, pp. 229–30

INDENTATION:
1 = ll. 1, 4, 6, 9, 12, 15
2 = ll. 2, 3, 5, 10
3 = ll. 7, 11, 13, 18–25
4 = ll. 8, 14, 16, 17, 26 MS

AT last I entered a long dark gallery,
Catacomb-lined; and ranged at the side
Were the bodies of men from far and wide
Who, motion past, were nevertheless not dead.

'The sense of waiting here strikes strong;
Everyone's waiting, waiting, it seems to me;
What are you waiting for so long? –
What is to happen?' I said.

'O we are waiting for one called God,' said they,
'(Though by some the Will, or Force, or Laws;
And, vaguely, by some, the Ultimate Cause);
Waiting for him to see us before we are clay.
Yes; waiting, waiting, for God *to know it*.' . . .
'To know what?' questioned I.
'To know how things have been going on earth and below it:
It is clear he must know some day.'
I thereon asked them why.
'Since he made us humble pioneers
Of himself in consciousness of Life's tears,
It needs no mighty prophecy
To tell that what he could mindlessly show
His creatures, he himself will know.

I Thought, My Heart
20–2] That you will swear/With heart laid bare/No wounds are there.' DCM *before revision*
22 no!] no. MS, DCM
The third stanza in MS reads as follows:
23 That kiss so strange, so stark, I'll take
24 When the world sleeps sound, and no noise will scare,
25 And a moon-touch whitens each stone and stake,
26 Yes; I will meet her there –
27 Just at the time she calls 'to-morrow,'
28 But I call 'after the shut of sorrow –'
29 And with her dwell,
30 Her parallel
31 In quit of pain
32 And frost, and rain,
33 And Life's inane.
RH has the following variants: l. 25 stake: l. 27 *'to-morrow'* l. 28 *'after the shut of sorrow,'* l. 29 dwell – l. 31 In cease of pain, l. 32 frost l. 33 life's

Fragment
4 motion past] motionless MS, MV1
13–14 Stanza break in CHP, CP4
19 himself] himself, MS
19 Life's] men's MS
22–3 Stanza break in all editions

'By some still close-cowled mystery
We have reached feeling faster than he,
But he will overtake us anon,
If the world goes on.'

465 *Midnight on the Great Western*

In the third-class seat sat the journeying boy,
And the roof-lamp's oily flame
Played down on his listless form and face,
Bewrapt past knowing to what he was going,
Or whence he came.

In the band of his hat the journeying boy
Had a ticket stuck; and a string
Around his neck bore the key of his box,
That twinkled gleams of the lamp's sad beams
Like a living thing.

What past can be yours, O journeying boy
Towards a world unknown,
Who calmly, as if incurious quite
On all at stake, can undertake
This plunge alone?

Knows your soul a sphere, O journeying boy,
Our rude realms far above,
Whence with spacious vision you mark and mete
This region of sin that you find you in,
But are not of?

TITLE:
Honeymoon-time at an Inn MS

466 *Honeymoon Time at an Inn*

At the shiver of morning, a little before the false dawn,
The moon was at the window-square,
Deedily brooding in deformed decay –
The curve hewn off her cheek as by an adze;
At the shiver of morning a little before the false dawn
So the moon looked in there.

Fragment
23 close-cowled] close-cloaked MS

Midnight on the Great Western
3 Played] Shone MS
13 incurious] indifferent MS, MV1, PE
14 On] To MS, MV1, PE
18 mark] measure MS

Honeymoon Time at an Inn
3 decay –] decay, MS

Her speechless eyeing reached across the chamber,
Where lay two souls opprest,
One a white lady sighing, 'Why am I sad!'
To him who sighed back, 'Sad, my Love, am I!'
And speechlessly the old moon conned the chamber,
And these two reft of rest.

While their large-pupilled vision swept the scene there,
Nought seeming imminent,
Something fell sheer, and crashed, and from the floor
Lay glittering at the pair with a shattered gaze,
While their large-pupilled vision swept the scene there,
And the many-eyed thing outleant.

With a start they saw that it was an old-time pier-glass
Which had stood on the mantel near,
Its silvering blemished, – yes, as if worn away
By the eyes of the countless dead who had smirked at it
Ere these two ever knew that old-time pier-glass
And its vague and vacant leer.

As he looked, his bride like a moth skimmed forth, and kneeling
Quick, with quivering sighs,
Gathered the pieces under the moon's sly ray,
Unwitting as an automaton what she did;
Till he entreated, hasting to where she was kneeling,
'Let it stay where it lies!'

'Long years of sorrow this means!' breathed the lady
As they retired. 'Alas!'
And she lifted one pale hand across her eyes.
'Don't trouble, Love; it's nothing,' the bridegroom said.
'Long years of sorrow for us!' murmured the lady,
'Or ever this evil pass!'

And the Spirits Ironic laughed behind the wainscot,
And the Spirits of Pity sighed.
'It's good,' said the Spirits Ironic, 'to tickle their minds
With a portent of their wedlock's aftergrinds.'
And the Spirits of Pity sighed behind the wainscot,
'It's a portent we cannot abide!

Honeymoon Time at an Inn
19 With a] In their MS
21 Its silvering] Quicksilver MS
28 Unwitting] Unconscious MS, MV1, PE
31 breathed] said MS, MV1, PE
33 pale] small MS
40 aftergrinds] after-woes MS: after-grinds WE, ME [MV, PE have line break]

'More, what shall happen to prove the truth of the portent?'
– 'Oh; in brief, they will fade till old,
And their loves grow numbed ere death, by the cark of care.'
– 'But nought see we that asks for portents there? –
'Tis the lot of all.' – 'Well, no less true is a portent
That it fits all mortal mould.'

467 The Robin

WHEN up aloft
I fly and fly,
I see in pools
The shining sky,
And a happy bird
Am I, am I!

When I descend
Towards their brink
I stand, and look,
And stoop, and drink,
And bathe my wings,
And chink and prink.

When winter frost
Makes earth as steel
I search and search
But find no meal,
And most unhappy
Then I feel.

But when it lasts,
And snows still fall,
I get to feel
No grief at all,
For I turn to a cold stiff
Feathery ball!

The Robin
1 aloft] aloft, WE, ME
2 fly] fly, MS
6 I!] I. MS
21–2] I soon escape/My troubles all, MS *before revision*

468 *I Rose and Went to Rou'tor Town*

(*She, alone*)

TITLE:
'I rose and went to Rou'tor Town' MS
(*She, alone*)] Not in MS, MV1, PE

I ROSE and went to Rou'tor Town
  With gaiety and good heart,
  And ardour for the start,
That morning ere the moon was down
That lit me off to Rou'tor Town
  With gaiety and good heart.

When sojourn soon at Rou'tor Town
  Wrote sorrows on my face,
  I strove that none should trace
The pale and gray, once pink and brown,
When sojourn soon at Rou'tor Town
  Wrote sorrows on my face.

The evil wrought at Rou'tor Town
  On him I'd loved so true
  I cannot tell anew:
But nought can quench, but nought can drown
The evil wrought at Rou'tor Town
  On him I'd loved so true!

469 *The Nettles*

  THIS, then, is the grave of my son,
  Whose heart she won! And nettles grow
Upon his mound; and she lives just below.

  How he upbraided me, and left,
  And our lives were cleft, because I said
She was hard, unfeeling, caring but to wed.

  Well, to see this sight I have fared these miles,
  And her firelight smiles from her window there,
Whom he left his mother to cherish with tender care!

I Rose and Went to Rou'tor Town
14–15] To thoughts I'd cherished well/'Tis not in me to tell, MS *before revision*
18] To thoughts I'd cherished well! MS *before revision*

It is enough. I'll turn and go;
Yes, nettles grow where lone lies he,
Who spurned me for seeing what he could not see.

TITLE:
In a Waiting Room MS

470 *In a Waiting-Room*

ON a morning sick as the day of doom
With the drizzling gray
Of an English May,
There were few in the railway waiting-room.
About its walls were framed and varnished
Pictures of liners, fly-blown, tarnished.
The table bore a Testament
For travellers' reading, if suchwise bent.

I read it on and on,
And, thronging the Gospel of Saint John,
Were figures – additions, multiplications –
By some one scrawled, with sundry emendations;
Not scoffingly designed,
But with an absent mind, –
Plainly a bagman's counts of cost,
What he had profited, what lost;
And whilst I wondered if there could have been
Any particle of a soul
In that poor man at all,
To cypher rates of wage
Upon that printed page,
There joined in the charmless scene
And stood over me and the scribbled book
(To lend the hour's mean hue
A smear of tragedy too)
A soldier and wife, with haggard look
Subdued to stone by strong endeavour;
And then I heard
From a casual word
They were parting as they believed for ever.

In a Waiting-Room
10 thronging] mixed with MS
22 charmless] dreary MS, MV1, PE
23 book] book, MS
30–1 Stanza break in all editions except WE where there is a page turn

But next there came
Like the eastern flame
Of some high altar, children – a pair –
Who laughed at the fly-blown pictures there.
'Here are the lovely ships that we,
Mother, are by and by going to see!
When we get there it's 'most sure to be fine,
And the band will play, and the sun will shine!'

It rained on the skylight with a din
As we waited and still no train came in;
But the words of the child in the squalid room
Had spread a glory through the gloom.

471 *The Clock-Winder*

TITLE:
The Clockwinder MS

IT is dark as a cave,
Or a vault in the nave
When the iron door
Is closed, and the floor
Of the church relaid
With trowel and spade.

But the parish-clerk
Cares not for the dark
As he winds in the tower
At a regular hour
The rheumatic clock
Whose dilatory knock
You can hear when praying
At the day's decaying,
Or at any lone while
From a pew in the aisle.

Up, up from the ground
Around and around
In the turret stair
He clambers, to where

In a Waiting-Room
33 Of. . . altar] Of morning in April MS, MV1, PE
40 in;] in, MS
41–2] But a glory had been brought into the room/By the faith of the child amid the gloom. MS *before revision*
41 room] gloom MS
42 gloom] room MS

The Clock-Winder
11 clock] clock, MS, MV, WE, PE ME
20–1 No stanza break

The wheelwork is,
With its tick, click, whizz,
Reposefully measuring
Each day to its end
That mortal men spend
In sorrowing and pleasuring.
Nightly thus does he climb
To the trackway of Time.

Him I followed one night
To this place without light,
And, ere I spoke, heard
Him say, word by word,
At the end of his winding,
The darkness unminding: –

'So I wipe out one more,
My Dear, of the sore
Sad days that still be,
Like a drying Dead Sea,
Between you and me!'

Who she was no man knew:
He had long borne him blind
To all womankind;
And was ever one who
Kept his past out of view.

EXTRA MANUSCRIPT:
In the Dorset County Museum = DCM

472 *Old Excursions*

'WHAT'S the good of going to Ridgeway,
    Cerne, or Sydling Mill,
    Or to Yell'ham Hill,
Blithely bearing Casterbridge-way
    As we used to do?
She will no more climb up there,
Or be visible anywhere
    In those haunts we knew.'

The Clock-Winder
21 wheelwork] machinery MS, MV1, PE
23 Reposefully] Deliberately MS, MV1, PE
29–44 Not in MS

Old Excursions
1 'What's] What's MS, DCM
2 Sydling] Sutton MS, DCM
6 there,] there MS
8 knew.'] knew. MS, DCM

But to-night, while walking weary,
Near me seemed her shade,
Come as 'twere to upbraid
This my mood in deeming dreary
Scenes that used to please;
And, if she did come to me,
Still solicitous, there may be
Good in going to these.

So, I'll care to roam to Ridgeway,
Cerne, or Sydling Mill,
Or to Yell'ham Hill,
Blithely bearing Casterbridge-way
As we used to do,
Since her phasm may flit out there,
And may greet me anywhere
In those haunts we knew.

April 1913

473 The Masked Face

I FOUND me in a great surging space,
At either end a door,
And I said: 'What is this giddying place,
With no firm-fixéd floor,
That I knew not of before?'
'It is Life,' said a mask-clad face.

I asked: 'But how do I come here,
Who never wished to come;
Can the light and air be made more clear,
The floor more quietsome,
And the doors set wide? They numb
Fast-locked, and fill with fear.'

Old Excursions
9 weary,] weary MS, DCM
17 So,] So DCM
18 Sydling] Sutton MS, DCM
22] If her phantom flits out there, MS, DCM
23 greet] meet MS, DCM
Below date DCM has: (copied)

The Masked Face
3 place,] place MV2, WE, ME
5] That I've never seen before?' MS
8 come;] come, MS

The mask put on a bleak smile then,
And said, 'O vassal-wight,
There once complained a goosequill pen
To the scribe of the Infinite
Of the words it had to write
Because they were past its ken.'

474 *In a Whispering Gallery*

THAT whisper takes the voice
Of a Spirit's compassionings,
Close, but invisible,
And throws me under a spell
At the kindling vision it brings;
And for a moment I rejoice,
And believe in transcendent things
That would mould from this muddy earth
A spot for the splendid birth
Of everlasting lives,
Whereto no night arrives;
And this gaunt gray gallery
A tabernacle of worth
On this drab-aired afternoon,
When you can barely see
Across its hazed lacune
If opposite aught there be
Of fleshed humanity
Wherewith I may commune;
Or if the voice so near
Be a soul's voice floating here.

EXTRA PRINTING:
Chosen Poems, pp. 216–17

TITLE:
The Something that saved him MS

475 *The Something that Saved Him*

IT was when
Whirls of thick waters laved me
Again and again,
That something arose and saved me;
Yea, it was then.

In a Whispering Gallery
1 takes] seems MS
2] Of a Spirit, speaking to me, MS, MV, WE, PE, CP1
8 mould from] make of MS, MV1, PE
10 lives,] lives MS, WE, ME
11 arrives;] arrives, MS
12] And from this gaunt gallery MV2, WE, ME
14 drab-aired] drab-fogged MS
15 barely] scarcely MS

In that day
Unseeing the azure went I
On my way,
And to white winter bent I,
Knowing no May.

Reft of renown,
Under the night clouds beating
Up and down,
In my needfulness greeting
Cit and clown.

Long there had been
Much of a murky colour
In the scene,
Dull prospects meeting duller;
Nought between.

Last, there loomed
A closing-in blind alley,
Though there boomed
A feeble summons to rally
Where it gloomed.

The clock rang;
The hour brought a hand to deliver;
I upsprang,
And looked back at den, ditch and river,
And sang.

476 The Enemy's Portrait

HE saw the portrait of his enemy, offered
At auction in a street he journeyed nigh,
That enemy, now late dead, who in his lifetime
Had injured deeply him the passer-by.
'To get that picture, pleased be God, I'll try,
And utterly destroy it; and no more
Shall be inflicted on man's mortal eye
A countenance so sinister and sore!'

The Something that Saved Him
14 needfulness] wistfulness MS, MV, WE, PE, ME
29 river,] river WE, ME

The Enemy's Portrait
1 enemy,] enemy MS

And so he bought the painting. Driving homeward,
'The frame will come in useful,' he declared,
'The rest is fuel.' On his arrival, weary,
Asked what he bore with him, and how he fared,
He said he had bid for a picture, though he cared
For the frame only: on the morrow he
Would burn the canvas, which could well be spared,
Seeing that it portrayed his enemy.

Next day some other duty found him busy:
The foe was laid his face against the wall;
But on the next he set himself to loosen
The straining-strips. And then a casual call
Prevented his proceeding therewithal;
And thus the picture waited, day by day,
Its owner's pleasure, like a wretched thrall,
Until a month and more had slipped away.

And then upon a morn he found it shifted,
Hung in a corner by a servitor.
'Why did you take on you to hang that picture?
You know it was the frame I bought it for.'
'It stood in the way of every visitor,
And I just hitched it there.' – 'Well, it must go:
I don't commemorate men whom I abhor.
Remind me 'tis to do. The frame I'll stow.'

But things become forgotten. In the shadow
Of the dark corner hung it by its string,
And there it stayed – once noticed by its owner,
Who said, 'Ah me – I must destroy that thing!'
But when he died, there, none remembering,
It hung, till moved to prominence, as one sees;
And comers pause and say, examining,
'I thought they were the bitterest enemies?'

The Enemy's Portrait
9 homeward,] homeward MS
12 bore] brought MS
13 bid for] bought MS
20 straining-strips] straining strips ME
36 Ah] Dear MS, MV1, PE
40 'I . . . the] 'Strange, I thought they were ME

477 *Imaginings*

SHE saw herself a lady
With fifty frocks in wear,
And rolling wheels, and rooms the best,
And faithful maidens' care,
And open lawns and shady
For weathers warm or drear.

She found herself a striver,
All liberal gifts debarred,
With days of gloom, and movements stressed,
And early visions marred,
And got no man to wive her
But one whose lot was hard.

Yet in the moony night-time
She steals to stile and lea
During his heavy slumberous rest
When homecome wearily,
And dreams of some blest bright-time
She knows can never be.

478 *On the Doorstep*

TITLE:
Staying and Going MS *before revision.* Hardy used a similar title for poem 528

THE rain imprinted the step's wet shine
With target-circles that quivered and crossed
As I was leaving this porch of mine;
When from within there swelled and paused
A song's sweet note;
And back I turned, and thought,
'Here I'll abide.'

On the Doorstep
7–8 Stanza break in all editions

The step shines wet beneath the rain,
Which prints its circles as heretofore;
I watch them from the porch again,
But no song-notes within the door
Now call to me
To shun the dripping lea;
And forth I stride.

Jan. 1914

479 *Signs and Tokens*

SAID the red-cloaked crone
In a whispered moan:

'The dead man was limp
When laid in his chest;
Yea, limp; and why
But to signify
That the grave will crimp
Ere next year's sun
Yet another one
Of those in that house –
It may be the best –
For its endless drowse!'

Said the brown-shawled dame
To confirm the same:

'And the slothful flies
On the rotting fruit
Have been seen to wear
While crawling there
Crape scarves, by eyes
That were quick and acute;
As did those that had pitched
On the cows by the pails,
And with flaps of their tails
Were far away switched.'

On the Doorstep
13 lea;] lea MV2, PE

Signs and Tokens
2 moan] tone MS

Said the third in plaid,
Each word being weighed:

'And trotting does
In the park, in the lane,
And just outside
The shuttered pane,
Have also been heard –
Quick feet as light
As the feet of a sprite –
And the wise mind knows
What things may betide
When such has occurred.'

Cried the black-craped fourth,
Cold faced as the north:

'O, though giving such
Some head-room, I smile
At your falterings
When noting those things
Round your domicile!
For what, what can touch
One whom, riven of all
That makes life gay,
No hints can appal
Of more takings away!'

480 Paths of Former Time

TITLE:
The old Paths MS *before revision*

No; no;
It must not be so:
They are the ways we do not go.

Still chew
The kine, and moo
In the meadows we used to wander through;

Signs and Tokens
43 Round] In MS

Still purl
The rivulets and curl
Towards the weirs with a musical swirl;

Haymakers
As in former years
Rake rolls into heaps that the pitchfork rears;

Wheels crack
On the turfy track
The waggon pursues with its toppling pack.

'Why then shun –
Since summer's not done –
All this because of the lack of one?'

Had you been
Sharer of that scene
You would not ask while it bites in keen

Why it is so
We can no more go
By the summer paths we used to know!

1913

TITLE:
The Clock of Time MS *before revision*

481 *The Clock of the Years*

'A spirit passed before my face; the hair of my flesh stood up.'

AND the Spirit said,
'I can make the clock of the years go backward,
But am loth to stop it where you will.'
And I cried, 'Agreed
To that. Proceed:
It's better than dead!'

He answered, 'Peace;'
And called her up – as last before me;
Then younger, younger she freshed, to the year
I first had known
Her woman-grown,
And I cried, 'Cease! –

Paths of Former Time
21 bites in] lingers MS
Copied from notes of 1912–13 MS *before revision*

The Clock of the Years
9 freshed] grew MS, MV1, PE

'Thus far is good –
It is enough – let her stay thus always!'
But alas for me – He shook his head:
No stop was there;
And she waned child-fair,
And to babyhood.

Still less in mien
To my great sorrow became she slowly,
And smalled till she was nought at all
In his checkless griff;
And it was as if
She had never been.

'Better,' I plained,
'She were dead as before! The memory of her
Had lived in me; but it cannot now!'
And coldly his voice:
'It was your choice
To mar the ordained.'

1916

482 *At the Piano*

A WOMAN was playing,
A man looking on;
And the mould of her face,
And her neck, and her hair,
Which the rays fell upon
Of the two candles there,
Sent him mentally straying
In some fancy-place
Where pain had no trace.

A cowled Apparition
Came pushing between;
And her notes seemed to sigh;
And the lights to burn pale,

The Clock of the Years
15 me –] me. MS, MV, WE, PE, ME
28 coldly] again MS: sternly MV1

At the Piano
3 face,] face MS
4 neck,] neck MS
12 sigh;] sigh, MS, MV, WE, PE, ME

As a spell numbed the scene.
But the maid saw no bale,
And the man no monition;
And Time laughed awry,
And the Phantom hid nigh.

483 *The Shadow on the Stone*

I WENT by the Druid stone
That broods in the garden white and lone,
And I stopped and looked at the shifting shadows
That at some moments fall thereon
From the tree hard by with a rhythmic swing,
And they shaped in my imagining
To the shade that a well-known head and shoulders
Threw there when she was gardening.

I thought her behind my back,
Yea, her I long had learned to lack,
And I said: 'I am sure you are standing behind me,
Though how do you get into this old track?'
And there was no sound but the fall of a leaf
As a sad response; and to keep down grief
I would not turn my head to discover
That there was nothing in my belief.

Yet I wanted to look and see
That nobody stood at the back of me;
But I thought once more: 'Nay, I'll not unvision
A shape which, somehow, there may be.'
So I went on softly from the glade,
And left her behind me throwing her shade,
As she were indeed an apparition –
My head unturned lest my dream should fade.

Begun 1913: finished 1916

At the Piano
18 hid nigh] passed by MS *before revision*

The Shadow on the Stone
2 broods] stands MS, MV1
4 fall thereon] there are thrown MS, MV, WE, PE, CP1
17] I felt I must look to see MS
At end MS first had 'From old notes'. This was corrected to 'From an old note' and then to the present reading

484 In the Garden

(M.H.)

WE waited for the sun
To break its cloudy prison
(For day was not yet done,
And night still unbegun)
Leaning by the dial.

After many a trial –
We all silent there –
It burst as new-arisen,
Throwing a shade to where
Time travelled at that minute.

Little saw we in it,
But this much I know,
Of lookers on that shade,
Her towards whom it made
Soonest had to go.

1915

485 The Tree and the Lady

I HAVE done all I could
For that lady I knew! Through the heats I have shaded her,
Drawn to her songsters when summer has jaded her,
Home from the heath or the wood.

At the mirth-time of May,
When my shadow first lured her, I'd donned my new bravery
Of greenth: 'twas my all. Now I shiver in slavery,
Icicles grieving me gray.

Plumed to every twig's end
I could tempt her chair under me. Much did I treasure her
During those days she had nothing to pleasure her;
Mutely she used me as friend.

TITLE:
(*M.H.*)] Not in MS

In the Garden
9] Shading its finger where MV2, WE, ME

The Tree and the Lady
7 greenth] green MS

I'm a skeleton now,
And she's gone, craving warmth. The rime sticks like a skin to me;
Through me Arcturus peers; Nor'lights shoot into me;
Gone is she, scorning my bough!

TITLE:
MS has 'gentle' inserted in pencil after 'An' and then erased

486 An Upbraiding

NOW I am dead you sing to me
The songs we used to know,
But while I lived you had no wish
Or care for doing so.

Now I am dead you come to me
In the moonlight, comfortless;
Ah, what would I have given alive
To win such tenderness!

When you are dead, and stand to me
Not differenced, as now,
But like again, will you be cold
As when we lived, or how?

TITLE:
The Young Glass-stainer MS

487 The Young Glass-Stainer

'THESE Gothic windows, how they wear me out
With cusp and foil, and nothing straight or square,
Crude colours, leaden borders roundabout,
And fitting in Peter here, and Matthew there!

'What a vocation! Here do I draw now
The abnormal, loving the Hellenic norm;
Martha I paint, and dream of Hera's brow,
Mary, and think of Aphrodite's form.'

Nov. 1893

The Young Glass-Stainer
4 in Peter] MS had first tried 'Christ in' and 'Luke in'
4 Matthew] John in MS *before revision*

488 *Looking at a Picture on an Anniversary*

TITLE:
Looking at her Picture MS *before revision*

BUT don't you know it, my dear,
Don't you know it,
That this day of the year
(What rainbow-rays embow it!)
We met, strangers confessed,
But parted – blest?

Though at this query, my dear,
There in your frame
Unmoved you still appear,
You must be thinking the same,
But keep that look demure
Just to allure.

And now at length a trace
I surely vision
Upon that wistful face
Of old-time recognition,
Smiling forth, 'Yes, as you say,
It is the day.'

For this one phase of you
Now left on earth
This great date must endue
With pulsings of rebirth? –
I see them vitalize
Those two deep eyes!

But if this face I con
Does not declare
Consciousness living on
Still in it, little I care
To live myself, my dear,
Lone-labouring here!

Spring 1913

ooking at a Picture on an Anniversary
) same,] same WE
7 say,] say WE
19 phase] shape MS
22 rebirth?] rebirth! ME
Spring 1913] (March *del*) 1913 MS

TITLE:
The Choirmaster's Funeral MS *before revision*

489 *The Choirmaster's Burial*

HE often would ask us
That, when he died,
After playing so many
To their last rest,
If out of us any
Should here abide,
And it would not task us,
We would with our lutes
Play over him
By his grave-brim
The psalm he liked best –
The one whose sense suits
'Mount Ephraim' –
And perhaps we should seem
To him, in Death's dream,
Like the seraphim.

As soon as I knew
That his spirit was gone
I thought this his due,
And spoke thereupon.

'I think,' said the vicar,
'A read service quicker
Than viols out-of-doors
In these frosts and hoars.
That old-fashioned way
Requires a fine day,
And it seems to me
It had better not be.'

Hence, that afternoon,
Though never knew he
That his wish could not be,
To get through it faster
They buried the master
Without any tune.

The Choirmaster's Burial
20–1 MS has a stanza break here, but there was a page turn in MV, PE. There is no stanza break in WE, ME, CP1–4. On the authority of MS and in the knowledge that WE and CP1 were set up from MV, a stanza break has been introduced in this edition.
23 viols] a hymn MS
34–5 Stanza break in all editions

But 'twas said that, when
At the dead of next night
The vicar looked out,
There struck on his ken
Thronged roundabout,
Where the frost was graying
The headstoned grass,
A band all in white
Like the saints in church-glass,
Singing and playing
The ancient stave
By the choirmaster's grave.

Such the tenor man told
When he had grown old.

490 *The Man Who Forgot*

TITLE:
The Man who forgot MS

AT a lonely cross where bye-roads met
I sat upon a gate;
I saw the sun decline and set,
And still was fain to wait.

A trotting boy passed up the way
And roused me from my thought;
I called to him, and showed where lay
A spot I shyly sought.

'A summer-house fair stands hidden where
You see the moonlight thrown;
Go, tell me if within it there
A lady sits alone.'

He half demurred, but took the track,
And silence held the scene;
I saw his figure rambling back;
I asked him if he had been.

he Choirmaster's Burial
7 tenor] treble MS, MV1, PE

The Man Who Forgot
8] A neighbouring spot I sought. MS
Note Erased pencil workings in MS show that Hardy considered putting the poem into the third person. MS has the whole poem in quotes

'I went just where you said, but found
No summer-house was there:
Beyond the slope 'tis all bare ground;
Nothing stands anywhere.

'A man asked what my brains were worth;
The house, he said, grew rotten,
And was pulled down before my birth,
And is almost forgotten!'

My right mind woke, and I stood dumb;
Forty years' frost and flower
Had fleeted since I'd used to come
To meet her in that bower.

491 *While Drawing in a Churchyard*

TITLE:
Architecture in a Churchyard MS *before revision*

'It is sad that so many of worth,
Still in the flesh,' soughed the yew,
'Misjudge their lot whom kindly earth
Secludes from view.

'They ride their diurnal round
Each day-span's sum of hours
In peerless ease, without jolt or bound
Or ache like ours.

'If the living could but hear
What is heard by my roots as they creep
Round the restful flock, and the things said there,
No one would weep.'

' "Now set among the wise,"
They say: "Enlarged in scope,
That no God trumpet us to rise
We truly hope." '

I listened to his strange tale
In the mood that stillness brings,
And I grew to accept as the day wore pale
That show of things.

The Man Who Forgot
25 dumb] numb MS

While Drawing in a Churchyard
1 worth,] worth MS
11 there,] there CP1–4
13–16 A late insertion on MS
15] That no official trump call *Rise*! MS
15 God] god MV, WE, PE, CP1
20 show] view MS, MV1, PE

492 *For Life I Had Never Cared Greatly*

FOR Life I had never cared greatly,
As worth a man's while;
Peradventures unsought,
Peradventures that finished in nought,
Had kept me from youth and through manhood till lately
Unwon by its style.

In earliest years – why I know not –
I viewed it askance;
Conditions of doubt,
Conditions that leaked slowly out,
May haply have bent me to stand and to show not
Much zest for its dance.

With symphonies soft and sweet colour
It courted me then,
Till evasions seemed wrong,
Till evasions gave in to its song,
And I warmed, until living aloofly loomed duller
Than life among men.

Anew I found nought to set eyes on,
When, lifting its hand,
It uncloaked a star,
Uncloaked it from fog-damps afar,
And showed its beams burning from pole to horizon
As bright as a brand.

And so, the rough highway forgetting,
I pace hill and dale
Regarding the sky,
Regarding the vision on high,
And thus re-illumed have no humour for letting
My pilgrimage fail.

TITLE:
'For Life I had never cared greatly' MS

INDENTATION:
1 = l. 5
2 = ll. 1, 4
3 = ll. 2, 3, 6
} and so throughout MS, MV, WE, PE, ME

For Life I Had Never Cared Greatly
1 greatly,] greatly MS
3 Peradventures] Adventures MS
4 Peradventures] Adventures MS
17 loomed] seemed MS
25 forgetting,] forgetting MS
26 pace] pad MS

POEMS OF WAR AND PATRIOTISM

493 Men Who March Away

(*Song of the Soldiers*)

WHAT of the faith and fire within us
    Men who march away
    Ere the barn-cocks say
    Night is growing gray,
Leaving all that here can win us;
What of the faith and fire within us
    Men who march away?

Is it a purblind prank, O think you,
    Friend with the musing eye,
    Who watch us stepping by
    With doubt and dolorous sigh?
Can much pondering so hoodwink you!
Is it a purblind prank, O think you,
    Friend with the musing eye?

Nay. We well see what we are doing,
    Though some may not see –
    Dalliers as they be –
    England's need are we;
Her distress would leave us rueing:
Nay. We well see what we are doing,
    Though some may not see!

In our heart of hearts believing
    Victory crowns the just,
    And that braggarts must
    Surely bite the dust,
Press we to the field ungrieving,
In our heart of hearts believing
    Victory crowns the just.

EXTRA MANUSCRIPTS:

(1) After its appearance in *The Times* this poem was collected in *Satires of Circumstance*. In 1919 Hardy transferred it to the Wessex Edition of *Moments of Vision*. The manuscript of the poem was withdrawn from the MS collection of *Satires of Circumstance* and sold at the Red Cross Sale at Christie's, 26 April 1915. It is that manuscript, present whereabouts unknown and checked from the facsimile in *A Bibliography of the Works of Thomas Hardy* by A. P. Webb (London, 1916), which is referred to here as MSSC.

(2) Another manuscript is in the possession of the University of Texas = UT

Note When the manuscripts of the *Satires of Circumstance* poems were bound up, the place of the missing manuscript was taken by a cutting of the poem from *The Times Literary Supplement*. This has alterations in Hardy's hand and is referred to here as TLSH. A further copy of the manuscript was required for the binding up of the *Moments of Vision* poems. This, in accordance with the practice of this Variorum Edition, is referred to as MS

EXTRA PRINTINGS:

(1) *The Times*, 9 Sept 1914, p. 9 = T

(2) *The Times Literary Supplement*, 10 Sept 1914, p. 413 [Identical with T except for omission of footnote]

(3) *The New York Times*, 10 Sept 1914, p. 5 = NYT

(4) Privately printed by Clement Shorter, 12 Sept 1914 = CS

(5) Privately printed by E. Williams, bookseller, 37 New Town Road, Hove, 16 Sept 1914 = EWP [The 1915 reprint is identical except that the comma found after 'believing' (l. 27) in 1914 has been deleted]

(6) *Selected Poems*, pp. 199–200

(7) *Chosen Poems*, pp. 253–4

Men Who March Away
1 us] us, NYT
2 away] away, MSSC, NYT
3 barn-cocks] barncocks NYT
5] To hazards whence no tears can win us; (us? NYT) MSSC, T, NYT, CS, EWP, TLSH, SC, SP
5 can] could UT
6 us] us, NYT
8 O] O! NYT
8 you,] you? NYT
9 eye,] eye MSSC, UT, T, CS, EWP, TLSH
10 by] by, T, CS, EWP, TLSH
11 doubt] doubts NYT
12 you!] you; NYT
13 O] O! NYT
13 you,] you? NYT
14 eye?] eye. NYT
15 Nay. We] Nay; we MS: Nay, we NYT
15 well see] see well T, NYT, CS, EWP
15 doing,] doing UT
16 see –] see, UT
17 they be –] they may be NYT
17 be –] be. – MS: be: UT: be! – T, CS, EWP
18 we;] we: MSSC: we, NYT
19 leave] set T, NYT, EWP
19 rueing:] rueing; NYT
20 Nay. We] Nay; we MS: Nay, we NYT
20 well see] see well T, NYT, CS, EWP
20 we are] we're NYT
21 see!] see. NYT
26 Press] March T, NYT, EWP
26 ungrieving,] ungrieving MS
27 believing] believing, EWP

Hence the faith and fire within us
        Men who march away
        Ere the barn-cocks say
        Night is growing gray,
Leaving all that here can win us;
Hence the faith and fire within us
        Men who march away.

5 September 1914

PLACING:
In the 1914 first edition of *Satires of Circumstance* printed last in the book under the heading 'Postscript'. In MS it is placed between 'Written before the War' and 'England to Germany in 1914'. It is omitted from MV and PE. In WE it is the first poem of 'Poems of War and Patriotism'.

TITLE:
(A NYT) Song of the Soldiers T, NYT, CS, EWP
'Men who march away' MS
Men Who March Away] Not in T, NYT, CS, EWP
(*Song* . . .)] Not in UT

His Country

Note In MS, MV, PE printed first in the 'Poems of War and Patriotism'

494 *His Country*

I JOURNEYED from my native spot
        Across the south sea shine,
And found that people in hall and cot
Laboured and suffered each his lot
        Even as I did mine.

He travels southward, and looks around;

Thus noting them in meads and marts
        It did not seem to me
That my dear country with its hearts,
Minds, yearnings, worse and better parts
        Had ended with the sea.

and cannot discover the boundary

I further and further went anon,
        As such I still surveyed,
And further yet – yea, on and on,
And all the men I looked upon
        Had heart-strings fellow-made.

of his native country;

I traced the whole terrestrial round,
        Homing the other side;
Then said I, 'What is there to bound
My denizenship? It seems I have found
        Its scope to be world-wide.'

or where his duties to his fellow-creatures end;

Men Who March Away
29 us] us, NYT
30 away] away, NYT
31 barn-cocks] barncocks NYT
33] To hazards whence no tears can win us; (us: EWP: us, NYT) MSSC, T, NYT, CS, EWP, TLSH, SC, SP
33 can] could UT
33 us;] us: MS
34 us] us, NYT
35 away.] away! MS

5 September 1914] Not in T, NYT, CS, EWP
MS has footnote in red ink: This poem first appeared (in volume form) as a postscript to "Satires of Circumstance"
T has footnote: Neither Mr Hardy nor *The Times* reserves copyright in the poem printed above.
TLSH has footnote: '[Originally printed from type-written copy, the rough draft having been destroyed]'

His Country
5] As did myself and mine. MS
9 parts] parts, MS, MV1, WE, ME
11 anon,] anon MS
17 Homing] And back MS

nor who are his enemies.

I asked me: 'Whom have I to fight,
    And whom have I to dare,
And whom to weaken, crush, and blight?
My country seems to have kept in sight
    On my way everywhere.'

1913

EXTRA PRINTING:
Privately printed by Florence Hardy, Feb 1917 = FH

TITLE:
England to Germany FH

Note In MS, MV, PE printed second in the 'Poems of War and Patriotism'

495 *England to Germany in 1914*

'O ENGLAND, may God punish thee!'
– Is it that Teuton genius flowers
Only to breathe malignity
Upon its friend of earlier hours?
– We have eaten your bread, you have eaten ours,
We have loved your burgs, your pines' green moan,
Fair Rhine-stream, and its storied towers;
Your shining souls of deathless dowers
Have won us as they were our own:

We have nursed no dreams to shed your blood,
We have matched your might not rancorously
Save a flushed few whose blatant mood
You heard and marked as well as we
To tongue not in their country's key;
But yet you cry with face aflame,
'O England, may God punish thee!'
And foul in onward history,
And present sight, your ancient name.

Autumn 1914

EXTRA PRINTING:
King Albert's Book, ed. Hall Caine (London, 1914), p. 21 = KA

TITLE:
Sonnet on the Belgian Expatriation KA

496 *On the Belgian Expatriation*

I DREAMT that people from the Land of Chimes
Arrived one autumn morning with their bells,
To hoist them on the towers and citadels
Of my own country, that the musical rhymes

His Country
MS, MV1, PE have extra stanza:
'Ah, you deceive you by such pleas!'/Said one with pitying eye./'Foreigners – not like us – are these;/Stretch country-love (country love MS) beyond the seas? –/Too Christian!' – 'Strange,' said I./(No never!' – 'Ah,' said I. MS)
Note in margin for extra stanza reads: But he is set right by a wise man who pities his blindness.
MS, MV1, PE have footnote: Written before the war.

England to Germany in 1914
6 burgs . . . moan] cities, forests (landscapes FH) lone MS, FH
8 souls] ones FH
11 rancorously] rancorously, MS, FH, MV, PE
12 flushed few] few fools, MS, FH
13 heard and marked] recognized FH
13 heard] read MS
14 tongue] ring MS, FH
15 aflame,] aflame FH

On the Belgian Expatriation
4–5 Stanza break in all editions

Rung by them into space at meted times
Amid the market's daily stir and stress,
And the night's empty star-lit silentness,
Might solace souls of this and kindred climes.

Then I awoke; and lo, before me stood
The visioned ones, but pale and full of fear;
From Bruges they came, and Antwerp, and Ostend,

No carillons in their train. Foes of mad mood
Had shattered these to shards amid the gear
Of ravaged roof, and smouldering gable-end.

18 October 1914

497 An Appeal to America on Behalf of the Belgian Destitute

SEVEN millions stand
Emaciate, in that ancient Delta-land: –
We here, full-charged with our own maimed and dead
And coiled in throbbing conflicts slow and sore,
Can poorly soothe these ails unmerited
Of souls forlorn upon the facing shore! –
Where naked, gaunt, in endless band on band
Seven millions stand.

No man can say
To your great country that, with scant delay,
You must, perforce, ease them in their loud need:
We know that nearer first your duty lies;
But – is it much to ask that you let plead
Your lovingkindness with you – wooingwise –
Albeit that aught you owe, and must repay,
No man can say?

December 1914

EXTRA PRINTINGS:
(1) *The New York Times*, 4 Jan 1915, p. 10 = NYT [and in other American and British newspapers]
(2) *The Need of Belgium, Handbook* = NBH
(3) Privately printed by Florence Hardy, May 1917 = FH

PROOFS:
It has not been possible to trace the proofs once in the possession of Sir Sydney Cockerell

On the Belgian Expatriation
5 meted] measured MS, KA, MV1, PE
7 star-lit] starlit KA
9 awoke;] awoke: KA
12 Foes of mad mood] Vicissitude KA
13] Had left these tinkling to the invaders' ear, KA
14 Of ravaged roof] And ravaged street KA
18 October 1914] Not in KA

An Appeal to America on Behalf of the Belgian Destitute
3 full-charged] full charged NYT, NBH
3 dead] dead, MS, NYT, FH, MV, WE, PE, ME
5 poorly soothe] soothe how slight NYT, NBH
6 shore! –] shore! NYT
8 millions] million NBH
11 loud] sore NYT, NBH
12 lies;] lies: NBH
14 lovingkindness] loving kindness NYT: loving-kindness NBH
14 wooing-wise] wooingwise WE, ME: wooing wise NYT [Line break in NBH, MV, PE]
15 owe,] owe NYT, NBH
15 repay,] repay NYT

498 The Pity of It

I WALKED in loamy Wessex lanes, afar
From rail-track and from highway, and I heard
In field and farmstead many an ancient word
Of local lineage like 'Thu bist', 'Er war',

'Ich woll', 'Er sholl', and by-talk similar,
Nigh as they speak who in this month's moon gird
At England's very loins, thereunto spurred
By gangs whose glory threats and slaughters are.

Then seemed a Heart crying: 'Whosoever they be
At root and bottom of this, who flung this flame
Between kin folk kin tongued even as are we,

'Sinister, ugly, lurid, be their fame;
May their familiars grow to shun their name,
And their brood perish everlastingly.'

April 1915

EXTRA MANUSCRIPT:
Presented by Hardy to Dr Caleb Saleeby and now in the possession of the University of Texas. On the back of the picture-frame was a note which read: Presented to Dr Caleb Williams Saleeby by Thomas Hardy, as the poem was inspired by reading an article on "Eugenics" written by Dr Saleeby during the Great War. The alteration of 'small talk' to 'bye-talk' was made to please Dr Saleeby. This alteration has been made in the MS. In the printed version it reads 'by-talk' = UT

TYPESCRIPT:
It has not been possible to trace the typescript once in the possession of Sir Sydney Cockerell

EXTRA PRINTINGS:
(1) *The Fortnightly Review*, April 1915, p. [567] = FR
(2) Privately printed by Florence Hardy, Feb 1917 = FH

499 In Time of Wars and Tumults

'WOULD that I'd not drawn breath here!' some one said,
'To stalk upon this stage of evil deeds,
Where purposelessly month by month proceeds
A play so sorely shaped and blood-bespread.'

Yet had his spark not quickened, but lain dead
To the gross spectacles of this our day,
And never put on the proffered cloak of clay,
He had but known not things now manifested;

Life would have swirled the same. Morns would have dawned
On the uprooting by the night-gun's stroke
Of what the yester noonshine brought to flower;

EXTRA PRINTINGS:
(1) *The Sphere*, 24 Nov 1917, p. 164 = S
(2) Signed off-print in the Miriam Lutcher Stark Library of the University of Texas = UT

TITLE:
In the Time of Wars and Tumults UT, S

INDENTATION:
ll. 2, 3, 6, 7 in UT and S are indented right of their position here

The Pity of It
1 lanes,] lanes FR, FH
4 lineage] lineage, UT
5 by-talk] bye-talk UT
6 Nigh] Even MS, UT, FR, FH, MV1, PE
12 lurid,] lurid UT, FH
12 fame;] fame: FR, FH
14 brood] breed MS, UT, FR, FH, MV, WE, PE, ME
April 1915] February 1915 MS, FH: 1915 UT: Not in FR
MV1, PE add '(*Fortnightly Review*')' after date
Note Erased pencil workings in MS show that Hardy considered altering 'they' in l. 9 to 'he', and 'their' in ll. 12, 13 and 14 to 'his'

In Time of Wars and Tumults
3 month by month] year by year MS
8 known not] not known UT, S, MV1, PE
11 noonshine brought] sunlight made MS
11–12 Stanza break in all editions

Brown martial brows in dying throes have wanned
Despite his absence; hearts no fewer been broke
By Empery's insatiate lust of power.

1915

500 In Time of 'The Breaking of Nations' [1]

I

ONLY a man harrowing clods
  In a slow silent walk
With an old horse that stumbles and nods
  Half asleep as they stalk.

II

Only thin smoke without flame
  From the heaps of couch-grass;
Yet this will go onward the same
  Though Dynasties pass.

III

Yonder a maid and her wight
  Come whispering by:
War's annals will cloud into night
  Ere their story die.

1915

EXTRA MANUSCRIPTS:
(1) It has not been possible to trace the MS once in the possession of Mr Paul Lemperly.
(2) In the Bancroft Library of the University of California at Berkeley = BL
(3) In Sir Edward Marsh's Manuscript Album. There are no variants

EXTRA PRINTINGS:
(1) *The Saturday Review*, 29 Jan 1916, p. 108 = SR
(2) Privately printed by Clement Shorter, 1 Feb 1916 = CS
(3) *Selected Poems*, p. 203
(4) *Chosen Poems*, p. 259

Note This was one of nine poems chosen by Hardy for the Library of the Royal Dolls' House at Windsor Castle. The copy there has 'couch-grass:' (l. 6), 'by;' (l. 10) and 'fade' (l. 11)

501 Cry of the Homeless

After the Prussian Invasion of Belgium

'INSTIGATOR of the ruin –
  Whichsoever thou mayst be
Of the masterful of Europe
  That contrived our misery –
Hear the wormwood-worded greeting
  From each city, shore, and lea
    Of thy victims:
  "Conqueror, all hail to thee!"

[1] Jer., LI 20.

EXTRA MANUSCRIPT:
In the Library of Congress [I have not been able to check this]

EXTRA PRINTINGS:
(1) *The Book of the Homeless*, ed. Edith Wharton (London, 1916), p. 16 = BH
(2) Privately printed by Florence Hardy, Feb 1917 = FH

TITLE:
After . . . Belgium] Not in BH: After the German Invasion of France and Belgium FH

In Time of Wars and Tumults
14] By monarchisms unnatural greed of power. MS *before revision*
1915] Not in UT, S

In Time of 'The Breaking of Nations'
1 man] hind BL
6 couch-grass;] couch grass: BL, SR, CS, SP
7 Yet] – Yet SR, CS
7 onward] on just SR, CS
8 Dynasties] dynasties SR, CS
10 by:] by; MS, SR, CS, SP
11 cloud] fade MS, BL, SR, CS, SP, CP3 [Hardy's copy of SP (1917) has been corrected to 'cloud']
1915] Not in BL, SR, CS, SP
Jer., LI 20.] Not in SP: CS adds 'Thou *art* my battle axe *and* weapons of war: for with thee will I break in pieces the nations, and with thee will I destroy kingdoms.'
BL, SR add below title: No Copyright Reserved

Cry of the Homeless
2 mayst] mayest FH
3 masterful] mastering minds BH
4 misery] misery, FH
6 lea] lea, FH
8 Conqueror] Enemy BH

'Yea: "All hail!" we grimly shout thee
That wast author, fount, and head
Of these wounds, whoever proven
When our times are throughly read.
"May thy loved be slighted, blighted,
And forsaken," be it said
By thy victims,
"And thy children beg their bread!"

'Nay: a richer malediction! –
Rather let this thing befall
In time's hurling and unfurling
On the night when comes thy call;
That compassion dew thy pillow
And bedrench thy senses all
For thy victims,
Till death dark thee with his pall.'

August 1915

502 *Before Marching and After*

(*In Memoriam F.W.G.*)

ORION swung southward aslant
Where the starved Egdon pine-trees had thinned,
The Pleiads aloft seemed to pant
With the heather that twitched in the wind;
But he looked on indifferent to sights such as these,
Unswayed by love, friendship, home joy or home sorrow,
And wondered to what he would march on the morrow.

The crazed household-clock with its whirr
Rang midnight within as he stood,
He heard the low sighing of her
Who had striven from his birth for his good;
But he still only asked the spring starlight, the breeze,
What great thing or small thing his history would borrow
From that Game with Death he would play on the morrow.

EXTRA MANUSCRIPTS:
(1) In the Miriam Lutcher Stark Library of the University of Texas = UT [This is the copy sold at Sotheby's in Dec 1937 to Lady Cynthia Asquith, and subsequently in the Bliss Collection. At top right in pencil it bears the inscription: (Original MS.)]
(2) In the Miriam Lutcher Stark Library of the University of Texas. This is a later fair copy, identical with UT except for the omission of the comma in the title

PROOF:
It has not been possible to trace the proof once in the possession of Sir Sydney Cockerell

EXTRA PRINTINGS:
(1) *The Fortnightly Review*, 1 Oct 1915, p. [609] = FR
(2) Privately printed by Clement Shorter, Dec (?) 1915 = CS
(3) *Selected Poems*, pp. 201–2
(4) *Chosen Poems*, pp. 255–6

TITLE:
Before Marching, and After UT, FR, SP

Cry of the Homeless
13] "May thy dearest ones be blighted BH
17] Nay: too much the malediction. – BH
17 richer] lesser FH
19] In the unfurling of the future, BH
19 time's] Time's FH
20 call;] call: BH, FH
22 bedrench] absorb MS, BH, FH, MV1, PE, CP1
Note There are variations in the use of quotes which have not been recorded above. The only one of importance is the omission of quotes in BH, FH at the beginnings of the stanzas and the end of stanza 3.

Before Marching and After
6 home joy] home-joy WE, ME
6 home sorrow] home-sorrow WE, ME
8 household-clock] household clock MS, UT, FR, CS, SP

When the heath wore the robe of late summer,
And the fuchsia-bells, hot in the sun,
Hung red by the door, a quick comer
Brought tidings that marching was done
For him who had joined in that game overseas
Where Death stood to win, though his name was to borrow
A brightness therefrom not to fade on the morrow.

September 1915

503 *Often When Warring*

EXTRA PRINTING:
The Sphere, 10 Nov 1917, p. 134 = S

TITLE:
'Often when Warring' MS

INDENTATION:
ll. 2, 3, 6, 7, 10, 12 in S are indented right of their position here

OFTEN when warring for he wist not what,
An enemy-soldier, passing by one weak,
Has tendered water, wiped the burning cheek,
And cooled the lips so black and clammed and hot;

Then gone his way, and maybe quite forgot
The deed of grace amid the roar and reek;
Yet larger vision than loud arms bespeak
He there has reached, although he has known it not

For natural mindsight, triumphing in the act
Over the throes of artificial rage,
Has thuswise muffled victory's peal of pride,
Rended to ribands policy's specious page
That deals but with evasion, code, and pact,
And war's apology wholly stultified.

1915

504 *Then and Now*

EXTRA PRINTING:
The Times, 11 July 1917, p. 7 = T

WHEN battles were fought
With a chivalrous sense of Should and Ought,
In spirit men said,
'End we quick or dead,
Honour is some reward!
Let us fight fair – for our own best or worst;
So, Gentlemen of the Guard,
Fire first!'

Before Marching and After
19 game] Game UT, CS
19 overseas] over-seas CP [MV, PE have line break]
20 win,] win; UT, FR, CS, SP
20 name was to] memory would FR, SP
21 fade] die FR, SP

Often When Warring
7 loud arms bespeak] the tongue can speak MS, S, MV1, PE, CP1
8 there] thus S
8 not] not. MS, S, MV, WE, PE, ME
11 thuswise] thereby MS, S, MV1
1915] Not in S

Then and Now
2 Should and Ought] should and ought MS, T

In the open they stood,
Man to man in his knightlihood:
They would not deign
To profit by a stain
On the honourable rules,
Knowing that practise perfidy no man durst
Who in the heroic schools
Was nurst.

But now, behold, what
Is warfare wherein honour is not!
Rama laments
Its dead innocents:
Herod breathes: 'Sly slaughter
Shall rule! Let us, by modes once called accurst,
Overhead, under water,
Stab first.'

1915

505 *A Call to National Service*

EXTRA PRINTINGS:
(1) *The Times*, 12 March 1917, p. 9 = T
(2) *The Morning Post*, 12 March 1917, p. 9 = MP
(3) *The Times Literary Supplement*, 15 March 1917, p. 127 = TLS
(4) Privately printed by Florence Hardy, May 1917 = FH

TITLE:
For National Service MS *before revision*
For National Service MP
National Service TLS
T has no title

UP and be doing, all who have a hand
To lift, a back to bend. It must not be
In times like these that vaguely linger we
To air our vaunts and hopes; and leave our land

Untended as a wild of weeds and sand.
– Say, then, 'I come!' and go, O women and men
Of palace, ploughshare, easel, counter, pen;
That scareless, scathless, England still may stand.

Would years but let me stir as once I stirred
At many a dawn to take the forward track,
And with a stride plunged on to enterprize,

I now would speed like yester wind that whirred
Through yielding pines; and serve with never a slack,
So loud for promptness all around outcries!

March 1917

Then and Now
18 warfare wherein] war with those where T
20 innocents:] innocents; T
21 Herod] Despots MS
21 breathes] nod MS: howls T
22 Shall rule] Rules now T
1915] Written 1915: published 1917 MS: not in T
Written 1915: *published in 'The Times'*, 1917 MV1, PE

A Call to National Service
6 – Say] Say MP, FH
7 pen;] pen: T, TLS, MP
8] It will enray your names to dates unscanned T, MP, TLS
13 yielding] breaking T, MP, TLS
14 outcries!] outcries. FH
T has footnote: Copyright not reserved
Note There are no stanza breaks in MP: the onl[y] stanza break in FH is between ll. 8 and 9

506 *The Dead and the Living One*

The dead woman lay in her first night's grave,
And twilight fell from the clouds' concave,
And those she had asked to forgive forgave.

The woman passing came to a pause
By the heaped white shapes of wreath and cross,
And looked upon where the other was.

And as she mused there thus spoke she:
'Never your countenance did I see,
But you've been a good good friend to me!'

Rose a plaintive voice from the sod below:
'O woman whose accents I do not know,
What is it that makes you approve me so?'

'O dead one, ere my soldier went,
I heard him saying, with warm intent,
To his friend, when won by your blandishment:

'"I would change for that lass here and now!
And if I return I may break my vow
To my present Love, and contrive somehow

'"To call my own this new-found pearl,
Whose eyes have the light, whose lips the curl
I always have looked for in a girl!"

' – And this is why that by ceasing to be –
Though never your countenance did I see –
You prove you a good good friend to me;

'And I pray each hour for your soul's repose
In gratitude for your joining those
No lover will clasp when his campaigns close.'

Away she turned, when arose to her eve
A martial phantom of gory dye,
That said, with a thin and far-off sigh:

PROOF:
In the Berg Collection of the New York Public Library = B

EXTRA PRINTINGS:
(1) *The Sphere*, 25 Dec 1915, p. 346 = S
(2) *The New York World*, 2 Jan 1916, p. 2 = NYW

The Dead and the Living One
2 clouds'] sky's S, NYW
5 cross,] cross WE, ME
10 Rose] Came MS, S, NYW, MV1, PE, CP1
10 sod] grave S, NYW
11 woman] woman, S
15 friend,] friend NYW
19 new-found] new found S, NYW
29 martial] soldier's S, NYW
30 said,] said NYW

'O sweetheart, neither shall I clasp you!
For the foe this day has pierced me through,
And sent me to where she is. Adieu! –

'And forget not when the night-wind's whine
Calls over this turf where her limbs recline,
That it travels on to lament by mine.'

There was a cry by the white-flowered mound,
There was a laugh from underground,
There was a deeper gloom around.

1915

507 *A New Year's Eve in War Time*

EXTRA PRINTINGS:
(1) *The Sphere*, 6 Jan 1917, p. 10 = S
(2) Privately printed by Florence Hardy, Feb 1917 = FH

PROOF, ETC.:
It has not been possible to trace the proof, and the printing cut from *The Sphere* and revised by Hardy, which were once in the possession of Sir Sydney Cockerell

I

PHANTASMAL fears,
And the flap of the flame,
And the throb of the clock,
And a loosened slate,
And the blind night's drone,
Which tiredly the spectral pines intone!

II

And the blood in my ears
Strumming always the same,
And the gable-cock
With its fitful grate,
And myself, alone.

III

The twelfth hour nears
Hand-hid, as in shame;
I undo the lock,
And listen, and wait
For the Young Unknown.

The Dead and the Living One
31 you!] you, MS, S, NYW, MV, WE, PE, ME
32 through,] through MS
33 is.] is! S
33 Adieu! –] Adieu!' B, S, NYW
34–9 Not in B, S, NYW: 34–6 are a late addition to MS
35 recline] decline MS, MV, PE
MV1, PE add: ('The Sphere.')

A New Year's Eve in War Time
5 drone,] drone S: drone; FH
5–6 S has a row of three dots between these two lines
6 Which] While S
6 intone!] intone, MS [Could be a stop]: intone S, FH
11 myself] ourselves S, FH
12 nears] nears, S, FH
14 lock,] lock S, FH
15 listen,] listen S, FH

IV

In the dark there careers –
As if Death astride came
To numb all with his knock –
A horse at mad rate
Over rut and stone.

V

No figure appears,
No call of my name,
No sound but 'Tic-toc'
Without check. Past the gate
It clatters – is gone.

VI

What rider it bears
There is none to proclaim;
And the Old Year has struck,
And, scarce animate,
The New makes moan.

VII

Maybe that 'More Tears! –
More Famine and Flame –
More Severance and Shock!'
Is the order from Fate
That the Rider speeds on
To pale Europe; and tiredly the pines intone.

1915–1916

508 *I Met a Man*

I MET a man when night was nigh,
Who said, with shining face and eye
Like Moses' after Sinai: –

I Met a Man
PROOF:
It has not been possible to trace the proof once in the possession of Sir Sydney Cockerell

EXTRA PRINTINGS:
(1) *The Fortnightly Review*, Feb 1917, pp. [187]–188 = FR
(2) Privately printed by Florence Hardy, Feb 1917 = FH

TITLE:
'I met a Man' MS

A New Year's Eve in War Time
20 horse] horse, S, FH
21–2 S has an extra line here, indented with ll. 6, 37. It reads: While tiredly the spectral pines intone.
23 my] our S
32 Tears!] Tears FH
33 Flame] Flame! S
36] That he carries to prone FH
36 speeds] bears MS, S
37 To] And FH
1915–1916] 1916 MS: *January* 1917 S, FH

I Met a Man
3–4 Stanza break in all editions, and between ll. 39 and 40. These two three-line stanzas are lined up with the first lines of the intermediate stanzas

'I have seen the Moulder of Monarchies,
Realms, peoples, plains and hills,
Sitting upon the sunlit seas! –
And, as He sat, soliloquies
Fell from Him like an antiphonic breeze
That pricks the waves to thrills.

'Meseemed that of the maimed and dead
Mown down upon the globe, –
Their plenteous blooms of promise shed
Ere fruiting-time – His words were said,
Sitting against the western web of red
Wrapt in His crimson robe.

'And I could catch them now and then:
– "Why let these gambling clans
Of human Cockers, pit liege men
From mart and city, dale and glen,
In death-mains, but to swell and swell again
Their swollen All-Empery plans,

' "When a mere nod (if my malign
Compeer but passive keep)
Would mend that old mistake of mine
I made with Saul, and ever consign
All Lords of War whose sanctuaries enshrine
Liberticide, to sleep?

' "With violence the lands are spread
Even as in Israel's day,
And it repenteth me I bred
Chartered armipotents lust-led
To feuds. . . . Yea, grieves my heart, as then I said,
To see their evil way!"

– 'The utterance grew, and flapped like flame,
And further speech I feared;
But no Celestial tongued acclaim,
And no huzzas from earthlings came,
And the heavens mutely masked as 'twere in shame
Till daylight disappeared.'

I Met a Man
5 plains] plains, FR, FH
7 And,] And MS
7 He] It FR, FH
8 Him] It FR, FH
8 an antiphonic] a fitful lyric FR
13 fruiting-time] fruiting time FR, FH
13 His] Its FR, FH
14 web] webs FR
15 His] Its FR, FH
17 gambling] dominant FR
18 human Cockers] human-Cockers FR, FH
22 mere] fleet FR
22 malign] Malign MS, FR, FH
26] All Lords of war with scutcheoned Rights-Divine FR
26 War] war FH
27 Liberticide] Of Liberticide FR
31 Chartered] Caste-mad FR
31 lust-led] court-fed FR
32 To feuds. . . .] For feud . . . FR
32 feuds. . . .] feuds. . . . . MS: feuds . . . FH
34 – 'The] ' – The FR, FH
36 acclaim,] acclaim MS

Thus ended he as night rode high –
The man of shining face and eye,
Like Moses' after Sinai.

1916

509 *I Looked Up from My Writing*

TITLE:
'I looked up from my Writing' MS

I LOOKED up from my writing,
   And gave a start to see,
As if rapt in my inditing,
   The moon's full gaze on me.

Her meditative misty head
   Was spectral in its air,
And I involuntarily said,
   'What are you doing there?'

'Oh, I've been scanning pond and hole
   And waterway hereabout
For the body of one with a sunken soul
   Who has put his life-light out.

'Did you hear his frenzied tattle?
   It was sorrow for his son
Who is slain in brutish battle,
   Though he has injured none.

'And now I am curious to look
   Into the blinkered mind
Of one who wants to write a book
   In a world of such a kind.'

Her temper overwrought me,
   And I edged to shun her view,
For I felt assured she thought me
   One who should drown him too.

I Looked Up from My Writing
3 inditing,] inditing MS
15 brutish] booming MS

FINALE

510 *The Coming of the End*

How it came to an end!
The meeting afar from the crowd,
And the love-looks and laughters unpenned,
The parting when much was avowed,
How it came to an end!

It came to an end;
Yes, the outgazing over the stream,
With the sun on each serpentine bend,
Or, later, the luring moon-gleam;
It came to an end.

It came to an end,
The housebuilding, furnishing, planting,
As if there were ages to spend
In welcoming, feasting, and jaunting;
It came to an end.

It came to an end,
That journey of one day a week:
('It always goes on,' said a friend,
'Just the same in bright weathers or bleak;')
But it came to an end.

'*How* will come to an end
This orbit so smoothly begun,
Unless some convulsion attend?'
I often said. 'What will be done
When it comes to an end?'

Well, it came to an end
Quite silently – stopped without jerk;
Better close no prevision could lend;
Working out as One planned it should work
Ere it came to an end.

The Coming of the End
21 *How*] How MS
Note On the verso of f. 139 ('He Revisits His First School') of MS is the following, with the title 'Afterwards', crossed through:

How it came to an end!/The meeting afar in the west,/And the lovedreams and laughters unpenned,/How it came to an end.

It came to an end,/Yes, the outgazing over the stream/With the sun on each serpentine bend

On the verso of f. 9 ('Apostrophe to an Old Psalm Tune') of MS is the following canceled:

How it came to an end!/The meeting near to the crest/And the love and the laughter unpenned,/The parting when much was confessed

511 *Afterwards*

EXTRA PRINTING:
Chosen Poems, pp. 140–1

WHEN the Present has latched its postern behind my tremulous stay,
And the May month flaps its glad green leaves like wings,
Delicate-filmed as new-spun silk, will the neighbours say,
'He was a man who used to notice such things'?

If it be in the dusk when, like an eyelid's soundless blink,
The dewfall-hawk comes crossing the shades to alight
Upon the wind-warped upland thorn, a gazer may think,
'To him this must have been a familiar sight.'

If I pass during some nocturnal blackness, mothy and warm,
When the hedgehog travels furtively over the lawn,
One may say, 'He strove that such innocent creatures should come to no harm,
But he could do little for them; and now he is gone.'

If, when hearing that I have been stilled at last, they stand at the door,
Watching the full-starred heavens that winter sees,
Will this thought rise on those who will meet my face no more,
'He was one who had an eye for such mysteries'?

And will any say when my bell of quittance is heard in the gloom,
And a crossing breeze cuts a pause in its outrollings,
Till they rise again, as they were a new bell's boom,
'He hears it not now, but used to notice such things'?

Afterwards
1] When night has closed its shutters on my dismantled day, MS
2 wings,] wings MS, ME
3 neighbours] people MS, MV1
4 such things'?] these things.'? MS
7 wind-warped] nibbled MS
7 a gazer may] will a gazer MS, MV1, PE
8 sight.'] sight'? MV1, PE
11 One may] Will they MS, MV1, PE
11 come to no] not come to MS
12 gone.'] gone'? MV, PE
17 bell of quittance] parting bell MS
18 cuts . . . outrollings] makes a blank in its utterings, MS *before revision*
19 rise] swell WE, ME
20 things'?] things?' CP1–3
MS has stops in place of queries at ends of ll. 16, 20

Best Times. ~~[illegible]~~

We went a day's excursion to the stream,
And climbed the bank, & looked at the rippled gleam,
And I did not know
That life would show,
However it might bloom, no finer glow.

I walked in the Sunday sunshine by the road
That wound towards the gate of your abode,
And I did not think
That life would shrink
To nothing ere it shed a rosier pink.

Unlooked for I arrived on a rainy night,
And you hailed me at the door by the swaying light,
And I quite forgot
That life might not
Again be touching that ecstatic height.

And that calm evening when you climbed the stair,
After a gaiety prolonged and rare ~~[illegible]~~
No thought soever
That you might never
Walk down again, struck me as I stood there.

Rewritten from an old draft.

See page 683

LATE LYRICS AND EARLIER

Abbreviations Specific to 'Late Lyrics and Earlier'

MS = The bound-up volume of manuscripts in the Dorset County Museum

LL1 = *Late Lyrics and Earlier* (First Printing: May 1922)

LL2 = *Late Lyrics and Earlier* (Second Printing: Aug 1922)

LL = Found in both LL1 and LL2

UE = Uniform Edition (The Third Printing of *Late Lyrics and Earlier* was published in Dec 1922 in the Uniform Edition format)

PE = Pocket Edition 1923

UPE = Found in both UE and PE

WE = Wessex Edition 1926

Note The above editions all add to the title:

With Many Other Verses

APOLOGY

ABOUT half the verses that follow were written quite lately. The rest are older, having been held over in MS. when past volumes were published, on considering that these would contain a sufficient number of pages to offer readers at one time, more especially during the distractions of the war. The unusually far back poems to be found here are, however, but some that were overlooked in gathering previous collections. A freshness in them, now unattainable, seemed to make up for their inexperience and to justify their inclusion. A few are dated; the dates of others are not discoverable.

The launching of a volume of this kind in neo-Georgian days by one who began writing in mid-Victorian, and has published nothing to speak of for some years, may seem to call for a few words of excuse or explanation. Whether or no, readers may feel assured that a new book is submitted to them with great hesitation at so belated a date. Insistent practical reasons, however, among which were requests from some illustrious men of letters who are in sympathy with my productions, the accident that several of the poems have already seen the light, and that dozens of them have been lying about for years, compelled the course adopted, in spite of the natural disinclination of a writer whose works have been so frequently regarded askance by a pragmatic section here and there, to draw attention to them once more.

I do not know that it is necessary to say much on the contents of the book, even in deference to suggestions that will be mentioned presently. I believe that those readers who care for my poems at all – readers to whom no passport is required – will care for this new instalment of them, perhaps the last, as much as for any that have preceded them. Moreover, in the eyes of a less friendly class the pieces, though a very mixed collection indeed, contain, so far as I am able to see, little or nothing in technic or teaching that can be considered a Star-Chamber matter, or so much as agitating to a ladies' school; even though, to use Wordsworth's observation in his Preface to *Lyrical Ballads*, such readers may suppose 'that by the act of writing in verse an author makes a formal engagement that he will gratify certain known habits of

Apology
20 pragmatic section] section of opinion MS
23 mentioned] explained MS
28 contain] may contain MS
31 observation] phrase MS

association: that he not only thus apprises the reader that certain classes of ideas and expressions will be found in his book, but that others will be carefully excluded.'

It is true, nevertheless, that some grave, positive, stark, delineations are interspersed among those of the passive, lighter, and traditional sort presumably nearer to stereotyped tastes. For – while I am quite aware that a thinker is not expected, and, indeed, is scarcely allowed, now more than heretofore, to state all that crosses his mind concerning existence in this universe, in his attempts to explain or excuse the presence of evil and the incongruity of penalizing the irresponsible – it must be obvious to open intelligences that, without denying the beauty and faithful service of certain venerable cults, such disallowance of 'obstinate questionings' and 'blank misgivings' tends to a paralysed intellectual stalemate. Heine observed nearly a hundred years ago that the soul has her eternal rights; that she will not be darkened by statutes, nor lullabied by the music of bells. And what is to-day, in allusions to the present author's pages, alleged to be 'pessimism' is, in truth, only such 'questionings' in the exploration of reality, and is the first step towards the soul's betterment, and the body's also.

If I may be forgiven for quoting my own old words, let me repeat what I printed in this relation more than twenty years ago, and wrote much earlier, in a poem entitled 'In Tenebris':

> If way to the Better there be, it exacts a full look at the Worst:

that is to say, by the exploration of reality, and its frank recognition stage by stage along the survey, with an eye to the best consummation possible: briefly, evolutionary meliorism. But it is called pessimism nevertheless; under which word, expressed with condemnatory emphasis, it is regarded by many as some pernicious new thing (though so old as to underlie the Gospel scheme, and even to permeate the Greek drama); and the subject is charitably left to decent silence, as if further comment were needless.

Happily there are some who feel such Levitical passing-by to be, alas, by no means a permanent dismissal of the matter; that comment on where the world stands is very much the reverse of needless in these disordered years of our prematurely afflicted century: that amendment and not madness lies that way. And looking down the future these few hold fast to the same: that whether the human and kindred animal races

Apology
12 venerable] old MS
24 frank] full MS
25 survey] journey MS
27 condemnatory] terminative MS
28 regarded . . . 30 subject is] Not in MS
29 Gospel scheme] Christian idea LL1
36 future these few] whole long future they MS

survive till the exhaustion or destruction of the globe, or whether these races perish and are succeeded by others before that conclusion comes, pain to all upon it, tongued or dumb, shall be kept down to a minimum by loving-kindness, operating through scientific knowledge, and actuated by the modicum of free will conjecturally possessed by organic life when the mighty necessitating forces – unconscious or other – that have 'the balancings of the clouds', happen to be in equilibrium, which may or may not be often.

To conclude this question I may add that the argument of the so-called optimists is neatly summarized in a stern pronouncement against me by my friend Mr Frederic Harrison in a late essay of his, in the words: 'This view of life is not mine.' The solemn declaration does not seem to me to be so annihilating to the said 'view' (really a series of fugitive impressions which I have never tried to co-ordinate) as is complacently assumed. Surely it embodies a too human fallacy quite familiar in logic. Next, a knowing reviewer, apparently a Roman Catholic young man, speaks, with some rather gross instances of the *suggestio falsi* in his whole article, of 'Mr Hardy refusing consolation', the 'dark gravity of his ideas', and so on. When a Positivist and a Romanist agree there must be something wonderful in it, which should make a poet sit up. But . . . O that 'twere possible!

I would not have alluded in this place or anywhere else to such casual personal criticisms – for casual and unreflecting they must be – but for the satisfaction of two or three friends in whose opinion a short answer was deemed desirable, on account of the continual repetition of these criticisms, or more precisely, quizzings. After all, the serious and truly literary inquiry in this connection is: Should a shaper of such stuff as dreams are made on disregard considerations of what is customary and expected, and apply himself to the real function of poetry, the application of ideas to life (in Matthew Arnold's familiar phrase)? This bears more particularly on what has been called the 'philosophy' of these poems – usually reproved as 'queer'. Whoever the author may be that undertakes such application of ideas in this 'philosophic' direction – where it is specially required – glacial judgments must inevitably fall upon him amid opinion whose arbiters largely decry individuality, to whom *ideas* are oddities to smile at, who are moved by a yearning the reverse of that of the Athenian inquirers on Mars Hill; and stiffen their

Apology
4 loving-kindness] lovingkindness MS, LL, UPE
7 that . . . clouds',] Not in MS
16 Next . . . 18 article,] A knowing young man, apparently a Roman-Catholic, speaks, too, in a recent periodical MS
17 whole] Not in LL, UE
19 on.] on, with sportive pity. MS
19 Romanist] Catholic MS, LL, UE
35 to . . . 36 who] Not in MS
37 and] who MS

features not only at sound of a new thing, but at a restatement of old things in new terms. Hence should anything of this sort in the following adumbrations seem 'queer' – should any of them seem to good Panglossians to embody strange and disrespectful conceptions of this best of all possible worlds, I apologize; but cannot help it.

Such divergences, which, though piquant for the nonce, it would be affectation to say are not saddening and discouraging likewise, may, to be sure, arise sometimes from superficial aspect only, writer and reader seeing the same thing at different angles. But in palpable cases of divergence they arise, as already said, whenever a serious effort is made towards that which the authority I have cited – who would now be called old-fashioned, possibly even parochial – affirmed to be what no good critic could deny as the poet's province, the application of ideas to life. One might shrewdly guess, by the by, that in such recommendation the famous writer may have overlooked the cold-shouldering results upon an enthusiastic disciple that would be pretty certain to follow his putting the high aim in practice, and have forgotten the disconcerting experience of Gil Blas with the Archbishop.

To add a few more words to what has already taken up too many, there is a contingency liable to miscellanies of verse that I have never seen mentioned, so far as I can remember; I mean the chance little shocks that may be caused over a book of various character like the present and its predecessors by the juxtaposition of unrelated, even discordant, effusions; poems perhaps years apart in the making, yet facing each other. An odd result of this has been that dramatic anecdotes of a satirical and humorous intention following verse in graver voice, have been read as misfires because they raise the smile that they were intended to raise, the journalist, deaf to the sudden change of key, being unconscious that he is laughing with the author and not at him. I admit that I did not foresee such contingencies as I ought to have done, and that people might not perceive when the tone altered. But the difficulties of arranging the themes in a graduated kinship of moods would have been so great that irrelation was almost unavoidable with efforts so diverse. I must trust for right note-catching to those finely-touched spirits who can divine without half a whisper, whose intuitiveness is proof against all the accidents of inconsequence. In respect of the less

Apology

3 'queer' – should] 'queer' (to use again the favourite word of a critic) – should MS

3–4 Panglossians] philistines MS

4 this . . . 5 it.] life, so they must. MS

6 piquant] piquant and MS

7 likewise] too MS

25 this has] this, more grievous to the author than little shocks, has MS

26 intention following] intention (such e.g., as 'Royal Sponsors') following MS, LL, UE

27 misfires] failures MS

28 deaf] blind MS

28 of key] Not in MS

31 tone] key MS

alert, however, should any one's train of thought be thrown out of gear by a consecutive piping of vocal reeds in jarring tonics, without a semiquaver's rest between, and be led thereby to miss the writer's aim and meaning in one out of two contiguous compositions, I shall deeply regret it.

Having at last, I think, finished with the personal points that I was recommended to notice, I will forsake the immediate object of this Preface; and, leaving *Late Lyrics* to whatever fate it deserves, digress for a few moments to more general considerations. The thoughts of any man of letters concerned to keep poetry alive cannot but run uncomfortably on the precarious prospects of English verse at the present day. Verily the hazards and casualties surrounding the birth and setting forth of almost every modern creation in numbers are ominously like those of one of Shelley's paper-boats on a windy lake. And a forward conjecture scarcely permits the hope of a better time, unless men's tendencies should change. So indeed of all art, literature, and 'high thinking' nowadays. Whether owing to the barbarizing of taste in the younger minds by the dark madness of the late war, the unabashed cultivation of selfishness in all classes, the plethoric growth of knowledge simultaneously with the stunting of wisdom, 'a degrading thirst after outrageous stimulation' (to quote Wordsworth again), or from any other cause, we seem threatened with a new Dark Age.

I formerly thought, like other much exercised writers, that so far as literature was concerned a partial cause might be impotent or mischievous criticism; the satirizing of individuality, the lack of whole-seeing in contemporary estimates of poetry and kindred work, the knowingness affected by junior reviewers, the overgrowth of meticulousness in their peerings for an opinion, as if it were a cultivated habit in them to scrutinize the tool-marks and be blind to the building, to hearken for the key-creaks and be deaf to the diapason, to judge the landscape by a nocturnal exploration with a flash-lantern. In other words, to carry on the old game of sampling the poem or drama by quoting the worst line or worst passage only, in ignorance or not of Coleridge's proof that a versification of any length neither can be nor ought to be all poetry; of reading meanings into a book that its author never dreamt of writing there. I might go on interminably.

But I do not now think any such temporary obstructions to be the

Apology

2 a consecutive piping] an abrupt succession MS

18 dark madness] curse MS

23 other much exercised] so many roughly handled MS, LL, UE

33 in . . . of] when well acquainted with MS

36 there. I] there. Carelessness, too, I adduced, (of which might be given one curiously iterated instance; the statement that this writer's verse is bad, he being a novice of the eleventh hour therein: his prose good, he being a practised hand at it; when by reference to dates it could be seen that he has written verse thirty years, and prose twentyfive at the outside). I MS

36 interminably] indefinitely MS

cause of the hazard, for these negligences and ignorances, though they may have stifled a few true poets in the run of generations, disperse like stricken leaves before the wind of next week, and are no more heard of again in the region of letters than their writers themselves. No: we may be convinced that something of the deeper sort mentioned must be the cause.

In any event poetry, pure literature in general, religion – I include religion, in its essential and undogmatic sense, because poetry and religion touch each other, or rather modulate into each other; are, indeed, often but different names for the same thing – these, I say, the visible signs of mental and emotional life, must like all other things keep moving, becoming; even though at present, when belief in witches of Endor is displacing the Darwinian theory and 'the truth that shall make you free', men's minds appear, as above noted, to be moving backwards rather than on. I speak somewhat sweepingly, and should except many thoughtful writers in verse and prose; also men in certain worthy but small bodies of various denominations, and perhaps in the homely quarter where advance might have been the very least expected a few years back – the English Church – if one reads it rightly as showing evidence of 'removing those things that are shaken', in accordance with the wise Epistolary recommendation to the Hebrews. For since the historic and once august hierarchy of Rome some generation ago lost its chance of being the religion of the future by doing otherwise, and throwing over the little band of New Catholics who were making a struggle for continuity by applying the principle of evolution to their own faith, joining hands with modern science, and outflanking the hesitating English instinct towards liturgical restatement (a flank march which I at the time quite expected to witness, with the gathering of many millions of waiting agnostics into its fold); since then, one may ask, what other purely English establishment than the Church, of sufficient dignity and footing, with such strength of old association, such scope for transmutability, such architectural spell, is left in this country to keep the shreds of morality together?[1]

It may indeed be a forlorn hope, a mere dream, that of an alliance

[1] However, one must not be too sanguine in reading signs, and since the above was written evidence that the Church will go far in the removal of 'things that are shaken' has not been encouraging.

Apology
2 true] good MS
8 religion,] religion MS, LL
8 in . . . sense,] Not in MS, LL
8 essential and] Not in UPE, CP2 [Hardy's copy of CP2 has been corrected to include these words]
15 speak somewhat] speak, of course, somewhat MS, LL
16 thoughtful . . . also] isolated minds; also the minds of MS, LL
24 New Catholics] Neo-Catholics MS, LL
27 restatement] reform MS, LL
29 many] tens of MS
31 with] and with MS, LL
32 such . . . transmutability,] Not in MS, LL
33 together?[1]] The footnote does not appear in MS, LL, UPE, CP2 [Hardy's copy of CP2 has been corrected to include the note]
34 indeed] Not in MS, LL, UPE, CP2 [Hardy's copy of CP2 has been corrected to include the word]

between religion, which must be retained unless the world is to perish, and complete rationality, which must come, unless also the world is to perish, by means of the interfusing effect of poetry – 'the breath and finer spirit of all knowledge; the impassioned expression of science', as it was defined by an English poet who was quite orthodox in his ideas. But if it be true, as Comte argued, that advance is never in a straight line, but in a looped orbit, we may, in the aforesaid ominous moving backward, be doing it *pour mieux sauter*, drawing back for a spring. I repeat that I forlornly hope so, notwithstanding the supercilious regard of hope by Schopenhauer, von Hartmann, and other philosophers down to Einstein who have my respect. But one dares not prophesy. Physical, chronological, and other contingencies keep me in these days from critical studies and literary circles

> Where once we held debate, a band
> Of youthful friends, on mind and art

(if one may quote Tennyson in this century). Hence I cannot know how things are going so well as I used to know them, and the aforesaid limitations must quite prevent my knowing henceforward.

I have to thank the editors and owners of *The Times*, *Fortnightly*, *Mercury*, and other periodicals in which a few of the poems have appeared for kindly assenting to their being reclaimed for collected publication.

February 1922 T.H.

Apology
8 *pour*] Not in MS
10 von . . . respect] and other philosophers MS
16 century] century of 'free verse' (free verse LL, UE) MS, LL, UE
19 *The* . . . 20 other] Not in MS
21 kindly] Not in MS
Note Minor variants, such as the change of a colon to a semi-colon, have been ignored in the Apology

512 *Weathers*

EXTRA PRINTINGS:
(1) *Good Housekeeping*, May 1922, p. 5 = GH
(2) *Chosen Poems*, p. 97

I

THIS is the weather the cuckoo likes,
        And so do I;
When showers betumble the chestnut spikes,
        And nestlings fly:
And the little brown nightingale bills his best,
And they sit outside at 'The Travellers' Rest',
And maids come forth sprig-muslin drest,
And citizens dream of the south and west,
        And so do I.

II

This is the weather the shepherd shuns,
        And so do I;
When beeches drip in browns and duns,
        And thresh, and ply;
And hill-hid tides throb, throe on throe,
And meadow rivulets overflow,
And drops on gate-bars hang in a row,
And rooks in families homeward go,
        And so do I.

513 *The Maid of Keinton Mandeville*

(*A Tribute to Sir H. Bishop*)

I HEAR that maiden still
Of Keinton Mandeville
Singing, in flights that played
As wind-wafts through us all,
Till they made our mood a thrall
To their aery rise and fall,
        'Should he upbraid!'

PROOFS, ETC:
The Berg Collection of the New York Public Library has:
(1) A proof dated 19–4–20 = B1
(2) A proof dated 26–4–20 marked 'Revise' = B2
(3) A typescript marked 'For Friday, April 30' = BT

EXTRA PRINTING:
The Athenaeum, 30 April 1920, p. [565] = A

TITLE:
H. Bishop)] Henry Bishop on the sixty-fifth anniversary of his death: April 30, 1855.) A, B1, B2, BT

Weathers
3 chestnut spikes] chestnut-spikes GH
5 bills] sings MS, GH
11 I;] I. GH
13 thresh,] thresh GH
14 hill-hid tides throb,] from the sea throbs MS
14 hill-hid] distant GH
14 throe,] throe; GH

The Maid of Keinton Mandeville
7 upbraid!] upbraid. MS, B1, B2, BT, A, LL

Rose-necked, in sky-gray gown,
From a stage in Stower Town
Did she sing, and singing smile
As she blent that dexterous voice
With the ditty of her choice,
And banished our annoys
    Thereawhile.

One with such song had power
To wing the heaviest hour
Of him who housed with her.
Who did I never knew
When her spoused estate ondrew,
And her warble flung its woo
    In his ear.

Ah, she's a beldame now,
Time-trenched on cheek and brow,
Whom I once heard as a maid
From Keinton Mandeville
Of matchless scope and skill
Sing, with smile and swell and trill,
    'Should he upbraid!'

1915 or 1916

514 *Summer Schemes*

WHEN friendly summer calls again,
    Calls again
Her little fifers to these hills,
We'll go – we two – to that arched fane
Of leafage where they prime their bills
Before they start to flood the plain
With quavers, minims, shakes, and trills.
    '– We'll go,' I sing; but who shall say
    What may not chance before that day!

The Maid of Keinton Mandeville
15] Such song, such lure (sleight B1, BT), were power B1, B2, BT, A
16 wing] fledge B1, B2, BT, A
17 her.] her: B1, B2, BT, A
19 ondrew] on-drew B1, B2, A
22 a beldame] an ancient B1, B2, BT, A
26 scope] mood B1: vein BT: mien B2, A
1915 or 1916] Not in B1, B2, BT, A

Summer Schemes
9–10 Stanza break in all editions except CP where there is a page turn

And we shall see the waters spring,
        Waters spring
From chinks the scrubby copses crown;
And we shall trace their oncreeping
To where the cascade tumbles down
And sends the bobbing growths aswing,
And ferns not quite but almost drown.
    ' – We shall,' I say; but who may sing
    Of what another moon will bring!

515 *Epeisodia*

EXTRA PRINTING:
Chosen Poems, pp. 98–9

I

PAST the hills that peep
Where the leaze is smiling,
On and on beguiling
Crisply-cropping sheep;
Under boughs of brushwood
Linking tree and tree
In a shade of lushwood,
        There caressed we!

II

Hemmed by city walls
That outshut the sunlight,
In a foggy dun light,
Where the footstep falls
With a pit-pat wearisome
In its cadency
On the flagstones drearisome
        There pressed we!

III

Where in wild-winged crowds
Blown birds show their whiteness
Up against the lightness
Of the clammy clouds;

Summer Schemes
10 spring,] spring; MS

Epeisodia
15 drearisome] drearisome, MS, WE
18 Blown birds] Stormbirds MS *before revision*
20 clouds;] clouds, MS

By the random river
Pushing to the sea,
Under bents that quiver
There shall rest we.

516 *Faintheart in a Railway Train*

EXTRA MANUSCRIPT:
In Colby College Library. This MS is not in Hardy's normal hand and may not be his. It is identical with LM

EXTRA PRINTING:
The London Mercury, Jan 1920, p. 265 = LM

TITLE:
A Glimpse from the Train = LM

AT nine in the morning there passed a church,
At ten there passed me by the sea,
At twelve a town of smoke and smirch,
At two a forest of oak and birch,
And then, on a platform, she:

A radiant stranger, who saw not me.
I said, 'Get out to her do I dare?'
But I kept my seat in my search for a plea,
And the wheels moved on. O could it but be
That I had alighted there!

517 *At Moonrise and Onwards*

I THOUGHT you a fire
On Heath-Plantation Hill,
Dealing out mischief the most dire
To the chattels of men of hire
There in their vill.

But by and by
You turned a yellow-green,
Like a large glow-worm in the sky;
And then I could descry
Your mood and mien.

How well I know
Your furtive feminine shape!
As if reluctantly you show
You nude of cloud, and but by favour throw
Aside its drape. . . .

Epeisodia
23 quiver] quiver, MS, WE
24 shall] Not in MS, LL, UPE, CP2 [Hardy's copy of CP2 has been corrected to include 'shall']

Faintheart in a Railway Train
5 she:] she. LM
6] Her I could see, though she saw not me: LM
6 radiant] matchless MS
7 said] queried MS, LM, LL, UPE, CP2 [Hardy's copy of CP2 has been corrected to 'said']

At Moonrise and Onwards
2 Heath-Plantation] Heron-Plantation MS, LL

– How many a year
Have you kept pace with me,
Wan Woman of the waste up there,
Behind a hedge, or the bare
Bough of a tree!

No novelty are you,
O Lady of all my time,
Veering unbid into my view
Whether I near Death's mew,
Or Life's top cyme!

518 *The Garden Seat*

EXTRA PRINTING:
Chosen Poems, p. 224

Its former green is blue and thin,
And its once firm legs sink in and in;
Soon it will break down unaware,
Soon it will break down unaware.

At night when reddest flowers are black
Those who once sat thereon come back;
Quite a row of them sitting there,
Quite a row of them sitting there.

With them the seat does not break down,
Nor winter freeze them, nor floods drown,
For they are as light as upper air,
They are as light as upper air!

519 *Barthélémon at Vauxhall*

EXTRA PRINTING:
The Times, 23 July 1921, p. 11 = T

François Hippolite Barthélémon, first-fiddler at Vauxhall Gardens, composed what was probably the most popular morning hymn-tune ever written. It was formerly sung, full-voiced, every Sunday in most churches, to Bishop Ken's words, but is now seldom heard.

He said: 'Awake my soul, and with the sun,' . . .
And paused upon the bridge, his eyes due east,
Where was emerging like a full-robed priest
The irradiate globe that vouched the dark as done.

Barthélémon at Vauxhall
Bishop] not in T
At end of introductory note MS has *deleted* 'The circumstances of the following lines have no claim to be more than supposititious'
1 sun,' . . .] sun . . .' T
4–5 Stanza break in all editions

It lit his face – the weary face of one
Who in the adjacent gardens charged his string,
Nightly, with many a tuneful tender thing,
Till stars were weak, and dancing hours outrun.

And then were threads of matin music spun
In trial tones as he pursued his way:
'This is a morn,' he murmured, 'well begun:
This strain to Ken will count when I am clay!'

And count it did; till, caught by echoing lyres,
It spread to galleried naves and mighty quires.

EXTRA MANUSCRIPT:
In the Dorset County Museum. It has no variants.

TITLE:
'I sometimes think' MS

520 I Sometimes Think

(For F.E.H.)

I SOMETIMES think as here I sit
 Of things I have done,
Which seemed in doing not unfit
 To face the sun:
Yet never a soul has paused a whit
 On such – not one.

There was that eager strenuous press
 To sow good seed;
There was that saving from distress
 In the nick of need;
There were those words in the wilderness:
 Who cared to heed?

Yet can this be full true, or no?
 For one did care,
And, spiriting into my house, to, fro,
 Like wind on the stair,
Cares still, heeds all, and will, even though
 I may despair.

Barthélémon at Vauxhall
6 string,] string T
7 Nightly,] Nightly T
7 thing,] thing MS
8 weak,] weak T
11 well begun] well-begun MS
T adds: To-day is the anniversary of his death in 1808. The circumstances of the following lines have no claim to be more than supposititious.

I Sometimes Think
13 be full] Hardy's copy of CP2 has 'be full' underlined and 'quite be' written in margin

521 *Jezreel*

On Its Seizure by the English under Allenby, September 1918

DID they catch as it were in a Vision at shut of the day –
When their cavalry smote through the ancient Esdraelon Plain,
And they crossed where the Tishbite stood forth in his enemy's way –
His gaunt mournful Shade as he bade the King haste off amain?

On war-men at this end of time – even on Englishmen's eyes –
Who slay with their arms of new might in that long-ago place,
Flashed he who drove furiously? . . . Ah, did the phantom arise
Of that queen, of that proud Tyrian woman who painted her face?

Faintly marked they the words 'Throw her down!' from the Night
 eerily,
Spectre-spots of the blood of her body on some rotten wall?
And the thin note of pity that came: 'A King's daughter is she,'
As they passed where she trodden was once by the chargers' footfall?

Could such be the hauntings of men of to-day, at the cease
Of pursuit, at the dusk-hour, ere slumber their senses could seal?
Enghosted seers, kings – one on horseback who asked 'Is it peace?' . . .
Yea, strange things and spectral may men have beheld in Jezreel!

24 September 1918

PROOF, ETC:
It has not been possible to trace the proof and typescript once in the possession of Sir Sydney Cockerell

EXTRA PRINTINGS:
(1) *The Times*, 27 Sept 1918, p. 7 = T
(2) *Air Pie*, the Royal Air Force Annual (London, 1919), p. 44 = AP
(3) Privately printed by Florence Hardy, Sept 1919 = FH
(4) *Chosen Poems*, pp. 257–8

TITLE:
On . . . 1918] Not in MS, T, AP, FH

INDENTATION:
1 = ll. 1, 3 } and so throughout
2 = ll. 2, 4 } T, AP, FH

522 *A Jog-Trot Pair*

WHO were the twain that trod this track
 So many times together
 Hither and back,
In spells of certain and uncertain weather?

Commonplace in conduct they
 Who wandered to and fro here
 Day by day:
Two that few dwellers troubled themselves to know here.

TITLE:
A Jog-trot Pair MS

Jezreel
4 gaunt] gaunt, T, AP, FH
4 King] king T, AP, FH
7 furiously? . . .] furiously? . . T
8 queen,] queen – T, AP, FH
9 Faintly marked] Faint-marked T, AP, FH
9 words] words, T, AP, FH
9 down!] down, T, AP, FH
9 from the] rise from MS, T, AP, FH, LL, UPE, WE, CP2 [Hardy's copy of CP2 has been corrected to 'from the']
9 Night] Time T, AP, FH
11 King's] king's T, AP, FH
12 footfall] foot-fall T, AP, FH
15 kings] kings, T, AP, FH
15 asked] asks T, AP, FH
15 peace?' . . .] peace?' MS
24 September 1918] Not in T, AP: 25 *September* 1918 FH
T adds: (No copyright)

A Jog-Trot Pair
7 day:] day; MS

The very gravel-path was prim
That daily they would follow:
Borders trim:
Never a wayward sprout, or hump, or hollow.

Trite usages in tamest style
Had tended to their plighting.
'It's just worth while,
Perhaps,' they had said. 'And saves much sad good-nighting.'

And petty seemed the happenings
That ministered to their joyance:
Simple things,
Onerous to satiate souls, increased their buoyance.

Who could those common people be,
Of days the plainest, barest?
They were we;
Yes; happier than the cleverest, smartest, rarest.

523 *The Curtains Now Are Drawn*

(*Song*)

EXTRA PRINTING:
Chosen Poems, pp. 106–7

TITLE:
'The Curtains now are drawn' MS
(*Song*)] MS adds 'Major and Minor' and then *deletes*

I

THE curtains now are drawn,
And the spindrift strikes the glass,
Blown up the jaggèd pass
By the surly salt sou'-west,
And the sneering glare is gone
Behind the yonder crest,
While she sings to me:
'O the dream that thou art my Love, be it thine,
And the dream that I am thy Love, be it mine,
And death may come, but loving is divine.'

II

I stand here in the rain,
With its smite upon her stone,

A Jog-Trot Pair
12 sprout, or hump,] growth or hump MS
16 good-nighting] goodnighting MS

The Curtains Now Are Drawn
3 jaggèd] jagged MS, LL
8 art] are MS
II followed in MS by 'Minor' *deleted*
12 stone,] stone MS

And the grasses that have grown
Over women, children, men,
And their texts that 'Life is vain;'
But I hear the notes as when
Once she sang to me:
'O the dream that thou art my Love, be it thine,
And the dream that I am thy Love, be it mine,
And death may come, but loving is divine.'

1913

524 *'According to the Mighty Working'*

I

WHEN moiling seems at cease
In the vague void of night-time,
And heaven's wide roomage stormless
Between the dusk and light-time,
And fear at last is formless,
We call the allurement Peace.

II

Peace, this hid riot, Change,
This revel of quick-cued mumming,
This never truly being,
This evermore becoming,
This spinner's wheel onfleeing
Outside perception's range.

1917

PROOFS, ETC:
The Berg Collection of the New York Public Library has:
(1) A typescript with the *deleted* title 'Transmutation' = BT
(2) A page proof = B1
(3) A page proof marked 'revised proof', 'Press when corrected' = B2

EXTRA PRINTINGS:
(1) *The Athenaeum*, 4 April 1919, p. [129] = A
(2) *Chosen Poems*, p. 218

INDENTATION:
All lines have same indentation in BT, A

525 *I Was Not He*

(Song)

I WAS not he – the man
Who used to pilgrim to your gate,
At whose smart step you grew elate,
And rosed, as maidens can,
For a brief span.

TITLE:
'I was not he' MS

'According to the Mighty Working'
1 at] to BT
2 night-time] night time BT
3] And earth's high arch is stormless BT
3 wide] lamped B1
4 dusk] dark BT, B1
4 light-time] light time MS, BT, B1, B2, A
5 formless,] formless B1
6 allurement] picture BT
6 Peace] peace BT, B1
7 Peace,] Peace – BT, B1, B2, A
7 Change] change BT
8 quick-cued] wordless BT
10 evermore] steadfastly BT
12 Outside] Past all BT
12 perception's] conception's B1, B2, A

It was not I who sang
Beside the keys you touched so true
With note-bent eyes, as if with you
It counted not whence sprang
The voice that rang. . . .

Yet though my destiny
It was to miss your early sweet,
You still, when turned to you my feet,
Had sweet enough to be
A prize for me!

EXTRA MANUSCRIPT:
Plymouth Public Library was presented with a copy of the MS by Hardy in 1923, but this is reported as having been destroyed in the Second World War.

526 *The West-of-Wessex Girl*

A VERY West-of-Wessex girl,
As blithe as blithe could be,
Was once well-known to me,
And she would laud her native town,
And hope and hope that we
Might sometime study up and down
Its charms in company.

But never I squired my Wessex girl
In jaunts to Hoe or street
When hearts were high in beat,
Nor saw her in the marbled ways
Where market-people meet
That in her bounding early days
Were friendly with her feet.

Yet now my West-of-Wessex girl,
When midnight hammers slow
From Andrew's, blow by blow,
As phantom draws me by the hand
To the place – Plymouth Hoe –
Where side by side in life, as planned,
We never were to go!

Begun in Plymouth, March 1913

The West-of-Wessex Girl
1 girl,] girl WE

527 *Welcome Home*

Back to my native place
Bent upon returning,
Bosom all day burning
To be where my race
Well were known, 'twas keen with me
There to dwell in amity.

Folk had sought their beds,
But I hailed: to view me
Under the moon, out to me
Several pushed their heads,
And to each I told my name,
Plans, and that therefrom I came.

'Did you? . . . Ah, 'tis true,'
Said they, 'back a long time,
Here had spent his young time,
Some such man as you. . . .
Good-night.' The casement closed again,
And I was left in the frosty lane.

528 *Going and Staying*

EXTRA PRINTINGS:
(1) *The London Mercury*, Nov 1919, p. 7 = LM
(2) *Modern British Poetry*, ed. Louis Untermeyer (New York, 1920), p. 4 = MBP

I

The moving sun-shapes on the spray,
The sparkles where the brook was flowing,
Pink faces, plightings, moonlit May,
These were the things we wished would stay;
But they were going.

II

Seasons of blankness as of snow,
The silent bleed of a world decaying,
The moan of multitudes in woe,
These were the things we wished would go;
But they were staying.

Welcome Home
1 Back to] To MS, LL, UPE, CP2
5 keen with] planned by MS
5 keen] much LL, UPE, CP2 [Hardy's copy of CP2 is corrected to 'keen']
13 true,'] true MS, LL, UPE, CP2, WE
14 Said they, 'back] I once heard, back MS, LL, UPE, CP2 [Hardy's copy of CP2 has been corrected to 'Said they, 'back]
14 'back] back WE
17 Good-night] Good night MS

Going and Staying
3 May,] May, – MBP
8 woe,] woe, – MBP
Note No stanza numbers in LM, MBP

III

Then we looked closelier at Time,
And saw his ghostly arms revolving
To sweep off woeful things with prime,
Things sinister with things sublime
Alike dissolving.

529 *Read by Moonlight*

I PAUSED to read a letter of hers
By the moon's cold shine,
Eyeing it in the tenderest way,
And edging it up to catch each ray
Upon her light-penned line.
I did not know what years would flow
Of her life's span and mine
Ere I read another letter of hers
By the moon's cold shine!

I chance now on the last of hers,
By the moon's cold shine;
It is the one remaining page
Out of the many shallow and sage
Whereto she set her sign.
Who could foresee there were to be
Such missives of pain and pine
Ere I should read this last of hers
By the moon's cold shine!

530 *At a House in Hampstead*

Sometime the Dwelling of John Keats

O POET, come you haunting here
Where streets have stolen up all around,
And never a nightingale pours one
Full-throated sound?

EXTRA MANUSCRIPTS:
(1) In the Ashley Library in the British Library = A
(2) At Keats's House, Wentworth Place, Hampstead: presented by Hardy in 1925. It contains no variants

EXTRA PRINTING:
The John Keats Memorial Volume (London, 1921), pp. 89–90 = JK

Going and Staying
11–15 Not in LM, MBP

Read by Moonlight
16 missives] letters MS, LL

At a House in Hampstead
2 stolen] crept A, JK
2 around,] around A
4 Full-throated] Full throated A

Drawn from your drowse by the Seven famed Hills,
Thought you to find all just the same
Here shining, as in hours of old,
    If you but came?

What will you do in your surprise
At seeing that changes wrought in Rome
Are wrought yet more on the misty slope
    One time your home?

Will you wake wind-wafts on these stairs?
Swing the doors open noisily?
Show as an umbraged ghost beside
    Your ancient tree?

Or will you, softening, the while
You further and yet further look,
Learn that a laggard few would fain
    Preserve your nook? . . .

– Where the Piazza steps incline,
And catch late light at eventide,
I once stood, in that Rome, and thought,
    ' 'Twas here he died.'

I drew to a violet-sprinkled spot,
Where day and night a pyramid keeps
Uplifted its white hand, and said,
    ' 'Tis there he sleeps.'

Pleasanter now it is to hold
That here, where sang he, more of him
Remains than where he, tuneless, cold,
    Passed to the dim.

July 1920

At a House in Hampstead
5 Seven famed Hills] far Gaunt Gate A, JK
7 hours] days JK
11 slope] hill A, JK
13 wind-wafts] windwafts A, JK
15 an umbraged] a troubled A, JK
18 look,] look; A
20 nook? . . .] nook? . . . . A
22 eventide,] eventide A
July 1920] Not in JK

531 *A Woman's Fancy*

'Ah, Madam; you've indeed come back here?
'Twas sad – your husband's so swift death,
And you away! You shouldn't have left him:
It hastened his last breath.'

'Dame, I am not the lady you think me;
I know not her, nor know her name;
I've come to lodge here – a friendless woman;
My health my only aim.'

She came; she lodged. Wherever she rambled
They held her as no other than
The lady named; and told how her husband
Had died a forsaken man.

So often did they call her thuswise
Mistakenly, by that man's name,
So much did they declare about him,
That his past form and fame

Grew on her, till she pitied his sorrow
As if she truly had been the cause –
Yea, his deserter; and came to wonder
What mould of man he was.

'Tell me my history!' would exclaim she;
'*Our* history,' she said mournfully.
'But *you* know, surely, Ma'am?' they would answer,
Much in perplexity.

Curious, she crept to his grave one evening,
And a second time in the dusk of the morrow;
Then a third time, with crescent emotion
Like a bereaved wife's sorrow.

No gravestone rose by the rounded hillock;
– 'I marvel why this is?' she said.
– 'He had no kindred, Ma'am, but you near.'
– She set a stone at his head.

A Woman's Fancy
20 mould] make MS

She learnt to dream of him, and told them:
'In slumber often uprises he,
And says: "I am joyed that, after all, Dear,
You've not deserted me!" '

At length died too this kinless woman,
As he had died she had grown to crave;
And at her dying she besought them
To bury her in his grave.

Such said, she had paused; until she added:
'Call me by his name on the stone,
As I were, first to last, his dearest,
Not she who left him lone!'

And this they did. And so it became there
That, by the strength of a tender whim,
The stranger was she who bore his name there,
Not she who wedded him.

532 Her Song

I SANG that song on Sunday,
To witch an idle while,
I sang that song on Monday,
As fittest to beguile;
I sang it as the year outwore,
And the new slid in;
I thought not what might shape before
Another would begin.

I sang that song in summer,
All unforeknowingly,
To him as a new-comer
From regions strange to me:
I sang it when in afteryears
The shades stretched out,
And paths were faint; and flocking fears
Brought cup-eyed care and doubt.

Sings he that song on Sundays
  In some dim land afar,
On Saturdays, or Mondays,
  As when the evening star
Glimpsed in upon his bending face,
  And my hanging hair,
And time untouched me with a trace
  Of soul-smart or despair?

533 *A Wet August*

NINE drops of water bead the jessamine,
And nine-and-ninety smear the stones and tiles:
– 'Twas not so in that August – full-rayed, fine –
When we lived out-of-doors, sang songs, strode miles.

Or was there then no noted radiancy
Of summer? Were dun clouds, a dribbling bough,
Gilt over by the light I bore in me,
And was the waste world just the same as now?

It can have been so: yea, that threatenings
Of coming down-drip on the sunless gray,
By the then golden chances seen in things
Were wrought more bright than brightest skies to-day.

1920

534 *The Dissemblers*

TITLE:
The Evaders MS

'IT was not you I came to please,
  Only myself,' flipped she;
'I like this spot of phantasies,
  And thought you far from me.'
But O, he was the secret spell
  That led her to the lea!

Her Song
21 face,] face LL, UPE, WE

A Wet August
2 nine-and-ninety] nine and ninety MS
11 golden chances seen] possibilities MS, LL

The Dissemblers
6–7 Stanza break in all editions

'It was not she who shaped my ways,
Or works, or thoughts,' he said.
'I scarcely marked her living days,
Or missed her much when dead.'
But O, his joyance knew its knell
When daisies hid her head!

535 *To a Lady Playing and Singing in the Morning*

TITLE:
To a Lady playing and singing in the Morning MS

JOYFUL lady, sing!
And I will lurk here listening,
Though nought be done, and nought begun,
And work-hours swift are scurrying.

Sing, O lady, still!
Aye, I will wait each note you trill,
Though duties due that press to do
This whole day long I unfulfil.

'– It is an evening tune;
One not designed to waste the noon,'
You say. I know: time bids me go –
For daytide passes too, too soon!

But let indulgence be,
This once, to my rash ecstasy:
When sounds nowhere that carolled air
My idled morn may comfort me!

536 *A Man Was Drawing Near to Me*

TITLE:
'A Man was drawing near to me' MS
Beneath title MS has *deleted*: (Woman's song)

ON that gray night of mournful drone,
Apart from aught to hear, to see,
I dreamt not that from shires unknown
In gloom, alone,
By Halworthy,
A man was drawing near to me.

To a Lady Playing and Singing in the Morning
10 not designed] undesigned MS

I'd no concern at anything,
No sense of coming pull-heart play;
Yet, under the silent outspreading
    Of even's wing
    Where Otterham lay,
A man was riding up my way.

I thought of nobody – not of one,
But only of trifles – legends, ghosts –
Though, on the moorland dim and dun
    That travellers shun
    About these coasts,
The man had passed Tresparret Posts.

There was no light at all inland,
Only the seaward pharos-fire,
Nothing to let me understand
    That hard at hand
    By Hennett Byre
The man was getting nigh and nigher.

There was a rumble at the door,
A draught disturbed the drapery,
And but a minute passed before,
    With gaze that bore
    My destiny,
The man revealed himself to me.

537 *The Strange House*

(Max Gate, A.D. 2000)

'I HEAR the piano playing –
  Just as a ghost might play.'
'– O, but what are you saying?
  There's no piano to-day;
Their old one was sold and broken;
  Years past it went amiss.'
'– I heard it, or shouldn't have spoken:
    A strange house, this!

A Man Was Drawing Near to Me
9] Yet, through the silent darkening MS *before revision*

The Strange House
2] Just as she used to play.' MS *before revision*
4–6] It's never touched today;/Some of its wires are broken;/Some of its keys amiss.' MS *before revision*

'I catch some undertone here,
From some one out of sight.'
' – Impossible; we are alone here,
And shall be through the night.'
' – The parlour-door – what stirred it?'
' – No one: no soul's in range.'
' – But, anyhow, I heard it,
And it seems strange!

'Seek my own room I cannot –
A figure is on the stair!'
' – What figure? Nay, I scan not
Any one lingering there.
A bough outside is waving,
And that's its shade by the moon.'
' – Well, all is strange! I am craving
Strength to leave soon.'

' – Ah, maybe you've some vision
Of showings beyond our sphere;
Some sight, sense, intuition
Of what once happened here?
The house is old; they've hinted
It once held two love-thralls,
And they may have imprinted
Their dreams on its walls?

'They were – I think 'twas told me –
Queer in their works and ways;
The teller would often hold me
With weird tales of those days.
Some folk can not abide here,
But we – we do not care
Who loved, laughed, wept, or died here,
Knew joy, or despair.'

The Strange House
10 some one] someone MS
20 Any one] Anyone MS
40] Or loved here to despair,' MS *before revision*

EXTRA PRINTING:
Chosen Poems, p. 108

TITLE:
'As 'twere to-night' MS

538 *As 'Twere To-night*

(*Song*)

As 'twere to-night, in the brief space
Of a far eventime,
My spirit rang achime
At vision of a girl of grace;
As 'twere to-night, in the brief space
Of a far eventime.

As 'twere at noontide of to-morrow
I airily walked and talked,
And wondered as I walked
What it could mean, this soar from sorrow;
As 'twere at noontide of to-morrow
I airily walked and talked.

As 'twere at waning of this week
Broke a new life on me;
Trancings of bliss to be
In some dim dear land soon to seek;
As 'twere at waning of this week
Broke a new life on me!

539 *The Contretemps*

A FORWARD rush by the lamp in the gloom,
And we clasped, and almost kissed;
But she was not the woman whom
I had promised to meet in the thawing brume
On that harbour-bridge; nor was I he of her tryst.

So loosening from me swift she said:
'O why, why feign to be
The one I had meant! – to whom I have sped
To fly with, being so sorrily wed!'
– 'Twas thus and thus that she upbraided me.

As 'Twere To-night
10 sorrow;] sorrow, MS

My assignation had struck upon
Some others' like it, I found.
And her lover rose on the night anon;
And then her husband entered on
The lamplit, snowflaked, sloppiness around.

'Take her and welcome, man!' he cried:
'I wash my hands of her.
I'll find me twice as good a bride!'
– All this to me, whom he had eyed,
Plainly, as his wife's planned deliverer.

And next the lover: 'Little I knew,
Madam, you had a third!
Kissing here in my very view!'
– Husband and lover then withdrew.
I let them; and I told them not they erred.

Why not? Well, there faced she and I –
Two strangers who'd kissed, or near,
Chancewise. To see stand weeping by
A woman once embraced, will try
The tension of a man the most austere.

So it began; and I was young,
She pretty, by the lamp,
As flakes came waltzing down among
The waves of her clinging hair, that hung
Heavily on her temples, dark and damp.

And there alone still stood we two;
She one cast off for me,
Or so it seemed: while night ondrew,
Forcing a parley what should do
We twain hearts caught in one catastrophe.

In stranded souls a common strait
Wakes latencies unknown,
Whose impulse may precipitate
A life-long leap. The hour was late,
And there was the Jersey boat with its funnel agroan.

The Contretemps
20 Plainly] Hardy's copy of CP2 has 'Plainly' underlined and ' 'Twas clear' written in margin

'Is wary walking worth much pother?'
It grunted, as still it stayed.
'One pairing is as good as another
Where all is venture! Take each other,
And scrap the oaths that you have aforetime made.' . . .

– Of the four involved there walks but one
On earth at this late day.
And what of the chapter so begun?
In that odd complex what was done?
Well; happiness comes in full to none:
Let peace lie on lulled lips: I will not say.

Weymouth

TITLE:
A Gentleman's Epitaph on himself and a Lady, who were buried together MS

540 *A Gentleman's Epitaph on Himself and a Lady, Who Were Buried Together*

I DWELT in the shade of a city,
She far by the sea,
With folk perhaps good, gracious, witty;
But never with me.

Her form on the ballroom's smooth flooring
I never once met,
To guide her with accents adoring
Through Weippert's 'First Set'.[1]

I spent my life's seasons with pale ones
In Vanity Fair,
And she enjoyed hers among hale ones
In salt-smelling air.

Maybe she had eyes of deep colour,
Maybe they were blue,
Maybe as she aged they got duller;
That never I knew.

[1] Quadrilles danced early in the nineteenth century.

The Contretemps
50 made.' . . .] made.' . . . . . MS
54 odd] queer MS

A Gentleman's Epitaph
1 shade] Shade MS
Quadrilles] Much MS

She may have had lips like the coral,
But I never kissed them,
Saw pouting, nor curling in quarrel,
Nor sought for, nor missed them.

Not a word passed of love all our lifetime,
Between us, nor thrill;
We'd never a husband-and-wife time,
For good or for ill.

Yet as one dust, through bleak days and vernal
Lie I and lies she,
This never-known lady, eternal
Companion to me!

541 *The Old Gown*

(*Song*)

I HAVE seen her in gowns the brightest,
Of azure, green, and red,
And in the simplest, whitest,
Muslined from heel to head;
I have watched her walking, riding,
Shade-flecked by a leafy tree,
Or in fixed thought abiding
By the foam-fingered sea.

In woodlands I have known her,
When boughs were mourning loud,
In the rain-reek she has shown her
Wild-haired and watery-browed.
And once or twice she has cast me
As she pomped along the street
Court-clad, ere quite she had passed me,
A glance from her chariot-seat.

But in my memoried passion
For evermore stands she
In the gown of fading fashion
She wore that night when we,

A Gentleman's Epitaph
21 lifetime,] lifetime MS
25 vernal] vernal, MS, LL, UPE, WE

Doomed long to part, assembled
   In the snug small room; yea, when
She sang with lips that trembled,
   'Shall I see his face again?'

EXTRA PRINTING:
Chosen Poems, p. 219

542 *A Night in November*

I MARKED when the weather changed,
And the panes began to quake,
And the winds rose up and ranged,
That night, lying half-awake.

Dead leaves blew into my room,
And alighted upon my bed,
And a tree declared to the gloom
Its sorrow that they were shed.

One leaf of them touched my hand,
And I thought that it was you
There stood as you used to stand,
And saying at last you knew!

(?) 1913

TITLE:
(The *del*) A Duettist to her Pianoforte MS

543 *A Duettist to Her Pianoforte*

Song of Silence

(E.L.H.-H.C.H.)

SINCE every sound moves memories,
      How can I play you
Just as I might if you raised no scene,
By your ivory rows, of a form between
My vision and your time-worn sheen,
      As when each day you
Answered our fingers with ecstasy?
So it's hushed, hushed, hushed, you are for me!

A Night in November
4 night, lying] night I lay MS

A Duettist to Her Pianoforte
7 our] her MS *before revision*

And as I am doomed to counterchord
Her notes no more
In those old things I used to know,
In a fashion, when we practised so,
'Good-night! – Good-bye!' to your pleated show
Of silk, now hoar,
Each nodding hammer, and pedal and key,
For dead, dead, dead, you are to me!

I fain would second her, strike to her stroke,
As when she was by,
Aye, even from the ancient clamorous 'Fall
Of Paris', or 'Battle of Prague' withal,
To the 'Roving Minstrels', or 'Elfin Call'
Sung soft as a sigh:
But upping ghosts press achefully,
And mute, mute, mute, you are for me!

Should I fling your polyphones, plaints, and quavers
Afresh on the air,
Too quick would the small white shapes be here
Of the fellow twain of hands so dear;
And a black-tressed profile, and pale smooth ear;
– Then how shall I bear
Such heavily-haunted harmony?
Nay: hushed, hushed, hushed, you are for me!

544 *Where Three Roads Joined*

TITLE:
'Where Three Roads (met *del*) joined' MS
Below title MS has *deleted*: (Near Tresparret Posts, Cornwall)

WHERE three roads joined it was green and fair,
And over a gate was the sun-glazed sea,
And life laughed sweet when I halted there;
Yet there I never again would be.

I am sure those branchways are brooding now,
With a wistful blankness upon their face,
While the few mute passengers notice how
Spectre-beridden is the place;

A Duettist to Her Pianoforte
15] And nodding hammers, and pedal, and key, MS
16 dead, you] dead you MS
23 achefully,] achefully WE
24 mute, you] mute you MS
32 hushed, you] hushed you MS, LL, UE

Where Three Roads Joined
2 was] gleamed MS *before revision*
2 sun-glazed] sun-stroked MS

Which nightly sighs like a laden soul,
And grieves that a pair, in bliss for a spell
Not far from thence, should have let it roll
Away from them down a plumbless well

While the phasm of him who fared starts up,
And of her who was waiting him sobs from near
As they haunt there and drink the wormwood cup
They filled for themselves when their sky was clear.

Yes, I see those roads – now rutted and bare,
While over the gate is no sun-glazed sea;
And though life laughed when I halted there,
It is where I never again would be.

545 *'And There Was a Great Calm'*

(On the Signing of the Armistice, 11 Nov. 1918)

EXTRA MANUSCRIPT:
In the Miriam Lutcher Stark Library of the University of Texas = UT

TYPESCRIPT:
In the Library of the University of Yale = UY

PROOF:
In the Library of the University of Yale. It is identical with FH

EXTRA PRINTINGS:
(1) *The Times* (Special Armistice Day Section, p. iii), 11 Nov 1920 = T
(2) Privately printed by Florence Hardy, Dec 1920 = FH

TITLE:
(On . . . Armistice,] Not in MS, UT, UY, T, FH

I

THERE had been years of Passion – scorching, cold,
And much Despair, and Anger heaving high,
Care whitely watching, Sorrows manifold,
Among the young, among the weak and old,
And the pensive Spirit of Pity whispered, 'Why?'

II

Men had not paused to answer. Foes distraught
Pierced the thinned peoples in a brute-like blindness,
Philosophies that sages long had taught,
And Selflessness, were as an unknown thought,
And 'Hell!' and 'Shell!' were yapped at Lovingkindness.

III

The feeble folk at home had grown full-used
To 'dug-outs', 'snipers', 'Huns', from the war-adept
In the mornings heard, and at evetides perused;
To day-dreamt men in millions, when they mused –
To nightmare-men in millions when they slept.

Where Three Roads Joined
12 well] well; MS
14 near] near, MS, LL, UPE
18 is] shines MS *before revision*
18 sun-glazed] sun-stroked MS

'And There Was a Great Calm'
1 scorching] caustic T
1 cold,] cold – UY, T, FH
3 watching,] watching T
4 old,] old; UY, FH: old; – T
5 pensive Spirit of Pity] Spirit of Compassion T
5 whispered,] whispered UY, FH
10 Lovingkindness] Loving-kindness UY, T
11 full-used] full used UY, FH
13 perused;] perused. UY, T
15 millions] millions, UT, UY, T, FH

IV

Waking to wish existence timeless, null,
Sirius they watched above where armies fell;
He seemed to check his flapping when, in the lull
Of night a boom came thencewise, like the dull
Plunge of a stone dropped into some deep well.

V

So, when old hopes that earth was bettering slowly
Were dead and damned, there sounded 'War is done!'
One morrow. Said the bereft, and meek, and lowly,
'Will men some day be given to grace? yea, wholly,
And in good sooth, as our dreams used to run?'

VI

Breathless they paused. Out there men raised their glance
To where had stood those poplars lank and lopped,
As they had raised it through the four years' dance
Of Death in the now familiar flats of France;
And murmured, 'Strange, this! How? All firing stopped?'

VII

Aye; all was hushed. The about-to-fire fired not,
The aimed-at moved away in trance-lipped song.
One checkless regiment slung a clinching shot
And turned. The Spirit of Irony smirked out, 'What?
Spoil peradventures woven of Rage and Wrong?'

VIII

Thenceforth no flying fires inflamed the gray,
No hurtlings shook the dewdrop from the thorn,
No moan perplexed the mute bird on the spray;
Worn horses mused: 'We are not whipped to-day;'
No weft-winged engines blurred the moon's thin horn.

And There Was a Great Calm'
17 fell;] fell: UY, T, FH
20 Plunge] Echo T
22 sounded] sounded, UY, T, FH
23 morrow.] morrow. – MS, UT, UY, T, FH
29 Death] Death, UY, T, FH
29 flats] mud T
31 not,] not. UY, T, FH
34 smirked out,] smirked, MS, UT: smirked UY, T, FH
34 What?] What? – UY, FH

IX

Calm fell. From Heaven distilled a clemency;
There was peace on earth, and silence in the sky;
Some could, some could not, shake off misery:
The Sinister Spirit sneered: 'It had to be!'
And again the Spirit of Pity whispered, 'Why?'

546 Haunting Fingers

A Phantasy in a Museum of Musical Instruments

'ARE you awake,
Comrades, this silent night?
Well 'twere if all of our glossy gluey make
Lay in the damp without, and fell to fragments quite!'

'O viol, my friend,
I watch, though Phosphor nears.
And I fain would drowse away to its utter end
This dumb dark stowage after our loud melodious years!'

And they felt past handlers clutch them,
Though none was in the room,
Old players' dead fingers touch them,
Shrunk in the tomb.

' 'Cello, good mate,
You speak my mind as yours:
Doomed to this voiceless, crippled, corpselike state,
Who, dear to famed Amphion, trapped here, long endures?'

'Once I could thrill
The populace through and through,
Wake them to passioned pulsings past their will.' . . .
(A contra-basso spake so, and the rest sighed anew.)

And they felt old muscles travel
Over their tense contours,
And with long skill unravel
Cunningest scores.

EXTRA MANUSCRIPT:
In the Dorset County Museum = DCM [It is marked 'Sent to New Republic Nov 7 1921']

EXTRA PRINTINGS:
(1) *The New Republic* (New York), 21 Dec 1921, p. 103 = NR
(2) Privately printed by Florence Hardy, Feb 1922 = FH

TITLE:
The Dead Fingers DCM *before revision*
The Haunting Fingers NR

INDENTATION:
MS, DCM, FH have stanzas 3, 6, 9, 12, 15 lined up so that l. 1 of these stanzas is lined up with l. 2 of the remaining stanzas. NR has l. 1 of these stanzas lined up with l. 1 of the remaining stanzas

'And There Was a Great Calm'
42] There was Peace on earth; and Silence in the sky: UY, T, FH
45 And . . . Pity] And the Spirit of Compassion MS *before revision*
45 whispered,] whispered MS, UT, UY, T, FH

Haunting Fingers
6 watch] sleep not NR
6 Phosphor] dawn NR
11 them,] them MS
15 corpselike] corpse-like FH
16] Who here, (here DCM, FH) of Ariel-lineage, (Ariel-lineage FH) trapped so, (so FH) long endures?' MS, DCM, FH: What vibrant frame so trapped and taken long endures?' NR
19 will.' . . .] will' . . . . NR, FH
20 contra-basso] contrabasso MS, DCM, NR
20 spake] spoke MS, NR
21 old muscles] dead touches NR
21 muscles] Hardy in DCM had previously tried 'fingers' and 'touches'
23 long] old NR

'The tender pat
Of her aery finger-tips
Upon me daily – I rejoiced thereat!'
(Thuswise a harpsichord, as 'twere from dampered lips.)

'My keys' white shine,
Now sallow, met a hand
Even whiter. . . . Tones of hers fell forth with mine
In sowings of sound so sweet no lover could withstand!'

And its clavier was filmed with fingers
Like tapering flames – wan, cold –
Or the nebulous light that lingers
In charnel mould.

'Gayer than most
Was I,' reverbed a drum;
'The regiments, marchings, throngs, hurrahs! What a host
I stirred – even when crape mufflings gagged me well-nigh dumb!'

Trilled an aged viol:
'Much tune have I set free
To spur the dance, since my first timid trial
Where I had birth – far hence, in sun-swept Italy!'

And he feels apt touches on him
From those that pressed him then;
Who seem with their glance to con him,
Saying, 'Not again!'

'A holy calm,'
Mourned a shawm's voice subdued,
'Steeped my Cecilian rhythms when hymn and psalm
Poured from devout souls met in Sabbath sanctitude.'

'I faced the sock
Nightly,' twanged a sick lyre,
'Over ranked lights! O charm of life in mock,
O scenes that fed love, hope, wit, rapture, mirth, desire!'

Haunting Fingers
27 thereat!'] thereat!' – NR
28 (Thuswise] Thuswise NR
28 'twere] Not in DCM, NR, FH, LL, UE
28 lips.)] lips. NR
31 whiter. . . .] whiter. . . . . MS: whiter . . . NR
32 sweet] sweet, FH
34] Like weak wan flames in the air, NR
35 the nebulous light] a phosphorous gleam NR
36] In mould laid bare. NR
40 well-nigh] wellnigh FH
41 Trilled] Thrilled NR
45 feels] feels the MS, DCM, FH
45 apt touches] the dead fingers NR
46 From] Of MS, DCM, NR, FH
46 that] who DCM, NR, FH
51] Would steep my rhythms when Sabbath hymn and psalm NR
52 Sabbath] sabbath DCM: weekly NR
54 twanged] (twanged MS, DCM, NR, FH
54 lyre,] lyre) MS: lyre,) DCM, NR: lyre), FH

Thus they, till each past player
Stroked thinner and more thin,
And the morning sky grew grayer
And day crawled in.

547 The Woman I Met

TYPESCRIPT:
In the Miriam Lutcher Stark Library of the University of Texas = UT

EXTRA PRINTING:
The London Mercury, April 1921, pp. 584–6 = LM

TITLE:
The Woman I met MS

A STRANGER, I threaded sunken-hearted
A lamp-lit crowd;
And anon there passed me a soul departed,
Who mutely bowed.
In my far-off youthful years I had met her,
Full-pulsed; but now, no more life's debtor,
Onward she slid
In a shroud that furs half-hid.

'Why do you trouble me, dead woman,
Trouble me;
You whom I knew when warm and human?
– How it be
That you quitted earth and are yet upon it
Is, to any who ponder on it,
Past being read!'
'Still, it is so,' she said.

'These were my haunts in my olden sprightly
Hours of breath;
Here I went tempting frail youth nightly
To their death;
But you deemed me chaste – me, a tinselled sinner!
How thought you one with pureness in her
Could pace this street
Eyeing some man to greet?

'Well; your very simplicity made me love you
Mid such town dross,
Till I set not Heaven itself above you,
Who grew my Cross;

Haunting Fingers
57 past] dead NR
59 grayer] grayer, MS, DCM, NR, FH, WE
60 crawled] looked NR

The Woman I Met
10 me;] me: LM
25 Well;] Well, LM
26 Mid] 'Mid LM
27 you,] you; UT
28] But you were my Cross, UT

For you'd only nod, despite how I sighed for you;
So you tortured me, who fain would have died for you!
– What I suffered then
Would have paid for the sins of ten!

'Thus went the days. I feared you despised me
To fling me a nod
Each time, no more: till love chastised me
As with a rod
That a fresh bland boy of no assurance
Should fire me with passion beyond endurance,
While others all
I hated, and loathed their call.

'I said: "It is his mother's spirit
Hovering around
To shield him, maybe!" I used to fear it,
As still I found
My beauty left no least impression,
And remnants of pride withheld confession
Of my true trade
By speaking; so I delayed.

'I said: "Perhaps with a costly flower
He'll be beguiled."
I held it, in passing you one late hour,
To your face: you smiled,
Keeping step with the throng; though you did not see there
A single one that rivalled me there! ...
Well: it's all past.
I died in the Lock at last.'

So walked the dead and I together
The quick among,
Elbowing our kind of every feather
Slowly and long;
Yea, long and slowly. That a phantom should stalk there
With me seemed nothing strange, and talk there
That winter night
By flaming jets of light.

The Woman I Met
30 So you] Yea, UT, LM
35 more:] more; MS
55 Well:] Well, LM

She showed me Juans who feared their call-time,
    Guessing their lot;
She showed me her sort that cursed their fall-time,
    And that did not.
Till suddenly murmured she: 'Now, tell me,
Why asked you never, ere death befell me,
    To have my love,
  Much as I dreamt thereof?'

I could not answer. And she, well weeting
    All in my heart,
Said: 'God your guardian kept our fleeting
    Forms apart!'
Sighing and drawing her furs around her
Over the shroud that tightly bound her,
    With wafts as from clay
  She turned and thinned away.

London, 1918

TITLE:
'If it's ever spring again' MS

548 *If It's Ever Spring Again*

(*Song*)

If it's ever spring again,
    Spring again,
I shall go where went I when
Down the moor-cock splashed, and hen,
Seeing me not, amid their flounder,
Standing with my arm around her;
If it's ever spring again,
    Spring again,
I shall go where went I then.

If it's ever summer-time,
    Summer-time,
With the hay crop at the prime,
And the cuckoos – two – in rhyme,

The Woman I Met
67 sort] kind UT
69 Now,] Now UT, LM
76 Forms] Hardy's copy of CP2 has been corrected to read 'Flesh']
London, 1918] London; (about *del*) 1918 MS

As they used to be, or seemed to,
We shall do as long we've dreamed to,
If it's ever summer-time,
        Summer-time,
With the hay, and bees achime.

549 The Two Houses

EXTRA PRINTING:
The Dial (New York), Aug 1921, pp. [127]–129 = D

    In the heart of night,
  When farers were not near,
The left house said to the house on the right,
'I have marked your rise, O smart newcomer here.'

    Said the right, cold-eyed:
  'Newcomer here I am,
Hence haler than you with your cracked old hide,
Loose casements, wormy beams, and doors that jam.

    'Modern my wood,
  My hangings fair of hue;
While my windows open as they should,
And water-pipes thread all my chambers through.

    'Your gear is gray,
  Your face wears furrows untold.'
' – Yours might,' mourned the other, 'if you held, brother,
The Presences from aforetime that I hold.

    'You have not known
  Men's lives, deaths, toils, and teens;
You are but a heap of stick and stone:
A new house has no sense of the have-beens.

    'Void as a drum
  You stand: I am packed with these,
Though, strangely, living dwellers who come
See not the phantoms all my substance sees!

The Two Houses
4 newcomer] new-comer MS, D [Line break in LL, UPE]
4 here.] here! D
5] The other replied, D
6 Newcomer] New-comer MS, D
7 haler] stronger D
15 mourned] said D
24 sees!] sees. D

'Visible in the morning
Stand they, when dawn drags in;
Visible at night; yet hint or warning
Of these thin elbowers few of the inmates win.

'Babes new-brought-forth
Obsess my rooms; straight-stretched
Lank corpses, ere outborne to earth;
Yea, throng they as when first from the 'Byss upfetched.

'Dancers and singers
Throb in me now as once;
Rich-noted throats and gossamered flingers
Of heels; the learned in love-lore and the dunce.

'Note here within
The bridegroom and the bride,
Who smile and greet their friends and kin,
And down my stairs depart for tracks untried.

'Where such inbe,
A dwelling's character
Takes theirs, and a vague semblancy
To them in all its limbs, and light, and atmosphere.

'Yet the blind folk
My tenants, who come and go
In the flesh mid these, with souls unwoke,
Of such sylph-like surrounders do not know.'

' – Will the day come,'
Said the new one, awestruck, faint,
'When I shall lodge shades dim and dumb –
And with such spectral guests become acquaint?'

' – That will it, boy;
Such shades will people thee,
Each in his misery, irk, or joy,
And print on thee their presences as on me.'

The Two Houses
26 drags] crawls D
29 new-brought-forth] new-brought forth MS, D
32 'Byss] void MS, D
32 upfetched.] upfetched! D
44 limbs, and light,] limbs and light MS, D
50 Said] (From MS
50 new one] new-built D
50 faint,] faint) MS
56 me.] me! D

550 *On Stinsford Hill at Midnight*

I GLIMPSED a woman's muslined form
Sing-songing airily
Against the moon; and still she sang,
And took no heed of me.

Another trice, and I beheld
What first I had not scanned,
That now and then she tapped and shook
A timbrel in her hand.

So late the hour, so white her drape,
So strange the look it lent
To that blank hill, I could not guess
What phantastry it meant.

Then burst I forth: 'Why such from you?
Are you so happy now?'
Her voice swam on; nor did she show
Thought of me anyhow.

I called again: 'Come nearer; much
That kind of note I need!'
The song kept softening, loudening on,
In placid calm unheed.

'What home is yours now?' then I said;
'You seem to have no care.'
But the wild wavering tune went forth
As if I had not been there.

'This world is dark, and where you are,'
I said, 'I cannot be!'
But still the happy one sang on,
And had no heed of me.

NOTE. – It was said that she belonged to a body of religious enthusiasts.

On Stinsford Hill at Midnight
NOTE . . . enthusiasts.] Note. – The girl was learnt to be one of the Salvation Army. MS: Not in LL, UPE, CP2

EXTRA MANUSCRIPT:
In Cheltenham College Library. There are no variants

EXTRA PRINTING:
Chosen Poems, p. 220

551 *The Fallow Deer at the Lonely House*

ONE without looks in to-night
    Through the curtain-chink
From the sheet of glistening white;
One without looks in to-night
    As we sit and think
    By the fender-brink.

We do not discern those eyes
    Watching in the snow;
Lit by lamps of rosy dyes
We do not discern those eyes
    Wondering, aglow,
    Fourfooted, tiptoe.

EXTRA PRINTING:
Chosen Poems, p. 221

552 *The Selfsame Song*

A BIRD sings the selfsame song,
With never a fault in its flow,
That we listened to here those long
    Long years ago.

A pleasing marvel is how
A strain of such rapturous rote
Should have gone on thus till now
    Unchanged in a note!

– But it's not the selfsame bird. –
No: perished to dust is he. . . .
As also are those who heard
    That song with me.

The Selfsame Song
1 sings] bills MS, LL
11 are those] is she MS *before revision*

553 The Wanderer

THERE is nobody on the road
    But I,
And no beseeming abode
    I can try
For shelter, so abroad
    I must lie.

The stars feel not far up,
    And to be
The lights by which I sup
    Glimmeringly,
Set out in a hollow cup
    Over me.

They wag as though they were
    Panting for joy
Where they shine, above all care,
    And annoy,
And demons of despair –
    Life's alloy.

Sometimes outside the fence
    Feet swing past,
Clock-like, and then go hence,
    Till at last
There is a silence, dense,
    Deep, and vast.

A wanderer, witch-drawn
    To and fro,
To-morrow, at the dawn,
    On I go,
And where I rest anon
    Do not know!

TITLE:
'The Benighted Traveller' MS *del*

Yet it's meet – this bed of hay
And roofless plight;
For there's a house of clay,
My own, quite,
To roof me soon, all day
And all night.

TITLE:
A Wife comes back MS

554 *A Wife Comes Back*

THIS is the story a man told me
Of his life's one day of dreamery.

A woman came into his room
Between the dawn and the creeping day:
She was the years-wed wife from whom
He had parted, and who lived far away,
As if strangers they.

He wondered, and as she stood
She put on youth in her look and air,
And more was he wonderstruck as he viewed
Her form and flesh bloom yet more fair
While he watched her there;

Till she freshed to the pink and brown
That were hers on the night when first they met,
When she was the charm of the idle town,
And he the pick of the club-fire set....
His eyes grew wet,

And he stretched his arms: 'Stay – rest! – '
He cried. 'Abide with me so, my own!'
But his arms closed in on his hard bare breast;
She had vanished with all he had looked upon
Of her beauty: gone.

He clothed, and drew downstairs,
But she was not in the house, he found;
And he passed out under the leafy pairs
Of the avenue elms, and searched around
To the park-pale bound.

A Wife Comes Back
5 years-wed] years'-wed MS
6 away,] away MS
16 set. . . .] set. . . . . MS
23 clothed] Hardy's copy of CP2 has been corrected to 'drest'

He mounted, and rode till night
To the city to which she had long withdrawn,
The vision he bore all day in his sight
Being her young self as pondered on
In the dim of dawn.

' – The lady here long ago –
Is she now here? – young – or such age as she is?'
' – She is still here.' – 'Thank God. Let her know;
She'll pardon a comer so late as this
Whom she'd fain not miss.'

She received him – an ancient dame,
Who hemmed, with features frozen and numb,
'How strange! – I'd almost forgotten your name! –
A call just now – is troublesome;
Why did you come?'

555 *A Young Man's Exhortation*

TITLE:
An Exhortation MS *before revision*

CALL off your eyes from care
By some determined deftness; put forth joys
Dear as excess without the core that cloys,
And charm Life's lourings fair.

Exalt and crown the hour
That girdles us, and fill it full with glee,
Blind glee, excelling aught could ever be
Were heedfulness in power.

Send up such touching strains
That limitless recruits from Fancy's pack
Shall rush upon your tongue, and tender back
All that your soul contains.

For what do we know best?
That a fresh love-leaf crumpled soon will dry,
And that men moment after moment die,
Of all scope dispossest.

A Wife Comes Back
38 received him] entered MS
40 strange] queer MS

If I have seen one thing
It is the passing preciousness of dreams;
That aspects are within us; and who seems
Most kingly is the King.

1867: Westbourne Park Villas

TITLE:
At Lulworth Cove a Century back MS

556 *At Lulworth Cove a Century Back*

HAD I but lived a hundred years ago
I might have gone, as I have gone this year,
By Warmwell Cross on to a Cove I know,
And Time have placed his finger on me there:

'*You see that man?*' – I might have looked, and said,
'O yes: I see him. One that boat has brought
Which dropped down Channel round Saint Alban's Head.
So commonplace a youth calls not my thought.'

'*You see that man?*' – 'Why yes; I told you; yes:
Of an idling town-sort; thin; hair brown in hue;
And as the evening light scants less and less
He looks up at a star, as many do.'

'*You see that man?*' – 'Nay, leave me!' then I plead,
'I have fifteen miles to vamp across the lea,
And it grows dark, and I am weary-kneed:
I have said the third time; yes, that man I see!'

'Good. That man goes to Rome – to death, despair;
And no one notes him now but you and I:
A hundred years, and the world will follow him there,
And bend with reverence where his ashes lie.'

September 1920

NOTE. – In September 1820 Keats, on his way to Rome, landed one day on the Dorset coast, and composed the sonnet, 'Bright Star! would I were steadfast as thou art.' The spot of his landing is judged to have been Lulworth Cove.

A Young Man's Exhortation
Westbourne Park Villas] Not in MS which has '(recopied)' *deleted*

At Lulworth Cove a Century Back
14 fifteen] twenty MS *before revision*
19 years, and the world] years hence folk MS

557 *A Bygone Occasion*

(Song)

THAT night, that night,
That song, that song!
Will such again be evened quite
Through lifetimes long?

No mirth was shown
To outer seers,
But mood to match has not been known
In modern years.

O eyes that smiled,
O lips that lured;
That such would last was one beguiled
To think ensured!

That night, that night,
That song, that song;
O drink to its recalled delight,
Though tears may throng!

558 *Two Serenades*

I

On Christmas Eve

LATE on Christmas Eve, in the street alone,
Outside a house, on the pavement-stone,
I sang to her, as we'd sung together
On former eves ere I felt her tether. –
Above the door of green by me
Was she, her casement seen by me;
But she would not heed
What I melodied
In my soul's sore need –
She would not heed.

Cassiopeia overhead,
And the Seven of the Wain, heard what I said
As I bent me there, and voiced, and fingered
Upon the strings. . . . Long, long I lingered:
Only the curtains hid from her
One whom caprice had bid from her;
But she did not come,
And my heart grew numb
And dull my strum;
She did not come.

II

A Year Later

I SKIMMED the strings; I sang quite low;
I hoped she would not come or know
That the house next door was the one now dittied,
Not hers, as when I had played unpitied;
– Next door, where dwelt a heart fresh stirred,
My new Love, of good will to me,
Unlike my old Love chill to me,
Who had not cared for my notes when heard:
Yet that old Love came
To the other's name
As hers were the claim;
Yea, the old Love came.

My viol sank mute, my tongue stood still,
I tried to sing on, but vain my will:
I prayed she would guess of the later, and leave me;
She stayed, as though, were she slain by the smart,
She would bear love's burn for a newer heart.
The tense-drawn moment wrought to bereave me
Of voice, and I turned in a dumb despair
At her finding I'd come to another there.
Sick I withdrew
At love's grim hue
Ere my last Love knew;
Sick I withdrew.

From an old copy

Two Serenades
13 voiced,] voiced MS
14 strings. . . .] strings. . . . . MS
18 numb] numb, MS
Note ll. 9, 19, 31, 42 are later additions to MS

559 *The Wedding Morning*

TABITHA dressed for her wedding: –
'Tabby, why look so sad?'
'– O I feel a great gloominess spreading, spreading,
Instead of supremely glad! . . .

'I called on Carry last night,
And he came whilst I was there,
Not knowing I'd called. So I kept out of sight,
And I heard what he said to her:

'" – Ah, I'd far liefer marry
You, Dear, to-morrow!" he said,
"But that cannot be." – O I'd give him to Carry,
And willingly see them wed,

'But how can I do it when
His baby will soon be born?
After that I hope I may die. And then
She can have him. I shall not mourn!'

560 *End of the Year 1912*

TITLE:
End of the Old Year MS *before revision*

YOU were here at his young beginning,
You are not here at his agèd end;
Off he coaxed you from Life's mad spinning,
Lest you should see his form extend
Shivering, sighing,
Slowly dying,
And a tear on him expend.

So it comes that we stand lonely
In the star-lit avenue,
Dropping broken lipwords only,
For we hear no songs from you,
Such as flew here
For the new year
Once, while six bells swung thereto.

The Wedding Morning
10 Dear] dear MS

End of the Year 1912
2 agèd] aged MS

EXTRA PRINTING:
Chosen Poems, p. 126

TITLE:
The Chimes play 'Life's a Bumper' MS

561 The Chimes Play 'Life's a Bumper!'

'AWAKE! I'm off to cities far away,'
I said; and rose, on peradventures bent.
The chimes played 'Life's a Bumper!' long that day
To the measure of my walking as I went:
Their sweetness frisked and floated on the lea,
As they played out 'Life's a Bumper!' there to me.

'Awake!' I said. 'I go to take a bride!'
– The sun arose behind me ruby-red
As I journeyed townwards from the countryside,
The chiming bells saluting near ahead.
Their sweetness swelled in tripping tings of glee
As they played out 'Life's a Bumper!' there to me.

'Again arise.' I seek a turfy slope,
And go forth slowly on an autumn noon,
And there I lay her who has been my hope,
And think, 'O may I follow hither soon!'
While on the wind the chimes come cheerily,
Playing out 'Life's a Bumper!' there to me.

1913

TITLE:
'I worked no wile to meet you' MS

562 I Worked No Wile to Meet You

(*Song*)

I WORKED no wile to meet you,
    My sight was set elsewhere,
I sheered about to shun you,
    And lent your life no care.
I was unprimed to greet you
    At such a date and place,
Constraint alone had won you
    Vision of my strange face!

The Chimes Play 'Life's a Bumper!'
3 Bumper!] Bumper MS
3 long] on MS, LL
6 Bumper!] Bumper MS
12 Bumper!] Bumper MS
13 arise.] arise! MS
18 Bumper!] Bumper MS

You did not seek to see me
  Then or at all, you said,
– Meant passing when you neared me,
  But stumbling-blocks forbade.
You even had thought to flee me,
  By other mindings moved;
No influent star endeared me,
  Unknown, unrecked, unproved!

What, then, was there to tell us
  The flux of flustering hours
Of their own tide would bring us
  By no device of ours
To where the daysprings well us
  Heart-hydromels that cheer,
Till Time enearth and swing us
  Round with the turning sphere.

563 *At the Railway Station, Upway*

INDENTATION:
MS has l. 2 lined up with l. 1

'THERE is not much that I can do,
  For I've no money that's quite my own!'
  Spoke up the pitying child –
A little boy with a violin
At the station before the train came in, –
'But I can play my fiddle to you,
And a nice one 'tis, and good in tone!'

  The man in the handcuffs smiled;
The constable looked, and he smiled, too,
  As the fiddle began to twang;
And the man in the handcuffs suddenly sang
      With grimful glee:
      'This life so free
      Is the thing for me!'
And the constable smiled, and said no word,
As if unconscious of what he heard;
And so they went on till the train came in –
The convict, and boy with the violin.

I Worked No Wile to Meet You
12 stumbling-blocks] stumblingblocks MS, LL, UPE

At the Railway Station, Upway
12] Uproariously: MS, LL, UE

564 Side by Side

So there sat they,
The estranged two,
Thrust in one pew
By chance that day;
Placed so, breath-nigh,
Each comer unwitting
Who was to be sitting
In touch close by.

Thus side by side
Blindly alighted,
They seemed united
As groom and bride,
Who'd not communed
For many years –
Lives from twain spheres
With hearts distuned.

Her fringes brushed
His garment's hem
As the harmonies rushed
Through each of them:
Her lips could be heard
In the creed and psalms,
And their fingers neared
At the giving of alms.

And women and men,
The matins ended,
By looks commended
Them, joined again.
Quickly said she,
'Don't undeceive them –
Better thus leave them:'
'Quite so,' said he.

Slight words! – the last
Between them said,
Those two, once wed,
Who had not stood fast.
Diverse their ways
From the western door,
To meet no more
In their span of days.

565 *Dream of the City Shopwoman*

'TWERE sweet to have a comrade here,
Who'd vow to love this garreteer,
By city people's snap and sneer
Tried oft and hard!

We'd rove a truant cock and hen
To some snug solitary glen,
And never be seen to haunt again
This teeming yard.

Within a cot of thatch and clay
We'd list the flitting pipers play,
Our lives a twine of good and gay
Enwreathed discreetly;

Our blithest deeds so neighbouring wise
That doves should coo in soft surprise,
'These must belong to Paradise
Who live so sweetly.'

Our clock should be the closing flowers,
Our sprinkle-bath the passing showers,
Our church the alleyed willow bowers,
The truth our theme;

And infant shapes might soon abound:
Their shining heads would dot us round
Like mushroom balls on grassy ground. . . .
– But all is dream!

O God, that creatures framed to feel
A yearning nature's strong appeal
Should writhe on this eternal wheel
In rayless grime;

And vainly note, with wan regret,
Each star of early promise set;
Till Death relieves, and they forget
Their one Life's time!

Westbourne Park Villas, 1866

566 *A Maiden's Pledge*

(*Song*)

I DO not wish to win your vow
To take me soon or late as bride,
And lift me from the nook where now
I tarry your farings to my side.
I am blissful ever to abide
In this green labyrinth – let all be,
If but, whatever may betide,
You do not leave off loving me!

Your comet-comings I will wait
With patience time shall not wear through;
The yellowing years will not abate
My largened love and truth to you,
Nor drive me to complaint undue
Of absence, much as I may pine,
If never another 'twixt us two
Shall come, and you stand wholly mine.

567 *The Child and the Sage*

YOU say, O Sage, when weather-checked,
'I have been favoured so
With cloudless skies, I must expect
This dash of rain or snow.'

Dream of the City Shopwoman
Below address MS has '(From old MS.)' *deleted*

A Maiden's Pledge
12 MS shows that this line went through the following stages of revision:
1. My large and deathless love for you,
2. My largening love and temper true,
3. My largening love and truth to you,
4. My largening love and truth in you,
5. Back to 3

12 largened] largening MS
16 stand] keep MS

'Since health has been my lot,' you say,
 'So many months of late,
I must not chafe that one short day
 Of sickness mars my state.'

You say, 'Such bliss has been my share
 From Love's unbroken smile,
It is but reason I should bear
 A cross therein awhile.'

And thus you do not count upon
 Continuance of joy;
But, when at ease, expect anon
 A burden of annoy.

But, Sage – this Earth – why not a place
 Where no reprisals reign,
Where never a spell of pleasantness
 Makes reasonable a pain?

21 December 1908

568 Mismet

I

HE was leaning by a face,
He was looking into eyes,
And he knew a trysting-place,
And he heard seductive sighs;
  But the face,
  And the eyes,
  And the place,
  And the sighs,
Were not, alas, the right ones – the ones meet for him –
Though fine and sweet the features, and the feelings all abrim.

The Child and the Sage
Below date MS has '(recopied)' *deleted*

Mismet
10 fine] soft MS

II

She was looking at a form,
She was listening for a tread,
She could feel a waft of charm
When a certain name was said;
    But the form,
    And the tread,
    And the charm,
    And name said,
Were the wrong ones for her, and ever would be so,
While the heritor of the right it would have saved her soul to know!

EXTRA PRINTING:
The Fortnightly Review, 1 Dec 1921, p. [881] = FR

TITLE:
A December Rain-Scene FR

569 *An Autumn Rain-Scene*

THERE trudges one to a merry-making
    With a sturdy swing,
  On whom the rain comes down.

To fetch the saving medicament
    Is another bent,
  On whom the rain comes down.

One slowly drives his herd to the stall
    Ere ill befall,
  On whom the rain comes down.

This bears his missives of life and death
    With quickening breath,
  On whom the rain comes down.

One watches for signals of wreck or war
    From the hill afar,
  On whom the rain comes down.

No care if he gain a shelter or none,
    Unhired moves one,
  On whom the rain comes down.

Mismet
17 charm,] charm MS, LL
18 And] Of the MS: Of LL

An Autumn Rain-Scene
1 merry-making] merrymaking MS, FR, [line break in LL, UPE]
16 No care] Hardy's copy of CP2 has been corrected to 'Careless'
17] Unhired, moves one FR

And another knows nought of its chilling fall
Upon him at all,
On whom the rain comes down.

October 1904

570 *Meditations on a Holiday*

(A New Theme to an Old Folk-Measure)

'TIS a May morning,
All-adorning,
No cloud warning
Of rain to-day.
Where shall I go to,
Go to, go to? –
Can I say No to
Lyonnesse-way?

Well – what reason
Now at this season
Is there for treason
To other shrines?
Tristram is not there,
Isolt forgot there,
New eras blot there
Sought-for signs!

Stratford-on-Avon –
Poesy-paven –
I'll find a haven
There, somehow! –
Nay – I'm but caught of
Dreams long thought of,
The Swan knows nought of
His Avon now!

What shall it be, then,
I go to see, then,
Under the plea, then,
Of votary?

TITLE:
A Meditation on a Holiday MS *before revision* (*A* . . .)] (A new chime to an old folk-metre) MS
Folk-Measure] Folk-Jingle LL, UE

An Autumn Rain-Scene
October 1904] Not in FR

Meditations on a Holiday
2] All things adorning, MS
15 eras] aeras MS
16 Sought-for] Sought for MS
28 votary] poesy MS

I'll go to Lakeland,
Lakeland, Lakeland,
Certainly Lakeland
Let it be.

But – why to that place,
That place, that place,
Such a hard come-at place
Need I fare?
When its bard cheers no more,
Loves no more, fears no more,
Sees no more, hears no more
Anything there!

Ah, there is Scotland,
Burns's Scotland,
And Waverley's. To what land
Better can I hie? –
Yet – if no whit now
Feel those of it now –
Care not a bit now
For it – why I?

I'll seek a town street,
Aye, a brick-brown street,
Quite a tumbledown street,
Drawing no eyes.
For a Mary dwelt there,
And a Percy felt there
Heart of him melt there,
A Claire likewise.

Why incline to *that* city,
Such a city, *that* city,
Now a mud-bespat city! –
Care the lovers who
Now live and walk there,
Sit there and talk there,
Buy there, or hawk there,
Or wed, or woo?

Meditations on a Holiday
35] That nigh-forgat place MS
37 more,] more MS
43 And Waverley's] Scott's too MS
58 Such a] *That* MS
60 the lovers] those MS
63 Buy there,] Buy there MS

Laughters in a volley
Greet so fond a folly
As nursing melancholy
        In this and that spot,
Which, with most endeavour,
Those can visit never,
But for ever and ever
        Will now know not!

If, on lawns Elysian,
With a broadened vision
And a faint derision
        Conscious be they,
How they might reprove me
That these fancies move me,
Think they ill behoove me,
        Smile, and say:

'What! – our hoar old houses,
Where the bygone drowses,
Nor a child nor spouse is
        Of our name at all?
Such abodes to care for,
Inquire about and bear for,
And suffer wear and tear for –
        How weak of you and small!'

May 1921

571 *An Experience*

WIT, weight, or wealth there was not
    In anything that was said,
    In anything that was done;
All was of scope to cause not
    A triumph, dazzle, or dread
    To even the subtlest one,
            My friend,
To even the subtlest one.

Meditations on a Holiday
65 Laughters] Curses MS
68 spot,] spot MS
70 visit] call up MS
81 hoar] gray MS
82 bygone drowses] past dead-drowses LL, UPE, CP2 [Hardy's copy of CP2 has been corrected to read 'bygone' for 'past dead–']
82 bygone] past now MS
May] April 21 MS *before revision*

An Experience
2 anything] any speech MS
2 said] sped MS
3 anything] any deed MS
6 and 8 subtlest] gentlest MS *before revision*

But there was a new afflation –
An aura zephyring round
That care infected not:
It came as a salutation,
And, in my sweet astound,
I scarcely witted what
Might pend,
I scarcely witted what.

The hills in samewise to me
Spoke, as they grayly gazed,
– First hills to speak so yet!
The thin-edged breezes blew me
What I, though cobwebbed, crazed,
Was never to forget,
My friend,
Was never to forget!

572 *The Beauty*

O DO not praise my beauty more,
In such word-wild degree,
And say I am one all eyes adore;
For these things harass me!

But do for ever softly say:
'From now unto the end
Come weal, come wanzing, come what may,
Dear, I will be your friend.'

I hate my beauty in the glass:
My beauty is not I:
I wear it: none cares whether, alas,
Its wearer live or die!

An Experience
9 a new afflation –] an exhalation MS
10] Of some new aura round, MS
10 round] round, LL, UPE

The inner I O care for, then,
Yea, me and what I am,
And shall be at the gray hour when
My cheek begins to clam.

NOTE. – 'The Regent Street beauty, Miss Verrey, the Swiss confectioner's daughter, whose personal attractions have been so mischievously exaggerated, died of fever on Monday evening, brought on by the annoyance she had been for some time subject to.' – London paper, October 1828.

573 *The Collector Cleans His Picture*

TITLE:
The Collector cleans his Picture MS

Fili hominis, ecce ego tollo a te desiderabile oculorum tuorum in plaga. – EZECH., XXIV 16

How I remember cleaning that strange picture! . . .
I had been deep in duty for my sick neighbour –
His besides my own – over several Sundays,
Often, too, in the week; so with parish pressures,
Baptisms, burials, doctorings, conjugal counsel –
All the whatnots asked of a rural parson –
Faith, I was well-nigh broken, should have been fully
Saving for one small secret relaxation,
One that in mounting manhood had grown my hobby.

This was to delve at whiles for easel-lumber,
Stowed in the backmost slums of a soon-reached city,
Merely on chance to uncloak some worthy canvas,
Panel, or plaque, blacked blind by uncouth adventure,
Yet under all concealing a precious artfeat.
Such I had found not yet. My latest capture
Came from the rooms of a trader in ancient house-gear
Who had no scent of beauty or soul for brushcraft.
Only a tittle cost it – murked with grimefilms,
Gatherings of slow years, thick-varnished over,
Never a feature manifest of man's painting.

So, one Saturday, time ticking hard on midnight
Ere an hour subserved, I set me upon it.
Long with coiled-up sleeves I cleaned and yet cleaned,

The Collector Cleans His Picture
plaga] plagâ MS
1 possibly a late insertion in MS. It is lined up with ll. 3–9, while l. 2 is lined up with the opening lines of later stanzas
1 picture! . . .] picture! . . . . . MS
8 Saving] Save MS
14 artfeat] art-feat MS [line break in LL, UPE]
18 grimefilms] grime-films MS [line break in LL, UPE]
19 thick-varnished] thick varnished MS
23 coiled-up] rolled up MS

Till a first fresh spot, a high light, looked forth,
Then another, like fair flesh, and another;
Then a curve, a nostril, and next a finger,
Tapering, shapely, significantly pointing slantwise.
'Flemish?' I said. 'Nay, Spanish. . . . But, nay, Italian!'
– Then meseemed it the guise of the ranker Venus,
Named of some Astarte, of some Cotytto.
Down I knelt before it and kissed the panel,
Drunk with the lure of love's inhibited dreamings.

Till the dawn I rubbed, when there leered up at me
A hag, that had slowly emerged from under my hands there,
Pointing the slanted finger towards a bosom
Eaten away of a rot from the lusts of a lifetime . . .
– I could have ended myself at the lashing lesson!
Stunned I sat till roused by a clear-voiced bell-chime,
Fresh and sweet as the dew-fleece under my luthern.
It was the matin service calling to me
From the adjacent steeple.

574 *The Wood Fire*

(*A Fragment*)

'THIS is a brightsome blaze you've lit, good friend, to-night!'
' – Aye, it has been the bleakest spring I have felt for years,
And nought compares with cloven logs to keep alight:
I buy them bargain-cheap of the executioners,
As I dwell near; and they wanted the crosses out of sight
By Passover, not to affront the eyes of visitors.

'Yes, they're from the crucifixions last week-ending
At Kranion. We can sometimes use the poles again,
But they get split by the nails, and 'tis quicker work than mending
To knock together new; though the uprights now and then
Serve twice when they're let stand. But if a feast's impending,
As lately, you've to tidy up for the comers' ken.

The Collector Cleans His Picture
28 Spanish. . . .] Spanish. . . . . MS
29 ranker] warmer MS
33 leered] gazed LL
35 Pointing . . . finger] The significant finger pointed MS
36 lifetime. . .] lifetime. . . . . MS: lifetime. . . . LL, UPE
37 – I] I MS
37 at . . . lesson!] in heart-shook horror. MS, LL
37 lesson!] lesson. UPE

'Though only three were impaled, you may know it didn't pass off
So quietly as was wont? That Galilee carpenter's son
Who boasted he was king, incensed the rabble to scoff:
I heard the noise from my garden. This piece is the one he was on. . . .
Yes, it blazes up well if lit with a few dry chips and shroff;
And it's worthless for much else, what with cuts and stains thereon.'

575 *Saying Good-bye*

(*Song*)

EXTRA PRINTING:
Chosen Poems, pp. 109–10

We are always saying
'Good-bye, good-bye!'
In work, in playing,
In gloom, in gaying:
At many a stage
Of pilgrimage
From youth to age
We say, 'Good-bye,
Good-bye!'

We are undiscerning
Which go to sigh,
Which will be yearning
For soon returning;
And which no more
Will dark our door,
Or tread our shore,
But go to die,
To die.

Some come from roaming
With joy again;
Some, who come homing
By stealth at gloaming,
Had better have stopped
Till death, and dropped
By strange hands propped,
Than come so fain,
So fain.

So, with this saying,
'Good-bye, good-bye,'
We speed their waying
Without betraying
Our grief, our fear
No more to hear
From them, close, clear,
Again: 'Good-bye,
Good-bye!'

TITLE:
On the tune called the Old-Hundred-and Fourth MS
On a tune by Ravenscroft MS *before revision*

576 On the Tune Called the Old-Hundred-and-Fourth

WE never sang together
Ravenscroft's terse old tune
On Sundays or on weekdays,
In sharp or summer weather,
At night-time or at noon.

Why did we never sing it,
Why never so incline
On Sundays or on weekdays,
Even when soft wafts would wing it
From your far floor to mine?

Shall we that tune, then, never
Stand voicing side by side
On Sundays or on weekdays? . . .
Or shall we, when for ever
In Sheol we abide,

Sing it in desolation,
As we might long have done
On Sundays or on weekdays
With love and exultation
Before our sands had run?

Saying Good-bye
28 saying,] saying MS

On a Tune Called the Old-Hundred-and-Fourth
2] Old Ravenscroft's terse tune MS
13 weekdays? . . .] weekdays? MS
15 Sheol] Hardy had previously tried in MS 'Tophet' and 'Haides'
20 run?] run! MS

577 *The Opportunity*

(*For H.P.*)

FORTY springs back, I recall,
  We met at this phase of the Maytime:
We might have clung close through all,
  But we parted when died that daytime.

We parted with smallest regret;
  Perhaps should have cared but slightly,
Just then, if we never had met:
  Strange, strange that we lived so lightly!

Had we mused a little space
  At that critical date in the Maytime,
One life had been ours, one place,
  Perhaps, till our long cold claytime.

– This is a bitter thing
  For thee, O man: what ails it?
The tide of chance may bring
  Its offer; but nought avails it!

578 *Evelyn G. of Christminster*

TITLE:
To Evelyn of Christminster MS *before revision*

I CAN see the towers
In mind quite clear
Not many hours'
Faring from here;
But how up and go,
And briskly bear
Thither, and know
That you are not there?

The Opportunity
1–4] Forty springs back, to a breath,/We met at this stroke of the daytime:/We might have clung close till death,/But we parted when passed that Maytime. MS *before revision*
4 died] passed MS
13 – This] This MS

Though the birds sing small,
And apple and pear
On your trees by the wall
Are ripe and rare,
Though none excel them,
I have no care
To taste them or smell them
And you not there.

Though the College stones
Are stroked with the sun,
And the gownsmen and Dons
Who held you as one
Of brightest brow
Still think as they did,
Why haunt with them now
Your candle is hid?

Towards the river
A pealing swells:
They cost me a quiver –
Those prayerful bells!
How go to God,
Who can reprove
With so heavy a rod
As your swift remove!

The chorded keys
Wait all in a row,
And the bellows wheeze
As long ago.
And the psalter lingers,
And organist's chair;
But where are your fingers
That once wagged there?

Shall I then seek
That desert place
This or next week,
And those tracks trace

Evelyn G. of Christminster
18 stroked] smit MS, LL, UE
19 gownsmen] Wardens MS: graduates LL

That fill me with cark
And cloy; nowhere
Being movement or mark
Of you now there!

579 The Rift

(*Song: Minor Mode*)

'TWAS just at gnat and cobweb-time,
When yellow begins to show in the leaf,
That your old gamut changed its chime
From those true tones – of span so brief! –
That met my beats of joy, of grief,
        As rhyme meets rhyme.

So sank I from my high sublime!
We faced but chancewise after that,
And never I knew or guessed my crime. . . .
Yes; 'twas the date – or nigh thereat –
Of the yellowing leaf; at moth and gnat
        And cobweb-time.

580 Voices from Things Growing in a Churchyard

THESE flowers are I, poor Fanny Hurd,
        Sir or Madam,
A little girl here sepultured.
Once I flit-fluttered like a bird
Above the grass, as now I wave
In daisy shapes above my grave,
        All day cheerily,
        All night eerily!

– I am one Bachelor Bowring, 'Gent',
        Sir or Madam;
In shingled oak my bones were pent;
Hence more than a hundred years I spent

TYPESCRIPT, ETC:
It has not been possible to trace the typescript, proof and revise once in the possession of Sir Sydney Cockerell

EXTRA PRINTINGS:
(1) *The London Mercury*, Dec 1921, pp. 119–20 = LM
(2) Privately printed by Florence Hardy, Feb 1922 = FH

TITLE:
Voices from Things Growing LM, FH

Voices from Things Growing in a Churchyard
5 grass] bents MS, LM, FH
8 eerily!] eerily. LM, FH

In my feat of change from a coffin-thrall
To a dancer in green as leaves on a wall,
All day cheerily,
All night eerily!

– I, these berries of juice and gloss,
Sir or Madam,
Am clean forgotten as Thomas Voss;
Thin-urned, I have burrowed away from the moss
That covers my sod, and have entered this yew,
And turned to clusters ruddy of view,
All day cheerily,
All night eerily!

– The Lady Gertrude, proud, high-bred,
Sir or Madam,
Am I – this laurel that shades your head;
Into its veins I have stilly sped,
And made them of me; and my leaves now shine,
As did my satins superfine,
All day cheerily,
All night eerily!

– I, who as innocent withwind climb,
Sir or Madam,
Am one Eve Greensleeves, in olden time
Kissed by men from many a clime,
Beneath sun, stars, in blaze, in breeze,
As now by glowworms and by bees,
All day cheerily,
All night eerily![1]

– I'm old Squire Audeley Grey, who grew,
Sir or Madam,
Aweary of life, and in scorn withdrew;
Till anon I clambered up anew
As ivy-green, when my ache was stayed,

[1] It was said her real name was Eve Trevillian or Trevelyan; and that she was the handsome mother of two or three illegitimate children, *circa* 1784–95.

Voices from Things Growing in a Churchyard
13 feat] growth MS, LM, FH [MS has 'growth' underlined and 'feat' written in margin]
16 eerily!] eerily. MS, LM, FH
24 eerily!] eerily. MS, LM, FH
32 eerily!] eerily. MS, LM, FH
35 Eve] Bet MS, LM, FH
38 glowworms] glow-worms LM, FH
39 cheerily,] cheerily LM
40 eerily!] eerily. MS, LM, FH
It . . . 1784–95] Not in LM, FH
two or three] several MS

And in that attire I have longtime gayed
All day cheerily,
All night eerily!

– And so these maskers breathe to each
Sir or Madam
Who lingers there, and their lively speech
Affords an interpreter much to teach,
As their murmurous accents seem to come
Thence hitheraround in a radiant hum,
All day cheerily,
All night eerily!

581 *On the Way*

THE trees fret fitfully and twist,
Shutters rattle and carpets heave,
Slime is the dust of yestereve,
And in the streaming mist
Fishes might seem to fin a passage if they list.

But to his feet,
Drawing nigh and nigher
A hidden seat,
The fog is sweet
And the wind a lyre.

A vacant sameness grays the sky,
A moisture gathers on each knop
Of the bramble, rounding to a drop,
That greets the goer-by
With the cold listless lustre of a dead man's eye.

But to her sight,
Drawing nigh and nigher
Its deep delight,
The fog is bright
And the wind a lyre.

Voices from Things Growing in a Churchyard
46 longtime] long time LM, FH
48 eerily!] eerily. MS, LM, FH
49] – And so they breathe, these growths (masks LL), to each MS, LM, FH, LL
54 hitheraround] hither around LM, FH
56 eerily!] eerily. MS, LM, FH

On the Way
1 fret] writhe MS
14 goer-by] goer by MS
15 eye.] The stop was missing from some copies of CP2–4, but Hardy's copy of CP2 has been corrected to include it

TITLE:
'She did not turn' MS

582 *She Did Not Turn*

SHE did not turn,
But passed foot-faint with averted head
In her gown of green, by the bobbing fern,
Though I leaned over the gate that led
From where we waited with table spread;
But she did not turn:
Why was she near there if love had fled?

She did not turn,
Though the gate was whence I had often sped
In the mists of morning to meet her, and learn
Her heart, when its moving moods I read
As a book – she mine, as she sometimes said;
But she did not turn,
And passed foot-faint with averted head.

583 *Growth in May*

I ENTER a daisy-and-buttercup land,
And thence thread a jungle of grass:
Hurdles and stiles scarce visible stand
Above the lush stems as I pass.

Hedges peer over, and try to be seen,
And seem to reveal a dim sense
That amid such ambitious and elbow-high green
They make a mean show as a fence.

Elsewhere the mead is possessed of the neats,
That range not greatly above
The rich rank thicket which brushes their teats,
And *her* gown, as she waits for her Love.

Near Chard

Growth in May
4 stems as] growths MS

584 The Children and Sir Nameless

SIR NAMELESS, once of Athelhall, declared:
'These wretched children romping in my park
Trample the herbage till the soil is bared,
And yap and yell from early morn till dark!
Go keep them harnessed to their set routines:
Thank God I've none to hasten my decay;
For green remembrance there are better means
Than offspring, who but wish their sires away.'

Sir Nameless of that mansion said anon:
'To be perpetuate for my mightiness
Sculpture must image me when I am gone.'
– He forthwith summoned carvers there express
To shape a figure stretching seven-odd feet
(For he was tall) in alabaster stone,
With shield, and crest, and casque, and sword complete:
When done a statelier work was never known.

Three hundred years hied; Church-restorers came,
And, no one of his lineage being traced,
They thought an effigy so large in frame
Best fitted for the floor. There it was placed,
Under the seats for schoolchildren. And they
Kicked out his name, and hobnailed off his nose;
And, as they yawn through sermon-time, they say,
'Who was this old stone man beneath our toes?'

EXTRA PRINTINGS:
(1) *The Salisbury Times*, 21 April 1922 = ST [A broadside preprint was distributed by the publishers in April. This printing would seem to be the result of that]
(2) *Nash's and Pall Mall Magazine*, May 1922, p. 198 = NPM

TITLE:
The Children versus Sir Nameless MS *before revision*

585 At the Royal Academy

THESE summer landscapes – clump, and copse, and croft –
Woodland and meadowland – here hung aloft,
Gay with limp grass and leafery new and soft,

The Children and Sir Nameless
1 Nameless] Nicholas MS *before revision* [and l. 9]
6 I've] I have ST, NPM
6 decay;] decay: NPM, ST
10 mightiness] mightiness, ST, NPM
12 – He] He ST, NPM
12 summoned carvers there] called an architect MS
13 shape] limn MS
15 casque] ruff MS
15 complete:] complete. ST, NPM
16 statelier] nobler MS
17 Three] Two MS
17 Church-restorers] church-restorers ST, NPM
18 And,] And ST, NPM
22 nose;] nose: ST: nose. NPM
23 sermon-time, they say,] sermon-time they say: ST, NPM

Seem caught from the immediate season's yield
I saw last noonday shining over the field,
By rapid snatch, while still are uncongealed

The saps that in their live originals climb;
Yester's quick greenage here set forth in mime
Just as it stands, now, at our breathing-time.

But these young foils so fresh upon each tree,
Soft verdures spread in sprouting novelty,
Are not this summer's though they feign to be.

Last year their May to Michaelmas term was run,
Last autumn browned and buried every one,
And no more know they sight of any sun.

586 *Her Temple*

DEAR, think not that they will forget you:
  – If craftsmanly art should be mine
I will build up a temple, and set you
    Therein as its shrine.

They may say: 'Why a woman such honour?'
  – Be told, 'O, so sweet was her fame,
That a man heaped this splendour upon her;
    None now knows his name.'

587 *A Two-Years' Idyll*

EXTRA MANUSCRIPT:
On the verso of f. 158 of the Yale University bound-up MS of *Human Shows* are found, cancelled, the title and first four lines of this poem. The wording is identical: the punctuation cannot be guaranteed, but it seems probable that there is no comma at the end of l. 2, and after 'Moving' in l. 4

    YES; such it was;
  Just those two seasons unsought,
Sweeping like summertide wind on our ways;
    Moving, as straws,
  Hearts quick as ours in those days;
Going like wind, too, and rated as nought
  Save as the prelude to plays
  Soon to come – larger, life-fraught:
    Yes; such it was.

At the Royal Academy
6 snatch] touch MS
9 stands, now,] stands now MS
12 summer's] summer's, MS, LL, UPE

Her Temple
8 None now] Hardy's copy of CP2 has 'None now' underlined and '?But none' written in margin

'Nought' it was called,
Even by ourselves – that which springs
Out of the years for all flesh, first or last,
Commonplace, scrawled
Dully on days that go past.
Yet, all the while, it upbore us like wings
Even in hours overcast:
Aye, though this best thing of things,
'Nought' it was called!

What seems it now?
Lost: such beginning was all;
Nothing came after: romance straight forsook
Quickly somehow
Life when we sped from our nook,
Primed for new scenes with designs smart and tall....
– A preface without any book,
A trumpet uplipped, but no call;
That seems it now.

588 By Henstridge Cross at the Year's End

(From this centuries-old cross-road the highway leads east to London, north to Bristol and Bath, west to Exeter and the Land's End, and south to the Channel coast.)

WHY go the east road now?...
That way a youth went on a morrow
After mirth, and he brought back sorrow
Painted upon his brow:
Why go the east road now?

Why go the north road now?
Torn, leaf-strewn, as if scoured by foemen,
Once edging fiefs of my forefolk yeomen,
Fallows fat to the plough:
Why go the north road now?

TYPESCRIPT:
In the Lady Hoare Collection at Stourhead House. It is inscribed 'Sent me by Florence Hardy, from the great Poet, when just finished writing, Nov[r]. 10th 1919' = LH

EXTRA PRINTING:
The Fortnightly Review, Dec 1919, pp. [801]–802 = FR

TITLE:
By Mellstock Cross at the Year's End LH, FR

A Two-Years' Idyll
24 tall....] tall..... MS

By Henstridge Cross at the Year's End
(From ...)] Not in LH, FR
1 now?...] now?.... MS: now?...... LH
2 a youth went] went one LH
4 Painted] Graven LH
7 Torn] Scarred LH
7 foemen,] foemen – LH, FR
8 yeomen,] yeomen – LH, FR
9] Stalwart peers of the plough: LH, FR

Why go the west road now?
Thence to us came she, bosom-burning,
Welcome with joyousness returning. . . .
She sleeps under the bough:
Why go the west road now?

Why go the south road now?
That way marched they some are forgetting,
Stark to the moon left, past regretting
Loves who have falsed their vow. . . .
Why go the south road now?

Why go any road now?
White stands the handpost for brisk onbearers,
'Halt!' is the word for wan-cheeked farers
Musing on Whither, and How. . . .
Why go any road now?

'Yea: we want new feet now'
Answer the stones. 'Want chit-chat, laughter:
Plenty of such to go hereafter
By our tracks, we trow!
We are for new feet now.'

During the War

589 *Penance*

'WHY do you sit, O pale thin man,
At the end of the room
By that harpsichord, built on the quaint old plan?
– It is cold as a tomb,
And there's not a spark within the grate;
And the jingling wires
Are as vain desires
That have lagged too late.'

'Why do I? Alas, far times ago
A woman lyred here
In the evenfall; one who fain did so
From year to year;

By Henstridge Cross at the Year's End
13 Welcome] Welcomes LH
18 to the moon] in a trench LH
19 vow. . . .] vow. . . . . LH
22 onbearers] blithe farers LH
23 farers] carers LH
24 How. . . .] How. . . . . . LH
24 Whither,] Whither LH, FR
26–30] Roads are for others now; (Such are for new feet now; FR)/Hark there to chit-chat, kisses, laughter;/Yea, there be plenty to go hereafter/By these ways, I trow; . . . . . (trow! . . . FR)/Roads are for others now. (They are for new feet now. FR) LH, FR
26 now] now, MS
27 Answer the] Echo these MS
29 our tracks] each track MS
During the War] Not in LH, FR

Penance
1 pale thin man,] thin pale man MS
3 quaint] flat MS
10 lyred] played MS

And, in loneliness bending wistfully,
Would wake each note
In sick sad rote,
None to listen or see!

'I would not join. I would not stay,
But drew away,
Though the winter fire beamed brightly. . . . Aye!
I do to-day
What I would not then; and the chill old keys,
Like a skull's brown teeth
Loose in their sheath,
Freeze my touch; yes, freeze.'

590 I Look in Her Face

TITLE:
'I look in her face' MS

(*Song: Minor*)

I LOOK in her face and say,
'Sing as you used to sing
About Love's blossoming;'
But she hints not Yea or Nay.

'Sing, then, that Love's a pain,
If, Dear, you think it so,
Whether it be or no;'
But dumb her lips remain.

I go to a far-off room,
A faint song ghosts my ear;
Which song I cannot hear,
But it seems to come from a tomb.

591 After the War

LAST Post sounded
Across the mead
To where he loitered
With absent heed.

I Look in Her Face
5–8 Not in MS
9–12] I hasten out of the room,/And then from my far retreat/I hear her singing sweet,/And it seems to come from a tomb. MS

Five years before
In the evening there
Had flown that call
To him and his Dear.
'You'll never come back;
Good-bye!' she had said;
'Here I'll be living,
And my Love dead!'

Those closing minims
Had been as shafts darting
Through him and her pressed
In that last parting;
They thrilled him not now,
In the selfsame place
With the selfsame sun
On his war-seamed face.
'Lurks a god's laughter
In this?' he said,
'That I am the living
And she the dead!'

TITLE:
'If you had known' MS
'If I had known' MS *before revision*

592 *If You Had Known*

If you had known
When listening with her to the far-down moan
Of the white-selvaged and empurpled sea,
And rain came on that did not hinder talk,
Or damp your flashing facile gaiety
In turning home, despite the slow wet walk
By crooked ways, and over stiles of stone;
If you had known

You would lay roses,
Fifty years thence, on her monument, that discloses
Its graying shape upon the luxuriant green;
Fifty years thence to an hour, by chance led there,

If You Had Known
1 you] I MS *before revision* [and so throughout]
2 listening with her] we two listened MS *before revision*
2 far-down] far down MS

What might have moved you? – yea, had you foreseen
That on the tomb of the selfsame one, gone where
The dawn of every day is as the close is,
You would lay roses!

1920

593 *The Chapel-Organist*

(*A.D. 185–*)

I'VE been thinking it through, as I play here to-night, to play never again,
By the light of that lowering sun peering in at the window-pane,
And over the back-street roofs, throwing shades from the boys of the chore
In the gallery, right upon me, sitting up to these keys once more. . . .

How I used to hear tongues ask, as I sat here when I was new:
'Who is she playing the organ? She touches it mightily true!'
'She travels from Havenpool Town,' the deacon would softly speak,
'The stipend can hardly cover her fare hither twice in the week.'
(It fell far short of doing, indeed; but I never told,
For I have craved minstrelsy more than lovers, or beauty, or gold.)

'Twas so he answered at first, but the story grew different later:
'It cannot go on much longer, from what we hear of her now!'
At the meaning wheeze in the words the inquirer would shift his place
Till he could see round the curtain that screened me from people below.
'A handsome girl,' he would murmur, upstaring (and so I am).
'But – too much sex in her build; fine eyes, but eyelids too heavy;
A bosom too full for her age; in her lips too voluptuous a dye.'
(It may be. But who put it there? Assuredly it was not I.)

I went on playing and singing when this I had heard, and more,
Though tears half-blinded me; yes, I remained going on and on,
Just as I used me to chord and to sing at the selfsame time! . . .
For it's a contralto – my voice is; they'll hear it again here to-night
In the psalmody notes that I love far beyond every lower delight.

If You Had Known
13 you] me MS *before revision*

The Chapel-Organist
1 thinking] thinking and thinking MS
1 to-night,] to-night MS
1 to play never] Not in MS
2 By] In MS
6 touches] plays MS
7 She] – She MS
10 minstrelsy] music MS
15 upstaring] upstaring, MS, LL, UPE
17 lips] face MS
17 dye] look MS, LL
21 chord] play MS
21 time! . . .] time! . . . . MS
23 far . . . delight] more than world or than flesh or than life MS, LL, UE
23–4 Stanza break in all editions

Well, the deacon, in fact, that day had learnt new tidings about me;
They troubled his mind not a little, for he was a worthy man.
(He trades as a chemist in High Street, and during the week he had sought
His fellow-deacon, who throve as a bookbinder over the way.)
'These are strange rumours,' he said. 'We must guard the good name of the chapel.
If, sooth, she's of evil report, what else can we do but dismiss her?'
' – But get such another to play here we cannot for double the price!'
It settled the point for the time, and I triumphed awhile in their strait,
And my much-beloved grand semibreves went living on, pending my fate.

At length in the congregation more headshakes and murmurs were rife,
And my dismissal was ruled, though I was not warned of it then.
But a day came when they declared it. The news entered me as a sword;
I was broken; so pallid of face that they thought I should faint, they said.
I rallied. 'O, rather than go, I will play you for nothing!' said I.
'Twas in much desperation I spoke it, for bring me to forfeit I could not
Those melodies chorded so richly for which I had laboured and lived.
They paused. And for nothing I played at the chapel through Sundays again,
Upheld by that art which I loved more than blandishments lavished of men.

But it fell that murmurs anew from the flock broke the pastor's peace.
Some member had seen me at Havenpool, comrading close a sea-captain.
(O yes; I was thereto constrained, lacking means for the fare to and fro.)
Yet God knows, if aught He knows ever, I loved the Old-Hundredth, Saint Stephen's,
Mount Zion, New Sabbath, Miles-Lane, Holy Rest, and Arabia, and Eaton,
Above all embraces of body by wooers who sought me and won! . . .
Next week 'twas declared I was seen coming home with a swain ere the sun.

The Chapel-Organist
32 much-beloved] much beloved MS
32 on . . . fate] on under my fingers MS, LL, UE
40 again] anon MS, LL
42 anew] again MS, LL
44 O yes] Yes MS, LL
45 He] he MS
46] The Hundred-and Thirteenth, New Sabbath, Mount Ephraim, Arabia, and Eaton MS
47 won! . . .] won! . . . . MS
48 swain ere the sun] lover at dawn MS, LL, UE
48–9 No stanza break in MS: page turn in LL, UPE: stanza break in WE, CP2–4

49 The deacons insisted then, strong; and forgiveness I did not implore.
50 I saw all was lost for me, quite, but I made a last bid in my throbs.
51 My bent, finding victual in lust, men's senses had libelled my soul,
52 But the soul should die game, if I knew it! I turned to my masters and said:
53 'I yield, Gentlemen, without parlance. But – let me just hymn you *once* more!
54 It's a little thing, Sirs, that I ask; and a passion is music with me!'
55 They saw that consent would cost nothing, and show as good grace, as knew I,
56 Though tremble I did, and feel sick, as I paused thereat, dumb for their words.
57 They gloomily nodded assent, saying, 'Yes, if you care to. Once more,
58 And only once more, understand.' To that with a bend I agreed.
59 – 'You've a fixed and a far-reaching look,' spoke one who had eyed me awhile.
60 'I've a fixed and a far-reaching plan, and my look only showed it,' I smile.

61 This evening of Sunday is come – the last of my functioning here.
62 'She plays as if she were possessed!' they exclaim, glancing upward and round.
63 'Such harmonies I never dreamt the old instrument capable of!'
64 Meantime the sun lowers and goes; shades deepen; the lights are turned up,
65 And the people voice out the last singing: tune Tallis: the Evening Hymn.
66 (I wonder Dissenters sing Ken: it shows them more liberal in spirit
67 At this little chapel down here than at certain new others I know.)
68 I sing as I play. Murmurs some one: 'No woman's throat richer than hers!'
69 'True: in these parts,' think I. 'But, my man, never more will its richness outspread.'
70 And I sing with them onward: 'The grave dread as little do I as my bed.'

71 I lift up my feet from the pedals; and then, while my eyes are still wet
72 From the symphonies born of my fingers, I do that whereon I am set,
73 And draw from my 'full round bosom' (their words; how can *I* help its heave?)

The Chapel-Organist
51] High love had been beaten by lust; and the senses had conquered the soul, MS, LL
51 My bent,] High love UE
51 lust,] lust UE
60 I smile] said I MS, LL
69] 'True: in these parts, at least,' ponder I. 'But ('But, LL, UE) my man, you will hear it no more.' MS, LL, UE
73 bosom] bosom, MS, LL, UPE
73 heave] shape MS *before revision*
73–4 No stanza break

74 A bottle blue-coloured and fluted – a vinaigrette, they may conceive –
75 And before the choir measures my meaning, reads aught in my moves to and fro,
76 I drink from the phial at a draught, and they think it a pick-me-up; so.
77 Then I gather my books as to leave, bend over the keys as to pray.
78 When they come to me motionless, stooping, quick death will have whisked me away.

79 'Sure, nobody meant her to poison herself in her haste, after all!'
80 The deacons will say as they carry me down and the night shadows fall,
81 'Though the charges were true,' they will add. 'It's a case red as scarlet withal!'
82 I have never once minced it. Lived chaste I have not. Heaven knows it above! . . .
83 But past all the heavings of passion – it's music has been my life-love! . . .
84 That tune did go well – this last playing! . . . I reckon they'll bury me here. . . .
85 Not a soul from the seaport my birthplace – will come, or bestow me . . . a tear.

594 *Fetching Her*

1 An hour before the dawn,
2 My friend,
3 You lit your waiting bedside-lamp,
4 Your breakfast-fire anon,
5 And outing into the dark and damp
6 You saddled, and set on.

7 Thuswise, before the day,
8 My friend,
9 You sought her on her surfy shore,
10 To fetch her thence away
11 Unto your own new-builded door
12 For a staunch lifelong stay.

The Chapel-Organist
76 pick-me-up;] pick-me-up: MS
82 once minced] denied MS
82 above! . . .] above! . . . . MS
83 life-love! . . .] life-love! . . . . MS
84 here. . . .] here . . . MS
85 me . . .] me – MS

You said: 'It seems to be,
My friend,
That I were bringing to my place
The pure brine breeze, the sea,
The mews – all her old sky and space,
In bringing her with me!'

– But time is prompt to expugn,
My friend,
Such magic-minted conjurings:
The brought breeze fainted soon,
And then the sense of seamews' wings,
And the shore's sibilant tune.

So, it had been more due,
My friend,
Perhaps, had you not pulled this flower
From the craggy nook it knew,
And set it in an alien bower;
But left it where it grew!

595 *Could I but Will*

TITLE:
'Could I but Will' MS

(*Song: Verses 1, 3, key major; verse 2, key minor*)

COULD I but will,
Will to my bent,
I'd have afar ones near me still,
And music of rare ravishment,
In strains that move the toes and heels!
And when the sweethearts sat for rest
The unbetrothed should foot with zest
Ecstatic reels.

Could I be head,
Head-god, 'Come, now,
Dear girl,' I'd say, 'whose flame is fled,
Who liest with linen-banded brow,

Fetching Her
19 time] Time MS

Stirred but by shakes from Earth's deep core – '
I'd say to her: 'Unshroud and meet
That Love who kissed and called thee Sweet! –
Yea, come once more!'

Even half-god power
In spinning dooms
Had I, this frozen scene should flower,
And sand-swept plains and Arctic glooms
Should green them gay with waving leaves,
Mid which old friends and I would walk
With weightless feet and magic talk
Uncounted eves.

TITLE:
(A Lady *del*) She revisits alone the Church of her Marriage MS

596 *She Revisits Alone the Church of Her Marriage*

I HAVE come to the church and chancel,
Where all's the same!
– Brighter and larger in my dreams
Truly it shaped than now, meseems,
Is its substantial frame.
But, anyhow, I made my vow,
Whether for praise or blame,
Here in this church and chancel
Where all's the same.

Where touched the check-floored chancel
My knees and his?
The step looks shyly at the sun,
And says, ' 'Twas here the thing was done,
For bale or else for bliss!'
Of all those there I least was ware
Would it be that or this
When touched the check-floored chancel
My knees and his!

Could I but Will
20 sand-swept] desert MS

Here in this fateful chancel
Where all's the same,
I thought the culminant crest of life
Was reached when I went forth the wife
I was not when I came.
Each commonplace one of my race,
Some say, has such an aim –
To go from a fateful chancel
As not the same.

Here, through this hoary chancel
Where all's the same,
A thrill, a gaiety even, ranged
That morning when it seemed I changed
My nature with my name.
Though now not fair, though gray my hair,
He loved me, past proclaim,
Here in this hoary chancel,
Where all's the same.

597 *At the Entering of the New Year*

I

(OLD STYLE)

OUR songs went up and out the chimney,
And roused the home-gone husbandmen;
Our allemands, our heys, poussettings,
Our hands-across and back again,
Sent rhythmic throbbings through the casements
On to the white highway,
Where nighted farers paused and muttered,
'Keep it up well, do they!'

The contrabasso's measured booming
Sped at each bar to the parish bounds,
To shepherds at their midnight lambings,
To stealthy poachers on their rounds;

PROOFS:
In the Berg Collection of the New York Public Library there are three proofs:
(1) Marked 'Proof: The Athenaeum' and bearing date 16.12.20 = B1
(2) Bearing date 20.12.20 = B2
(3) Bearing date 24.12.20 and '2nd revise' = B3

EXTRA PRINTING:
The Athenaeum, 31 Dec 1920, p. [881] = A

She Revisits Alone the Church of Her Marriage
36 Where all's] Who's not MS

At the Entering of the New Year
8 well,] well B1–3, A
10] Sped, (Sped B1) as the old year touched his (its B1) bounds, B1–3, A
10 Sped] Sped, MS

And everybody caught full duly
    The notes of our delight,
As Time unrobed the Youth of Promise
    Hailed by our sanguine sight.

II

(NEW STYLE)

We stand in the dusk of a pine-tree limb,
As if to give ear to the muffled peal,
Brought or withheld at the breeze's whim;
But our truest heed is to words that steal
From the mantled ghost that looms in the gray,
And seems, so far as our sense can see,
To feature bereaved Humanity,
As it sighs to the imminent year its say: –

'O stay without, O stay without,
Calm comely Youth, untasked, untired;
Though stars irradiate thee about
Thy entrance here is undesired.
Open the gate not, mystic one;
Must we avow what we would close confine?
With thee, good friend, we would have converse none,
Albeit the fault may not be thine.'

31 December. During the War

TITLE:
They would not come MS

598 *They Would Not Come*

I TRAVELLED to where in her lifetime
    She'd knelt at morning prayer,
    To call her up as if there;
But she paid no heed to my suing,
As though her old haunt could win not
    A thought from her spirit, or care.

At the Entering of the New Year
14 delight,] delight MS
15–16] Except our heedless headstoned neighbours,/Mute in the moon's cold light. B1
15 Youth] youth B2, 3
15 Promise] promise B2, 3, A
21 ghost] form B1–3, A
23 Humanity] humanity B1–3, A
24 say: –] say: B1–3, A
26 Youth] youth B1–3
29 mystic] hopeful B1
29 one;] one: A
30 avow] unseal B1
31 No italics in B1–3, A
31 good] my B1
31 . . . War] Not in B1–3, A

They Would Not Come
6 spirit,] spirit MS

I went where my friend had lectioned
  The prophets in high declaim,
  That my soul's ear the same
Full tones should catch as aforetime;
But silenced by gear of the Present
  Was the voice that once there came!

Where the ocean had sprayed our banquet
  I stood, to recall it as then:
  The same eluding again!
No vision. Shows contingent
Affrighted it further from me
  Even than from my home-den.

When I found them no responders,
  But fugitives prone to flee
  From where they had used to be,
It vouched I had been led hither
As by night wisps in bogland,
  And bruised the heart of me!

599 *After a Romantic Day*

TITLE:
After a romantic day MS
Below title MS has *deleted* 'Your young men shall see visions.'

  THE railway bore him through
An earthen cutting out from a city:
  There was no scope for view,
Though the frail light shed by a slim young moon
  Fell like a friendly tune.

  Fell like a liquid ditty,
And the blank lack of any charm
  Of landscape did no harm.
The bald steep cutting, rigid, rough,
  And moon-lit, was enough
For poetry of place: its weathered face
Formed a convenient sheet whereon
The visions of his mind were drawn.

They Would Not Come
10 aforetime;] aforetime: MS
11 Present] present MS

After a Romantic Day
9 rigid] inflexible MS

TITLE:
(*Smoker's Club-Story*)] ((Grim *del*) smoker's club-story) MS

600 *The Two Wives*

(*Smoker's Club-Story*)

I WAITED at home all the while they were boating together –
My wife and my near neighbour's wife:
Till there entered a woman I loved more than life,
And we sat and sat on, and beheld the uprising dark weather,
With a sense that some mischief was rife.

Tidings came that the boat had capsized, and that one of the ladies
Was drowned – which of them was unknown:
And I marvelled – my friend's wife? – or was it my own
Who had gone in such wise to the land where the sun as the shade is?
– We learnt it was *his* had so gone.

Then I cried in unrest: 'He is free! But no good is releasing
To him as it would be to me!'
' – But it is,' said the woman I loved, quietly.
'How?' I asked her. ' – Because he has long loved me too without ceasing,
And it's just the same thing, don't you see.'

TITLE:
'I Knew a Lady' MS

601 *I Knew a Lady*

(*Club Song*)

I KNEW a lady when the days
Grew long, and evenings goldened;
But I was not emboldened
By her prompt eyes and winning ways.

And when old Winter nipt the haws,
'Another's wife I'll be,
And then you'll care for me,'
She said, 'and think how sweet I was!'

And soon she shone as another's wife:
As such I often met her,
And sighed, 'How I regret her!
My folly cuts me like a knife!'

And then, to-day, her husband came,
And moaned, 'Why did you flout her?
Well could I do without her!
For both our burdens you are to blame!'

602 A House with a History

THERE is a house in a city street
Some past ones made their own;
Its floors were criss-crossed by their feet,
And their babblings beat
From ceiling to white hearth-stone.

And who are peopling its parlours now?
Who talk across its floor?
Mere freshlings are they, blank of brow,
Who read not how
Its prime had passed before

Their raw equipments, scenes, and says
Afflicted its memoried face,
That had seen every larger phase
Of human ways
Before these filled the place.

To them that house's tale is theirs,
No former voices call
Aloud therein. Its aspect bears
Their joys and cares
Alone, from wall to wall.

603 *A Procession of Dead Days*

I SEE the ghost of a perished day;
I know his face, and the feel of his dawn:
'Twas he who took me far away
   To a spot strange and gray:
Look at me, Day, and then pass on,
But come again: yes, come anon!

Enters another into view;
His features are not cold or white,
But rosy as a vein seen through:
   Too soon he smiles adieu.
Adieu, O ghost-day of delight;
But come and grace my dying sight.

Enters the day that brought the kiss:
He brought it in his foggy hand
To where the mumbling river is,
   And the high clematis;
It lent new colour to the land,
And all the boy within me manned.

Ah, this one. Yes, I know his name,
He is the day that wrought a shine
Even on a precinct common and tame,
   As 'twere of purposed aim.
He shows him as a rainbow sign
Of promise made to me and mine.

The next stands forth in his morning clothes,
And yet, despite their misty blue,
They mark no sombre custom-growths
   That joyous living loathes,
But a meteor act, that left in its queue
A train of sparks my lifetime through.

A Procession of Dead Days
29 meteor act,] shaped act MS
29 left] Not in MS
30 A train of sparks] Left a star-track MS

I almost tremble at his nod –
This next in train – who looks at me
As I were slave, and he were god
  Wielding an iron rod.
I close my eyes; yet still is he
In front there, looking mastery.

In semblance of a face averse
The phantom of the next one comes:
I did not know what better or worse
  Chancings might bless or curse
When his original glossed the thrums
Of ivy, bringing that which numbs.

Yes; trees were turning in their sleep
Upon their windy pillows of gray
When he stole in. Silent his creep
  On the grassed eastern steep. . . .
I shall not soon forget that day,
And what his third hour took away!

604 He Follows Himself

TITLE:
He follows himself MS

In a heavy time I dogged myself
  Along a louring way,
Till my leading self to my following self
  Said: 'Why do you hang on me
    So harassingly?'

'I have watched you, Heart of mine,' I cried,
  'So often going astray
And leaving me, that I have pursued,
  Feeling such truancy
    Ought not to be.'

He said no more, and I dogged him on
  From noon to the dun of day
By prowling paths, until anew
  He begged: 'Please turn and flee! –
    What do you see?'

A Procession of Dead Days
37] In the similitude of a nurse MS, LL
47 not soon forget] forget not soon MS

'Methinks I see a man,' said I,
'Dimming his hours to gray.
I will not leave him while I know
Part of myself is he
Who dreams such dree!'

'I go to my old friend's house,' he urged,
'So do not watch me, pray!'
'Well, I will leave you in peace,' said I,
'Though of this poignancy
You should fight free:

'Your friend, O other me, is dead;
You know not what you say.'
– 'That do I! And at his green-grassed door
By night's bright galaxy
I bend a knee.'

– The yew-plumes moved like mockers' beards
Though only boughs were they,
And I seemed to go; yet still was there,
And am, and there haunt we
Thus bootlessly.

EXTRA PRINTING:
Chosen Poems, p. 121

605 *The Singing Woman*

THERE was a singing woman
Came riding across the mead
At the time of the mild May weather,
Tameless, tireless;
This song she sung: 'I am fair, I am young!'
And many turned to heed.

And the same singing woman
Sat crooning in her need
At the time of the winter weather;
Friendless, fireless,
She sang this song: 'Life, thou'rt too long!'
And there was none to heed.

He Follows Himself
20 dree!] dree. MS
21 friend's] Hardy's copy of CP2 has 'friend's' underlined and 'Qy love's?' in the margin
26 friend] Hardy's copy of CP2 has 'friend' underlined and 'Qy love?' in the margin
28 his] Hardy's copy of CP2 has 'his' underlined and 'Qy her?' in the margin
31 beards] beards, MS, LL, UPE
Note The revisions considered in CP2 have been pencilled in MS and then erased

606 *Without, Not Within Her*

TITLE:
Without, not Within her MS

It was what you bore with you, Woman,
Not inly were,
That throned you from all else human,
However fair!

It was that strange freshness you carried
Into a soul
Whereon no thought of yours tarried
Two moments at all.

And out from his spirit flew death,
And bale, and ban,
Like the corn-chaff under the breath
Of the winnowing-fan.

607 *O I Won't Lead a Homely Life*

EXTRA MANUSCRIPT:
It has not been possible to trace the MS once in the possession of Sir Sydney Cockerell

TITLE:
'O I won't lead a homely life' MS

(*To an old air*)

'O I won't lead a homely life
As father's Jack and mother's Jill,
But I will be a fiddler's wife,
With music mine at will!
Just a little tune,
Another one soon,
As I merrily fling my fill!'

And she became a fiddler's Dear,
And merry all day she strove to be;
And he played and played afar and near,
But never at home played he
Any little tune
Or late or soon;
And sunk and sad was she!

Without, Not Within Her
4 fair!] fair. MS
8] That did it all. MS *before revision*
8 Two moments] One moment MS
9 his] my MS *before revision*

O I Won't Lead a Homely Life
8 Dear] dear MS

608 In the Small Hours

I LAY in my bed and fiddled
 With a dreamland viol and bow,
And the tunes flew back to my fingers
 I had melodied years ago.
It was two or three in the morning
 When I fancy-fiddled so
Long reels and country-dances,
 And hornpipes swift and slow.

And soon anon came crossing
 The chamber in the gray
Figures of jigging fieldfolk –
 Saviours of corn and hay –
To the air of 'Haste to the Wedding',
 As after a wedding-day;
Yea, up and down the middle
 In windless whirls went they!

There danced the bride and bridegroom,
 And couples in a train,
Gay partners time and travail
 Had longwhiles stilled amain! . . .
It seemed a thing for weeping
 To find, at slumber's wane
And morning's sly increeping,
 That Now, not Then, held reign.

609 The Little Old Table

CREAK, little wood thing, creak,
When I touch you with elbow or knee;
That is the way you speak
Of one who gave you to me!

In the Small Hours
4 melodied] played far MS
20 amain! . . .] amain! . . . . . MS

You, little table, she brought –
Brought me with her own hand,
As she looked at me with a thought
That I did not understand.

– Whoever owns it anon,
And hears it, will never know
What a history hangs upon
This creak from long ago.

610 Vagg Hollow[1]

'WHAT do you see in Vagg Hollow,
Little boy, when you go
In the morning at five on your lonely drive?'
' – I see men's souls, who follow
Till we've passed where the road lies low,
When they vanish at our creaking!

'They are like white faces speaking
Beside and behind the waggon –
One just as father's was when here.
The waggoner drinks from his flagon,
(Or he'd flinch when the Hollow is near)
But he does not give me any.

'Sometimes the faces are many;
But I walk along by the horses,
He asleep on the straw as we jog;
And I hear the loud water-courses,
And the drops from the trees in the fog,
And watch till the day is breaking,

[1] Vagg Hollow is a marshy spot on the old Roman Road near Ilchester, where 'things' are seen. Merchandise was formerly fetched inland from the canal-boats at Load-Bridge by waggons this way.

Vagg Hollow
8 Beside] Before MS
9 just] Not in MS
11 Hollow] hollow MS
Merchandise . . . way.] Not in MS

'And the wind out by Tintinhull waking;
I hear in it father's call
As he called when I saw him dying,
And he sat by the fire last Fall,
And mother stood by sighing;
But I'm not afraid at all!'

TITLE:
The Dream is – which? MS
As if not there MS *before revision*

611 *The Dream Is – Which?*

I AM laughing by the brook with her,
  Splashed in its tumbling stir;
And then it is a blankness looms
  As if I walked not there,
Nor she, but found me in haggard rooms,
  And treading a lonely stair.

With radiant cheeks and rapid eyes
  We sit where none espies;
Till a harsh change comes edging in
  As no such scene were there,
But winter, and I were bent and thin,
  And cinder-gray my hair.

We dance in heys around the hall,
  Weightless as thistleball;
And then a curtain drops between,
  As if I danced not there,
But wandered through a mounded green
  To find her, I knew where.

March 1913

EXTRA PRINTINGS:
(1) Privately printed by Florence Hardy, Oct 1917 = FH
(2) *Cassell's Winter Annual 1921–2* (Nov 1921), pp. 67–8. It has not been possible to find a copy of this annual and check the poem

TITLE:
The Fiddler's Story FH

612 *The Country Wedding*

(*A Fiddler's Story*)

LITTLE fogs were gathered in every hollow,
But the purple hillocks enjoyed fine weather
As we marched with our fiddles over the heather
– How it comes back! – to their wedding that day.

The Dream Is – Which?
17 wandered] tottered MS

Our getting there brought our neighbours and all, O!
Till, two and two, the couples stood ready.
And her father said: 'Souls, for God's sake, be steady!'
And we strung up our fiddles, and sounded out 'A'.

The groomsman he stared, and said, 'You must follow!'
But we'd gone to fiddle in front of the party,
(Our feelings as friends being true and hearty)
And fiddle in front we did – all the way.

Yes, from their door by Mill-tail-Shallow,
And up Styles-Lane, and by Front-Street houses,
Where stood maids, bachelors, and spouses,
Who cheered the songs that we knew how to play.

I bowed the treble before her father,
Michael the tenor in front of the lady,
The bass-viol Reub – and right well played he! –
The serpent Jim; ay, to church and back.

I thought the bridegroom was flurried rather,
As we kept up the tune outside the chancel,
While they were swearing things none can cancel
Inside the walls to our drumstick's whack.

'Too gay!' she pleaded. 'Clouds may gather,
And sorrow come.' But she gave in, laughing,
And by supper-time when we'd got to the quaffing
Her fears were forgot, and her smiles weren't slack.

A grand wedding 'twas! And what would follow
We never thought. Or that we should have buried her
On the same day with the man that married her,
A day like the first, half hazy, half clear.

Yes: little fogs were in every hollow,
Though the purple hillocks enjoyed fine weather,
When we went to play 'em to church together,
And carried 'em there in an after year.

The Country Wedding
5–8 Not in FH
5 all,] all MS
8 sounded out] then sounded MS
9 he] Not in FH
9 said,] said FH
10 party,] party FH
11 hearty)] hearty), FH
16 how] Not in FH
21 rather,] rather MS, FH
22 chancel,] chancel MS, FH
24 Inside] Within FH
27 supper-time] supper-time, FH
27 quaffing] quaffing, FH
28 forgot,] forgot MS
32 hazy] hazed FH
33 Yes:] Yes; FH
36] And went to carry them there next year. FH
36 'em] them MS

613 First or Last

(Song)

IF grief come early
Joy comes late,
If joy come early
Grief will wait;
Aye, my dear and tender!

Wise ones joy them early
While the cheeks are red,
Banish grief till surly
Time has dulled their dread.

And joy being ours
Ere youth has flown,
The later hours
May find us gone;
Aye, my dear and tender!

614 Lonely Days

LONELY her fate was,
Environed from sight
In the house where the gate was
Past finding at night.
None there to share it,
No one to tell:
Long she'd to bear it,
And bore it well.

Elsewhere just so she
Spent many a day;
Wishing to go she
Continued to stay.
And people without
Basked warm in the air,
But none sought her out,
Or knew she was there.

Lonely Days
2 Environed] Screened MS
16–17 No stanza break

Even birthdays were passed so,
Sunny and shady:
Years did it last so
For this sad lady.
Never declaring it,
No one to tell,
Still she kept bearing it –
Bore it well.
The days grew chillier,
And then she went
To a city, familiar
In years forespent,
When she walked gaily
Far to and fro,
But now, moving frailly,
Could nowhere go.
The cheerful colour
Of houses she'd known
Had died to a duller
And dingier tone.
Streets were now noisy
Where once had rolled
A few quiet coaches,
Or citizens strolled.
Through the party-wall
Of the memoried spot
They danced at a ball
Who recalled her not.
Tramlines lay crossing
Once gravelled slopes,
Metal rods clanked,
And electric ropes.
So she endured it all,
Thin, thinner wrought,
Until time cured it all,
And she knew nought.

Versified from a Diary

Lonely Days
23 kept] went MS
35 died to] donned them MS
51] And had to bear it all, MS *before revision*

TITLE:
'What did it mean?'

615 *What Did It Mean?*

WHAT did it mean that noontide, when
  You bade me pluck the flower
Within the other woman's bower,
  Whom I knew nought of then?

I thought the flower blushed deeplier – aye,
And as I drew its stalk to me
It seemed to breathe: 'I am, I see,
Made use of in a human play.'

And while I plucked, upstarted sheer
As phantom from the pane thereby
A corpse-like countenance, with eye
That iced me by its baleful peer –
  Silent, as from a bier. . . .

When I came back your face had changed,
  It was no face for me;
O did it speak of hearts estranged,
  And deadly rivalry
      In times before
      I darked your door,
      To seise me of
      Mere second love,
Which still the haunting first deranged?

616 *At the Dinner-Table*

I SAT at dinner in my prime,
And glimpsed my face in the sideboard-glass,
And started as if I had seen a crime,
And prayed the ghastly show might pass.

Wrenched wrinkled features met my sight,
Grinning back to me as my own;
I well-nigh fainted with affright
At finding me a haggard crone.

What Did It Mean?
10 pane] shade MS
13 bier. . . .] bier. . . . . MS

My husband laughed. He had slily set
A warping mirror there, in whim
To startle me. My eyes grew wet;
I spoke not all the eve to him.

He was sorry, he said, for what he had done,
And took away the distorting glass,
Uncovering the accustomed one;
And so it ended? No, alas,

Fifty years later, when he died,
I sat me in the selfsame chair,
Thinking of him. Till, weary-eyed,
I saw the sideboard facing there;

And from its mirror looked the lean
Thing I'd become, each wrinkle and score
The image of me that I had seen
In jest there fifty years before.

617 *The Marble Tablet*

TITLE: The Marble Monument (At St. Juliot) MS

THERE it stands, though alas, what a little of her
    Shows in its cold white look!
Not her glance, glide, or smile; not a tittle of her
    Voice like the purl of a brook;
    Not her thoughts, that you read like a book.

It may stand for her once in November
    When first she breathed, witless of all;
Or in heavy years she would remember
    When circumstance held her in thrall;
    Or at last, when she answered her call!

Nothing more. The still marble, date-graven,
    Gives all that it can, tersely lined;
That one has at length found the haven
    Which every one other will find;
    With silence on what shone behind.

St Juliot: 8 September 1916

At the Dinner-Table
15 Uncovering] And put there MS
20 there;] there, MS

The Marble Tablet
St . . . 1916] September, 1916 MS

TYPESCRIPT, ETC:
It has not been possible to trace the typescript and proof once in the possession of Sir Sydney Cockerell

EXTRA PRINTINGS:
(1) *The Owl*, a Miscellany, May 1919, p. 5 = O
(2) Privately printed by Florence Hardy, Sept 1919 = FH

618 *The Master and the Leaves*

I

WE are budding, Master, budding,
We of your favourite tree;
March drought and April flooding
Arouse us merrily,
Our stemlets newly studding;
And yet you do not see!

II

We are fully woven for summer
In stuff of limpest green,
The twitterer and the hummer
Here rest of nights, unseen,
While like a long-roll drummer
The nightjar thrills the treen.

III

We are turning yellow, Master,
And next we are turning red,
And faster then and faster
Shall seek our rooty bed,
All wasted in disaster!
But you lift not your head.

IV

– 'I mark your early going,
And that you'll soon be clay,
I have seen your summer showing
As in my youthful day;
But why I seem unknowing
Is too sunk in to say!'

1917

The Master and the Leaves
1 Master] master MS, O, FH
4 merrily,] merrily. O
5 Our] The O, FH
5 newly] brightly O, FH
6 see!] see. O, FH
8 stuff] modes O, FH
10] Here rest their rounds between, O, FH
11 long-roll] 'long-roll' O, FH
12 nightjar] nighthawk MS: night-hawk O, FH
13 Master] master MS, O, FH
16 bed,] bed MS: bed – O, FH
17 disaster!] disaster O, FH
18] The magic show we spread! O, FH
19 – 'I] 'I O, FH
23 But why] But – why FH
24 Is too deep down to say.' O, FH
1917] Not in FH

619 *Last Words to a Dumb Friend*

PET was never mourned as you,
Purrer of the spotless hue,
Plumy tail, and wistful gaze
While you humoured our queer ways,
Or outshrilled your morning call
Up the stairs and through the hall –
Foot suspended in its fall –
While, expectant, you would stand
Arched, to meet the stroking hand;
Till your way you chose to wend
Yonder, to your tragic end.

Never another pet for me!
Let your place all vacant be;
Better blankness day by day
Than companion torn away.
Better bid his memory fade,
Better blot each mark he made,
Selfishly escape distress
By contrived forgetfulness,
Than preserve his prints to make
Every morn and eve an ache.

From the chair whereon he sat
Sweep his fur, nor wince thereat;
Rake his little pathways out
Mid the bushes roundabout;
Smooth away his talons' mark
From the claw-worn pine-tree bark,
Where he climbed as dusk embrowned,
Waiting us who loitered round.

Strange it is this speechless thing,
Subject to our mastering,
Subject for his life and food
To our gift, and time, and mood;

Last Words to a Dumb Friend
33 mood;] mood, MS

Timid pensioner of us Powers,
His existence ruled by ours,
Should – by crossing at a breath
Into safe and shielded death,
By the merely taking hence
Of his insignificance –
Loom as largened to the sense,
Shape as part, above man's will,
Of the Imperturbable.

As a prisoner, flight debarred,
Exercising in a yard,
Still retain I, troubled, shaken,
Mean estate, by him forsaken;
And this home, which scarcely took
Impress from his little look,
By his faring to the Dim
Grows all eloquent of him.

Housemate, I can think you still
Bounding to the window-sill,
Over which I vaguely see
Your small mound beneath the tree,
Showing in the autumn shade
That you moulder where you played.

2 October 1904

TITLE:
A (wet *del*) drizzling Easter Morning MS

620 *A Drizzling Easter Morning*

AND he is risen? Well, be it so. . . .
And still the pensive lands complain,
And dead men wait as long ago,
As if, much doubting, they would know
What they are ransomed from, before
They pass again their sheltering door.

Last Words to a Dumb Friend
40 This line was a late addition to MS

A Drizzling Easter Morning
6–7 Stanza break in all editions

I stand amid them in the rain,
While blusters vex the yew and vane;
And on the road the weary wain
Plods forward, laden heavily;
And toilers with their aches are fain
For endless rest – though risen is he.

621 *On One Who Lived and Died Where He Was Born*

TITLE:
On one who lived and died where he was born MS

WHEN a night in November
  Blew forth its bleared airs
An infant descended
  His birth-chamber stairs
  For the very first time,
  At the still, midnight chime;
All unapprehended
  His mission, his aim. –
Thus, first, one November,
An infant descended
    The stairs.

On a night in November
  Of weariful cares,
A frail aged figure
  Ascended those stairs
  For the very last time:
  All gone his life's prime,
All vanished his vigour,
  And fine, forceful frame:
Thus, last, one November
Ascended that figure
    Upstairs.

On those nights in November –
  Apart eighty years –
The babe and the bent one
  Who traversed those stairs

On One Who Lived and Died Where He Was Born
1 a night] an eve MS
2 bleared] moist MS
12 a night] an eve MS
23 nights] eves MS

From the early first time
To the last feeble climb –
That fresh and that spent one –
Were even the same:
Yea, who passed in November
As infant, as bent one,
Those stairs.

Wise child of November!
From birth to blanched hairs
Descending, ascending,
Wealth-wantless, those stairs;
Who saw quick in time
As a vain pantomime
Life's tending, its ending,
The worth of its fame.
Wise child of November,
Descending, ascending
Those stairs!

622 The Second Night

(*Ballad*)

I MISSED one night, but the next I went;
It was gusty above, and clear;
She was there, with the look of one ill-content,
And said: 'Do not come near!'

– 'I am sorry last night to have failed you here,
And now I have travelled all day;
And it's long rowing back to the West-Hoe Pier,
So brief must be my stay.'

– 'O man of mystery, why not say
Out plain to me all you mean?
Why you missed last night, and must now away
Is – another has come between!'

On One Who Lived and Died Where He Was Born
37 stairs;] stairs, MS

– 'O woman so mocking in mood and mien,
So be it!' I replied:
'And if I am due at a differing scene
Before the dark has died,

' 'Tis that, unresting, to wander wide
Has ever been my plight,
And at least I have met you at Cremyll side
If not last eve, to-night.'

– 'You get small rest – that read I quite;
And so do I, maybe;
Though there's a rest hid safe from sight
Elsewhere awaiting me!'

A mad star crossed the sky to the sea,
Wasting in sparks as it streamed,
And when I looked back at her wistfully
She had changed, much changed, it seemed:

The sparks of the star in her pupils gleamed,
She was vague as a vapour now,
And ere of its meaning I had dreamed
She'd vanished – I knew not how.

I stood on, long; each cliff-top bough,
Like a cynic nodding there,
Moved up and down, though no man's brow
But mine met the wayward air.

Still stood I, wholly unaware
Of what had come to pass,
Or had brought the secret of my new Fair
To my old Love, alas!

I went down then by crag and grass
To the boat wherein I had come.
Said the man with the oars: 'This news of the lass
Of Edgcumbe, is sharp for some!

The Second Night
16 dark] night MS
27 back at her wistfully] to where stood she MS, LL
28 seemed:] seemed. CP2–4 [But some evidence of print defect]
44 some!] some. MS

'Yes: found this daybreak, stiff and numb
On the shore here, whither she'd sped
To meet her lover last night in the glum,
And he came not, 'tis said.

'And she leapt down, heart-hit. Pity she's dead:
So much for the faithful-bent!' . . .
I looked, and again a star overhead
Shot through the firmament.

TITLE:
She who saw not MS

623 *She Who Saw Not*

'DID you see something within the house
That made me call you before the red sunsetting?
Something that all this common scene endows
With a richened impress there can be no forgetting?'

' – I have found nothing to see therein,
O Sage, that should have made you urge me to enter,
Nothing to fire the soul, or the sense to win:
I rate you as a rare misrepresenter!'

' – Go anew, Lady, – in by the right. . . .
Well: why does your face not shine like the face of Moses?'
' – I found no moving thing there save the light
And shadow flung on the wall by the outside roses.'

' – Go yet once more, pray. Look on a seat.'
' – I go. . . . O Sage, it's only a man that sits there
With eyes on the sun. Mute, – average head to feet.'
' – No more?' – 'No more. Just one the place befits there,

'As the rays reach in through the open door,
And he looks at his hand, and the sun glows through his fingers,
While he's thinking thoughts whose tenour is no more
To me than the swaying rose-tree shade that lingers.'

No more. And years drew on and on
Till no sun came, dank fogs the house enfolding;
And she saw inside, when the form in the flesh had gone,
As a vision what she had missed when the real beholding.

The Second Night
50 faithful-bent!' . . .] faithful-bent!' . . . . MS
51 looked,] looked MS

She Who Saw Not
9 right. . . .] right. . . . . MS
14 go. . . .] go. . . . . MS
16 there,] there MS

624 *The Old Workman*

TITLE:
The Old (Mason *del*) Workman MS

'WHY are you so bent down before your time,
Old mason? Many have not left their prime
So far behind at your age, and can still
        Stand full upright at will.'

He pointed to the mansion-front hard by,
And to the stones of the quoin against the sky;
'Those upper blocks,' he said, 'that there you see,
        It was that ruined me.'

There stood in the air up to the parapet
Crowning the corner height, the stones as set
By him – ashlar whereon the gales might drum
        For centuries to come.

'I carried them up,' he said, 'by a ladder there;
The last was as big a load as I could bear;
But on I heaved; and something in my back
        Moved, as 'twere with a crack.

'So I got crookt. I never lost that sprain;
And those who live there, walled from wind and rain
By freestone that I lifted, do not know
        That my life's ache came so.

'They don't know me, or even know my name,
But good I think it, somehow, all the same
To have kept 'em safe from harm, and right and tight,
        Though it has broke me quite.

'Yes; that I fixed it firm up there I am proud,
Facing the hail and snow and sun and cloud,
And to stand storms for ages, beating round
        When I lie underground.'

The Old Workman
1 time,] time MS
7 see,] see MS

EXTRA PRINTING:
The Anglo-Italian Review, Sept 1918, p. 1 = AIR

625 The Sailor's Mother

'O WHENCE do you come,
Figure in the night-fog that chills me numb?'

'I come to you across from my house up there,
And I don't mind the brine-mist clinging to me
That blows from the quay,
For I heard him in my chamber, and thought you unaware.'

'But what did you hear,
That brought you blindly knocking in this middle-watch so drear?'

'My sailor son's voice as 'twere calling at your door,
And I don't mind my bare feet clammy on the stones,
And the blight to my bones,
For he only knows of *this* house I lived in before.'

'Nobody's nigh,
Woman like a skeleton, with socket-sunk eye.'

'Ah – nobody's nigh! And my life is drearisome,
And this is the old home we loved in many a day
Before he went away;
And the salt fog mops me. And nobody's come!'

From 'To Please His Wife'

626 Outside the Casement

(*A Reminiscence of the War*)

WE sat in the room
And praised her whom
We saw in the portico-shade outside:
She could not hear
What was said of her,
But smiled, for its purport we did not hide.

The Sailor's Mother
7 hear,] hear AIR
8 so] Not in AIR
18 mops] smears AIR
From . . . Wife'] Not in AIR

Then in was brought
That message, fraught
With evil fortune for her out there,
Whom we loved that day
More than any could say,
And would fain have fenced from a waft of care.

And the question pressed
Like lead on each breast,
Should we cloak the tidings, or call her and tell?
It was too intense
A choice for our sense,
As we pondered and watched her we loved so well.

Yea, spirit failed us
At what assailed us;
How long, while seeing what soon must come,
Should we counterfeit
No knowledge of it,
And stay the stroke that would blanch and numb?

And thus, before
For evermore
Joy left her, we practised to beguile
Her innocence when
She now and again
Looked in, and smiled us another smile.

627 *The Passer-By*

(*L.H. Recalls Her Romance*)

HE used to pass, well-trimmed and brushed,
My window every day,
And when I smiled on him he blushed,
That youth, quite as a girl might; aye,
In the shyest way.

TITLE: The Passer-by
In Memoriam L—— H——
(She speaks) MS

The Passer-By
4 aye,] aye MS
5 way.] way! MS

Thus often did he pass hereby,
    That youth of bounding gait,
Until the one who blushed was I,
And he became, as here I sate,
        My joy, my fate.

And now he passes by no more,
    That youth I loved too true!
I grieve should he, as here of yore,
Pass elsewhere, seated in his view,
        Some maiden new!

If such should be, alas for her!
    He'll make her feel him dear,
Become her daily comforter,
Then tire him of her beauteous gear,
        And disappear!

TITLE:
'I was the midmost' MS

628 I Was the Midmost

I WAS the midmost of my world
    When first I frisked me free,
For though within its circuit gleamed
    But a small company,
And I was immature, they seemed
    To bend their looks on me.

She was the midmost of my world
    When I went further forth,
And hence it was that, whether I turned
    To south, east, west, or north,
Beams of an all-day Polestar burned
    From that new axe of earth.

Where now is midmost in my world?
    I trace it not at all:
No midmost shows it here, or there,
    When wistful voices call
'We are fain! We are fain!' from everywhere
    On Earth's bewildering ball!

The Passer-By
11 by] here MS

629 *A Sound in the Night*

(*Woodsford Castle: 17—*)

'WHAT do I catch upon the night-wind, husband? –
What is it sounds in this house so eerily?
It seems to be a woman's voice: each little while I hear it,
And it much troubles me!'

' 'Tis but the eaves dripping down upon the plinth-slopes:
Letting fancies worry thee! – sure 'tis a foolish thing,
When we were on'y coupled half an hour before the noontide,
And now it's but evening.'

'Yet seems it still a woman's voice outside the castle, husband,
And 'tis cold to-night, and rain beats, and this is a lonely place.
Didst thou fathom much of womankind in travel or adventure
Ere ever thou sawest my face?'

'It may be a tree, bride, that rubs his arms acrosswise,
If it is not the eaves-drip upon the lower slopes,
Or the river at the bend, where it whirls about the hatches
Like a creature that sighs and mopes.'

'Yet it still seems to me like the crying of a woman,
And it saddens me much that so piteous a sound
On this my bridal night when I would get agone from sorrow
Should so ghost-like wander round!'

'To satisfy thee, Love, I will strike the flint-and-steel, then,
And set the rush-candle up, and undo the door,
And take the new horn-lantern that we bought upon our journey,
And throw the light over the moor.'

He struck a light, and breeched and booted in the further chamber,
And lit the new horn-lantern and went from her sight,
And vanished down the turret; and she heard him pass the postern,
And go out into the night.

A Sound in the Night
21 flint-and-steel] flint and steel MS
26 horn-lantern] horn-lantern, MS

She listened as she lay, till she heard his step returning,
And his voice as he unclothed him: ' 'Twas nothing, as I said,
But the nor'-west wind a-blowing from the moor ath'art the river,
    And the tree that taps the gurgoyle-head.'

'Nay, husband, you perplex me; for if the noise I heard here,
Awaking me from sleep so, were but as you avow,
The rain-fall, and the wind, and the tree-bough, and the river,
    Why is it silent now?

'And why is thy hand and thy clasping arm so shaking,
And thy sleeve and tags of hair so muddy and so wet,
And why feel I thy heart a-thumping every time thou kissest me,
    And thy breath as if hard to get?'

He lay there in silence for a while, still quickly breathing,
Then started up and walked about the room resentfully:
'O woman, witch, whom I, in sooth, against my will have wedded,
    Why castedst thou thy spells on me?

'There was one I loved once: the cry you heard was her cry:
She came to me to-night, and her plight was passing sore,
As no woman. . . . Yea, and it was e'en the cry you heard, wife,
    But she will cry no more!

'And now I can't abide thee: this place, it hath a curse on't,
This farmstead once a castle: I'll get me straight away!'
He dressed this time in darkness, unspeaking, as she listened,
    And went ere the dawn turned day.

They found a woman's body at a spot called Rocky Shallow,
Where the Froom stream curves amid the moorland, washed aground,
And they searched about for him, the yeoman, who had darkly known her,
    But he could not be found.

And the bride left for good-and-all the farmstead once a castle,
And in a county far away lives, mourns, and sleeps alone,
And thinks in windy weather that she hears a woman crying,
    And sometimes an infant's moan.

A Sound in the Night
35 rain-fall,] rain-fall MS
39 a-thumping] thumping MS
47 As] Such as MS
50 farmstead] homestead MS
50 me straight] from it MS
55 him,] him MS
57 good-and-all] good and all MS
57 farmstead] homestead MS

630 *On a Discovered Curl of Hair*

TITLE:
On a discovered curl of hair MS

WHEN your soft welcomings were said,
This curl was waving on your head,
And when we walked where breakers dinned
It sported in the sun and wind,
And when I had won your words of grace
It brushed and clung about my face.
Then, to abate the misery
Of absentness, you gave it me.

Where are its fellows now? Ah, they
For brightest brown have donned a gray,
And gone into a caverned ark,
Ever unopened, always dark!

Yet this one curl, untouched of time,
Beams with live brown as in its prime,
So that it seems I even could now
Restore it to the living brow
By bearing down the western road
Till I had reached your old abode.

February 1913

631 *An Old Likeness*

(*Recalling R.T.*)

TITLE:
The Old Portrait MS *before revision*
(Recalling R.T.)] A late addition to title

WHO would have thought
That, not having missed her
Talks, tears, laughter
In absence, or sought
To recall for so long
Her gamut of song;
Or ever to waft her
Signal of aught
That she, fancy-fanned,
Would well understand,

On a Discovered Curl of Hair
14 prime,] prime WE

An Old Likeness
3 Talks] Words MS
5–6] A late addition in MS
5 recall] read MS
6 gamut] volume MS
9–10] Happening at hand/In her own land, MS

I should have kissed her
Picture when scanned
Yawning years after!

Yet, seeing her poor
Dim-outlined form
Chancewise at night-time,
Some old allure
Came on me, warm,
Fresh, pleadful, pure,
As in that bright time
At a far season
Of love and unreason,
And took me by storm
Here in this blight-time!

And thus it arose
That, yawning years after
Our early flows
Of wit and laughter,
And framing of rhymes
At idle times,
At sight of her painting,
Though she lies cold
In churchyard mould,
I took its feinting
As real, and kissed it,
As if I had wist it
Herself of old.

632 *Her Apotheosis*

'Secretum meum mihi'

(*Faded Woman's Song*)

THERE were years vague of measure,
  Needless the asking when;
No honours, praises, pleasure
  Reached common maids from men.

TITLE:
Faded] Not in MS

An Old Likeness
13 Yawning] (Forty *del*) Thirty MS
16] By chance at nighttime, MS
17 Some] The MS
19 pleadful,] sweet, and MS
21 far] far-off MS
26 yawning] (forty *del*) thirty MS
29–30 a late addition in MS
31 painting,] painting; MS

Her Apotheosis
1] There was a certain summer, MS:
There was a spell of leisure, LL:
There were blank years of leisure, UE
1 measure,] measure CP2–4 [Hardy's copy of CP2 has been corrected to include the comma]
2] No record vouches when; MS, LL, UE
3] With ailments, wars, and tumults MS:
With honours, praises, pleasure LL
4] As usual among men. MS:
To womankind from men. LL

And hence no lures bewitched them,
 No hand was stretched to raise,
No gracious gifts enriched them,
 No voices sang their praise.

Yet an iris at that season
 Amid the accustomed slight
From denseness, dull unreason,
 Ringed me with living light.

633 *'Sacred to the Memory'*

(*Mary H.*)

THAT 'Sacred to the Memory'
Is clearly carven there I own,
And all may think that on the stone
The words have been inscribed by me
In bare conventionality.

They know not and will never know
That my full script is not confined
To that stone space, but stands deep lined
Upon the landscape high and low
Wherein she made such worthy show.

TITLE:
(*Mary H.*)] (M.H.) MS

634 *To a Well-Named Dwelling*

GLAD old house of lichened stonework,
What I owed you in my lone work,
  Noon and night!
Whensoever faint or ailing,
Letting go my grasp and failing,
  You lent light.

How by that fair title came you?
Did some forward eye so name you
  Knowing that one,

TITLE:
To a well-named Dwelling MS

Her Apotheosis
5] No people did me honour, MS:
 But no such lures bewitched me, LL
5 them] me LL, UE [Hardy's copy of CP2 has '?me' in margin]
7] No enterprize enriched me, MS
7 them] me LL, UE [Hardy's copy of CP2 has '?me' in margin]
8 their] my MS, LL, UE [Hardy's copy of CP2 has '?my' in margin]
9 Yet an iris] But an aureole MS
10 slight] blight MS
11] Of scorn, offence, unreason, MS

'Sacred to the Memory'
5 bare] mere MS
7 my] the MS
10 such worthy] so fair a MS

To a Well-Named Dwelling
6 lent] shed MS

Stumbling down his century blindly,
Would remark your sound, so kindly,
And be won?

Smile in sunlight, sleep in moonlight,
Bask in April, May, and June-light,
Zephyr-fanned;
Let your chambers show no sorrow,
Blanching day, or stuporing morrow,
While they stand.

TITLE:
The Whipper-in MS

635 *The Whipper-In*

'MY father was the whipper-in, –
Is still – if I'm not misled?
And now I see, where the hedge is thin,
A little spot of red;
Surely it is my father
Going to the kennel-shed!

'I cursed and fought my father – aye,
And sailed to a foreign land;
And feeling sorry, I'm back, to stay,
Please God, as his helping hand.
Surely it is my father
Near where the kennels stand?'

' – True. Whipper-in he used to be
For twenty years or more;
And you did go away to sea
As youths have done before.
Yes, oddly enough that red there
Is the very coat he wore.

'But he – he's dead; was thrown somehow,
And gave his back a crick,
And though that is his coat, 'tis now
The scarecrow of a rick;
You'll see when you get nearer –
'Tis spread out on a stick.

To a Well-Named Dwelling
10 Stumbling] Sauntering MS, LL, UE
16 show] hold MS

The Whipper-In
9 sorry,] sorry MS

'You see, when all had settled down
      Your mother's things were sold,
And she went back to her own town,
      And the coat, ate out with mould,
      Is now used by the farmer
      For scaring, as 'tis old.'

636 *A Military Appointment*

TITLE:
(*Scherzando*)] (Scherzo) MS

(*Scherzando*)

'SO back you have come from the town, Nan, dear!
And have you seen him there, or near –
      That soldier of mine –
Who long since promised to meet me here?'

' – O yes, Nell: from the town I come,
And have seen your lover on sick-leave home –
      That soldier of yours –
Who swore to meet you, or Strike-him-dumb;

'But has kept himself of late away;
Yet, – in short, he's coming, I heard him say –
      That lover of yours –
To this very spot on this very day.'

' – Then I'll wait, I'll wait, through wet or dry!
I'll give him a goblet brimming high –
      This lover of mine –
And not of complaint one word or sigh!'

' – Nell, him I have chanced so much to see,
That – he has grown the lover of me! –
      That lover of yours –
And it's here our meeting is planned to be.'

A Military Appointment
1 Nan,] Ann MS
17 Nell,] But MS

TITLE:
The Milestone by the Rabbit-burrow MS

637 *The Milestone by the Rabbit-Burrow*

(*On Yell'ham Hill*)

IN my loamy nook
As I dig my hole
I observe men look
At a stone, and sigh
As they pass it by
To some far goal.

Something it says
To their glancing eyes
That must distress
The frail and lame,
And the strong of frame
Gladden or surprise.

Do signs on its face
Declare how far
Feet have to trace
Before they gain
Some blest champaign
Where no gins are?

TITLE:
The Lament of the Looking-glass MS

638 *The Lament of the Looking-Glass*

WORDS from the mirror softly pass
To the curtains with a sigh:
'Why should I trouble again to glass
These smileless things hard by,
Since she I pleasured once, alas,
Is now no longer nigh!

'I've imaged shadows of coursing cloud,
And of the plying limb
On the pensive pine when the air is loud
With its aerial hymn;
But never do they make me proud
To catch them within my rim!

The Lament of the Looking-Glass
7 coursing] dark MS
8 plying] swaying MS
9 On] Of MS
12 within] Hardy's copy of CP2 has '?in' in margin

'I flash back phantoms of the night
  That sometimes flit by me,
I echo roses red and white –
  The loveliest blooms that be –
But now I never hold to sight
  So sweet a flower as she.'

639 Cross-Currents

THEY parted – a pallid, trembling pair,
  And rushing down the lane
He left her lonely near me there;
  – I asked her of their pain.

'It is for ever,' at length she said,
  'His friends have schemed it so,
That the long-purposed day to wed
  Never shall we two know.'

'In such a cruel case,' said I,
  'Love will contrive a course?'
'– Well, no . . . A thing may underlie,
  Which robs that of its force;

'A thing I could not tell him of,
  Though all the year I have tried;
This: never could I have given him love,
  Even had I been his bride.

'So, when his kinsfolk stop the way
  Point-blank, there could not be
A happening in the world to-day
  More opportune for me!

'Yet hear – no doubt to your surprise –
  I am grieving, for his sake,
That I have escaped the sacrifice
  I was distressed to make!'

Cross-Currents
1 pallid] pensive MS
11 no . . .] no. . . . . MS
22 grieving] sorry MS, LL, UE
24 distressed] prepared MS, LL

640 *The Old Neighbour and the New*

'TWAS to greet the new rector I called here,
But in the arm-chair I see
My old friend, for long years installed here,
Who palely nods to me.

The new man explains what he's planning
In a smart and cheerful tone,
And I listen, the while that I'm scanning
The figure behind his own.

The newcomer urges things on me;
I return a vague smile thereto,
The olden face gazing upon me
Just as it used to do!

And on leaving I scarcely remember
Which neighbour to-day I have seen,
The one carried out in September,
Or him who but entered yestreen.

641 *The Chosen*

Ἅτινά ἐστιν ἀλληγορούμενα

'A WOMAN for whom great gods might strive!'
I said, and kissed her there:
And then I thought of the other five,
And of how charms outwear.

I thought of the first with her eating eyes,
And I thought of the second with hers, green-gray,
And I thought of the third, experienced, wise,
And I thought of the fourth who sang all day.

And I thought of the fifth, whom I'd called a jade,
And I thought of them all, tear-fraught;
And that each had shown her a passable maid,
Yet not of the favour sought.

The Old Neighbour and the New
1 rector] tenant MS *before revision*
11 olden face] old dweller MS
12 it] he MS

So I traced these words on the bark of a beech,
Just at the falling of the mast:
'After scanning five; yes, each and each,
I've found the woman desired – at last!'

' – I feel a strange benumbing spell,
As one ill-wished!' said she.
And soon it seemed that something fell
Was starving her love for me.

'I feel some curse. O, *five* were there?'
And wanly she swerved, and went away.
I followed sick: night numbed the air,
And dark the mournful moorland lay.

I cried: 'O darling, turn your head!'
But never her face I viewed;
'O turn, O turn!' again I said,
And miserably pursued.

At length I came to a Christ-cross stone
Which she had passed without discern;
And I knelt upon the leaves there strown,
And prayed aloud that she might turn.

I rose, and looked; and turn she did;
I cried, 'My heart revives!'
'Look more,' she said. I looked as bid;
Her face was all the five's.

All the five women, clear come back,
I saw in her – with her made one,
The while she drooped upon the track,
And her frail term seemed well-nigh run.

She'd half forgot me in her change;
'Who are you? Won't you say
Who you may be, you man so strange,
Following since yesterday?'

The Chosen
13 traced] cut MS
22 swerved] turned MS
23 numbed] chilled MS

I took the composite form she was,
And carried her to an arbour small,
Not passion-moved, but even because
In one I could atone to all.

And there she lies, and there I tend,
    Till my life's threads unwind,
A various womanhood in blend –
    Not one, but all combined.

TITLE:
The Words on the Brass MS *before revision*

642 *The Inscription*

(*A Tale*)

SIR JOHN was entombed, and the crypt was closed, and she,
Like a soul that could meet no more the sight of the sun,
Inclined her in weepings and prayings continually,
    As his widowed one.

And to pleasure her in her sorrow, and fix his name
As a memory Time's fierce frost should never kill,
She caused to be richly chased a brass to his fame,
    Which should link them still;

For she bonded her name with his own on the brazen page,
As if dead and interred there with him, and cold, and numb,
(Omitting the day of her dying and year of her age
    Till her end should come;)

And implored good people to pray **'Of their Charytie
For these twaine Soules,'** – yea, she who did last remain
Forgoing Heaven's bliss if ever with spouse should she
    Again have lain.

Even there, as it first was set, you may see it now,
Writ in quaint Church-text, with the date of her death left bare,
In the aged Estminster aisle, where the folk yet bow
    Themselves in prayer.

The Chosen
47 passion-moved] Hardy had previously tried 'passioned now' and 'for love' in MS

The Inscription
18 Church-text] Church text MS, LL, UPE
19 aged] well-known MS

Thereafter some years slid, till there came a day
When it slowly began to be marked of the standers-by
That she would regard the brass, and would bend away
        With a drooping sigh.

Now the lady was fair as any the eye might scan
Through a summer day of roving – a type at whose lip
Despite her maturing seasons, no meet man
        Would be loth to sip.

And her heart was stirred with a lightning love to its pith
For a newcomer who, while less in years, was one
Full eager and able to make her his own forthwith,
        Restrained of none.

But she answered Nay, death-white; and still as he urged
She adversely spake, overmuch as she loved the while,
Till he pressed for why, and she led with the face of one scourged
        To the neighbouring aisle,

And showed him the words, ever gleaming upon her pew,
Memorizing her there as the knight's eternal wife,
Or falsing such, debarred inheritance due
        Of celestial life.

He blenched, and reproached her that one yet undeceased
Should bury her future – that future which none can spell;
And she wept, and purposed anon to inquire of the priest
        If the price were hell

Of her wedding in face of the record. Her lover agreed,
And they parted before the brass with a shudderful kiss,
For it seemed to flash out on their impulse of passionate need,
        'Mock ye not this!'

Well, the priest, whom more perceptions moved than one,
Said she erred at the first to have written as if she were dead
Her name and adjuration; but since it was done
        Nought could be said

The Inscription
23 brass] script MS
26 lip] lip, MS, WE
28 sip.] sip; MS
33 death-white;] death-white, MS
49 whom . . . perceptions] whom, haply, more motives had MS

Save that she must abide by the pledge, for the peace of her soul,
And so, by her life, maintain the apostrophe good,
If she wished anon to reach the coveted goal
        Of beatitude.

To erase from the consecrate text her prayer as there prayed
Would aver that, since earth's joys most drew her, past doubt,
Friends' prayers for her joy above by Jesu's aid
        Could be done without.

Moreover she thought of the laughter, the shrug, the jibe
That would rise at her back in the nave when she should pass
As another's avowed by the words she had chosen to inscribe
        On the changeless brass.

And so for months she replied to her Love: 'No, no;'
While sorrow was gnawing her beauties ever and more,
Till he, long-suffering and weary, grew to show
        Less warmth than before.

And, after an absence, wrote words absolute:
That he gave her till Midsummer morn to make her mind clear;
And that if, by then, she had not said Yea to his suit,
        He should wed elsewhere.

Thence on, at unwonted times through the lengthening days
She was seen in the church – at dawn, or when the sun dipt
And the moon rose, standing with hands joined, blank of gaze,
        Before the script.

She thinned as he came not; shrank like a creature that cowers
As summer drew nearer; but yet had not promised to wed,
When, just at the zenith of June, in the still night hours,
        She was missed from her bed.

'The church!' they whispered with qualms; 'where often she sits.'
They found her: facing the brass there, else seeing none,
But feeling the words with her finger, gibbering in fits;
        And she knew them not one.

The Inscription
58 that . . . 59 Friends'] Hardy's copy of CP2 has been corrected to read 'that the joys of the earth had so wound her about,/That'
58 most drew her] drew her most MS
59 aid] aid, MS
68 before.] before, MS
78 yet] still MS, LL, UE
79 When,] When MS
82 her . . . else] her there: she faced the brass, MS
83 But] And was MS
83 fits;] fits, MS
84 she] Not in MS

And so she remained, in her handmaids' charge; late, soon,
Tracing words in the air with her finger, as seen that night –
Those incised on the brass – till at length unwatched one noon,
She vanished from sight.

And, as talebearers tell, thence on to her last-taken breath
Was unseen, save as wraith that in front of the brass made moan;
So that ever the way of her life and the time of her death
Remained unknown.

And hence, as indited above, you may read even now
The quaint Church-text, with the date of her death left bare,
In the aged Estminster aisle, where folk yet bow
Themselves in prayer.

30 October 1907

643 The Marble-Streeted Town

I REACH the marble-streeted town,
Whose 'Sound' outbreathes its air
Of sharp sea-salts;
I see the movement up and down
As when she was there.
Ships of all countries come and go,
The bandsmen boom in the sun
A throbbing waltz;
The schoolgirls laugh along the Hoe
As when she was one.

I move away as the music rolls:
The place seems not to mind
That she – of old
The brightest of its native souls –
Left it behind!
Over this green aforedays she
On light treads went and came,
Yea, times untold;
Yet none here knows her history –
Has heard her name.

Plymouth (1914?)

EXTRA MANUSCRIPT:
Plymouth Public Library was presented with a copy of the MS by Hardy in 1923 but this is reported as having been destroyed in the Second World War

TITLE:
The Marble-streeted Town MS

The Inscription
87 length] length, MS
94 Church-text] church-text MS, LL, UE
95 aged] well-known MS

The Marble-Streeted Town
7 boom] play MS
(*1914?*)] (1913?) MS

644 A Woman Driving

How she held up the horses' heads,
Firm-lipped, with steady rein,
Down that grim steep the coastguard treads,
Till all was safe again!

With form erect and keen contour
She passed against the sea,
And, dipping into the chine's obscure,
Was seen no more by me.

To others she appeared anew
At times of dusky light,
But always, so they told, withdrew
From close and curious sight.

Some said her silent wheels would roll
Rutless on softest loam,
And even that her steeds' footfall
Sank not upon the foam.

Where drives she now? It may be where
No mortal horses are,
But in a chariot of the air
Towards some radiant star.

645 A Woman's Trust

If he should live a thousand years
He'd find it not again
That scorn of him by men
Could less disturb a woman's trust
In him as a steadfast star which must
Rise scathless from the nether spheres:
If he should live a thousand years
He'd find it not again.

A Woman Driving
7 obscure,] obscure MS
11 always] slowly MS
12] Until she vanished quite. MS

A Woman's Trust
2] It could not happen again MS
4 Could] Should MS
5 steadfast star which] star which would and MS
8] It could not happen again. MS

She waited like a little child,
  Unchilled by damps of doubt,
  While from her eyes looked out
A confidence sublime as Spring's
When stressed by Winter's loiterings.
Thus, howsoever the wicked wiled,
She waited like a little child
  Unchilled by damps of doubt.

Through cruel years and crueller
  Thus she believed in him
  And his aurore, so dim;
That, after fenweeds, flowers would blow;
And above all things did she show
Her faith in his good faith with her;
Through cruel years and crueller
  Thus she believed in him!

646 Best Times

TITLE:
Best Times Not Again MS *before revision*

WE went a day's excursion to the stream,
Basked by the bank, and bent to the ripple-gleam,
    And I did not know
    That life would show,
However it might flower, no finer glow.

I walked in the Sunday sunshine by the road
That wound towards the wicket of your abode,
    And I did not think
    That life would shrink
To nothing ere it shed a rosier pink.

Unlooked for I arrived on a rainy night,
And you hailed me at the door by the swaying light,
    And I full forgot
    That life might not
Again be touching that ecstatic height.

A Woman's Trust
12 Spring's] spring's MS
13 Winter's] winter's MS

Best Times
2] And climbed the bank, and looked at the rippled gleam, MS
5 flower] bloom MS
7 wicket] gate MS
12 light,] light CP2–4 [but evidence of print defect]
13 full] quite MS

And that calm eve when you walked up the stair,
After a gaiety prolonged and rare,
No thought soever
That you might never
Walk down again, struck me as I stood there.

Rewritten from an old draft

647 *The Casual Acquaintance*

WHILE he was here with breath and bone,
To speak to and to see,
Would I had known – more clearly known –
What that man did for me

When the wind scraped a minor lay,
And the spent west from white
To gray turned tiredly, and from gray
To broadest bands of night!

But I saw not, and he saw not
What shining life-tides flowed
To me-ward from his casual jot
Of service on that road.

He would have said: ' 'Twas nothing new;
We all do what we can;
'Twas only what one man would do
For any other man.'

Now that I gauge his goodliness
He's slipped from human eyes;
And when he passed there's none can guess,
Or point out where he lies.

648 *Intra Sepulchrum*

WHAT curious things we said,
What curious things we did
Up there in the world we walked till dead,
Our kith and kin amid!

Best Times
16 eve] evening MS
16 walked up] climbed MS
17] After a languid rising from your chair, MS *before revision*

The Casual Acquaintance
1 with] in MS, LL

Intra Sepulchrum
3 dead,] dead MS, LL, UE

How we played at love,
And its wildness, weakness, woe;
Yes, played thereat far more than enough
As it turned out, I trow!

Played at believing in gods
And observing the ordinances,
I for your sake in impossible codes
Right ready to acquiesce.

Thinking our lives unique,
Quite quainter than usual kinds,
We held that we could not abide a week
The tether of typic minds.

– Yet people who day by day
Pass by and look at us
From over the wall in a casual way
Are of this unconscious;

And feel, if anything,
That none can be buried here
Removed from commonest fashioning,
Or lending note to a bier:

No twain who in heart-heaves proved
Themselves at all adept,
Who more than many laughed and loved,
Who more than many wept,

Or were as sprites or elves
Into blind matter hurled,
Or ever could have been to themselves
The centre of the world.

649 *The Whitewashed Wall*

EXTRA PRINTING:
Reveille, Nov 1918, p. [175] = R

WHY does she turn in that shy soft way
Whenever she stirs the fire,
And kiss to the chimney-corner wall,
As if entranced to admire

Intra Sepulchrum
12 ready] willing MS
14 kinds] lives MS
16] Like other men and their wives. MS
19 casual] musing MS
20 unconscious;] unconscious. MS, LL, UPE, CP2–4
27 loved,] loved CP2–4

Its whitewashed bareness more than the sight
Of a rose in richest green?
I have known her long, but this raptured rite
I never before have seen.

– Well, once when her son cast his shadow there,
A friend took a pencil and drew him
Upon that flame-lit wall. And the lines
Had a lifelike semblance to him.
And there long stayed his familiar look;
But one day, ere she knew,
The whitener came to cleanse the nook,
And covered the face from view.

'Yes,' he said: 'My brush goes on with a rush,
And the draught is buried under;
When you have to whiten old cots and brighten,
What else can you do, I wonder?'
But she knows he's there. And when she yearns
For him, deep in the labouring night,
She sees him as close at hand, and turns
To him under his sheet of white.

EXTRA PRINTING:
Chosen Poems, p. 124

650 *Just the Same*

I SAT. It all was past;
Hope never would hail again;
Fair days had ceased at a blast,
The world was a darkened den.

The beauty and dream were gone,
And the halo in which I had hied
So gaily gallantly on
Had suffered blot and died!

I went forth, heedless whither,
In a cloud too black for name:
– People frisked hither and thither;
The world was just the same.

The Whitewashed Wall
6 richest] a garden R
9 once when her son] her soldier-son R
10 A] And a R
15 nook,] nook MS
17 My] my R
17 rush,] rush; R
22 deep] lone R
22 labouring] moaning R
23 turns] turns, R
24] And kisses him under the white. R

651 The Last Time

EXTRA PRINTING:
Chosen Poems, p. 122

THE kiss had been given and taken,
  And gathered to many past:
It never could reawaken;
  But I heard none say: 'It's the last!'

The clock showed the hour and the minute,
  But I did not turn and look:
I read no finis in it,
  As at closing of a book.

But I read it all too rightly
  When, at a time anon,
A figure lay stretched out whitely,
  And I stood looking thereon.

652 The Seven Times

THE dark was thick. A boy he seemed at that time
  Who trotted by me with uncertain air;
'I'll tell my tale,' he murmured, 'for I fancy
    A friend goes there? . . .'

Then thus he told. 'I reached – 'twas for the first time –
  A dwelling. Life was clogged in me with care;
I thought not I should meet an eyesome maiden,
    But found one there.

'I entered on the precincts for the second time –
  'Twas an adventure fit and fresh and fair –
I slackened in my footsteps at the porchway,
    And found her there.

'I rose and travelled thither for the third time,
  The hope-hues growing gayer and yet gayer
As I hastened round the boscage of the outskirts,
    And found her there.

The Last Time
4 I] you MS, LL [and so in ll. 6, 7, 9, 12]
5 minute,] minute CP2–4

The Seven Times
3 tale,] tale MS
7] I thought not of a meeting with a maiden, MS

'I journeyed to the place again the fourth time
    (The best and rarest visit of the rare,
As it seemed to me, engrossed about these goings),
        And found her there.

'When I bent me to my pilgrimage the fifth time
    (Soft-thinking as I journeyed I would dare
A certain word at token of good auspice),
        I found her there.

'That landscape did I traverse for the sixth time,
    And dreamed on what we purposed to prepare;
I reached a tryst before my journey's end came,
        And found her there.

'I went again – long after – aye, the seventh time;
    The look of things was sinister and bare
As I caught no customed signal, heard no voice call,
        Nor found her there.

'And now I gad the globe – day, night, and any time,
    To light upon her hiding unaware,
And, maybe, I shall nigh me to some nymph-niche,
        And find her there!'

'But how,' said I, 'has your so little lifetime
    Given roomage for such loving, loss, despair?
A boy so young!' Forthwith I turned my lantern
        Upon him there.

His head was white. His small form, fine aforetime,
    Was shrunken with old age and battering wear,
An eighty-years long plodder saw I pacing
        Beside me there.

The Seven Times
17 time] time, MS
19 engrossed . . . goings),] embarked upon these goings) MS
21 time] time, MS
22 Soft-thinking] Soft thinking MS
43 eighty-years] eighty-years' MS: [*Before revision* MS read 'A ninety-years']

653 *The Sun's Last Look on the Country Girl*

TITLE:
The Sun's last Look on the Country Girl MS

(M.H.)

THE sun threw down a radiant spot
  On the face in the winding-sheet –
The face it had lit when a babe's in its cot;
And the sun knew not, and the face knew not
  That soon they would no more meet.

Now that the grave has shut its door,
  And lets not in one ray,
Do they wonder that they meet no more –
That face and its beaming visitor –
  That met so many a day?

December 1915

654 *In a London Flat*

TITLE:
In a London lodging MS *before revision*

I

'YOU look like a widower,' she said
Through the folding-doors with a laugh from the bed,
As he sat by the fire in the outer room,
Reading late on a night of gloom,
And a cab-hack's wheeze, and the clap of its feet
In its breathless pace on the smooth wet street,
Were all that came to them now and then. . . .
'You really do!' she quizzed again.

II

And the Spirits behind the curtains heard,
And also laughed, amused at her word,
And at her light-hearted view of him.
'Let's get him made so – just for a whim!'
Said the Phantom Ironic. ' 'Twould serve her right
If we coaxed the Will to do it some night.'
'O pray not!' pleaded the younger one,
The Sprite of the Pities. 'She said it in fun!'

The Sun's Last Look on the Country Girl
1 down] in MS

In a London Flat
10 also] likewise MS
11 light-hearted] lighthearted MS

III

But so it befell, whatever the cause,
That what she had called him he next year was;
And on such a night, when she lay elsewhere,
He, watched by those Phantoms, again sat there,
And gazed, as if gazing on far faint shores,
At the empty bed through the folding-doors
As he remembered her words; and wept
That she had forgotten them where she slept.

INDENTATION:
In MS, LL, UE ll. 8 and 16 are lined up with l. 1

655 *Drawing Details in an Old Church*

I HEAR the bell-rope sawing,
And the oil-less axle grind,
As I sit alone here drawing
What some Gothic brain designed;
And I catch the toll that follows
        From the lagging bell,
Ere it spreads to hills and hollows
        Where people dwell.

I ask not whom it tolls for,
Incurious who he be;
So, some morrow, when those knolls for
One unguessed, sound out for me,
A stranger, loitering under
        In nave or choir,
May think, too, 'Whose, I wonder?'
        But not inquire.

TITLE:
(The seducer *del*) Rake-hell muses MS

656 *Rake-Hell Muses*

YES; since she knows not need,
        Nor walks in blindness,
I may without unkindness
        This true thing tell:

In a London Flat
22 folding-doors] folding doors MS

Drawing Details in an Old Church
8 Where] Where the parish MS, LL: Where the UE
16] But care not to inquire. MS, LL

Rake-Hell Muses
4 This] A MS, LL, UE

Which would be truth, indeed,
Though worse in speaking,
Were her poor footsteps seeking
A pauper's cell.

I judge, then, better far
She now have sorrow,
Than gladness that to-morrow
Might know its knell. –

It may be men there are
Could make of union
A lifelong sweet communion
Or passioned spell;

But *I*, to save her name
And bring salvation
By altar-affirmation
And bridal bell;

I, by whose rash unshame
These tears come to her: –
My faith would more undo her
Than my farewell!

Chained to me, year by year
My moody madness
Would make her olden gladness
An intermell.

She'll take the ill that's near,
And bear the blaming.
'Twill pass. Full soon her shaming
They'll cease to yell.

Our unborn, first her moan,
Will grow her guerdon,
Until from blot and burden
A joyance swell;

Rake-Hell Muses
15 communion] communion – MS, LL, UE
16 Or] A MS, LL, UE
27 make her olden] wither her old MS, LL, UE
28] Like famine fell. MS, LL, UE
29 near,] near MS

In that therein she'll own
My good part wholly,
My evil staining solely
My own vile fell.

Of the disgrace, may be
'He shunned to share it,
Being false,' they'll say. I'll bear it;
Time will dispel

The calumny, and prove
This much about me,
That she lives best without me
Who would live well.

That, this once, not self-love
But good intention
Pleads that against convention
We two rebel.

For, is one moonlight dance,
One midnight passion,
A rock whereon to fashion
Life's citadel?

Prove they their power to prance
Life's miles together
From upper slope to nether
Who trip an ell?

– Years hence, or now apace,
May tongues be calling
News of my further falling
Sinward pell-mell:

Then this great good will grace
Our lives' division,
She's saved from more misprision
Though I plumb hell.

189–

Rake-Hell Muses
40 fell] vell MS, LL, UE

657 The Colour

(The following lines are partly original, partly remembered from a Wessex folk-rhyme)

'WHAT shall I bring you?
Please will white do
Best for your wearing
The long day through?'
' – White is for weddings,
Weddings, weddings,
White is for weddings,
And that won't do.'

'What shall I bring you?
Please will red do
Best for your wearing
The long day through?'
' – Red is for soldiers,
Soldiers, soldiers,
Red is for soldiers,
And that won't do.'

'What shall I bring you?
Please will blue do
Best for your wearing
The long day through?'
' – Blue is for sailors,
Sailors, sailors,
Blue is for sailors,
And that won't do.'

'What shall I bring you?
Please will green do
Best for your wearing
The long day through?'
' – Green is for mayings,
Mayings, mayings,
Green is for mayings,
And that won't do.'

TITLE:
original . . .)] made up of a Wessex folk-rhyme.) MS
original] made up LL, UPE

The Colour
7 weddings,] weddings MS
15 soldiers,] soldiers MS
23 sailors,] sailors MS

'What shall I bring you
Then? Will black do
Best for your wearing
    The long day through?'
' – Black is for mourning,
Mourning, mourning,
Black is for mourning,
    And black will do.'

658 *Murmurs in the Gloom*

(*Nocturne*)

I WAYFARED at the nadir of the sun
Where populations meet, though seen of none;
    And millions seemed to sigh around
    As though their haunts were nigh around,
    And unknown throngs to cry around
        Of things late done.

'O Seers, who well might high ensample show'
(Came throbbing past in plainsong small and slow),
    'Leaders who lead us aimlessly,
    Teachers who train us shamelessly,
    Why let ye smoulder flamelessly
        The truths ye trow?

'Ye scribes, that urge the old medicament,
Whose fusty vials have long dried impotent,
    Why prop ye meretricious things,
    Denounce the sane as vicious things,
    And call outworn factitious things
        Expedient?

'O Dynasties that sway and shake us so,
Why rank your magnanimities so low
    That grace can smooth no waters yet,
    But breathing threats and slaughters yet
    Ye grieve Earth's sons and daughters yet
        As long ago?

Murmurs in the Gloom
22 slaughters] slaughters, MS

'Live there no heedful ones of searching sight,
Whose accents might be oracles that smite
    To hinder those who frowardly
    Conduct us, and untowardly;
    To lead the nations vawardly
        From gloom to light?'

22 September 1899

659 *Epitaph*

I NEVER cared for Life: Life cared for me,
And hence I owed it some fidelity.
It now says, 'Cease; at length thou hast learnt to grind
Sufficient toll for an unwilling mind,
And I dismiss thee – not without regard
That thou didst ask no ill-advised reward,
Nor sought in me much more than thou couldst find.'

660 *An Ancient to Ancients*

PROOF:
In the Miriam Lutcher Stark Library of the University of Texas = UT

EXTRA PRINTING:
The Century Magazine (New York), May 1922, pp. [52–4] = CM

WHERE once we danced, where once we sang,
        Gentlemen,
The floors are sunken, cobwebs hang,
And cracks creep; worms have fed upon
The doors. Yea, sprightlier times were then
Than now, with harps and tabrets gone,
        Gentlemen!

Where once we rowed, where once we sailed,
        Gentlemen,
And damsels took the tiller, veiled
Against too strong a stare (God wot
Their fancy, then or anywhen!)
Upon that shore we are clean forgot,
        Gentlemen!

Murmurs in the Gloom
MS adds at end: (Copied)

Epitaph
3 says,] says MS

An Ancient to Ancients
4 creep;] creep: UT
5 sprightlier] brighter UT, CM
5 then] then, UT
7] Gentlemen. CM
12 fancy,] fancy . . . UT, CM
12 anywhen!)] any when!), CM
14] Gentlemen. CM

We have lost somewhat, afar and near,
Gentlemen,
The thinning of our ranks each year
Affords a hint we are nigh undone,
That we shall not be ever again
The marked of many, loved of one,
Gentlemen.

In dance the polka hit our wish,
Gentlemen,
The paced quadrille, the spry schottische,
'Sir Roger'. – And in opera spheres
The 'Girl' (the famed 'Bohemian'),
And 'Trovatore', held the ears,
Gentlemen.

This season's paintings do not please,
Gentlemen,
Like Etty, Mulready, Maclise;
Throbbing romance has waned and wanned;
No wizard wields the witching pen
Of Bulwer, Scott, Dumas, and Sand,
Gentlemen.

The bower we shrined to Tennyson,
Gentlemen,
Is roof-wrecked; damps there drip upon
Sagged seats, the creeper-nails are rust,
The spider is sole denizen;
Even she who voiced those rhymes is dust,
Gentlemen!

We who met sunrise sanguine-souled,
Gentlemen,
Are wearing weary. We are old;
These younger press; we feel our rout
Is imminent to Aïdes' den, –
That evening shades are stretching out,
Gentlemen!

An Ancient to Ancients
15 somewhat,] somewhat CM
22 hit] met CM
25 'Sir . . . And] 'Sir Roger'; and CM
25 'Sir Roger'. –] *Sir Roger* – UT
26] The 'Girl,' the famed 'Bohemian,' CM
26 'Girl'] 'Girl', MS: *Girl* UT
26 'Bohemian'),] *Bohemian*), UT
27 'Trovatore'] *Trovatore* UT
38 damps there] there damps CM
39 rust,] rust; UT, CM
41 voiced] read MS, UT, CM, LL, UE
42] Gentlemen. CM
45 wearing] getting MS, CM
47 Aïdes'] Haides' MS, CM
47 den, –] den – UT: den, CM
48 evening] evening's LL, UE
49] Gentlemen. CM

And yet, though ours be failing frames,
Gentlemen,
So were some others' history names,
Who trode their track light-limbed and fast
As these youth, and not alien
From enterprise, to their long last,
Gentlemen.

Sophocles, Plato, Socrates,
Gentlemen,
Pythagoras, Thucydides,
Herodotus, and Homer, – yea,
Clement, Augustin, Origen,
Burnt brightlier towards their setting-day,
Gentlemen.

And ye, red-lipped and smooth-browed; list,
Gentlemen;
Much is there waits you we have missed;
Much lore we leave you worth the knowing,
Much, much has lain outside our ken:
Nay, rush not: time serves: we are going,
Gentlemen.

661 *After Reading Psalms XXXIX, XL, etc.*

TITLE:
After reading Psalms XXXIX, XL, etc. MS

SIMPLE was I and was young;
Kept no gallant tryst, I;
Even from good words held my tongue,
Quoniam Tu fecisti!

Through my youth I stirred me not,
High adventure missed I,
Left the shining shrines unsought;
Yet – *me deduxisti!*

At my start by Helicon
Love-lore little wist I,
Worldly less; but footed on;
Why? *Me suscepisti!*

An Ancient to Ancients
50 failing] faltering UT, CM
53 trode] trod CM
53 track] track, CM
53 light-limbed] light-stepped MS, CM
57–60] Pythagoras, Homer, Socrates,/ Gentlemen,/With Aeschylus, Thucydides,/And Sophocles, and Plato, – yea, MS *before revision*
60 Homer, –] Homer, UT, CM
61 Augustin] Augustine CM
62 brightlier] brightliest MS
64 ye] you MS, CM
64 smooth-browed;] smooth-browed, CM
65 Gentlemen;] Gentlemen: CM
67 knowing,] knowing; CM
68 ken:] ken. CM
69 serves:] serves; CM

After Reading Psalms XXXIX, XL, etc.
2 tryst,] tryst MS
3 Even] Ev'n MS

When I failed at fervid rhymes,
　　'Shall,' I said, 'persist I?'
'*Dies*' (I would add at times)
　　'*Meos posuisti!*'

So I have fared through many suns;
　　Sadly little grist I
Bring my mill, or any one's,
　　Domine, Tu scisti!

And at dead of night I call:
　　'Though to prophets list I,
Which hath understood at all?
　　Yea: *Quem elegisti?*'

187–

662 *Surview*

'Cogitavi vias meas'

A CRY from the green-grained sticks of the fire
　　Made me gaze where it seemed to be:
'Twas my own voice talking therefrom to me
On how I had walked when my sun was higher –
　　My heart in its arrogancy.

'*You held not to whatsoever was true,*'
　　Said my own voice talking to me:
'*Whatsoever was just you were slack to see;*
Kept not things lovely and pure in view,'
　　Said my own voice talking to me.

'*You slighted her that endureth all,*'
　　Said my own voice talking to me;
'*Vaunteth not, trusteth hopefully;*
That suffereth long and is kind withal,'
　　Said my own voice talking to me.

'*You taught not that which you set about,*'
　　Said my own voice talking to me;
'*That the greatest of things is Charity. . . .*'
– And the sticks burnt low, and the fire went out,
　　And my voice ceased talking to me.

After Reading Psalms XXXIX, XL, etc.
MS has '[recopied]' at end *deleted*

Surview
5 in its arrogancy] where it best could be MS
7 me:] me; MS
18 Charity. . . .'] Charity.' . . . . MS
20 ceased] stopped MS

HUMAN SHOWS
FAR PHANTASIES
SONGS, AND TRIFLES

Abbreviations Specific to 'Human Shows'

MS = The bound-up volume of manuscripts in the Library of Yale University

HS1 = *Human Shows* (First Printing: Nov 1925)

HS2 = *Human Shows* (Second Printing: Nov 1925)

HS = Found in both HS1 and HS2

HSA = *Human Shows* (New York, 1925)

PE = Pocket Edition 1927

WE = Wessex Edition 1931

Song.

1.

Retty used to gaily sing
why a gloomy thing

2.

Retty used to shake her head
Look with wicked eyes
Say "I'll make you, idle Fred!"
If I cared to try"
But she'd colour scarlet red
Quickly haste away
much afraid that thing she'd said
Were saucy things to say.

3.

Retty used to fall in love
Every now & then,
With some hero written of or spoken
As handsomest of men:
Or a soldier passing by,
Or a sailor gay.

Night's she lie awake & cry
When he'd gone away.
Let her dream's decay.

4.

Retty used to think she loved,
(Just a little) me;

5.

Retty used to want to rest
When we'd walked a mile
And she'd whisper. "I were blest
Could I run awhile
As I ran on that dear old day
When you saw me wade
Through the pond that people say
Fairy shovels made.

— 6 —

— 7 —

Retty used to draw me down
To the green church-way
Where with yeoman, squire & clown
Her little body lay
Now her silent mouldering place
Scarce my footsteps know,
For when last I saw her face
Was so long ago.

or: —
For since last I saw her face
Times have altered so.

See page 790

663 *Waiting Both*

EXTRA MANUSCRIPT:
In Colby College Library = CL

EXTRA PRINTINGS:
(1) *The London Mercury*, Nov 1924, p. 7 = LM
(2) *Chosen Poems*, p. 215

A STAR looks down at me,
And says: 'Here I and you
Stand, each in our degree:
What do you mean to do, –
        Mean to do?'

I say: 'For all I know,
Wait, and let Time go by,
Till my change come.' – 'Just so,'
The star says: 'So mean I: –
        So mean I.'

664 *A Bird-Scene at a Rural Dwelling*

EXTRA PRINTING:
Chambers's Journal, Jan 1925 (6 Dec 1924), p. [1] = C

TITLE:
A Bird-scene at a Rural Dwelling MS

INDENTATION:
1 = ll. 1, 2, 7, 8, 11, 12, 13, 14
2 = ll. 5, 6
3 = ll. 3, 4
4 = ll. 9, 10 MS

1 = ll. 1, 2, 12, 13, 14
2 = ll. 5, 6, 7, 8, 11
3 = ll. 3, 4, 9, 10 C

WHEN the inmate stirs, the birds retire discreetly
From the window-ledge, whereon they whistled sweetly
        And on the step of the door,
        In the misty morning hoar;
    But now the dweller is up they flee
    To the crooked neighbouring codlin-tree;
And when he comes fully forth they seek the garden,
And call from the lofty costard, as pleading pardon
        For shouting so near before
        In their joy at being alive: –
Meanwhile the hammering clock within goes five.

I know a domicile of brown and green,
Where for a hundred summers there have been
Just such enactments, just such daybreaks seen.

Waiting Both
2 says:] says; CL
4 do,] do LM
9 says:] says; CL
9 I:] I, CL

A Bird-Scene at a Rural Dwelling
3 door,] door MS, C
6 crooked] long-armed C
8 pleading] asking C
10 alive:] alive C
11 hammering] halting MS, C
11 goes] strikes MS, C
14 daybreaks] day-breaks MS, C

EXTRA MANUSCRIPT:
In the Dorset County Museum. There are no variants.

EXTRA PRINTING:
Chosen Poems, p. 111

TITLE:
'Any Little Old Song' MS

665 *Any Little Old Song*

ANY little old song
Will do for me,
Tell it of joys gone long,
Or joys to be,
Or friendly faces best
Loved to see.

Newest themes I want not
On subtle strings,
And for thrillings pant not
That new song brings:
I only need the homeliest
Of heartstirrings.

TITLE:
In a former Resort after many years MS
In an old place of Resort after many years MS *before revision*

666 *In a Former Resort after Many Years*

DO I know these, slack-shaped and wan,
Whose substance, one time fresh and furrowless,
Is now a rag drawn over a skeleton,
As in El Greco's canvases? –
Whose cheeks have slipped down, lips become indrawn,
And statures shrunk to dwarfishness?

Do they know me, whose former mind
Was like an open plain where no foot falls,
But now is as a gallery portrait-lined,
And scored with necrologic scrawls,
Where feeble voices rise, once full-defined,
From underground in curious calls?

Any Little Old Song
8 strings,] strings MS

In a Former Resort after Many Years
4 El Greco's] Crivelli's MS

667 A Cathedral Façade at Midnight

ALONG the sculptures of the western wall
    I watched the moonlight creeping:
It moved as if it hardly moved at all,
    Inch by inch thinly peeping
Round on the pious figures of freestone, brought
And poised there when the Universe was wrought
To serve its centre, Earth, in mankind's thought.

The lunar look skimmed scantly toe, breast, arm,
    Then edged on slowly, slightly,
To shoulder, hand, face; till each austere form
    Was blanched its whole length brightly
Of prophet, king, queen, cardinal in state,
That dead men's tools had striven to simulate;
And the stiff images stood irradiate.

A frail moan from the martyred saints there set
    Mid others of the erection
Against the breeze, seemed sighings of regret
    At the ancient faith's rejection
Under the sure, unhasting, steady stress
Of Reason's movement, making meaningless
The coded creeds of old-time godliness.

668 The Turnip-Hoer

EXTRA PRINTING:
Cassell's Magazine, Aug 1925, pp. [28]–33 = C

INDENTATION:
1 = ll. 1, 3 } and so throughout C
2 = ll. 2, 4

  OF tides that toss the souls of men
Some are foreseen, and weathered warefully;
More burst at flood, none witting why or when,
    And are called Destiny.

  – Years past there was a turnip-hoer,
Who loved his wife and child, and worked amain
In the turnip-time from dawn till day out-wore
    And night bedimmed the plain.

A Cathedral Façade at Midnight
4 thinly] gently MS
1897 MS at end *deleted*

The Turnip-Hoer
2 foreseen,] foreseen C
2 warefully] wantonly MS, C
5 Years past] Years-past C
7 out-wore] outwore MS: outwore, C

The thronging plants of blueish green
Would fall in lanes before his skilful blade,
Which, as by sleight, would deftly slip between
Those spared and those low-laid.

'Twas afternoon: he hoed his best,
Unlifting head or eye, when, through the fence,
He heard a gallop dropping from the crest
Of the hill above him, whence,

Descending at a crashing pace,
An open carriage came, horsed by a pair:
A lady sat therein, with lilywhite face
And wildly windblown hair.

The man sprang over, and horse and horse
Faced in the highway as the pair ondrew;
Like Terminus stood he there, and barred their course,
And almost ere he knew

The lady was limp within his arms,
And, half-unconscious, clutched his hair and beard;
And so he held her, till from neighbouring farms
Came hinds, and soon appeared

Footman and coachman on the way: –
The steeds were guided back, now breath-bespent,
And the hoer was rewarded with good pay: –
So passed the accident.

'She was the Duchess of Southernshire,
They tell me,' said the second hoe, next day:
'She's come a-visiting not far from here;
This week will end her stay.'

The hoer's wife that evening set
Her hand to a crusted stew in the three-legged pot,
And he sat looking on in silence; yet
The cooking saw he not,

The Turnip-Hoer
9 blueish] bluest C
13 best,] best HSA
16 whence,] whence MS, C
17 pace,] pace MS, C
18 came,] came C
25 arms,] arms HSA
30 guided] soon brought MS, C
34 hoe,] hoe C

But a woman, with her arms around him,
Glove-handed, clasping his neck and clutching his blouse,
And ere he went to bed that night he found him
Outside a manor-house.

A page there smoking answered him:
'Her Grace's room is where you see that light;
By now she's up there slipping off her trim:
The Dook's is on the right.'

She was, indeed, just saying through the door,
'That dauntless fellow saved me from collapse:
I'd not much with me, or 'd have given him more:
'Twas not enough, perhaps!'

Up till she left, before he slept,
He walked, though tired, to where her window shined,
And mused till it went dark; but close he kept
All that was in his mind.

'What is it, Ike?' inquired his wife;
'You are not so nice now as you used to be.
What have I done? You seem quite tired of life!'
'Nothing at all,' said he.

In the next shire this lady of rank,
So 'twas made known, would open a bazaar:
He took his money from the savings-bank
To go there, for 'twas far.

And reached her stall, and sighted, clad
In her ripe beauty and the goodliest guise,
His Vision of late. He straight spent all he had,
But not once caught her eyes.

Next week he heard, with heart of clay,
That London held her for three months or so:
Fearing to tell his wife he went for a day,
Pawning his watch to go;

The Turnip-Hoer
50 dauntless] handsome MS, C
53 Up] On MS, C
64 far.] far, MS, C
65–8 A late addition to MS
65 sighted] saw there MS, C
66 guise] trim C
67 Vision] vision MS, C
67 had,] had; C
68] But she did not note him. C

And scanned the Square of her abode,
And timed her moves, as well as he could guess,
That he might glimpse her; till afoot by road
He came home penniless. . . .

– The Duke in Wessex once again,
Glanced at the Wessex paper, where he read
Of a man, late taken to drink, killed by a train
At a crossing, so it said.

'Why – he who saved your life, I think?'
– 'O no,' said she. 'It cannot be the same:
He was sweet-breath'd, without a taint of drink;
Yet it is like his name.'

EXTRA PRINTING:
Chosen Poems, p. 212

669 The Carrier

'THERE's a seat, I see, still empty?'
Cried the hailer from the road;
'No, there is not!' said the carrier,
Quickening his horse and load.

' – They say you are in the grave, Jane;
But still you ride with me!'
And he looked towards the vacant space
He had kept beside his knee.

And the passengers murmured: ' 'Tis where his wife
In journeys to and fro
Used always to sit; but nobody does
Since those long years ago.'

Rumble-mumble went the van
Past Sidwell Church and wall,
Till Exon Towers were out of scan,
And night lay over all.

The Turnip-Hoer
82 – 'O] 'O C
82 she. 'It] she, 'it C
83 sweet-breath'd] sweet breath'd C

The Carrier
3 No,] No MS, HSA

670 *Lover to Mistress*

(*Song*)

EXTRA PRINTING:
Chosen Poems, p. 112

BECKON to me to come
With handkerchief or hand,
Or finger mere or thumb;
Let forecasts be but rough,
Parents more bleak than bland,
'Twill be enough,
Maid mine,
'Twill be enough!

Two fields, a wood, a tree,
Nothing now more malign
Lies between you and me;
But were they bysm, or bluff,
Or snarling sea, one sign
Would be enough,
Maid mine,
Would be enough!

From an old copy

671 *The Monument-Maker*

EXTRA PRINTING:
Chosen Poems, pp. 127–8

TITLE:
The Monument-maker MS

I CHISELLED her monument
To my mind's content,
Took it to the church by night,
When her planet was at its height,
And set it where I had figured the place in the daytime.
Having niched it there
I stepped back, cheered, and thought its outlines fair,
And its marbles rare.

Then laughed she over my shoulder as in our Maytime:
'It spells not me!' she said:
'Tells nothing about my beauty, wit, or gay time
With all those, quick and dead,

Lover to Mistress
4 forecasts] prospects MS

The Monument-Maker
5 figured] marked MS
7 fair,] fair MS
10 It spells not] It is not like MS

Of high or lowlihead,
That hovered near,
Including you, who carve there your devotion;
But you felt none, my dear!'

And then she vanished. Checkless sprang my emotion
And forced a tear
At seeing I'd not been truly known by her,
And never prized! – that my memorial here,
To consecrate her sepulchre,
Was scorned, almost,
By her sweet ghost:
Yet I hoped not quite, in her very innermost!

1916

672 *Circus-Rider to Ringmaster*

EXTRA PRINTING:
Harper's Monthly Magazine (New York), June 1925, p. [10] = H

TITLE:
[Casterbridge Fair] H below title
(Casterbridge Fair: 188–) MS *deleted* below title

WHEN I am riding round the ring no longer,
Tell a tale of me;
Say, no steed-borne woman's nerve was stronger
Than used mine to be.
Let your whole soul say it; do:
O it will be true!

Should I soon no more be mistress found in
Feats I've made my own,
Trace the tan-laid track you'd whip me round in
On the cantering roan:
There may cross your eyes again
My lithe look as then.

Show how I, when clay becomes my cover,
Took the high-hoop leap
Into your arms, who coaxed and grew my lover, –
Ah, to make me weep
Since those claspings cared for so
Ever so long ago!

The Monument-Maker
17 emotion] emotion, MS, HS, HSA, PE

Circus-Rider to Ringmaster
15 lover, –] lover – H
17 claspings cared for] journeys joyed in H

Though not now as when you freshly knew me,
But a fading form,
Shape the kiss you'd briskly blow up to me
While our love was warm,
And my cheek unstained by tears,
As in these last years!

673 Last Week in October

THE trees are undressing, and fling in many places –
On the gray road, the roof, the window-sill –
Their radiant robes and ribbons and yellow laces;
A leaf each second so is flung at will,
Here, there, another and another, still and still.

A spider's web has caught one while downcoming,
That stays there dangling when the rest pass on;
Like a suspended criminal hangs he, mumming
In golden garb, while one yet green, high yon,
Trembles, as fearing such a fate for himself anon.

674 Come Not; Yet Come!

EXTRA PRINTING:
Chosen Poems, p. 113

TITLE:
Come not; yet come! MS

(*Song*)

IN my sage moments I can say,
Come not near,
But far in foreign regions stay,
So that here
A mind may grow again serene and clear.

But the thought withers. Why should I
Have fear to earn me
Fame from your nearness, though thereby
Old fires new burn me,
And lastly, maybe, tear and overturn me!

So I say, Come: deign again shine
Upon this place,
Even if unslackened smart be mine
From that sweet face,
And I faint to a phantom past all trace.

EXTRA PRINTING:
The Saturday Review, 28 Oct 1922, p. [633] = SR

675 *The Later Autumn*

GONE are the lovers, under the bush
Stretched at their ease;
Gone the bees,
Tangling themselves in your hair as they rush
On the line of your track,
Leg-laden, back
With a dip to their hive
In a prepossessed dive.

Toadsmeat is mangy, frosted, and sere;
Apples in grass
Crunch as we pass,
And rot ere the men who make cyder appear.
Couch-fires abound
On fallows around,
And shades far extend
Like lives soon to end

Spinning leaves join the remains shrunk and brown
Of last year's display
That lie wasting away,
On whose corpses they earlier as scorners gazed down
From their aery green height:
Now in the same plight
They huddle; while yon
A robin looks on.

The Later Autumn
1 Gone are the lovers,] No more lovers SR
3] No more bees SR
15] shades far] shades MS: shadows SR
1921 MS at end

676 *Let Me Believe*

(*Song*)

EXTRA PRINTING:
Chosen Poems, p. 114

TITLE:
'Let me' MS, HS, HSA

LET me believe it, dearest,
    Let it be
As just a dream – the merest –
    Haunting me,
That a frank full-souled sweetness
    Warmed your smile
And voice, to indiscreetness
    Once, awhile!

And I will fondly ponder
    Till I lie
Earthed up with others yonder
    Past a sigh,
That you may name at stray times
    With regret
One whom through green and gray times
    You forget!

677 *At a Fashionable Dinner*

WE sat with the banqueting-party
    By the table-end –
Unmarked, – no diners out
    Were we: scarce a friend
    Of our own mind's trend
Was there, though the welcome was hearty.
Then we noticed a shade extend
    By a distant screen,
And I said: 'What to you does it seem to mean,
    Lavine?'

' – It is like my own body lying
    Beyond the door
Where the servants glide in and about
    The carpeted floor;

Let Me Believe
7 indiscreetness] indiscreteness MS

At a Fashionable Dinner
10 Lavine] Emleen MS *before revision* [and so ll. 20, 30]

And it means my death hour! – '
' – What a fancy! Who feels like dying
While these smart sallies pour,
With laughter between!
To me it is more like satin sheen,
Lavine.'

' – That means your new bride, when you win her:
Yes, so it must be!
It's her satin dress, no doubt –
That shine you see –
My own corpse to me!'
And a gloom came over the dinner,
Where almost strangers were we,
As the spirit of the scene
Forsook her – the fairest of the whole thirteen –
Lavine!

678 Green Slates

(*Penpethy*)

It happened once, before the duller
Loomings of life defined them,
I searched for slates of greenish colour
A quarry where men mined them;

And saw, the while I peered around there,
In the quarry standing
A form against the slate background there,
Of fairness eye-commanding.

And now, though fifty years have flown me,
With all their dreams and duties,
And strange-pipped dice my hand has thrown me,
And dust are all her beauties,

Green slates – seen high on roofs, or lower
In waggon, truck, or lorry –
Cry out: 'Our home was where you saw her
Standing in the quarry!'

Green Slates
8] Of beauty all commanding. MS *before revision*

679 An East-End Curate

EXTRA PRINTINGS:
(1) *The London Mercury*, Nov 1924, p. 7 = LM
(2) *Chosen Poems, pp. 213—14*

INDENTATION:
MS, HS have l. 1 lined up with ll. 2, 3
MS, LM have l. 15 lined up with ll. 16, 17

A SMALL blind street off East Commercial Road;
    Window, door; window, door;
    Every house like the one before,
Is where the curate, Mr Dowle, has found a pinched abode.
Spectacled, pale, moustache straw-coloured, and with a long thin face,
Day or dark his lodgings' narrow doorstep does he pace.

A bleached pianoforte, with its drawn silk plaitings faded,
Stands in his room, its keys much yellowed, cyphering, and abraded,
'Novello's Anthems' lie at hand, and also a few glees,
And 'Laws of Heaven for Earth' in a frame upon the wall one sees.

He goes through his neighbours' houses as his own, and none regards,
And opens their back-doors off-hand, to look for them in their yards:
A man is threatening his wife on the other side of the wall,
But the curate lets it pass as knowing the history of it all.

Freely within his hearing the children skip and laugh and say:
    'There's Mister Dow-well! There's Mister Dow-well!' in their play;
    And the long, pallid, devoted face notes not,
But stoops along abstractedly, for good, or in vain, Got wot!

680 At Rushy-Pond

ON the frigid face of the heath-hemmed pond
    There shaped the half-grown moon:
Winged whiffs from the north with a husky croon
    Blew over and beyond.

And the wind flapped the moon in its float on the pool,
    And stretched it to oval form;
Then corkscrewed it like a wriggling worm;
    Then wanned it weariful.

An East-End Curate
8 abraded,] abraded; LM
15 skip and laugh and] Not in MS, LM

And I cared not for conning the sky above
　　Where hung the substant thing,
For my thought was earthward sojourning
　　On the scene I had vision of.

Since there it was once, in a secret year,
　　I had called a woman to me
From across this water, ardently –
　　And practised to keep her near;

Till the last weak love-words had been said,
　　And ended was her time,
And blurred the bloomage of her prime,
　　And white the earlier red.

And the troubled orb in the pond's sad shine
　　Was her very wraith, as scanned
When she withdrew thence, mirrored, and
　　Her days dropped out of mine.

681 *Four in the Morning*

AT four this day of June I rise:
The dawn-light strengthens steadily;
Earth is a cerule mystery,
As if not far from Paradise
　　　　　　At four o'clock,

Or else near the Great Nebula,
Or where the Pleiads blink and smile:
(For though we see with eyes of guile
The grisly grin of things by day,
　　　　　　At four o'clock

They show their best.) . . . In this vale's space
I am up the first, I think. Yet, no,
A whistling? and the to-and-fro
Wheezed whettings of a scythe apace
　　　　　　At four o'clock? . . .

At Rushy-Pond
13 secret] yearning MS (secret *del*)
15 ardently –] secretly, MS (ardently *del*)
16 near;] near! MS
20 white the earlier] waned to white the MS

Four in the Morning
6 near] in MS, HS, HSA

– Though pleasure spurred, I rose with irk:
Here is one at compulsion's whip
Taking his life's stern stewardship
With blithe uncare, and hard at work
                At four o'clock!

Bockhampton

682 *On the Esplanade*

Midsummer: 10 p.m.

The broad bald moon edged up where the sea was wide,
        Mild, mellow-faced;
Beneath, a tumbling twinkle of shines, like dyed,
        A trackway traced
To the shore, as of petals fallen from a rose to waste,
        In its overblow,
And fluttering afloat on inward heaves of the tide: –
All this, so plain; yet the rest I did not know.

The horizon gets lost in a mist new-wrought by the night:
        The lamps of the Bay
That reach from behind me round to the left and right
        On the sea-wall way
For a constant mile of curve, make a long display
        As a pearl-strung row,
Under which in the waves they bore their gimlets of light: –
All this was plain; but there was a thing not so.

Inside a window, open, with undrawn blind,
        There plays and sings
A lady unseen a melody undefined:
        And where the moon flings
Its shimmer a vessel crosses, whereon to the strings
        Plucked sweetly and low
Of a harp, they dance. Yea, such did I mark. That, behind,
My Fate's masked face crept near me I did not know!

On the Esplanade
3 like dyed] like-dyed MS
24 crept near] had neared MS

TITLE:
In St Paul's (1869 *del*) a while ago MS

INDENTATION:
MS has l. 22 lined up with ll. 19–21

683 In St Paul's a While Ago

SUMMER and winter close commune
On this July afternoon
As I enter chilly Paul's,
With its chasmal classic walls.
– Drifts of gray illumination
From the lofty fenestration
Slant them down in bristling spines that spread
Fan-like upon the vast dust-moted shade.

Moveless here, no whit allied
To the daemonian din outside,
Statues stand, cadaverous, wan,
Round the loiterers looking on
Under the yawning dome and nave,
Pondering whatnot, giddy or grave.
Here a verger moves a chair,
Or a red rope fixes there: –
A brimming Hebe, rapt in her adorning,
Brushes an Artemisia craped in mourning;
Beatrice Benedick piques, coquetting;
All unknowing or forgetting
That strange Jew, Damascus-bound,
Whose name, thereafter travelling round
To this precinct of the world,
Spread here like a flag unfurled:
Anon inspiring architectural sages
To frame this pile, writ his throughout the ages:
Whence also the encircling mart
Assumed his name, of him no part,
And to his vision-seeing mind
Charmless, blank in every kind;
And whose displays, even had they called his eye,
No gold or silver had been his to buy;
Whose haunters, had they seen him stand
On his own steps here, lift his hand

In St Paul's a While Ago
22 name,] name MS
24 unfurled:] unfurled; MS

In stress of eager, stammering speech,
And his meaning chanced to reach,
Would have proclaimed him as they passed
An epilept enthusiast.

684 *Coming Up Oxford Street: Evening*

EXTRA PRINTING:
The Nation & the Athenaeum, 13 June 1925, p. 324 = NA

THE sun from the west glares back,
And the sun from the watered track,
And the sun from the sheets of glass,
And the sun from each window-brass;
Sun-mirrorings, too, brighten
From show-cases beneath
The laughing eyes and teeth
Of ladies who rouge and whiten.
And the same warm god explores
Panels and chinks of doors;
Problems with chymists' bottles
Profound as Aristotle's
He solves, and with good cause,
Having been ere man was.

Also he dazzles the pupils of one who walks west,
A city-clerk, with eyesight not of the best,
Who sees no escape to the very verge of his days
From the rut of Oxford Street into open ways;
And he goes along with head and eyes flagging forlorn,
Empty of interest in things, and wondering why he was born.

As seen 4 July 1872

685 *A Last Journey*

INDENTATION:
There is some variation in MS and difficulty in interpreting Hardy's intention, but the following seems likely:
1 = ll. 2, 6, 9, 14, 19, 22, 23, 26, 32
2 = ll. 1, 8, 11, 12, 15, 17, 20, 25, 27, 28, 29, 31, 33, 34
3 = l. 4
4 = l. 3
5 = l. 5, 7, 10, 13, 16, 18, 21, 24, 30

'FATHER, you seem to have been sleeping fair?'
The child uncovered the dimity-curtained window-square
And looked out at the dawn,
And back at the dying man nigh gone,
And propped up in his chair,
Whose breathing a robin's 'chink' took up in antiphon.

Coming Up Oxford Street: Evening
3 sheets] plates NA
4 window-brass;] window-brass. NA
4–5 Stanza break in NA
8–9 Stanza break in NA
16 A] Me, NA
17 sees] see NA
17 verge of his] end of my NA
19 he goes] I go NA
19 flagging] drooping NA
20 Empty of] Taking no NA
20 he] I NA
1872] 18— NA

The open fireplace spread
Like a vast weary yawn above his head,
Its thin blue blower waved against his whitening crown,
For he could not lie down:
He raised him on his arms so emaciated: –

'Yes; I've slept long, my child. But as for rest,
Well, that I cannot say.
The whole night have I footed field and turnpike-way –
A regular pilgrimage – as at my best
And very briskest day!

' 'Twas first to Weatherb'ry, to see them there,
And thence to King's-Stag, where
I joined in a jolly trip to Weydon-Priors Fair:
I shot for nuts, bought gingerbreads, cream-cheese;
And, not content with these,
I went to London: heard the watchmen cry the hours.

'I soon was off again, and found me in the bowers
Of father's apple-trees,
And he shook the apples down: they fell in showers,
Whereon he turned, smiled strange at me, as ill at ease;
And then you pulled the curtain; and, ah me,
I found me back where I wished not to be!'

'Twas told the child next day: 'Your father's dead.'
And, struck, she questioned, 'O,
That journey, then, did father really go? –
Buy nuts, and cakes, and travel at night till dawn was red,
And tire himself with journeying, as he said,
To see those old friends that he cared for so?'

686 Singing Lovers

EXTRA PRINTING:
Chosen Poems, pp. 116–17

TITLE:
(in 1869.) MS *deleted* below title

I ROWED: the dimpled tide was at the turn,
And mirth and moonlight spread upon the bay:
There were two singing lovers in the stern;
But mine had gone away, –
Whither, I shunned to say!

A Last Journey
14 turnpike-way] turnpike way CP3–4
24 apple-trees] appletrees MS

The houses stood confronting us afar,
A livid line against the evening glare;
The small lamps livened; then out-stole a star;
But my Love was not there, –
Vanished, I sorrowed where!

His arm was round her, both full facing me
With no reserve. Theirs was not love to hide;
He held one tiller-rope, the other she;
I pulled – the merest glide, –
Looked on at them, and sighed.

The moon's glassed glory heaved as we lay swinging
Upon the undulations. Shoreward, slow,
The plash of pebbles joined the lovers' singing,
But she of a bygone vow
Joined in the song not now!

Weymouth

687 The Month's Calendar

TEAR off the calendar
Of this month past,
And all its weeks, that are
Flown, to be cast
To oblivion fast!

Darken that day
On which we met,
With its words of gay
Half-felt regret
That you'll forget!

The second day, too;
The noon I nursed
Well – thoughts; yes, through
To the thirty-first;
That was the worst.

The Month's Calendar
9] Half-regret MS
14 thirty-first] thirtyfirst MS [Could be two words]

For then it was
You let me see
There was good cause
Why you could not be
Aught ever to me!

TITLE:
A Sleeping Palace MS *before revision*

INDENTATION:
MS has ll. 10 and 20 lined up with l. 7

688 *A Spellbound Palace*

(Hampton Court)

On this kindly yellow day of mild low-travelling winter sun
The stirless depths of the yews
Are vague with misty blues:
Across the spacious pathways stretching spires of shadow run,
And the wind-gnawed walls of ancient brick are fired vermilion.

Two or three early sanguine finches tune
Some tentative strains, to be enlarged by May or June:
From a thrush or blackbird
Comes now and then a word,
While an enfeebled fountain somewhere within is heard.

Our footsteps wait awhile,
Then draw beneath the pile,
When an inner court outspreads
As 'twere History's own asile,
Where the now-visioned fountain its attenuate crystal sheds
In passive lapse that seems to ignore the yon world's clamorous clutch,
And lays an insistent numbness on the place, like a cold hand's touch.

And there swaggers the Shade of a straddling King, plumed, sworded, with sensual face,
And lo, too, that of his Minister, at a bold self-centred pace:
Sheer in the sun they pass; and thereupon all is still,
Save the mindless fountain tinkling on with thin enfeebled will.

A Spellbound Palace
14 asile] aisle HSA
17 numbness] stillness MS, HS, HSA

689 When Dead

To ——

It will be much better when
I am under the bough;
I shall be more myself, Dear, then,
Than I am now.

No sign of querulousness
To wear you out
Shall I show there: strivings and stress
Be quite without.

This fleeting life-brief blight
Will have gone past
When I resume my old and right
Place in the Vast.

And when you come to me
To show you true,
Doubt not I shall infallibly
Be waiting you.

690 Sine Prole

(*Mediaeval Latin Sequence-Metre*)

Forth from ages thick in mystery,
Through the morn and noon of history,
To the moment where I stand
Has my line wound: I the last one –
Outcome of each spectral past one
Of that file, so many-manned!

TITLE: (*Mediaeval* . . .)] (Medical (Latin *del*) sequence-Metre) MS

Sine Prole
4 wound:] wound; HSA

Nothing in its time-trail marred it:
As one long life I regard it
    Throughout all the years till now,
When it fain – the close seen coming –
After annals past all plumbing –
    Makes to Being its parting bow.

Unlike Jahveh's ancient nation,
Little in their line's cessation
    Moderns see for surge of sighs:
They have been schooled by lengthier vision,
View Life's lottery with misprision,
    And its dice that fling no prize!

TITLE:
Ten Years since MS

691 *Ten Years Since*

    'TIS ten years since
  I saw her on the stairs,
  Heard her in house-affairs,
  And listened to her cares;
And the trees are ten feet taller,
And the sunny spaces smaller
Whose bloomage would enthrall her;
And the piano wires are rustier,
The smell of bindings mustier,
And lofts and lumber dustier
  Than when, with casual look
  And ear, light note I took
  Of what shut like a book
    Those ten years since!

Nov. 1922

692 *Every Artemisia*

'YOUR eye-light wanes with an ail of care,
Frets freeze gray your face and hair.'

Sine Prole
9 Throughout] Down through MS

Every Artemisia
2–3 Stanza break in all editions

'I was the woman who met him,
Then cool and keen,
Whiling away
Time, with its restless scene on scene
Every day.'

'Your features fashion as in a dream
Of things that were, or used to seem.'

'I was the woman who won him:
Steadfast and fond
Was he, while I
Tepidly took what he gave, nor conned
Wherefore or why.'

'Your house looks blistered by a curse,
As if a wraith ruled there, or worse.'

'I was the woman who slighted him:
Far from my town
Into the night
He went. . . . My hair, then auburn-brown,
Pangs have wanned white.'

'Your ways reflect a monstrous gloom;
Your voice speaks from within a tomb.'

'I was the woman who buried him:
My misery
God laughed to scorn:
The people said: " 'Twere well if she
Had not been born!" '

'You plod to pile a monument
So madly that your breath is spent.'

'I am the woman who god him:
I build, to ease
My scalding fires,
A temple topping the Deities'
Fanes of my sires.'

Every Artemisia
35 Fanes of] Built by MS

693 *The Best She Could*

TITLE:
The Fall of the Leaf MS *deleted*
The Best she could MS

NINE leaves a minute
Swim down shakily;
Each one fain would spin it
Straight to earth; but, see,
How the sharp airs win it
Slantwise away! – Hear it say,
'Now we have finished our summer show
Of what we knew the way to do:
Alas, not much! But, as things go,
As fair as any. And night-time calls,
And the curtain falls!'

Sunlight goes on shining
As if no frost were here,
Blackbirds seem designing
Where to build next year;
Yet is warmth declining:
And still the day seems to say,
'Saw you how Dame Summer drest?
Of all God taught her she bethought her!
Alas, not much! And yet the best
She could, within the too short time
Granted her prime.'

8 Nov. 1923

694 *The Graveyard of Dead Creeds*

I LIT upon the graveyard of dead creeds
In wistful wanderings through old wastes of thought,
Where bristled fennish fungi, fruiting nought,
Amid the sepulchres begirt with weeds,

The Best She Could
20 Alas] Ah MS

Which stone by stone recorded sanct, deceased
Catholicons that had, in centuries flown,
Physicked created man through his long groan,
Ere they went under, all their potence ceased.

When in a breath-while, lo, their spectres rose
Like wakened winds that autumn summons up: –
'Out of us cometh an heir, that shall disclose
New promise!' cried they. 'And the caustic cup

'We ignorantly upheld to men, be filled
With draughts more pure than those we ever distilled,
That shall make tolerable to sentient seers
The melancholy marching of the years.'

695 There Seemed a Strangeness

TITLE:
The Great Adjustment MS *deleted*
'There seemed a Strangeness' MS

A Phantasy

THERE seemed a strangeness in the air,
Vermilion light on the land's lean face;
I heard a Voice from I knew not where: –
'The Great Adjustment is taking place!

'I set thick darkness over you,
And fogged you all your years therein;
    At last I uncloud your view,
Which I am weary of holding in.

'Men have not heard, men have not seen
Since the beginning of the world
    What earth and heaven mean;
But now their curtains shall be furled,

'And they shall see what is, ere long,
Not through a glass, but face to face;
And Right shall disestablish Wrong:
The Great Adjustment is taking place.'

The Graveyard of Dead Creeds
9 breath-while] breathwhile MS

There Seemed a Strangeness
15] And Good shall be established Wrong: MS *before revision*

696 *A Night of Questionings*

On the eve of All-Souls' Day
I heard the dead men say
Who lie by the tottering tower,
To the dark and doubling wind
At the midnight's turning hour,
When other speech had thinned:
  'What of the world now?'
The wind whiffed back: 'Men still
Who are born, do good, do ill
Here, just as in your time:
Till their years the locust hath eaten,
Leaving them bare, downbeaten;
Somewhiles in springtide rime,
Somewhiles in summer glow,
Somewhiles in winter snow: –
    No more I know.'

The same eve I caught cry
To the selfsame wind, those dry
As dust beneath the aisles
Of old cathedral piles,
Walled up in vaulted biers
Through many Christian years:
  'What of the world now?'
Sighed back the circuiteer:
'Men since your time, shrined here
By deserved ordinance,
Their own craft, or by chance,
Which follows men from birth
Even until under earth,
But little difference show
When ranged in sculptured row,
Different as dyes although: –
    No more I know.'

A Night of Questionings
29 earth,] earth MS
33–4 Stanza break in all editions

On the selfsame eve, too, said
Those swayed in the sunk sea-bed
To the selfsame wind as it played
With the tide in the starless shade
From Comorin to Horn,
And round by Wrath forlorn:
'What of the world now?'
And the wind for a second ceased,
Then whirred: 'Men west and east,
As each sun soars and dips,
Go down to the sea in ships
As you went – hither and thither;
See the wonders of the deep,
As you did, ere they sleep;
But few at home care whither
They wander to and fro;
Themselves care little also! –
No more I know.'

Said, too, on the selfsame eve
The troubled skulls that heave
And fust in the flats of France,
To the wind wayfaring over
Listlessly as in trance
From the Ardennes to Dover,
'What of the world now?'
And the farer moaned: 'As when
You mauled these fields, do men
Set them with dark-drawn breaths
To knave their neighbours' deaths
In periodic spasms!
Yea, fooled by foul phantasms,
In a strange cyclic throe
Backward to type they go: –
No more I know.'

That night, too, men whose crimes
Had cut them off betimes,
Who lay within the pales

A Night of Questionings
39 forlorn:] forlorn; MS
48 at home care] care why or MS

Of town and county jails
With the rope-groove on them yet,
Said to the same wind's fret,
  'What of the world now?'
And the blast in its brooding tone
Returned: 'Men have not shown,
Since you were stretched that morning,
A white cap your adorning,
More lovely deeds or true
Through thus neck-knotting you;
Or that they purer grow,
Or ever will, I trow! –
    No more I know.'

EXTRA PRINTING:
The Nineteenth Century, March 1924, pp. 315–17 = NC

697 *Xenophanes, the Monist of Colophon*

Ann: aet: suae XCII.–A: C: CCCCLXXX

'ARE You groping Your way?
Do You do it unknowing? –
Or mark Your wind blowing?
Night tell You from day,
O Mover? Come, say!'
    Cried Xenophanes.

'I mean, querying so,
Do You do it aware,
Or by rote, like a player,
Or in ignorance, nor care
Whether doing or no?'
    Pressed Xenophanes.

'Thus strive I to plumb
Your depths, O Great Dumb! –
Not a god, but the All
(As I read); yet a thrall
To a blind ritual,'
    Sighed Xenophanes.

A Night of Questionings
73 fret,] fret MS, HS, HSA, PE, WE

Xenophanes, the Monist of Colophon
2 unknowing? –] unknowing? NC
3 wind] wind's NC
9 rote,] rote NC

'If I only could bring
You to own it, close Thing,
I would write it again
With a still stronger pen
To my once neighbour-men!'
    Said Xenophanes.

– Quoth the listening Years:
'You ask It in vain;
You waste sighs and tears
On these callings inane,
Which It grasps not nor hears,
    O Xenophanes!

'When you penned what you thought
You were cast out, and sought
A retreat over sea
From aroused enmity:
So it always will be,
    Yea, Xenophanes!

'In the lone of the nights
At Elea unseen,
Where the swinging wave smites
Of the restless Tyrrhene,
You may muse thus, serene,
    Safe, Xenophanes.

'But write it not back
To your dear Colophon;
Brows still will be black
At your words, "All is One,"
From disputers thereon,
    Know, Xenophanes.

'Three thousand years hence,
Men who hazard a clue
To this riddle immense,
And still treat it as new,
Will be scowled at, like you,
    O Xenophanes!

Xenophanes, the Monist of Colophon
32 out,] out NC
38] Here at Velia unseen, NC
44 Colophon;] Colophon: NC

' "*Some day I may tell,*
When I've broken My spell,"
It snores in Its sleep
If you listen long, deep
At Its closely-sealed cell,
Wronged Xenophanes!

'Yea, on, near the end,
Its doings may mend;
Aye, when you're forgotten,
And old cults are rotten,
And bulky codes shotten,
Xenophanes!'

1921

698 Life and Death at Sunrise

(*Near Dogbury Gate, 1867*)

TITLE:
A Long ago Sunrise at Dogbury Gate: 1867 MS *before revision*

THE hills uncap their tops
Of woodland, pasture, copse,
And look on the layers of mist
At their foot that still persist:
They are like awakened sleepers on one elbow lifted,
Who gaze around to learn if things during night have shifted.

A waggon creaks up from the fog
With a laboured leisurely jog;
Then a horseman from off the hill-tip
Comes clapping down into the dip;
While woodlarks, finches, sparrows, try to entune at one time,
And cocks and hens and cows and bulls take up the chime.

With a shouldered basket and flagon
A man meets the one with the waggon,
And both the men halt of long use.
'Well,' the waggoner says, 'what's the news?'
' – 'Tis a boy this time. You've just met the doctor trotting back.
She's doing very well. And we think we shall call him "Jack".

Xenophanes, the Monist of Colophon
56 *My*] *my* MS, NC
58 deep] deep, NC
59 closely-sealed] closely sealed NC
61 the] my NC
1921] Not in MS, NC

Life and Death at Sunrise
4 foot] base MS
8] At the slowest possible jog; MS
9–10] And a trotting horse then nighs,/Slacks, passes on over the rise; MS *before revision*
10 clapping] trotting MS

'And what have you got covered there?'
He nods to the waggon and mare.
'Oh, a coffin for old John Thinn:
We are just going to put him in.'
' – So he's gone at last. He always had a good constitution.'
' – He was ninety-odd. He could call up the French Revolution.'

699 Night-Time in Mid-Fall

EXTRA PRINTING:
Chosen Poems, p. 225

TITLE:
(Autumn *del*) Night-time in Mid-Fall MS

IT is a storm-strid night, winds footing swift
Through the blind profound;
I know the happenings from their sound;
Leaves totter down still green, and spin and drift;
The tree-trunks rock to their roots, which wrench and lift
The loam where they run onward underground.

The streams are muddy and swollen; eels migrate
To a new abode;
Even cross, 'tis said, the turnpike-road;
(Men's feet have felt their crawl, home-coming late):
The westward fronts of towers are saturate,
Church-timbers crack, and witches ride abroad.

700 A Sheep Fair

EXTRA PRINTING:
Chosen Poems, pp. 226–7

THE day arrives of the autumn fair,
And torrents fall,
Though sheep in throngs are gathered there,
Ten thousand all,
Sodden, with hurdles round them reared:
And, lot by lot, the pens are cleared,
And the auctioneer wrings out his beard,
And wipes his book, bedrenched and smeared,
And rakes the rain from his face with the edge of his hand,
As torrents fall.

Life and Death at Sunrise
21 John] Andrew MS *before revision*

Night-Time in Mid-Fall
10 home-coming] homecoming MS
11 westward fronts] stormward stones MS

The wool of the ewes is like a sponge
With the daylong rain:
Jammed tight, to turn, or lie, or lunge,
They strive in vain.
Their horns are soft as finger-nails,
Their shepherds reek against the rails,
The tied dogs soak with tucked-in tails,
The buyers' hat-brims fill like pails,
Which spill small cascades when they shift their stand
In the daylong rain.

POSTSCRIPT

Time has trailed lengthily since met
At Pummery Fair
Those panting thousands in their wet
And woolly wear:
And every flock long since has bled,
And all the dripping buyers have sped,
And the hoarse auctioneer is dead,
Who 'Going – going!' so often said,
As he consigned to doom each meek, mewed band
At Pummery Fair.

EXTRA PRINTING:
Chosen Poems, p. 228

701 *Snow in the Suburbs*

EVERY branch big with it,
Bent every twig with it;
Every fork like a white web-foot;
Every street and pavement mute:
Some flakes have lost their way, and grope back upward, when
Meeting those meandering down they turn and descend again.
The palings are glued together like a wall,
And there is no waft of wind with the fleecy fall.

A sparrow enters the tree,
Whereon immediately
A snow-lump thrice his own slight size
Descends on him and showers his head and eyes,

A Sheep Fair
17 tucked-in] tucked in MS
27 hoarse] drenched MS
29 meek,] meek MS

Snow in the Suburbs
5 grope] float MS *before revision*
6 meandering] coming MS *before revision*
7 glued] joined MS *before revision*
8 there is no waft] there's not a whiff MS
12 eyes,] eyes. HS, PE, CP3–4, CHP
12–13 No stanza break

And overturns him,
And near inurns him,
And lights on a nether twig, when its brush
Starts off a volley of other lodging lumps with a rush.

The steps are a blanched slope,
Up which, with feeble hope,
A black cat comes, wide-eyed and thin;
And we take him in.

702 *A Light Snow-Fall after Frost*

ON the flat road a man at last appears:
How much his whitening hairs
Owe to the settling snow's mute anchorage,
And how much to a life's rough pilgrimage,
One cannot certify.

The frost is on the wane,
And cobwebs hanging close outside the pane
Pose as festoons of thick white worsted there,
Of their pale presence no eye being aware
Till the rime made them plain.

A second man comes by;
His ruddy beard brings fire to the pallid scene:
His coat is faded green;
Hence seems it that his mien
Wears something of the dye
Of the berried holm-trees that he passes nigh.

The snow-feathers so gently swoop that though
But half an hour ago
The road was brown, and now is starkly white,
A watcher would have failed defining quite
When it transformed it so.

Near Surbiton

Snow in the Suburbs
15 lights] falls MS *before revision*
15 nether] lower MS *before revision*
16 volley] cascade MS
16 lodging] waiting MS *before revision*
17 blanched] white MS *before revision*
19 wide-eyed] large-eyed MS *before revision*

A Light Snow-Fall after Frost
6–10 A late addition to MS

PROOF:
It has not been possible to trace the proof once in the possession of Sir Sydney Cockerell

EXTRA PRINTINGS:
(1) *Country Life*, 6 Dec 1924, p. 865 = CL
(2) Privately printed by Florence Hardy, Dec 1924 = FH

703 *Winter Night in Woodland*

(*Old Time*)

THE bark of a fox rings, sonorous and long: –
Three barks, and then silentness; 'wong, wong, wong!'
In quality horn-like, yet melancholy,
As from teachings of years; for an old one is he.
The hand of all men is against him, he knows; and yet, why?
That he knows not, – will never know, down to his death-halloo cry.

With clap-nets and lanterns off start the bird-baiters,
In trim to make raids on the roosts in the copse,
Where they beat the boughs artfully, while their awaiters
Grow heavy at home over divers warm drops.
The poachers, with swingels, and matches of brimstone, outcreep
To steal upon pheasants and drowse them a-perch and asleep.

Out there, on the verge, where a path wavers through,
Dark figures, filed singly, thrid quickly the view,
Yet heavily laden: land-carriers are they
In the hire of the smugglers from some nearest bay.
Each bears his two 'tubs', slung across, one in front, one behind,
To a further snug hiding, which none but themselves are to find.

And then, when the night has turned twelve the air brings
From dim distance, a rhythm of voices and strings:
'Tis the quire, just afoot on their long yearly rounds,
To rouse by worn carols each house in their bounds;
Robert Penny, the Dewys, Mail, Voss, and the rest; till anon
Tired and thirsty, but cheerful, they home to their beds in the dawn.

704 *Ice on the Highway*

SEVEN buxom women abreast, and arm in arm,
Trudge down the hill, tip-toed,
And breathing warm;
They must perforce trudge thus, to keep upright
On the glassy ice-bound road,

Winter Night in Woodland
1 long: –] long; CL, FH
6 not,] not CL, FH
6 death-halloo cry] death-hallo-cry CL, FH
8 trim] mode MS
8 make . . . roosts] spend most of the night CL, FH
9 beat . . . artfully] bivouac jollily CL, FH
10 divers] sundry CL, FH
11 outcreep] creep, creep CL, FH
12 a-perch] at roost CL, FH
19 twelve] twelve, MS, CL, FH
20 dim] far CL, FH
21 rounds,] rounds CL, FH
22 worn] quaint MS, CL, FH

Ice on the Highway
3 warm;] warm: [?] MS
5–6 No stanza break

And they must get to market whether or no,
    Provisions running low
    With the nearing Saturday night,
While the lumbering van wherein they mostly ride
        Can nowise go:
Yet loud their laughter as they stagger and slide!

Yell'ham Hill

705 *Music in a Snowy Street*

THE weather is sharp,
But the girls are unmoved:
One wakes from a harp,
The next from a viol,
A strain that I loved
When life was no trial.

The tripletime beat
Bounds forth on the snow,
But the spry springing feet
Of a century ago,
And the arms that enlaced
As the couples embraced,
Are silent old bones
Under graying gravestones.

The snow-feathers sail
Across the harp-strings,
Whose throbbing threads wail
Like love-satiate things.
Each lyre's grimy mien,
With its rout-raising tune,
Against the new white
Of the flake-laden noon,
Is incongruous to sight,
Hinting years they have seen
Of revel at night
Ere these damsels became
Possessed of their frame.

Ice on the Highway
10 In MS indented right of l. 3

Music in a Snowy Street
4 viol,] viol MS, HSA
5 strain] dance MS
27–8 Stanza break in MS, HS, HSA, PE: page turn in CP3–4, WE

O bygone whirls, heys,
Crotchets, quavers, the same
That were danced in the days
Of grim Bonaparte's fame,
Or even by the toes
Of the fair Antoinette, –
Yea, old notes like those
Here are living on yet! –
But of their fame and fashion
How little these know
Who strum without passion
For pence, in the snow!

706 *The Frozen Greenhouse*

(*St Juliot*)

'THERE was a frost
Last night!' she said,
'And the stove was forgot
When we went to bed,
And the greenhouse plants
Are frozen dead!'

By the breakfast blaze
Blank-faced spoke she,
Her scared young look
Seeming to be
The very symbol
Of tragedy.

The frost is fiercer
Than then to-day,
As I pass the place
Of her once dismay,
But the greenhouse stands
Warm, tight, and gay,

While she who grieved
At the sad lot
Of her pretty plants –
Cold, iced, forgot –
Herself is colder,
And knows it not.

707 Two Lips

EXTRA PRINTING:
Chosen Poems, p. 123

TITLE:
Two (red *del*) lips MS

I KISSED them in fancy as I came
Away in the morning glow:
I kissed them through the glass of her picture-frame:
She did not know.

I kissed them in love, in troth, in laughter,
When she knew all; long so!
That I should kiss them in a shroud thereafter
She did not know.

708 No Buyers

A Street Scene

A LOAD of brushes and baskets and cradles and chairs
Labours along the street in the rain:
With it a man, a woman, a pony with whiteybrown hairs. –
The man foots in front of the horse with a shambling sway
At a slower tread than a funeral train,
While to a dirge-like tune he chants his wares,
Swinging a Turk's-head brush (in a drum-major's way
When the bandsmen march and play).

A yard from the back of the man is the whiteybrown pony's nose:
He mirrors his master in every item of pace and pose:
He stops when the man stops, without being told,
And seems to be eased by a pause; too plainly he's old,
Indeed, not strength enough shows

Two Lips
2 morning glow] dark and snow MS
5 laughter,] laughter MS

No Buyers
8 the] his MS

To steer the disjointed waggon straight,
Which wriggles left and right in a rambling line,
Deflected thus by its own warp and weight,
And pushing the pony with it in each incline.

The woman walks on the pavement verge,
Parallel to the man:
She wears an apron white and wide in span,
And carries a like Turk's-head, but more in nursing-wise:
Now and then she joins in his dirge,
But as if her thoughts were on distant things.
The rain clams her apron till it clings. –
So, step by step, they move with their merchandize,
And nobody buys.

709 One Who Married Above Him

TITLE:
One who married above him MS

INDENTATION:
There has been some variation of this complex pattern. MS has:
1 = ll. 9, 10, 19–22, 25–7, 40
2 = ll. 7, 8, 11–14, 28–30, 32, 34, 37–9
3 = ll. 1–4, 17, 18, 23, 24, 31, 33, 36
4 = ll. 5, 6, 15, 16, 35

WE has:
1 = ll. 9, 10, 19–22, 25–7, 40
2 = ll. 7, 8, 11–14, 28–30, 32, 34, 37–9
3 = ll. 1–4, 17, 18, 31, 33, 36
4 = ll. 5, 6, 15, 16, 35
5 = ll. 23–4

' 'TIS you, I think? Back from your week's work, Steve?'

'It is I. Back from work this Christmas Eve.'

'But you seem off again? – in this night-rime?'

'I am off again, and thoroughly off this time.'

'What does that mean?'

'More than may first be seen. . . .

Half an hour ago I footed homeward here,
No wife found I, nor child, nor maid, indoors or near.
She has, as always, gone with them to her mother's at the farm,
Where they fare better far than here, and, maybe, meet less harm.
She's left no fire, no light, has cooked me nothing to eat,
Though she had fuel, and money to get some Christmas meat.
Christmas with them is grand, she knows, and brings good victual,
Other than how it is here, where it's but lean and little.
But though not much, and rough,
If managed neat there's enough.
She and hers are too highmade for me;
But she's whimmed her once too often, she'll see!

No Buyers
22 Now and then] Occasionally MS
26 nobody] nobody ever MS

One Who Married Above Him
3 in] and in MS
14 lean] lean, MS
18–19 No stanza break

Farmer Bollen's daughter should never have married a man that's poor;
And I can stand it no longer; I'm leaving; you'll see me no more, be sure.'

'But nonsense: you'll be back again ere bedtime, and lighting a fire,
And sizzling your supper, and vexing not that her views of supper are higher.'
'Never for me.'
'Well, we shall see.'

The sceptical neighbour and Stephen then followed their foredesigned ways,
And their steps dimmed into white silence upon the slippery glaze;
And the trees went on with their spitting amid the icicled haze.

The evening whiled, and the wife with the babies came home,
But he was not there, nor all Christmas Day did he come.
Christmastide went, and likewise went the New Year,
But no husband's footfall revived,
And month after month lapsed, graytime to green and to sere,
And other new years arrived,
And the children grew up: one husbanded and one wived. –
She wept and repented,
But Stephen never relented.
And there stands the house, and the sycamore-tree and all,
With its roots forming steps for the passers who care to call,
And there are the mullioned windows, and Ham-Hill door,
Through which Steve's wife was brought out, but which Steve re-entered no more.

710 The New Toy

SHE cannot leave it alone,
The new toy;
She pats it, smooths it, rights it, to show it's her own,
As the other train-passengers muse on its temper and tone,
Till she draws from it cries of annoy: –

One Who Married Above Him
19 poor;] poor: MS
30 Year,] Year. HSA

The New Toy
5–6 No stanza break

She feigns to appear as if thinking it nothing so rare
    Or worthy of pride, to achieve
This wonder a child, though with reason the rest of them there
    May so be inclined to believe.

TITLE:
Queen Caroline to her Guests MS

711 *Queen Caroline to Her Guests*

    DEAR friends, stay!
Lamplit wafts of wit keep sorrow
In the purlieus of to-morrow:
    Dear friends, stay!

    Haste not away!
Even now may Time be weaving
Tricks of ravage, wrack, bereaving:
    Haste not away!

    Through the pane,
Lurking along the street, there may be
Heartwrings, keeping hid till day be,
    Through the pane.

    Check their reign:
Since while here we are the masters,
And can barricade dim disasters:
    Check their reign!

    Give no ear
To those ghosts withoutside mumming,
Mouthing, threatening, 'We are coming!'
    Give no ear!

    Sheltered here
Care we not that next day bring us
Pains, perversions! No racks wring us
    Sheltered here.

Queen Caroline to Her Guests
3 to-morrow:] to-morrow; MS
7 bereaving:] bereaving, MS, HSA
15 disasters:] disasters; MS

Homeward gone,
Sleep will slay this merrymaking;
No resuming it at waking,
Homeward gone.

After dawn
Something sad may be befalling;
Mood like ours there's no recalling
After dawn!

Morrow-day
Present joy that moments strengthen
May be past our power to lengthen,
Morrow-day!

Dear friends, stay!
Lamplit wafts of wit keep sorrow
In the limbo of to-morrow:
Dear friends, stay!

712 Plena Timoris

THE lovers looked over the parapet-stone:
The moon in its southing directly blent
Its silver with their environment.
Her ear-rings twinkled; her teeth, too, shone
As, his arm around her, they laughed and leant.

A man came up to them; then one more.
'There's a woman in the canal below,'
They said; climbed over; slid down; let go,
And a splashing was heard, till an arm upbore,
And a dripping body began to show.

'Drowned herself for love of a man,
Who at one time used to meet her here,
Until he grew tired. But she'd wait him near,
And hope, till hopeless despair began.
So much for love in this mortal sphere!'

Queen Caroline to Her Guests
33] Morrowday MS
35 lengthen,] lengthen MS
36] Morrowday! MS
39 to-morrow:] to-morrow; MS, HSA

Plena Timoris
4 ear-rings] earrings MS
14 hopeless] hope died, and MS
15 much for] endeth MS

The girl's heart shuddered; it seemed as to freeze her
That here, at their tryst for so many a day,
Another woman's tragedy lay.
Dim dreads of the future grew slowly to seize her,
And her arm dropt from his as they wandered away.

TYPESCRIPT:
In the possession of James Gibson.
There are no variants

EXTRA PRINTING:
The Bermondsey Book, Dec 1925, p. 8 = BB

713 *The Weary Walker*

A PLAIN in front of me,
  And there's the road
Upon it. Wide country,
  And, too, the road!

Past the first ridge another,
  And still the road
Creeps on. Perhaps no other
  Ridge for the road?

Ah! Past that ridge a third,
  Which still the road
Has to climb furtherward –
  The thin white road!

Sky seems to end its track;
  But no. The road
Trails down the hill at the back.
  Ever the road!

Last Love-Word

EXTRA PRINTING:
Chosen Poems, p. 115

TITLE:
Last Love-word MS

INDENTATION:
That used here is identical with the first stanzas of MS, WE, CHP, and with the second stanzas of all editions. The first stanzas of HS, HSA, PE used
1 = l. 1
2 = l. 3
3 = ll. 2, 5
4 = ll. 4, 6

CP3, 4 used
1 = l. 1
2 = ll. 3, 5
3 = l. 2
4 = ll. 4, 6

714 *Last Love-Word*

(*Song*)

THIS is the last; the very, very last!
    Anon, and all is dead and dumb,
Only a pale shroud over the past,
      That cannot be
    Of value small or vast,
      Love, then to me!

The Weary Walker
9 Ah!] Ah. MS
13 track;] track: BB

Last Love-Word
1 very,] very MS
6–7 Stanza break in all editions

I can say no more: I have even said too much.
I did not mean that this should come:
I did not know 'twould swell to such –
Nor, perhaps, you –
When that first look and touch,
Love, doomed us two!

189–

715 Nobody Comes

TREE-LEAVES labour up and down,
And through them the fainting light
Succumbs to the crawl of night.
Outside in the road the telegraph wire
To the town from the darkening land
Intones to travellers like a spectral lyre
Swept by a spectral hand.

A car comes up, with lamps full-glare,
That flash upon a tree:
It has nothing to do with me,
And whangs along in a world of its own,
Leaving a blacker air;
And mute by the gate I stand again alone,
And nobody pulls up there.

9 October 1924

716 In the Street

(*Song*)

ONLY acquaintances
Seem do we,
Each of whom, meeting, says
Civilly
'Good morning.' – Yes: thus we appear to be!

Last Love-Word
8 come:] come. MS

But far, near, left and right,
Here or there,
By day or dingiest night,
Everywhere
I see you: one incomparably fair!

So do we wend our ways,
Beautiful girl,
Along our parallel days;
While unfurl
Our futures, and what there may whelm and whirl.

EXTRA PRINTING:
Nash's and Pall Mall Magazine, Nov 1924, p. 47
= NPM

717 *The Last Leaf*

'THE leaves throng thick above: –
Well, I'll come back, dear Love,
When they all are down!'

She watched that August tree,
(None now scorned summer as she),
Till it broidered it brown.

And then October came blowing,
And the leaves showed signs they were going,
And she saw up through them.

O how she counted them then!
– November left her but ten,
And started to strew them.

'Ah, when they all are gone,
And the skeleton-time comes on,
Whom shall I see!'

– When the fifteenth spread its sky
That month, her upturned eye
Could count but three.

In the Street
15 and whirl] or whirl MS

The Last Leaf
1 throng] are NPM
4 tree,] tree NPM
6 broidered] showed NPM
8 showed] gave NPM
10 O] O, NPM
11] November left but ten NPM
12 And started] After starting NPM
16 – When] When NPM

And at the close of the week
A flush flapped over her cheek:
    The last one fell.

But – he did not come. And, at length,
Her hope of him lost all strength,
    And it was as a knell. . . .

When he did come again,
Years later, a husband then,
    Heavy somewhat,

With a smile she reminded him:
And he cried: 'Ah, that vow of our whim! –
    Which I forgot,

'As one does! – And was that the tree?
So it was! – Dear me, dear me:
    Yes: I forgot.'

718 At Wynyard's Gap

SHE (*on horseback*)

THE hounds pass here?

HE (*on horseback*)

                They did an hour ago,
Just in full cry, and went down-wind, I saw,
Towards Pen Wood, where they may kill, and draw
A second time, and bear towards the Yeo.

SHE

How vexing! And I've crept along unthinking.

HE

Ah! – lost in dreams. Fancy to fancy linking!

SHE (*more softly*)

Not that, quite. . . . Now, to settle what I'll do.

The Last Leaf
20 flapped] passed NPM
24 knell. . . .] knell. . . . . MS
29 cried:] cried, NPM

At Wynyard's Gap
6 Ah!] Ah, MS

He

Go home again. But have you seen the view
From the top there? Not? It's really worth your while. –
You must dismount, because there is a stile.

They dismount, hitch their horses, and climb a few-score yards from the road.

There you see half South Wessex, – combe, and glen,
And down, to Lewsdon Hill and Pilsdon Pen.

She

Yes. It is fine. And I, though living out there
By Crewkerne, never knew it. (*She turns her head*) Well, I declare,
Look at the horses! – How shall I catch my mare?

The horses have got loose and scampered off.

Now that's your fault, through leading me up here!
You must have known 'twould happen –

He

No, my dear!

She

I'm not your dear.

He (*blandly*)

But you can't help being so,
If it comes to that. The fairest girl I've seen
Is of course dear – by her own fault, I mean.

She (*quickly*)

What house is that we see just down below?

He

Oh – that's the inn called 'Wynyard's Gap'. – I'll go
While you wait here, and catch those brutes. Don't stir.

He goes. She waits.

She

What a handsome man. Not local, I'll aver.

He comes back.

HE

I met a farmer's labourer some way on;
He says he'll bring them to us here anon,
If possible before the day is dim.
Come down to the inn: there we can wait for him.

They descend slowly in that direction.

SHE

What a lonely inn. Why is there such a one?

HE

For us to wait at. Thus 'tis things are done.

SHE

Thus things are done? Well – what things do you mean?

HE

Romantic things. Meetings unknown, unseen.

SHE

But ours is accident, and needn't have been,
And isn't what I'd plan with a stranger, quite,
Particularly at this time – nearly night.

HE

Nor I. But still, the tavern's loneliness
Is favourable for lovers in distress,
When they've eloped, for instance, and are in fear
Of being pursued. No one would find them here.

He goes to speak to the labourer approaching; and returns.

He says the horses long have passed the combe,
And cannot be overtaken. They'll go home.

SHE

And what's to be done? And it's beginning to rain.
'Tis always so. One trouble brings a train!

HE

It seems to me that here we'd better stay
And rest us till some vehicle comes this way:
In fact, we might put up here till the morning:
The floods are high, and night-farers have warning.

She

Put up? Do you think so!

He

I incline to such,
My *dear* (do you mind?)

She

Yes. – Well (*more softly*), I don't much,
If I seem like it. But I ought to tell you
One thing. I'm married. Being so, it's well you —

He

Oh, so am I. (*A silence, he regarding her*) I note a charming thing –
You stand so stock-still that your ear-ring shakes
At each pulsation which the vein there makes.

She

Does it? Perhaps because it's flustering
To be caught thus! (*In a murmur*) Why did we chance to meet here?

He

God knows! Perhaps to taste a bitter-sweet here. –
Still, let us enter. Shelter we must get:
The night is darkening and is growing wet.
So, anyhow, you can treat me as a lover
Just for this once. To-morrow 'twill be over!

They reach the inn. The door is locked, and they discern a board marked 'To Let'. While they stand stultified a van is seen drawing near, with passengers.

She

Ah, here's an end of it! The Crewkerne carrier.

He

So cynic circumstance erects its barrier!

She (*mischievously*)

To your love-making, which would have grown stronger,
No doubt, if we had stayed on here much longer?

The carrier comes up. Her companion reluctantly hails him.

At Wynyard's Gap
49 *dear*] dear; MS
49 don't much] don't – much MS
53 ear-ring] earring MS
56 here?] here! CP3, 4

HE

Yes. . . . And in which you might have shown some ruth,
Had but the inn been open! – Well, forsooth,
I'm sorry it's not. Are you? Now, dear, the truth!

SHE (*with gentle evasiveness*)

I am – almost. But best 'tis thus to be.
For – dear one – there I've said it! – you can see
That both at one inn (though roomed separately,
Of course) – so lone, too – might have been unfit,
Perfect as 'tis for lovers, I admit.

HE (*after a sigh*)

Carrier! A lift for my wife, please.

SHE (*in quick undertones*)

Wife? But nay —

HE (*continuing*)

Her horse has thrown her and has gone astray:
See she gets safe to Crewkerne. I've to stay.

CARRIER

I will, sir! I'm for Crookhorn straight away.

HE (*to her, aloud*)

Right now, dear. I shall soon be home. Adieu! (*Kisses her*)

SHE (*whispering confusedly*)

You shouldn't! Pretending you are my husband, too!
I now must act the part of wife to you!

HE (*whispering*)

Yes, since I've kissed you, dear. You see it's done
To silence tongues as we're found here alone
At night, by gossipers, and seem as shown
Staying together!

SHE (*whispering*)

Then must I, too, kiss?

HE

Yes: a mere matter of form, you know,
To check all scandal. People will talk so!

At Wynyard's Gap
84 together!] together. MS
85–6 A late addition to MS
85 Yes:] Yes; HSA
85 form,] form HSA

SHE

I'd no idea it would reach to this! (*Kisses him*)
What makes it worse is, I'm ashamed to say,
I've a young baby waiting me at home!

HE

Ah – there you beat me! – But, my dearest, play
The wife to the end, and don't give me away,
Despite the baby, since we've got so far,
And what we've acted feel we almost are!

SHE (*sighing*)

Yes. 'Tis so! And my conscience has gone dumb!
(*Aloud*)
'Bye, dear, awhile! I'll sit up till you come.
(*In a whisper*)
Which means Good-bye for ever, truly heard!
Upon to-night be silent!

HE

Never a word,
Till Pilsdon Pen by Marshwood wind is stirred!

He hands her up. Exeunt omnes.

719 At Shag's Heath

1685

(*Traditional*)

I GRIEVE and grieve for what I have done,
And nothing now is left to me
But straight to drown; yea, I have slain
The rarest soul the world shall see!
– My husband said: 'Now thou art wed
Thou must beware! And should a man
Cajole, mind, he means ill to thee,
Depend on't: fool him if ye can!'
But 'twas King Monmouth, he!

At Wynyard's Gap
92–4 A late addition to MS
92 far,] far MS
97 silent!] silent. MS

As truth I took what was not true:
Till darked my door just such a one.
He asked me but the way to go,
Though looking all so down and done.
And as he stood he said, unsued,
'The prettiest wife I've eyed to-day!'
And then he kissed me tenderly
Before he footed fast away
        Did dear King Monmouth, he!

Builded was he so beautiful! –
Why did I pout a pettish word
For what he'd done? – Then whisking off –
For his pursuers' feet were heard –
'Dear one, keep faith!' he turns and saith.
And next he vanished in the copse
Before I knew what such might be,
And how great fears and how great hopes
        Had rare King Monmouth – he!

Up rode the soldiers. 'Where's this man? –
He is the rebel Duke,' say they.
'And calls himself King Monmouth, sure!'
Then I believed my husband; aye,
Though he'd spoke lies in jealous-wise!
– To Shag's nigh copse beyond the road
I moved my finger mercilessly;
And there lay hidden where I showed:
        My dear King Monmouth, he!

The soldiers brought him by my door,
His elbows bound behind him, fast;
Passing, he me-ward cast his eyes –
What eyes of beauty did he cast!
Grieved was his glance at me askance:
'I wished all weal might thee attend,
But this is what th'st done to me,
O heartless woman, held my friend!'
        Said sweet King Monmouth, he!

At Shag's Heath
18 dear] sweet MS
23 saith.] saith, HSA
27 rare] sweet MS
36 dear] sweet MS

O then I saw he was no hind,
But a great lord of loftihood,
Come here to claim his rule and rights,
Who'd wished me, as he'd said, but good. –
With tug and jolt, then, out to Holt,
To Justice Ettricke, he was led,
And thence to London speedily,
Where under yester's headsman bled
    The rare King Monmouth, he!

Last night, the while my husband slept,
He rose up at the window there,
All blood and blear, and hacked about,
With heavy eyes, and rumpled hair;
And said: 'My Love, 'twas cruel of
A Fair like thee to use me so!
But now it's nought: from foes I'm free!
Sooner or later all must go,'
    Said dear King Monmouth, he!

'Yes, lovely cruel one!' he said
In through the mullioned pane, shroud-pale,
'I love you still, would kiss you now,
But blood would stain your nighty-rail!'
– That's all. And so to drown I go:
O wear no weeds, my friends, for me. . . .
When comes the waterman, he'll say,
'Who's done her thuswise?' – 'Twill be, yea,
    Sweet, slain King Monmouth – he!

720 *A Second Attempt*

THIRTY years after
I began again
An old-time passion:
And it seemed as fresh as when
The first day ventured on:

At Shag's Heath
54 rare] sweet MS
63 dear] sweet MS
72 Sweet, slain] My sweet MS

When mutely I would waft her
In Love's past fashion
Dreams much dwelt upon,
Dreams I wished she knew.

I went the course through,
From Love's fresh-found sensation –
Remembered still so well –
To worn words charged anew,
That left no more to tell:
Thence to hot hopes and fears,
And thence to consummation,
And thence to sober years,
Markless, and mellow-hued.

Firm the whole fabric stood,
Or seemed to stand, and sound
As it had stood before.
But nothing backward climbs,
And when I looked around
As at the former times,
There was Life – pale and hoar;
And slow it said to me,
'Twice-over cannot be!'

721 *Freed the Fret of Thinking*

EXTRA PRINTING:
The Adelphi, May 1925, p. 959 = A

TITLE:
'Freed the fret of Thinking' MS

FREED the fret of thinking,
  Light of lot were we,
Song with service linking
  Like to bird or bee:
Chancing bale unblinking,
Freed the fret of thinking
  On mortality!
Had not thought-endowment
  Beings ever known,

A Second Attempt
25 Life – pale and] a phantom MS *before revision*
About 1900 MS at end *deleted*

Freed the Fret of Thinking
7] Over things that be! MS, A
9] Ever mortals known, MS, A

What Life once or now meant
None had wanted shown –
Measuring but the moment –
Had not thought-endowment
Caught Creation's groan!

Loosed from wrings of reason,
We might blow like flowers,
Sense of Time-wrought treason
Would not then be ours
In and out of season;
Loosed from wrings of reason
We should laud the Powers!

EXTRA PRINTING:
The Nineteenth Century, Feb 1925, pp. 157–60
= NC

722 *The Absolute Explains*

I

'O NO,' said It: 'her lifedoings
Time's touch hath not destroyed:
They lie their length, with the throbbing things
Akin them, down the Void,
Live, unalloyed.

II

'Know, Time is toothless, seen all through;
The Present, that men but see,
Is phasmal: since in a sane purview
All things are shaped to be
Eternally.

III

'Your "Now" is just a gleam, a glide
Across your gazing sense:
With me, "Past", "Future", ever abide:
They come not, go not, whence
They are never hence.

The Absolute Explains
1 lifedoings] life-doings NC
2 Time's touch hath] Forsooth, I've NC
3 their length,] full length NC
3 throbbing] kindred NC
4] Of men, adown the Void, NC
5 Live,] Quite NC
6–7] 'Know, you are timeless, visioned true;/The Present that you see NC
8 phasmal:] phasmal; MS: phasmal, NC
8 sane] right NC
9 shaped] framed NC
11 gleam, a] flash and NC
13 me,] me NC

IV

'As one upon a dark highway,
Plodding by lantern-light,
Finds but the reach of its frail ray
Uncovered to his sight,
Though mid the night

V

'The road lies all its length the same,
Forwardly as at rear,
So, outside what you "Present" name,
Future and Past stand sheer,
Cognate and clear.'

VI

– Thus It: who straightway opened then
The vista called the Past,
Wherein were seen, as fair as when
They seemed they could not last,
Small things and vast.

VII

There were those songs, a score times sung,
With all their tripping tunes,
There were the laughters once that rung,
There those unmatched full moons,
Those idle noons!

VIII

There fadeless, fixed, were dust-dead flowers
Remaining still in blow;
Elsewhere, wild love-makings in bowers;
Hard by, that irised bow
Of years ago.

The Absolute Explains
18 Finds] Hath NC
20 mid] 'mid NC
20 night] night. HSA, WE
25] Equally clear.' NC
26 It:] It, NC
32 tunes,] tunes; NC
33 rung,] rung; NC
38 Elsewhere,] Elsewhere NC
38 wild] those MS *before revision*
39 that irised bow] the stream in flow MS *before revision*

IX

There were my ever memorable
  Glad days of pilgrimage,
Coiled like a precious parchment fell,
  Illumined page by page,
    Unhurt by age.

X

' – Here you see spread those mortal ails
  So powerless to restrain
Your young life's eager hot assails,
  With hazards then not plain
    Till past their pain.

XI

'Here you see her who, by these laws
  You learn of, still shines on,
As pleasing-pure as erst she was,
  Though you think she lies yon,
    Graved, glow all gone.

XII

'Here are those others you used to prize. –
  But why go further we?
The Future? – Well, I would advise
  You let the future be,
    Unshown by me!

XIII

' 'Twould harrow you to see undraped
  The scenes in ripe array
That wait your globe – all worked and shaped;
  And I'll not, as I say,
    Bare them to-day.

The Absolute Explains
46 ' – Here] – 'Here NC [As often, Hardy's dash is immediately below the quote in MS, and it has been variously interpreted by the printers]
48 eager] eager, NC
53 pleasing-pure] bright and blithe NC
55] To ashes gone. NC
59 future] Future NC
62 ripe] long NC
63 worked and] fully NC

XIV

'In fine, Time is a mock, – yea, such! –
    As he might well confess:
Yet hath he been believed in much,
    Though lately, under stress
        Of science, less.

XV

'And hence, of her you asked about
    At your first speaking: she
Hath, I assure you, not passed out
    Of continuity,
        But is in me.

XVI

'So thus doth Being's length transcend
    Time's ancient regal claim
To see all lengths begin and end.
    "The Fourth Dimension" fame
        Bruits as its name.'

New Year's Eve, 1922

723 So, Time

TITLE:
'So, Time' MS

(The same thought resumed)

    So, Time,
    Royal, sublime;
Heretofore held to be
Master and enemy,
Thief of my Love's adornings,
Despoiling her to scornings: –
The sound philosopher
Now sets him to aver
    You are nought
    But a thought
Without reality.

The Absolute Explains
66 mock,] myth NC
67 confess:] confess; NC
71 hence,] hence NC
75 in] with NC
New . . . 1922] Not in NC

So, Time
4 enemy] Enemy MS
6 scornings:] scornings; MS
11–12 Stanza break in all editions

Young, old,
Passioned, cold,
All the loved-lost thus
Are beings continuous,
In dateless dure abiding,
Over the present striding
With placid permanence
That knows not transience:
Firm in the Vast,
First, last;
Afar, yet close to us.

724 *An Inquiry*

A Phantasy

Circumdederunt me dolores mortis. – Ps. XVIII

I SAID to It: 'We grasp not what you meant,
(Dwelling down here, so narrowly pinched and pent)
By crowning Death the King of the Firmament:
– The query I admit to be
One of unwonted size,
But it is put you sorrowingly,
And not in idle-wise.'

'Sooth, since you ask me gravely,' It replied,
'Though too incisive questions I have decried,
This shows some thought, and may be justified.
I'll gauge its value as I go
Across the Universe,
And bear me back in a moment or so
And say, for better or worse.'

Many years later, when It came again,
'That matter an instant back which brought you pain,'
It said, 'and you besought me to explain:
Well, my forethoughtless modes to you
May seem a shameful thing,
But – I'd no meaning, that I knew,
In crowning Death as King!'

So, Time
12 old,] old MS

An Inquiry
1 you] You MS
13 so] so, MS
19 shameful] senseless MS: shameless HS, HSA

725 *The Faithful Swallow*

WHEN summer shone
Its sweetest on
An August day,
'Here evermore,'
I said, 'I'll stay;
Not go away
To another shore
As fickle they!'

December came:
'Twas not the same!
I did not know
Fidelity
Would serve me so.
Frost, hunger, snow;
And now, ah me,
Too late to go!

726 *In Sherborne Abbey*

INDENTATION:
All printed versions are as here, but MS has
1 = ll. 7, 8, 27, 28, 30
2 = ll. 1–6, 9, 10, 13, 14, 21, 22, 25, 26, 29
3 = ll. 11, 12, 15–20, 23, 24

(*17—*)

THE moon has passed to the panes of the south-aisle wall,
And brought the mullioned shades and shines to fall
On the cheeks of a woman and man in a pew there, pressed
Together as they pant, and recline for rest.

Forms round them loom, recumbent like their own,
Yet differing; for they are chiselled in frigid stone;
In doublets are some; some mailed, as whilom ahorse they leapt;
And stately husbands and wives, side by side as they anciently slept.

'We are not like those,' she murmurs. 'For ever here set!'
'True, Love,' he replies. 'We two are not marble yet.'

'And, worse,' said she; 'not husband and wife!'
'But we soon shall be' (from him) 'if we've life!'
A silence. A trotting of horses is heard without.
The lovers scarce breathe till its echo has quite died out.

'It was they! They have passed, anyhow!'
'Our horse, slily hid by the conduit,
They've missed, or they'd rushed to impound it!'
'And they'll not discover us now.'
'Will not, until 'tis too late,
And we can outface them straight!'

'Why did you make me ride in your front?' says she.
'To outwit the law. That was my strategy.
As I was borne off on the pillion behind you,
Th'abductor was you, Dearest, let me remind you;
And seizure of me by an heiress is no felony,
Whatever to do with me as the seizer may be.'

Another silence sinks. And a cloud comes over the moon:
The print of the panes upon them enfeebles, as fallen in a swoon,
Until they are left in darkness unbroke and profound,
As likewise are left their chill and chiselled neighbours around.

A Family tradition

TITLE:
The Pair he saw pass MS
The Bridegroom MS *before revision*

727 The Pair He Saw Pass

O SAD man, now a long dead man,
To whom it was so real,
I picture, as 'twere yesterday,
How you would tell the tale!

Just wived were you, you sad dead man,
And 'settling down', you'd say,
And had rigged the house you had reared for yourself
And the mate now yours alway.

In Sherborne Abbey
12 him)] him), MS
16 slily . . . conduit] sly hid in the close MS
17] They've seen not, we must suppose.' MS
27 sinks] falls MS, HS, HSA
Family] family MS

The Pair He Saw Pass
1 long dead] long-dead MS

You had eyed and tried each door and lock,
   And cupboard, and bell, and glass,
When you glanced across to the road without,
   And saw a carriage pass.

It bowled along from the old town-gate;
   Two forms its freight, and those
Were a just-joined pair, as you discerned
   By the favours and the bows.

And one of the pair you saw was a Fair
   Whom you had wooed awhile,
And the other you saw, with a creeping awe,
   Was yourself, in bridegroom style.

'And there we rode as man and wife
   In the broad blaze of the sun,'
Would you aver; yea, you with her
   You had left for another one.

'The morning,' you said, my friend long dead,
   'Was ordinary and fine;
And yet there gleamed, it somehow seemed,
   At moments, a strange shine.'

You hailed a boy from your garden-plot,
   And sent him along the way
To the parish church; whence word was brought
   No marriage had been that day.

You mused, you said; till you heard anon
   That at that hour she died
Whom once, instead of your living wife,
   You had meant to make your bride. . . .

You, dead man, dwelt in your new-built house
   With no great spirit or will,
And after your soon decease your spouse
   Re-mated: she lives there still.

Which should be blamed, if either can,
  The teller does not know
For your mismatch, O weird-wed man,
  Or what you thought was so.

From an old draft

728 *The Mock Wife*

It's a dark drama, this; and yet I know the house, and date;
That is to say, the where and when John Channing met his fate.
The house was one in High Street, seen of burghers still alive,
The year was some two centuries bygone; seventeen-hundred and five.

And dying was Channing the grocer. All the clocks had struck eleven,
And the watchers saw that ere the dawn his soul would be in Heaven;
When he said on a sudden: 'I should *like* to kiss her before I go, –
For one last time!' They looked at each other and murmured, 'Even so.'

She'd just been haled to prison, his wife; yea, charged with shaping his death:
By poison, 'twas told; and now he was nearing the moment of his last breath:
He, witless that his young housemate was suspect of such a crime,
Lay thinking that his pangs were but a malady of the time.

Outside the room they pondered gloomily, wondering what to do,
As still he craved her kiss – the dying man who nothing knew:
'Guilty she may not be,' they said; 'so why should we torture him
In these his last few minutes of life? Yet how indulge his whim?'

And as he begged there piteously for what could not be done,
And the murder-charge had flown about the town to every one,
The friends around him in their trouble thought of a hasty plan,
And straightway set about it. Let denounce them all who can.

'O will you do a kindly deed – it may be a soul to save;
At least, great misery to a man with one foot in the grave?'
Thus they to the buxom woman not unlike his prisoned wife;
'The difference he's past seeing; it will soothe his sinking life.'

The Mock Wife
1 this;] this, HSA
3 alive,] alive. HSA
4 seventeen-hundred and five] seventeen-hundred-five MS
18 murder-charge] murder charge MS

Well, the friendly neighbour did it; and he kissed her; held her fast;
Kissed her again and yet again. 'I – knew she'd – come at last! –
Where have you been? – Ah, kept away! – I'm sorry – overtried –
God bless you!' And he loosed her, fell back tiredly, and died.

His wife stood six months after on the scaffold before the crowd,
Ten thousand of them gathered there; fixed, silent, and hard-browed,
To see her strangled and burnt to dust, as was the verdict then
On women truly judged, or false, of doing to death their men.

Some of them said as they watched her burn: 'I am glad he never knew,
Since a few hold her as innocent – think such she could not do!
Glad, too, that (as they tell) he thought she kissed him ere he died.'
And they seemed to make no question that the cheat was justified.

729 The Fight on Durnover Moor

(183–)

WE'D loved, we two, some while,
And that had come which comes when men too much beguile;
And without more ado
My lady said: 'O shame! Get home, and hide!' But he was true.

Yes: he was true to me,
And helped me some miles homealong; and vowing to come
Before the weeks were three,
And do in church a deed should strike all scandal dumb.

And when we had traipsed to Grey's great Bridge, and pitched my box
On its cope, to breathe us there,
He cried: 'What wrangle's that in yonder moor? Those knocks,
Gad, seem not to be fair!

'And a woman on her knees! . . . I'll go. . . . There's surely something wrong!'
I said: 'You are tired and spent
With carrying my heavy things so far and long!'
But he would go, and went.

The Fight on Durnover Moor
13 knees! . . .] knees! . . . . MS
15 my heavy things] that heavy load MS

And there I stood, steadying my box, and screened from none,
Upon the crown of the bridge,
Ashamed o' my shape, as lower and lower slipped the sun
Down behind Pummery Ridge. . . .

'O you may long wait so!
Your young man's done – aye, dead!' they by and by ran and cried.
'You shouldn't have let him go
And join that whorage, but have kept him at your side!

'It was another wench,
Biggening as you, that he championed: yes, he came on straight
With a warmth no words could quench
For her helpless face, as soon as ever he eyed her state,

'And fought her fancy-lad, who had used her far from well,
So soon to make her moan,
Aye, closed with him in fight, till at a blow yours fell,
His skull against a stone.

'She'd followed him there, this man who'd won her, and overwon,
So, when he set to twit her
Yours couldn't abide him – him all other fighters shun,
For he's a practised hitter.

'Your man moved not, and the constables came for the other; so he,
He'll never make her his wife
Any more than yours will you; for they say that at least 'twill be
Across the water for life.'

'O what has she brought about!'
I groaned; 'this woman met here in my selfsame plight;
She's put another yielding heart's poor candle out
By dogging her man to-night!

'He might never have done her his due
Of amends! But mine had bidden the banns for marrying me!
Why did we rest on this bridge; why rush to a quarrel did he
With which he had nothing to do!'

The Fight on Durnover Moor
20 Ridge. . . .] Ridge. MS
42 groaned;] groaned: HSA

But vain were bursts of blame:
We twain stood like and like, though strangers till that hour,
Foredoomed to tread our paths beneath like gaze and glower,
Bear a like blushful name.

Almost the selfsame day
It fell that her time and mine came on, – a lad and a lass:
The father o' mine was where the worms waggle under the grass,
Of hers, at Botany Bay.

730 Last Look round St Martin's Fair

THE sun is like an open furnace door,
Whose round revealed retort confines the roar
Of fires beyond terrene;
The moon presents the lustre-lacking face
Of a brass dial gone green,
Whose hours no eye can trace.
The unsold heathcroppers are driven home
To the shades of the Great Forest whence they come
By men with long cord-waistcoats in brown monochrome.
The stars break out, and flicker in the breeze,
It seems, that twitches the trees. –
From its hot idol soon
The fickle unresting earth has turned to a fresh patroon –
The cold, now brighter, moon.
The woman in red, at the nut-stall with the gun,
Lights up, and still goes on:
She's redder in the flare-lamp than the sun
Showed it ere it was gone.
Her hands are black with loading all the day,
And yet she treats her labour as 'twere play,
Tosses her ear-rings, and talks ribaldry
To the young men around as natural gaiety,
And not a weary work she'd readily stay,
And never again nut-shooting see,
Though crying, 'Fire away!'

The Fight on Durnover Moor
55 waggle] glide MS

Last Look round St Martin's Fair
2 confines] contains MS, HS, HSA
14–15 Stanza break in MS: page turn in HS, HSA, PE: no break in WE, CP3–4
24 A late addition in MS and indented midway between ll. 23 and 25 in a line of indentation found nowhere else. It so appeared in HS, HSA, PE, WE
25 In MS, HS, HSA, PE, WE lined up with ll. 16, 18

731 *The Caricature*

Of the Lady Lu there were stories told,
For she was a woman of comely mould,
In heart-experience old.

Too many a man for her whimful sake
Had borne with patience chill and ache,
And nightly lain awake!

This epicure in pangs, in her tooth
For more of the sweet, with a calm unruth
Cast eyes on a painter-youth.

Her junior he; and the bait of bliss
Which she knew to throw – not he to miss –
She threw, till he dreamed her his.

To her arts not blind, he yet sued long,
As a songster jailed by a deed of wrong
Will shower the doer with song;

Till tried by tones now smart, now suave,
He would flee in ire, to return a slave
Who willingly forgave.

When no! One day he left her door,
'I'll ease mine agony!' he swore,
'And bear this thing no more!

'I'll practise a plan!' Thereon he took
Her portrait from his sketching-book,
And, though his pencil shook,

He moulded on the real its mock;
Of beauteous brow, lip, eye, and lock
Composed a laughingstock.

Amazed at this satire of his long lure,
Whenever he scanned it he'd scarce endure
His laughter. 'Twas his cure.

The Caricature
7 tooth] drouth MS
8 For . . . sweet] To replace her last MS
29 it he'd] he could MS

And, even when he woke in the night,
And chanced to think of the comic sight,
He laughed till exhausted quite.

'Why do you laugh?' she said one day
As he gazed at her in a curious way.
'Oh – for nothing,' said he. 'Mere play.'

– A gulf of years then severed the twain;
Till he heard – a painter of high attain –
She was dying on her domain.

'And,' dryly added the friend who told,
'You may know or not that, in semblance cold,
She loved once, loved whole-souled;

'And that you were the man? Did you break your vow?
Well, well; she is good as gone by now . . .
But you hit her, all allow!'

Ah, the blow past bearing that he received!
In his bachelor quiet he grieved and grieved;
How cruel; how self-deceived!

Did she ever know? . . . Men pitied his state
As the curse of his own contrivance ate
Like canker into his fate.

For ever that thing of his evil craft
Uprose on his grief – his mocking draught –
Till, racked, he insanely laughed.

Thence onward folk would muse in doubt
What gloomed him so as he walked about,
But few, or none, found out.

732 A Leader of Fashion

EXTRA PRINTING:
The Adelphi, Nov 1925, p. 395. There are no variants

TITLE:
The Fine Lady MS *before revision*

NEVER has she known
The way a robin will skip and come,
With an eye half bold, half timorsome,
To the table's edge for a breakfast crumb:

The Caricature
31 And] Thence MS
44 now . . .] now. . . . MS
49 know? . . .] know? . . . . MS
56 about,] about WE
About 1890 MS *deleted* at end

Nor has she seen
A streak of roseate gently drawn
Across the east, that means the dawn,
When, up and out, she foots it on:

Nor has she heard
The rustle of the sparrow's tread
To roost in roof-holes near her head
When dusk bids her, too, seek her bed:

Nor has she watched
Amid a stormy eve's turmoil
The pipkin slowly come to boil,
In readiness for one at toil:

Nor has she hearkened
Through the long night-time, lone and numb,
For sounds of sent-for help to come
Ere the swift-sinking life succumb:

Nor has she ever
Held the loved-lost one on her arm,
Attired with care his straightened form,
As if he were alive and warm:

Yea, never has she
Known, seen, heard, felt, such things as these,
Haps of so many in their degrees
Throughout their count of calvaries!

733 *Midnight on Beechen, 187–*

ON Beechen Cliff self-commune I
This night of mid-June, mute and dry;
When darkness never rises higher
Than Bath's dim concave, towers, and spire,
Last eveglow loitering in the sky

To feel the dawn, close lurking by,
The while the lamps as glow-worms lie
In a glade, myself their lonely eyer
On Beechen Cliff:

Midnight on Beechen, 187–
9–10 Stanza break in all editions

The city sleeps below. I sigh,
For there dwells one, all testify,
To match the maddest dream's desire:
What swain with her would not aspire
To walk the world, yea, sit but nigh
                    On Beechen Cliff!

734 *The Aërolite*

I THOUGHT a germ of Consciousness
Escaped on an aërolite
        Aions ago
From some far globe, where no distress
Had means to mar supreme delight;

But only things abode that made
The power to feel a gift uncloyed
        Of gladsome glow,
And life unendingly displayed
Emotions loved, desired, enjoyed.

And that this stray, exotic germ
Fell wanderingly upon our sphere,
        After its wingings,
Quickened, and showed to us the worm
That gnaws vitalities native here,

And operated to unblind
Earth's old-established ignorance
        Of stains and stingings,
Which grin no griefs while not opined,
But cruelly tax intelligence.

'How shall we,' then the seers said,
'Oust this awareness, this disease
        Called sense, here sown,
Though good, no doubt, where it was bred,
And wherein all things work to please?'

Midnight on Beechen, 187–
11 one,] one MS
11 testify,] testify MS

The Aërolite
17 ignorance] wise unsense MS: innocence HS, HSA, WE
19 Which grin no griefs] Innocuous MS
19 opined,] opined HSA
20] Dismaying to intelligence. MS

Others cried: 'Nay, we rather would,
Since this untoward gift is sent
    For ends unknown,
Limit its registerings to good,
And hide from it all anguishment.'

I left them pondering. This was how
(Or so I dreamed) was waked on earth
    The mortal moan
Begot of sentience. Maybe now
Normal unwareness waits rebirth.

735 The Prospect

THE twigs of the birch imprint the December sky
    Like branching veins upon a thin old hand;
I think of summer-time, yes, of last July,
    When she was beneath them, greeting a gathered band
        Of the urban and bland.

Iced airs wheeze through the skeletoned hedge from the north,
    With steady snores, and a numbing that threatens snow,
And skaters pass; and merry boys go forth
    To look for slides. But well, well do I know
        Whither I would go!

December 1912

736 Genitrix Laesa

(Measure of a Sarum Sequence)

NATURE, through these generations
You have nursed us with a patience
Cruelly crossed by malversations,
    Marring mother-ministry

The Aërolite
35 unwareness waits] conditions wait MS *before revision*
35 unwareness] unawareness HSA

The Prospect
8 pass;] pass, MS

To your multitudes, so blended
By your processes, long-tended,
And the painstaking expended
    On their chording tunefully.

But this stuff of slowest moulding,
In your fancy ever enfolding
Life that rhythmic chime is holding:
    (Yes; so deem it you, Ladye –
This 'concordia discors'!) – truly,
Rather, as if some imp unruly
Twitched your artist-arm when newly
    Shaping forth your scenery!

Aye. Yet seem you not to know it.
Hence your world-work needs must show it
Good in dream, in deed below it:
    (Lady, yes: so sight it we!)
Thus, then, go on fondly thinking:
Why should man your purblind blinking
Crave to cure, when all is sinking
    To dissolubility?

737 The Fading Rose

I SAW a rose, in bloom, but sad,
Shedding the petals that still it had,
And I heard it say: 'O where is she
Who used to come and muse on me?

'The pruner says she comes no more
Because she loves another flower,
The weeder says she's tired of me
Because I droop so suddenly.

'Because of a sweetheart she comes not,
Declares the man with the watering-pot;
"She does not come," says he with the rake,
"Because all women are fickle in make."

Genitrix Laesa
14 Rather,] Rather MS
24] Solved by time's dark alchemy. MS *before revision*
24 dissolubility?] dissolubility. MS, HS, HSA, PE, WE

'He with the spade and humorous leer
Says: "Know, I delve elsewhere than here,
Mid text-writ stones and grassy heaps,
Round which a curious silence creeps.

' "She must get to you underground
If any way at all be found,
For, clad in her beauty, marble's kin,
'Tis there I have laid her and trod her in." '

TITLE:
When Oats were reaped MS

738 When Oats Were Reaped

THAT day when oats were reaped, and wheat was ripe, and barley ripening,
The road-dust hot, and the bleaching grasses dry,
I walked along and said,
While looking just ahead to where some silent people lie:

'I wounded one who's there, and now know well I wounded her;
But, ah, she does not know that she wounded me!'
And not an air stirred,
Nor a bill of any bird; and no response accorded she.

August 1913

739 Louie

I AM forgetting Louie the buoyant;
Why not raise her phantom, too,
Here in daylight
With the elect one's?
She will never thrust the foremost figure out of view!

Mid this heat, in gauzy muslin
See I Louie's life-lit brow
Here in daylight
By the elect one's. –
Long two strangers they and far apart; such neighbours now!

July 1913

The Fading Rose
15 text-writ] storied MS

740 *She Opened the Door*

TITLE:
'She opened the Door' MS

SHE opened the door of the West to me,
With its loud sea-lashings,
And cliff-side clashings
Of waters rife with revelry.

She opened the door of Romance to me,
The door from a cell
I had known too well,
Too long, till then, and was fain to flee.

She opened the door of a Love to me,
That passed the wry
World-welters by
As far as the arching blue the lea.

She opens the door of the Past to me,
Its magic lights,
Its heavenly heights,
When forward little is to see!

1913

741 *What's There to Tell?*

TITLE:
'What's there to tell?' MS

(*Song*)

WHAT'S there to tell of the world
More than is told?
– Into its vortex hurled,
Out of it rolled,
Can we yet more of the world
Find to be told?
Lalla-la, lu!

She Opened the Door
4 rife with] wild in MS
14–16 Its times intense,/Its heights immense,/When nothing onward is to see! MS *before revision*

If some could last alive
Much might be told;
Yes, gladness might survive;
But they go cold –
Each and each late alive –
All their tale told.
Lalla-la, lu!

There's little more of the world,
Then, to be told;
Had ever life unfurled
Joys manifold,
There had been more of the world
Left to be told.
Lalla-la, lalla-la, lalla-la, lu!

190–

742 *The Harbour Bridge*

FROM here, the quay, one looks above to mark
The bridge across the harbour, hanging dark
Against the day's-end sky, fair-green in glow
Over and under the middle archway's bow:
It draws its skeleton where the sun has set,
Yea, clear from cutwater to parapet;
On which mild glow, too, lines of rope and spar
Trace themselves black as char.

Down here in shade we hear the painters shift
Against the bollards with a drowsy lift,
As moved by the incoming stealthy tide.
High up across the bridge the burghers glide
As cut black-paper portraits hastening on
In conversation none knows what upon:
Their sharp-edged lips move quickly word by word
To speech that is not heard.

What's There to Tell?
18 manifold,] manifold MS, HSA

There trails the dreamful girl, who leans and stops,
There presses the practical woman to the shops,
There is a sailor, meeting his wife with a start,
And we, drawn nearer, judge they are keeping apart.
Both pause. She says: 'I've looked for you. I thought
We'd make it up.' Then no words can be caught.
At last: 'Won't you come home?' She moves still nigher:
' 'Tis comfortable, with a fire.'

'No,' he says gloomily. 'And, anyhow,
I can't give up the other woman now:
You should have talked like that in former days,
When I was last home.' They go different ways.
And the west dims, and yellow lamplights shine:
And soon above, like lamps more opaline,
White stars ghost forth, that care not for men's wives,
Or any other lives.

Weymouth

743 *Vagrant's Song*

(*With an Old Wessex Refrain*)

EXTRA PRINTING:
Nash's and Pall Mall Magazine, Jan 1925, p. 39
= NPM

I

WHEN a dark-eyed dawn
Crawls forth, cloud-drawn,
And starlings doubt the night-time's close;
And 'three months yet,'
They seem to fret,
'Before we cease us slaves of snows,
And sun returns
To loose the burns,
And this wild woe called Winter goes!' –
O a hollow tree
Is as good for me
As a house where the back-brand[1] glows!
Che-hane, mother; che-hane, mother,
As a house where the back-brand glows!

[1] 'back-brand' – the log which used to be laid at the back of a wood fire.

The Harbour Bridge
25 No,] No MS

Vagrant's Song
9 Winter goes!' –] winter goes!' NPM
10 O] – O NPM
13–14 Not in NPM

II

When autumn brings
A whirr of wings
Among the evergreens around,
And sundry thrills
About their quills
Awe rooks, and misgivings abound,
And the joyless pines
In leaning lines
Protect from gales the lower ground,
O a hollow tree
Is as good for me
As a house of a thousand pound!
Che-hane, mother; che-hane, mother,
As a house of a thousand pound!

744 *Farmer Dunman's Funeral*

'BURY me on a Sunday,'
He said; 'so as to see
Poor folk there. 'Tis their one day
To spare for following me.'

With forethought of that Sunday,
He wrote, while he was well,
On ten rum-bottles one day,
'*Drink for my funeral.*'

They buried him on a Sunday,
That folk should not be balked
His wish, as 'twas their one day:
And forty couple walked.

They said: 'To have it Sunday
Was always his concern;
His meaning being that one day
He'd do us a good turn.

Vagrant's Song
23 ground,] ground; NPM
24 O] – O NPM
27–8 Not in NPM

Farmer Dunman's Funeral
4 me.'] me. MS
5–8 A late addition to MS
5 With forethought] 'Being mindful MS: And mindful HS, HSA
6 He] I MS
6 he] I MS
7 rum-bottles] rum-bottles, MS
8 '*Drink*] *Drink* MS

'We must, had it been Monday,
Have got it over soon,
But now we gain, being Sunday,
A jolly afternoon.'

745 *The Sexton at Longpuddle*

HE passes down the churchyard track
On his way to toll the bell;
And stops, and looks at the graves around,
And notes each finished and greening mound
Complacently,
As their shaper he,
And one who can do it well,
And, with a prosperous sense of his doing,
Thinks he'll not lack
Plenty such work in the long ensuing
Futurity.
For people will always die,
And he will always be nigh
To shape their cell.

746 *The Harvest-Supper*

(*Circa 1850*)

NELL and the other maids danced their best
With the Scotch-Greys in the barn;
These had been asked to the harvest-feast;
Red shapes amid the corn.

Nell and the other maids sat in a row
Within the benched barn-nook;
Nell led the songs of long ago
She'd learnt from never a book.

EXTRA PRINTING:
The New Magazine, Dec 1925, pp. 308–9 = NM

TITLE:
The Harvest-supper MS
The Harvest Supper NM

The Sexton at Longpuddle
5 Complacently,] Complacently MS
7 well,] well. MS, HS, HSA, PE, WE
12 die,] die WE

The Harvest-Supper
2 barn;] barn, MS, NM
3 These] (These MS, NM
4 amid] mid the brown of MS: amongst NM
4 corn.] corn.) MS, NM
6 benched barn-nook] barn's benched nook MS, NM

She sang of the false Sir John of old,
  The lover who witched to win,
And the parrot, and cage of glittering gold;
  And the other maids joined in.

Then whispered to her a gallant Grey,
  'Dear, sing that ballet again!
For a bonnier mouth in a bonnier way
  Has sung not anywhen!'

As she loosed her lips anew there sighed
  To Nell through the dark barn-door
The voice of her Love from the night outside,
  Who was buried the month before:

'O Nell, can you sing ballets there,
  And I out here in the clay,
Of lovers false of yore, nor care
  What you vowed to me one day!

'O can you dance with soldiers bold,
  Who kiss when dancing's done,
Your little waist within their hold,
  As ancient troth were none!'

She cried: 'My heart is pierced with a wound!
  There's something outside the wall
That calls me forth to a greening mound:
  I can sing no more at all!

'My old Love rises from the worms,
  Just as he used to be,
And I must let gay gallants' arms
  No more encircle me!'

They bore her home from the merry-making;
  Bad dreams disturbed her bed:
'Nevermore will I dance and sing,'
  Mourned Nell; 'and never wed!'

The Harvest-Supper
9 false Sir John] lover false NM
10] Who falsely lured to win, NM
17 loosed] parted NM
20 before:] before. MS
25 soldiers] gallants NM
35 gallants'] soldiers' NM
37 merry-making] merrymaking MS, NM
38] 'Twas long ere she grew well; NM
38 bed:] bed; MS
39 sing,'] sing, NM
40] And never wed!' said Nell. NM
40 Mourned] groaned MS [MS is revised from NM, and the lower-case 'g' results from this]

747 *At a Pause in a Country Dance*

(Middle of Last Century)

THEY stood at the foot of the figure,
And panted: they'd danced it down through –
That 'Dashing White Serjeant' they loved so: –
A window, uncurtained, was nigh them
That end of the room. Thence in view

Outside it a valley updrew,
Where the frozen moon lit frozen snow:
At the furthermost reach of the valley
A light from a window shone low.
'They are inside that window,' said she,

As she looked. 'They sit up there for me;
And baby is sleeping there, too.'
He glanced. 'Yes,' he said. 'Never mind,
Let's foot our way up again; do!
And dance down the line as before.

'What's the world to us, meeting once more!'
' – Not much, when your husband full trusts you,
And thinks the child his that I bore!'
He was silent. The fiddlers six-eighted
With even more passionate vigour.

The pair swept again up the figure,
The child's cuckoo-father and she,
And the next couples threaded below,
And the twain wove their way to the top
Of 'The Dashing White Serjeant' they loved so,
Restarting: right, left, to and fro.

– From the homestead, seen yon, the small glow
Still adventured forth over the white,
Where the child slept, unknowing who sired it,
In the cradle of wicker tucked tight,
And its grandparents, nodding, admired it
In elbow-chairs through the slow night.

At a Pause in a Country Dance
12 sleeping there] there sleeping MS
13 said.] said, MS
13 mind,] mind. HS, PE, WE
22 cuckoo-father] cuckoo father MS

748 On the Portrait of a Woman about to be Hanged

PROOF:
In the Dorset County Museum = DCM

EXTRA PRINTING:
The London Mercury, Feb 1923, p. 344 = LM

TITLE:
On the Portrait of a Woman about to be hanged MS

COMELY and capable one of our race,
Posing there in your gown of grace,
    Plain, yet becoming;
        Could subtlest breast
        Ever have guessed
What was behind that innocent face,
    Drumming, drumming!

Would that your Causer, ere knoll your knell
For this riot of passion, might deign to tell
    Why, since It made you
        Sound in the germ,
        It sent a worm
To madden Its handiwork, when It might well
    Not have assayed you,

Not have implanted, to your deep rue,
The Clytaemnestra spirit in you,
    And with purblind vision
        Sowed a tare
        In a field so fair,
And a thing of symmetry, seemly to view,
    Brought to derision!

6 January 1923

749 The Church and the Wedding

PROOF:
It has not been possible to trace the proof once in the Bliss Collection

EXTRA PRINTING:
The Chapbook, March 1923, p. 26 = CH

'I'LL restore this old church for our marriage:
    I've ordered the plans:
Style of wedding your choice – foot or carriage –
    By licence, or banns.'

On the Portrait of a Woman about to be Hanged
1 Comely] fair LM
3 Plain,] Plain DCM, LM
19 field so] garden LM
20 symmetry . . . view,] symmetry to the view LM
20 symmetry,] symmetry MS, DCM
20 view,] view DCM

He restored it, as though built newly:
    The bishop was won
To preach, who pronounced it truly
    A thing well done.

But the wedding waits; long, long has waited;
    And guesswork is dumb
Why those who were there to have mated
    Do not come.

And when the nights moan like the wailings
    Of souls sore-tried,
The folk say who pass the church-palings
    They hear inside

Strange sounds as of anger and sadness
    That cut the heart's core,
And shaken words bitter to madness;
    And then no more.

750 *The Shiver*

FIVE lone clangs from the house-clock nigh,
    And I woke with a sigh:
Stars wore west like a slow tide flowing,
And my lover had told yesternight of his going, –
That at this gray hour he'd be hasting by,

Starting betimes on a journey afar: –
    So, casement ajar,
I eyed in the upland pasture his figure,
A dim dumb speck, growing darker and bigger,
Then smalling to nought where the nut-trees are.

He could not bend his track to my window, he'd said,
    Being hurried ahead:
But I wished he had tried to! – and then felt a shiver,
Corpse-cold, as he sank toward the town by the river;
And back I went sadly and slowly to bed.

The Church and the Wedding
5 it,] it CH
7 truly] duly CH
14 sore-tried] hell-hied MS: fiend-led CH
15 say] think CH
15 church-palings] church palings, CH
16] 'False, or dead?' CH
17] Others say they hear sounds as of sadness, CH
17 sadness] sadness, MS
18] And tears over sore, MS, CH

The Shiver
1 lone] long HSA

What meant my shiver while seeing him pass
As a dot on the grass
I surmised not then. But later I knew it
When came again he; and my words outdrew it,
As said he: 'It's hard for your bearing, alas!

'But I've seen, I have clasped, where the smart ships plough,
One of far brighter brow.
A sea-goddess. Shiver not. One far rarer
In gifts than I find thee; yea, warmer and fairer: –
I seek her again; and I love you not now.'

TITLE:
'Not only I' MS

751 *Not Only I*

NOT only I
Am doomed awhile to lie
In this close bin with earthen sides;
But the things I thought, and the songs I sang,
And the hopes I had, and the passioned pang
For people I knew
Who passed before me,
Whose memory barely abides;
And the visions I drew
That daily upbore me!

And the joyous springs and summers,
And the jaunts with blithe newcomers,
And my plans and appearances; drives and rides
That fanned my face to a lively red;
And the grays and blues
Of the far-off views,
That nobody else discerned outspread;
And little achievements for blame or praise;
Things left undone; things left unsaid;
In brief, my days!

The Shiver
19 came] home MS
20 he:] he, MS
20] While cold waved the winds on the laurels, alas! MS *before revision*

Not Only I
12 newcomers] new-comers MS

Compressed here in six feet by two,
In secrecy
To lie with me
Till the Call shall be,
Are all these things I knew,
Which cannot be handed on;
Strange happenings quite unrecorded,
Lost to the world and disregarded,
That only thinks: 'Here moulders till Doom's-dawn
A woman's skeleton.'

752 She Saw Him, She Said

TITLE:
She saw him, she said MS

'WHY, I saw you with the sexton, outside the church-door,
So I did not hurry me home,
Thinking you'd not be come,
Having something to him to say. –
Yes: 'twas you, Dear, though you seemed sad, heart-sore;
How fast you've got therefrom!'

'I've not been out. I've watched the moon through the birch,
And heard the bell toll. Yes,
Like a passing soul in distress!'
' – But no bell's tolled to-day?' . . .
His face looked strange, like the face of him seen by the church,
And she sank to musefulness.

753 Once at Swanage

THE spray sprang up across the cusps of the moon,
And all its light loomed green
As a witch-flame's weirdsome sheen
At the minute of an incantation scene;
And it greened our gaze – that night at demilune.

She Saw Him, She Said
3 come,] come MS
10 to-day?' . . .] to-day?' . . . . . . MS

Once at Swanage
5–6 Stanza break in all editions

Roaring high and roaring low was the sea
    Behind the headland shores:
    It symboled the slamming of doors,
Or a regiment hurrying over hollow floors. . . .
And there we two stood, hands clasped; I and she!

754 *The Flower's Tragedy*

IN the bedchamber window, near the glass,
Stood the little flower in the little vase,
        Unnoticed quite
        For a whole fortnight,
And withered for lack of watering
To a skeleton mere – a mummied thing.

But it was not much, mid a world of teen,
That a flower should waste in a nook unseen!

One needed no thought to ascertain
How it happened; that when she went in the rain
        To return here not,
        She was mindless what
She had left here to perish. – Ah, well: for an hour
I wished I had not found the flower!

Yet it was not much. And she never had known
Of the flower's fate; nor it of her own.

755 *At the Aquatic Sports*

WITH their backs to the sea two fiddlers stand
Facing the concourse on the strand,
    And a third man who sings.
The sports proceed; there are crab-catchings;
The people laugh as levity spreads;
Yet these three do not turn their heads
    To see whence the merriment springs.

The Flower's Tragedy
8 waste in a nook] fust, unsought, MS
About 1910 MS *deleted* at end

At the Aquatic Sports
7–8 Stanza break in all editions

They cease their music, but even then
They stand as before, do those three men,
    Though pausing, nought to do:
They never face to the seaward view
To enjoy the contests, add their cheer,
So wholly is their being here
    A business they pursue.

756 A Watcher's Regret

J.E.'s Story

I SLEPT across the front of the clock,
    Close to the long case-door;
The hours were brought by their brazen knock
    To my ear as the slow nights wore.

Thus did I, she being sick to death,
    That each hour as it belled
Should wake me to rise, and learn by her breath
    Whether her strength still held.

Yet though throughout life's midnights all
    I would have watched till spent
For her dear sake, I missed the call
    Of the hour in which she went.

757 Horses Aboard

TITLE: Horses aboard MS

HORSES in horsecloths stand in a row
On board the huge ship, that at last lets go:
Whither are they sailing? They do not know,
Nor what for, nor how. –
                    They are horses of war,
And are going to where there is fighting afar;
But they gaze through their eye-holes unwitting they are,

Horses Aboard
2 ship,] ship CP4 [Almost certainly print deterioration]
4 war,] war MS
6 But they gaze] But gaze MS
6–7 No stanza break

And that in some wilderness, gaunt and ghast,
Their bones will bleach ere a year has passed,
And the item be as 'war-waste' classed. –
And when the band booms, and the folk say 'Good-bye!'
And the shore slides astern, they appear wrenched awry
From the scheme Nature planned for them, – wondering why.

758 *The History of an Hour*

VAIN is the wish to try rhyming it, writing it!
Pen cannot weld into words what it was;
Time will be squandered in toil at inditing it;
        Clear is the cause!

Yea, 'twas too satiate with soul, too ethereal;
June-morning scents of a rose-bush in flower
Catch in a clap-net of hempen material;
        So catch that hour!

759 *The Missed Train*

        HOW I was caught
Hieing home, after days of allure,
And forced to an inn – small, obscure –
        At the junction, gloom-fraught.

        How civil my face
To get them to chamber me there –
A roof I had scorned, scarce aware
        That it stood at the place.

        And how all the night
I had dreams of the unwitting cause
Of my lodgment. How lonely I was;
        How consoled by her sprite!

EXTRA PRINTINGS:
(1) *The Owl*, Winter 1923, p. 3 = O
(2) *The Best Poems of 1924*, ed. L. A. G. Strong (Boston, 1924), p. 111 = BP

INDENTATION:
1 = ll. 1, 4 } and so throughout BP
2 = ll. 2, 3 }

Horses Aboard
7–9 A late addition to MS
7 And] Or MS
12 them,] them MS

The Missed Train
3 forced] driven O
4 gloom-fraught.] fret-fraught! O, BP
7 scorned,] passed O, BP

Thus onetime to me . . .
Dim wastes of dead years bar away
Then from now. But such happenings to-day
Fall to lovers, may be!

Years, years as shoaled seas,
Truly, stretch now between! Less and less
Shrink the visions then vast in me. – Yes,
Then in me: Now in these.

760 Under High-Stoy Hill

TITLE:
Under High Stoy Hill MS

FOUR climbed High-Stoy from Ivelwards,
Where hedge meets hedge, and cart-ruts wind,
Chattering like birds,
And knowing not what lay behind.

We laughed beneath the moonlight blink,
Said supper would be to our mind,
And did not think
Of Time, and what might lie behind. . . .

The moon still meets that tree-tipped height,
The road – as then – still trails inclined;
But since that night
We have well learnt what lay behind!

For all of the four then climbing here
But one are ghosts, and he brow-lined;
With him they fare,
Yet speak not of what lies behind.

761 At the Mill

O MILLER KNOX, whom we knew well,
And the mill, and the floury floors,
And the corn, – and those two women,
And infants – yours!

The Missed Train
13 onetime] one time BP
13 me . . .] me. . . . MS, BP: me. . . . . O
15 now.] now! O, BP
15 such happenings] the like haps O
16 Fall to] To young O
16 be!] be. O, BP
17 shoaled] gray O, BP
19 vast] great O, BP
19 me. –] me. BP
20 me:] me. MS, O, BP

Under High-Stoy Hill
1 High-Stoy] High Stoy MS
1 Ivelwards] Ivel-wards MS
8 behind. . . .] behind. . . . . MS
13 For all] For, MS
13 here] here, MS

The sun was shining when you rode
  To market on that day:
The sun was set when home-along
  You ambled in the gray,
And gathered what had taken place
    While you were away.

O Miller Knox, 'twas grief to see
  Your good wife hanging there
By her own rash and passionate hand,
    In a throe of despair;

And those two children, one by her,
  And one by the waiting-maid,
Borne the same hour, and you afar,
    And she past aid.

And though sometimes you walk of nights,
  Sleepless, to Yalbury Brow,
And glance the graveyard way, and grunt,
  ' 'Twas not much, anyhow:
She shouldn't ha' minded!' nought it helps
    To say that now.

And the water dribbles down your wheel,
  Your mead blooms green and gold,
And birds 'twit in your apple-boughs
    Just as of old.

TITLE:
She speaks MS *deleted* below '(Great Orme's Head)'

762 Alike and Unlike

(*Great-Orme's Head*)

We watched the selfsame scene on that long drive,
Saw the magnificent purples, as one eye,
Of those near mountains; saw the storm arrive;
Laid up the sight in memory, you and I,
As if for joint recallings by and by.

At the Mill
13 hand,] hand MS
27 'twit] twit HSA

Alike and Unlike
5–6 Stanza break in all editions

But our eye-records, like in hue and line,
Had superimposed on them, that very day,
Gravings on your side deep, but slight on mine! –
Tending to sever us thenceforth alway;
Mine commonplace; yours tragic, gruesome, gray.

763 The Thing Unplanned

THE white winter sun struck its stroke on the bridge,
The meadow-rills rippled and gleamed
As I left the thatched post-office, just by the ridge,
And dropped in my pocket her long tender letter,
With: 'This must be snapped! it is more than it seemed;
And now is the opportune time!'

But against what I willed worked the surging sublime
Of the thing that I did – the thing better!

764 The Sheep-Boy

A YAWNING, sunned concave
Of purple, spread as an ocean wave
Entroughed on a morning of swell and sway
After a night when wind-fiends have been heard to rave:
Thus was the Heath called 'Draäts', on an August day.

Suddenly there intunes a hum:
This side, that side, it seems to come.
From the purple in myriads rise the bees
With consternation mid their rapt employ.
So headstrongly each speeds him past, and flees,
As to strike the face of the shepherd-boy.
Awhile he waits, and wonders what they mean;
Till none is left upon the shagged demesne.

INDENTATION:
There is some variation, the most important being MS and WE
1 = ll. 4, 17, 20, 21
2 = ll. 5, 9, 10, 12, 13, 14, 16, 24
3 = ll. 2, 3, 6, 7, 8, 11, 15
4 = l. 1
5 = ll. 18, 19, 22, 23 MS

1 = ll. 4, 17, 20, 21, 24
2 = ll. 5, 9, 10, 12, 13, 14, 16, 18, 19
3 = ll. 3, 6, 7, 8, 11, 15
4 = ll. 1, 2, 22, 23 WE

Alike and Unlike
8–9] Events your track affecting much – not mine! – / Sharply dividing us thence on alway; MS *before revision*

The Sheep-Boy
3 morning] morn MS
5 'Draäts',] 'Draäts' MS
13–14 Stanza break in all editions

To learn what ails, the sheep-boy looks around;
  Behind him, out of the sea in swirls
Flexuous and solid, clammy vapour-curls
Are rolling over Pokeswell Hills to the inland ground.
  Into the heath they sail,
  And travel up the vale
Like the moving pillar of cloud raised by the Israelite: –
In a trice the lonely sheep-boy seen so late ago,
    Draäts'-Hollow in gorgeous blow,
    And Kite-Hill's regal glow,
Are viewless – folded into those creeping scrolls of white.

On Rainbarrows

765 *Retty's Phases*

I

RETTY used to shake her head,
  Look with wicked eye;
Say, 'I'd tease you, simple Ned,
  If I cared to try!'
Then she'd hot-up scarlet red,
  Stilly step away,
Much afraid that what she'd said
  Sounded bold to say.

II

Retty used to think she loved
  (Just a little) me.
Not untruly, as it proved
  Afterwards to be.
For, when weakness forced her rest
  If we walked a mile,
She would whisper she was blest
  By my clasp awhile.

EXTRA MANUSCRIPT:

There is an early draft, with the title 'Song', in the Dorset County Museum. (See illustration on p. 700.) It is reproduced in Prof. R. L. Purdy's *Thomas Hardy: A Bibliographical Study* (facing p. 242) where it is described as 'the earliest MS of a poem by Hardy'. There is a fair copy of this draft inserted in Hardy's copy of *Human Shows* in the Dorset County Museum. 'Retty' appears as 'Hetty' throughout this fair copy, and it is clear from the draft that Hetty was Hardy's first thought. In so far as the draft can be accurately given, it is printed below:

June 22. 1868

Song

1

Retty used to gaily sing
  why a gloomy thing &c

. . . . . .

2

Retty used to shake her head
  Look with wicked eye
Say 'I'd match you, idle Fred!'
  If I cared to try'
But she'd colour scarlet red
  Quickly haste away
much afraid that things she'd said
  Were saucy things to say.

The Sheep-Boy
16 Flexuous] Opaque MS
17 ground.] ground, CP3, 4
24 creeping] Not in MS

Retty's Phases
3 simple Ned] simplehead MS, HS, HSA
10 me.] me, MS

III

Retty used at last to say
  When she neared the Vale,
'Mind that you, Dear, on that day
  Ring my wedding peal!'
And we all, with pulsing pride,
  Vigorous sounding gave
Those six bells, the while outside
  John filled in her grave.

IV

Retty used to draw me down
  To the turfy heaps,
Where, with yeoman, squire, and clown
  Noticeless she sleeps.
Now her silent slumber-place
  Seldom do I know,
For when last I saw her face
  Was so long ago!

From an old draft of 1868

Note. – In many villages it was customary after the funeral of an unmarried young woman to ring a peal as for her wedding while the grave was being filled in, as if Death were not to be allowed to balk her of bridal honours. Young unmarried men were always her bearers.

3
Retty used to fall in love
  Every now and then
With some hero written/spoken of
  As handsomest of men:
Or a soldier passing by,
  Or a sailor gay,
Nights she'd lie awake and cry
  When he went/he'd gone away.
/At her dream's decay:

4
Retty used to think she loved,
  (Just a little) me;

. . . . . .

5
Retty used to want to rest
  When we'd walked a mile
And she'd whisper, 'I were blest
  Could I run awhile
As I ran on that dear/old day
  When you saw me wade
Through the pond that people say
  Fairy shovels made.

6
. . . . . .

7
Retty used to draw me down
  To the green church-hay
Where with yeoman squire and clown
  Her little body lay
Now her silent mouldering place
  Scarce my footsteps know
For when last I saw her face
  Was so long ago.
/For since last I saw her face
  Times have altered so.

766 *A Poor Man and a Lady*

We knew it was not a valid thing,
And only sanct in the sight of God
(To use your phrase), as with fervent nod
You swore your assent when I placed the ring
On your pale slim hand. Our whispering
Was soft as the fan of a turtledove
That round our heads might have seemed to wing;
So solemn were we; so sincere our love.

Retty's Phases
19 Dear] dear MS
26 heaps,] heaps MS
27 clown] clown, WE

From old note-book MS at end *before revision*
June 22. 1868 MS at end *deleted*
many] remote Wessex MS *before revision*

A Poor Man and a Lady
6 fan of a] rustle of MS

We could do no better; and thus it stood
Through a time of timorous secret bliss,
Till we were divided, and never a kiss
Of mine could touch you, or likelihood
Illumed our sky that we might, or should
Be each to each in the world's wide eye
What we were unviewed; and our vows make good
In the presence of parents and standers by.

I was a striver with deeds to do,
And little enough to do them with,
And a comely woman of noble kith,
With a courtly match to make, were you;
And we both were young; and though sterling-true
You had proved to our pledge under previous strains,
Our 'union', as we called it, grew
Less grave to your eyes in your town campaigns.

Well: the woeful neared, you needn't be told:
The current news-sheets clarioned soon
That you would be wived on a summer noon
By a man of illustrious line and old:
Nor better nor worse than the manifold
Of marriages made, had there not been
Our faith-swearing when fervent-souled,
Which, to me, seemed a breachless bar between.

We met in a Mayfair church, alone:
(The request was mine, which you yielded to).
'But we were not married at all!' urged you:
'Why, of course we were!' I said. Your tone,
I noted, was world-wise. You went on:
' 'Twas sweet while it lasted. But you well know
That law is law. He'll be, anon,
My husband *really*. You, Dear, weren't so.'

'I wished – but to learn if — ' faltered I,
And stopped. 'But I'll sting you not. Farewell!'
And we parted. – Do you recall the bell
That tolled by chance as we said good-bye? . . .

A Poor Man and a Lady
9 better;] better, MS
24 town] Town MS
44 good-bye? . . .] Good-bye? . . . . . MS

I saw you no more. The track of a high,
Sweet, liberal lady you've doubtless trod.
– All's past! No heart was burst thereby,
And no one knew, unless it was God.

NOTE. – The foregoing was intended to preserve an episode in the story of 'The Poor Man and the Lady', written in 1868, and, like these lines, in the first person; but never printed, and ultimately destroyed.

767 An Expostulation

WHY want to go afar
Where pitfalls are,
When all we swains adore
Your featness more and more
As heroine of our artless masquings here,
And count few Wessex' daughters half so dear?

Why paint your appealing face,
When its born grace
Is such no skill can match
With powder, puff, or patch,
Whose every touch defames your bloomfulness,
And with each stain increases our distress?

Yea, is it not enough
That (rare or rough
Your lines here) all uphold you,
And as with wings enfold you,
But you must needs desert the kine-cropt vale
Wherein your foredames gaily filled the pail?

768 To a Sea-Cliff

(Durlston Head)

LEND me an ear
While I read you here
A page from your history,

An Expostulation
11 bloomfulness] freshfulness MS

Old cliff – not known
To your solid stone,
Yet yours inseparably.

Near to your crown
There once sat down
A silent listless pair;
And the sunset ended,
And dark descended,
And still the twain sat there.

Past your jutting head
Then a line-ship sped,
Lit brightly as a city;
And she sobbed: 'There goes
A man who knows
I am his, beyond God's pity!'

He slid apart
Who had thought her heart
His own, and not aboard
A bark, sea-bound. . . .
That night they found
Between them lay a sword.

TITLE:
The Echo-elf answers (Impromptu *del* below) MS
The Echo Elf Answers HSA

769 *The Echo-Elf Answers*

How much shall I love her?
For life, or not long?
'Not long.'

Alas! When forget her?
In years, or by June?
'By June.'

And whom woo I after?
No one, or a throng?
'A throng.'

To a Sea-Cliff
5 solid] stolid MS
13 head] Head MS
22 sea-bound. . . .] sea-bound. . . . . MS

Of these shall I wed one
Long hence, or quite soon?
　　'Quite soon.'

And which will my bride be?
The right or the wrong?
　　'The wrong.'

And my remedy – what kind?
Wealth-wove, or earth-hewn?
　　'Earth-hewn.'

770 *Cynic's Epitaph*

EXTRA PRINTINGS:
(1) *The London Mercury*, Sept 1925, p. 456 = LM
(2) *Chosen Poems*, p. 231

INDENTATION:
1 = ll. 1, 3, 5, 7
2 = ll. 2, 4, 6, 8, LM

A RACE with the sun as he downed
　　I ran at evetide,
Intent who should first gain the ground
　　And there hide.

He beat me by some minutes then,
　　But I triumphed anon,
For when he'd to rise up again
　　I stayed on.

771 *A Beauty's Soliloquy during Her Honeymoon*

TITLE:
A Beauty's soliloquy during her Honeymoon MS

TOO late, too late! I did not know my fairness
　　Would catch the world's keen eyes so!
How the men look at me! My radiant rareness
　　I deemed not they would prize so!

That I was a peach for any man's possession
　　Why did not some one say
Before I leased myself in an hour's obsession
　　To this dull mate for aye!

Cynic's Epitaph
1 sun] sun, MS
1 downed] downed, MS
2 evetide] eve-tide LM
3 ground] ground, MS

A Beauty's Soliloquy during Her Honeymoon
6 some one] someone MS

His days are mine. I am one who cannot steal her
  Ahead of his plodding pace:
As he is, so am I. One doomed to feel her
  A wasted form and face!

I was so blind! It did sometimes just strike me
  All girls were not as I,
But, dwelling much alone, how few were like me
  I could not well descry;

Till, at this Grand Hotel, all looks bend on me
  In homage as I pass
To take my seat at breakfast, dinner, – con me
  As poorly spoused, alas!

I was too young. I dwelt too much on duty:
  If I had guessed my powers
Where might have sailed this cargo of choice beauty
  In its unanchored hours!

Well, husband, poor plain man; I've lost life's battle! –
  Come – let them look at me.
O damn, don't show in your looks that I'm your chattel
  Quite so emphatically!

In a London Hotel, 1892

772 Donaghadee

EXTRA MANUSCRIPT:
In the Miriam Lutcher Stark Library of the University of Texas = UT

(*Song*)

I'VE never gone to Donaghadee,
That vague far townlet by the sea;
In Donaghadee I shall never be:
Then why do I sing of Donaghadee,
That I know not in a faint degree? . . .
– Well, once a woman wrote to me
With a tender pen from Donaghadee.

A Beauty's Soliloquy during Her Honeymoon
13 blind!] blind. MS
19 dinner,] dinner MS

Donaghadee
5 degree? . . .] degree? . . . . MS: degree? . . . . . UT
7–8 Stanza break in all editions

'Susan', I've sung, 'Pride of Kildare',
Because I'd heard of a Susan there,
The 'Irish Washerwoman's' capers
I've shared for hours to midnight tapers,
And 'Kitty O'Linch' has made me spin
Till dust rose high, and day broke in:
That other 'Kitty, of Coleraine',
Too, set me aching in heart and brain:
While 'Kathleen Mavourneen', of course, would ring
When that girl learnt to make me sing.
Then there was 'Irish Molly O'
I tuned as 'the fairest one I know',
And 'Nancy Dawson', if I remember,
Rhymed sweet in moonlight one September.

But the damsel who once wrote so free
And tender-toned from Donaghadee,
Is a woman who has no name for me –
Moving sylph-like, mysteriously,
(For doubtless, of that sort is she)
In the pathways of her destiny;
But that is where I never shall be; –
And yet I sing of Donaghadee!

773 *He Inadvertently Cures His Love-Pains*

(*Song*)

TITLE:
He inadvertently cures his love-pains MS

I SAID: 'O let me sing the praise
Of her who sweetly racks my days, –
    Her I adore;
Her lips, her eyes, her moods, her ways!'

In miseries of pulse and pang
I strung my harp, and straightway sang
    As none before: –
To wondrous words my quavers rang!

Donaghadee
8 Susan',] Susan' MS, UT
8 Pride] the Pride UT
13 in:] in; UT
15 brain:] brain; UT
16 Mavourneen',] Mavourneen' MS
17 that] *that* UT
21 September.] September. . . . . UT
23] In a tender tone from Donaghadee, (Donaghadee UT) MS, UT
23 tender-toned] tender toned HS, HSA, PE, WE
25] A fair sylph, moving mysteriously MS, UT
26 For] For, MS
26 doubtless,] doubtless UT
27 destiny;] destiny! UT
28 be;] be: UT
29 Donaghadee!] Donaghadee. UT

Thus I let heartaches lilt my verse,
Which suaged and soothed, and made disperse
    The smarts I bore
To stagnance like a sepulchre's.

But, eased, the days that thrilled ere then
Lost value; and I ask, O when,
    And how, restore
Those old sweet agonies again!

EXTRA PRINTING:
The Graphic, Jubilee Christmas Number, 24 Nov 1919, p. 22 = G

TITLE:
The Peach Peal HSA (!)
Four] Not in G

774 *The Peace Peal*

(*After Four Years of Silence*)

SAID a wistful daw in Saint Peter's tower,
High above Casterbridge slates and tiles,
'Why do the walls of my Gothic bower
Shiver, and shrill out sounds for miles?
    This gray old rubble
    Has scorned such din
    Since I knew trouble
    And joy herein.
    How still did abide them
    These bells now swung,
    While our nest beside them
    Securely clung! . . .
    It means some snare
    For our feet or wings;
    But I'll be ware
    Of such baleful things!'
And forth he flew from his louvred niche
To take up life in a damp dark ditch.
– So mortal motives are misread,
And false designs attributed,
In upper spheres of straws and sticks,
Or lower, of pens and politics.

At the end of the War

He Inadvertently Cures His Love-Pains
12 stagnance] lentor MS: quiet HS, HSA

The Peace Peal
1 daw in Saint] sparrow in G
4 Shiver,] Shiver G
8 And] Or G
10 swung,] swung MS, G
12 clung! . . .] clung! . . . . MS
19 – So] So G
At . . . War] Not in G

775 *Lady Vi*

THERE goes the Lady Vi. How well,
How well I know the spectacle
  The earth presents
  And its events
  To her sweet sight
  Each day and night!

'Life is a wheeling show, with *me*
As its pivot of interest constantly.
Below in the hollows of towns is sin,
Like a blue brimstone mist therein,
Which makes men lively who plunge amid it,
But wrongfully, and wives forbid it.
London is a place for prancing
Along the Row and, later, dancing
Till dawn, with tightening arm-embowments
As hours warm up to tender moments.

'Travel is piquant, and most thrilling
If, further, joined to big-game killing:
At home, too, hunting, hounds full cry,
When Reynard nears his time to die,
'Tis glee to mark his figure flag,
And how his brush begins to drag,
Till, his earth reached by many a wend,
He finds it *stopped*, and meets his end.

'Religion is good for all who are meek;
It stays in the Bible through the week,
And floats about the house on Sundays,
But does not linger on till Mondays.
The ten Commandments in one's prime
Are matter for another time,
While griefs and graves and things allied
In well-bred talk one keeps outside.'

Lady Vi

1 Vi] From deletions here and in title it seems probable that the name was first 'Clo'

2 In CP3, 4 this line was indented with ll. 3–6. In MS, WE, it was lined up with l. 1, as here. The CP indentation was almost certainly a mistake arising from the displacement of l. 2 of HS by the large capital 'T' from l. 1

15 arm-embowments] arm-elbowments HSA (!)

29–32 Death one dismisses in one's prime/To think of at another time;/In short the grave and things allied/In social talk one keeps outside. MS

EXTRA PRINTING:
The Flying Carpet, ed. Cynthia Asquith (London, 1925), pp. 9–10 = FC

INDENTATION:
1 = ll. 1, 3 } and so throughout
2 = ll. 2, 4 } FC

776 A Popular Personage at Home

'I LIVE here: "Wessex" is my name:
I am a dog known rather well:
I guard the house; but how that came
To be my whim I cannot tell.

'With a leap and a heart elate I go
At the end of an hour's expectancy
To take a walk of a mile or so
With the folk I let live here with me.

'Along the path, amid the grass
I sniff, and find out rarest smells
For rolling over as I pass
The open fields towards the dells.

'No doubt I shall always cross this sill,
And turn the corner, and stand steady,
Gazing back for my mistress till
She reaches where I have run already,

'And that this meadow with its brook,
And bulrush, even as it appears
As I plunge by with hasty look,
Will stay the same a thousand years.'

Thus 'Wessex'. But a dubious ray
At times informs his steadfast eye,
Just for a trice, as though to say,
'Yet, will this pass, and pass shall I?'

1924

777 Inscriptions for a Peal of Eight Bells

After a Restoration

I. THOMAS TREMBLE new-made me
Eighteen hundred and fifty-three:
Why he did I fail to see.

A Popular Personage at Home
1 name:] name, FC
4 whim] lot FC
5 go] go, FC
6 expectancy] expectancy, FC
7 so] so, FC
8 I let live here] who share the house FC
9 path,] path FC
16 already,] already. FC
18 even] just FC
19 by] past FC
21 But] Yet FC
23 say,] say: FC
24] 'Will these things, after all, go by?' FC

II. I was well-toned by William Brine,
Seventeen hundred and twenty-nine;
Now, re-cast, I weakly whine!

III. Fifteen hundred used to be
My date, but since they melted me
'Tis only eighteen fifty-three.

IV. Henry Hopkins got me made,
And I summon folk as bade;
Not to much purpose, I'm afraid!

V. I likewise; for I bang and bid
In commoner metal than I did,
Some of me being stolen and hid.

VI. I, too, since in a mould they flung me,
Drained my silver, and rehung me,
So that in tin-like tones I tongue me.

VII. In nineteen hundred, so 'tis said,
They cut my canon off my head,
And made me look scalped, scraped, and dead.

VIII. I'm the peal's tenor still, but rue it!
Once it took two to swing me through it:
Now I'm rehung, one dolt can do it.

778 A Refusal

SAID the grave Dean of Westminster:
Mine is the best minster
Seen in Great Britain,
As many have written:
So therefore I cannot
Rule here if I ban not
Such liberty-taking
As movements for making
Its grayness environ
The memory of Byron,

Inscriptions for a Peal of Eight Bells
16 I,] I MS

A Refusal
10–11 No Stanza break

Which some are demanding
Who think them of standing,
But in my own viewing
Require some subduing
For tendering suggestions
On Abbey-wall questions
That must interfere here
With my proper sphere here,
And bring to disaster
This fane and its master,
Whose dict is but Christian
Though nicknamed Philistian.

A lax Christian charity –
No mental clarity
Ruling its movements
For fabric improvements –
Demands admonition
And strict supervision
When bent on enshrining
Rapscallions, and signing
Their names on God's stonework,
As if like His own work
Were their lucubrations:
And passed is my patience
That such a creed-scorner
(Not mentioning horner)
Should claim Poets' Corner.

'Tis urged that some sinners
Are here for worms' dinners
Already in person;
That he could not worsen
The walls by a name mere
With men of such fame here.
Yet nay; they but leaven
The others in heaven
In just true proportion,
While more mean distortion.

A Refusal
31 God's] my MS *before revision*
38–47 A late addition to MS
47–8 Stanza break in MS, HS, HSA, PE, WE: page turn in CP3, 4

'Twill next be expected
That I get erected
To Shelley a tablet
In some niche or gablet.
Then – what makes my skin burn,
Yea, forehead to chin burn –
That I ensconce Swinburne!

August 1924

779 *Epitaph on a Pessimist*

EXTRA PRINTING:
The London Mercury, Sept 1925, p. 456 = LM

I'M Smith of Stoke, aged sixty-odd,
I've lived without a dame
From youth-time on; and would to God
My dad had done the same.

From the French and Greek

780 *The Protean Maiden*

(*Song*)

TITLE:
The Protean (Lady *del*) Maiden MS

THIS single girl is two girls:
How strange such things should be!
One noon eclipsed by few girls,
The next no beauty she.

And daily cries the lover,
In voice and feature vext:
'My last impression of her
Is never to be the next!

'She's plain: I will forget her!
She's turned to fair. Ah no,
Forget? – not I! I'll pet her
With kisses swift and slow.'

Epitaph on a Pessimist
3 on;] on: LM
and Greek] Not in MS, LM, HS, HSA

TITLE:
A Watering-place Lady inventoried MS

781 *A Watering-Place Lady Inventoried*

A SWEETNESS of temper unsurpassed and unforgettable,
A mole on the cheek whose absence would have been regrettable,
A ripple of pleasant converse full of modulation,
A bearing of inconveniences without vexation,
Till a cynic would find her amiability provoking,
Tempting him to indulge in mean and wicked joking.

Flawlessly oval of face, especially cheek and chin,
With a glance of a quality that beckoned for a glance akin,
A habit of swift assent to any intelligence broken,
Before the fact to be conveyed was fully spoken
And she could know to what her colloquist would win her, –
This from a too alive impulsion to sympathy in her, –
All with a sense of the ridiculous, keen yet charitable;
In brief, a rich, profuse attractiveness unnarratable.

I should have added her hints that her husband prized her but slenderly,
And that (with a sigh) 'twas a pity she'd no one to treat her tenderly.

782 *The Sea Fight*

31 May: 1916

In Memoriam Captain Prowse

DOWN went the grand 'Queen Mary',
'Queen Mary's' captain, and her crew;
The brunt of battle bare he,
And he died;
And he died, as heroes do.

More really now we view him,
More really lives he, moves with men,
Than while on earth we knew him
As our fellow,
As our fellow-denizen.

A Watering-Place Lady Inventoried
5 Till] Till, MS
9 any intelligence] intelligence quickly MS

Maybe amid the changes
Of ocean's caverned dim profound,
Gaily his spirit ranges
With his comrades,
With his comrades all around.

1916

783 Paradox

(M.H.)

THOUGH out of sight now, and as 'twere not the least to us;
Comes she in sorrows, as one bringing peace to us?
Lost to each meadow, each hill-top, each tree around,
Yet the whole truth may her largened sight see around?
Always away from us
She may not stray from us!
Can she, then, know how men's fatings befall?
Yea indeed, may know well; even know thereof all.

784 The Rover Come Home

TITLE:
The Rover come home MS

HE's journeyed through America
From Canso Cape to Horn,
And from East Indian Comorin
To Behring's Strait forlorn;
He's felled trees in the backwoods,
In swamps has gasped for breath;
In Tropic heats, in Polar ice,
Has often prayed for death.

He has fought and bled in civil wars
Of no concern to him,
Has shot his fellows – beasts and men –
At risk of life and limb.
He has suffered fluxes, fevers,
Agues, and ills allied,
And now he's home. You look at him
As he talks by your fireside.

Paradox
1 as 'twere] gone quiet; MS

And what is written in his glance
  Stressed by such foreign wear,
After such alien circumstance
  What does his face declare?
His mother's; she who saw him not
  After his starting year,
Who never left her native spot,
  And lies in the churchyard near.

TITLE: 'Known had I' MS

785 *Known Had I*

(*Song*)

KNOWN had I what I knew not
  When we met eye to eye,
That thenceforth I should view not
  Again beneath the sky
So truefooted a farer
  As you who faced me then,
My path had been a rarer
  Than it figures among men!

I would have trod beside you
  To guard your feet all day,
And borne at night to guide you
  A lantern on your way:
Would not have left you lonely
  With wringing doubt, to cow
Old hope, if I could only
  Have known what I know now.

786 *The Pat of Butter*

ONCE, at the Agricultural Show,
  We tasted – all so yellow –
  Those butter-pats, cool and mellow!
Each taste I still remember, though
  It was so long ago.

Known Had I
2 eye,] eye; MS
6 you who] just had MS *before revision*
9 you] her MS before revision [and 'her' in ll. 10, 11, 12, 13]

This spoke of the grass of Netherhay,
    And this of Kingcomb Hill,
    And this of Coker Rill:
Which was the prime I could not say
    Of all those tried that day,

Till she, the fair and wicked-eyed,
    Held out a pat to me:
    Then felt I all Yeo-Lea
Was by her sample sheer outvied;
    And, 'This is the best,' I cried.

787 *Bags of Meat*

    'HERE's a fine bag of meat,'
    Says the master-auctioneer,
    As the timid, quivering steer,
    Starting a couple of feet
    At the prod of a drover's stick,
    And trotting lightly and quick,
    A ticket stuck on his rump,
Enters with a bewildered jump.

    'Where he's lived lately, friends,
    I'd live till lifetime ends:
    They've a whole life everyday
    Down there in the Vale, have they!
    He'd be worth the money to kill
And give away Christmas for good-will.'

    'Now here's a heifer – worth more
    Than bid, were she bone-poor;
    Yet she's round as a barrel of beer;'
'She's a plum,' said the second auctioneer.

Bags of Meat
16 Than] Than you MS
18–19 Stanza break in all editions

'Now this young bull – for thirty pound?
Worth that to manure your ground!'
'Or to stand,' chimed the second one,
'And have his picter done!'
The beast was rapped on the horns and snout
To make him turn about.
'Well,' cried a buyer, 'another crown –
Since I've dragged here from Taunton Town!'

'That calf, she sucked three cows,
Which is not matched for bouse
In the nurseries of high life
By the first-born of a nobleman's wife!'
The stick falls, meaning, 'A true tale's told,'
On the buttock of the creature sold,
And the buyer leans over and snips
His mark on one of the animal's hips.

Each beast, when driven in,
Looks round at the ring of bidders there
With a much-amazed reproachful stare,
As at unnatural kin,
For bringing him to a sinister scene
So strange, unhomelike, hungry, mean;
His fate the while suspended between
A butcher, to kill out of hand,
And a farmer, to keep on the land;
One can fancy a tear runs down his face
When the butcher wins, and he's driven from the place.

788 The Sundial on a Wet Day

I DRIP, drip here
In Atlantic rain,
Falling like handfuls
Of winnowed grain,
Which, tear-like, down
My gnomon drain,

Bags of Meat
21–2 A late addition to MS
21 stand,' chimed] stand' said MS
25 buyer,] buyer MS
26 Taunton] Toneborough MS *before revision*
30 first-born] firstborn MS
Wimborne MS *deleted* at end

And dim my numerals
With their stain, –
Till I feel useless,
And wrought in vain!

And then I think
In my despair
That, though unseen,
He is still up there,
And may gaze out
Anywhen, anywhere;
Not to help clockmen
Quiz and compare,
But in kindness to let me
My trade declare.

St Juliot

789 Her Haunting-Ground

TITLE:
Her Haunting-ground MS

CAN it be so? It must be so,
That visions have not ceased to be
In this the chiefest sanctuary
Of her whose form we used to know.
– Nay, but her dust is far away,
And 'where her dust is, shapes her shade,
If spirit clings to flesh,' they say:
Yet here her life-parts most were played!

Her voice explored this atmosphere,
Her foot impressed this turf around,
Her shadow swept this slope and mound,
Her fingers fondled blossoms here;
And so, I ask, why, why should she
Haunt elsewhere, by a slighted tomb,
When here she flourished sorrow-free,
And, save for others, knew no gloom?

790 *A Parting-Scene*

THE two pale women cried,
But the man seemed to suffer more,
Which he strove hard to hide.
They stayed in the waiting-room, behind the door,
Till startled by the entering engine-roar,
As if they could not bear to have unfurled
Their misery to the eyes of all the world.

A soldier and his young wife
Were the couple; his mother the third,
Who had seen the seams of life.
He was sailing for the East I later heard.
– They kissed long, but they did not speak a word;
Then, strained, he went. To the elder the wife in tears
'Too long; too long!' burst out. ('Twas for five years.)

791 *Shortening Days at the Homestead*

TITLE:
Before choosing 'Shortening Days' Hardy in MS had tried 'Autumn' and 'October'

THE first fire since the summer is lit, and is smoking into the room:
The sun-rays thread it through, like woof-lines in a loom.
Sparrows spurt from the hedge, whom misgivings appal
That winter did not leave last year for ever, after all.
Like shock-headed urchins, spiny-haired,
Stand pollard willows, their twigs just bared.

Who is this coming with pondering pace,
Black and ruddy, with white embossed,
His eyes being black, and ruddy his face,
And the marge of his hair like morning frost?
It's the cider-maker,
And appletree-shaker,
And behind him on wheels, in readiness,
His mill, and tubs, and vat, and press.

Shortening Days at the Homestead
2 it through] through it MS
3 spurt] spurt up MS
9 face,] face CP3, 4
11–12] It is Mr Baker
The cider-maker, MS

792 Days to Recollect

Do you recall
That day in Fall
When we walked towards Saint Alban's Head,
On thistledown that summer had shed,
Or must I remind you?
Winged thistle-seeds which hitherto
Had lain as none were there, or few,
But rose at the brush of your petticoat-seam
(As ghosts might rise of the recent dead),
And sailed on the breeze in a nebulous stream
Like a comet's tail behind you:
You don't recall
That day in Fall?

Then do you remember
That sad November
When you left me never to see me more,
And looked quite other than theretofore,
As if it could not *be* you?
And lay by the window whence you had gazed
So many times when blamed or praised,
Morning or noon, through years and years,
Accepting the gifts that Fortune bore,
Sharing, enduring, joys, hopes, fears!
Well: I never more did see you. –
Say you remember
That sad November!

INDENTATION:
In HS, HSA, PE, CP3, 4, ll. 12, 13 are indented farther right, but MS and WE make it clear that the intended pattern was the one used here

793 To C.F.H.

On Her Christening-Day

Fair Caroline, I wonder what
You think of earth as a dwelling-spot,
And if you'd rather have come, or not?

EXTRA MANUSCRIPT:
It has not been possible to trace the MS given by Hardy to his godchild, Caroline Fox Hanbury [see *The Life of Thomas Hardy*, p. 414]

Days to Recollect
4 On] Over MS, HS1, HSA
4 shed,] shed? MS
19 lay by] faced MS
22 bore,] bore MS

To-day has laid on you a name
That, though unasked for, you will claim
Lifelong, for love or praise or blame.

May chance and change impose on you
No heavier burthen than this new
Care-chosen one your future through!

Dear stranger here, the prayer is mine
That your experience may combine
Good things with glad. . . . Yes, Caroline!

794 *The High-School Lawn*

GRAY prinked with rose,
White tipped with blue,
Shoes with gay hose,
Sleeves of chrome hue;
Fluffed frills of white,
Dark bordered light;
Such shimmerings through
Trees of emerald green are eyed
This afternoon, from the road outside.

They whirl around:
Many laughters run
With a cascade's sound;
Then a mere one.

A bell: they flee:
Silence then: –
So it will be
Some day again
With them, – with me.

The High-School Lawn
10 around:] around; MS

795 *The Forbidden Banns*

A Ballad of the Eighteen-Thirties

I

'O WHAT's the gain, my worthy Sir,
In stopping the banns to-day!
Your son declares he'll marry her
If a thousand folk say Nay.'

'I'll do't; I'll do't; whether or no!
And, if I drop down dead,
To church this morning I will go,
And say they shall not wed!'

That day the parson clear outspoke
The maid's name and the man's:
His father, mid the assembled folk,
Said, 'I forbid the banns!'

Then, white in face, lips pale and cold,
He turned him to sit down,
When he fell forward; and behold,
They found his life had flown.

II

'Twas night-time, towards the middle part,
When low her husband said,
'I would from the bottom of my heart
That father was not dead!'

She turned from one to the other side,
And a sad woman was she
As he went on: 'He'd not have died
Had it not been for me!'

She brought him soon an idiot child,
And then she brought another:
His face waned wan, his manner wild
With hatred of their mother.

The Forbidden Banns
2 In stopping] To stop MS
5 no!] no, MS
9 clear] due MS
11 folk,] folk MS, HS, HSA, PE, WE
24 me!'] me!' . . . . MS

'Hearken to me, my son. No: no:
There's madness in her blood!'
Those were his father's words; and lo,
Now, now he understood.

What noise is that? One noise, and two
Resound from a near gun.
Two corpses found; and neighbours knew
By whom the deed was done.

EXTRA PRINTING:
McCall's Magazine (New York), Dec 1924, pp. 8–9 = MM

TITLE:
The Midnight Revel MM
Another] A MM

796 The Paphian Ball

Another Christmas Experience of the Mellstock Quire

WE went our Christmas rounds once more,
With quire and viols as theretofore.

Our path was near by Rushy-Pond,
Where Egdon-Heath outstretched beyond.

There stood a figure against the moon,
Tall, spare, and humming a weirdsome tune.

'You tire of Christian carols,' he said:
'Come and lute at a ball instead.

' 'Tis to your gain, for it ensures
That many guineas will be yours.

'A slight condition hangs on't, true,
But you will scarce say nay thereto:

'That you go blindfold; that anon
The place may not be gossiped on.'

They stood and argued with each other:
'Why sing from one house to another

'These ancient hymns in the freezing night,
And all for nought? 'Tis foolish, quite!'

The Paphian Ball
2] To viol carols as of yore. MM
3 near by Rushy-Pond] hard by Rushy Pond MM
4 Egdon-Heath] Egdon Heath MS, MM
4 outstretched] meets land MM
11 hangs on't,] hangs, it's MS, MM

'– 'Tis serving God, and shunning evil:
Might not elsedoing serve the devil?'

'But grand pay!' . . . They were lured by his call,
Agreeing to go blindfold all.

They walked, he guiding, some new track,
Doubting to find the pathway back.

In a strange hall they found them when
They were unblinded all again.

Gilded alcoves, great chandeliers,
Voluptuous paintings ranged in tiers,

In brief, a mansion large and rare,
With rows of dancers waiting there.

They tuned and played; the couples danced;
Half-naked women tripped, advanced,

With handsome partners footing fast,
Who swore strange oaths, and whirled them past.

And thus and thus the slow hours wore them:
While shone their guineas heaped before them.

Drowsy at length, in lieu of the dance
'*While Shepherds watched* . . .' they bowed by chance;

And in a moment, at a blink,
There flashed a change; ere they could think

The ball-room vanished and all its crew:
Only the well-known heath they view –

The spot of their crossing overnight,
When wheedled by the stranger's sleight.

There, east, the Christmas dawn hung red,
And dark Rainbarrow with its dead

Bulged like a supine negress' breast
Against Clyffe-Clump's faint far-off crest.

The Paphian Ball
19 ' – 'Tis] – ' 'Tis MS
20 elsedoing] else-doing MM
21 But] – But MM
21 pay!' . . .] pay!' . . . . MS: pay!' . . MM
28 paintings ranged] paintings, gauds MM
28 tiers,] tiers. HSA
32 Half-naked] Lightly-clad MM
34 oaths,] oaths MS
34 past.] past,[?] MS
37 Drowsy] Weary MS, MM
37 in . . . dance] dazed by the dance, MM
38 *watched* . . .'] *watched*. . . .' MS: *watched*' MM

Yea; the rare mansion, gorgeous, bright,
The ladies, gallants, gone were quite.

The heaped-up guineas, too, were gone
With the gold table they were on.

'Why did not grasp we what was owed!'
Cried some, as homeward, shamed, they strode.

Now comes the marvel and the warning:
When they had dragged to church next morning,

With downcast heads and scarce a word,
They were astound at what they heard.

Praises from all came forth in showers
For how they'd cheered the midnight hours.

'We've heard you many times,' friends said,
'But like *that* never have you played!

'*Rejoice, ye tenants of the earth,*
And celebrate your Saviour's birth,

'Never so thrilled the darkness through,
Or more inspired us so to do!' . . .

– The man who used to tell this tale
Was the tenor-viol, Michael Mail;

Yes; Mail the tenor, now but earth! –
I give it for what it may be worth.

797 *On Martock Moor*

TITLE:
On Durnover Moor MS *before revision*

I

MY deep-dyed husband trusts me,
He feels his mastery sure,
Although I leave his evening hearth
To walk upon the moor.

The Paphian Ball
51 gone] gone, MM
52 gold] jewelled MS: ivory MM
53 did not grasp we] was not quick-grasped MM
54 some] they MM
57 heads] heads, MM
63 *Rejoice,*] *Rejoice* MS, MM, HS, HSA, PE, WE
63 *ye*] *Ye* MM
63 *earth*] *Earth* MM
64 *celebrate your*] *Celebrate Your* MM
64 *birth*] *Birth* MM
66 do!' . . .] do!' . . . . . MS: do!' . . . . MM
68 Michael] old Michael MM
Note. The foregoing was composed several years ago; but, being cast in a familiar medieval mould was not printed till now, when it has been considered to have some qualities worth preserving. MS *deleted* at end

On Martock Moor
1 deep-dyed] dark-dyed MS

II

– I had what wealth I needed,
And of gay gowns a score,
And yet I left my husband's house
To muse upon the moor.

III

O how I loved a dear one
Who, save in soul, was poor!
O how I loved the man who met
Me nightly on the moor.

IV

I'd feather-beds and couches,
And carpets for the floor,
Yet brighter to me was, at eves,
The bareness of the moor.

V

There was a dogging figure,
There was a hiss of 'Whore!'
There was a flounce at Weir-water
One night upon the moor. . . .

VI

Yet do I haunt there, knowing
By rote each rill's low pour,
But only a fitful phantom now
Meets me upon the moor.

1899

798 That Moment

TITLE:
The misery of that Moment MS *before revision*

THE tragedy of that moment
Was deeper than the sea,
When I came in that moment
And heard you speak to me!

On Martock Moor
19 Weir-water] Black Water MS *before revision*

That Moment
4–5 Stanza break in all editions

What I could not help seeing
  Covered life as a blot;
Yes, that which I was seeing,
  And knew that you were not!

799 *Premonitions*

TITLE:
Forebodings MS *before revision*

'THE bell went heavy to-day
At afternoon service, they say,
And a screech-owl cried in the boughs,
And a raven flew over the house,
And Betty's old clock with one hand,
That's worn out, as I understand,
And never goes now, never will,
Struck twelve when the night was dead still,
Just as when my last loss came to me. . . .
Ah! I wonder who next it will be!'

800 *This Summer and Last*

UNHAPPY summer you,
    Who do not see
What your yester-summer saw!
Never, never will you be
    Its match to me,
  Never, never draw
  Smiles your forerunner drew,
    Know what it knew!

  Divine things done and said
    Illumined it,
Whose rays crept into corn-brown curls,
Whose breezes heard a humorous wit
    Of fancy flit. –
  Still the alert brook purls,
  Though feet that there would tread
    Elsewhere have sped.

Premonitions
9 me. . . .] me. . . . . MS

So, bran-new summer, you
Will never see
All that yester-summer saw!
Never, never will you be
In memory
Its rival, never draw
Smiles your forerunner drew,
Know what it knew!

1913?

801 *Nothing Matters Much*

TITLE:
'Nothing Matters Much' MS

(*B.F.L.*)

'NOTHING matters much,' he said
Of something just befallen unduly:
He, then active, but now dead,
Truly, truly!

He knew the letter of the law
As voiced by those of wig and gown,
Whose slightest syllogistic flaw
He hammered down.

And often would he shape in word
That nothing needed much lamenting;
And she who sat there smiled and heard,
Sadly assenting.

Facing the North Sea now he lies,
Toward the red altar of the East,
The Flamborough roar his psalmodies,
The wind his priest.

And while I think of his bleak bed,
Of Time that builds, of Time that shatters,
Lost to all thought is he, who said
'Nothing much matters.'

Nothing Matters Much
2 something] some ill, MS

EXTRA PRINTINGS:
The Times, 5 Jan 1924, p. 11 = T
The Dorset Year-Book 1924, p. 3 = DY

TITLE:
'In the Evening' T
2 Jan. 1924] Not in T

INDENTATION:
1 = ll. 1, 3
2 = ll. 2, 5 } and so throughout T
3 = l. 4

802 *In the Evening*

In Memoriam Frederici Treves, 1853–1923
(Dorchester Cemetery, 2 Jan. 1924)

IN the evening, when the world knew he was dead,
He lay amid the dust and hoar
Of ages; and to a spirit attending said:
'This chalky bed? –
I surely seem to have been here before?'

'O yes. You have been here. You knew the place,
Substanced as you, long ere your call;
And if you cared to do so you might trace
In this gray space
Your being, and the being of men all.'

Thereto said he: 'Then why was I called away?
I knew no trouble or discontent:
Why did I not prolong my ancient stay
Herein for aye?'
The spirit shook its head. 'None knows: you went.

'And though, perhaps, Time did not sign to you
The need to go, dream-vision sees
How Aesculapius' phantom hither flew,
With Galen's, too,
And his of Cos – plague-proof Hippocrates,

'And beckoned you forth, whose skill had read as theirs,
Maybe, had Science chanced to spell
In their day, modern modes to stem despairs
That mankind bears! . . .
Enough. You have returned. And all is well.'

803 *The Six Boards*

SIX boards belong to me:
I do not know where they may be;
If growing green, or lying dry
In a cockloft nigh.

In the Evening
1 when . . . knew] shortly after T
3 ages;] ages, T
3 said:] said, T
5 surely] Not in T
6 have] *have* T
6 place,] place,' T
7 Substanced as you, long] The sprite replied, 'long T
7 call;] call. MS
9 gray] white T
10] Your quality, your substance, and your all.' T
11 Thereto . . . why] Thereat he said: 'Why T
12 knew] felt T
12 discontent:] discontent. T
15 spirit shook its head] sprite looked vague T
15 knows:] knows! T
16–25 'True, Time has not as yet revealed to you/Your need to go. But, some men tell,/A marvellous Deftness called you forth – to do/Much that was due./Good. You have returned. And all is well.' T
16 sign] show MS, DY
17 The] Your MS, DY
21 beckoned] touched DY
22 spell] excel DY
23 modern modes] with its scope DY
24 bears! . . .] bears! . . . . MS, DY

Some morning I shall claim them,
And who may then possess will aim them
To bring to me those boards I need
With thoughtful speed.

But though they hurry so
To yield me mine, I shall not know
How well my want they'll have supplied
When notified.

Those boards and I – how much
In common we, of feel and touch
Shall share thence on, – earth's far core-quakings,
Hill-shocks, tide-shakings –

Yea, hid where none will note,
The once live tree and man, remote
From mundane hurt as if on Venus, Mars,
Or furthest stars.

804 *Before My Friend Arrived*

TITLE:
Before my Friend arrived MS

I SAT on the eve-lit weir,
Which gurgled in sobs and sighs;
I looked across the meadows near
To the towered church on the rise.
Overmuch cause had my look!
I pulled out pencil and book,
And drew a white chalk mound,
Outthrown on the sepulchred ground.

Why did I pencil that chalk?
It was fetched from the waiting grave,
And would return there soon,
Of one who had stilled his walk
And sought oblivion's cave.
He was to come on the morrow noon
And take a good rest in the bed so hewn.

Before My Friend Arrived
15–16 Stanza break in all editions

He came, and there he is now, although
This was a wondrous while ago.
And the sun still dons a ruddy dye;
    The weir still gurgles nigh;
    The tower is dark on the sky.

PROOF:
In the Dorset County Museum. It is identical with FH

EXTRA PRINTINGS:
(1) *The Times*, 16 June 1924, p. 15 = T
(2) *A Century of Work for Animals* by Edward G. Fairholme and Wellesley Pain (London, 1924), pp. xv–xvi = CWA
(3) Privately printed by Florence Hardy, June 1924 = FH
(4) *The First Edition and Book Collector*, 16 June 1924 = FE [This was one of a number of private printings resulting from the 'No copyright' announcement in *The Times*]

TITLE:
An Ode . . . Animals] Not in FE

805 Compassion

An Ode

In Celebration of the Centenary of the Royal Society for the Prevention of Cruelty to Animals

I

  BACKWARD among the dusky years
  A lonesome lamp is seen arise,
  Lit by a few fain pioneers
      Before incredulous eyes. –
  We read the legend that it lights:
'Wherefore beholds this land of historied rights
Mild creatures, despot-doomed, bewildered, plead
Their often hunger, thirst, pangs, prisonment,
  In deep dumb gaze more eloquent
      Than tongues of widest heed?'

II

  What was faint-written, read in a breath
  In that year – ten times ten away –
  A larger louder conscience saith
      More sturdily to-day. –
  But still those innocents are thralls
To throbless hearts, near, far, that hear no calls
Of honour towards their too-dependent frail,
And from Columbia Cape to Ind we see
  How helplessness breeds tyranny
      In power above assail.

Compassion
1 among] amid T, FE
4 eyes. –] eyes. T, CWA, FH, FE
6 'Wherefore beholds] 'Why must (should CWA) throughout T, CWA, FE
10 tongues of widest] tongue of highest T, FE
11 faint-written] faintwritten FE
12 ten times ten] ten-times-ten T, CWA, FH, FE
13 louder] clearer T, CWA, FE
14 to-day. –] to-day. T, CWA, FH, FE
17 too-dependent] too dependent FE
17 frail,] frail; T, CWA, FH, FE
20 above] beyond T, FE

III

Cries still are heard in secret nooks,
Till hushed with gag or slit or thud;
And hideous dens whereon none looks
Are sprayed with needless blood.
But here, in battlings, patient, slow,
Much has been won – more, maybe, than we know –
And on we labour hopeful. 'Ailinon!'
A mighty voice calls: 'But may the good prevail!'
And 'Blessed are the merciful!'
Calls a yet mightier one.

22 January 1924

806 *Why She Moved House*

TITLE:
'Why she moved house' MS

(*The Dog Muses*)

WHY she moved house, without a word,
I cannot understand;
She'd mirrors, flowers, she'd book and bird,
And callers in a band.

And where she is she gets no sun,
No flowers, no book, no glass;
Of callers I am the only one,
And I but pause and pass.

807 *Tragedian to Tragedienne*

SHALL I leave you behind me
When I play
In earnest what we've played in mock to-day?

Why, yes; most surely shall I
Leave you behind
In yet full orbit, when my years upwind.

Compassion
24 sprayed] blotched CWA
24 needless] spurting T, FE
27 hopeful] stressful CWA
27 Ailinon!] Ailinon, T, FE
28] Outcalls one great of old: 'May good have rule!' T, FE
30 a yet] yet a T, CWA, FH, FE
30 mightier] greater T, FE
T adds: (No copyright)

Why She Moved House
7 one,] one. CP3, 4

Tragedian to Tragedienne
6 yet full] vigorous MS
6 upwind] unwind HS1, HSA

I may creep off in the night-time,
And none know
Till comes the morning, bringing news 'tis so.

Will you then turn for a moment
White or red,
Recall those spells of ours; things done, things said?

Aye, those adventurous doings
And those days
Of stress, when I'd the blame and you the praise?

Still you will meet adventure –
None knows what –
Still you will go on changing: I shall not.

Still take a call at the mummings
Daily or nightly,
Yielding to custom, calmly, gloomily, brightly.

Last, you will flag, and finish
Your masquings too:
Yes: end them: I not there to succour you.

808 The Lady of Forebodings

'WHAT do you so regret, my lady,
Sitting beside me here?
Are there not days as clear
As this to come – ev'n shaped less shady?'
'O no,' said she. 'Come what delight
To you, by voice or pen,
To me will fall such day, such night,
Not, not again!'

The lamps above and round were fair,
The tables were aglee,
As if 'twould ever be
That we should smile and sit on there.

The Lady of Forebodings
1 regret] regard HSA
4 As this] Of cloud MS

But yet she said, as though she must,
'Yes: it will soon be gone,
And all its dearness leave but dust
To muse upon.'

809 The Bird-Catcher's Boy

EXTRA MANUSCRIPT:
In the Miriam Lutcher Stark Library of the University of Texas = UT

PROOF:
In the Miriam Lutcher Stark Library of the University of Texas = P

EXTRA PRINTING:
The Sphere, 4 Jan 1913, p. 21 = S

'FATHER, I fear your trade:
Surely it's wrong!
Little birds limed and made
Captive life-long.

'Larks bruise and bleed in jail,
Trying to rise;
Every caged nightingale
Soon pines and dies.'

'Don't be a dolt, my boy!
Birds must be caught;
My lot is such employ,
Yours to be taught.

'Soft shallow stuff as that
Out from your head!
Just learn your lessons pat,
Then off to bed.'

Lightless, without a word
Bedwise he fares;
Groping his way is heard
Seek the dark stairs

Through the long passage, where
Hang the caged choirs:
Harp-like his fingers there
Sweep on the wires.

The Bird-Catcher's Boy
1] 'I don't like your trade, father, UT, P, S
2 wrong!] wrong – UT, P, S
3–5] Prisoning those little birds/All their lives long. (long! UT)/'The larks bruise their tender crowns UT, P, S
6 rise;] rise, UT, P, S
7–8] Every year every caged/Nightingale dies.' UT, P, S
9 dolt, my boy!] fool, my boy. UT, P, S
10 caught;] caught: UT
11] My business 'tis to earn, UT, P, S
13] 'Keep such cursed sentiment UT, P, S
14 from your head!] of your head; UT, P, S
15 lessons pat,] lessons, then UT, P, S
16 Then] March UT, P, S
16 bed.] bed! UT
17–19] Softly (– Softly UT) and lightless/To bed he repairs,/Groping he feels his way UT: They hear him feel his way P, S
18 Bedwise] Bedward MS
20 Seek] Toward UT, P, S
20 stairs] stairs, S
21 passage,] passage UT, P, S
22 choirs:] choirs; P, S
23–4] Groping, (They hear UT) his fingers sweep/Over the wires. UT, P, S
23 Harp-like] Feeling, MS

Next day, at dye of dawn,
  Freddy was missed:
Whither the boy had gone
  Nobody wist.

That week, the next one, whiled:
  No news of him:
Weeks up to months were piled:
  Hope dwindled dim.

Yet not a single night
  Locked they the door,
Waiting, heart-sick, to sight
  Freddy once more.

Hopping there long anon
  Still the birds hung:
Like those in Babylon
  Captive, they sung.

One wintry Christmastide
  Both lay awake;
All cheer within them dried,
  Each hour an ache.

Then some one seemed to flit
  Soft in below;
'Freddy's come!' Up they sit,
  Faces aglow.

Thereat a groping touch
  Dragged on the wires
Lightly and softly – much
  As they were lyres;

'Just as it used to be
  When he came in,
Feeling in darkness the
  Stairway to win!'

The Bird-Catcher's Boy
25 Next (– Next UT) day at ruddy dawn UT, P, S
26 missed:] missed, UT, P, S
28 Nobody] No parent UT, P, S
29–31] That week and next week,/And nothing of him;/Weeks grew to months and more, UT, P, S
35] Waiting, heartsick, to see UT, P, S
37–40 Not in UT, P, S
41–4] One winter midnight/The twain lay awake,/No cheer within them,/Their days one long ache. UT, P, S
45 some one] someone MS, UT, P, S
45 flit] be UT, P, S
46] Entering below. UT, P, S
47 sit,] sit MS, HS, HSA, PE, WE
49–60] Over the bird-cage wires/Fingers swept light (light, UT)/As when he felt his way/Stairward at night, (night. UT)

Sounding the wires by touch/Like a light broom: (broom; UT)/Both parents rose and sought/Freddy's old room. UT, P, S

49 Thereat] Sudden MS
52 lyres;] lyres. MS

Waiting a trice or two
  Yet, in the gloom,
Both parents pressed into
  Freddy's old room.

There on the empty bed
  White the moon shone,
As ever since they'd said,
  'Freddy is gone!'

That night at Durdle-Door[1]
  Foundered a hoy,
And the tide washed ashore
  One sailor boy.

21 November 1912

810 A Hurried Meeting

It is August moonlight in the tall plantation,
Whose elms, by aged squirrels' footsteps worn,
  Outscreen the noon, and eve, and morn.
On the facing slope a faint irradiation
  From a mansion's marble front is borne,
    Mute in its woodland wreathing.
  Up here the night-jar whirrs forlorn,
And the trees seem to withhold their softest breathing.

To the moonshade slips a woman in muslin vesture:
Her naked neck the gossamer-web besmears,
  And she sweeps it away with a hasty gesture.
Again it touches her forehead, her neck, her ears,
    Her fingers, the backs of her hands.
    She sweeps it away again
    Impatiently, and then
She takes no notice; and listens, and sighs, and stands.

[1] Durdle-Door, a rock on the south coast

The Bird-Catcher's Boy
63–4] All was as ever since/Freddy had gone. UT, P, S
65 Durdle-Door[1]] Portland Race UT, P, S
21 November 1912] Not in UT, P, S
[1]Durdle-Door . . . coast] Not in UT, P, S

A Hurried Meeting
7 forlorn,] forlorn MS

The night-hawk stops. A man shows in the obscure:
They meet, and passively kiss,
And he says: 'Well, I've come quickly. About this –
Is it really so? You are sure?'
'I am sure. In February it will be.
That such a thing should come to me!
We should have known. We should have left off meeting.
Love is a terrible thing: a sweet allure
That ends in heart-outeating!'

'But what shall we do, my Love, and how?'
'You need not call me by that name now.'
Then he more coldly: 'What is your suggestion?'
'I've told my mother, and she sees a way,
Since of our marriage there can be no question.
We are crossing South – near about New Year's Day
The event will happen there.
It is the only thing that we can dare
To keep them unaware!'
'Well, you can marry me.'
She shook her head. 'No: that can never be.

' 'Twill be brought home as hers. She's forty-one,
When many a woman's bearing is not done,
And well might have a son. –
We should have left off specious self-deceiving:
I feared that such might come,
And knowledge struck me numb.
Love is a terrible thing: witching when first begun,
To end in grieving, grieving!'

And with one kiss again the couple parted:
Inferior clearly he; she haughty-hearted.
He watched her down the slope to return to her place,
The marble mansion of her ancient race,
And saw her brush the gossamers from her face
As she emerged from shade to the moonlight ray.
And when she had gone away
The night-jar seemed to imp, and say,

A Hurried Meeting
18 kiss,] kiss MS

'You should have taken warning:
Love is a terrible thing: sweet for a space,
And then all mourning, mourning!'

811 Discouragement

To see the Mother, naturing Nature, stand
All racked and wrung by her unfaithful lord,
Her hopes dismayed by his defiling hand,
Her passioned plans for bloom and beauty marred.

Where she would mint a perfect mould, an ill;
Where she would don divinest hues, a stain,
Over her purposed genial hour a chill,
Upon her charm of flawless flesh a blain:

Her loves dependent on a feature's trim,
A whole life's circumstance on hap of birth,
A soul's direction on a body's whim,
Eternal Heaven upon a day of Earth,
Is frost to flower of heroism and worth,
And fosterer of visions ghast and grim.

Westbourne Park Villas, 1863–7
(From old MS.)

812 A Leaving

Knowing what it bore
I watched the rain-smitten back of the car –
(Brown-curtained, such as the old ones were) –
When it started forth for a journey afar
Into the sullen November air,
And passed the glistening laurels and round the bend.

EXTRA MANUSCRIPT:
In possession of Prof. R. L. Purdy [It has been checked from the facsimile in *English Handwriting* by R. Fry and E. A. Lowe (Oxford, 1926), S.P.E. Tract No. xxiii, plate 22] = RLP

TITLE:
A Last Leaving RLP

Discouragement
1863–7] 1865–7 MS

A Leaving
2 car –] car RLP
3 were) –] were) RLP
6–7 Stanza break in all editions

I have seen many gayer vehicles turn that bend
In autumn, winter, and summer air,
Bearing for journeys near or afar
Many who now are not, but were,
But I don't forget that rain-smitten car,
Knowing what it bore!

EXTRA PRINTING:
Chosen Poems, pp. 131–2

813 Song to an Old Burden

THE feet have left the wormholed flooring,
That danced to the ancient air,
The fiddler, all-ignoring,
Sleeps by the gray-grassed 'cello player:
Shall I then foot around around around,
As once I footed there!

The voice is heard in the room no longer
That trilled, none sweetlier,
To gentle stops or stronger,
Where now the dust-draped cobwebs stir:
Shall I then sing again again again,
As once I sang with her!

The eyes that beamed out rapid brightness
Have longtime found their close,
The cheeks have wanned to whiteness
That used to sort with summer rose:
Shall I then joy anew anew anew,
As once I joyed in those!

O what's to me this tedious Maying,
What's to me this June?
O why should viols be playing
To catch and reel and rigadoon?
Shall I sing, dance around around around,
When phantoms call the tune!

A Leaving
7 turn] pass RLP
9 Bearing] Bearing, MS
9 for] on RLP
9 afar] afar, MS
10 were,] were; RLP
11 I don't] who shall RLP
12 Knowing] And MS, RLP

814 *Why Do I?*

EXTRA PRINTING:
Chosen Poems, p. 133

TITLE:
'Why do I?' MS

WHY do I go on doing these things?
Why not cease?
Is it that you are yet in this world of welterings
And unease,
And that, while so, mechanic repetitions please?

When shall I leave off doing these things? –
When I hear
You have dropped your dusty cloak and taken you wondrous wings
To another sphere,
Where no pain is: Then shall I hush this dinning gear.

Why Do I?
2 cease?] cease? – WE, CHP

The Two Tall Men

1

"What's that tapping at night – tack, tack,
In some one's house in the street at the back?"

"O it's a man who, when he has leisure,
Is making himself a coffin to measure.
He's so very tall that no carpenter
Will make it long enough, ~~for him, he fears~~ ~~he believes~~ is his fear."

~~carpenter,~~
~~he's in fear.~~

His father's was short for a man of his limbs,
And it made a great impression on him."

2

"That tapping has begun again
That ceased (some months ago, I ken" / months back – I can't say when" / a year back – or near then";

"Yes; 'tis the man you heard before
Making his coffin. The first scarce
'Twas hardly done,
His brother died – his only one,
And, being of his own height ~~as tall as he~~ ~~quite of his height~~, or more,
He gave it to him, being much afraid / for he was afraid
He'd not get a fit one hastily made:
~~And~~ He's making a second now, to fit
Himself when there shall be need for it."

3

Many years later was brought to me
News that the man had died at sea.

See page 853

WINTER WORDS
IN VARIOUS MOODS AND METRES

Abbreviations Specific to 'Winter Words'

MS = The bound-up volume of manuscripts in the Library of The Queen's College, Oxford
WW1 = *Winter Words* (First Printing: Oct 1928)
WW2 = *Winter Words* (Second Printing: Oct 1928)
WW = Found in both WW1 and WW2
WWA = *Winter Words* (New York, 1928)
PE = Pocket Edition 1930
WE = Wessex Edition 1931

[*'Winter Words', though prepared for the press, would have undergone further revision, had the author lived to issue it on the birthday of which he left the number uninserted below.*]

INTRODUCTORY NOTE

So far as I am aware, I happen to be the only English poet who has brought out a new volume of his verse on his . . . birthday, whatever may have been the case with the ancient Greeks, for it must be remembered that poets did not die young in those days.

This, however, is not the point of the present few preliminary words. My last volume of poems was pronounced wholly gloomy and pessimistic by reviewers – even by some of the more able class. My sense of the oddity of this verdict may be imagined when, in selecting them, I had been, as I thought, rather too liberal in admitting flippant, not to say farcical, pieces into the collection. However, I did not suppose that the licensed tasters had wilfully misrepresented the book, and said nothing, knowing well that they could not have read it.

As labels stick, I foresee readily enough that the same perennial inscription will be set on the following pages, and therefore take no trouble to argue on the proceeding, notwithstanding the surprises to which I could treat my critics by uncovering a place here and there to them in the volume.

This being probably my last appearance on the literary stage, I would say, more seriously, that though, alas, it would be idle to pretend that the publication of these poems can have much interest for me, the track having been adventured so many times before to-day, the pieces themselves have been prepared with reasonable care, if not quite with the zest of a young man new to print.

I also repeat what I have often stated on such occasions, that no harmonious philosophy is attempted in these pages – or in any bygone pages of mine, for that matter.

T.H.

815 *The New Dawn's Business*

WHAT are you doing outside my walls,
    O Dawn of another day?
I have not called you over the edge
        Of the heathy ledge,
    So why do you come this way,
With your furtive footstep without sound here,
    And your face so deedily gray?

'I show a light for killing the man
    Who lives not far from you,
And for bringing to birth the lady's child,
        Nigh domiciled,
    And for earthing a corpse or two,
And for several other such odd jobs round here
    That Time to-day must do.

'But you he leaves alone (although,
    As you have often said,
You are always ready to pay the debt
        You don't forget
    You owe for board and bed):
The truth is, when men willing are found here
    He takes those loth instead.'

EXTRA PRINTING:
The Daily Telegraph, 20 March 1928 = DT

TITLE:
The new Dawn's Business MS

816 *Proud Songsters*

THE thrushes sing as the sun is going,
And the finches whistle in ones and pairs,
And as it gets dark loud nightingales
        In bushes
Pipe, as they can when April wears,
    As if all Time were theirs.

EXTRA MANUSCRIPT:
Permission was refused to see the MS in the possession of Mr Frederick B. Adams, Jnr

EXTRA PRINTING:
The Daily Telegraph, 9 April 1928 = DT

INDENTATION:
The indentation of l. 2 adopted here is that found in MS, WE. CP4 may have gone wrong in lining it up with l. 6 because of the displacement resulting from the capital 'T' in l. 1 of WW

The New Dawn's Business
1 walls,] walls DT

Proud Songsters
6–7 Stanza break in all editions

These are brand-new birds of twelve-months' growing,
Which a year ago, or less than twain,
No finches were, nor nightingales,
Nor thrushes,
But only particles of grain,
And earth, and air, and rain.

EXTRA MANUSCRIPT:
In the Library of King's College, Cambridge = KC

817 *Thoughts at Midnight*

MANKIND, you dismay me
When shadows waylay me! –
Not by your splendours
Do you affray me,
Not as pretenders
To demonic keenness,
Not by your meanness,
Nor your ill-teachings,
Nor your false preachings,
Nor your banalities
And immoralities,
Nor by your daring
Nor sinister bearing;
But by your madnesses
Capping cool badnesses,
Acting like puppets
Under Time's buffets;
In superstitions
And ambitions
Moved by no wisdom,
Far-sight, or system,
Led by sheer senselessness
And presciencelessness
Into unreason
And hideous self-treason. . . .
God, look he on you,
Have mercy upon you!

Part written 25 May 1906

Proud Songsters
7 brand-new] brand new MS, DT, WW, WWA, PE, WE

Thoughts at Midnight
2 When shadows] Till grim ghosts KC *before revision*
3] A late addition in KC
3 splendours] splendours, KC
4 me,] me; KC
6 keenness,] keenness; KC
13 bearing;] bearing, KC
14 madnesses] madnesses, KC
17 buffets;] buffets: – KC
18–19] A late addition in KC
25 self-treason. . . .] self-treason. . . . . MS
26 God,] God – KC
26 you,] you – KC

818 I Am the One

EXTRA PRINTING:
The Daily Telegraph, 2 April 1928 = DT

TITLE:
'I am the One MS

I AM the one whom ringdoves see
Through chinks in boughs
When they do not rouse
In sudden dread,
But stay on cooing, as if they said:
'Oh; it's only he.'

I am the passer when up-eared hares,
Stirred as they eat
The new-sprung wheat,
Their munch resume
As if they thought: 'He is one for whom
Nobody cares.'

Wet-eyed mourners glance at me
As in train they pass
Along the grass
To a hollowed spot,
And think: 'No matter; he quizzes not
Our misery.'

I hear above: 'We stars must lend
No fierce regard
To his gaze, so hard
Bent on us thus, –
Must scathe him not. He is one with us
Beginning and end.'

819 The Prophetess

I

'NOW shall I sing
That pretty thing
"The Mocking-Bird"?' – And sing it straight did she.

I Am the One
16 hollowed] hallowed DT
22 thus,] thus DT
23 us] us, DT

I had no cause
To think it was
A Mocking-bird in truth that sang to me.

2

Not even the glance
She threw askance
Foretold to me, nor did the tune or rhyme,
That the words bore
A meaning more
Than that they were a ditty of the time.

3

But after years
Of hopes and fears,
And all they bring, and all they take away,
I found I had heard
The Mocking-bird
In person singing there to me that day.

EXTRA PRINTING:
The Daily Telegraph, 5 July 1928.
There are no variants

820 *A Wish for Unconsciousness*

If I could but abide
As a tablet on a wall,
Or a hillock daisy-pied,
Or a picture in a hall,
And as nothing else at all,
I should feel no doleful achings,
I should hear no judgment-call,
Have no evil dreams or wakings,
No uncouth or grisly care;
In a word, no cross to bear.

The Prophetess
7–12 A late addition to MS

821 The Bad Example

FIE, Aphrodite, shamming you are no mother,
And your maternal markings trying to smother,
As you were maiden, now you love another! . . .
If one like you need such pretence to noose him,
Indulgence in too early fires beware you,
All girls yet virgin, and have constant care you
Become not staled by use as she has, ere you
Meet your most-loved; lest, tumbled, you should lose him.

Partly from Meleager

822 To Louisa in the Lane

EXTRA PRINTING:
The Daily Telegraph, 26 April 1928.
There are no variants

MEET me again as at that time
In the hollow of the lane;
I will not pass as in my prime
I passed at each day's wane.
– Ah, I remember!
To do it you will have to see
Anew this sorry scene wherein you have ceased to be!

But I will welcome your aspen form
As you gaze wondering round
And say with spectral frail alarm,
'Why am I still here found?
– Ah, I remember!
It is through him with blitheful brow
Who did not love me then, but loves and draws me now!'

And I shall answer: 'Sweet of eyes,
Carry me with you, Dear,
To where you donned this spirit-guise;
It's better there than here!'

The Bad Example
3 another! . . .] another! . . . . MS
4] If such as you have need to so abuse him, MS *before revision*
5 you,] you MS

– Till I remember
Such is a deed you cannot do:
Wait must I, till with flung-off flesh I follow you.

TITLE:
Love watches a Window MS

823 Love Watches a Window

'HERE in the window beaming across
Is he – the lineaments like him so! –
The saint whose name I do not know,
With the holy robe and the cheek aglow.
Here will I kneel as if worshipping God
When all the time I am worshipping you,
Whose Love I was –
You that with me will nevermore tread anew
The paradise-paths we trod!'

She came to that prominent pew each day,
And sat there. Zealously she came
And watched her Love – looking just the same
From the rubied eastern tracery-frame –
The man who had quite forsaken her
And followed another, it was thought. –
Be 't as it may,
Thinner, more thin, was the lady's figure wrought
By some ache, year on year.

Well, now she's dead, and dead is he
From whom her heart once drew delight,
Whose face glowed daily, lover-bright,
High in the glass before her sight.
And still the face is seen as clear
In the rubied eastern window-gleam
As formerly;
But not seen now is a passioned woman's dream
Glowing beside it there.

824 The Love-Letters

(*In Memoriam H.R.*)

I MET him quite by accident
In a bye-path that he'd frequent.
And, as he neared, the sunset glow
Warmed up the smile of pleasantry
Upon his too thin face, while he
Held a square packet up to me,
    Of what, I did not know.

'Well,' said he then; 'they are my old letters.
Perhaps she – rather felt them fetters. . . .
You see, I am in a slow decline,
And she's broken off with me. Quite right
To send them back, and true foresight;
I'd got too fond of her! To-night
    I burn them – stuff of mine!'

He laughed in the sun – an ache in his laughter –
And went. I heard of his death soon after.

EXTRA MANUSCRIPT:
There is a fragment of an early draft in the possession of Prof. R. L. Purdy. It has not been available for checking

TITLE:
The Love-letters MS

825 An Unkindly May

A SHEPHERD stands by a gate in a white smock-frock:
He holds the gate ajar, intently counting his flock.

The sour spring wind is blurting boisterous-wise,
And bears on it dirty clouds across the skies;
Plantation timbers creak like rusty cranes,
And pigeons and rooks, dishevelled by late rains,
Are like gaunt vultures, sodden and unkempt,
And song-birds do not end what they attempt:
The buds have tried to open, but quite failing
Have pinched themselves together in their quailing.

EXTRA PRINTING:
The Daily Telegraph, 23 April 1928.
There are no variants

TITLE:
(1877) MS *deleted* below title

The Love-Letters
9 fetters. . . .] fetters. . . . . MS
15–16] He smiled again in the sun, and went:/I'd met him quite by accident. MS *before revision*

An Unkindly May
1 smock-frock] smockfrock MS
3 boisterous-wise] boisterouswise WE [line break in WW, WWA, PE]
10–11 No stanza break

The sun frowns whitely in eye-trying flaps
Through passing cloud-holes, mimicking audible taps.
'Nature, you're not commendable to-day!'
I think. 'Better to-morrow!' she seems to say.

That shepherd still stands in that white smock-frock,
Unnoting all things save the counting his flock.

EXTRA PRINTING:
The Daily Telegraph, 5 April 1928.
There are no variants

826 *Unkept Good Fridays*

THERE are many more Good Fridays
Than this, if we but knew
The names, and could relate them,
Of men whom rulers slew
For their goodwill, and date them
As runs the twelvemonth through.

These nameless Christs' Good Fridays,
Whose virtues wrought their end,
Bore days of bonds and burning,
With no man to their friend,
Of mockeries, and spurning;
Yet they are all unpenned.

When they had their Good Fridays
Of bloody sweat and strain
Oblivion hides. We quote not
Their dying words of pain,
Their sepulchres we note not,
Unwitting where they have lain.

No annual Good Fridays
Gained they from cross and cord,
From being sawn asunder,
Disfigured and abhorred,

Unkept Good Fridays
4] Of those their fellows slew MS *before revision*

Smitten and trampled under:
Such dates no hands have scored.

Let be. Let lack Good Fridays
These Christs of unwrit names;
The world was not even worthy
To taunt their hopes and aims,
As little of earth, earthy,
As his mankind proclaims.

Good Friday, 1927

827 The Mound

For a moment pause: –
Just here it was;
And through the thin thorn hedge, by the rays of the moon,
I can see the tree in the field, and beside it the mound –
Now sheeted with snow – whereon we sat that June
When it was green and round,
And she crazed my mind by what she coolly told –
The history of her undoing,
(As I saw it), but she called 'comradeship',
That bred in her no rueing:
And saying she'd not be bound
For life to one man, young, ripe-yeared, or old,
Left me – an innocent simpleton to her viewing;
For, though my accompt of years outscored her own,
Hers had more hotly flown. . . .
We never met again by this green mound,
To press as once so often lip on lip,
And palter, and pause: –
Yes; here it was!

828 Liddell and Scott

On the Completion of their Lexicon

(Written after the death of Liddell in 1898. Scott had died some ten years earlier.)

'WELL, though it seems
Beyond our dreams,'
Said Liddell to Scott,
'We've really got
To the very end,
All inked and penned
Blotless and fair
Without turning a hair,
This sultry summer day, A.D.
Eighteen hundred and forty-three.

'I've often, I own,
Belched many a moan
At undertaking it,
And dreamt forsaking it.
– Yes, on to Pi,
When the end loomed nigh,
And friends said: "You've as good as done,"
I almost wished we'd not begun.
Even now, if people only knew
My sinkings, as we slowly drew
Along through Kappa, Lambda, Mu,
They'd be concerned at my misgiving,
And how I mused on a College living
Right down to Sigma,
But feared a stigma
If I succumbed, and left old Donnegan
For weary freshmen's eyes to con again:
And how I often, often wondered
What could have led me to have blundered

Liddell and Scott
11 own,] own MS

So far away from sound theology
To dialects and etymology;
Words, accents not to be breathed by men
Of any country ever again!'

'My heart most failed,
Indeed, quite quailed,'
Said Scott to Liddell,
'Long ere the middle! . . .
'Twas one wet dawn
When, slippers on,
And a cold in the head anew,
Gazing at Delta
I turned and felt a
Wish for bed anew,
And to let supersedings
Of Passow's readings
In dialects go.
"That German has read
More than we!" I said;
Yea, several times did I feel so! . . .

'O that first morning, smiling bland,
With sheets of foolscap, quills in hand,
To write ἀάατος and ἀαγής,
Followed by fifteen hundred pages,
What nerve was ours
So to back our powers,
Assured that we should reach ὠώδης
While there was breath left in our bodies!'

Liddell replied: 'Well, that's past now;
The job's done, thank God, anyhow.'

'And yet it's not,'
Considered Scott,
'For we've to get
Subscribers yet

Liddell and Scott
49 so! . . .] so! . . . . MS

We must remember;
Yes; by September.'

'O Lord; dismiss that. We'll succeed.
Dinner is my immediate need.
I feel as hollow as a fiddle,
Working so many hours,' said Liddell.

829 Christmastide

THE rain-shafts splintered on me
As despondently I strode;
The twilight gloomed upon me
And bleared the blank high-road.
Each bush gave forth, when blown on
By gusts in shower and shower,
A sigh, as it were sown on
In handfuls by a sower.

A cheerful voice called, nigh me,
'A merry Christmas, friend!' –
There rose a figure by me,
Walking with townward trend,
A sodden tramp's, who, breaking
Into thin song, bore straight
Ahead, direction taking
Toward the Casuals' gate.

830 Reluctant Confession

'WHAT did you do? Cannot you let me know?'
'Don't ask! . . . 'Twas midnight, and I'd lost at cards.'
'Ah. Was it crime – or seemed it to be so?'
'No – not till afterwards.'
'But *what*, then, did you do?'
'Well – that was the beginning – months ago;
You see, I had lost, and could not pay but – so.

Liddell and Scott
64 remember;] remember: [?] MS

Christmastide
13 who,] who MS

Reluctant Confession
2 ask! . . .] ask! . . . . MS
7–8 No stanza break

And there flashed from him strange and strong regards
That you only see when scruples smash to shards;
And thus it happened – O it rained and blew! –
But I can't tell. 'Twas all so lurid in hue!
And what was worst came after, when I knew
    What first crossed not my mind,
    And he has never divined!' . . .
'But he must have, if he proposed it you?'
'I mean, that – I got rid of what resulted
In a way a woman told me I consulted:
    'Tis that he does not know;
    Great God, it harrows me so!
    I did not mean to. Every night –
        In hell-dark dreams
    I see an appealing figure in white –
        That somehow seems
A newborn child in the clothes I set to make,
But left off, for my own depraved name's sake!'

831 *Expectation and Experience*

'I HAD a holiday once,' said the woman –
    Her name I did not know –
'And I thought that where I'd like to go,
Of all the places for being jolly,
And getting rid of melancholy,
    Would be to a good big fair:
And I went. And it rained in torrents, drenching
Every horse, and sheep, and yeoman,
    And my shoulders, face and hair;
And I found that I was the single woman
    In the field – and looked quite odd there!
Everything was spirit-quenching:
I crept and stood in the lew of a wall
To think, and could not tell at all
    What on earth made me plod there!'

Reluctant Confession
14 The indentation adopted here is that of MS, WW, WWA, PE, WE
14 divined!' . . .] divined!' . . . . . MS

Expectation and Experience
9 face] face, MS

832 Aristodemus the Messenian

(Dramatic Hendecasyllabics)

Scene: BEFORE THE STRONGHOLD OF ITHOME,

MESSENIA, 735 B.C.

His daughter's lover discovered, in the disguise of a soothsayer; to whom enters ARISTODEMUS.

ARISTODEMUS (*apostrophically*)

Straightway let it be done!

LOVER

Let what be done, chief?

ARISTODEMUS

Who art thou that art speaking? Some sage prophet? –
She, my daughter's to perish on the altar!

LOVER

Thou called hero! – a myth thy vaunted power,
If it fail to redeem thy best beloved.

ARISTODEMUS

Power is nought to the matter. What the Sibyl
Bids, must be!

LOVER

But I doubt such bidding thereto.

ARISTODEMUS

Nay. White lippings above the Delphic tripod
Mangle never their message! And they lip such.
Thriving, conquering shall Messene be forthwith –
Future worthy my gift of this intact one.
Yea, and who of the Aépýtids' renowned house
Weigh can greater with Zeus than she my offspring?
Shall these Spartiats sway to save me reavement?
What is fatherhood when they march in hearing?
Hark! E'en now they are here!

(*Marching soldiers heard afar.*)

Aristodemus the Messenian
735 B.C.] B.C. 72 MS

LOVER (*after a silence*)

And mean you to warn her?

ARISTODEMUS

Not till evening shades can cover pallor.

[*Exit.*

Lover stands motionless. Enter the daughter of ARISTODEMUS.

DAUGHTER

Ah! Thou comest to me, Love, not as earlier!

Lover, as it were waking, approaches, unhoods his face, and embraces her.

Why not speak to me?

LOVER

Sweetest, thou'rt a doomed one!

DAUGHTER

How?

LOVER

Thy sacrifice by thy father waits thee –
Thee, as offering for the State's salvation.

DAUGHTER

Not the slaying of me?

LOVER

Fail I to stay him –

(*She droops in his arms*)

Whereto bursts in a flame a means upon me!

DAUGHTER

How? My father is mighty. Thou'rt so powerless.

LOVER

Thus and now it adumbrates. Haste I to him,
Vowing love for thee!

DAUGHTER

Which he'll value wryly –
Less than nought, as I know.

LOVER

Till comes my sequel;
This, to wit. Thou art got with child by me. Ay,
List: the Sibylline utterance asks a virgin;
So th'rt saved!

DAUGHTER

But a maid's the thing I am, Love!
Gods! With child I am not, but veriest virgin –
Who knows surer than thou?

LOVER

I'll make him think so,
Though no man upon earth more knows its falseness,
Such will I.

DAUGHTER

But alas, thou canst not make him:
Me he knows to the core. He'll not believe thee.

LOVER

Then thou canst. He'll accept thy vouching, sure, Sweet,
And another intact one, equal serving,
Straightway find for the knife.

DAUGHTER

My Love, I must not!

LOVER

Not? And yet there is pending for thee, elsewise,
Dark destruction, and all thy burning being
Dungeoned in an eternal nescientness!

She shudders, but weepingly shows unwillingness.

Stay. I'll make the asseverance first. Thou'lt clinch it?

DAUGHTER (*with white cheeks, after a pause*)

Be it so! . . .

The Messenian army is heard going out to meet the Spartans. Lover hoods himself as ARISTODEMUS *enters from the stronghold.*

Aristodemus the Messenian
43 so! . . .] so! . . . . . MS

ARISTODEMUS (*looking strangely at his daughter*)

Stay you yet at the gate? The old man also?
Hath indeed he disclosed the sore pronouncement?

DAUGHTER (*falteringly*)

Sore pronouncement? And what is, sire, its substance?

Messenger enters.

MESSENGER

King Euphaes is just found slain in combat:
Thereby King is the Chief, Aristodemus,
E'en ere falters the strife – still hard against us!

ARISTODEMUS

Ha! And is it in balance yet! – The deed, then!

Daughter looks at her lover, who throws off his disguise; and they go up to ARISTODEMUS *together.*

Who's this man? And to what tends all this feigning?

DAUGHTER

He – my lover – who thinks to be my husband –
O my father, thy pardon! Know a secret!

ARISTODEMUS

Lover? Secret? And what? But such is nought now:
Husband he nor another can be to thee,
Let him think as he may! And though I meant not
Death to broach till the eve, let doom be dealt now.
Hark, the Spartan assays! It straight behoves me,
Cost it what to my soul, to give deliverance
To my country the instant. Thou, my daughter,
Foremost maiden of all the maidens round us —

DAUGHTER

O but save me, I pray, sire! And to that end
There has now to be spoke a thing immediate,
And I fain would be speaker. But I cannot!
What he now will reveal, receive as vouched for!

(*She rushes into the castle.*)

ARISTODEMUS (*to lover*)

What means this in her? Reads she what's impending?

LOVER

King, its meaning is much! That she's with child. Yea,
By me! Hence there is called for immolation
One who's what she is not – a sure-sealed virgin –
If you'd haste to deliver stressed Ithome,
Bulking yet overhead as though unweakened!

ARISTODEMUS *sinks on to a projection of the rock, and covers his eyes.*

ARISTODEMUS (*brokenly*)

Better had she been made the purposed victim
Than that this should have so befallen to save her!
Foul disaster of fatherhood and home-pride!...
Let this citadel fall; the Spartan army
Trample over its dust, and enter in here!
She is worse than a martyr for the State-weal,
I than one of the slain. And king to-morrow!

(*He pauses*)

'Tis not true!

He makes as if to fall upon her lover with his sword. Lover defends himself with his dagger. ARISTODEMUS *turns to rush into the castle after his daughter.*

I misdoubt it! They speak falsely!

[*Exit* ARISTODEMUS.

Lover walks up and down in strained suspense. Interval. A groan is heard. Lover is about to rush out, but re-enter ARISTODEMUS *sword in hand, now bloody.*

ARISTODEMUS

I have proved me her honour, shown the falsehood
Ye twain both have declared me!

LOVER

That canst not do!

ARISTODEMUS

I say I have outshown it; proved her even
Until death very virgin pure and spotless!

Enter Attendants.

Aristodemus the Messenian
74 home-pride! . . .] home-pride! . . . . . MS

ATTENDANTS (*severally*)

Horror, horror indeed! He's ripped her up – yea,
With his sword! He hath split her beauteous body
To prove her maid!

ARISTODEMUS (*to lover*)

Now diest thou for thy lying, like as she died!

He turns his sword on lover, but falls from exhaustion. Lover seizes ARISTODEMUS' *sword, and is about to run him through with it; but he checks his hand, and turns the sword upon himself.*

(*Lover dies.*)

833 Evening Shadows

EXTRA PRINTING:
The Daily Telegraph, 7 May 1928.
There are no variants

THE shadows of my chimneys stretch afar
Across the plot, and on to the privet bower,
And even the shadows of their smokings show,
And nothing says just now that where they are
They will in future stretch at this same hour,
Though in my earthen cyst I shall not know.

And at this time the neighbouring Pagan mound,
Whose myths the Gospel news now supersede,
Upon the greensward also throws its shade,
And nothing says such shade will spread around
Even as to-day when men will no more heed
The Gospel news than when the mound was made.

834 The Three Tall Men

EXTRA MANUSCRIPTS:
(1) In Colby College Library there is a rough-draft MS of a poem called 'The Two Tall Men', later revised and expanded into 'The Three Tall Men'. (See illustration on p. 832.) The text is given below.
(2) In the Dorset County Museum = DCM

EXTRA PRINTING:
The Daily Telegraph, 9 Aug 1928 = DT

THE FIRST TAPPING

'WHAT'S that tapping at night: tack, tack,
In some house in the street at the back?'

Evening Shadows
8 news] MS has 'tidings' written in pencil above

The Three Tall Men
1 night:] night; DCM
2–3 Stanza break in all editions

'O, 'tis a man who, when he has leisure,
Is making himself a coffin to measure.
He's so very tall that no carpenter
Will make it long enough, he's in fear.
His father's was shockingly short for his limb –
And it made a deep impression on him.'

The Second Tapping

'That tapping has begun again,
Which ceased a year back, or near then?'

'Yes, 'tis the man you heard before
Making his coffin. The first scarce done
His brother died – his only one –
And, being of his own height, or more,
He used it for him; for he was afraid
He'd not get a long enough one quick made.
He's making a second now, to fit
Himself when there shall be need for it.
Carpenters work so by rule of thumb
That they make mistakes when orders come.'

The Third Tapping

'It's strange, but years back, when I was here,
I used to notice a tapping near;
A man was making his coffin at night,
And he made a second, if I am right?
I have heard again the self-same tapping –
Yes, late last night – or was I napping?'

'O no. It's the same man. He made one
Which his brother had; and a second was done –
For himself, as he thought. But lately his son,
As tall as he, died; aye, and as trim,
And his sorrowful father bestowed it on him.
And now the man is making a third,
To be used for himself when he is interred.'

'Many years later was brought to me
News that the man had died at sea.'

The Two Tall Men

1

"What's that tapping at night – tack, tack,/In someone's house in the street at the back?"

"O its a man who, when he has leisure,/Is making himself a coffin to measure./He's so very tall that no carpenter/Will make it long enough is his fear."/His father's was short for a man of his limb,/And it made a great impression on him"

2

"That tapping has begun again/That ceased [months back – I can't say when"] [some months ago, I ken."] [a year back – or near then."]/"Yes; 'tis the man you heard before/Making his coffin./[The first scarce] ['Twas hardly] done,/[His] [When his] brother died – his only one,/And, being of his own height, or more,/He gave it to him, being much (for he was) afraid/He'd not get a fit one hastily made:/He's making a second now, to fit/Himself when there shall be need for it."

3

Many years later was brought to me/News that the man had died at sea.

The Three Tall Men
7 limb –] limb, DCM
8 made a deep] left a great DCM
9 again,] again DCM
11 before] before, DCM
13 one –] one, DCM
15 used it for him;] gave it to him, DCM
16 one] one, DCM
18 Himself] Himself, DCM
19 work so] work DT
21 here,] here DCM
23 night,] night; DCM
26 Yes, late] 'Twas late DCM
27 no] No DCM
30 trim,] trim; DCM
31 him.] him: DCM
32 third,] third DCM
34 'Many] Many DCM
35 sea.'] sea. DCM
34–6] Later I paused in the town for a space;/ Of the too tall man I could find no trace:/I hoped he secured his well-earned (at last his) place. DCM *deleted*

835 *The Lodging-House Fuchsias*

EXTRA PRINTING:
The Daily Telegraph, 13 Aug 1928 = DT

TITLE:
The Lodging-house Fuchsias MS

MRS MASTERS'S fuchsias hung
Higher and broader, and brightly swung,
Bell-like, more and more
Over the narrow garden-path,
Giving the passer a sprinkle-bath
In the morning.

She put up with their pushful ways,
And made us tenderly lift their sprays,
Going to her door:
But when her funeral had to pass
They cut back all the flowery mass
In the morning.

836 *The Whaler's Wife*

I NEVER pass that inn 'The Ring of Bells'
Without recalling what its signpost tells
To recollection:
A tale such as all houses yield, maybe,
That ever have known of fealties, phantasy,
Hate, or affection.

He has come from a whaling cruise to settle down
As publican in his small native town,
Where his wife dwells.
It is a Sunday morning; she has gone
To church with others. Service still being on,
He seeks 'The Bells'.

'Yes: she's quite thriving; very much so, they say.
I don't believe in tales; 'tis not my way!
I hold them stuff.

The Lodging-House Fuchsias
2 swung,] swung DT
6 and 12] MS has written above in pencil 'Peremptorily'

The Whaler's Wife
11 on,] on MS

But – as you press me – certainly we know
He visits her once at least each week or so,
Fair weather or rough.

'And, after all, he's quite a gentleman,
And lonely wives must friend them where they can.
She'll tell you all,
No doubt, when prayers are done and she comes home.
I'm glad to hear your early taste to roam
Begins to pall.'

'I'll stroll out and await her,' then said he.
Anon the congregation passed, and she
Passed with the rest,
Unconscious of the great surprise at hand
And bounding on, and smiling – fair and bland –
In her Sunday best.

Straight she was told. She fainted at the news,
But rallied, and was able to refuse
Help to her home.
There she sat waiting all day – with a look –
A look of joy, it seemed, if none mistook . . .
But he did not come.

Time flew: her husband kept him absent still,
And by slow slips the woman pined, until,
Grown thin, she died –
Of grief at loss of him, some would aver,
But how could that be? They anyway buried her
By her mother's side.

And by the grave stood, at the funeral,
A tall man, elderly and grave withal;
Gossip grew grim:
He was the same one who had been seen before;
He paid, in cash, all owing; and no more
Was heard of him.

At the pulling down of her house, decayed and old,
Many years after, was the true tale told

The Whaler's Wife
35 mistook . . .] mistook. . . . MS
46 before;] before: [?] MS

By an ancient swain.
The tall man was the father of the wife.
He had beguiled her mother in maiden life,
And to cover her stain,

Induced to wive her one in his service bred,
Who brought her daughter up as his till wed.
– This the girl knew,
But hid it close, to save her mother's name,
Even from her seaman spouse, and ruined her fame
With him, though true.

837 Throwing a Tree

New Forest

THE two executioners stalk along over the knolls,
Bearing two axes with heavy heads shining and wide,
And a long limp two-handled saw toothed for cutting great boles,
And so they approach the proud tree that bears the death-mark on its side.

Jackets doffed they swing axes and chop away just above ground,
And the chips fly about and lie white on the moss and fallen leaves;
Till a broad deep gash in the bark is hewn all the way round,
And one of them tries to hook upward a rope, which at last he achieves.

The saw then begins, till the top of the tall giant shivers:
The shivers are seen to grow greater each cut than before:
They edge out the saw, tug the rope; but the tree only quivers,
And kneeling and sawing again, they step back to try pulling once more.

Then, lastly, the living mast sways, further sways: with a shout
Job and Ike rush aside. Reached the end of its long staying powers
The tree crashes downward: it shakes all its neighbours throughout,
And two hundred years' steady growth has been ended in less than two hours.

EXTRA PRINTING:
Commerce (Paris), Winter 1927 (1928), pp. [5]–9 = C [There is an accompanying translation by Paul Valéry and a note which reads 'Ce poème nous a été communiqué par Madame Hardy. Il est le dernier qui fut écrit par Thomas Hardy, peu de temps avant sa mort.]

TITLE:
Felling a Tree C

INDENTATION:
C has all lines equally indented

The Whaler's Wife
52 wife.] wife: MS
54 stain,] stain MS

Throwing a Tree
16] And seventy-odd years steady growth has been ended in less than an hour. MS *before revision*

EXTRA PRINTING:
The Daily Telegraph, 21 June 1928 = DT

TITLE:
The War-wife of Catknoll MS

838 *The War-Wife of Catknoll*

'WHAT crowd is this in Catknoll Street,
Now I am just come home?
What crowd is this in my old street,
That flings me such a glance?
A stretcher – and corpse? A sobering sight
To greet me, when my heart is light
With thoughts of coming cheer to-night
Now I am back from France.'

'O 'tis a woman, soldier-man,
Who seem to be new come:
O 'tis a woman, soldier-man,
Found in the river here,
Whither she went and threw her in,
And now they are carrying her within:
She's drowned herself for a sly sin
Against her husband dear.

' 'A said to me, who knew her well,
"O why was I so weak!"
'A said to me, who knew her well,
And have done all her life,
With a downcast face she said to me,
"O why did I keep company
Wi' them that practised gallantry,
When vowed a faithful wife!"

' "O God, I'm driven mad!" she said,
"To hear he's coming back;
I'm fairly driven mad!" she said:
"He's been two years agone,
And now he'll find me in this state,
And not forgive me. Had but fate
Kept back his coming three months late,
Nothing of it he'd known!"

The War-Wife of Catknoll
10 seem] seems MS, DT, WWA
19 me,] me DT
23 gallantry,] There is some doubt as to whether the comma in MS *is intended*

'We did not think she meant so much,
And said: "He may forgive."
O never we thought she meant so much
As to go doing this.
And now she must be crowned! – so fair! –
Who drew men's eyes so everywhere! –
And love-letters beyond compare
For coaxing to a kiss.

'She kept her true a year or more
Against the young men all;
Yes, kept her true a year or more,
And they were most to blame.
There was Will Peach who plays the flute,
And Waywell with the dandy suit,
And Nobb, and Knight. . . . But she's been mute
As to the father's name.'

NOTE: verse 5. – 'She must be crowned.' Old English for 'there must be a coroner's inquest over her'.

839 Concerning His Old Home

EXTRA MANUSCRIPT:
In the Dorset County Museum = DCM

EXTRA PRINTING:
The Daily Telegraph, 16 Aug 1928.
There are no variants

TITLE:
Moods concerning an old House DCM *before revision*
Concerning his old Home MS

MOOD I

I WISH to see it never –
That dismal place
With cracks in its floor –
I would forget it ever!

MOOD II

To see it once, that sad
And memoried place –
Yes, just once more –
I should be faintly glad!

MOOD III

To see it often again –
That friendly place
With its green low door –
I'm willing anywhen!

The War-Wife of Catknoll
39 love-letters] loveletters MS
47 Knight. . . .] Knight. . . . . MS

MOOD IV

I'll haunt it night and day –
    That loveable place,
    With its flowers' rich store
That drives regret away!

EXTRA PRINTING:
The Daily Telegraph, 23 July 1928 = DT

TITLE:
Her Second Husband hears her Story MS

840 Her Second Husband Hears Her Story

'STILL, Dear, it is incredible to me
    That here, alone,
You should have sewed him up until he died,
And in this very bed. I do not see
How you could do it, seeing what might betide.'

'Well, he came home one midnight, liquored deep –
    Worse than I'd known –
And lay down heavily, and soundly slept:
Then, desperate driven, I thought of it, to keep
Him from me when he woke. Being an adept

'With needle and thimble, as he snored, click-click
    An hour I'd sewn,
Till, had he roused, he couldn't have moved from bed,
So tightly laced in sheet and quilt and tick
He lay. And in the morning he was dead.

'Ere people came I drew the stitches out,
    And thus 'twas shown
To be a stroke.' – 'It's a strange tale!' said he.
'And this same bed?' – 'Yes, here it came about.'
'Well, it sounds strange – told here and now to me.

'Did you intend his death by your tight lacing?'
    'O, that I cannot own.
I could not think of else that would avail
When he should wake up, and attempt embracing.' –
    'Well, it's a cool queer tale!'

Concerning His Old Home
15 store] store, DCM

Her Second Husband Hears Her Story
16 out,] out. DT

841 *Yuletide in a Younger World*

WE believed in highdays then,
And could glimpse at night
On Christmas Eve
Imminent oncomings of radiant revel –
Doings of delight: –
Now we have no such sight.

We had eyes for phantoms then,
And at bridge or stile
On Christmas Eve
Clear beheld those countless ones who had crossed it
Cross again in file: –
Such has ceased longwhile!

We liked divination then,
And, as they homeward wound
On Christmas Eve,
We could read men's dreams within them spinning
Even as wheels spin round: –
Now we are blinker-bound.

We heard still small voices then,
And, in the dim serene
Of Christmas Eve,
Caught the far-time tones of fire-filled prophets
Long on earth unseen. . . .
– Can such ever have been?

EXTRA PRINTINGS:
(1) As No. 1 of the *Ariel Poems* (London, 1927) = AP [There was a limited edition of 350 and an ordinary edition of 5000 copies. They are identical in text]
(2) In a limited edition by William Edwin Rudge, Mount Vernon, New York, Dec 1927. It has not been possible to trace and check a copy.

Note MS has written in pencil top right '[For Mr de la Mare] published by Faber & Gwyn as Xmas Card Aug. 27'

842 *After the Death of a Friend*

YOU died, and made but little of it! –
Why then should I, when called to doff it,
Drop, and renounce this worm-holed raiment,
Shrink edgewise off from its grey claimant?

EXTRA PRINTING:
The Daily Telegraph, 10 July 1928 = DT

Yuletide in a Younger World
4 revel] revel, AP
5 delight: –] delight: AP
11 file: –] file: AP
12 longwhile!] longwhile. AP
17 round: –] round: AP
23 unseen. . . .] unseen. . . . . . MS, AP

After the Death of a Friend
1 it! –] it! DT
4–5 No stanza break

Rather say, when I am Time-outrun,
As you did: Take me, and have done,
Inexorable, insatiate one!

Note MS has in pencil '[Sent to Macmillan 23.3.24 for American period[?]]'

843 *The Son's Portrait*

I WALKED the streets of a market town,
　And came to a lumber-shop,
Which I had known ere I met the frown
　　Of fate and fortune,
　And habit led me to stop.

In burrowing mid this chattel and that,
　High, low, or edgewise thrown,
I lit upon something lying flat –
　　A fly-flecked portrait,
　Framed. 'Twas my dead son's own.

'That photo? . . . A lady – I know not whence –
　Sold it me, Ma'am, one day,
With more. You can have it for eighteenpence:
　　The picture's nothing;
　It's but for the frame you pay.'

He had given it her in their heyday shine,
　When she wedded him, long her wooer:
And then he was sent to the front-trench-line,
　　And fell there fighting;
　And she took a new bridegroom to her.

I bought the gift she had held so light,
　And *buried it* – as 'twere he. –
Well, well! Such things are trifling, quite,
　　But when one's lonely
　How cruel they can be!

The Son's Portrait
17 wooer:] wooer; [?] MS
18 front-trench-line] front-trenchline WE: [WW, PE have line break]

844 Lying Awake

YOU, Morningtide Star, now are steady-eyed, over the east,
    I know it as if I saw you;
You, Beeches, engrave on the sky your thin twigs, even the least;
    Had I paper and pencil I'd draw you.

You, Meadow, are white with your counterpane cover of dew,
    I see it as if I were there;
You, Churchyard, are lightening faint from the shade of the yew,
    The names creeping out everywhere.

EXTRA PRINTING:
The Saturday Review, 3 Dec 1927, p. 769 = SR

Note MS has in pencil '[Copy sent to Saturday Review 23 Nov. 1927]'

845 The Lady in the Furs

'I'M a lofty lovely woman,'
    Says the lady in the furs,
In the glance she throws around her
    On the poorer dames and sirs:
'This robe, that cost three figures,
    Yes, is mine,' her nod avers.

'True, my money did not buy it,
    But my husband's, from the trade;
And they, they only got it
    From things feeble and afraid
By murdering them in ambush
    With a cunning engine's aid.

'True, my hands, too, did not shape it
    To the pretty cut you see,
But the hands of midnight workers
    Who are strangers quite to me:
It was fitted, too, by dressers
    Ranged around me toilsomely.

EXTRA PRINTINGS:
(1) *The Saturday Review*, 4 Dec 1926, p. 669 = SR
(2) *The Daily Telegraph*, 26 July 1928 = DT

Note MS has in pencil 'Sent to Ed of Saturday Review 22 Nov. 1926'

TITLE:
The Lady in the Christmas Furs SR

Lying Awake
1 steady-eyed,] steady-eyed SR
4 paper and pencil] pencil and paper SR
6 there;] there: SR

'But I am a lovely lady,
Though sneerers say I shine
By robbing Nature's children
Of apparel not mine,
And that I am but a broom-stick,
Like a scarecrow's wooden spine.'

1925

MANUSCRIPT:
The MS of this poem is missing from the bound-up volume in the Library of The Queen's College, Oxford, and is now owned by Mr Frederick B. Adams, Jnr. Permission to see and check this MS has been refused

EXTRA PRINTING:
The Daily Telegraph, 29 March 1928 = DT

846 Childhood among the Ferns

I SAT one sprinkling day upon the lea,
Where tall-stemmed ferns spread out luxuriantly,
And nothing but those tall ferns sheltered me.

The rain gained strength, and damped each lopping frond,
Ran down their stalks beside me and beyond,
And shaped slow-creeping rivulets as I conned,

With pride, my spray-roofed house. And though anon
Some drops pierced its green rafters, I sat on,
Making pretence I was not rained upon.

The sun then burst, and brought forth a sweet breath
From the limp ferns as they dried underneath:
I said: 'I could live on here thus till death;'

And queried in the green rays as I sate:
'Why should I have to grow to man's estate,
And this afar-noised World perambulate?'

847 A Countenance

HER laugh was not in the middle of her face quite,
As a gay laugh springs,
It was plain she was anxious about some things
I could not trace quite.

The Lady in the Furs
1925] Not in DT, SR

Childhood among the Ferns
11 underneath:] underneath; DT

A Countenance
4–5 No stanza break

Her curls were like fir-cones – piled up, brown –
   Or rather like tight-tied sheaves:
It seemed they could never be taken down. . . .

And her lips were too full, some might say:
I did not think so. Anyway,
The shadow her lower one would cast
Was green in hue whenever she passed
      Bright sun on midsummer leaves.
Alas, I knew not much of her,
And lost all sight and touch of her!

If otherwise, should I have minded
The shy laugh not in the middle of her mouth quite,
And would my kisses have died of drouth quite
      As love became unblinded?

1884

848 A Poet's Thought

EXTRA MANUSCRIPT:
In the Dorset County Museum = DCM

IT sprang up out of him in the dark,
And took on the lightness of a lark:
It went from his chamber along the city strand,
Lingered awhile, then leapt all over the land.

It came back maimed and mangled. And the poet
When he beheld his offspring did not know it:
Yea, verily, since its birth Time's tongue had tossed to him
Such travesties that his old thought was lost to him.

849 Silences

THERE is the silence of a copse or croft
         When the wind sinks dumb,
         And of a belfry-loft
When the tenor after tolling stops its hum.

A Countenance
7 down. . . .] down. . . . . MS
10 lower] bottom MS
18] As I slowly grew unblinded? MS *before revision*

A Poet's Thought
7–8] Since it had taken form, Time's tongue had brought to him/So many Nays that his old Yea was nought to him.
DCM *before revision*

And there's the silence of a lonely pond
Where a man was drowned,
Nor nigh nor yond
A newt, frog, toad, to make the merest sound.

But the rapt silence of an empty house
Where oneself was born,
Dwelt, held carouse
With friends, is of all silences most forlorn!

Past are remembered songs and music-strains
Once audible there:
Roof, rafters, panes
Look absent-thoughted, tranced, or locked in prayer.

It seems no power on earth can waken it
Or rouse its rooms,
Or its past permit
The present to stir a torpor like a tomb's.

850 I Watched a Blackbird

EXTRA PRINTING:
The Daily Telegraph, 2 July 1928.
There are no variants

TITLE:
'I watched a blackbird' MS

I WATCHED a blackbird on a budding sycamore
One Easter Day, when sap was stirring twigs to the core;
I saw his tongue, and crocus-coloured bill
Parting and closing as he turned his trill;
Then he flew down, seized on a stem of hay,
And upped to where his building scheme was under way,
As if so sure a nest were never shaped on spray.

851 A Nightmare, and the Next Thing

TITLE:
A Nightmare, and the next Thing MS

ON this decline of Christmas Day
The empty street is fogged and blurred:
The house-fronts all seem backwise turned
As if the outer world were spurned:

Voices and songs within are heard,
Whence red rays gleam when fires are stirred,
Upon this nightmare Christmas Day.

The lamps, just lit, begin to outloom
Like dandelion-globes in the gloom;
The stonework, shop-signs, doors, look bald;
Curious crude details seem installed,
And show themselves in their degrees
As they were personalities
Never discerned when the street was bustling
With vehicles, and farmers hustling.

Three clammy casuals wend their way
To the Union House. I hear one say:
'Jimmy, this is a treat! Hay-hay!'

Six laughing mouths, six rows of teeth,
Six radiant pairs of eyes, beneath
Six yellow hats, looking out at the back
Of a waggonette on its slowed-down track
Up the steep street to some gay dance,
Suddenly interrupt my glance.

They do not see a gray nightmare
Astride the day, or anywhere.

852 To a Tree in London

(Clement's Inn)

HERE you stay
Night and day,
Never, never going away!

Do you ache
When we take
Holiday for our health's sake?

A Nightmare, and the Next Thing
15–16 Stanza break in MS, WWA, WE: page turn in WW, PE: no break in CP4

To a Tree in London
3 Never,] Never MS

Wish for feet
When the heat
Scalds you in the brick-built street,

That you might
Climb the height
Where your ancestry saw light,

Find a brook
In some nook
There to purge your swarthy look?

No. You read
Trees to need
Smoke like earth whereon to feed....

Have no sense
That far hence
Air is sweet in a blue immense,

Thus, black, blind,
You have opined
Nothing of your brightest kind;

Never seen
Miles of green,
Smelt the landscape's sweet serene.

192–

EXTRA MANUSCRIPT:
It has not been possible to trace the MS once in the possession of Mrs St John Hornby

TITLE:
The Thrown Elm and She MS *before revision*

853 The Felled Elm and She

WHEN you put on that inmost ring
She, like you, was a little thing:
When your circles reached their fourth,
Scarce she knew life's south from north:
When your year-zones counted twenty
She had fond admirers plenty:
When you'd grown your twenty-second
She and I were lovers reckoned:

To a Tree in London
19–21 A late addition to MS. The pencilled workings provide variants of 'expands to a' for 'is sweet in', and 'light intense' for 'a blue immense'

The Felled Elm and She
7 twenty-second] twentysecond MS [possibly two words]
8–9 No stanza break

When you numbered twenty-three
She went everywhere with me:
When you, at your fortieth line,
Showed decay, she seemed to pine:
When you were quite hollow within
She was felled – mere bone and skin:
You too, lacking strength to grow
Further trunk-rings, were laid low,
Matching her; both unaware
That your lives formed such a pair.

854 He Did Not Know Me

(Woman's Sorrow Song)

HE said: 'I do not know you;
You are not she who came
And made my heart grow tame?'
I laughed: 'The same!'

Still said he: 'I don't know you.'
'But I am your Love!' laughed I:
'Yours – faithful ever – till I die,
And pulseless lie!'

Yet he said: 'I don't know you.'
Freakful, I went away,
And met pale Time, with 'Pray,
What means his Nay?'

Said Time: 'He does not know you
In your mask of Comedy.'
'But,' said I, 'that I have chosen to be:
Tragedy he.'

'True; hence he did not know you.'
'But him I could recognize?'
'Yea. Tragedy is true guise,
Comedy lies.'

EXTRA MANUSCRIPT:
The present whereabouts of the MS once in the possession of Sir Newman Flower and sold at Sotheby's on 12 March 1968 are unknown. It has been checked from the facsimile in *English Poetical Autographs* ed. Desmond Flower and A. N. L. Munby (London, 1938), plate 38 = EPA

EXTRA PRINTING:
The Daily Telegraph, 17 May 1928 = DT

INDENTATION:
EPA, DT have:
1 = ll. 1, 2, 3 }
2 = l. 4 } and so throughout

TITLE:
He did not know me MS, EPA
(*Woman's* . . .)] Not in EPA

Note EPA has '[best]' written top right

The Felled Elm and She
9 twenty-three] twentythree MS [possibly two words]

He Did Not Know Me
6 Love!' laughed] Love,' said EPA
7 ever] not in EPA
8 lie!] lie. EPA
10 Freakful] Soul-sunk EPA
11 pale] grey EPA
12 Nay] nay EPA
14 of] as EPA
15 'But,' said I, 'that] – 'But that EPA
15 'But] – 'But MS, WWA
15 that] That MS
15 be:] be; EPA
17 'True] – 'True MS, WWA: – 'And EPA
18 'But] – 'But MS, EPA, WWA
19 'Yea] – 'Yea MS, EPA, WWA

EXTRA MANUSCRIPT:
It has not been possible to trace the rough draft of the last three stanzas once in the possession of Sir Sydney Cockerell

EXTRA PRINTING:
The Daily Telegraph, 22 March 1928 = DT

855 So Various

YOU may have met a man – quite young –
A brisk-eyed youth, and highly strung:
One whose desires
And inner fires
Moved him as wires.

And you may have met one stiff and old,
If not in years; of manner cold;
Who seemed as stone,
And never had known
Of mirth or moan.

And there may have crossed your path a lover,
In whose clear depths you could discover
A staunch, robust,
And tender trust,
Through storm and gust.

And you may have also known one fickle,
Whose fancies changed as the silver sickle
Of yonder moon,
Which shapes so soon
To demilune!

You entertained a person once
Whom you internally deemed a dunce: –
As he sat in view
Just facing you
You saw him through.

You came to know a learned seer
Of whom you read the surface mere:
Your soul quite sank;
Brain of such rank
Dubbed yours a blank.

So Various
22 dunce: –] dunce: DT

Anon you quizzed a man of sadness,
Who never could have known true gladness:
Just for a whim
You pitied him
In his sore trim.

You journeyed with a man so glad
You never could conceive him sad:
He proved to be
Indubitably
Good company.

You lit on an unadventurous slow man,
Who, said you, need be feared by no man;
That his slack deeds
And sloth must needs
Produce but weeds.

A man of enterprise, shrewd and swift,
Who never suffered affairs to drift,
You eyed for a time
Just in his prime,
And judged he might climb.

You smoked beside one who forgot
All that you said, or grasped it not.
Quite a poor thing,
Not worth a sting
By satirizing!

Next year you nearly lost for ever
Goodwill from one who forgot slights never;
And, with unease,
Felt you must seize
Occasion to please. . . .

Now. . . . All these specimens of man,
So various in their pith and plan,
Curious to say
Were *one* man. Yea,
I was all they.

So Various
32 gladness:] gladness. MS, WWA: gladness DT, WW, PE, WE
60 please. . . .] please . . . MS
61 Now. . . .] Now. . . . . MS

856 A Self-Glamourer

TITLE:
A Self-glamourer MS

MY little happiness,
How much I have made of it! –
As if I had been not less
Than a queen, to be straight obeyed of it.
'Life, be fairer far,'
I said, 'than you are.'

So I counted my springtime-day's
Dream of futurity
Enringed with golden rays
To be quite a summer surety;
And my trustful daring undoubt
Brought it about!

Events all human-wrought
Had look of divinity,
And what I foreframed in thought
Grew substanced, by force of affinity:
Visions to verities came,
Seen as the same.

My years in trusting spent
Make to shape towardly,
And fate and accident
Behave not perversely or frowardly.
Shall, then, Life's winter snow
To me be so?

857 The Dead Bastard

EXTRA PRINTING:
The Daily Telegraph, 7 Sept 1928.
There are no variants

TITLE:
The Bastard MS *before revision*

MANY and many a time I thought,
'Would my child were in its grave!'
Such the trouble and shame it brought.

The Dead Bastard
3–4 Stanza break in all editions

Now 'tis there. And now I'd brave
Opinion's worst, in word or act,
To have that child alive; yes, slave

To dress and flaunt it to attract;
Show it the gossips brazenly,
And let as nothing be the fact
That never its father married me.

858 The Clasped Skeletons

Surmised Date 1800 B.C.

(*In an Ancient British barrow near the writer's house*)

O WHY did we uncover to view
So closely clasped a pair?
Your chalky bedclothes over you,
This long time here!

Ere Paris lay with Helena –
The poets' dearest dear –
Ere David bedded Bathsheba
You two were bedded here.

Aye, even before the beauteous Jael
Bade Sisera doff his gear
And lie in her tent; then drove the nail,
You two lay here.

Wicked Aholah, in her youth,
Colled loves from far and near
Until they slew her without ruth;
But you had long colled here.

Aspasia lay with Pericles,
And Philip's son found cheer
At eves in lying on Thais' knees
While you lay here.

EXTRA MANUSCRIPT:
In the Dorset County Museum = DCM
[This MS shows that the poem was previously written with 'there' as the final word in l. 4 of each stanza, and with l. 2 rhyming with it. But a substantial revision has taken place with 'here' substituted for 'there' throughout, and 'there' has not always been deleted]

EXTRA PRINTING:
The Daily Telegraph, 2 Aug 1928 = DT

INDENTATION:
MS, DCM have:
1 = ll. 1, 3
2 = l. 2
3 = l. 4
} Stanzas 1, 3, 5, 7, 9, 11

1 = ll. 1, 3
2 = ll. 2, 4
} Stanzas 2, 4, 6, 8, 10

The Clasped Skeletons
6] The world's so famous Fair – DCM *before revision*
6 dear] Dear DCM, DT, WWA
10] Won Sisera by a snare DCM *before revision* ['by a snare' remains undeleted]
11] To lie with her; then drove a nail; DCM *before revision*
14] Colled lovers and to spare, DCM *before revision*
14 loves] Loves MS, DCM, DT
17 Pericles,] Pericles; DCM
18] And Philip's conquering heir (son, wardrear,) DCM
19] Much loved to lie on Thais' knees DCM

Cleopatra with Antony,
   Resigned to dalliance sheer,
Lay, fatuous he, insatiate she,
      Long after you'd lain here.

Pilate by Procula his wife
   Lay tossing at her tear
Of pleading for an innocent life;
      You tossed not here.

Ages before Monk Abélard
   Gained tender Héloïse' ear,
And loved and lay with her till scarred,
      Had you lain loving here.

So long, beyond chronology,
   Lovers in death as 'twere,
So long in placid dignity
      Have you lain here!

Yet what is length of time? But dream!
   Once breathed this atmosphere
Those fossils near you, met the gleam
      Of day as you did here;

But so far earlier theirs beside
   Your life-span and career,
That they might style of yestertide
      Your coming here!

859 *In the Marquee*

IT was near last century's ending,
   And, though not much to rate
In a world of getting and spending,
      To her it was great.

In the Marquee

EXTRA MANUSCRIPTS:
(1) In the Dorset County Museum [stanzas 1–5 only] = DCM
(2) In the Miriam Lutcher Stark Library of the University of Texas = UT

EXTRA PRINTING:
The Daily Telegraph, 16 July 1928 = DT

INDENTATION:
There is some difficulty in interpreting the indentation of UT because of the tendency of Hardy's writing to drift right, but it seems almost certain that it was intended to be:
1 = ll. 1, 3 } and so throughout
2 = ll. 2, 4 }

The Clasped Skeletons
21 Antony,] Antony DCM
22] (Who all for love could dare) DCM *before revision*
22 sheer,] sheer DCM
24 you'd lain] you lay DCM
26] Lay sleepless at her prayer DCM *before revision*
26 tear] tears DT
27 Of pleading for] To him to save DCM *before revision*
27 Of] In DCM
28] But you slept there. DCM *before revision*
30] Of Héloise grew aware, DCM *before revision*
33 So] – So DCM
35 long] long, DCM
38] Once moved in earth and air DCM *before revision*
42] Your day and what it bare, DCM *before revision*

In the Marquee
1–4] It was in the century vanished/And, if what none would rate/To be much as things are reckoned,/To her it was great UT [A late addition]
1 ending,] ending DT
4 great.] great. . . . DCM

The scene was a London suburb
On a night of summer weather,
And the villas had back gardens
Running together.

Her neighbours behind were dancing
Under a marquee;
Two violoncellos played there,
And violins three.

She had not been invited,
Although her lover was;
She lay beside her husband,
Perplexed at the cause.

Sweet after sweet quadrille rang:
Absence made her weep;
The tears dried on her eyelids
As she fell asleep.

She dreamt she was whirling with him
In this dance upon the green
To which she was not invited
Though her lover had been.

All night she danced as he clasped her –
That is, in the happy dream
The music kept her dreaming
Till the first daybeam.

'O damn those noisy fiddles!'
Her husband said as he turned:
'Close to a neighbour's bedroom:
I'd like them burned!'

At intervals thus all night-long
Her husband swore. But she
Slept on, and danced in the loved arms,
Under the marquee.

In the Marquee
5–8 Not in UT: a late addition to DCM
9] Behind her house they were dancing UT
17 rang:] rang; DCM, UT
18 weep;] weep: UT: weep! DT
28 Till] Till near UT [But 'near' ringed as if to be deleted]
30 turned:] turned. UT
33 all] Not in UT
35 arms,] arms UT

Next day she found that her lover,
Though asked, had gone elsewhere,
And that she had possessed him in absence
More than if there.

EXTRA MANUSCRIPT:
In the Dorset County Museum = DCM

860 *After the Burial*

THE family had buried him,
Their bread-bringer, their best:
They had returned to the house, whose hush a dim
Vague vacancy expressed.

There sat his sons, mute, rigid-faced,
His daughters, strained, red-eyed,
His wife, whose wan, worn features, vigil-traced,
Bent over him when he died.

At once a peal bursts from the bells
Of a large tall tower hard by:
Along the street the jocund clangour swells,
And upward to the sky.

Probably it was a wedding-peal,
Or possibly for a birth,
Or townsman knighted for political zeal,
This resonant mark of mirth.

The mourners, heavy-browed, sat on
Motionless. Well they heard,
They could not help it; nevertheless thereon
Spoke not a single word,

Nor window did they close, to numb
The bells' insistent calls
Of joy; but suffered the harassing din to come
And penetrate their souls.

In the Marquee
37 lover,] lover UT
39 possessed him] UT seems to offer 'enjoyed' as an alternative

After the Burial
2 bread-bringer] breadbringer DCM
7 wan,] wan DCM
9 bursts] burst DCM
10 large tall tower] tower that rose DCM
10 by:] by; [?] DCM
17 heavy-browed] heavy browed DCM
19 it;] it: [?] DCM
21 numb] dumb DCM

861 *The Mongrel*

EXTRA PRINTING:
The Daily Telegraph, 25 June 1928 = DT

In Havenpool Harbour the ebb was strong,
And a man with a dog drew near and hung,
And taxpaying day was coming along,
    So the mongrel had to be drowned.
The man threw a stick from the paved wharf-side
Into the midst of the ebbing tide,
And the dog jumped after with ardent pride
    To bring the stick aground.

But no: the steady suck of the flood
To seaward needed, to be withstood,
More than the strength of mongrelhood
    To fight its treacherous trend.
So, swimming for life with desperate will,
The struggler with all his natant skill
Kept buoyant in front of his master, still
    There standing to wait the end.

The loving eyes of the dog inclined
To the man he held as a god enshrined,
With no suspicion in his mind
    That this had all been meant.
Till the effort not to drift from shore
Of his little legs grew slower and slower,
And, the tide still outing with brookless power,
    Outward the dog, too, went.

Just ere his sinking what does one see
Break on the face of that devotee?
A wakening to the treachery
    He had loved with love so blind?
The faith that had shone in that mongrel's eye
That his owner would save him by and by
Turned to much like a curse as he sank to die,
    And a loathing of mankind.

The Mongrel
13 will,] will DT
15 master,] master CP4

EXTRA PRINTING:
The Daily Telegraph, 21 May 1928 = DT

862 *Concerning Agnes*

I AM stopped from hoping what I have hoped before –
Yes, many a time! –
To dance with that fair woman yet once more
As in the prime
Of August, when the wide-faced moon looked through
The boughs at the faery lamps of the Larmer Avenue.

I could not, though I should wish, have over again
That old romance,
And sit apart in the shade as we sat then
After the dance
The while I held her hand, and, to the booms
Of contrabassos, feet still pulsed from the distant rooms.

I could not. And you do not ask me why.
Hence you infer
That what may chance to the fairest under the sky
Has chanced to her.
Yes. She lies white, straight, features marble-keen,
Unapproachable, mute, in a nook I have never seen.

There she may rest like some vague goddess, shaped
As out of snow;
Say Aphrodite sleeping; or bedraped
Like Kalupso;
Or Amphitrite stretched on the Mid-sea swell,
Or one of the Nine grown stiff from thought. I cannot tell!

863 *Henley Regatta*

SHE looks from the window: still it pours down direly,
And the avenue drips. She cannot go, she fears;
And the Regatta will be spoilt entirely;
And she sheds half-crazed tears.

Concerning Agnes
24 tell!] tell. DT

Regatta Day and rain come on together
Again, years after. Gutters trickle loud;
But Nancy cares not. She knows nought of weather,
    Or of the Henley crowd:

She's a Regatta quite her own. Inanely
She laughs in the asylum as she floats
Within a water-tub, which she calls 'Henley',
    Her little paper boats.

864 *An Evening in Galilee*

SHE looks far west towards Carmel, shading her eyes with her hand,
And she then looks east to the Jordan, and the smooth Tiberias' strand.
'Is my son mad?' she asks; and never an answer has she,
Save from herself, aghast at the possibility.
'He professes as his firm faiths things far too grotesque to be true,
And his vesture is odd – too careless for one of his fair young hue! . . .

'He lays down doctrines as if he were old – aye, fifty at least:
In the Temple he terrified me, opposing the very High-Priest!
Why did he say to me, "Woman, what have I to do with thee?"
O it cuts to the heart that a child of mine thus spoke to me!
And he said, too, "Who is my mother?" – when he knows so very well.
He might have said, "Who is my father?" – and I'd found it hard to tell!
That no one knows but Joseph and – one other, nor ever will;
One who'll not see me again. . . . How it chanced! – I dreaming no ill! . . .

'Would he'd not mix with the lowest folk – like those fishermen –
The while so capable, culling new knowledge, beyond our ken! . . .
That woman of no good character, ever following him,
Adores him if I mistake not: his wish of her is but a whim
Of his madness, it may be, outmarking his lack of coherency;
After his "Keep the Commandments!" to smile upon such as she!
It is just what all those do who are wandering in their wit.
I don't know – dare not say – what harm may grow from it.

An Evening in Galilee
6 hue! . . .] hue! . . . . MS
10–11 Stanza break in WE: page turn in WW, PE: no break in MS, WWA, CP4
14 again. . . .] again. . . . . MS
14 ill! . . .] ill! . . . . MS
16 ken! . . .] ken! . . . . MS
18 Adores] She loves MS *before revision*
22–3 No stanza break

O a mad son is a terrible thing; it even may lead
To arrest, and death! . . . And how he can preach, expound, and read!

'Here comes my husband. Shall I unveil him this tragedy-brink?
No. He has nightmares enough. I'll pray, and think, and think.' . . .
She remembers she's never put on any pot for his evening meal,
And pondering a plea looks vaguely to south of her – towards Jezreel.

865 The Brother

O KNOW you what I have done
To avenge our sister? She,
I thought, was wantoned with
By a man of levity:

And I lay in wait all day,
All day did I wait for him,
And dogged him to Bollard Head
When twilight dwindled dim,

And hurled him over the edge
And heard him fall below:
O would I were lying with him,
For the truth I did not know!

'O where's my husband?' she asked,
As evening wore away:
'Best you had one, forsooth,
But never had you!' I say.

'Yes, but I have!' says she,
'My Love made it up with me,
And we churched it yesterday
And mean to live happily.'

And now I go in haste
To the Head, before she's aware,
To join him in death for the wrong
I've done them both out there!

An Evening in Galilee
24–5 MS, WWA, WE have stanza break: WW, PE have page turn: CP4 has no break
24 death! . . .] death! . . . . MS
26 think.' . . .] think.' . . . . MS

866 We Field-Women

EXTRA MANUSCRIPT:
It has not been possible to trace the MS once in the Bliss Collection

How it rained
When we worked at Flintcomb-Ash,
And could not stand upon the hill
Trimming swedes for the slicing-mill.
The wet washed through us – plash, plash, plash:
How it rained!

How it snowed
When we crossed from Flintcomb-Ash
To the Great Barn for drawing reed,
Since we could nowise chop a swede. –
Flakes in each doorway and casement-sash:
How it snowed!

How it shone
When we went from Flintcomb-Ash
To start at dairywork once more
In the laughing meads, with cows three-score,
And pails, and songs, and love – too rash:
How it shone!

867 A Practical Woman

'O WHO'LL get me a healthy child: –
I should prefer a son –
Seven have I had in thirteen years,
Sickly every one!

'Three mope about as feeble shapes;
Weak; white; they'll be no good.
One came deformed; an idiot next;
And two are crass as wood.

We Field-Women
10 Since] Since, WE
16 three-score] threescore MS

'I purpose one not only sound
    In flesh, but bright in mind:
And duly for producing him
    A means I've now to find.'

She went away. She disappeared,
    Years, years. Then back she came:
In her hand was a blooming boy
    Mentally and in frame.

'I found a father at last who'd suit
    The purpose in my head,
And used him till he'd done his job,'
    Was all thereon she said.

EXTRA PRINTING:
The Daily Telegraph, 12 April 1928.
There are no variants

868 Squire Hooper

HOOPER was ninety. One September dawn
    He sent a messenger
For his physician, who asked thereupon
    What ailed the sufferer
Which he might circumvent, and promptly bid begone.

'Doctor, I summoned you,' the squire replied –
    'Pooh-pooh me though you may –
To ask what's happened to me – burst inside,
    It seems – not much, I'd say –
But awkward with a house-full here for a shoot to-day.'

And he described the symptoms. With bent head
    The listener looked grave.
'H'm. . . . *You're a dead man in six hours,*' he said. –
    'I speak out, since you are brave –
And best 'tis you should know, that last things may be sped.'

'Right,' said the squire. 'And now comes – what to do?
    One thing: on no account
Must I now spoil the sport I've asked them to –
    My guests are paramount –
They must scour scrub and stubble; and big bags bring as due.'

Squire Hooper
13 H'm. . . .] H'm. . . . MS

He downed to breakfast, and bespoke his guests: –
'I find I have to go
An unexpected journey, and it rests
With you, my friends, to show
The shoot can go off gaily, whether I'm there or no.'

Thus blandly spoke he; and to the fields they went,
And Hooper up the stair.
They had a glorious day; and stiff and spent
Returned as dusk drew near. –
'Gentlemen,' said the doctor, 'he's not back as meant,

To his deep regret!' – So they took leave, each guest
Observing: 'I dare say
Business detains him in the town: 'tis best
We should no longer stay
Just now. We'll come again anon;' and they went their way.

Meeting two men in the obscurity
Shouldering a box a thin
Cloth-covering wrapt, one sportsman cried: 'Damn me,
I thought them carrying in,
At first, a coffin; till I knew it could not be.'

869 *'A Gentleman's Second-Hand Suit'*

EXTRA MANUSCRIPT:
In the Dorset County Museum = DCM

EXTRA PRINTING:
Harper's Monthly Magazine (New York), March 1928, p. [443] = H

TITLE:
'A Gentleman's second-hand suit' MS
A gentleman's second-hand suit DCM

Note MS has in pencil 'Harper's Magazine through Mr [?] Wells Dec – 1927'

HERE it is hanging in the sun
By the pawn-shop door,
A dress-suit – all its revels done
Of heretofore.
Long drilled to the waltzers' swing and sway,
As its tokens show:
What it has seen, what it could say
If it did but know!

The sleeve bears still a print of powder
Rubbed from her arms
When she warmed up as the notes swelled louder
And livened her charms –

'A Gentleman's Second-Hand Suit'
2 pawn-shop] pawnshop H
3 revels] DCM has 'gay days' as alternative
5] Well used to the dancers' spin and sway, DCM
5 Long drilled] Long-drilled H
6 its] Not in DCM
6 show:] show; DCM
9 a print of powder] some print ('old puffs' given as alternative) of powder DCM
10 arms] arms, DCM

Or rather theirs, for beauties many
Leant there, no doubt,
Leaving these tell-tale traces when he
Spun them about.

Its cut seems rather in bygone style
On looking close,
So it mayn't have bent it for some while
To the dancing pose:
Anyhow, often within its clasp
Fair partners hung,
Assenting to the wearer's grasp
With soft sweet tongue.

Where is, alas, the gentleman
Who wore this suit?
And where are his ladies? Tell none can:
Gossip is mute.
Some of them may forget him quite
Who smudged his sleeve,
Some think of a wild and whirling night
With him, and grieve.

870 *We Say We Shall Not Meet*

EXTRA MANUSCRIPT:
In the Library of King's College, Cambridge = KC

EXTRA PRINTING:
The Daily Telegraph, 11 Sept 1928.
There are no variants

TITLE:
'We say we shall not meet' MS
No title in KC

WE say we shall not meet
Again beneath this sky,
And turn with leaden feet,
Murmuring 'Good-bye!'

But laugh at how we rued
Our former time's adieu
When those who went for good
Are met anew.

We talk in lightest vein
On trifles talked before,
And part to meet again,
But meet no more.

'A Gentleman's Second-Hand Suit'
14 Leant] Pressed DCM *before revision*
14 there,] there H
15 tell-tale] telltale H
16 Spun] Whirled DCM
18 close,] close DCM
19 bent] lent DCM ['bent' has been deleted]
21–4] Anyhow, one time within its hold/Were casual guests,/Who gave them to the gentle souled/And panting breasts. DCM *before revision*
27 are] Not in DCM
30 smudged] DCM gives 'brushed' as alternative
32 him,] him H

We Say We Shall Not Meet
2 beneath] under KC
3 leaden] MS has 'heavy' in ink, and 'leaden' in pencil
3 leaden feet,] heavy feet KC
4 Murmuring] Murmuring, KC
6 former time's] Could be one word in KC
6 adieu] adieu, KC
10 talked before] KC has as undeleted alternatives 'at the door' and 'by the score'

871 Seeing the Moon Rise

EXTRA MANUSCRIPT:
In the Dorset County Museum = DCM

TITLE:
At Moonrise, or 'We used to go' DCM

INDENTATION:
DCM has l. 6 indented farther right

WE used to go to Froom-hill Barrow
        To see the round moon rise
        Into the heath-rimmed skies,
Trudging thither by plough and harrow
Up the pathway, steep and narrow,
        Singing a song.
Now we do not go there. Why?
        Zest burns not so high!

Latterly we've only conned her
        With a passing glance
        From window or door by chance,
Hoping to go again, high yonder,
As we used, and gaze, and ponder,
        Singing a song.
Thitherward we do not go:
        Feet once quick are slow!

August 1927

872 Song to Aurore

EXTRA PRINTING:
The Daily Telegraph, 3 May 1928.
There are no variants

WE'LL not begin again to love,
    It only leads to pain;
The fire we now are master of
    Has seared us not in vain.
Any new step of yours I'm fain
    To hear of from afar,
And even in such may find a gain
    While lodged not where you are.

No: that must not be done anew
    Which has been done before;
I scarce could bear to seek, or view,
    Or clasp you any more!

Seeing the Moon Rise
2 the round moon] Diana DCM [MS has 'Diana' in ink, and 'the round moon' in pencil]
5 pathway,] pathway – DCM
8] Zest fails – tends to die! DCM [in pencil, while 'Zest burns not so high!' is in ink and has been *deleted*]
12 yonder,] yonder DCM
16 slow!] slow. DCM
August 1927] Not in DCM

Life is a labour, death is sore,
And lonely living wrings;
But go your courses, Sweet Aurore,
Kisses are caresome things!

873 He Never Expected Much

[*or*]

A Consideration

[*A reflection*] *on My Eighty-Sixth Birthday*

WELL, World, you have kept faith with me,
Kept faith with me;
Upon the whole you have proved to be
Much as you said you were.
Since as a child I used to lie
Upon the leaze and watch the sky,
Never, I own, expected I
That life would all be fair.

'Twas then you said, and since have said,
Times since have said,
In that mysterious voice you shed
From clouds and hills around:
'Many have loved me desperately,
Many with smooth serenity,
While some have shown contempt of me
Till they dropped underground.

'I do not promise overmuch,
Child; overmuch;
Just neutral-tinted haps and such,'
You said to minds like mine.
Wise warning for your credit's sake!
Which I for one failed not to take,
And hence could stem such strain and ache
As each year might assign.

EXTRA MANUSCRIPT:
In the British Library = BL

EXTRA PRINTING:
The Daily Telegraph, 19 March 1928.
There are no variants apart from the omission of 'A Consideration' in the title

TITLE:
He never expected much MS
A Reconsideration/On my eighty sixth birthday BL

INDENTATION:
CP4 had ll. 2, 10, 18 lined up with ll. 4, 8, but MS and all earlier editions were as printed here

Song to Aurore
15 Sweet] sweet MS, WW, WWA, PE, WE
16 caresome] perilous MS *before revision*

He Never Expected Much
2 Kept] Yes, BL
8] A smooth life-thoroughfare. BL *before revision*
23–4] And hence could cope with strain and ache/In each year's twist and twine. BL *before revision*
24 might] MS has 'might' in ink, and 'would' in pencil

874 *Standing by the Mantelpiece*

(*H.M.M., 1873*)

THIS candle-wax is shaping to a shroud
To-night. (They call it that, as you may know) –
By touching it the claimant is avowed,
And hence I press it with my finger – so.

To-night. To me twice night, that should have been
The radiance of the midmost tick of noon,
And close around me wintertime is seen
That might have shone the veriest day of June!

But since all's lost, and nothing really lies
Above but shade, and shadier shade below,
Let me make clear, before one of us dies,
My mind to yours, just now embittered so.

Since you agreed, unurged and full-advised,
And let warmth grow without discouragement,
Why do you bear you now as if surprised,
When what has come was clearly consequent?

Since you have spoken, and finality
Closes around, and my last movements loom,
I say no more: the rest must wait till we
Are face to face again, yonside the tomb.

And let the candle-wax thus mould a shape
Whose meaning now, if hid before, you know,
And how by touch one present claims its drape,
And that it's I who press my finger – so.

875 *Boys Then and Now*

TITLE:
Boys then and now MS

'MORE than one cuckoo?'
And the little boy

Standing by the Mantelpiece
10 below,] below MS

Seemed to lose something
Of his spring joy.

When he'd grown up
He told his son
He'd used to think
There was only one,

Who came each year
With the trees' new trim
On purpose to please
England and him:

And his son – old already
In life and its ways –
Said yawning: 'How foolish
Boys were in those days!'

876 *That Kiss in the Dark*

EXTRA MANUSCRIPTS:
In the Miriam Lutcher Stark Library of the University of Texas there are two manuscripts = UT1, UT2

EXTRA PRINTING:
The Daily Telegraph, 13 Sept 1928.
There are no variants

TITLE:
A Kiss in the dark UT1 *before revision*

RECALL it you? –
Say you do! –
When you went out into the night,
In an impatience that would not wait,
From that lone house in the woodland spot,
And when I, thinking you had gone
For ever and ever from my sight,
Came after, printing a kiss upon
Black air
In my despair,
And my two lips lit on your cheek
As you leant silent against a gate,
Making my woman's face flush hot
At what I had done in the dark, unware
You lingered for me but would not speak:
Yes, kissed you, thinking you were not there!
Recall it you? –
Say you do!

That Kiss in the Dark
1 you? –] you? UT1, UT2
2 do! –] do, UT1
2–3 UT1 has extra line here 'Say you do!'
4 wait,] wait UT1
5] At that lorn lonely country spot (spot, UT2) UT1, UT2
11 cheek] cheek, – UT1
12 leant silent] were leaning UT1
12 gate,] gate UT1
13 hot] hot – UT1
14] All, in the dark, quite unaware UT1
15 lingered] waited UT1
17 you? –] you? UT1, UT2
18 Repeated in UT1 and becomes that MS's l. 20

877 *A Necessitarian's Epitaph*

A WORLD I did not wish to enter
Took me and poised me on my centre,
Made me grimace, and foot, and prance,
As cats on hot bricks have to dance
Strange jigs to keep them from the floor,
Till they sink down and feel no more.

878 *Burning the Holly*

EXTRA MANUSCRIPT:
In the Dorset County Museum = DCM
[The state of this MS is such that the completeness of the variants given here cannot be guaranteed]

EXTRA PRINTING:
The Daily Telegraph, 20 Aug 1928 = DT

O YOU are sad on Twelfth Night,
I notice: sad on Twelfth Night;
You are as sad on Twelfth Night
  As any that I know.

'Yes: I am sad on that night,
Doubtless I'm sad on that night:
Yes; I am sad on that night,
  For we all loved her so!'

Why are you sad on Twelfth Night,
Especially on Twelfth Night?
Why are you sad on Twelfth Night
  When wit and laughter flow?

– 'She'd been a famous dancer,
Much lured of men; a dancer.
She'd been a famous dancer,
  Facile in heel and toe. . . .

'And we were burning the holly
On Twelfth Night; the holly,
As people do: the holly,
  Ivy, and mistletoe.

Burning the Holly
5 Yes:] Yes; DCM
6] It's certain! Sad on that night; DCM
7 Yes; I am] I am as DCM
7 night,] night DCM
8] And well I may be so!' DCM
14 Much lured of men] Till latterly DCM
15 dancer,] dancer DCM
16 Facile] DCM gives 'Graceful' as an alternative
16 in] with DCM
16 toe. . . .] toe. DCM
19 do: the holly,] do – the holly – DCM

'And while it popped and crackled,
(She being our lodger), crackled;
And while it popped and crackled,
    Her face caught by the glow,

'In he walked and said to her,
In a slow voice he said to her;
Yes, walking in he said to her,
    "We sail before cock-crow."

' "Why did you not come on to me,
As promised? Yes, come on to me?
Why did you not come on to me,
    Since you had sworn to go?"

'His eyes were deep and flashing,
As flashed the holm-flames: flashing;
His eyes were deep, and flashing
    In their quick, keen upthrow.

'As if she had been ready,
Had furtively been ready;
As if she had been ready
    For his insistence – lo! –

'She clasped his arm and went with him
As his entirely: went with him.
She clasped his arm and went with him
    Into the sprinkling snow.

'We saw the prickly leaves waste
To ashes: saw the leaves waste;
The burnt-up prickly leaves waste....
    The pair had gone also.

– 'On Twelfth Night, two years after –
Yes, Twelfth Night, two years after;
On Twelfth Night, two years after,
    We sat – our spirits low –

Burning the Holly
21 crackled,] crackled DCM
22] Amid the hearth-logs: crackled: DCM
24 Her . . . by] And sputtered [?] in DCM
26 her;] her, DCM
27 her,] her DCM
29 on to me,] out to me DCM
30 on] out DCM
31 on to me,] out to me DCM
33 deep and flashing,] dark and flashing DCM
34 holm-flames: flashing;] holm-flame. Flashing, DCM
35 deep,] dark DCM
36 quick,] quick DCM
40 insistence – lo! –] insistence, lo! DCM
47 burnt-up] burning DCM
49 – 'On] On DCM
50 Yes,] Yes DCM
50 after;] after – DCM
51 after,] after DCM
52 sat –] sat, DCM
52 low –] low, DCM

'Musing, when back the door swung
Without a knock. The door swung;
Thought flew to her. The door swung,
And in she came, pale, slow;

'Against her breast a child clasped;
Close to her breast a child clasped;
She stood there with the child clasped,
Swaying it to and fro.

'Her look alone the tale told;
Quite wordless was the tale told;
Her careworn eyes the tale told
As larger they seemed to grow. . . .

'One day next spring she disappeared,
The second time she disappeared.
And that time, when she'd disappeared
Came back no more. Ah, no!

'But we still burn the holly
On Twelfth Night; burn the holly
As people do: the holly,
Ivy, and mistletoe.'

879 Suspense

EXTRA MANUSCRIPT:
In the Dorset County Museum = DCM

A CLAMMINESS hangs over all like a clout,
The fields are a water-colour washed out,
The sky at its rim leaves a chink of light,
Like the lid of a pot that will not close tight.

She is away by the groaning sea,
Strained at the heart, and waiting for me:
Between us our foe from a hid retreat
Is watching, to wither us if we meet. . . .

But it matters little, however we fare –
Whether we meet, or I get not there;
The sky will look the same thereupon,
And the wind and the sea go groaning on.

Burning the Holly
55 flew to] flashed on DCM
56 slow;] slow. DCM
57 clasped;] clasped DCM
60 Swaying] And swayed DCM
62 Quite wordless] Without words DCM
63 told] told, DCM
64] And larger seemed to grow DCM
64 grow. . . .] grow. . . . . MS
66 disappeared.] disappeared. . . . DCM
67 time,] time DCM
68 Came . . . more] DCM offers 'Came not again' as an alternative
68 no!] no!' DT
69 'But] But MS, DCM, DT
72 Ivy,] Ivy DCM
72 mistletoe.'] mistletoe. MS, DCM, DT

Suspense
2 out,] out DCM
3 rim] edge DCM
6 me:] me; DCM
8 meet. . . .] meet. DCM

EXTRA PRINTING:
The Daily Telegraph, 31 May 1928 = DT

880 The Second Visit

1 CLACK, clack, clack, went the mill-wheel as I came,
2 And she was on the bridge with the thin hand-rail,
3 And the miller at the door, and the ducks at mill-tail;
4 I come again years after, and all there seems the same.

5 And so indeed it is: the apple-tree'd old house,
6 And the deep mill-pond, and the wet wheel clacking,
7 And a woman on the bridge, and white ducks quacking,
8 And the miller at the door, powdered pale from boots to brows.

9 But it's not the same miller whom long ago I knew,
10 Nor are they the same apples, nor the same drops that dash
11 Over the wet wheel, nor the ducks below that splash,
12 Nor the woman who to fond plaints replied, 'You know I do!'

TITLE:
Our old friend Dualism MS

881 Our Old Friend Dualism

1 ALL hail to him, the Protean! A tough old chap is he:
2 Spinoza and the Monists cannot make him cease to be.
3 We pound him with our 'Truth, Sir, please!' and quite appear to still
him:
4 He laughs; holds Bergson up, and James; and swears we cannot kill
him.
5 We argue them pragmatic cheats. 'Aye,' says he. 'They're deceiving:
6 But I must live; for flamens plead I am all that's worth believing!'

1920

EXTRA PRINTING:
The Daily Telegraph, 16 April 1928.
There are no variants

882 Faithful Wilson

1 'I SAY she's handsome, by all laws
2 Of beauty, if wife ever was!'
3 Wilson insists thus, though each day
4 The years fret Fanny towards decay.

The Second Visit
4–5 No stanza break in DT
6 mill-pond] mill pond MS, WW, WWA, PE, WE
8–9 No stanza break in DT

Faithful Wilson
4–5 No stanza break

'She *was* once beauteous as a jewel,'
Hint friends; 'but Time, of course, is cruel.'
Still Wilson does not quite feel how,
Once fair, she can be different now.

Partly from Strato of Sardis

883 Gallant's Song

WHEN the maiden leaves off teasing,
Then the man may leave off pleasing:
        Yea, 'tis sign,
        Wet or fine,
She will love him without ceasing
With a love there's no appeasing.
        Is it so?
        Ha-ha. Ho!

Nov. 1868
From an old notebook

884 A Philosophical Fantasy

'Milton . . . made God argue.' – WALTER BAGEHOT

'WELL, if you wilt, then, ask me;
To answer will not task me:
I've a response, I doubt not,
And quite agree to flout not
Thy question, if of reason,
Albeit not quite in season:
A universe to marshal,
What god can give but partial
Eye to frail Earth – life-shotten
Ere long, extinct, forgotten! –
But seeing indications
That thou read'st my limitations,
And since my lack of forethought
Aggrieves thy more and more thought,
I'll hearken to thy pleading:

EXTRA MANUSCRIPT:
In the Dorset County Museum = DCM

EXTRA PRINTING:
The Fortnightly Review, 1 Jan 1927, pp. [1]–4 = FR

TITLE:
In the Matter of an Intent
A conversational Fantasy DCM

Note MS has in pencil: [Published in Fortnightly Review, slightly abridged Jan. 1927]

A Philosophical Fantasy
6 season:] season. DCM, FR
7–15] Since never my lack of forethought/ Copes with thy more and more thought./So hasten with thy pleading: DCM
9 frail Earth –] this Earth, FR
10 forgotten! –] forgotten! FR
11–12 Not in FR
13 And] But FR
14 Aggrieves] Meets not FR
15] E'en hasten with thy pleading: FR
15–16 No stanza break

Some lore may lie in heeding
Thy irregular proceeding.'

' 'Tis this *unfulfilled intention*,
O Causer, I would mention: –
Will you, in condescension
This evening, ere we've parted,
Say why you felt fainthearted,
And let your aim be thwarted,
Its glory be diminished,
Its concept stand unfinished? –
Such I ask you, Sir or Madam,
(I know no more than Adam,
Even vaguely, what your sex is, –
Though feminine I had thought you
Till seers as "Sire" besought you; –
And this my ignorance vexes
Some people not a little,
And, though not me one tittle,
It makes me sometimes choose me
Call you "It", if you'll excuse me?)'

'Call me "It" with a good conscience,
And be sure it is all nonsense
That I mind a fault of manner
In a pigmy towards his planner!
Be I, be not I, sexless,
I am in nature vexless.
– How vain must clay-carved man be
To deem such folly can be
As that freaks of my own framing
Can set my visage flaming –
Start me volleying interjections
Against my own confections,
As the Jews and others limned me,
And in fear and trembling hymned me!
Call me "but dream-projected",
I shall not be affected;
Call me "blind force persisting",

A Philosophical Fantasy
18 ' 'Tis this] 'This DCM
19] Ruler, I'm fain to mention: – DCM
19 O] O! FR
19 mention: –] mention: FR
20 you,] you DCM
22 fainthearted] faint-hearted FR
25 unfinished? –] unfinished? DCM
26 Madam,] Madam FR
28 is, –] is, DCM, FR
29–30 Not in DCM, FR
31] An ignorance that still vexes DCM, FR
32 little,] little,) DCM
33 And,] And DCM
33 tittle,] tittle DCM
35 "It"] It DCM
35 me?)'] me?' DCM
36 "It"] It DCM
40–62 Call me blind ('blind FR) force persisting, (persisting,' FR)/I shall remain unlisting;/Call me but ('but FR) dream projected, (projected,' FR)/I shall not be affected; (affected. . . . FR)/How mean (vain FR) must clay-wrought man be/To dream (deem FR) such folly can be/As that freaks of my own framing/Indifferent, and unaiming [Not in FR]/Can set my visage flaming –/Start me volleying interjections/Against my own confections,/As the Jews and others limned me,/And in fear and trembling hymned me! DCM, FR [Stanza break here in DCM, FR]

I shall remain unlisting;
(A few have done it lately,
And, maybe, err not greatly).
– Another such a vanity
In witless weak humanity
Is thinking that of those all
Through space at my disposal,
Man's shape must needs resemble
Mine, that makes zodiacs tremble!

'Continuing where we started: –
As for my aims being thwarted,
Wherefore I feel fainthearted,
Aimless am I, revealing
No heart-scope for faint feeling.
– But thy mistake I'll pardon,
And, as Adam's mentioned to me,
(Though in timeless truth there never
Was a man like him whatever),
I'll meet thee in thy garden,
As I did not him, beshrew me!
In the sun of so-called daytime –
Say, just about the Maytime
Of my next, or next, Creation?
(I love procrastination,
To use the words in thy sense,
Which have no hold on my sense)
Or at any future stray-time. –
One of thy representatives
In some later incarnation
I mean, of course, well knowing
Thy present conformation
But a unit of my tentatives,
Whereof such heaps lie blowing
As dust, where thou art going;
Yea, passed to where suns glow not,
Begrieved of those that go not,
(Though what grief is, I know not).

A Philosophical Fantasy
63–6 Not in DCM
63 As] 'As FR
64–6] Aimless am I, disparted! FR
67] 'Forsooth, then, that I'll pardon: DCM
67 – But] But FR
67 pardon,] pardon; FR
68 as] since DCM, FR
68 me,] me FR
69 Though] Though, DCM, FR
69 truth] truth, DCM, FR
71 thy] the DCM
71 garden,] garden DCM, FR
72 As] (As DCM, FR
72 me!] me!) DCM, FR
73] In the cool of a future (of so-called FR) daytime – DCM, FR
76 procrastination,] procrastination) DCM
77–8 Not in DCM
77 words] word FR
77 sense,] sense FR
78 have] hath FR
78 sense)] sense) – FR
79 at] Not in DCM, FR
79 future] passing DCM
79 stray-time. –] stray-time – DCM, FR, WWA
85 Whereof] Of which DCM
88 not,] not! FR: not CP4
89 is,] *is*, DCM: is FR
89–90 Stanza break in all editions except FR, which has page turn

'Perhaps I may inform thee,
In case I should alarm thee,
That no dramatic stories
Like ancient ones whose core is
A mass of superstition
And monkish imposition
Will mark my explanation
Of the world's sore situation
(As thou tell'st), with woes that shatter;
Though from former aions to latter
To me 'tis malleable matter
For treatment scientific
More than sensitive and specific –
Stuff without moral features,
Which I've no sense of ever,
Or of ethical endeavour,
Or of justice to Earth's creatures,
Or how Right from Wrong to sever:

'Let these be as men learn such;
For me, I don't discern such,
And – real enough I daresay –
I know them but by hearsay
As something Time hath rendered
Out of substance I engendered,
Time, too, being a condition
Beyond my recognition.
– I would add that, while unknowing
Of this justice earthward owing,
Nor explanation offering
Of what is meant by suffering,
Thereof I'm not a spurner,
Or averse to be a learner.

'To return from wordy wandering
To the question we are pondering;
Though, viewing the world in *my* mode,
I fail to see it in *thy* mode
As "unfulfilled intention",

A Philosophical Fantasy
93 Like] Like those FR
98 DCM is not clear
103 features,] features FR
104 Which] (Such DCM, FR
106 Earth's creatures,] earth's creatures,) DCM
107–8 MS, CP4 have no stanza break: WW, WWA, PE have page turn: WE has stanza break
107–9 Not in DCM, FR which have no stanza break until ll. 121–2
110–11] Which, though right enough, (enough FR) I daresay,/To me's but known by hearsay, (hearsay FR) DCM, FR
112 hath] has DCM, FR
114] Time being a definition DCM, FR
115] Quite beyond my recognition.) DCM: Beyond my recognition) . . . FR
116 – I] I DCM
117 earthward owing] earthward-owing FR
120 Thereof I'm not] Hold me not thereof DCM: I'm not thereof FR
123 are] were DCM, FR
124] Though in viewing world-work *my* way, (way FR) DCM, FR
125] I do not see it *thy* way DCM
125 in *thy* mode] *thy* way FR
126–7 No stanza break

Which is past my comprehension
Being unconscious in my doings
So largely, (whence thy rueings); –
Aye, to human tribes nor kindlessness
Nor love I've given, but mindlessness,
Which state, though far from ending,
May nevertheless be mending.

'However, I'll advise him –
Him thy scion, who will walk here
When Death hath dumbed thy talk here –
In phrase that may surprise him,
What thing it was befel me,
(A thing that my confessing
Lack of forethought helps thy guessing),
And acted to compel me
By that *purposeless propension*
Which is mine, and not intention,
Along lines of least resistance,
Or, in brief, unsensed persistence,
That saddens thy existence
To think my so-called scheming
Not that of my first dreaming.'

1920 and 1926

885 *A Question of Marriage*

EXTRA PRINTING:
The Daily Telegraph, 26 Sept 1928 = DT

'I YIELD you my whole heart, Countess,' said he;
'Come, Dear, and be queen of my studio.'
'No, sculptor. You're merely my friend,' said she:
'We dine our artists; but marry them – no.'

'Be it thus,' he replied. And his love, so strong,
He subdued as a stoic should. Anon
He wived some damsel who'd loved him long,
Of lineage noteless; and chiselled on.

A Philosophical Fantasy
127 comprehension] comprehension, DCM
129 largely,] largely FR
129 rueings); –] rueings.) DCM: rueings) – FR
130 Aye, to] Nay to DCM: Nay, to FR
131 given,] given DCM
131 mindlessness,] mindlessness DCM
133 nevertheless] even now DCM
134 'However] However DCM
138 me,] me FR
140 guessing),] guessing DCM
142 *purposeless propension*] purposeless propension DCM
144] To that line of least resistance DCM, FR
145] Which men call inconsistence, DCM: That seers call rapt persistence, FR
146–7] And saddens thy existence,/And makes thee think my scheming DCM, FR
1920 and 1926] 1925 DCM: not in FR

A Question of Marriage
3 sculptor] MS has in pencil in margin 'Why not painter?'
3 she:] she; DT

And a score years passed. As a master-mind
The world made much of his marching fame,
And his wife's little charms, with his own entwined,
Won day after day increased acclaim.

The countess-widow had closed with a mate
In rank and wealth of her own degree,
And they moved among the obscurely great
Of an order that had no novelty.

And oldening – neither with blame nor praise –
Their stately lives begot no stir,
And she saw that when death should efface her days
All men would abandon thought of her;

And said to herself full gloomily:
'Far better for me had it been to shine
The wench of a genius such as he
Than rust as the wife of a spouse like mine!'

886 The Letter's Triumph

(*A Fancy*)

EXTRA PRINTING:
The Daily Telegraph, 19 July 1928.
There are no variants

YES: I perceive it's to your Love
You are bent on sending me. That this is so
Your words and phrases prove!

And now I am folded, and start to go,
Where you, my writer, have no leave to come:
My entry none will know!

And I shall catch her eye, and dumb
She'll keep, should my unnoised arrival be
Hoped for, or troublesome.

My face she'll notice readily:
And, whether she care to meet you, or care not,
She will perforce meet me;

Take me to closet or garden-plot
And, blushing or pouting, bend her eyes quite near,
Moved much, or never a jot.

And while you wait in hope and fear,
Far from her cheeks and lips, snug I shall stay
In close communion there,

And hear her heart-beats, things she may say,
As near her naked fingers, sleeve, or glove
I lie – ha-ha! – all day.

887 A Forgotten Miniature

THERE you are in the dark,
Deep in a box
Nobody ever unlocks,
Or even turns to mark;
– Out of mind stark.

Yet there you have not been worsed
Like your sitter
By Time, the Fair's hard-hitter;
Your beauties, undispersed,
Glow as at first.

Shut in your case for years,
Never an eye
Of the many passing nigh,
Fixed on their own affairs,
Thinks what it nears!

– While you have lain in gloom,
A form forgot,
Your reign remembered not,
Much life has come to bloom
Within this room.

The Letter's Triumph
Based on an incident] MS *deleted* at end

Yea, in Time's cyclic sweep
    Unrest has ranged:
Women and men have changed:
Some you knew slumber deep;
    Some wait for sleep.

EXTRA PRINTING:
The Daily Telegraph, 4 June 1928 = DT

TITLE:
Whispered at the Church-opening MS

888 *Whispered at the Church-Opening*

IN the bran-new pulpit the bishop stands,
And gives out his text, as his gaze expands
To the people, the aisles, the roof's new frame,
And the arches, and ashlar with coloured bands.

'Why – he's the man,' says one, 'who came
To preach in my boyhood – a fashion then –
In a series of sermons to working-men
On week-day evenings, a novelty
Which brought better folk to hear and see.
They preached each one each week, by request:
Some were eloquent speakers, among the best
Of the lot being this, as all confessed.'

'I remember now. And reflection brings
Back one in especial, sincerest of all;
Whose words, though unpicked, gave the essence of things; –
And where is he now, whom I well recall?'

'Oh, he'd no touches of tactic skill:
His mind ran on charity and good will:
He's but as he was, a vicar still.'

889 *In Weatherbury Stocks*

(1850)

'I SIT here in these stocks,
And Saint-Mary's moans eleven;
The sky is dark and cold:
I would I were in heaven!

A Forgotten Miniature
21–5 Yea, since your durance there/Life has changed:/Men's hearts and hopes have changed:/One you knew slumbered deep;/Some wait for sleep. MS *during revision*

Whispered at the Church-Opening
15 things; –] things: – MS: things; DT

'What footsteps do I hear?
Ah, you do not forget,
My Sophy! O, my dear,
We may be happy yet!

'But —. Mother, is't your voice?
You who have come to me? –
It did not cross my thought:
I was thinking it was she.'

'She! Foolish simple son!
She says: "I've finished quite
With him or any one
Put in the stocks to-night."

'She's gone to Blooms-End dance,
And will not come back yet:
Her new man sees his chance,
And is teaching her to forget.

'Jim, think no other woman
To such a fellow is true
But the mother you have grieved so,
Or cares for one like you!'

890 A Placid Man's Epitaph

EXTRA PRINTING:
The Daily Telegraph, 19 April 1928 = DT

As for my life, I've led it
With fair content and credit:
It said: 'Take this.' I took it.
Said: 'Leave.' And I forsook it.
If I had done without it
None would have cared about it,
Or said: 'One has refused it
Who might have meetly used it.'

1925

In Weatherbury Stocks
7 Sophy] Celia MS *before revision*

A Placid Man's Epitaph
3 it.] it: MS, DT
4 Said:] Said; MS
7–8] MS has pencilled alternatives:

Or commented upon it
'A pity he did not don it!'

and

Or said this man has scorned it
Who well might have adorned it

891 The New Boots

'THEY are his new boots,' she pursued;
'They have not been worn at all:
They stay there hung on the wall,
And are getting as stiff as wood.
He bought them for the wet weather,
And they are of waterproof leather.'

'Why does her husband,' said I,
'Never wear those boots bought new?'
To a neighbour of hers I knew;
Who answered: 'Ah, those boots. Aye,
He bought them to wear whenever
It rained. But there they hang ever.

' "Yes," he laughed, as he hung them up,
"I've got them at last – a pair
I can walk in anywhere
Through rain and slush and slop.
For many a year I've been haunted
By thoughts of how much they were wanted."

'And she's not touched them or tried
To remove them. . . . Anyhow,
As you see them hanging now
They have hung ever since he died
The day after gaily declaring:
"Ha-ha! Now for wet wayfaring.
They're just the chaps for my wearing!" '

TITLE:
The Imaginative Maiden MS *before revision*

892 The Musing Maiden

'WHY so often, silent one,
Do you steal away alone?'
Starting, half she turned her head,
And guiltily she said: –

'When the vane points to his far town
I go upon the hog-backed down,
And think the breeze that stroked his lip
Over my own may slip.

'When he walks at close of day
I ramble on the white highway,
And think it reaches to his feet:
A meditation sweet!

'When coasters hence to London sail
I watch their puffed wings waning pale;
His window opens near the quay;
Their coming he can see.

'I go to meet the moon at night;
To mark the moon was our delight;
Up there our eyesights touch at will
If such he practise still.'

W.P.V.
October 1866 (recopied)

893 Lorna the Second

LORNA! Yes, you are sweet,
But you are not your mother,
Lorna the First, frank, feat,
Never such another! –
Love of her could smother
Griefs by day or night;
Nor could any other,
Lorna, dear and bright,
Ever so well adorn a
Mansion, coach, or cot,
Or so make men scorn a
Rival in their sight;
Even you could not!
Hence I have to mourn a
Loss ere you were born; a
Lorna!

The Musing Maiden
19 touch] touched WWA

EXTRA PRINTING:

The Daily Telegraph, 30 July 1928. There are no variants

Note. This poem derives from an earlier poem called 'The Forsaking of the Nest' which was published in *Nash's Magazine*, Feb 1912, p. 584 = NM. There is a MS of this in the Library of Congress = LC. It is given in full below:

'The hoers quit the mangel-field,/The firelight flecks the loam,/It is the minute of the hour/She named to start for home.

– 'I ('I NM) see her step forth from the town/ And leave the lamps behind,/And trot along the eastern road/Where elms stand, double-lined.

'And now she nears the branching path,/And takes the quicker way/Across the meadows where the brooks/Glide gurgling night and day.

'By now she clacks the kissing-gate (kissing gate NM)/Beneath the storm-tried trees,/ And passes to the second mead/That fringes Mellstock Leaze.

'And soon she swings the wicket next/The grey brick garden wall,/And sees the third mead stretching down/Towards the water-fall.

'When, (When NM) through the third-reached kissing-gate,/Still nearer and more near/She draws to me; and, as 'tis eight,/ She should be almost here.

'And now she should approach the door,/Unlatch it with her thumb,/And show the form I have reared and roofed –/But ah – (ah! NM) she does not come.'. . . . . (.' . . . NM)

What chanced by that third kissing-gate/When the hushed mead grew dun?/Lo – (Lo! NM) two dark figures clasped and closed/As if they were but one.

The waiting father counts the clock,/And still no footstep nighs,/For new delight has come to mock/All early filial ties! LC, NM

[The indentation of LC and NM is that of 'The Third Kissing-Gate']

894 A Daughter Returns

I LIKE not that dainty-cut raiment, those earrings of pearl,
 I like not the light in that eye;
I like not the note of that voice. Never so was the girl
 Who a year ago bade me good-bye!

Hadst but come bare and moneyless, worn in the vamp, weather-gray,
 But innocent still as before,
How warmly I'd lodged thee! But sport thy new gains far away;
 I pray thee now – come here no more!

And yet I'll not try to blot out every memory of thee;
 I'll think of thee – yes, now and then:
One who's watched thee since Time called thee out o' thy mother and
  me
 Must think of thee; aye, I know when! . . .

When the cold sneer of dawn follows night-shadows black as a hearse,
 And the rain filters down the fruit tree,
And the tempest mouths into the flue-top a word like a curse,
 Then, then I shall think, think of thee!

17 December 1901

895 The Third Kissing-Gate

SHE foots it forward down the town,
 Then leaves the lamps behind,
And trots along the eastern road
 Where elms stand double-lined.

She clacks the first dim kissing-gate
 Beneath the storm-strained trees,
And passes to the second mead
 That fringes Mellstock Leaze.

A Daughter Returns
12 when! . . .] when! . . . . MS

She swings the second kissing-gate
Next the gray garden-wall,
And sees the third mead stretching down
Towards the waterfall.

And now the third-placed kissing-gate
Her silent shadow nears,
And touches with; when suddenly
Her person disappears.

What chanced by that third kissing-gate
When the hushed mead grew dun?
Lo – two dark figures clasped and closed
As if they were but one.

896 Drinking Song

ONCE on a time when thought began
Lived Thales: he
Was said to see
Vast truths that mortals seldom can;
It seems without
A moment's doubt
That everything was made for man.

Chorus

Fill full your cups: feel no distress
That thoughts so great should now be less!

Earth mid the sky stood firm and flat,
He held, till came
A sage by name
Copernicus, and righted that.
We trod, he told,
A globe that rolled
Around a sun it warmed it at.

Chorus

Fill full your cups: feel no distress;
'Tis only one great thought the less!

EXTRA PRINTING:
The Daily Telegraph, 14 June 1928 = DT

TITLE:
MS adds in pencil 'on Great Thoughts belittled (?)'

But still we held, as Time flew by
And wit increased,
Ours was, at least,
The only world whose rank was high:
Till rumours flew
From folk who knew
Of globes galore about the sky.

Chorus

Fill full your cups: feel no distress;
'Tis only one great thought the less!

And that this earth, our one estate,
Was no prime ball,
The best of all,
But common, mean; indeed, tenth-rate:
And men, so proud,
A feeble crowd,
Unworthy any special fate.

Chorus

Fill full your cups: feel no distress;
'Tis only one great thought the less!

Then rose one Hume, who could not see,
If earth were such,
Required were much
To prove no miracles could be:
'Better believe
The eyes deceive
Than that God's clockwork jolts,' said he.

Chorus

Fill full your cups: feel no distress;
'Tis only one great thought the less!

Next this strange message Darwin brings,
(Though saying his say
In a quiet way);

We all are one with creeping things;
And apes and men
Blood-brethren,
And likewise reptile forms with stings.

Chorus

Fill full your cups: feel no distress;
'Tis only one great thought the less!

And when this philosoph had done
Came Doctor Cheyne:
Speaking plain he
Proved no virgin bore a son.
'Such tale, indeed,
Helps not our creed,'
He said. 'A tale long known to none.'

Chorus

Fill full your cups: feel no distress;
'Tis only one great thought the less!

And now comes Einstein with a notion –
Not yet quite clear
To many here –
That's there's no time, no space, no motion,
Nor rathe nor late,
Nor square nor straight,
But just a sort of bending-ocean.

Chorus

Fill full your cups: feel no distress;
'Tis only one great thought the less!

So here we are, in piteous case:
Like butterflies
Of many dyes
Upon an Alpine glacier's face:
To fly and cower
In some warm bower
Our chief concern in such a place.

Drinking Song
70 bending-ocean] MS has 'ether-ocean' in ink, and 'bending-ocean' in pencil

Chorus

Fill full your cups: feel no distress
At all our great thoughts shrinking less:
We'll do a good deed nevertheless!

897 The Tarrying Bridegroom

WILDLY bound the bells this morning
For the glad solemnity;
        People are adorning
        Chancel and canopy;
But amid the peal a warning
Under-echo calls to me.

Where the lane divides the pasture
Long I watch each bend and stone,
        Why not now as last year,
        When he sought me – lone?
Come, O come, and see, and cast here
Light and love on one your own!

How it used to draw him to me,
When I piped a pretty tune;
        Yes, when first he knew me
        In my pink shalloon:
Little I guessed 'twould so undo me
Lacking him this summer noon!

898 The Destined Pair

EXTRA PRINTING:
The Daily Telegraph, 7 June 1928.
There are no variants

TWO beings were drifting
Each one to the other:
No moment's veil-lifting
Or hint from another
        Led either to weet
        That the tracks of their feet
        Were arcs that would meet.

Drinking Song
80 cups:] cups; MS
80 distress] distress; DT
81] That all our great thoughts have shrunk less: MS *before revision*

One moved in a city,
And one in a village,
Where many a ditty
He tongued when at tillage
 On dreams of a dim
 Figure fancy would limn
 That was viewless to him.

Would Fate have been kinder
To keep night between them? –
Had he failed to find her
And time never seen them
 Unite; so that, caught
 In no burning love-thought,
 She had faded unsought?

899 A Musical Incident

WHEN I see the room it hurts me
As with a pricking blade,
Those women being the memoried reason why my cheer deserts me. –
'Twas thus. One of them played
To please her friend, not knowing
That friend was speedily growing,
Behind the player's chair,
Somnolent, unaware
Of any music there.

I saw it, and it distressed me,
For I had begun to think
I loved the drowsy listener, when this arose to test me
And tug me from love's brink.
'Beautiful!' said she, waking
As the music ceased. 'Heart-aching!'
Though never a note she'd heard
To judge of as averred –
Save that of the very last word.

A Musical Incident
15 Heart-aching] Heartaching WWA
18–19 Stanza break in MS, WWA, WE, CP4: page turn in WW, PE

All would have faded in me,
But that the sleeper brought
News a week thence that her friend was dead. It stirred
within me
Sense of injustice wrought
That dead player's poor intent –
So heartily, kindly meant –
As blandly added the sigher:
'How glad I am I was nigh her,
To hear her last tune!' – 'Liar!'
I lipped. – This gave love pause,
And killed it, such as it was.

EXTRA PRINTING:
The Daily Telegraph, 28 June 1928 = DT

900 June Leaves and Autumn

I

LUSH summer lit the trees to green;
But in the ditch hard by
Lay dying boughs some hand unseen
Had lopped when first with festal mien
They matched their mates on high.
It seemed a melancholy fate
That leaves but brought to birth so late
Should rust there, red and numb,
In quickened fall, while all their race
Still joyed aloft in pride of place
With store of days to come.

II

At autumn-end I fared that way,
And traced those boughs fore-hewn
Whose leaves, awaiting their decay
In slowly browning shades, still lay
Where they had lain in June
And now, no less embrowned and curst

June Leaves and Autumn
16 June] June, [?] MS
17–22 Not in DT

Than if they had fallen with the first,
Nor known a morning more,
Lay there alongside, dun and sere,
Those that at my last wandering here
Had length of days in store.

19 November 1898

901 No Bell-Ringing

A Ballad of Durnover

THE little boy legged on through the dark,
To hear the New-Year's ringing:
The three-mile road was empty, stark,
No sound or echo bringing.

When he got to the tall church tower
Standing upon the hill,
Although it was hard on the midnight hour
The place was, as elsewhere, still;

Except that the flag-staff rope, betossed
By blasts from the nor'-east,
Like a dead man's bones on a gibbet-post
Tugged as to be released.

'Why is there no ringing to-night?'
Said the boy to a moveless one
On a tombstone where the moon struck white;
But he got answer none.

'No ringing in of New Year's Day.'
He mused as he dragged back home;
And wondered till his head was gray
Why the bells that night were dumb.

And often thought of the snowy shape
That sat on the moonlit stone,
Nor spoke nor moved, and in mien and drape
Seemed like a sprite thereon.

PROOF:
In the Dorset County Museum. It is identical with S

EXTRA PRINTINGS:
(1) Privately printed by Florence Hardy, Feb 1925 = FH
(2) *The Sphere*, 23 Nov 1925, p. 14 = S
(3) *The Ladies' Home Journal* (USA) Dec 1925 = LHJ

Note In MS this poem follows 'The Tarrying Bridegroom', and has in pencil '[Copy made for Mr Shorter's Christmas number – Sent Feb 1925 – appeared Xmas 1925]'

No Bell-Ringing
2 New-Year's] New Year's S, LHJ
2 ringing:] ringing; FH, LHJ
8 still;] still, LHJ
9 flag-staff] flagstaff LHJ
10 nor'-east] nor' east FH
11 gibbet-post] gibbet post LHJ
17 Day.] Day, FH, S, LHJ
20 bells] peal FH, S, LHJ
20 were] was FH, S, LHJ
21–4 A late addition to MS

And then he met one left of the band
  That had treble-bobbed when young,
And said: 'I never could understand
  Why, that night, no bells rung.'

'True. There'd not happened such a thing
  For half a century; aye,
And never I've told why they did not ring
  From that time till to-day. . . .

'Through the week in bliss at *The Hit or Miss*[1]
  We had drunk – not a penny left;
What then we did – well, now 'tis hid, –
  But better we'd stooped to theft!

'Yet, since none other remains who can,
  And few more years are mine,
I may tell you,' said the cramped old man.
  'We – swilled the Sacrament-wine.

'Then each set-to with the strength of two,
  Every man to his bell;
But something was wrong we found ere long
  Though what, we could not tell.

'We pulled till the sweat-drops fell around,
  As we'd never pulled before,
An hour by the clock, but not one sound
  Came down through the bell-loft floor.

'On the morrow all folk of the same thing spoke,
  They had stood at the midnight time
On their doorsteps near with a listening ear,
  But there reached them never a chime.

'We then could read the dye of our deed,
  And we knew we were accurst;
But we broke to none the thing we had done,
  And since then never durst.'

[1] An old tavern now demolished. The full legend over the door ran, 'Hit or Miss: Luck's All!'

No Bell-Ringing
32 to-day. . . .] to-day. . . . . . MS
33 'Through] – Through MS
33 *The Hit or Miss*] the 'Hit or Miss' S, LHJ
35 hid, –] hid, S, LHJ
39 man.] man, FH, S, LHJ
40 Sacrament-wine.] Sacrament-wine. . . . . FH: sacrament wine. LHJ
41 set-to] set to S, LHJ
43 long] long, FH, S, LHJ
44 what,] what LHJ
45 pulled] rang FH
45 sweat-drops] sweat drops LHJ
46 pulled] rung FH

902 I Looked Back

I LOOKED back as I left the house,
And, past the chimneys and neighbour tree,
The moon upsidled through the boughs: –
I thought: 'I shall a last time see
This picture; when will that time be?'

I paused amid the laugh-loud feast,
And selfward said: 'I am sitting where,
Some night, when ancient songs have ceased,
"Now is the last time I shall share
Such cheer," will be the thought I bear.'

An eye-sweep back at a look-out corner
Upon a hill, as forenight wore,
Stirred me to think: 'Ought I to warn her
That, though I come here times three-score,
One day 'twill be I come no more?'

Anon I reasoned there had been,
Ere quite forsaken was each spot,
Bygones whereon I'd lastly seen
That house, that feast, that maid forgot;
But when? – Ah, I remembered not!

EXTRA PRINTING:
The Daily Telegraph, 24 May 1928 = DT

TITLE:
'I looked back' MS

INDENTATION:
1 = ll. 1, 3 } and so throughout DT
2 = ll. 2, 4, 5 }

903 The Aged Newspaper Soliloquizes

YES; yes; I am old. In me appears
The history of a hundred years;
Empires', kings', captives', births and deaths,
Strange faiths, and fleeting shibboleths.
– Tragedy, comedy, throngs my page
Beyond all mummed on any stage:
Cold hearts beat hot, hot hearts beat cold,
And I beat on. Yes; yes; I am old.

The Aged Newspaper Soliloquizes

EXTRA PRINTINGS:
(1) *The Observer*, 14 March 1926, p. 16 = O
(2) *The New York Times*, 11 April 1926 = NYT
[With this accompanying note: Thomas Hardy, the 'grand old man of English letters', recently wrote a poem entitled 'The Aged Newspaper Soliloquizes', which was published in The London Observer and THE NEW YORK TIMES on March 14. So great was the interest aroused by the poem among American readers that Mr Hardy was asked whether he would lend the manuscript to THE NEW YORK TIMES for reproduction. He responded by mailing it from his home in Dorchester.]

TITLE:
The Aged Newspaper soliloquizes MS
The Newspaper Soliloquises O

I Looked Back
2 And,] And WWA
2 tree,] tree. MS, WW, WWA, PE, WE
14 That,] That DT
14 three-score] three score MS [Could be one word]

The Aged Newspaper Soliloquizes
3 captives',] captives' O, NYT
3 deaths,] deaths; O
4 shibboleths.] shibboleths: O
5 – Tragedy] Tragedy O
6 stage:] stage: – O

EXTRA PRINTING:
The Daily Telegraph, 18 June 1928 = DT

TITLE:
'Peace Upon Earth'
(These lines were written at Christmas, 1924)
DT

904 Christmas: 1924

'PEACE upon earth!' was said. We sing it,
And pay a million priests to bring it.
After two thousand years of mass
We've got as far as poison-gas.

1924

905 The Single Witness

'DID no one else, then, see them, man,
Lying among the whin?
Did no one else, behold them at all
Commit this shameless sin,
But you, in the hollow of the down
No traveller's eye takes in?'

'Nobody else, my noble lord,
Saw them together there –
Your young son's tutor and she. I made
A short cut from the fair,
And lit on them. I've said no word
About it anywhere.'

'Good. . . . Now, you see my father's sword,
Hanging up in your view;
No hand has swung it since he came
Home after Waterloo.
I'll show it you. . . . There is the sword:
And this is what I'll do.'

He ran the other through the breast,
Ere he could plead or cry.
'It is a dire necessity,
But – since no one was nigh
Save you and they, my historied name
Must not be smirched thereby.'

Christmas: 1924
1924] Not in DT

The Single Witness
13 Good. . . .] Good. . . . MS

906 *How She Went to Ireland*

Dora's gone to Ireland
 Through the sleet and snow;
Promptly she has gone there
 In a ship, although
Why she's gone to Ireland
 Dora does not know.

That was where, yea, Ireland,
 Dora wished to be:
When she felt, in lone times,
 Shoots of misery,
Often there, in Ireland,
 Dora wished to be.

Hence she's gone to Ireland,
 Since she meant to go,
Through the drift and darkness
 Onward labouring, though
That she's gone to Ireland
 Dora does not know.

TITLE:
How she went to Ireland MS

907 *Dead 'Wessex' the Dog to the Household*

Do you think of me at all,
 Wistful ones?
Do you think of me at all
 As if nigh?
Do you think of me at all
At the creep of evenfall,
Or when the sky-birds call
 As they fly?

EXTRA MANUSCRIPT:
In the Dorset County Museum = DCM

EXTRA PRINTING:
The Daily Telegraph, 10 May 1928 = DT

TITLE:
Dead 'Wessex' To The Household MS *before revision*
Dead 'Wessex'/To the Household DCM
Dead 'Wessex'/To the wondering Ones DCM *before revision*

Dead 'Wessex' the Dog to the Household
2 Wistful] Wondering DCM *before revision*
[Likewise ll. 10, 18, 26]

Do you look for me at times,
Wistful ones?
Do you look for me at times
Strained and still?
Do you look for me at times,
When the hour for walking chimes,
On that grassy path that climbs
Up the hill?

You may hear a jump or trot,
Wistful ones,
You may hear a jump or trot –
Mine, as 'twere –
You may hear a jump or trot
On the stair or path or plot;
But I shall cause it not,
Be not there.

Should you call as when I knew you,
Wistful ones,
Should you call as when I knew you,
Shared your home;
Should you call as when I knew you,
I shall not turn to view you,
I shall not listen to you,
Shall not come.

908 *The Woman Who Went East*

EXTRA PRINTING:
The Daily Telegraph, 14 May 1928 = DT

TITLE:
The Woman who went East MS
The Woman of the West MS *before revision*

'WHERE is that woman of the west,
Good Sir, once friends with me,
In rays of her own rareness drest,
And fired by sunset from the sea?
Yes, she – once friends with me.'

' – She went to sojourn in the east,
O stranger Dame, one day;

Dead 'Wessex' the Dog to the Household
11 times] times, DCM
17–32 A late addition to MS: not in DT
22 stair] stairs DCM
29 you,] you MS, DCM

The Woman Who Went East
6 east] East DT
7 stranger] Stranger DT

Her own west land she reckoned least
Of all lands, with its weird old way,
So left it, Dame, one day:

'Doubtless they prized her marvellous mould
At its right worth elsewhere,
Yea, Dame, and kept her shrined in gold,
So speaking, as one past compare;
Aye, prized her worth elsewhere!'

– 'Must, must I then a story tell,
Old native, here to you,
Of peradventures that befel
Her eastward – shape it as 'twere new,
Old native, here to you?

'O unforgotten day long back,
When, wilful, east she sped
From you with her new Love. Alack,
Her lips would still be ripe and red
Had she not eastward sped!

'For know, old lover, dull of eyes,
That woman, I am she:
This skeleton that Time so tries
Your rose of rareness used to be;
Yes, sweetheart, I am she.'

909 Not Known

THEY know the wilings of the world,
The latest flippancy;
They know each jest at hazard hurled,
But know not me.

They know a phasm they name as me,
In whom I should not find
A single self-held quality
Of body or mind.

The Woman Who Went East
10 it,] it MS, DT
13 Yea,] Yea MS
16 – 'Must] ' – Must DT, WWA
21 back,] back MS
23] All pulsing, flushed, not one look back! – MS *before revision*

Not Known
1914 After reading criticism MS *deleted* at end

EXTRA PRINTING:
The Daily Telegraph, 12 July 1928.
There are no variants

910 *The Boy's Dream*

PROVINCIAL town-boy he, – frail, lame,
His face a waning lily-white,
A court the home of his wry, wrenched frame,
Where noontide shed no warmth or light.

Over his temples – flat, and wan,
Where bluest veins were patterned keen,
The skin appeared so thinly drawn
The skull beneath was almost seen.

Always a wishful, absent look
Expressed it in his face and eye;
At the strong shape this longing took
One guessed what wish must underlie.

But no. That wish was not for strength,
For other boys' agility,
To race with ease the field's far length,
Now hopped across so painfully.

He minded not his lameness much,
To shine at feats he did not long,
Nor to be best at goal and touch,
Nor at assaults to stand up strong.

But sometimes he would let be known
What the wish was: – to have, next spring,
A real green linnet – his very own –
Like that one he had late heard sing.

And as he breathed the cherished dream
To those whose secrecy was sworn,
His face was beautified by the theme,
And wore the radiance of the morn.

The Boy's Dream
5 flat,] flat CP4

911 *The Gap in the White*

(178–)

SOMETHING had cracked in her mouth as she slept,
Having danced with the Prince long, and sipped his gold tass;
And she woke in alarm, and quick, breathlessly, leapt
Out of bed to the glass.

And there, in the blue dawn, her mouth now displayed
To her woe, in the white
Level line of her teeth, a black gap she had made
In a dream's nervous bite.

'O how can I meet him to-morrow!' she said.
'I'd won him – yes, yes! Now, alas, he is lost!'
(That age knew no remedy.) Duly her dread
Proved the truth, to her cost.

And if you could go and examine her grave
You'd find the gap there,
But not understand, now that science can save,
Her unbounded despair.

912 *Family Portraits*

THREE picture-drawn people stepped out of their frames –
The blast, how it blew!
And the white-shrouded candles flapped smoke-headed flames;
– Three picture-drawn people came down from their frames,
And dumbly in lippings they told me their names,
Full well though I knew.

The first was a maiden of mild wistful tone,
Gone silent for years,
The next a dark woman in former time known;

EXTRA PRINTINGS:
(1) *Nash's and Pall Mall Magazine*, Dec 1924, p. 27 = NPM [NPM has seven stanzas: stanzas 1–4 match stanzas 1–4 here: stanza 5 matches stanza 7: stanzas 6 and 7 (which is close to stanza 8) are given below]
(2) *The Daily Telegraph*, 6 Aug 1928 = DT

TITLE:
The Portraits = NPM

Note MS has in pencil '[Sent to Macm – for serial pubn in America]'

The Gap in the White
4 glass.] glass, MS

Family Portraits
2 blew!] blew! – NPM
4 – Three . . . people] The picture-drawn past ones NPM
4 – Three] Three DT
6 Full] So NPM
6 knew.] knew! NPM
9 in . . . known;] aforetime well known: NPM

But the first one, the maiden of mild wistful tone,
So wondering, unpractised, so vague and alone,
    Nigh moved me to tears.

The third was a sad man – a man of much gloom;
    And before me they passed
In the shade of the night, at the back of the room,
The dark and fair woman, the man of much gloom,
Three persons, in far-off years forceful, but whom
    Death now fettered fast.

They set about acting some drama, obscure,
    The women and he,
With puppet-like movements of mute strange allure;
Yea, set about acting some drama, obscure,
Till I saw 'twas their own lifetime's tragic amour,
    Whose course begot me;

Yea – a mystery, ancestral, long hid from my reach
    In the perished years past,
That had mounted to dark doings each against each
In those ancestors' days, and long hid from my reach;
Which their restless enghostings, it seemed, were to teach
    Me in full, at this last.

But fear fell upon me like frost, of some hurt
    If they entered anew
On the orbits they smartly had swept when expert
In the law-lacking passions of life, – of some hurt
To their souls – and thus mine – which I fain would avert;
    So, in sweat cold as dew,

'Why wake up all this?' I cried out. 'Now, so late!
    Let old ghosts be laid!'
And they stiffened, drew back to their frames and numb state,
Gibbering: 'Thus are your own ways to shape, know too late!'
Then I grieved that I'd not had the courage to wait
    And see the play played.

Stanzas 6 and 7 of NPM read:

For why should it not have been? Could it have hurt,/Had they paced again through/Those orbits that once they had trod when expert/In the labouresome passions of life – of deep hurt/To them, maybe to me? But I found them inert,/And the blast again blew.

I have grieved ever since; for I fed my own pain/By the interdict thrown:/Years long night by night stretched awake I have lain/Perplexed in endeavours to heal my own pain/By uncovering the drift of their drama. In vain!/Yet they called it my own.

Family Portraits
19 obscure,] obscure – NPM
21] With puppet-like movement of mute, strange allure: – NPM
22 drama, obscure,] drama obscure – NPM
24] Largely bearing on me; MS *before revision*: Strangely bearing on me. NPM
25–36 Not in NPM
35 avert;] avert CP4
37 cried out] inquired NPM
40 'Thus . . . shape] 'Such your own story will be NPM
41 courage to wait] patience to wait, NPM

I have grieved ever since: to have balked future pain,
    My blood's tendance foreknown,
Had been triumph. Nights long stretched awake I have lain
Perplexed in endeavours to balk future pain
By uncovering the drift of their drama. In vain,
    Though therein lay my own.

913 *The Catching Ballet of the Wedding Clothes*

(*Temp. Guliel. IV*)

'A GENTLEMAN'S coming
    To court me, they say;
The ringers are told,
    And the band is to play.
O why should he do it
    Now poor Jack's away?
I surely shall rue it:
    Come, white witch, and say!'

'The gentleman's coming
    To marry you, dear;
They tell at the turnpikes
    That he has been here!
He rode here in secret,
    To gain eye of you: –
Throw over the sailor,
    Is what I should do!'

'I will not throw over
    Poor Jack: no, indeed,
For a new unknown lover
    Who loves at such speed,
And writes to the ringers,
    And orders the band,
As if I could only
    Obey his command!

'La! now here is something
   Close packed in a box,
And strapped up and corded,
   And held with two locks!'
'Dear, that's from him, surely,
   As we may suppose?
Ay, through the chink shining
   I spy wedding clothes!'

'Yes – here's a drawn bonnet,
   And tortoiseshell combs,
And a silk gown, silk stockings,
   And scents of rare blooms;
And shoes, too, of satin,
   Quite past all my pride:
O, how will it end, witch;
   I can't be his bride!'

'Don't waste you in weeping:
   Not worth it is man!
Beshrew me, my deary,
   I've shaped a new plan.
Wear the clothes of the rich one,
   Since he will not see,
But marry the poor one
   You love faithfully.'

'Here's a last packet. . . . Never!
   It knocks me to bits –
The ring! "*Just to try on,*
   To see if it fits."
O I cannot!' . . . But Jack said,
   Quite cool, when he came,
'Well, it will save money,
   And be just the same.'

The marriage took place,
   Yes; as vowed, she was true
To her dear sailor Jack
   Ere the gentleman knew;

The Catching Ballet of the Wedding Clothes
49–56 A late addition to MS
49 packet. . . .] packet. . . . . MS
53 cannot!' . . .] cannot!' . . . . MS

But she wore the rich clothing,
Much joyed at such guise,
Yet fearing and trembling
With tears in her eyes.

And at midnight, between her
And him she had wed,
The gentleman's figure
Arose up and said:
'My too-cruel darling,
In spite of your oaths,
You have married the man
Of the ring and the clothes!'

Thence on, would confront her,
When sleep had grown slack,
His face on the pillow
Between her and Jack;
And he nightly kept whispering:
'You surely must see,
Though your tongue-tip took him, Love,
Your body took me.'

Till she sighed: 'Yes, my word,
It must be confessed o' me,
Jack has; but this man
Can claim all the rest o' me!
And off to go with him
Bewitched am I now:
I'd fain not be two men's,
And won't, anyhow!'

So she pleaded and pleaded
From daybreak till dark,
Converting the parish
(Save parson and clerk).
She then wrote to Jack thus:
'I'm torn with mind-strife:
She who wears a man's bride-clothes
Must be the man's wife!'

And still she kept plaining,
Till Jack he wrote: 'Aye!'
And the villagers gathered,
And, on a fixed day,
They went out alertly
And stood in a row,
Quite blithe with excitement
To see John's wife go.

Some were facing her dwelling,
And some on the bridge,
And some at the corner,
And some by the ridge.
With a nod and a word
The coach stopped at her door,
And she upped like a bird,
And they saw her no more.

'Twas told that, years after,
When autumn winds wave,
A wealthy old lady
Stood long at Jack's grave,
The while her coach waited: –
She mused there; and then
She stepped in, and never
Came thither again.

1919

914 *A Winsome Woman*

(*Song*)

THERE's no winsome woman so winsome as she;
Some are flower-like in mouth,
Some have fire in the eyes,
Some feed a soul's drouth
Trilling words music-wise;
But where are these gifts all in one found to be
Save in her known to me?

The Catching Ballet of the Wedding Clothes
100 And,] And CP4
117 The] And CP4

A Winsome Woman
7–8 Stanza break in all editions

What her thoughts are I read not, but this much I know,
That she, too, will pass
From the sun and the air
To her cave under grass;
And the world will declare,
'No such woman as his passioned utterances show
Walked this planet, we trow!'

915 *The Ballad of Love's Skeleton*

(179–)

'COME, let's to Culliford Hill and Wood,
And watch the squirrels climb,
And look in sunny places there
For shepherds' thyme.'

– 'Can I have heart for Culliford Wood,
And hill and bank and tree,
Who know and ponder over all
Things done by me!'

– 'Then Dear, don hat, and come along:
We'll strut the Royal strand;
King George has just arrived, his Court,
His guards, and band.'

– 'You are a Baron of the King's Court
From Hanover lately come,
And can forget in song and dance
What chills me numb.

'Well be the royal scenes for you,
And band beyond compare,
But how is she who hates her crime
To frolic there?

'O why did you so urge and say
'Twould soil your noble name! –
I should have prized a little child,
And faced the shame.

The Ballad of Love's Skeleton
9 Then] Then, CP4
13–16 A late addition to MS

'I see the child – *that should have been,*
But was not, born alive;
With such a deed in a woman's life
A year seems five.

'I asked not for the wifely rank,
Nor maiden honour saved;
To call a nestling thing my own
Was all I craved.

'For what's the hurt of shame to one
Of no more note than me?
Can littlest life beneath the sun
More littled be?'

– 'Nay, never grieve. The day is bright,
Just as it was ere then:
In the Assembly Rooms to-night
Let's joy again!

'The new Quick-Step is the sweetest dance
For lively toes and heels;
And when we tire of that we'll prance
Bewitching reels.

'Dear, never grieve! As once we whirled
So let us whirl to-night,
Forgetting all things save ourselves
Till dawning light.

'The King and Queen, Princesses three,
Have promised to meet there
The mayor and townsfolk. I've my card
And One to spare.

'The Court will dance at the upper end;
Only a cord between
Them and the burgher-throng below;
A brilliant scene!'

– 'I'll go. You've still my heart in thrall:
Save you, all's dark to me.
And God knows what, when love is all,
The end will be!'

916 *A Private Man on Public Men*

EXTRA PRINTING:
The Daily Telegraph, 26 March 1928.
There are no variants

WHEN my contemporaries were driving
Their coach through Life with strain and striving,
And raking riches into heaps,
And ably pleading in the Courts
With smart rejoinders and retorts,
Or where the Senate nightly keeps
Its vigils, till their fames were fanned
By rumour's tongue throughout the land,
I lived in quiet, screened, unknown,
Pondering upon some stick or stone,
Or news of some rare book or bird
Latterly bought, or seen, or heard,
Not wishing ever to set eyes on
The surging crowd beyond the horizon,
Tasting years of moderate gladness
Mellowed by sundry days of sadness,
Shut from the noise of the world without,
Hearing but dimly its rush and rout,
Unenvying those amid its roar,
Little endowed, not wanting more.

917 *Christmas in the Elgin Room*

British Museum: Early Last Century

EXTRA MANUSCRIPT:
In Magdalene College Library, Cambridge = MC

EXTRA PRINTINGS:
(1) *The Times*, 24 Dec 1927, p. 9.
There are no variants
(2) Privately printed by Florence Hardy, Dec 1927.
There are no variants
(3) *The Daily Telegraph*, 11 June 1928 = DT

'WHAT is the noise that shakes the night,
And seems to soar to the Pole-star height?'
– 'Christmas bells,
The watchman tells
Who walks this hall that blears us captives with its blight.'

Christmas in the Elgin Room
2 height?'] height?' – MC
3 – 'Christmas] ' – Christmas MS
4 watchman] Watchman MS

'And what, then, mean such clangs, so clear?'
' – 'Tis said to have been a day of cheer,
And source of grace
To the human race
Long ere their woven sails winged us to exile here.

'We are those whom Christmas overthrew
Some centuries after Pheidias knew
How to shape us
And bedrape us
And to set us in Athena's temple for men's view.

'O it is sad now we are sold –
We gods! for Borean people's gold,
And brought to the gloom
Of this gaunt room
Which sunlight shuns, and sweet Aurore but enters cold.

'For all these bells, would I were still
Radiant as on Athenai's Hill.'
– 'And I, and I!'
The others sigh,
'Before this Christ was known, and we had men's good will.'

Thereat old Helios could but nod,
Throbbed, too, the Ilissus River-god,
And the torsos there
Of deities fair,
Whose limbs were shards beneath some Acropolitan clod:

Demeter too, Poseidon hoar,
Persephone, and many more
Of Zeus' high breed, –
All loth to heed
What the bells sang that night which shook them to the core.

1905 and 1926

Christmas in the Elgin Room
6 what, then,] what then MS
6 clangs,] clangs MS
6 clear?'] clear?' – MS, MC
7 cheer,] cheer MS
14 bedrape] to drape MS
22 Hill.'] Hill.' – MC
25 good will] good-will MS
27 Throbbed,] Throbbed MS
31–5 And Proserpine, and Neptune hoar,/Iris, and Ceres, and many more/And none of the band/Could understand/What the bells sang that night which shook them to the core. MS *before revision*
1905 and 1926] Not in DT

918 We Are Getting to the End

EXTRA PRINTING:
The Daily Telegraph, 28 May 1928 = DT

TITLE:
'We are getting to the end' MS

WE are getting to the end of visioning
The impossible within this universe,
Such as that better whiles may follow worse,
And that our race may mend by reasoning.

We know that even as larks in cages sing
Unthoughtful of deliverance from the curse
That holds them lifelong in a latticed hearse,
We ply spasmodically our pleasuring.

And that when nations set them to lay waste
Their neighbours' heritage by foot and horse,
And hack their pleasant plains in festering seams,
They may again, – not warely, or from taste,
But tickled mad by some demonic force. –
Yes. We are getting to the end of dreams!

919 He Resolves to Say No More

EXTRA MANUSCRIPTS:
(1) In the Dorset County Museum = DCM1
(2) In the Dorset County Museum = DCM2

EXTRA PRINTING:
The Daily Telegraph, 18 Sept 1928.
There are no variants

TITLE:
He resolves to say no more DCM1, DCM2

O MY soul, keep the rest unknown!
It is too like a sound of moan
            When the charnel-eyed
            Pale Horse has nighed:
Yea, none shall gather what I hide!

Why load men's minds with more to bear
That bear already ails to spare?
            From now alway
            Till my last day
What I discern I will not say.

We Are Getting to the End
4–5 No stanza break in DT
5 sing] sing, DT
11 seams,] seams WE

He Resolves to Say No More
1 soul] heart DCM2; both MS and DCM1 had 'heart' *before revision*
1 unknown!] unknown; DCM2
2–4] It comes too near a sound of moan/At Death's grey glide/To mortal's side DCM2 *before revision*

Let Time roll backward if it will;
(Magians who drive the midnight quill
With brain aglow
Can see it so,)
What I have learnt no man shall know.

And if my vision range beyond
The blinkered sight of souls in bond,
– By truth made free –
I'll let all be,
And show to no man what I see.

He Resolves to Say No More
12 Magians] DCM2 offers 'Sages' as alternative
12–13] (And some who dip the midnight quill/By genius aglow DCM2 *before revision*

PREVIOUSLY UNCOLLECTED POEMS AND FRAGMENTS

A Victorian ~~the~~ Rehearsal.

A single shine broods sloomily
Where footlight flares are wont to be;
The stalls are swathed in holland shrounds,
Imaging lifeless first-night dowds;
The scene-cloths sway each feeble while
Like fusty banners in an aisle;
A daylight arrow shoots down through
Some inlet, of a steely blue,
Dappling, at minutes, the rehearsings,
Mutterings, crossings, & reversings
Done by a queer little group dull-dressed,
~~Let~~ As ~~the~~ 'twere some children's game unguessed;
Town dwellers who affect them clowns,
Or villains fierce with oaths & frowns;
Among them being the leading lady,
Whose private life is whispered shady,
But who's ~~to~~ divorce her spouse, they say,
Adding, "it should be the other way":
Yet haggarded in the morning light,
By too late-houring overnight,
In frowzed fur jacket, donned in haste,
A sweetheart not to every taste.

So much for what the gossips tell,
Truly, or liker falsely. — Well,
Anyhow, here are throbbing natures,
Arrived to take feigned nomenclatures,
Unheeding what warm complications
May issue from new, forced relations,
Wherein may lie more tragedy
Than in the play the town's ~~will~~ to see.

See page 935

920 *When Wearily We Shrink Away*

Printed here from an untitled manuscript in the Dorset County Museum. The tone, style and handwriting make it almost certainly Hardy's. Written on it is 'Suggested by M.H.'

WHEN wearily we shrink away
  From comrades forward striving,
And drop behind where once we strove
  High schemes no more contriving
Though feeling but chance contact bred
  Their slight concern about us,
Still seems it sad they all whirl on
  Nor think they whirl without us.

When worn by fondness unrepaid,
  We class all friends together,
As passage-birds who leave us lone
  At close of summer weather;
Nor ask or hear of them, and they
  Ne'er ask or hear about us,
The punishment is hard, to see
  They love so well without us.

'Tis not that, lacking us, they love
  Which touches then most keenly,
But that, un-noting whom they lack
  They still love on serenely;
That e'en they fail to note they lack
  Their own old thoughts about us;
That hardly would they, might they note
  They thus love on without us.

921 *The Unplanted Primrose*

Printed here from a manuscript in the Dorset County Museum. This and poems 922, 924, 927 and 945 were previously printed in *The London Magazine* Jan 1956, in an article by Evelyn Hardy entitled 'Some Unpublished Poems by Thomas Hardy'. Title in MS is 'The unplanted Primrose'

'A PINK primrose from the plant he knows
  Let me send him in his far spot,
From the root I brought to his garden-knot
When he dwelt herefrom but a little mile;

A root I had reared at that time of love,
And of all my stock the best that throve,
  Which he took with so warm a smile.'

Such she sang and said, and aflush she sped
  To her Love's old home hard by
Ere he left that nook for the wider sky
Of a southern country unassayed.
And she crept to the border of early stocks,
Of pansies, pinks, and hollyhocks,
  Where their vows and the gift were made.

'It has not bloomed!' And her glances gloomed
  As she missed the expected hue.
'Yet the rest are in blow the border through;
Nor is leaf or bud of it evident.
Ah, can it have died of an over-care
In its tendance, sprung of his charge to spare
  No pains for its nourishment?'

She turned her round from the wrong ones found
  To the seat where a year before
She had brought it him as the best of her store,
And lo, on a ledge of the wall she neared,
Lay its withered skeleton, dry and brown,
Untouched since there he had laid it down
  When she waved and disappeared.

1865–67 Westbourne Park Villas
(From old MS.)

Printed here from a manuscript in the Dorset County Museum

922 To a Bridegroom

SWEAR to love and cherish her?
She might moan were beauty's throne
  Beauty's sepulchre.

Think her not so new as now,
Staid, with here and there a blur
  On her cheek and brow.

Fancy men to change and say,
'No great gods with gifts endow
    This fine-feathered jay.'

Should infirmity succeed,
Who will each and every day
    Rush to his invalid?

Think her little fingers rough,
Tresses thin; her satin brede
    Serest sorriest stuff.

Spread a tale that wronged her fame,
Who'd not feel 'Of her enough!
    Love is a foolish game?'

Grew her love too wild to own,
Who'd not, with some sense of shame,
    Hide a secret groan?

Swear to love and cherish her?
She might moan were beauty's throne
    Beauty's sepulchre.

***1866** (abridged)*

923 *A Victorian Rehearsal*

Printed here from a manuscript in the Dorset County Museum. A facsimile of the MS was published in *The Times Literary Supplement*, 2 June 1966, with a comment by Evelyn Hardy. *Before revision* the title was 'The Rehearsal'

A SINGLE shine broods gloomily
Where footlight flares are wont to be;
The stalls are swathed in holland shrouds,
Imaging lifeless first-night dowds;
The scene-cloths sway each feeble while
Like fusty banners in an aisle;
A daylight arrow shoots down through
Some inlet, of a steely blue,
Dappling at minutes the rehearsings,
Mutterings, crossings, and reversings
Done by a queer little group dull-dressed,
As 'twere some children's game unguessed;

A Victorian Rehearsal
12–13 No stanza break

Town dwellers who affect them clowns,
Or villains fierce with oaths and frowns;
Among them being the leading lady,
Whose private life is whispered shady,
But who's to divorce her spouse, they say,
Adding, 'it should be the other way;'
Yet haggarded, in the morning light,
By too late-houring overnight,
In frowzed fur jacket, donned in haste,
A sweetheart not to every taste.

So much for what the gossips tell,
Truly, or liker falsely. – Well,
Anyhow, here are throbbing natures,
Arrived to take feigned nomenclatures,
Unheeding what warm complications
May issue from new, forced relations,
Wherein may lie more tragedy
Than in the play the town's to see.

Printed here from a manuscript in the Dorset County Museum

924 *Thoughts from Sophocles*

(*Oed. Col.* 1200–1250)

WHO would here sojourn for an outstretched spell
Has senseless promptings, to the thinking gaze,
Since pain comes nigh and nigher with lengthening days,
And nothing shows that joy will ever upwell.

Death is the remedy that cures at call
The doubtful jousts of black and white assays.
What are song, laughter, what the footed maze,
Beside the good of knowing no birth at all?

Gaunt age is as some blank upstanding beak
Chafed by the billows of a northern shore
And facing friendless cold calamity
That strikes upon its features worn and weak
Where sunshine bird and bloom frequent no more,
And cowls of cloud wrap the stars' radiancy.

Thoughts from Sophocles
2 Has] Feels MS *as alternative*
4 upwell] Hardy's intentions are not clear. The word was 'upswell', but the 's' was deleted and the 'up' ringed but not deleted
5 cures at call] winds up well MS *as alternative*
6 doubtful] sorry MS *as alternative*
9 blank] gray MS *as alternative*

925 *Eunice*

Printed here from the 1912 Wessex Edition of *Desperate Remedies*, p. 352, where it is supposed to have been written by the character Manston

Whoso for hours or lengthy days
Shall catch her aspect's changeful rays,
Then turn away, can none recall
Beyond a galaxy of all
In hazy portraiture;
Lit by the light of azure eyes
Like summer days by summer skies:
Her sweet transitions seem to be
A pinkly pictured melody,
And not a set contour.

From 'Desperate Remedies'

926 *Epigraph to 'The Woodlanders'*

Printed here from the title-page of the 1912 Wessex Edition of *The Woodlanders*. Hardy in a letter to Florence Henniker, 12 Aug 1895, wrote: 'I have been looking for a motto for the title page of *The Woodlanders* and not being able to find one, composed it'

'Not boskiest bow'r,
When hearts are ill affin'd,
Hath tree of pow'r
To shelter from the wind!'

927 *She Would Welcome Old Tribulations*

Printed here from a manuscript in the Dorset County Museum, where the title is written: 'She would welcome old Tribulations'. It has in pencil '[not used]'

I see a fresh-cheeked figure,
Rising but three feet high,
Shrink on the stony track here
From the sea-swell lifting nigh:
The little one is I.
Ah, could the time come back here,
Shrinking and all, I cry!

I see the bathing woman,
Sturdy and stout and browned:
She swings me by the shoulder,
And flouts my gasps, half-drowned;

Eunice
6 eyes] eyes, *Desperate Remedies* 1871
7 skies:] skies, *Desperate Remedies* 1871
9] A kind of pictured melody, *Desperate Remedies* 1871, 1896

O now for that swishing sound,
The sea's slap, cold and colder;
Could it again come round!

I pause beside these places,
Under no eye, but free;
I have no childish terror
Of hands to capture me
By discipline's decree;
I am not chid for error,
Yet – could it once more be!

About 1900

Printed here from the manuscript in the bound-up volume of manuscripts of *Time's Laughingstocks* in the Fitzwilliam Museum, Cambridge. It was first printed in Prof. R. L. Purdy's *Thomas Hardy: A Bibliographical Study* (London, 1954), p. 149

928 Looking Back

WHEN formerly we thought, Dear,
Of how our souls were set
On spousals doomed to nought, Dear,
We sickened with regret.

When now we think thereof, Dear,
Although our eyes are wet,
We know what quenches love, Dear,
And we do not regret.

From *The Dynasts*, Pt I, Act v, sc. vii. Printed here from the 1927 Limited Edition. For this poem and poems 930–4 the First Edition (= 1st Ed) and the Wessex Edition (= WE) of *The Dynasts* have been collated. There is a MS of 929 in the Bancroft Library of the University of California at Berkeley = BL

929 The Night of Trafalgár

(*Boatman's Song*)

I

IN the wild October night-time, when the wind raved round the land,
And the Back-sea met the Front-sea, and our doors were blocked with sand,
And we heard the drub of Dead-man's Bay, where bones of thousands are,
We knew not what the day had done for us at Trafalgár.
Had done,
Had done,
For us at Trafalgár!

The Night of Trafalgár
3 Dead-man's] Deadman's BL
4 Trafalgár] Trafalgar 1st Ed
6 done,] done BL
7 Trafalgár] Trafalgar 1st Ed

II

'Pull hard, and make the Nothe, or down we go!' one says, says he.
We pulled; and bedtime brought the storm; but snug at home slept we.
Yet all the while our gallants after fighting through the day,
Were beating up and down the dark, sou'-west of Cadiz Bay.
The dark,
The dark,
Sou'-west of Cadiz Bay!

III

The victors and the vanquished then the storm it tossed and tore,
As hard they strove, those worn-out men, upon that surly shore;
Dead Nelson and his half-dead crew, his foes from near and far,
Were rolled together on the deep that night at Trafalgár!
The deep,
The deep,
That night at Trafalgár!

From 'The Dynasts'

930 Budmouth Dears
(*Hussar's Song*)

From *The Dynasts*, Pt III, Act II, sc. i. Printed here from the 1927 Limited Edition

I

WHEN we lay where Budmouth Beach is,
O, the girls were fresh as peaches,
With their tall and tossing figures and their eyes of blue and brown!
And our hearts would ache with longing
As we paced from our sing-songing,
With a smart *Clink! Clink!* up the Esplanade and down.

II

They distracted and delayed us
By the pleasant pranks they played us,
And what marvel, then, if troopers, even of regiments of renown,
On whom flashed those eyes divine, O,
Should forget the countersign, O,
As we tore *Clink! Clink!* back to camp above the town.

The Night of Trafalgár
8 hard,] hard BL
8 he.] he: BL
9 pulled;] pulled, BL
9 we.] we: BL
10 day,] day BL
14 Bay!] Bay. BL
17 far,] far BL
18 Trafalgár] Trafalgar 1st Ed
19 deep,] deep BL
20 deep,] deep BL
21 Trafalgár!] Trafalgár. BL: Trafalgar! 1st Ed

III

Do they miss us much, I wonder,
Now that war has swept us sunder,
And we roam from where the faces smile to where the faces frown?
And no more behold the features
Of the fair fantastic creatures,
And no more *Clink! Clink!* past the parlours of the town?

IV

Shall we once again there meet them?
Falter fond attempts to greet them?
Will the gay sling-jacket glow again beside the muslin gown? –
Will they archly quiz and con us
With a sideway glance upon us,
While our spurs *Clink! Clink!* up the Esplanade and down?

From 'The Dynasts'

From *The Dynasts*, Pt III, Act v, vi. Printed here from the 1927 Limited Edition

931 *My Love's Gone a-Fighting*

(*Country-Girl's Song*)

I

My Love's gone a-fighting
Where war-trumpets call,
The wrongs o' men righting
Wi' carbine and ball,
And sabre for smiting,
And charger, and all!

II

Of whom does he think there
Where war-trumpets call?
To whom does he drink there,
Wi' carbine and ball
On battle's red brink there,
And charger, and all?

Budmouth Dears
20 Falter fond attempts] Risk a fond attempt 1st Ed

III

Her, whose voice he hears humming
  Where war-trumpets call,
'I wait, Love, thy coming
  Wi' carbine and ball,
And bandsmen a-drumming
  Thee, charger and all!'

From 'The Dynasts'

932 The Eve of Waterloo

From *The Dynasts*, Pt III, Act VI, sc. viii. Printed here from the 1927 Limited Edition

(*Chorus of Phantoms*)

THE eyelids of eve fall together at last,
And the forms so foreign to field and tree
Lie down as though native, and slumber fast!

Sore are the thrills of misgiving we see
In the artless champaign at this harlequinade,
Distracting a vigil where calm should be!

The green seems opprest, and the Plain afraid
Of a Something to come, whereof these are the proofs, –
Neither earthquake, nor storm, nor eclipse's shade!

Yea, the coneys are scared by the thud of hoofs,
And their white scuts flash at their vanishing heels,
And swallows abandon the hamlet-roofs.

The mole's tunnelled chambers are crushed by wheels,
The lark's eggs scattered, their owners fled;
And the hedgehog's household the sapper unseals.

The snail draws in at the terrible tread,
But in vain; he is crushed by the felloe-rim;
The worm asks what can be overhead,

And wriggles deep from a scene so grim,
And guesses him safe; for he does not know
What a foul red flood will be soaking him!

The Eve of Waterloo
2 field] plain 1st Ed
7 green] trees 1st Ed
14 fled;] fled, 1st Ed
15 hedgehog's household] hare's hid litter 1st Ed
21 flood] rain WE
21 be soaking] soak down to 1st Ed

Beaten about by the heel and toe
Are butterflies, sick of the day's long rheum
To die of a worse than the weather-foe.

Trodden and bruised to a miry tomb
Are ears that have greened but will never be gold,
And flowers in the bud that will never bloom.

So the season's intent, ere its fruit unfold,
Is frustrate, and mangled, and made succumb,
Like a youth of promise struck stark and cold! . . .

And what of these who to-night have come?
The young sleep sound; but the weather awakes
In the veterans, pains from the past that numb;

Old stabs of Ind, old Peninsular aches,
Old Friedland chills, haunt their moist mud bed,
Cramps from Austerlitz; till their slumber breaks.

And each soul shivers as sinks his head
On the loam he's to lease with the other dead
From tomorrow's mist-fall till Time be sped!

From 'The Dynasts'

933 *Chorus of the Pities*

From *The Dynasts*, Pt III, After Scene. Printed here from the 1927 Limited Edition

(*After the Battle*)

To Thee whose eye all Nature owns,
Who hurlest Dynasts from their thrones,
And liftest those of low estate
We sing, with Her men consecrate!

Yea, Great and Good, Thee, Thee we hail,
Who shak'st the strong, Who shield'st the frail,
Who hadst not shaped such souls as we
If tendermercy lacked in Thee!

The Eve of Waterloo
22 toe] the toe 1st Ed
23 rheum] rheum, 1st Ed, WE
33 veterans] veteran 1st Ed
34 Ind,] Ind., 1st Ed
35 their] his 1st Ed
36 their] his 1st Ed

Though times be when the mortal moan
Seems unascending to Thy throne,
Though seers do not as yet explain
Why Suffering sobs to Thee in vain;

We hold that Thy unscanted scope
Affords a food for final Hope,
That mild-eyed Prescience ponders nigh
Life's loom, to lull it by and by.

Therefore we quire to highest height
The Wellwiller, the kindly Might
That balances the Vast for weal,
That purges as by wounds to heal.

The systemed suns the skies enscroll
Obey Thee in their rhythmic roll,
Ride radiantly at Thy command,
Are darkened by Thy Masterhand!

And these pale panting multitudes
Seen surging here, their moils, their moods,
All shall 'fulfil their joy' in Thee,
In Thee abide eternally!

Exultant adoration give
The Alone, through Whom all living live,
The Alone, in Whom all dying die,
Whose means the End shall justify! Amen.

From 'The Dynasts'

934 Last Chorus

From *The Dynasts*, Pt III, After Scene. Printed here from the 1927 Limited Edition

The Years

LAST as first the question rings
Of the Will's long travailings;
Why the All-mover,
Why the All-prover
Ever urges on and measures out the chordless chime of Things.

Chorus of the Pities
15 Prescience ponders] Consciousness stands 1st Ed

Last Chorus
5 chordless chime] droning tune 1st Ed, WE

Heaving dumbly
As we deem,
Moulding numbly
As in dream,
Apprehending not how fare the sentient subjects of Its scheme.

The Pities

Nay; – shall not Its blindness break?
Yea, must not Its heart awake,
Promptly tending
To Its mending
In a genial germing purpose, and for loving-kindness' sake?

Should It never
Curb or cure
Aught whatever
Those endure
Whom It quickens, let them darkle to extinction swift and sure.

Chorus

But – a stirring thrills the air
Like to sounds of joyance there
That the rages
Of the ages
Shall be cancelled, and deliverance offered from the darts that were,
Consciousness the Will informing, till It fashion all things fair!

From 'The Dynasts'

First printed in *The Fortnightly Review*, 1 April 1911 (= FR), but subsequently omitted from the 'Satires of Circumstance' sequence in *Satires of Circumstance* (1914). The manuscript of the poem appears in the bound-up volume of manuscripts in the Dorset County Museum, but it has been crossed through. As it appears to be a later version than FR, it is the one printed here

935 On the Doorstep

SHE sits in her night-dress without the door,
And her father comes up: 'He at it again?'
He mournfully cries. 'Poor girlie!' and then
Comes her husband to fetch her in, shamed and sore.
The elder strikes him. He falls head-bare
On the edge of the step, and lies senseless there.

On the Doorstep
1 night-dress] nightdress FR
3 He hoarsely cries – 'A villain!' and then FR
4 fetch] drag FR
6–7 Stanza break in MS: page turn in FR

She, seeing him stretched like a corpse at length,
Cries out to her father, who stands aghast,
'I hate you with all my soul and strength!
You've killed him. And if this word's my last
I hate you. . . . O my husband dear –
Live – do as you will! None shall interfere!'

936 *The Calf*

Printed here from *The Book of Baby Beasts*, Pictures in Colour by E. J. Detmold, Descriptions by Florence E. Dugdale (London, 1911), p. 105. Ascribed to Hardy by Mrs Hardy's sisters. No MS is known to have survived

YOU may have seen, in road or street
  At times, when passing by,
A creature with bewildered bleat
Behind a milcher's tail, whose feet
  Went pit-pat. That was I.

Whether we are of Devon kind,
  Shorthorns, or Herefords,
We are in general of one mind
That in the human race we find
  Our masters and our lords.

When grown up (if they let me live)
  And in a dairy-home,
I may less wonder and misgive
Than now, and get contemplative,
  And never wish to roam.

And in some fair stream, taking sips,
  May stand through summer noons,
With water dribbling from my lips
And rising halfway to my hips,
  And babbling pleasant tunes.

937 *A.H., 1855–1912*

Printed here from *Arthur Henniker, A Little Book for His Friends* (London, 1912), p. 58

A LAURELLED soldier he; yet who could find
In camp or court a less vainglorious mind?

On the Doorstep
9 hate] curse FR
11 hate] curse FR

Sincere as bold, one read as in a book
His modest spirit in his candid look.

At duty's beckoning alert as brave,
We could have wished for him a later grave!
A season ere the setting of his sun
To rest upon the honours he had won . . .

Yet let us not lament. We do not weep
When our best comrade sinks in fitful sleep,
And why indulge regrets if he should fall
At once into the sweetest sleep of all?

938 The Yellow-Hammer

Printed here from *The Book of Baby Birds*, Illustrations by E. J. Detmold, Descriptions by Florence E. Dugdale (London, 1912), p. 75. There is a manuscript in the possession of Prof. R. L. Purdy, which has not been available for checking

WHEN, towards the summer's close,
  Lanes are dry,
And unclipt the hedgethorn rows,
  There we fly!

While the harvest waggons pass
  With their load,
Shedding corn upon the grass
  By the road.

In a flock we follow them,
  On and on,
Seize a wheat-ear by the stem,
  And are gone. . . .

With our funny little song,
  Thus you may
Often see us flit along,
  Day by day.

939 A Jingle on the Times

Printed here from the edition privately printed by Florence Hardy, Oct 1917. There are a manuscript, typescript and proof in the possession of Prof. R. L. Purdy, which have not been available for checking

1

'I AM a painter
  Of Earth's pied hue;
What can my pencil
  Do for you?'
' – You can do nothing,
  Nothing, nothing,
Nations want nothing
  That you can do.'

2

'I am a sculptor,
  A worker who
Preserves dear features
  The tombs enmew.' –
' – Sculpture, sculpture!
  More than sculpture
For dear remembrance
  Have we to do.'

3

' I am a poet,
  And set in view
Life and its secrets
  Old and new.' –
' – Poets we read not,
  Heed not, feed not,
Men now need not
  What they do.'

4

'I'm a musician,
  And balm I strew

On the passions people
Are prone unto.' –
' – Music? Passions
Calmed by music?
Nothing but passions
Today will do!'

5

'I am an actor;
The world's strange crew
In long procession
My masques review.'
' – O it's not acting,
Acting, acting
And glassing nature
That's now to do!'

6

'I am an architect;
Once I drew
Glorious buildings,
And built them too.' –
' – That was in peace-time,
Peace-time, peace-time,
Nought but demolishing
Now will do.'

7

'I am a preacher:
I would ensue
Whatsoever things are
Lovely, true.' –
' – Preachers are wordy,
Wordy, wordy;
Prodding's the preaching
We've now to do.'

8

'How shall we ply, then,
  Our old mysteries?' –
' – Silly ones! Must we
  Show to you
What is the only
  Good, artistic,
Cultured, Christian
  Thing to do?

9

'To manners, amenities,
  Bid we adieu, –
To the old lumber
  Of Right and True!
Fighting, smiting,
  Running through;
That's now the civilized
  Thing to do.'

December 1914

940 *Prologue*

Written for Granville-Barker's production of *The Dynasts* at the Kingsway Theatre, London, in 1914. It is printed here from the programme of that production, and was reprinted in *The Sphere*, 5 Dec 1916, p. viii, with the title 'A Poem on the War'. No MS is known to have survived

IN these stern times of ours, when crimson strife
Throws shade on every thoroughfare of life,
Disfigures comely countries with its gore,
And sends back mangled heroes to our shore,
The gift of gifts is sturdy hardihood,
That holds it firm through each vicissitude,
Not only hour by hour, but year by year,
If need be, till life's lurid skies are clear.

Arrested by perceptions such as this,
We gather that it may not be amiss, –
During the few brief minutes you can spare
From the innumerous claims that call your care, –

To raise up visions of historic wars
Which taxed the endurance of our ancestors;
That such reminders of the feats they did
May stouten hearts now strained by issues hid;

Therefore have we essayed to represent,
By our faint means, event upon event
That Europe saw a hundred years ago.....
– What matters that Napoleon was our foe?
Fair France herself had no ambitious ends;
And we are happy in a change that tends
To make of nearest neighbours closest friends.

Epilogue

Written for Granville-Barker's production of *The Dynasts* at the Kingsway Theatre, London, in 1914. It is printed here from the programme of that production. No MS is known to have survived

WE have now set forth, in our imperfect way,
Ten years of history as a three hours' play,
Leaving to your quick fancy all, or much,
That made a stern reality of such!

Yet how should art, even thus, call clearly back
Court, camp, and council, battle and bivouac,
The din and uproar of that crashing time
By the mere conjurings of masque and rhyme,
Were it not helped today in saddest wise
By sudden sharp events beneath our eyes!
Nation at war with nation, cruel wrong
Inflicted on the weaker by the strong!

May such reminders soon for ever pass,
And war be but a shade on memory's glass,
May Might uphold the injured people's cause,
And Europe move again to genial laws;
May soon succumb all influences malign,
And still the Star of England proudly shine!

Written for the production of '*The Dynasts*'
at The Kingsway Theatre.

941 *A Hundred Years Since*

Printed here from the manuscript in the University of Texas Library, where it has the title 'A hundred years since' and is marked 'Original MS'. First printed in *The North American Review*, Feb 1915, pp. [173]–174 = NAR

WHEN first you fluttered on this scene
In a May month just growing green,
And a young century turned fifteen,

What did the people say of you
As dubiously they glanced you through,
O North American Review?

You had come to go? You had come to stay?
Or neither? Be that as it may
We know some things they did not say:

They did not say that you would see
The surging nations bond and free
Shape in this wise their history.

They did not say that in your run
Some deeds for freedom would be done
To pale the glory arms had won.

Nor did they, on the other hand,
Deem that some brass gods still would stand
When a whole century had been spanned.

Even you, a young philosopher,
Did not, perhaps, at all infer
That scientific massacre

For empire, step by step would climb
To horrors at this latter time
Undreamt of in your early prime.

What sane mind could suppose, indeed,
Blunt force again would supersede
The sway of grace, art, cult, and creed.

– Yet some may here and there be fraught
With things humane you long have taught
Unwitting if they effected aught.

A Hundred Years Since
6] O NORTH AMERICAN REVIEW? NAR

For when we take good seed to throw
Broadcast afar, how much may grow,
How much may fail, we do not know;

And of your influence, what may dwell,
What die and work no kindly spell
In minds around, tongues fail to tell.

But may it still expand and last,
And make for binding Satan fast
Ere one more hundred years be passed!

942 *The Lizard*

Printed here from *The Book of Baby Pets*, Illustrations by E. J. Detmold, Descriptions by Florence E. Dugdale (London, 1915), p. 75. There is a manuscript in the possession of Prof. R. L. Purdy, which has not been available for checking

IF on any warm day when you ramble around
Among moss and dead leaves, you should happen to see
A quick trembling thing dart and hide on the ground,
And you search in the leaves, you would uncover me.

943 *They Are Great Trees*

Printed here from *The Later Years of Thomas Hardy 1892–1928* by Florence Emily Hardy (London, 1930), p. 187. There it is followed by 'Whether any more of this poem was written is not known.'

THEY are great trees, no doubt, by now,
  That were so thin in bough –
    That row of limes –
When we housed there; I'm loth to reckon when;
  The world has turned so many times,
    So many, since then!

From 'The Life of Thomas Hardy'

944 *At a Rehearsal of One of J.M.B.'s Plays*

Printed here from the manuscript in the Houghton Library of the University of Harvard. A facsimile of this appears in Sotheby's Sale Catalogue, 20–2 Dec 1937, facing p. 7. It was first printed in *The Plays of J. M. Barrie* (London, 1928) below the frontispiece portrait of Barrie = JMB. In JMB all lines are indented equally, there is no title and Hardy's name after the poem is followed by 'at a rehearsal of "Mary Rose"'

IF any day a promised play
  Should be in preparation
You never see friend J.M.B.
  Depressed, or in elation.

A Hundred Years Since
39 be] have NAR

At a Rehearsal of One of J.M.B.'s Plays
2 preparation] preparation, JMB
4 Depressed,] Depressed JMB
4–5 Stanza break in MS, JMB

But with a stick rough, crook'd, and thick,
  You may sometimes discern him
Standing as though a mumming show
  Did not at all concern him.

At a rehearsal of 'Mary Rose'

945 *The Hatband*

Printed here from the manuscript in the Dorset County Museum

SHE held it out. 'But you can't both have it,' she said;
And hesitating they stood. The boom of the bell
For the maiden came across as her fond farewell: –
  That one was the friend of the dead,
The second her lover, there needed no words to tell.

They looked at the object – a hatband the parish folk
Would borrow at times of the well-to-do woman who spoke:
Its trailing two-yards' length had grown rusty and bare
  From much promiscuous wear.

'Decide between you,' she added, and handed it over,
Whereon their faces appeared as much stressed at the choice
As the one at the loss of his friend, of his sweetheart the lover:
And still did the bell throb forth, as with querying voice,
  Which head the crape symbol should cover?

'You take it,' at last said the friend, standing back with a sigh:
  'You were dearer to her than was I.'
The streamer was tied on the hat with a love-knot of white,
And they hurried away, and shared in the last sad rite.

Next Sunday came; and pending the due church-hour
There stood, hot, playing at fives, by the western tower,
The ruddy young lover, as often aforetime there:
And the long black love-knotted hatband blew wild in the air
  With his rushings everywhere.

At a Rehearsal of One of J.M.B.'s Plays
5 stick] stick, JMB
5 crook'd,] crooked JMB
6 him] him, JMB
7 mumming] mummery JMB

Then murmured her friend, as he slowly drew near that day,
'I might just as well, truly, have had it! Alas, could not he
Refrain him for one little week, out of bare loyalty?
    But young love is brief; let him play:
Yet never *this* sight, had the sad sign been worn here by me!'

NOTE. – It should be remembered that hatbands were formerly worn hanging down behind to the waist, and tied with a bow of white ribbon when the deceased was a young unmarried woman. It was retained for the service on the Sunday following the funeral.

946 *Epitaph for G. K. Chesterton*

Printed here from the manuscript in the Dorset County Museum. This and poem 947 are contained in an inner envelope labelled 'Last lines dicated [sic] by T.H., referring to George Moore and G. K. Chesterton', with an outer envelope inscribed 'Two epitaphs on G. Moore and G. K. Chesterton – dictated by Hardy on his death-bed.' The inner envelope is signed 'F. E. Hardy'

HERE lies nipped in this narrow cyst
The literary contortionist
Who prove and never turn a hair
That Darwin's theories were a snare
He'd hold as true with tongue in jowl,
That Nature's geocentric rule
. . . true and right
And if one with him could not see
He'd shout his choice word 'Blasphemy'.

947 *Epitaph for George Moore*

Printed here from the manuscript in the Dorset County Museum

On one who thought no other could write such English as himself

'No mortal man beneath the sky
Can write such English as can I
They say it holds no thought my own
What then, such beauty (perfection) is not known.'

Heap dustbins on him:
They'll not meet
The apex of his self conceit.

Index of Titles

Figures refer to poem numbers

Index of First Lines

Figures refer to poem numbers